Linux®
Troubleshooting
Bible

Christopher Negus and Thomas Weeks

WILEY

Wiley Publishing, Inc.

Linux® Troubleshooting Bible

Published by
Wiley Publishing, Inc.
10475 Crosspoint Boulevard
Indianapolis, IN 46256
www.wiley.com

Copyright © 2004 by Wiley Publishing, Inc., Indianapolis, Indiana

Published simultaneously in Canada

ISBN: 0-7645-6997-X

Manufactured in the United States of America

10 9 8 7 6 5 4 3 2 1

About the Authors

Christopher Negus is the author of *Red Hat Linux Bible* (all editions), *Linux Toys*, and dozens of other books on Linux and UNIX systems. Chris began his career writing about UNIX systems at AT&T more than two decades ago. His work with AT&T included an 8-year run with Bell Laboratories and UNIX System Laboratories, where he worked directly with the developers of the UNIX System V operating system. Later, Chris followed the UNIX source code to Novell, Inc., in Utah, where he helped develop UnixWare documentation and wrote several books on UNIX and UnixWare.

Thomas ("Tweeks") Weeks holds a BS-EET/Telecom degree from Texas A&M, has worked for several large government and IT/security contractors in the positions of Test and Integration lab coordinator and general sysadmin, sysadmin technical trainer and course developer, as well as electrical and systems engineer. He has been working with Rackspace Managed Hosting since 1999 in the roles of Sys-Admin, Corporate Technical Trainer, and has acted as liaison between customer support/security/product/engineering departments. Tweeks has also been president of the San Antonio user group, X-otic Computer Systems of San Antonio (xcssa.org) since 1996.

Credits

Acquisitions Editor
Debra Williams Cauley

Development Editor
Sara Shlaer

Production Editor
Eric Newman

Technical Editor
François Caen

Contributing Author
Jesse Keating

Editorial Manager
Mary Beth Wakefield

Vice President & Executive Group Publisher
Richard Swadley

Vice President and Executive Publisher
Bob Ipsen

Vice President and Publisher
Joseph B. Wikert

Executive Editorial Director
Mary Bednarek

Permissions Editor
Laura Moss

Media Development Specialist
Kit Malone

As always, I dedicate this book to my wife, Sheree.
—C.N.

To my loving and supporting wife, Teri,
who likes firewalls, especially green ones.
Without her, I would be an incomplete geek.
—T.W.

Preface

Simplified install screens, rich desktop interfaces, and GUI administration tools have made Linux an easy operating system to use . . . unless something goes wrong.

If installation fails, you might find yourself figuring out what kernel options to add at an installation boot prompt. If you check a Linux forum with a server problem, most times your friends will push aside your graphical tools and have you type shell commands and hand-edit configuration file.

With official support options disappearing for Red Hat Linux, and Red Hat's free Fedora Project offered with no long-term official Red Hat support, some people continuing to use free Linux distributions are feeling left out in the cold. If you are devoted to the idea of using free Linux distributions that don't have commercial support options, you have another option—learn to troubleshoot Linux yourself.

Getting in Deeper

Troubleshooting is an often-neglected area of system administration. After books and manuals have gone through the steps to configure and use a feature, usually they've filled up their chapter and are on to the next topic. So what happens if you get to the end of a setup procedure and the feature doesn't work?

Linux Troubleshooting Bible was created to help you troubleshoot failures that you may encounter as you use Linux. For most features covered in *Linux Troubleshooting Bible*, we take you through some quick, basic steps of setting up that feature. In many cases, running the basic setup will uncover some step you forgot to do. For more details on basic uses of the feature, we point you to books (such as the latest edition of *Red Hat Fedora Linux Bible*), mailing lists, and websites.

After you have done what should have worked, and found that it didn't work, we tell you how to go a bit deeper. For example, nearly every type of Linux service outputs messages to log files. Daemon processes have verbose or debug modes to spew out reams of messages for tracing down a problem. There are commands that come with many software packages that let you check the status of a feature and see what is broken. The trick is to know where the troubleshooting tools are and how to use them.

Troubleshooting Fedora and Red Hat Linux

We chose Fedora Core 1 as the Linux operating system to illustrate Linux troubleshooting. We go through some of the reasoning behind this choice in more depth in Chapter 1. Basically, however, we chose Fedora because we felt it was the best free Linux you could use to learn troubleshooting techniques that would span from home desktop systems to corporate enterprise computers.

Despite many people's fear that Fedora Linux might lack quality without official long-term support from Red Hat, Inc., we found the first release of Fedora (Fedora Core 1) to be quite reliable. There is also a strong (and growing) community to support Fedora Linux distributions.

If your goal is to be a professional Linux system administrator, learning Fedora will help you learn skills that are immediately transferable to Red Hat Linux (versions 8 and 9 in particular) as well as Red Hat Enterprise Linux (version 3 in particular). All of those operating systems use the same installer (Anaconda), graphical administration tools, and desktops (bluecurve theme on KDE or GNOME desktop environments).

You may want to build a business around providing computers installed with Fedora distributions to small businesses, schools, or nonprofit organizations, as many people are doing today. Or, you may want to learn skills that will transfer easily to large Red Hat Enterprise Linux installations. By going through the procedures and learning the tips in this book, you will learn tools and techniques to help you trace down and repair problems with Linux, as well as learn how to prevent problems before they occur.

Transitioning to SUSE or Debian Linux

You need a Fedora or other Red Hat Linux system in front of you to make best use of the procedures and tips in this book. However, given the turmoil surrounding Red Hat's changes to the name, support options, documentation, and training for its free Linux system, we recognize that some previously faithful Red Hat supporters are now exploring other Linux systems.

Whether you plan to drop Red Hat Linux distributions altogether or simply have requirements (or desire) to use other Linuxes, we want to help transition your troubleshooting skills to those Linux systems. In particular, we want to help you understand the challenges you will face moving to SUSE and Debian Linux systems.

SUSE Linux

SUSE is an obvious alternative to Red Hat Linux distributions for those with an eye toward the enterprise. Since the acquisition of SUSE Linux by Novell, Inc., in January 2004, SUSE has become hooked in with the strong, established international sales, marketing, and development resources of Novell. SUSE is also RPM-based, so the tools for managing software packages are the same as those in Fedora and other Red Hat Linux systems.

As a Red Hat Linux troubleshooter transitioning your skills to SUSE, you will need to learn about differences in software packaging, system administration and installation tools (provided by the YaST facility in SUSE), and licensing and support issues. These and other features that you need to understand to transition from Fedora and Red Hat troubleshooting practices to SUSE troubleshooting are covered in Appendix B.

Debian Linux

When Red Hat, Inc., dropped the official Red Hat Linux product, Debian Linux was one of the first distributions that people evaluated as an alternative to Red Hat,—particularly for small business servers. The Debian "stable" distribution (with the code name *Woody*), has a reputation for being rock solid, if slightly slow in implementing the latest Linux software.

Despite its stability, however, some consider Debian to be less suited for mission-critical applications because it doesn't have big-company support behind it (such as Red Hat and Novell). Installation is not as simplified as you will find in Red Hat distributions. Likewise, hardware detection can require more manual activity than it does in Red Hat. On the whole, Debian has a stronger draw for people who are more technically inclined. You won't find as many books or support options available with Debian as you will with Red Hat systems—but that's okay, since most Debian users prefer to read man pages anyway.

Appendix C covers Debian troubleshooting issues that will help you understand what you will face if you want to transition your Fedora and Red Hat Linux troubleshooting skills to Debian.

Using *Linux Troubleshooting Bible*

Our primary goal with *Linux Troubleshooting Bible* is to give you the resources you need to overcome any problems you might have using and administering Fedora Linux (primarily), as well as other Red Hat Linux systems. We take two approaches to attaining this goal:

+ Teaching you how to troubleshoot Fedora on your own

+ Getting you in touch with other Fedora resources

By focusing mostly on command-line tools and text-based configuration files, you'll learn basic troubleshooting techniques that will apply to most Linux distributions. For example, whether you use an Apache web server from Fedora, RHEL, SUSE, or another Linux distribution, the `httpd.conf` file will still be the basic file you will troubleshoot if something goes wrong with your web server.

For the features we cover, we try to give you multiple commands and options to try out. Because we know we can't cover every issue that might come up, for most subjects we will point you to mailing lists, FAQs, or other online resources you can turn to for more information.

Approaching Linux troubleshooting

You can use this book as a reference (check it when you have a problem) or a guide (step through the procedure, to learn how to troubleshoot a feature). We have divided the book into six major parts.

+ *Part I: Getting Going*—Part I contains the most Fedora-specific information in the book. In addition to an introductory chapter (Chapter 1), the two other chapters in this part describe how to troubleshoot problems installing Fedora Core 1 (Chapter 2) and how to get the updates and do upgrades you need to keep Fedora patched and secure (Chapter 3).

+ *Part II: Preventing Problems*—The two chapters in this part focus on how to prevent problems from happening in the first place. Chapter 4 describes how to lock down both desktop and server Fedora systems before you deploy them. Chapter 5 focuses on how to prepare good backup policies to protect your data.

+ *Part III: Troubleshooting Basic Features*—Many features that apply to troubleshooting both desktop and server systems are covered in this part. Basic tips and tools that can be used to troubleshoot many different Linux features are described in Chapter 6. Chapter 7 tells how to troubleshoot your video, mouse, and keyboard. Tools for managing your software packages and correcting problems are described in Chapter 8. Troubleshooting disks and file systems is covered in Chapter 9.

✦ *Part IV: Troubleshooting the Network*—Techniques for making your network secure and keep it running smoothly are contained in this part. Security issues are covered in Chapter 10. Chapter 11 tells how to troubleshoot your firewalls. Chapter 12 describes how to troubleshoot problems with serving domain names from a DNS server. Chapter 13 covers how to troubleshoot modem problems.

✦ *Part V: Troubleshooting Internal Services*—Network services that are typically offered behind a company firewall are covered in this part. The part includes chapters for troubleshooting printers (Chapter 14), Samba (Chapter 15), and NFS (Chapter 16).

✦ *Part VI: Troubleshooting External Services*—Popular services that are often made available on public networks are covered in this part. Troubleshooting techniques are described for web servers (Chapter 17), file transfer servers, such as FTP (Chapter 18), and e-mail servers (Chapter 19).

In addition, the book contains three appendixes.

✦ *Appendix A: Fedora Software Repositories* describes several repositories for Fedora packages.

✦ *Appendix B: Troubleshooting SUSE Linux* is intended to help transition the Fedora and Red Hat Linux troubleshooting techniques learned in this book to SUSE Linux systems.

✦ *Appendix C: Troubleshooting Debian/GNU Linux* aims at helping Fedora troubleshooters transition their skills to Debian Linux.

Many of the chapters in *Linux Troubleshooting Bible* will cover the same basic types of information. This information includes the following:

✦ *Overview*—Provides an overview of the feature being covered in the chapter. This often includes a quick review of the steps needed to get each basic feature running.

✦ *Procedures*—Provides step-by-step procedures for walking through techniques for troubleshooting a feature. When you are done, you should have a good sense of how to feel your way around a feature and look for potential problems.

✦ *Tools*—Provides additional commands, options, and interfaces for working with a particular feature. Once you understand the basic tools needed to work with a feature, you should be able to refer to man pages and info pages to get more options you can use with those tools.

✦ *Tips*—Provides tips for troubleshooting some of the most common problems you might encounter.

✦ *References*—Provides refererence information to help you find things like the location of mailing lists, project home pages, and FAQS for the feature being described.

If you find that you are stuck on a problem, you might try one of the many Fedora and Red Hat Linux online forums listed in Chapter 1 for further information.

Conventions Used in This Book

Throughout the book, a special typeface indicates code or commands. Commands and code are shown in monospace type:

```
This is how code looks.
```

In the event that an example includes both input and output, monospace is still used, but input is presented in bold type to distinguish the two. Here is an example:

```
$ ftp ftp.linuxtoys.net
Name (home:jake): jake
Password: ******
```

The following special mark-up is used to call your attention to points that are particularly important.

A Note provides extra information to which you need to pay special attention.

A Tip shows a special way of performing a particular task, or introduces a shortcut to ease your way.

A Caution alerts you to take special care when executing a procedure, or damage to your computer hardware or software could result.

A Cross-Reference refers you to further information on a subject that you can find outside the current chapter.

Reach Out

The FedoraTrouble.com website contains updates and errata information for *Linux Troubleshooting Bible*. You can also go to that site to download some of the code examples that are contained in this book.

If you have any questions or comments about this book, feel free to contact Chris by e-mail at chris@linuxtoys.net. **Thomas (Tweeks) can be reached at** tweeks-bible@theweeks.org.

Acknowledgments

Chris Negus: With the change from Red Hat Linux to Fedora Core and a rampant feeling that those using free Linux systems weren't going to get any official support if things went wrong, we wanted to get a Linux troubleshooting book out to you quickly. To that end, we asked a lot of people to work really hard in a short period of time.

I was thrilled when Thomas Weeks agreed to coauthor this book. His years of experience working with and training the people who support thousands of Red Hat Linux systems at Rackspace Managed Hosting (www.rackspace.com) have added incredible depth to the content of this book. I'd like to thank him for the long hours, late nights, and weekends he consumed to get this book out to you.

Getting Jesse Keating to write the chapter on upgrading and updating, as well as an appendix on Fedora software repositories, was another coup. As leader of the Fedora Legacy project, there is no better authority than Jesse on getting the critical software updates you need to continue to use free Red Hat Linux and Fedora distributions as reliable operating systems. My thanks to Jesse for the countless hours spent outside his day job to make this book a reality.

Special thanks go to François Caen (spidermaker.com), whose RHCE skills added a wonderful dimension to his technical editing of the book. Rounding out the writing team, Kate and Joe Merlino have shown the value of having technically savvy professional writers on a Linux book project. The Kate and Joe team had to work through large amounts of raw material from Thomas and myself, which I feel they did with great success.

As any Linux book should, I would like to acknowledge Linux kernel developers (kernel.org) and the GNU Project (gnu.org) as major contributors to Linux and the whole open source movement. Likewise, I would like to thank Red Hat, Inc., (www.redhat.com) and members of the Fedora Project (http://fedora.redhat.com) for producing high-quality Linux distributions.

I'd like to thank Debra Williams Cauley at Wiley for suggesting that I do this project, instead of just working on more Linux Toys (www.linuxtoys.net). Thanks to Sara Shlaer for keeping us on track with a tight schedule. Thanks to Margot Maley Hutchison at Waterside Productions for contracting the book with Wiley and the other writers on this project.

And finally, thanks to my wife, Sheree, for being my rock, and Caleb and Seth for being the best boys a dad could ask for.

Thomas Weeks: I am honored to have been asked by Chris to participate in this project. He's a great resource to the Linux community, and he and I have really come to know each other well during this frenzied project. Technical Editor François Caen and I used to work together at Rackspace Managed Hosting and have been good friends for years. Between our long hours of work during the early years at Rackspace, I would try to get his wife to let him come to my ubergeeky LUG-ish user group here in town: X-otic Computer Systems of San Antonio (xcssa.org). But now that François has settled into the Tacoma, Washington, area, he has become heavily involved with his own local LUG there, taclug.org, and has been elected president!

My point here is that I am a strong believer in that people who use and love Open Source products (and specifically GPL products) need to contribute back to this planet-wide, utopian, software development model that we've built in whatever form they can. If you have programming skills, get involved by joining an Open Source/GPL-based project development group that interests you (sourceforge.net). For others, you might just join and support your local user group, assist at Linux Install-Fests, College LinuxFest events, or work for an incredible company that believes in and supports Open Source, such as Rackspace.

I could not have done this book without all the others that did their part. I would like to thank Chris for having the faith (or sheer workload-induced stupor) to ask for my help on this impossibly quick, monstrous undertaking. Working with him and Francois, both on the book and on helping to host the Linux Toys site (linuxtoys.net) community effort has been a lot of fun. I'm very glad that our paths all crossed when they did.

Also big thanks go to Joe Merlino and Kate Wrightson for spending countless hours trying to interpret and mold my raw research into something usable, to Sara for listening to my mail list whining about timelines, and to Debra for all her work in getting all this contract material worked out for me.

I would like to thank Rackspace—working there is the most fun I've ever had while getting paid! Plus it's such a super-rich learning environment to boot! It's been a wild ride since 1999. Thanks Rackspace, for allowing us to get some of our "in the trenches" expertise from the Fanatical Support™ Department in this book. This is a great way to give back to the community! Dirk, Pat, Richard—keep on "doing the needful" guys.

I would also be remiss if I didn't thank my parents and my Creator. Mom, Dad, thank you for bringing me up, keeping me engaged, challenged, and always supporting me. Thank you, God, for carrying me though the rough parts. It's to you I give all glory.

Most of all, I want to thank my wife, Teri, for giving up all the evenings and weekends that it took me to complete my portion of this work. Teri, I love you, and yes, I would marry you all over again.

Contents at a Glance

Contents

●●

Part III: Troubleshooting Basic Features · 137

Chapter 6: Troubleshooting Tools . . . . · 139

Part IV: Troubleshooting the Network   239

Chapter 10: Detecting and Responding to Intrusions 241

Chapter 11: Firewall Troubleshooting 265

Getting Going

Introduction to Linux Troubleshooting

Linux troubleshooting skills that were once useful only for hackers and ubergeeks have become necessities for computer professionals and serious technology enthusiasts. Once confined to the computers of free software proponents, Linux systems have found their way into desktop computers, small office servers, hand-held computers, enterprise operations, and anywhere else computer processors might be found.

If you can troubleshoot Linux, demand for your skills will grow exponentially in the time to come.

Despite the fact that there are now scores of different Linux systems, the core components of those systems are still strikingly similar. The kernel, hundreds of basic commands, and the approach you need to take to track down problems are very much the same among most Linux systems.

The goals of *Linux Troubleshooting Bible* are to help you:

✦ Set up and fix Linux desktop, laptop, workstation, and server systems.

✦ Develop Linux troubleshooting expertise that can easily transition to many different Linux systems.

To provide detailed, working instructions to learn Linux troubleshooting, we chose Fedora Core 1 as the example Linux distribution for this book. In fact, we are strong proponents of Fedora for those who want to:

✦ Become proficient in a free Linux distribution that can be used in the same ways that Red Hat Linux was traditionally used.

✦ Learn how to dig up resources that can help you maintain Linux systems yourself, without paying expensive subscription fees.

✦ Develop a set of troubleshooting skills that will transition up to enterprise-quality Linux distributions.

Most of the techniques described in this book will work exactly the same on Red Hat Enterprise and Red Hat Linux (versions 8 and 9, in particular) as well. In the next section, we explain why we believe Fedora is an excellent choice for both learning Linux troubleshooting and for using as desktop and server systems, in many situations.

Once you have studied the troubleshooting techniques in chapters of this book, you may find that you want to spread those skills to other Linux distributions. For that reason, we provide two appendixes (Appendixes B and C) to help you understand the challenges you will face transitioning to two other popular Linux distributions: SUSE and Debian.

For the moment, however, I recommend that you have a Fedora Core system in front of you (or a Red Hat Enterprise Linux system) if you care to step through the information laid out in this book.

Introducing Fedora Linux

In September 2003, while in the middle of developing the successor to Red Hat Linux 9 (presumably Red Hat Linux 10), Red Hat, Inc., made a startling announcement. It was merging its Red Hat Linux development with Fedora Linux (www.fedora.us) into a new initiative: *The Fedora Project*.

Suddenly, it seemed, there was no flagship Red Hat Linux product anymore. Users would have to choose between the subscription-based Red Hat Enterprise Linux and the community-supported Fedora Project. The Red Hat Linux product in development was renamed and eventually released as Fedora Core 1.

Common reactions to the abandonment of Red Hat Linux for Fedora ranged from surprise, to confusion, to anger. As the dust settles, however, the logic of this move and the potential upside for the open-source community has already begun to emerge.

Learning Linux Troubleshooting with Fedora

The Fedora Project is being touted as a Red Hat–sponsored and community-supported open-source project. Its mission is to produce a Linux distribution called Fedora Core (sometimes also referred to as Fedora Linux), which in its first release was built from the Red Hat Linux code base. The distribution would be re-released every 4 to 6 months.

With the name change and its association with Red Hat, Inc., changing so suddenly, there has been a lot of speculation about what exactly Fedora is and how well it can be relied upon. Let's start by separating the facts from the speculation about Fedora:

✦ *Fedora is essentially Red Hat Linux 10*—A good case can be made for this statement. Up until the last 2 months of the development process, what is now called Fedora Core 1 was being developed as the next release of Red Hat Linux. Most of the last-minute changes had to do with changing logos and expanding access to software repositories (which we will discuss later).

✦ *Fedora Core 1 is a solid Linux system*—Hundreds of bug fixes and improvements were made during the development process. There were not a tremendous number of new features added to the Red Hat Linux 9 base. By most accounts, Fedora Core 1 is a rock-solid Linux distribution.

✦ *Red Hat, Inc., supports Fedora*—It is clear that Red Hat, Inc., wants to create high-quality software from the Fedora Project. Most of the technology in Red Hat Enterprise Linux 3 matches almost exactly the same software packages in Fedora Core 1. Red Hat, Inc., plans to use Fedora as a proving ground for its enterprise products. It doesn't have the resources to maintain and enhance the entire Linux operating system and related applications itself. Fedora is critical to Red Hat's success.

✦ *Fedora is a path to Red Hat Enterprise*—Some people like to use a freely distributed Linux as a means of showing a reluctant boss or IT department that Linux will work in their business. With Fedora Core 1, you can demonstrate many of the same features that are in Red Hat Enterprise Linux 3. Future releases of Fedora could be used to evaluate new technologies in which a company may be interested. (See the description of Fedora Core 2 later in this chapter.)

✦ *Fedora offers more software*—For someone interested in trying software that is outside of the corporate software model (such as games, audio, and video), Fedora Core offers dozens more packages than does Red Hat Enterprise Linux. It also contains tools, such as yum, for downloading complete sets of applications from software repositories in Red Hat RPM format.

✦ *Fedora has the latest technology*—Here's where some of the risks (and opportunities) lie with Fedora. Because Fedora is slated to come out two to three times per year, it can incorporate the latest software available for Linux. This should make Fedora Core a great operating system for keeping your knowledge and troubleshooting skills up to date. However, this should also have the effect of making some releases of Fedora less stable. You might find yourself picking and choosing a Fedora Core release to use as your server.

✦ *Fedora offers critical updates and patches*—This has been the biggest concern for those who have been using Red Hat Linux as a server for their businesses or organizations. The amount of time that critical updates will be officially supported by Red Hat for Fedora Core is shorter than it was for Red Hat Linux. The Fedora Legacy Project (www.fedoralegacy.org), as well as other organizations, is stepping up to deal with this issue. (See Chapter 3 for discussions of how to solve the update and upgrade issues with Fedora.)

The bottom line is that Fedora offers great technology in a freely distributed Linux system. Yes, there are fewer guarantees from Red Hat, Inc., if you want to bet your business on Fedora. However, if the prospect of going it alone with Fedora is exciting but somewhat daunting to you, we are here to tell you that you don't have to go it alone. If you decide to go with Fedora (or at least look into it further), *Linux Troubleshooting Bible* is here to give you (or help you find) the resources you need to support it.

Finding Opportunities with Fedora

If you take the time to learn how to troubleshoot Fedora, what kinds of Linux systems can you support with your new skills? The short answer is: any kind of system you could set up with Red Hat Linux. The software in Fedora supports desktop, workstation, and server systems, and is being used for a variety of specialty uses.

Fedora Linux Desktop

As with most Linux and UNIX systems, Fedora Core uses the X Window System as the foundation for its graphical user interface (GUI). It also offers the GNOME and KDE desktop environments. If you don't want to use a full-blown desktop environment, you can use other window managers that come with Fedora instead, such as the Tab Window manager and Motif Window manager.

Figure 1-1 illustrates the GNOME desktop, including two panels, the Nautilus graphical shell and the Konqueror web browser/file manager.

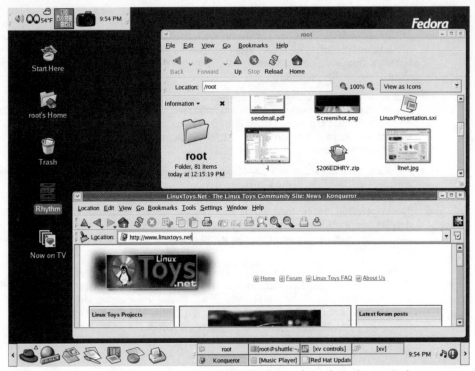

Figure 1-1: Choose between GNOME and KDE desktops, based on the X Window System.

Fedora comes with all the basic desktop applications you would expect to find on a Linux desktop: editors, web browsers, office productivity applications, music players, and graphics programs. Using yum and apt repositories, you can add to the hundreds of desktop applications that come with Fedora Core.

Whether you are supporting dozens of desktop systems or just a few, this book covers how to troubleshoot installation (Chapter 2), your video card, mouse, and keyboard (Chapter 7), and software packages (Chapter 8). Chapter 4 tells how to lock down a Fedora desktop system, and Chapter 3 describes how to get critical updates for your desktop system.

Fedora Linux Servers

All the basic server features that came with Red Hat Linux are in Fedora Core. Graphical configuration tools developed for Red Hat Linux are included in Fedora Core, as are a variety of commands and graphical utilities for troubleshooting your servers.

Figure 1-2 illustrates the categories of server software in Fedora from the Package Management window.

Despite the lack of guarantees from Red Hat, Inc., for supporting more than a short update period for Fedora systems, a group of people committed to using Fedora as a server have rallied around the Fedora Legacy Project (see Chapter 3 for details). Their goal is to provide the long-term support for Fedora that it needs to be a viable server operating system.

Servers

☑ **Server Configuration Tools** [12/12] Details

This group contains all of Red Hat's custom server configuration tools.

☑ **Web Server** [17/17] Details

These tools allow you to run a Web server on the system.

☑ **Mail Server** [8/8] Details

These packages allow you to configure an IMAP or Postfix mail server.

☑ **Windows File Server** [2/2] Details

This package group allows you to share files between Linux and MS Windows(tm) systems.

☑ **DNS Name Server** [3/3] Details

This package group allows you to run a DNS name server (BIND) on the system.

☑ **FTP Server** [1/1] Details

These tools allow you to run an FTP server on the system.

☑ **SQL Database Server** [5/5] Details

This package group allows you to run an SQL server on the system.

☑ **News Server** [1/1] Details

This group allows you to configure the system as a news server.

☑ **Network Servers** [17/17] Details

These packages include network-based servers such as CIPE, DHCP, and telnet.

Figure 1-2: Advanced network server software once in Red Hat Linux is included in Fedora.

Most of the troubleshooting skills you will gain from this book are aimed at server troubleshooting. While we briefly touch on Red Hat–specific graphical administration tools, techniques for working with server configuration files and command-line tools will help you develop a skill set that applies to most Linux and UNIX systems.

For small office servers and personal servers, you can probably use Fedora Core. For larger installations, you might consider purchasing Red Hat Enterprise Linux server subscriptions. In either case, the skills for troubleshooting both distributions will be the same.

In terms of how server topics are covered in this book, we have divided the chapters into three major sections. The chapters in Part IV focus on how to troubleshoot your network with an eye toward security (Chapter 10 covers how to detect and deal with intruders), and then describe specific techniques to troubleshoot your firewalls (Chapter 11), domain name system server (Chapter 12), and modems (Chapter 13).

Fedora Linux Workstation

A Linux workstation is basically thought of as a desktop system used for software development. There are well over 100 software packages that come with Fedora Core that fall under the heading of development packages (see Figure 1-3 for an illustration of software development package groups in Fedora).

Development		
☑ **Development Tools**	**[50/50]**	Details
These tools include core development tools such as automake, gcc, perl, python, and debuggers.		
☑ **Kernel Development**	**[5/5]**	Details
Install these packages to recompile the kernel.		
☑ **X Software Development**	**[20/20]**	Details
These packages allow you to develop applications for the X Window System.		
☑ **GNOME Software Development**	**[44/44]**	Details
Install these packages in order to develop GTK+ and GNOME graphical applications.		
☑ **KDE Software Development**	**[20/20]**	Details
Install these packages to develop QT and KDE graphical applications.		

Figure 1-3: Software development tools are spread across more than 100 software packages in Fedora.

Troubleshooting skills needed to support Fedora Linux workstations are pretty much the same skills you would need to support any desktop system.

Specialty Fedora Linux Systems

Because there are no licensing fees associated with Fedora Core, people have already begun using it to create their own specialized Linux systems. For example, bootable live CD Linux distributions created from Fedora include ADIOS Linux Boot CD (http://dc.qut.edu.au/adios) and RPM Live Linux CD (http://nwst.de/livelinuxcd).

Many companies creating devices that use embedded Linux systems have leaned toward Red Hat Linux in the past. According to the 2003 LinuxDevices.com Embedded Linux Market Survey, Red Hat Linux was the preferred Linux source/vendor for embedded Linux systems. With 14.4 percent of embedded Linux systems being based on Red Hat Linux (with only homegrown Linux systems beating it, with an 18 percent share), Red Hat Linux captured a substantial share of the embedded systems market. The fact that most surveyed (63.9 percent) considered no royalties as being the most important feature for choosing a Linux distribution for creating their embedded systems means that we can expect Fedora to carry on that tradition.

Whether you hope to build your own embedded or other specialty Linux system some day, the skills you learn in *Linux Troubleshooting Bible* will help you not only get your systems working, but understand the range of features that lie beneath the surface of Linux. Even if it's just in the area of fun projects, such as those included with Linux Toys (www.linuxtoys.net), learning to troubleshoot Fedora can be a useful skill. Figure 1-4 illustrates the Linux Toys Television Recorder/Player.

Figure 1-4: Linux Toys and other hobbyist applications will run on Fedora Core.

Going with Fedora (Without Going It Alone)

What some seem to forget as they worry about how well Red Hat, Inc., will support Fedora is that Linux was originally created and supported by a community of open-source developers, administrators, and integrators. Right now, the community of people and companies out there that are ready and able to support the software that comes in Fedora is as strong as ever.

While calling Red Hat, Inc., for every problem with Fedora may not be an option, the trick is to know what the Fedora Project itself is offering (with the support of Red Hat, Inc.) and how to look elsewhere for the help you need. The first thing to do, however, is to get your hands on Fedora.

Choosing a Fedora Version

By the time this book is released, Fedora Core 1 would have been available for several months and Fedora Core 2 would just be hitting the market. Although versions 1 and 2 are similar in many ways, we based most of this book on Fedora Core 1 for the following reasons:

✦ Fedora Core 1 had gone through nearly a full Red Hat testing cycle before becoming Fedora Core 1. There were not major feature additions over Red Hat Linux 9, while there were many bug fixes that were included.

✦ Fedora Core 2 included many major new features and hadn't been out long enough to know if all the major bugs had been fully shaken out yet.

For these reasons, we felt that Fedora Core 1 made a more stable environment for those who wanted to use the skill taught in this book to set up and use reliable desktop and server systems. If, however, you want to use Fedora Core 2 instead with this book, here are some of the differences you can expect:

✦ Fedora Core 2 includes the new 2.6 kernel by default. While there are not many features about the new kernel that change how you use Linux, it's possible that support for some hardware drivers may not have been carried over to the 2.6 kernel yet. The new kernel also has brought some changes in the types of boot media you can use with Fedora Core 2. (Refer to `http://fedora.redhat.com/download` for details on installation media and install procedures.)

✦ All the `redhat-config-*` graphical administration utilities had their names changed to `system-config-*`. So, anywhere in the book that we discuss the commands that launch graphical administration tools, you should change `redhat` to `system` when you type the command.

✦ The XFree86 X server used in Fedora Core 1 has been replaced by a new X server from X.org. During descriptions of troubleshooting video in Chapter 7, you may find differences in how some of the X-related commands behave.

Likewise, in the course of normal improvements to Linux software (such as new versions of KDE and GNOME desktops in Fedora Core 2), some of the steps and options described in this book (which was based on Fedora Core 1) may differ.

Getting Fedora

You need Fedora Core Linux operating system to use this book. When Red Hat, Inc., transitioned its operating system from Red Hat Linux to Fedora, it stopped producing boxed sets of that product. To follow along with this book, you should get the three-CD Fedora Core 1 set in one of the following ways:

✦ *Red Hat Linux Bible: Fedora and Enterprise Edition*—The complete three-CD installation set for Fedora Core 1 comes with this edition of *Red Hat Linux Bible*. If you are new to Red Hat Linux, Fedora, or Linux in general, *Red Hat Linux Bible* covers the basics you need to use, administer, and set up servers for Fedora Core. *Linux Troubleshooting Bible* builds on those basics.

✦ *Downloading*—You can download the ISO images of the CDs from the Fedora Project website (`http://fedora.redhat.com/download/`). The site describes the process of downloading, verifying, and burning the CD images.

✦ *Find a friend*—Many Linux enthusiasts or Linux user groups will be happy to get you a copy of Fedora Core, or any other Linux that you desire. Remember, Fedora is free and distributable.

Fedora Core can be installed on most Pentium class PCs. Unless otherwise noted, all the software needed in this book is available on the Fedora distribution CDs.

Note   Chapter 2 contains information on installing Fedora Core and tips on troubleshooting installation.

To learn about what is new in Fedora Core, especially if you want to know the differences between Fedora Core and Red Hat Linux 9, you can refer to the Release Notes document. That document describes the hardware requirements for running Fedora, provides notes on installing and using Fedora Core, and lists new and removed software packages. You can get the Release Notes on the first disk of the three-CD Fedora Core set or from the Fedora Project website (`http://fedora.redhat.com/docs/release-notes`).

Connecting with the Fedora Project

The best resource for the latest news and policies relating to Fedora is the Fedora Project website: `http://fedora.redhat.com`. From that site, you can get the latest information on release schedules, project objectives, and ways of participating in the project.

You should read the Fedora Project FAQ (click the FAQ link from the home page). You can also click the About link to learn about the people and structure that supports the project.

Getting Fedora Documentation

The Red Hat Linux documentation is one component that didn't come across to the Fedora Project. In fact, one of the major reasons for this book is to fill the void left by the lack of official documentation coming out of Red Hat, Inc., for Fedora.

Instead of porting the Red Hat Linux Documentation to Fedora, the Fedora Docs project is focusing its first efforts on producing an Installation Guide. Beyond that, the Fedora Docs project hopes to produce (and encourage others to produce) smaller tutorial and HOWTO documents.

Because the first Fedora release (Fedora Core 1) was very similar in many ways to the previous release (Red Hat Linux 9) and the recent enterprise release (Red Hat Enterprise Linux 3), you can find answers to many questions in existing Red Hat documentation for those products. Another resource for Fedora documentation is documents that come with each software package in the Fedora distribution itself. Here are some places to look:

✦ *Red Hat Linux 9 Doc Set*—Manuals for installing, customizing, and administering Red Hat Linux 9 are on the Red Hat website (`www.redhat.com/docs/manuals/linux`). You can download the Installation Guide, Getting Started Guide, Customization Guide, Reference Guide, Security Guide, System Administration Primer, Glossary, and Release Notes. Most of the documents are available in PDF, RPM, and HTML (tarball) formats.

✦ *Red Hat Enterprise Linux Doc Set*—Manuals for the Red Hat Enterprise Linux products are also available online (`www.redhat.com/docs/manuals/enterprise`). Several of these manuals are quite generic. So most of the content in, for example, Introduction to System Administration, System Administration Guide, Reference Guide, Security Guide, and Step by Step Guide would be appropriate for Fedora as well.

✦ */usr/share/doc*—Software packages that come with documentation often put that documentation in subdirectories of the `/usr/share/doc` directory. Much of the documentation is in HTML format, and so you can read it from your web browser.

✦ *Man pages*—Traditional UNIX and Linux documentation was done on per component documents referred to as *man pages*. For a Fedora troubleshooter, man pages are a great resource for understanding all the options that come with each command. Man pages are typically stored in the `/usr/share/man` subdirectories for commands (man1), system calls (man2), programming functions (man3), special files (man4), file formats (man5), games (man6), miscellaneous components (man7), and administration commands (man8).

✦ *Info pages*—Like man pages, info pages are text-based descriptions of components in Fedora. However, the info utility, which displays info pages, is more menu-oriented than are man pages.

Checking Documents with man and info

The man and info commands are used to display man pages and info pages, respectively. For example, to see the man page for the cat command, type

```
#   man cat
```

To start the info utility, you can simply type the info command. From there, scroll up and down to find the command or other component that interests you. With the cursor on the item you want, press Enter to display the information.

Finding Documents in Software Packages

If you would like to see what documentation is included with a particular software package, you can use the rpm command. For example, to see what documentation comes with the bash shell software (bash package), you could type the following:

```
#  rpm -qd bash |less
```

This command will show you any manual pages, HOWTOs, release notes, or other documents associated with a Fedora software package.

Checking Project Sites

Nearly every project represented by software packages in Fedora has its own website, at which you can find further information and documentation on the project. You can usually find the address of a project's website by checking the README file or the RPM description that comes with the software package in Fedora.

For example, to find out about the Rhythmbox multimedia player in Fedora, I paged through the Rhythmbox README file:

```
# less /usr/share/doc/rhythmbox-*/README
```

In that file, I saw that the official website is http://web.rhythmbox.org and that there is a mailing list at http://lists.gnome.org/mailman/listinfo/rhythmbox-devel. If you can't find information about the project's website from its README file, you can try listing information about the package to find the site. For example, to list information about the rdesktop package (a Windows NT terminal server client), you could type the following:

```
# rpm -qi rdesktop
```

Besides showing a description of the package, this command showed that the rdesktop website is at www.rdesktop.org. Links from this site point you to documents that describe the protocols used in rdesktop, if you want to research further how the software works.

Getting on Fedora Mailing Lists

Many of the resources slated to support the Fedora Project were created to suit its charter to be a community-supported Linux. While Fedora mailing lists have been churning away happily from the get-go, community involvement in other areas will, by their nature, take more time to develop.

The Fedora Project has an active set of mailing lists that are available through Red Hat, Inc. To access the mailing lists (both archives and e-mailed versions are available to everyone), visit the following site:

```
http://redhat.com/mailman/listinfo/
```

There is very active participation from Red Hat, Inc., developers on all of these lists, so you can often get information straight from those people developing and making decisions about the direction of Fedora. Here's a rundown of what you can expect from each of the Fedora mailing lists:

✦ *General Fedora questions (fedora-list)*—The fedora-list is for general questions about Fedora. Of the available mailing lists, fedora-list is the most active. If you sign up for this list, you can expect 100 to 200 posts per day (or more) devoted to questions about Fedora. Although there are all types of Fedora questions on this list, the list is especially good for "how do I get" and "where do I find" types of questions.

✦ *Fedora testing discussions (fedora-test-list)*—The fedora-test-list tracks the development of Fedora software. For the troubleshooter, this is a good list to talk about software that has broken down and is in the process of being fixed.

✦ *Fedora announcements (fedora-announce-list)*—If you are using Fedora, you should at least subscribe to fedora-announce-list. This list announces the availability of critical updates for your Fedora systems.

✦ *Fedora desktop (fedora-desktop-list)*—For issues related to troubleshooting desktop problems or discussing desktop enhancements, the fedora-desktop-list is a good place to start.

✦ *Fedora software updates (fedora-legacy-list)*—To get in on discussions of how updates will be available for Fedora (and older Red Hat Linux systems as well) beyond the officially supported update plans from Red Hat, Inc., you should join the fedora-legacy-list.

To keep up with the ongoing development of Fedora, there are also other lists that might interest you. Fedora-devel-list contains information on newly built packages and lets people comment on feature changes. For development issues related directly to configuration tools, there is fedora-config-list. If you want to contribute to the Fedora documentation effort, you can join fedora-docs-list.

Getting on Fedora Internet Relay Chat

If you have never used Internet Relay Chat (IRC) before, it offers a great way to participate in (or just watch) discussions by typing messages to a scrolling list. Messages are transferred in real time, so anyone on the IRC channel can participate right at the moment.

The Fedora Project offers several IRC channels through the Freenode IRC Network (www.freenode.net). Channels include:

✦ *Fedora general chat (#fedora)*—Open to end users or any participants in the Fedora Project.

✦ *Fedora development chat (#fedora-devel)*—For chatting about problems and suggestions related to Fedora software development.

✦ *Fedora problem reporting chat (#fedora-bugs)*—To talk about bugs you encounter while using Fedora and find out if workarounds or fixes are available.

There is also a Spanish language chat channel (#fedora-es) and other public and private channels associated with Fedora projects. If you have not used IRC before, refer to an IRC tutorial, such as the one at www.irchelp.org/irchelp/irctutorial.htm.

Here's a quick procedure for getting into a Fedora IRC channel:

1. With a computer connected to the Internet, open an IRC client. For example, in Fedora you can open an X-Chat window by clicking the Red Hat menu and selecting Internet ⇨ More Internet Applications ⇨ IRC Client.

2. Add a Nick Name (and two alternate nicknames, in case yours is taken), a User Name, and a Real Name, and click Connect.

3. Once you are connected to the server, join the list you choose by typing /join and the channel name. For example, to join the general Fedora chat channel, type

   / join # fedora

Getting More Software

While the plans to broaden the range of software available for Fedora are still being developed, new features in Fedora already make it easier to get additional software packages for Fedora than it was for Red Hat Linux. Right now, you can:

✦ *Use up2date*—The up2date facility that you used to get software updates for Red Hat Linux has been enhanced for Fedora Core. Beginning with Fedora Core 1, software repositories created for the yum or apt package managers can be accessed through the up2date facility. By default, up2date is configured to use yum repositories to get updates for Fedora systems, while Red Hat Enterprise Linux systems still use the Red Hat Network to get official updates from Red Hat, Inc.

✦ *Use yum or apt*—The yum package manager (which comes with Fedora Core) and apt package manager (which is easily attainable) can be used to get additional software packages that are not in Fedora Core.

High-quality software packages, in RPM format, are already available from yum and apt repositories. The www.fedora.us site (which merged with Red Hat Linux to form the Fedora Project) has software repositories built for Fedora (www.fedora.us/wiki/ FedoraPackageLists). The Freshrpms.net site is the first place many Fedora users go to get additional software packages. There are also other repositories that contain more software that may not meet Fedora's or Red Hat's standards of quality (or legality).

There is a Fedora Project Developer's Guide (http://fedora.redhat.com/participate/ developers-guide) for those who want to contribute their software to the Fedora Project. Plans for software packages that don't make it into the main Fedora Core distribution, but still want to be sanctioned to some extent by the Fedora Project, can be added to Fedora repositories in one of the following ways:

✦ *Fedora Extras*—These are additional software packages that don't replace any of the basic Fedora Core packages. Eventually, the www.fedora.us site is slated to hold an official set of Fedora Extras packages.

✦ *Fedora Alternatives*—These are software packages that can replace existing software packages that are in the Fedora Core.

✦ *Fedora Legacy*—These are packages that contain fixes to older versions of Fedora Core software.

The guidelines for submitting Fedora software packages, and having them sanctioned by the Fedora Project, are still being developed. For more on software package definitions, visit the Fedora Project Terminology page (http://fedora.redhat.com/participate/terminology.html). As I noted earlier, you should also keep in mind that there are some (and will be more) software repositories that will be available that won't fall under Fedora Project guidelines. You will be on your own to evaluate the quality and legality of those packages.

Cross-Reference See Chapter 3 for more complete information on getting Fedora software packages and updates. See Appendix A for a list of popular third-party software repositories.

Giving Back to Fedora

Contributing to the open-source community is the best way to ensure that Linux, in general, and Fedora, in particular, will continue to improve and grow in the future. Even if you are not a kernel hacker, or a software developer at all, there are plenty of other ways you can contribute.

Finding Bugs and Filing Reports

The easiest way that anyone using Fedora can help improve it is to report problems. As you use Fedora, you will certainly bump into things that don't exactly work right. Using a facility called *Bugzilla*, which is maintained by Red Hat, Inc., for the Fedora Project, you can:

✦ *Search*—You can search the Bugzilla database to see if anyone has encountered the same problem you have. If someone has, there may already be a workaround or software fix available to overcome the problem. If you can't find the exact bug you encountered in the database, you might also want to check a Fedora mailing list on the topic to see if the problem has been encountered, before you file a bug report. To search Bugzilla, go to the Red Hat Bugzilla site (http://bugzilla.redhat.com/bugzilla/) and enter a search term.

✦ *Report*—If you feel that the bug has not been reported yet, you can enter a Bugzilla report into the database. When you do, make sure that you have as many details available about the problem as possible before you enter the report.

To enter a bug report, you need to give a valid e-mail address and password. To get an account, or just log in to enter a bug report, go to the following web address: http://bugzilla.redhat.com/bugzilla/enter_bug.cgi.

Once you log in, check the frequently reported bug list and check the latest errata updates to see if your bug has already been dealt with. Then select Fedora Core to enter a new bug report by selecting the component (software package), severity, platform, priority, summary, description, and other information about the bug.

Note If you have never entered a bug report before, click the bug writing guidelines link from the Enter New Bug page. Those guidelines will give you good advice on how to pass on the most important information about your bug to help the developers reproduce and fix the problem.

✦ *Fix*—If you believe that you have a code fix or other solution to the problem, it's a good idea to submit that fix along with the bug report. Red Hat, Inc., recommends that most fixes be delivered in the form of unified diffs (so the maintainer can see exactly what code changes you are suggesting).

After you have entered the bug report, you are given an opportunity to attach a patch or other text to the bug report. Select Create an Attachment and enter the filename of your patch (and a brief summary description) along with the attachment.

I can't stress enough how important it is to enter bug reports to get important fixes done. When a package maintainer goes through the list of fixes needed to a software package, a report entered into Bugzilla will carry a lot more weight than ranting in a mailing list or just firing off e-mails to the maintainer. Bug reports make for orderly fixes.

Joining Fedora Projects

The Fedora Project website already lists a variety of software projects you can become involved with. Signing on to one of the Fedora mailing lists (described earlier in this chapter) is a great way to connect up with the people at Red Hat, Inc., who are running the ongoing Fedora projects.

Some of the best features of Red Hat Linux that have made their transition over to Fedora are the Red Hat installation program, the graphically oriented redhat-config tools (called system-config in Fedora Core 2), and the Red Hat desktop. Current projects being sponsored by Red Hat as part of the Fedora Project that include these features are:

✦ *Red Hat Installation Program (Anaconda)*—Its installation program named Anaconda, with both graphical and text-based versions, has been one of the strong points of Red Hat Linux for the past few years. Anaconda also includes a kick-start feature that lets someone installing Fedora preconfigure installation selections so that the install can be done with little or no live input. Anaconda is written in Python.

Currently, the Fedora Project is asking for bug reports and requests for enhancements for Anaconda. If you are interested in contributing to this project, I recommend that you join the anaconda-devel-list and/or kickstart-list mailing lists to see how you can become involved.

✦ *Configuration Tools*—Red Hat's own home-grown graphical configuration tools (many of which also have text-based interfaces) have made great strides in recent Red Hat Linux (and now Fedora) releases toward simplifying Linux system administration. These let you configure your network, file sharing, video cards, printers, and many other features.

While I count about 40 Red Hat configuration tools, there is still room to simplify many other administrative features. The Fedora Configuration Tools Project is recommending a list of features that could benefit from a GUI. These include GUI tools for partitioning your disks, scheduling tasks, configuring more refined firewalls, and setting up boot servers (such as DHCP and NIS).

To find out how you can contribute to the Configuration Tools Project, you can start by joining the fedora-config-list mailing list.

✦ *Desktop Project*—Red Hat brought the concept of a standard look-and-feel across the two major desktop environments (GNOME and KDE) to Fedora in the form of the Fedora Desktop Project. The standard Red Hat look-and-feel is referred to as Blue Curve. Particular areas where Red Hat is looking for input related to the Desktop Project is in the area of creating desktop themes, creating splash screens, and choosing which applications are set up as defaults.

If you are fond of writing, or have enough insight into a feature that you could write a tutorial on it, the Fedora Docs Project is looking for contributors. As noted earlier, you could join the fedora-docs-list mailing list to find out more. There is also an ongoing effort to find people to translate Fedora into different languages. The fedora-trans-list mailing list is a good way to get further information.

Moving to Fedora Core 2

Fedora Core 2 reflects Red Hat's commitment to making the Fedora Project a platform for rapid development and adoption of Linux technology. Although we are recommending Fedora Core 1 as a more stable Linux distribution to follow along with this book, you may want to use Fedora Core 2 to take advantage of some of its new features.

If you are sitting down to use this book with Fedora Core 2, you should be aware of several differences from Fedora Core 1. Here are some of the major ones:

✦ *Linux 2.6.5 kernel*—The Linux 2.6 kernel is a major upgrade from the 2.4.22 kernel included in Fedora Core 1. New features should result in improved performance, more supported hardware, and better scalability. For the most part, the new kernel shouldn't change how you use this book. However, visible reflections of the new kernel include a new /sys file system (where you can view and change kernel information) and device files represented by .ko instead of .o suffixes.

✦ *Advanced Linux Sound Architecture (ALSA)*—The underlying mechanism for sound in Fedora Core 2 is ALSA, replacing the Open Source Sound system (OSS) used in Fedora Core 1 and earlier Red Hat Linux distributions.

✦ *system-config tools*—To give a more generic feel, commands to launch graphical administration tools that previously began with redhat-config now begin with system-config. For example, the redhat-config-network command is now system-config-network. Anytime you encounter a command beginning with redhat-config, try system-config in Fedora Core 2 instead.

✦ *Security Enhanced Linux*—The SE Linux feature pervades many aspects of the Fedora Core 2 operating system. This new security model can be used to overcome the monolithic "root owns the world" approach to security in earlier Linux and UNIX systems. Using access control lists (ACLs), a system with SE Linux enabled can finely define administrative control over the files, processes, and devices in that system. By default, SE Linux is turned off in Fedora Core 2.

✦ *X.org X server*—The X server delivered with Fedora Core 2 changed from the XFree86 server to the X server software available from X.org. While this shouldn't have much impact on the average desktop user (who sees mostly the GNOME or KDE desktop environment, colored by the metacity window manager and Bluecurve theme), it does change some of the tools available for configuring your video cards from the command line.

✦ *Many new packages*—More than 200 new packages were added to Fedora Core 2 after Fedora Core 1. While many of these packages were added to improve support for application development (especially Java applications), some new administrative features were added such as IPSEC (VPN software replacing cipe) and the exim mail transfer agent (which could be used instead of sendmail or postfix).

Summary

Despite the change in both name and how it is produced, the Linux operating system referred to as Fedora Core is a good, free Linux operating system for learning Linux troubleshooting. Red Hat's flagship Red Hat Linux product formed the foundation for the new Fedora Core distribution that is available today.

Linux Troubleshooting Bible is dedicated to bringing you the skills you need to prevent, find, and fix problems with Fedora Core, in particular. The same skills you learn in troubleshooting Fedora can be used for troubleshooting older Red Hat Linux systems and newer Red Hat Enterprise Linux systems, as well as a variety of other Linux systems.

Besides the information in this book, there are many other resources available if you want to support Fedora Core systems. The Fedora Project itself sponsors several very active mailing lists where you can ask questions about Fedora features, development, and software fixes. And despite not having a full documentation set dedicated to Fedora, there are many useful documents from Red Hat Linux 9, Red Hat Enterprise Linux, and from individual software projects (included on the Fedora Core CDs) that can be used to find information that applies to Fedora.

Because Fedora is a community-supported distribution, there are many ways you can contribute to the project itself. You can start by filing bug reports when you encounter problems. The Fedora Project also encourages you to contribute code fixes and request for enhancements to help improve Fedora going forward.

Troubleshooting Installation

A failed Linux installation will stop you cold. I've heard too many stories of people giving up on Linux because they couldn't get it to install. In many cases, just knowing a few tricks can get you through.

Installation is one of the most distribution-specific features described in this book. The topics in this chapter cover how to fix or avoid problems when installing Fedora Core. However, because the same installer is used with Red Hat Linux 9 (as well as earlier versions) and Red Hat Enterprise Linux, most of the information contained here will cover those issues as well.

For other versions of Linux, such as SUSE and Debian, the installation process is much different. However, many of the installation troubleshooting concepts (passing options to the kernel, dealing with unsupported hardware, and so on) will help you know what to do if you have trouble installing those other Linux distributions. (See Appendixes B and C for descriptions of SUSE and Debian, respectively.)

Understanding Installation

Each Red Hat Linux distribution (Fedora Core, Red Hat Linux 9, or Red Hat Enterprise Linux) is made up of groups of RPM packages, bootable images, and other assorted software and README files. These files are commonly gathered together in one of the following forms:

✦ *Sets of CDs or DVDs*—CDs are the most common medium for installing Red Hat Linux systems, although in the coming years DVDs will probably become more popular. Fedora Core 1 and Red Hat Linux 9 each consists of three installation CDs and three source code CDs. Red Hat Enterprise Linux is packaged in different CD combinations for WS, AS, and ES installations.

✦ *ISO images*—These are images created to fit on a particular medium, such as CD or DVD. Typically, users can download a set of ISO images and burn them to CD or DVD themselves to use for installation. This creates, bit-for-bit, the same CDs or DVDs that were packaged with Red Hat Linux 9 boxed set or books on Fedora.

As an alternative to burning ISO images to CD or DVD, you can copy these images to hard disk. The Red Hat installation procedures allow you to install images from a local hard disk or by using a network protocol, such as NFS.

✦ *Software repositories*—The directory structure of a Red Hat Linux distribution can also be copied into a network server and installed using NFS, HTTP, or FTP protocols. RPM packages that would be on multiple CDs are merged into a single `RedHat` or `Fedora` directory (depending on which distribution used).

With the installation CDs in hand (or available on a server), you begin the installation process by booting from a CD or floppy disk. The installation program used on Fedora and all other Red Hat Linux distributions is referred to as Anaconda. Here's what happens when you start the installation process:

✦ A kernel is started with a minimum set of installed drivers, and then additional modules are loaded from the initrd (initial RAM disk).

✦ Installation begins using default values (graphical install from CD) or in a mode you enter at the boot prompt. The modes you enter determine if the install is run in text or graphical mode, if installation is done interactively or from a kickstart file, and whether the software is installed from the CD, network server (NFS, HTTP, or FTP), to name a few choices.

You can choose the modes Anaconda can run in to suit your situation. For example, installation normally runs in graphical mode, but you can run it in text mode to skip over any problems you might have with a video card. You can also add kernel options from the installation boot prompt. This can help you overcome some of the most common factors related to installation failures, which are due to unsupported, improperly probed, or buggy computer hardware.

Books such as *Red Hat Linux Bible* and the installation manuals that come with Fedora or Red Hat Linux do a good job of taking you through the steps to install Red Hat Linux distribution. Because our aim here is to help you troubleshoot, the following list is just to remind you of the choices you'll face during Fedora or Red Hat Linux installation:

✦ *Check media*—You are given the option to verify the integrity of each of the CDs in your installation set before starting installation.

✦ *Language*—You need to choose which language to use during installation. You can add other languages later.

✦ *Keyboard*—Different languages and countries use different keyboards. Choosing the wrong keyboard type can result in letters not being where you expect and special characters you need (such as an umlaut or a circumflex not being available).

✦ *Mouse*—Generic mouse selections based on your mouse type (serial, USB, and so on) will probably work in most cases. However, if your mouse device offers a wheel or special buttons, look for an exact match by manufacturer and model to get those features working correctly. Figure 2-1 shows an example of the Mouse Configuration window during Fedora Core installation.

✦ *Monitor*—If you can't find an exact match for your monitor, consider using a generic selection based on screen resolution and monitor type (such as CRT or LCD). If you can't get a selection to work, try some of the options suggested in the troubleshooting tips ahead (such as `vga=`). After that, consider running installation in text mode and dealing with the issue later (see Chapter 7 for information on troubleshooting video cards and monitors). Figure 2-2 shows the Monitor Configuration screen during installation.

✦ *Upgrade or new install*—Issues related to upgrading to Fedora from an earlier Red Hat Linux distribution are described in Chapter 3. Figure 2-3 shows the Upgrade Examine screen during installation.

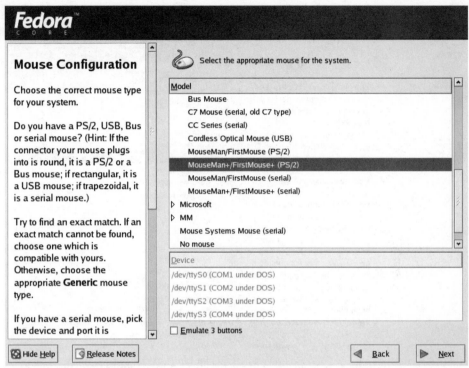

Figure 2-1: When configuring a mouse during installation, select the manufacturer and model number when possible.

✦ *Install type*—Fedora offers special software package groups and configuration settings for Personal Desktop, Workstation, and Server installs. Advanced users typically choose Custom install where they can install everything, a minimum set of packages, or any combination of packages they choose. (Advanced users who repeat the same install process multiple times can use the kickstart feature described in Chapter 4.)

✦ *Disk partitioning*—The Disk Druid screen lets you add, modify, or delete partitions on any of your hard disks. Advanced users can switch to a different virtual console (type Ctrl+Alt+F2) to get to a shell and then use the fdisk command to work with disk partitions. Disk Druid also supports RAID and LVM partitions. If you want to resize a partition as well, you can use the parted command.

✦ *GRUB boot loader*—The GRUB boot loader can be configured so you can launch any bootable partition when you boot your computer. You can add a password to the boot loader (to protect from one who can boot your system) and you can include kernel boot options for special hardware needs. (Kernel boot options are described later in this chapter.)

The LILO boot loader is no longer offered as an option, although you can replace GRUB with LILO by installing the lilo RPM package from CD 3 of the Fedora Core 1 installation set.

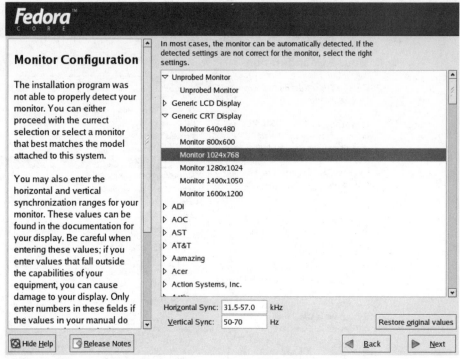

Figure 2-2: If your monitor isn't listed on the Monitor Configuration screen, choose a generic CRT or LCD display option.

✦ *Configure networking*—If your computer has an ethernet interface, you can configure that at install time. You can just leave the defaults in place, so that the computer will be set up as a DHCP client (and automatically start up if there is a DHCP server on the network).

✦ *Firewall*—Red Hat Linux distributions presently all use iptables, by default, to configure firewalls. Selections during installation let you get a same set of rules to begin with (with high, medium, or no firewall security). See Chapter 11 for more information on firewalls. All firewall features on Red Hat Linux distributions use the iptables service by default.

✦ *Additional languages*—You can select to have more languages supported than just the one you chose during installation

✦ *Date and time zone*—If the computer has an Internet connection, you can use network time protocol (NTP) to automatically keep your computer's clock correct. You need to choose your time zone.

✦ *Root password*—At least one user (root) is required for every Linux system. You enter (and verify) the root password here.

✦ *Packages*—With custom installs, you can go through and select the exact set of software packages you want to install.

✦ *Boot disk*—If your computer has a floppy disk drive, you have the option of creating a boot disk (which is recommended).

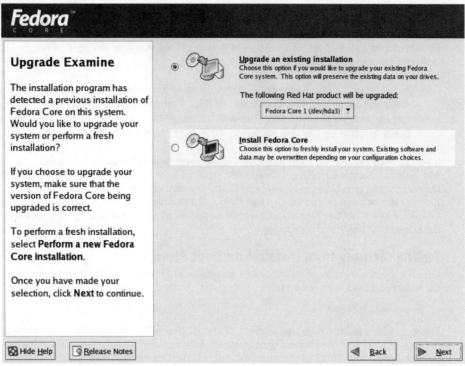

Figure 2-3: Fedora detects an earlier Fedora or Red Hat Linux installation and gives you the option of upgrading.

If installation failed at some point, go through the sections on choosing hardware and troubleshooting installation problems to help track down and solve the problem.

Choosing Hardware

By using computer hardware that is both supported and contains the recommended amount of power (RAM, CPU, and so forth), you have the best chance of successfully installing a Red Hat Linux system. This section presents some of the issues related to making sure you have computer hardware that will work for Fedora and Red Hat Linux systems.

Random Access Memory (RAM)

Having enough RAM installed on your computer is critical to a successful installation of Fedora or Red Hat Linux. Recommended memory amounts for Fedora Core are as follows:

✦ Text mode: 64MB (minimum)

✦ Graphical mode: 192MB (mimimum)

✦ Graphical mode: 256MB (recommended)

If you are running in graphical mode with less than 192MB, you will almost certainly be unhappy with performance at some point. To run a Red Hat Linux system on less than 64MB of RAM, you might consider looking into the RULE project (www.rule-project.org). RULE (Run Up2date Linux Everywhere) is a version of Red Hat Linux that was modified to run on less powerful computers.

> **Note**   According to the RULE project (speaking on an earlier version), Red Hat Linux will absolutely not install with less than 20MB of RAM. Using RULE, the project claims that you can install on a Pentium 200 MHz with 12MB of RAM in about 1 hour. So, if you are trying to install on low-end hardware, RULE might be the way to go.

If you meet or exceed the minimum RAM requirement, in most cases the Anaconda installer will detect it. So, the installation should just work without any special consideration of RAM. However, there are some cases where the kernel cannot detect the actual amount of RAM. In these cases, you can run a memory test to find out how much RAM you actually have (as explained in the next section), then provide an option when you boot the install process to tell the kernel how much memory to use.

Testing Memory from Installation Boot Prompt

To run a memory test, boot from the first installation CD (Fedora or Red Hat Linux). Then type the following at the boot prompt:

```
boot: memtest86
```

The memtest86 feature runs the memtest86 stand-alone memory diagnostic utility. Besides accurately reporting the total amount of available memory, memtest86 also tests for memory failures, level 1 and level2 cache memory, and reserved memory. It also reports on the memory chipset and method used to find memory size (e820 by default). For more information on memtest86, refer to www.memtest86.com.

Checking Memory After Installation

After Fedora or Red Hat Linux is installed, you can find out how much memory is being used by checking /proc/meminfo as follows:

```
$ cat /proc/meminfo
```

> **Note**   You can also view the contents of /proc/meminfo using the free command or the top command.

If you are about to do an upgrade or a fresh install, you can compare the amount shown in the cache size line to the Memory line shown in the memtest86 output. If not all the memory is being detected, you might consider providing the higher amount of RAM as an option when you boot Fedora or Red Hat Linux installation. (See the *Selecting Memory Sizes* section later in this chapter.)

Installation Media (CD-ROM)

CD-ROMs are still the most common medium for installing Linux systems. Red Hat Linux 9 and Fedora Core 1 each comes on a set of three CDs that you can get by downloading from the Internet or with books such as *Red Hat Linux Bible*. If you download the CD ISO images on your own, then burn them on to CDs, here are a few tips to help insure that you make good copies of those media:

✦ Consider purchasing media or getting copies from a friend if you have a dial-up connection. Even a broadband connection will take 1 to 3 hours for each CD to download.

✦ Run the md5sum command on each ISO image. For example, if you downloaded Fedora Core 1 (code-named yarrow), with the images in the current directory, type

```
# md5sum yarrow*iso > myMD5SUM
```

Compare the contents of myMD5SUM to the MD5SUM you downloaded along with the ISO images (MD5SUM is a small text file contained in the same directory as the ISOs).

✦ The most recent recommendation from Red Hat, Inc., for a command line to burn CD is to use the cdrecord command in dao mode. Here's that command line showing how to burn the first Fedora Core 1 CD from the current directory (repeat this step for the other two CDs in the installation set):

```
# cdrecord -v -dao -eject -pad padsize=150s yarrow-i386-disc1.iso
```

✦ If you are burning bad copies, slow down the burn process (even as low as 2× or 4×).

✦ Use CD-R instead of CD-RW media.

Video Cards

If your video card or monitor is improperly detected, the screen may be too garbled to be able to complete installation. Here are some suggestions if the install process is not able to properly probe and configure your video hardware:

✦ *Run the install in text mode (linux text)*—After you boot the computer, you can fix the GUI using redhat-config-xfree86 or the XFree86 tools. As long as you are able to see the screen in text mode, you can continue with the installation. (This issue is addressed in *Failing to Start the Install Process* section later in this chapter.)

✦ *Try setting the vga=option*—If you have a nonstandard size monitor or undetectable video card, you can try to set the vga= option at the boot prompt when you run the install. Laptop computers are particularly at risk for not being detected properly.

Using the vga= option at the boot prompt, Anaconda can use the video BIOS to modify the display mode being used. This takes place before the kernel is even booted to start the install process. To display a list of available VGA settings to choose from, you can boot the install process using the following vga= option:

```
boot: linux vga=ask
```

When you see the first message, press Enter to see a list of VGA settings you can choose from and it will appear as follows:

```
Press <RETURN> to see video modes available.
SPACE to continue or wait 30 secs
Video adapter: VESA VGA
Mode: COLSxROWS:
0    0F00 80x25
1    0F01 80x50
2    0F02 80x43
3    0F03 80x28
```

```
4     OF05 80x30
5     OF06 80x34
6     OF07 80x60
7     0100 40x25
Enter node number or 'scan':
```

You can type scan to scan for additional modes or type a mode number (from 0 to 7 in the example above) to choose a particular mode. As an alternative, you can choose a video mode directly with the vga= option. Table 2-1 contains some examples of vga options and the values they represent.

Table 2-1: VESA Framebuffer Console

VGA Value	Video Modes Each Represents
vga=769	640 × 480 × 256K
vga=771	800 × 600 × 256
vga=773	1024 × 768 × 256K
vga=784	640 × 480 × 32K
vga=785	640 × 480 × 64K
vga=787	800 × 600 × 32K
vga=788	800 × 600 × 64K
vga=790	1024 × 768 × 32K
vga=791	1024 × 768 × 64K

The vga values can also be entered as hexadecimal numbers. Table 2-2 shows the hexadecimal values for different resolutions and numbers of colors (this table is from the Framebuffer HOWTO).

Table 2-2: Setting VGA Modes

Colors	640 × 400	640 × 480	800 × 600	1024 × 768	1152 × 864	1280 × 1024	1600 × 1200
4 bits	?	?	0 × 302	?	?	?	?
8 bits	0 × 300	0 × 301	0 × 303	0 × 305	0 × 161	0 × 307	0 × 31C
15 bits	?	0 × 310	0 × 313	0 × 316	0 × 162	0 × 319	0 × 31D
16 bits	?	0 × 311	0 × 314	0 × 317	0 × 163	0 × 31A	0 × 31E
24 bits	?	0 × 312	0 × 315	0 × 318	?	0 × 31B	0 × 31F
32 bits	?	?	?	?	0 × 164	?	

For more information on VGA modes, refer to the svga.txt file in /usr/src/linux-2.*/ Documentation directory. Refer to Chapter 7 for more in-depth coverage on troubleshooting video cards.

Laptop Problems

Some specific problems known to cause laptop installations to fail in Fedora Core 1 include the following:

✦ *Boot fails on LCD displays*—Some LCD displays may prevent the installation process from starting. To get around the problem you can try disabling the frame buffer as follows:

```
boot: linux nofb
```

✦ *Installation not starting on Sony VAIO notebooks*—You may need to temporarily disable some PCI devices on Sony VAIO notebooks to get Fedora to install properly. Here are options you can try to add to the boot prompt to get installation to work:

```
boot:  linux pci=off idel=0x180,0x386
```

If All Else Fails...

Even the sections you just read will help you take you through the type of hardware and media you should have used to install Fedora or Red Hat Linux; it's quite possible that some hardware that is up to specifications will not work. If you have gone through the information in this chapter and are still having failures installing Linux, I suggest you do the following:

✦ *Bugzilla*—For now, Fedora and other Red Hat Linux distributions all log bug reports into Bugzilla database of Red Hat, Inc.: http://bugzilla.redhat.com. Try searching the Bugzilla database for your computer hardware to see if someone else has had trouble installing on it. If nothing turns up, consider entering a bug report yourself. Then track the bug to see how people on the project respond to the report.

✦ *Google*—Use www.google.com or your favorite search engine to search for the word Linux, along with the name of your motherboard, chipset, or computer model. Although you may not be able to get Linux to install on your particular PC hardware, chances are someone else has tried and has shared their experiences on a website or mailing list somewhere. Googling might tell you about other peoples' results installing on the hardware you have.

✦ *Installation mailing lists*—There are mailing lists devoted to answering questions about Fedora and Red Hat Linux. You can access the Red Hat installation list from www.redhat.com/mailman/listinfo/redhat-install-list. For Fedora, try the general list: www.redhat.com/mailman/listinfo/fedora-list.

Overcoming Installation Problems

This section takes you through common (and some uncommon) failures that can occur during installation and provides advice to get through those problems.

Note   Many of the features for installing Fedora Core or Red Hat Linux are described in detail in *Red Hat Linux Bible*. If you are not familiar with techniques for installing over the network, creating install servers, making boot floppies, doing kickstart installations, and other installation topics, you can find these and other installation topics covered in *Red Hat Linux Bible*. Information on doing kickstart installations is included in Chapter 4.

Failing to Start the Install Process

There are some cases where you don't even make it to the `boot:` prompt on the installation screen. If that's the case, here are a few things you can try:

✦ *CD drive not booting*—Some computers are not set up to boot from a CD. This is more often true of older PCs where you were expected to boot from a floppy disk. You can often fix this problem by changing the BIOS.

To change the BIOS, boot the computer and look early on for a message that tells you how to enter setup (usually by pressing Del, F1, or F2). After entering setup, look for a place to change the boot order so that your CD drive is first on the list of media to boot (at least, before hard disk).

✦ *CD drive not found*—It is possible that the installation process might be able to boot the CD from your IDE (ATAPI) CD drive, but not find the drive when it goes to install Fedora. To get around this problem, you can identify the CD drive from the installation boot prompt. For example, if your CD driverwere the slave drive on your first IDE controller, you could enter the following line to identify your CD drive:

```
boot: linux hdb=cdrom
```

The master on the first IDE controller would be `hda`; the master on the second IDE controller, `hdc`; and the slave on the second IDE controller would be `hdd`.

✦ *Not bootable CD drive*—If there is no way to make your CD drive bootable, you can create a bootable floppy disk image from the Red Hat Linux or Fedora installation media. You can find the bootable floppy disk images on the first Fedora Core CD in the images directory. The README file in that same directory provides a brief description of each image.

✦ *No bootable CD drive or floppy*—An even slimmer possibility is that you have a computer with a nonbootable CD drive and no floppy disk drive at all. In that case, you might be able to boot installation from MS-DOS (that's MS-DOS directly and not from a DOS window in Windows). With DOS running, insert the CD into the CD drive and type the following:

```
C:\ >  D:
D:\ >  cd \ dosutils
D:\ DOSUTILS>  autoboot.bat
```

Another alternative if your computer has a network connection is a Preboot eXecution Environment (PXE) install. To be able to do a PXE install, you must first set up a boot server to let the client boot the necessary install image. (PXE install images are contained on CD 1 for Fedora and Red Hat Linux systems in the images/pxeboot directory.) Then set up an install server (as described in *Red Hat Linux Bible*). If PXE support is built into the network interface card on the machine you want to install from, you can enable PXE in that computer's BIOS. When you boot the computer, select to boot from PXE. When prompted, identify the install method you want to use, and continue as you would with any network install.

Note

There is a white paper from HP on doing a PXE install. You can find it here: http://h18000.www1.hp.com/products/servers/linux/redhat-whitepapers .html. **The Linux on an IBM ThinkPad page** (www.solarblue.net/docs/x31.htm) provides a good description of how to do a PXE install, including how to set up the PXE boot server.

✦ *No CD drive*—If there is no CD drive on the computer, you can install from any of several other media types. By first creating a floppy boot disk (as mentioned in the previous point), you can install from software that is located on an HTTP, FTP, or NFS server. An ethernet card is required for each of those network install types. If you can get copies on to the hard disk, you can install from that medium as well.

✦ *Checking media*—The media could be so bad that you may not even get to a boot prompt. To find out if the medium is truly damaged beyond repair, try inserting the first boot CD into any running computer (Linux or Windows) and try to browse the contents of the CD. If you can access the CD and some of the files on that CD, chances are that you should be able to boot the CD. (The CD could still be corrupted, but you can find that out with a media check when you boot the install process.)

✦ *Screen is unreadable*—My first suggestion to installing on a machine where the GUI is unreadable is to run the installation in text mode:

```
boot: linux text
```

Some experienced system administrators prefer text-based installs because it allows them to deal with their video cards after the operating system is installed. Instead of having the system boot to runlevel 5 with a GUI that may or may not work, the computer will boot runlevel 3 (text login prompt) and let the administrator get the GUI going on a working system.

Note

I always do a text-based install when I have an NVIDIA-based card since I know I'm going to replace the video driver after installation with an NVIDIA proprietary driver.

If you are having trouble with the screen not being readable in text mode, there are some ways of telling the install process something about your graphical hardware. See the description of the `vga=` option earlier in this chapter for further information.

From the Boot Prompt

If you are able to successfully boot the Fedora Core or Red Hat Linux CD, you should see the installation boot screen (with a `boot:` prompt at the bottom). In most cases, you will choose from one of the following two installation types:

✦ *Graphical installation*—If you just press Enter (or wait a few seconds for it to start automatically), Fedora Core 1 will start up the graphical installation process and expect to install the software from the three-CD set. This is the default way to install Red Hat Linux systems.

✦ *Text-based install*—If you have a low memory computer, unsupported graphics card, or simply don't feel the need for colors and icons, you can do a text-based install. To start a text-based install, type `linux text` from the boot prompt.

Starting the installation process essentially means booting a small Linux kernel that, in turn, runs the Anaconda installer. Because you are starting an install process, there are several different install-related options you can add to direct how the installation process should behave. Likewise, you can also pass options to the kernel that can specifically tell the kernel about how to deal with your hardware (especially if the installation process is unable to properly detect your hardware).

Trying Red Hat Installation Options

The following points describe different problems that can arise during installation and that you might be able to correct by trying different options from the installation boot prompt.

✦ *Corrupted CDs*—Before you install Fedora Core or Red Hat Linux from CD, you can verify that the contents of the CD have not been damaged by running mediacheck from the boot prompt. Even if you have no reason to suspect that the CDs are bad, checking the entire set of CDs can help you avoid having to deal with a partially completed installation.

The mediacheck performs an md5sum checksum of the contents of any of the Red Hat installation CDs you provide. Because the exact same content (an ISO image) is used in an NFS or hard disk install, mediacheck allows you to validate those installation media as well. To start mediacheck from a boot prompt, type

```
boot:  linux mediacheck
```

✦ *CD-ROM installation hangs transferring disk image*—When booting from a CD, it is possible that your computer will hang with the message "Transferring Install Image to Hard Disk." There are two recommended courses to try: Turning on DMA for your CD or turning it off completely for your system. To turn on DMA for your CD, type the following from the installation boot prompt:

```
boot:  linux allowcddma
```

Note

To run the same option for a text-based install, type `linux text allowcddma`. **This also applies to any other option you want to add to a text-based install type.**

To try turning off DMA (during installation at least) to fix the problem, type the following at the boot prompt:

```
boot:  linux nodma
```

With DMA turned off, installation will go slower, but failures may be less likely to occur. After Linux is installed, you may want to remove the `nodma` option from the `/boot/grub/grub.conf` file to see if your computer can run with DMA on (to improve performance).

One reported fix for this problem is also to reduce the amount of memory on computers (either by physically removing one of the RAM sticks or by making less memory available using the `mem=` option). See the *Selecting Memory Sizes* section later in this chapter for information on the `mem` option.

✦ *Hangs when installing on SMP system*—If your computer hangs while trying to install on a system with multiple processors, you can try disabling IO-APIC. The `noapic` option causes an SMP kernel to disable some interrupt controller features on multiprocessor computers. Here's how to disable IO-APIC:

```
boot:  linux noapic
```

If your board doesn't create a working multiprocessor table, you might be able to create one manually using the pirq boot option. For information on how to do this, refer to the `IO-APIC.txt` file in the `/usr/src/linux-2.*/Documentation` directory.

✦ *Hangs probing PCMCIA devices*—You can disable the probing of PCMCIA devices by adding the `nopcmcia` option as follows:

```
boot:  linux nopcmcia
```

✦ *Hangs probing Firewire devices*—You can disable the probing of Firewire devices by adding the `nofirewire` option as follows:

```
boot:  linux nofirewire
```

✦ *Hardware not detected (or improperly detected)*—The Anaconda installer does an amazingly good job of probing and identifying your computer's hardware. However, if you have reason to suspect that your hardware is not being properly identified, you can boot using the `noprobe` option.

Before you start a noprobe install, you should know what hardware you have in your computer. If the drivers are not on the CD, you need to have the drivers you need available on floppy. Here's how to start a noprobe install:

```
boot:  linux noprobe
```

When prompted, you need to select the drivers to match your hardware or provide the drivers yourself on a floppy.

✦ *No floppy to start network or hard disk install*—Earlier releases of Red Hat Linux required that you create a boot floppy to start an FTP, HTTP, NFS, or hard disk install (assuming, I suppose, that if you have a CD-ROM drive you can just install from there). In Fedora Core 1 (and other recent Red Hat Linux distributions), you can start a network or hard disk install from the first installation CD boot prompt using the `askmethod` option as follows:

```
boot:  linux askmethod
```

After entering your language and keyboard type, the installation screen asks you to select the type of install (HTTP, FTP, NFS, or hard disk). You might want to do this to save yourself from the trouble of inserting each CD.

✦ *Unable to upgrade*—Any change to the `/etc/fedora-release` or `/etc/redhat-release` files (depending on which system you are upgrading from) may cause the upgrade process to fail to offer you the chance to upgrade your system to your chosen version of Fedora. If that is the case, you can force Fedora to allow you to upgrade by entering the `upgradeany` option at the boot prompt as follows:

```
boot:  linux upgradeany
```

Trying Kernel Installation Options

There are literally hundreds of options you can pass to the kernel when you begin installation. While we go over some of those options here, you can find a more complete list in the documentation that comes with the kernel source code. For Fedora Core 1, refer to the following file for descriptions of kernel options:

```
/usr/src/linux-2.*/Documentation/kernel-parameters.txt
```

Options you can pass to the kernel are also described, in some detail, in the BootPrompt HOWTO. You can find that document here

```
http://www.ibiblio.org/mdw/HOWTO/text/BootPrompt-HOWTO
```

Documentation associated with particular drivers can be found in files and subdirectories of the /usr/src/linux-2*/Documentation directory. For the most part, you will not need to add module-specific options to the installation boot prompt. Special settings that need to be done to individual drivers can be done after installation (see Chapter 6 for information on adding loadable modules).

Caution   While most options that you can pass to the kernel from the boot prompt will cause no harm, some have the potential for damaging your hardware. For example, some improper video settings can damage your video card and options that effect CPU activity (such as no-hlt) can result in overheating.

In most cases, you don't need to enter any kernel options to get the Fedora or Red Hat Linux installation to work. Hardware will be detected properly and same defaults will be set. However, cases where you would want to add kernel parameters include the following:

✦ *Not able to probe*—In some cases, the kernel is not able to properly identify the hardware you are using or fully determine the features it does or doesn't support.

✦ *Extra tuning*—Some options that can be passed to the kernel can be used to tune your kernel to make most efficient use of your hardware.

✦ *Override the defaults*—You may want to access hardware in a different way than it is used by default (for example, to change the default screen resolution).

Once you find kernel options that work during installation, write down those options. You may need to add those same options to the kernel boot process after Fedora or Red Hat Linux is installed so that your system can boot properly (see the *Adding Kernel Options After Installation* section later in this chapter).

The following sections break down different kernel options you can use at the boot prompt for Fedora and Red Hat Linux installation.

Selecting Memory Sizes

Sometimes CPU bugs, old BIOS limitations, and other issues can prevent Linux from properly detecting the amount of memory available on your computer. Not having all available memory useable by the install process can considerably slow down the install process. The cachesize= and mem= options can be used to tell the kernel how much memory to use during the install process.

Note   Before you start installing, you can test the amount of available memory using the memory test feature. See the *Random Access Memory* section earlier in this chapter for information on using the memtest feature from the installation boot prompt.

✦ *Set CPU cache size*—If the kernel can't determine the cache size correctly from the CPU (typically because of a CPU bug), you can override the level two CPU cache size and enter the proper amount in kilobytes. Here's an example where the level two cache is set to 512kB:

```
boot:  linux cachesize=512k
```

Be sure to not set this number higher than the actual available level two CPU cache size.

✦ *Set memory size*—If you have added memory to an older machine (beyond the 64MB limit originally defined in PC BIOS), the boot process may not detect that fact. Using the mem= option, you can set how much memory the kernel has available to it. Don't set this number higher than the actual amount of RAM available or your computer will crash at some point.

Changing Power Mode Options

The `hlt` instructions tell CPU to change modes to use less power. The CPU essentially goes to sleep during some periods of disuse. Some older processors, particularly 486 processors, had problems coming out of this low-power mode. If you think this is the case for you, try entering `no-hlt` to the linux boot prompt as follows:

```
boot:  linux no-hlt
```

One downside to using the `no-hlt` option is that the CPU stays on continuously. This could cause the CPU to overheat, especially in situations where you are overclocking the processor.

Some laptops have bugs in battery query support. If the machine crashes while entering a graphical install, you can try turning off advanced power management support as follows:

```
boot:  linux apm=off
```

Partitioning Problems

When you create the disk partitions on which you install your Fedora or Red Hat Linux system, you need to make sure that those partitions provide enough space not only for the current installation, but also for the space you need for data. Here are some tips related to partitioning your hard disk:

✦ *Allow enough total space*—An Everything installation of Fedora Core 1 can take up about 5GB of disk space. So, you need to allow at least that much space plus room for your data if you do a complete installation.

✦ *Allow enough space for installation on each partition*—If you separate your hard disk into multiple partitions to keep areas of the files system, be sure to allow enough space in each partition to handle the data needed. For example, some parts of the file system you may want to assign to their own partitions are /bin, /var, /home, /usr, and /tmp.

   If you have 5GB available for a full install, but separate that space evenly across several partitions, chances are you will not have enough disk space where you need it. For example, /usr can require most of that 5GB of disk space itself, while /bin may require about 5MB of disk space.

✦ *Allow enough space for data on each partition*—If you are splitting up partitions on your hard disk, be sure that you have taken account of the amount of space you need for data. Typically, content for your Web server, FTP server, and other data servers are contained under your /var directory. User data tends to be store under the /home directory.

✦ *Allow for overhead*—An ext3 journaling file system (the default file system typed used by Fedora and Red Hat Linux systems), requires about 30MB of overhead for each partition. You need to take that into account if you are creating multiple partitions for your Linux installation.

✦ *The /boot partition*—Although a 100MB partition is recommended for Fedora, you can get by with a much smaller boot partition if you are tight on space. A typical bootable linux kernel will consume between 1 and 4MB of disk space. So even with several different kernels, if the space is tight you can probably get by with as little as 20MB of space in /boot.

General Installation Troubleshooting Tips

This section contains some random tips to help you through the installation process.

✦ *Escaping to virtual consoles*—During installation, it's possible to find out more about what is happening with the installation process than you can see from the main install screens. Using a set of Ctrl+Alt keystrokes, you can switch to different virtual terminals to see installation-related messages or even go to a shell prompt to run commands. Table 2-3 shows different key sequences (hold Ctrl and Alt keys as you press a function key).

Note   You can use these same key sequences to switch between virtual consoles after installation is completed. You can use these virtual consoles to have multiple login sessions, even while a graphical desktop is running.

Table 2-3: Keys for Switching Virtual Terminals

Keys	Terminal
Ctrl+Alt+F1	Virtual console 1: Contains running installation dialog
Ctrl+Alt+F2	Virtual console 2: Offers shell prompt to run commands as root user
Ctrl+Alt+F3	Virtual console 3: Shows install log messages from installation program
Ctrl+Alt+F4	Virtual console 4: Displays system-related messages
Ctrl+Alt+F5	Virtual console 5: Displays other messages
Ctrl+Alt+F7	Virtual console 7: Return to graphical installation screen

✦ *Changing partitions with* fdisk *or* parted—Advanced users can use the parted, fdisk, or sfdisk commands to change partitions during the installation process itself. You do this by changing to a virtual console (Ctrl+Alt+F2) to get to a shell, then simply typing the command. Some features available through fdisk are not offered with Disk Druid; for example, more file system types are available through fdisk. Disk Druid also cannot resize partitions as parted can.

✦ *Getting help during installation*—During the installation process, you can view online help text by pressing F1, F2, F3, F4, F5, or F6 buttons. Each provides a different type of help information.

✦ *Reading Release Notes*—There is a lot of excellent information about the installation process in the Fedora Release Notes. To view the Release Notes from within any GUI install screen, click the Release Notes button on the bottom of the screen.

✦ *Grabbing install screens*—During graphical installs you can grab screenshots of any installation screen. To do this, press Shift+Print Screen to save the current screen to hard disk. You can repeat this as many times as you like. When installation is completed, you can find the screenshot(s) in the /root/anaconda-screenshots directory. (This feature is not supported in text-based installs.)

✦ *Get the* `ks.cfg` *file for kickstart*—You can use a kickstart file to answer installation questions, so you can run unattended installations of Fedora Core or Red Hat Linux distributions. After you have installed Fedora or Red Hat Linux, a file named `anaconda-ks.cfg` is created in the `/root` directory. You can use that kickstart file to reproduce the installation you just completed on another computer.

Later, you can edit the `anaconda-ks.cfg` file with any text editor. You can also use the `redhat-config-kickstart` window to modify that file or create a new kickstart file.

Note

Refer to Chapter 4 for information on using the kickstart feature to create your own custom installs that you can use to automate the installation process for many computers.

Getting Linux to Boot After Installation

You may find that after you have finished installing Fedora or Red Hat Linux, your system will not boot. There are several things you can try if that is the case. The first suggestion would be to pass options to the kernel. After that, you can try to go into rescue mode to correct the problem.

Adding Kernel Options After Installation

If you need to add options to the kernel to get the installation process to work, you may also need to pass those same options to the kernel after the operating system is installed. Otherwise, some piece of hardware may not work properly or the entire boot process may fail. You can try out kernel options before you add them permanently to your boot loader configuration file. Procedures for adding kernel options temporarily and permanently are described in the following two sections.

Adding Options at Boot Time

To try out kernel options before adding them permanently, do the following:

1. Reboot your computer.

2. When you see the boot screen (GRUB by default), quickly press the arrow key to highlight the operating system you want to boot.

3. Press e to be able to edit the boot lines for that operating system.

4. Move the cursor to highlight the kernel line and press e to edit the kernel line.

5. With the cursor at the end of the kernel line, type the options you want to add and press Enter.

6. Press b to continue the boot process, including the new options.

If the options you added fixed your problem, you can consider adding them to your boot loader configuration file so that they can be used permanently. The following section describes how to add kernel options to the GRUB boot loader.

Adding Options to the GRUB Boot Loader

If you have decided that you want to permanently add boot options to your computer, and you are using the GRUB boot loader, you can put those options directly into the `/boot/grub/grub.conf` file. The following example shows what a grub.conf looks like:

```
# grub.conf generated by anaconda
#
# Note that you do not have to rerun grub after making changes to this file
# NOTICE: You have a /boot partition. This means that
#         all kernel and initrd paths are relative to /boot/, eg.
#         root (hd0,0)
#         kernel /vmlinuz-version ro root=/dev/hda6
#         initrd /initrd-version.img
#boot=/dev/hda
default=0
timeout=13
splashimage=(hd0,0)/grub/splash.xpm.gz
title Fedora Core (2.4.22-1.2115.nptl)
root (hd0,0)
kernel /vmlinuz-2.4.22-1.2115.nptl ro root=LABEL=/ hdb=ide-scsi
initrd /initrd-2.4.22-1.2115.nptl.img
```

If you want to add boot options to this file, you can put them right at the end of the kernel line. For example, if you wanted to tell the kernel to use 256MB of RAM, you could add the mem=256M option to the end of the kernel line so that it appears as follows:

```
kernel /vmlinuz-2.4.22-1.2115.nptl ro root=LABEL=/ hdb=ide-scsi mem=256M
```

When Fedora boots, the mem= values will be read and the kernel will attempt to use the assigned amount of memory.

Entering Rescue Mode

The same boot CD you used to install Fedora Core or Red Hat Linux can be used to boot your computer in rescue mode. To enter rescue mode, insert the CD and boot the computer as you would start a regular installation. When the boot prompt appears, type the following:

```
boot: linux rescue
```

Rescue mode does what it can to start up a network connection for your computer, locate your Fedora or Red Hat Linux installation, and mount the file system so that you access your files. If you can access your computer file system at that point, you can try to modify your configuration files to get Fedora to boot.

The first thing you should do is change the root directory to /mnt/sysimage (where the rescue CD should have put the root directory of your Fedora Core installation). To do that, type

```
# chroot /mnt/sysimage
```

With your file system now accessible as it would be during a regular system boot, you can try to correct whatever problem is preventing your system from starting up properly. The things you might want to do include the following:

✦ *Disabling services that may be hanging the computer*—If there is a service keeping your computer from booting, you can simply disable it. For example, once you have access to a shell, you could disable the Samba service by typing

```
# chkconfig smb off
```

The next time you boot your computer, it will not try to start the Samba service.

✦ *Change the default run level*—If the GUI is not starting up or crashing, you can edit the /etc/inittab file to make the default a text-based login. If the initdefault line is booting to state 5, change the line to read as follows so it will boot to init 3:

```
id:3:initdefault:
```

✦ *Add boot options*—You can edit the /etc/grub/grub.conf file to add options to the kernel line, as described in the preceding section.

Installation Troubleshooting Reference

Table 2-4 lists some resources where you can find more information on troubleshooting Fedora and Red Hat Linux installation.

Table 2-4: Red Hat Linux and Fedora Installation Information

Resource	Location
Anaconda installer project	http://fedora.redhat.com/projects/anaconda-installer
Installation guides	**Red Hat Enterprise Linux Installation Guides:** www.redhat.com/docs/manuals/enterprise
	Red Hat Linux Installation Guides: www.redhat.com/docs/manuals/linux
Red Hat installation mailing lists	www.redhat.com/mailman/listinfo/redhat-install-list
Anaconda documentation in Fedora	/usr/share/doc/anaconda-9.2/
Anaconda development mailing list	www.redhat.com/mailman/listinfo/anaconda-devel-list
Kickstart mailing list	www.redhat.com/mailman/listinfo/kickstart-list

Summary

Fedora and Red Hat Linux operating systems rely on the Anaconda installer to handle the installation of the operating system. Both graphical and text-based installation processes are supported, as are different installation methods (including CD, NFS, HTTP, FTP, and hard disk installs).

Linux has improved dramatically in recent years in its ability to properly probe and configure hardware during installation. In those cases where Linux cannot detect your hardware or you want to fine-tune how hardware is configured, you can pass options to the installation process from the boot prompt.

Updating and Upgrading Fedora

One of the most overlooked aspects of running a Linux system is keeping it up to date. Keeping a system up to date involves installing new versions of the software on your system. This can seem like a daunting task, given the huge amount of software included with Fedora Core. Luckily, there are automated updating systems both included with Fedora Core and available for Fedora Core as a third-party add-on.

Another process that needs attention is upgrading of your existing Red Hat Linux to Fedora Core. This process involves obtaining the installation media, performing the upgrade, and verifying your software.

Sometimes upgrading a system is more of a challenge than you want to handle, or maybe you've just gotten too comfortable with your current version to change to a new one. This chapter provides some information that helps you keep your legacy Red Hat Linux system running strong.

Keeping Fedora Core Up to Date

Because no software is perfect, software developers are constantly trying to find ways to improve and enhance their products. The two most important reasons you should be vigilant about updating your system are *security* and *stability*.

- ✦ *Security*—With the ever-growing popularity of Linux, discovering and correcting the security vulnerabilities of the software used on Linux systems becomes paramount. The fixes that emerge are made available to the community by your distribution vendor in the package format chosen for that distribution. Fedora Core is no different. Updates are provided in RPM format for end-user consumption.

- ✦ *Stability*—Bugfix updates, while of lower priority than are security updates, are still very important as they directly affect the stability of your system. For the most part, minor bugs are fixed upstream by the software developers and do not spawn an update rpm for the current Fedora Core release. As the severity of the bug increases, so does the possibility of an update rpm being issued for the current Fedora Core release.

There are many ways to keep your Fedora Core system up to date. These include:

✦ *Automated updates*—Using tools that automate the installation of updates, as well as resolving dependencies for the updates. These methods can be totally automated (with scheduled times for automatically processing updates), or triggered manually.

✦ *Manual updates*—Manually seeking out available updates and processing them by hand. This method is satisfactory for single updates, but becomes tiresome when you need to handle lots of updates and/or large numbers of systems.

✦ *Source updates*—Using source code to update existing software. This method may be useful when you need an update before a new package is made available, but it is also highly discouraged as it will lead to the irrelevance (what's actually on your system doesn't match what's in your RPM database) of your package management system as it's only able to track what you install/update in RPM format.

Caution

While it may seem on the surface that source installs will make only that package irrelevant in your RPM database, all the packages that rely on this package or interact with it will also suffer from expecting one version of the package while a newer version is installed via source. This can cause a cascading effect as you gradually replace more and more packaged software with source to overcome the irrelevance of that first single package. While this may not happen with every user or package, it's necessary to warn against it.

Using Automated Updates

The preferred method of keeping your Fedora Core system up to date is with automated update tools. Two such tools are included with Fedora Core: up2date and yum.

up2date

up2date is the familiar Red Hat-developed tool that has both a command-line interface and a graphical user interface (GUI). up2date has been given some pretty significant enhancements with Fedora Core, including the ability to access yum, apt-rpm, and dir repositories. (yum and apt-rpm are discussed later in this chapter.) While up2date is technically able to communicate with Red Hat Network (RHN), currently there are no Fedora Core channels available at RHN and thus this functionality is wholly unused.

To go along with these new features, up2date has a new configuration file. Given that RHN functionality is no longer used in Fedora Core, you can safely ignore all other up2date configuration files, save the new one. This file holds a list of the yum/apt-rpm/dir repository you wish to use. The format is one repository entry per line. The first word on each line reflects the type of repository. The `/etc/sysconfig/rhn/sources` file contains the following active entries:

```
yum fedora-core-1 http://fedora.redhat.com/releases/fedora- core-1
yum updates-released
http://fedora.redhat.com/updates/released/fedora-core-1
```

The first line shows a yum style repository named `fedora-core-1` for the base OS packages (all the packages you'd find on Fedora Core CDs 1–3). The second line shows another yum style repository named `updates-released` for the released updates for Fedora Core 1. You can add as many repository lines as you wish, even linking to third-party repository for all your extra software.

Note

> There's a line in /etc/sysconfig/rhn/sources **that contains** up2date default. **It is safe to ignore this line, which is a vestigial artifact of the development process. If you want the full explanation, read on.**
>
> **The line is for use with RHN servers. It is included, and the client supports RHN servers, because at the time of the initial beta cycles, the decision had not yet been made as to whether RHN would carry Fedora content. The decision was later made not to carry Fedora content, but the application still supports RHN protocol.**

Each repository type has its own syntax. The syntax of each repository that can appear in the sources file used by up2date is covered in Table 3-1.

Table 3-1: up2date Sources Syntax

Repository Type	Syntax	Example*
yum	Type + channel-label + url	yum fedora-core-1 http://fedora.redhat.com/releases/ fedora-core-1
apt	Type + channel-label + service:server + path + repo-name	apt arjan-2.6-kernel http://people .redhat.com~arjan/2.5 kernel
dir	Type + repo-label + path	dir my-local-rpms /home/buildman/RPMS/

* Each repository name should be one line, with no breaks.

Multiple versions of all repositories can be used, aside from RHN repositories. Dependencies can be resolved *cross-repository* if need be, meaning that if you wish to install a package from one configured repository, and it requires a package located in a different repository, the second package can be found and installed from within its repository. This means that each repository does not have to be self-hosting, and can depend on other repositories to fulfill package requirements.

By default, up2date is configured to use the yum repository at fedora.redhat.com. If you've used up2date in the past, the usage syntax has not changed, even though the backend repository has. To check for available updates, type

```
#  /usr/sbin/up2date -l
```

or

```
#  /usr/sbin/up2date --list
```

If you are using a GUI when you first call up2date, it will bring up a screen to help you configure up2date. Each option is self-explanatory, and most often the defaults will suffice. It will also bring up a box asking you to import the Fedora GPG key into your rpm keyring. This will allow rpm to make an extra check of the package validity.

The next time you run up2date (configured for yum) it will need some time to download all the available package headers from the repository. Do not be alarmed if up2date seems to stall; check for network activity before killing any processes.

If there are any updates available, up2date will list them for you. You can update them individually, or choose to install all available updates. To update a single package, type

```
#   /usr/sbin/up2date -u  package
```

where *package* is the update you want to install.

Caution   When using up2date to update single packages, beware that if the package you pass to up2date is not currently installed, up2date will install that package, and any dependencies it may need.

If you wish to process all the available updates at once, just type

```
#   /usr/sbin/up2date -u
```

If you use the GNOME or KDE desktop environments, you'll have a panel icon that can look like a blue ball with a white checkmark, or like a red ball with a white exclamation point, depending on whether any updates are available. This is the Red Hat Network Alert Notification Tool. This tool uses the repositories configured in /etc/sysconfig/rhn/sources to periodically check for available updates, changing from the blue check (no updates available) to the red exclamation point (updates available). Clicking the icon brings up a window that shows available updates and allows you to launch a graphical up2date interface to process the available updates.

This interface does not offer as much functionality as the command-line interface, but can be used to check for updates and install individual updates or all available updates. Figure 3-1 shows the graphical up2date with an update available, and Figure 3-2 shows the graphical up2date downloading an update.

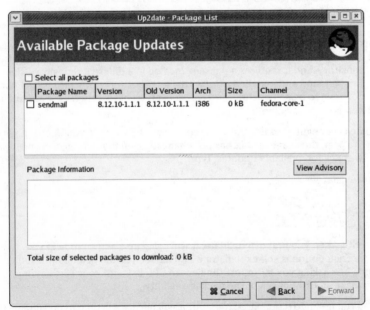

Figure 3-1: Graphical up2date with an update available.

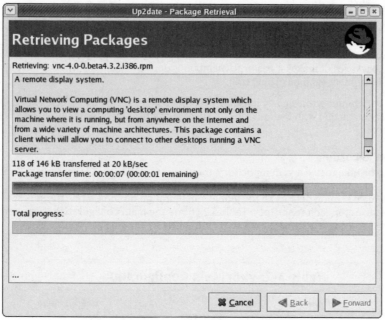

Figure 3-2: Graphical up2date downloading an update.

Once you understand the basics of what up2date does, you might want to look into some of the extra features that come with it. Here are a few tips and tricks that might interest you:

✦ *Package search*—up2date has the ability to display all the packages available for download. The command to see this is up2date—showall. You can pipe the output of this through grep to search for a specific package or packages.

✦ *Source package retrival*—up2date can retrieve a given srpm without trying to resolve dependencies. This option is -get-src.

✦ *Force install*—up2date by default is set to skip kernel packages. To override this setting without editing the /etc/sysconfig/rhn/up2date configuration file, you can supply the -f flag on the command line. This will force up2date to ignore package exclusion rules and install/update what you ask it to.

✦ *Test run*—up2date can be ran in a test mode, where it will process its task without actually doing the task. This can help you see the expected outcome of a complicated task without actually making any changes. The option for this is -dry-run.

There are many more options and configurations for up2date. Consult the up2date man page and the core configuration file /etc/sysconfig/rhn/up2date for more information.

yum

yum stands for *Yellowdog Updater, Modified*. You could say that yum started its life as a tool called *yup* or *Yellowdog Updater* for the Yellowdog Linux distribution. Yellowdog Linux is a

Linux distribution built for Apple hardware and based on Red Hat Linux. The description of yum from its home page (http://linux.duke.edu/projects/yum) is:

> yum is an automatic updater and package installer/remover for rpm systems. It automatically computes dependencies and figures out what things should occur to install packages. It makes it easier to maintain groups of machines without having to manually update each one using rpm.

Originally a very popular third-party package management tool, yum was officially included in Red Hat systems starting with Fedora Core 1. One of yum's best features is how easy it is to set up a yum server.

Using a yum Repository

For clients to be able to use a yum repository, they need to define that repository in their /etc/yum.conf configuration file. There are two sections to this configuration file: main and servers. The main section defines all the global configuration options, while the server section defines the entries for each repository. Table 3-2 shows the main configuration items and their default values. You can read more about these and other options on the yum.conf man page.

Table 3-2: yum Main Configuration

Options	Usage	Default Value
Cachedir	Directory that holds the cached header info	/var/cache/yum
Debuglevel	Controls the amount of debug output	2
Logfile	File that yum log into	/var/log/yum.log
Pkgpolicy	Package sorting order (for use with multiple repositories)	newest (install the newest version found)
Distroverpkg	Package used to determine distribution release	fedora-release
Tolerant	How to treat errors on the command-line options	0 (not tolerant)
Exactarch	Force yum to be strict with package archs	1 (enabled)

Following the main options is the repository configuration section. This section lists the repositories one by one, each usually in a three-line set per repository. The first line is the serverid, contained in square ([ ]) brackets. This must be a unique name, all one word. The next line holds the human readable name for the repository. This is the name you'll see on the command line. The syntax for this line is name=My Repository Name. The final line is the actual URL to the repository. This can be in the form of http://, ftp://, or file://. The syntax is baseurl=url://server/path/to/repository.

Note   Don't forget the third slash (/) when defining a file-based repository, for example, baseurl=file:///var/packages.

You can also specify more than one URL, to set up a failover array of URLs, by just adding more URL lines. (Don't add another `baseurl` line or you'll get bizarre results from yum) By default, there are two servers configured for your Fedora system.

See Appendix A for a list of third-party repositories you can use with your Fedora Core system and yum. yum repositories can be added to your `/etc/yum.conf` file. Please consult the yum.conf man page as well as `/etc/yum.conf` for examples.

Now that you have your configuration file just the way you like it, it's time to actually use the application. yum is incredibly simple to use; simplicity is one of its strong points, and one of the goals behind the development of yum. To check for available updates, type the following:

```
# /usr/bin/yum list updates
```

If there are any updates available, yum will list them for you. You can update them individually, or choose to install all available updates. To update a single package type

```
# /usr/bin/yum update  package
```

where *package* is the update you want to install. In order to process all the available updates at once, type

```
# /usr/bin/yum update
```

This command will ask you to verify that you wish to install each update. This can get very tiresome if there are a lot of updates available. To assume yes for every question, pass yum the `-y` option. This will make yum fully automatic.

Setting Up a yum Server

Setting up your own yum server has many benefits. Updates can be downloaded once to a local system, and then other local systems can update from it, saving wasted bandwidth from duplicate downloads. Custom repositories can be created with special content. Repositories can be created for systems that don't ship with yum.

There is no specific protocol for yum. yum supports http, ftp, local directory, and just about any remote file system protocol. There is no specific directory structure either. You can create any kind of file structure, and just make the top directory (and the subdirectories) available by one of the available protocols. The following instructions show how to set up a yum repository on an HTTP server.

1. Copy the software packages to the directory structure you want to use. Assuming the packages you want are in the current directory, you could type

   ```
   # mkdir /var/www/html/mypackages-1
   # cp *.rpm /var/www/html/mypackages-1
   ```

2. Create the metadata needed by the yum client as follows:

   ```
   # yum-arch /var/www/html/mypackages-1/
   ```

3. Enable the httpd server if you haven't already done so.

As shown in the code example, `yum-arch` takes one main argument: the location of the RPMS you want to scan for. This argument will scan from the argument directory down through all its subdirectories, gathering information about all the RPMs it finds along the way. `yum-arch` will create a directory named `headers/`. This directory holds the compressed RPM header information. This directory tree is now ready to be a yum repository.

Tips on Using yum

Although on the surface yum appears to be a simple tool, it is remarkably powerful and useful. Here are a few neat things that yum supports:

✦ *Package information*—yum has the ability to display a package summary and description, even if the package is not installed. The option for this is `info`. It takes a package name or names as arguments, for example, `# /usr/bin/yum info kernel`.

✦ *Package removal*—yum has the ability to remove packages, as well as any other packages that might depend on the package you're trying to remove. This can be extremely handy when trying to slim down an installation base. This option is `remove`. It takes a package name or names as arguments, for example, `# /usr/bin/yum remove gimp`.

✦ *Alternative configuration file*—yum can be told to use an alternative configuration file for an operation. This comes in handy when you need to use a separate repository that is not normally used. Also, with yum's ability to read a configuration file over the Internet (http/ftp), you can maintain a single configuration file for an entire work group of computers, minimizing maintenance tasks when needing to make changes to yum's configuration. The option to use a different configuration file is `-c` and it takes a file location or an http/ftp file location as its argument, for example, `# /usr/bin/yum -c http://mywebserver/myyumconf.conf update`.

yum also supports some advanced features like package group operations and package listing options. For more information consult the yum and yum.conf man pages and the `/etc/yum.conf` configuration file.

Manual Updates

In some situations, you may prefer manual updates to automatic updates. This could be because you wish to quickly update a critical package without waiting for a possibly lengthy update program to run, or you wish to update a system that does not have any external Internet access.

In order to update your system manually, you'll need to know what updates are available and where you can download them from. Typically you can use the location of available updates to glean what updates are available, just by looking at the packages within the updates directory. There is also a Red Hat-sponsored mailing list setup for update announcements at `www.redhat.com/mailman/listinfo/fedora-announce-list`. This page also has an archive of past messages sent to the list.

Messages sent to this list have two main formats. One format is for security-related updates, and the other format is for non-security-related updates. Listing 3-1 shows a security update for the Linux kernel, and Listing 3-2 shows a nonsecurity update for the kernel as well.

Listing 3-1: **Security-Related Update**

```
From: Dave Jones <davej redhat com>
To: fedora-announce-list redhat com
```

Subject: [SECURITY] Updated kernel resolves security vulnerability
Date: Tue, 6 Jan 2004 13:18:20 +0000

Fedora Update Notification
FEDORA-2003-046
2004-01-05

Name   : kernel
Version   : 2.4.22
Release   : 1.2138.nptl
Summary   : The Linux kernel (the core of the Linux operating system)
Description :The kernel package contains the Linux kernel (vmlinuz), the
core of your Red Hat Linux operating system. The kernel handles the basic
functions of the operating system: memory allocation, process allocation,
device input and output, etc.

Paul Starzetz discovered a flaw in bounds checking in mremap() in the Linux
kernel versions 2.4.23 and previous which may allow a local attacker to
gain root privileges. No exploit is currently available; however, it is
believed that this issue is exploitable (although not trivially.) The
Common Vulnerabilities and Exposures project (cve.mitre.org) has assigned
the name CAN-2003-0985 to this issue.

All users are advised to upgrade to these errata packages, which contain a
backported security patch that corrects this issue.

Red Hat would like to thank Paul Starzetz from ISEC for disclosing this
issue as well as Andrea Arcangeli and Solar Designer for working on the
patch.

These packages also contain a fix for a minor information leak in the real
time clock (rtc) routines. The Common Vulnerabilities and Exposures project
(cve.mitre.org) has assigned the name CAN-2003-0984 to this issue.

----
* Wed Dec 24 2003 Dave Jones <davej redhat com>
- Fix mremap corner case.

* Tue Dec 23 2003 Dave Jones <davej redhat com>
- Numerous USB fixes (#110307, #90442, #107929, #110872)

* Tue Dec 16 2003 Dave Jones <davej redhat com>
- Fix leak in CDROM IOCTL. (#112249)

This update can be downloaded from:
  http://download.fedora.redhat.com/pub/fedora/linux/core/updates/1/

Continued

Listing 3-1: *(continued)*

```
c9a94fe6d6a3cffb2604a17bf42839e2 SRPMS/kernel-2.4.22-1.2138.nptl.src.rpm
841d46869237a9acce1c5e667e13807e i386/kernel-source-2.4.22-
1.2138.nptl.i386.rpm
ad2e530db065ddc5cceef49ff825d606 i386/kernel-doc-2.4.22-
1.2138.nptl.i386.rpm
ed345bd737557d25437d8a06ff10c6ed i386/kernel-BOOT-2.4.22-
1.2138.nptl.i386.rpm
bc4dab2573386726679014c6fa2eb059 i386/debug/kernel-debuginfo-2.4.22-
1.2138.nptl.i386.rpm
88bb242a1d86c54674c8be1b2a5d918e i386/kernel-2.4.22-1.2138.nptl.i586.rpm
e5f61174a8586eb7487453dae7ea1875 i386/debug/kernel-debuginfo-2.4.22-
1.2138.nptl.i586.rpm
ee7ac4ffefdfa5ceff18e10d9c5b776b i386/kernel-2.4.22-1.2138.nptl.i686.rpm
50a7aabcbb8642c878714e3c58a49dff i386/kernel-smp-2.4.22-
1.2138.nptl.i686.rpm
fdd33ad20548d78295e59a3d3c7d1f5b i386/debug/kernel-debuginfo-2.4.22-
1.2138.nptl.i686.rpm
8b6ee386df3bcb68dd1c149c91f677e5 i386/kernel-2.4.22-1.2138.nptl.athlon.rpm
01af9cea1186fefc4e844c4d78cc7a06 i386/kernel-smp-2.4.22-
1.2138.nptl.athlon.rpm
01592b67d16d33f577c4de864f3799e5 i386/debug/kernel-debuginfo-2.4.22-
1.2138.nptl.athlon.rpm

This update can also be installed with the Update Agent; you can
launch the Update Agent with the 'up2date' command.
-------------------------------------------------------------------
References:
http://cve.mitre.org/cgi-bin/cvename.cgi?name=CAN-2003-0985
http://isec.pl/vulnerabilities/isec-0013-mremap.txt
```

Listing 3-2: **Non-Security-Related Update**

```
From    : Dave Jones <davej redhat com>
To      : fedora-announce-list redhat com
Subject : Fedora Core 1 kernel update.
Date    : Tue, 13 Jan 2004 20:24:56 +0000
-------------------------------------------------------------------
Fedora Update Notification
FEDORA-2003-048
2004-01-13
-------------------------------------------------------------------
Name       : kernel
```

```
Version     : 2.4.22
Release     : 1.2149.nptl
Summary     : The Linux kernel (the core of the Linux operating system)
Description :
The kernel package contains the Linux kernel (vmlinuz), the core of your
Fedora Core Linux operating system. The kernel handles the basic functions
of the operating system: memory allocation, process allocation, device
input and output, etc.

-----------------------------------------------------------------


* Wed Jan 07 2004 Dave Jones <davej redhat com>

- Merge several EXT2/3 fixes from 2.4.25pre
  - EXT2/3 fixes.
   - Reclaim pages in truncate
   - 2.6 EA symlink compatibility
   - forward-compatibility: online resizing
   - Allow filesystems with expanded inodes to be mounted
   - Handle j_commit_interval == 0
  - IDE timeout race fix
- Merge some 2.4.23pre patches that were missed.
  - Make root a special case for per-user process limits.
  - out_of_memory() locking
  - Drop module count if lockd reclaimer thread failed to start
  - Fix potential fsync() race condition
- s/Red Hat/Fedora/ in specfile (#112992)
- Add PCI ident for new Intel e1000 card. (#105046)
- Actually wire up 3c59x ethtool ioctl.
- Fix up numeric sysctls to match mainline.

-----------------------------------------------------------------


This update can be downloaded from:
  http://download.fedora.redhat.com/pub/fedora/linux/core/updates/1/

0528ff2ef4b077e34a6e9f0bdc4c4c43   SRPMS/kernel-2.4.22-1.2149.nptl.src.rpm
cf2da4c300650d6a68aeb3141e8de93e   i386/kernel-source-2.4.22-
1.2149.nptl.i386.rpm
b6ffe91b11cb64af23f08de19c965677   i386/kernel-doc-2.4.22-
1.2149.nptl.i386.rpm
37bdb02f23cd936fc6a68c8b2f176275   i386/kernel-BOOT-2.4.22-
1.2149.nptl.i386.rpm
fe89710f267b238c9e5fcdf3d2658383   i386/debug/kernel-debuginfo-2.4.22-
1.2149.nptl.i386.rpm
68de6d015862dfc63d40b68a8fa1affa   i386/kernel-2.4.22-1.2149.nptl.i586.rpm
9714ae57c042a42400336c06ae07f2c3   i386/debug/kernel-debuginfo-2.4.22-
1.2149.nptl.i586.rpm
```

Continued

Listing 3-2: *(continued)*

```
ccc831fbb9ffa04ed7504f058411febc    i386/kernel-2.4.22-1.2149.nptl.i686.rpm
257145cc01f1ea38fbcf22304b93d566    i386/kernel-smp-2.4.22-
1.2149.nptl.i686.rpm
baff2d70eb4e24b626511b9f3feacccd    i386/debug/kernel-debuginfo-2.4.22-
1.2149.nptl.i686.rpm
70b1314d932ff4283cab39a289b7aedc    i386/kernel-2.4.22-1.2149.nptl.athlon.rpm
af27b81477979c6ff42a9e1475adaf3b    i386/kernel-smp-2.4.22-
1.2149.nptl.athlon.rpm
307fb0efbbc54a55e3d0c2a4b134c691    i386/debug/kernel-debuginfo-2.4.22-
1.2149.nptl.athlon.rpm


This update can also be installed with the Update Agent; you can launch the
Update Agent with the 'up2date' command.
```

The main differences between the two formats are the subject lines, the update description, and the references. Security updates get a special [SECURITY] prefix to their subject lines. This makes it easier for an administrator to pay close attention to security-based updates. The nature of a security update means there is more information given in the update description. The security flaw is described, and any external security tracking cases are referenced as well (like CVE or Common Vulnerabilities and Exposures). At the bottom of the notification, the external references are listed once more, with specific URLs.

These messages provide URLs to the updated packages, and you can find a mirror list at http://fedora.redhat.com/download/mirrors.html. You can manually download the packages and install them, using the -Uvh option, to rpm:

```
# rpm -Uvh gaim-0.74-5.i386.rpm
```

Updating packages manually means that you'll have to resolve the dependencies manually as well. This can sometimes be tricky. Thankfully, Fedora Core's rpm system is now able to make package suggestions for missing dependencies if you have the rpmdb-fedora package installed. (If you don't have this package installed, and you plan on manually updating your system, I highly recommend you install it.) Here's an example of rpm's ability to suggest resolutions:

```
# rpm -ivh xsane-gimp-0.91-1.i386.rpm
error: Failed dependencies:
        libieee1284.so.3 is needed by xsane-gimp-0.91-1
        libsane.so.1 is needed by xsane-gimp-0.91-1
    Suggested resolutions:
        libieee1284-0.2.8-1.i386.rpm
        sane-backends-1.0.12-4.i386.rpm
```

The output suggests that we install libieee1284 and sane-backends to satisfy the dependency requirements of xsane-gimp.

Source Updates

Source updates, while technically possible, are highly discouraged. Updating via source tarballs involves downloading the latest source from a project website, compiling the source, and installing over the current software set. This method is not very clean, as the default source install may not put files in the same places that the previous package did, does not update your rpm database, and may be missing critical patches that are necessary for operation on your Fedora Core system.

If you must go the source route, I recommend that you use a tool that will keep your RPM database up to date. Checkinstall (`http://asic-linux.com.mx/~izto/checkinstall/`) provides a way to take a set of sources and build RPMs out of them. It's still not as clean as RPM updates provided by the Fedora Project, but it is cleaner than straight source installs.

Troubleshooting Update Problems

Many problems can occur when updating your system. Many of the errors involve network problems of one kind or another. When you do run into update problems, make sure you can access the server you have configured. Try using mirrors of the server. If you are using a development tree, beware that the tree can sometimes be inconsistent and not all dependency resolutions are complete.

Upgrading to Fedora Core

Upgrading may seem like a daunting task. "Will my programs be ok?" "Will I lose my settings?" "Will I lose my custom applications?" These are some of the questions that get asked over and over again when preparing for an upgrade. Answers to these questions and many more can be found in the following sections.

Before you upgrade your system, there are a few things you should do:

✦ *Back up your data*—One thing that can't be stressed enough is the importance of backing up your data prior to performing an upgrade. This step will ensure that in the case of upgrade failure, you can still recover your data. In most cases, your entire data set is held within your home directory, so making a backup of your home directory will suffice. If you've stored data elsewhere on the file system, you must back it up as well prior to upgrading your system.

✦ *Remove unnecessary software*—Removing unused or unnecessary software will greatly reduce the time needed to complete your upgrade. Running `/bin/rpm -qa |sort |less` will give you an alphabetical list of all the RPMs that are installed on your system that you can page through. Removing the packages you no longer need is recommended.

✦ *Obtain the proper media*—Once an upgrade has begun, you cannot roll back to your previous Red Hat Linux release. Thus, it is vital that you have all the media that you will need to perform your upgrade. Upgrades can be done over any of the media that installs can be done from.

The process of upgrading to Fedora Core can be performed in many different ways. This chapter covers the three ways:

✦ Upgrading using the Fedora Core installer (Anaconda)

✦ Upgrading using Yellowdog Updater, Modified (yum)

✦ Upgrading using apt-rpm (apt-get)

I also touch on some issues that may come up as you upgrade your system.

The process of upgrading differs from a new installation in that all the packages on the system are upgraded to the new version, but none of the settings are overwritten. This provides a way for you to get the new release installed without spending a lot of time reconfiguring your system to the settings it had prior to the upgrade.

Upgrading Using the Fedora Core Installer

The Fedora Core installer, like previous incarnations of Red Hat Linux, offers the capability to upgrade from previous Red Hat Linux systems to Fedora Core. This method is arguably the most tested and most supported way of upgrading your system.

Starting the Upgrade

To start an upgrade process using the Fedora Core installer, boot your PC to the installation media (CD-ROM, DVD-ROM, floppy, PXE). This will bring up Anaconda, much like a normal Fedora Core install. After selecting your language, your mouse and keyboard, and your monitor, Anaconda will search for existing Red Hat Linux installs. If it finds any, you'll be given the choice to either upgrade or do a fresh install. Figure 3-3 shows the Anaconda screen where you can choose to upgrade an existing Red Hat Linux install.

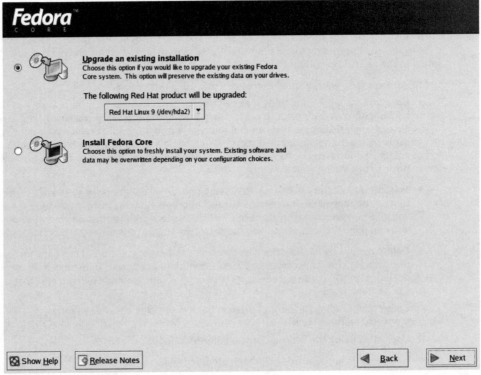

Figure 3-3: Upgrade an existing Red Hat Linux install.

Once you choose to upgrade your existing install, you'll see some different screens and choices than you would with a standard install. The first screen you may see asks if you'd like to migrate your ext2 partitions to ext3. Migration is safe and causes no data loss. Figure 3-4 shows this screen, asking if I'd like to migrate my ext2 /boot partition to ext3.

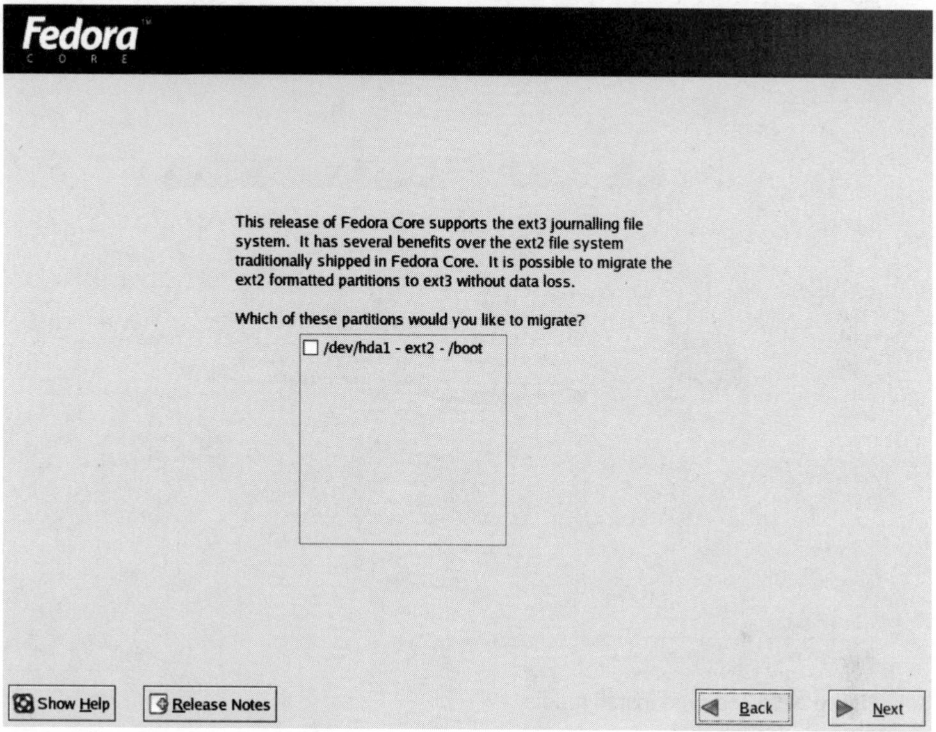

Figure 3-4: Migrate ext2 to ext3.

The next screen asks you how you'd like to handle the boot loader. You have a few options:

✦ *Update your boot loader*—This will update your current boot loader. This is the recommended option.

✦ *Skip boot loader updating*—This will make no changes to boot loader configuration. If you are using a third-party boot loader (like Microsoft Windows), you should choose this.

✦ *Creat new boot loader configuration*—This will let you create a new boot loader configuration. If you wish to switch boot loaders, you should choose this.

Next the installer will check your installed packages for things that it needs to upgrade. This process may take a while so don't get worried if you don't see anything happen on the screen other than the hourglass rotating.

On the next screen, click Next to upgrade to Fedora Core. A complete log of your upgrade will be saved to /root/upgrade.log. Based upon the package set Anaconda found to upgrade, you'll get a pop-up window showing which CDs you'll need to have to complete the upgrade. Figure 3-5 shows this screen.

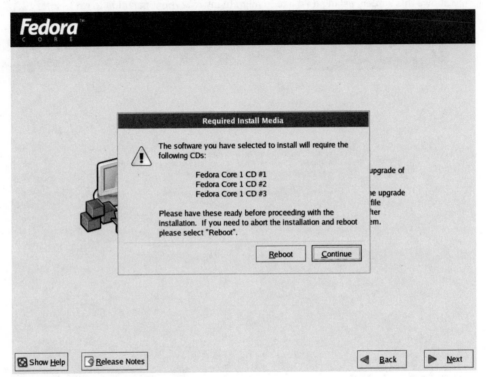

Figure 3-5: Required install media.

If you don't have the required media handy, choose the reboot option to cancel the upgrade process, and start over when you have all the required media. If you click Continue, Anaconda will display a progress screen where you can track the progress of the upgrade process, as well as see the individual package names that are upgraded. Be sure to watch for requests to insert the next CD.

After all the packages are updated, you'll see two brief pop-up windows: the first tells you that the post-install configuration is being done, and the second notifies you that Anaconda is installing the boot loader. After these processes are complete, you'll see a screen that lets you know that the upgrade has finished, and you can reboot. Now you can reboot into your freshly upgraded Fedora Core 1.

Note Because of the nature of upgrades, you will not see any new software, such as the graphical boot screens of Fedora Core 1. An upgrade will only upgrade existing packages, and only install new packages if they are a dependency of an upgraded package. If you wish to add newly available software after you perform the upgrade, use the redhat-config-packages tool after you have completed the upgrade.

Checking the Upgrade

All that's left now is playing with your new Fedora Core system, and configuring everything just the way you like it. Be sure to review your upgrade log files. Your /root directory will contain an upgrade.log file, and possibly an upgrade.log.syslog file. upgrade.log is a log file of how many packages were upgraded, which ones, and all the packages that were available on the Fedora Core CDs that were not used as part of the upgrade process. You can quickly look through the packages that did not get used to see what you might be missing. Within the section of packages that did get upgraded, there may be some comments about configuration files and how the new ones were treated during installation. For example:

```
Upgrading openldap-2.1.22-8.i386.
warning: /etc/openldap/ldap.conf created as
/etc/openldap/ldap.conf.rpmnew
```

This lets you know that the ldap.conf file that came with the new ldap server package was saved with the .rpmnew extension, so as to not overwrite your current configuration. While this is normally a good thing, there may be key elements to that new file that you need to replicate in your existing file. It's a good practice to compare the two files and make the appropriate changes.

An upgrade.log.syslog file is created if any of the package upgrades caused a message to get logged to the syslog facility. Here's an excerpt from an upgrade that I recently did:

```
<21>Jan 24 12:54:47 sendmail[1191]: alias database
/etc/aliases rebuilt by root

<22>Jan 24 12:54:47 sendmail[1191]: /etc/aliases: 63 aliases,
longest 10 bytes, 625 bytes total

<86>Jan 24 12:55:53 useradd[1259]: new group: name=dbus,
gid=81

<86>Jan 24 12:55:53 useradd[1259]: new user: name=dbus,
uid=81, gid=81, home=/, shell=/sbin/nologin
```

These are messages that would have normally appeared in /var/log/messages, but were added to the upgrade.log.syslog file for you to review after the upgrade was complete.

Upgrading Using yum

A very popular, although not supported, method of upgrading your system is using the yum system. This allows "live" upgrades to happen, often without a reboot. At the most basic levels, you fool yum into thinking that the system it's installed on is actually Fedora Core, and then just tell yum to install all available updates.

Caution

Given the unsupported nature of this type of upgrade, I cannot stress the importance of making a good backup of your data prior to attempting an upgrade.

An advantage to this upgrade method is that you upgrade automatically to the latest updates available, instead of upgrading to the initially released packages, then processing all the available updates. If you use any third-party package repositories, then with the proper configuration, you can update all the non-Red Hat packages on your system to the proper version along with your Red Hat packages.

When upgrading a Red Hat Linux 9 system to Fedora Core, it's best to use the yum that is included with Fedora Core, as the configuration will already be pointing to Fedora Core repositories. This RPM can be found at:

```
http://download.fedora.redhat.com/pub/fedora/linux/core/1/i38
6/os/Fedora/RPMS/yum-2.0.4-2.noarch.rpm
```

Download this file and install it with rpm. You may have to install the libxml2-python package from your Red Hat 9 media. Now that you have yum installed, you need to fool yum into thinking that you are running Fedora Core. To accomplish this, you need to install the fedora-release package from the same directory listed above. For this package you'll want to use the `rpm -Uvh` command as it will be upgrading the redhat-release package already on your system.

Once the fedora-release package is installed, you can issue the standard yum update command:

```
#  /usr/bin/yum update
```

After yum spends some time downloading all the header files for all the new RPMs (and updates), it will try to solve the dependency tree. Once it has done that, it will begin to gather all the RPMs. This can be quite a lengthy task, depending on how many packages you have installed, and where you're getting the updated packages from. If you're going to do this task for more than one system, it's a good idea to set up a local yum repository with all the necessary content to avoid the lengthy download multiple times. After yum gathers all the RPMs, it will attempt a test transaction. If this passes, it will proceed into updating all your packages. As each package transaction occurs, you'll see a comment to the right, something like syslinux 100 % done 143/929. The numbers indicate how many actions have occurred versus how many are left to process. An action can be a package installation, a package removal, or a package %post script completing. A log of the upgrade process can be found at /var/log/yum.log. Once yum completes its task, you should reboot to the new kernel and your new Fedora Core system.

Upgrading Using apt-rpm (apt-get)

Upgrading to Fedora Core using apt-get is very similar to using yum. You have to install the apt package, upgrade to the fedora-release package, and tell apt to update your system. This method is also unsupported, although nearly as popular, maybe even more so, than yum-based upgrades. Debian folk have been upgrading their systems with the Debian version of apt-get for many years, and swear by this method. Although apt-rpm and Debian's apt-get share a lot of the same syntaxes and theories, the methods by which packages are installed are quite different. This stems from the inherent differences between Debian's package platform (.deb) and Red Hat's RPM. Because of these differences, apt-rpm has to do a lot of different work to reach the same goal as apt-get. While this is not necessarily a bad thing, it is a new method, and thus shouldn't be as trusted as the tried-and-true Debian system. So again, make backups before you attempt to upgrade your system via apt-get.

Use the following instructions to upgrade with apt-rpm:

1. Make a backup of your system in case of problems.

2. The next step is to obtain apt-get. I recommend the apt package that Fedora.us provides, available at the following URL (which should be one line, with no spaces):

```
http://download.fedora.us/fedora/redhat/9/i386/
RPMS.stable/apt-0.5.5cnc6-0.fdr.8.rh90.i386.rpm.
```

3. To fool apt into thinking it is on a Fedora Core system, you need to edit its sources configuration file, /etc/apt/sources.list. In this file find these two uncommented lines:

```
rpm http://download.fedora.us/fedora redhat/9/i386
os updates stable


rpm-src http://download.fedora.us/fedora redhat/9/i386
os updates stable
```

Change these to point to the Fedora Core 1 repository, as follows:

```
rpm http://download.fedora.us/fedora fedora/1/i386
os updates stable


rpm-src http://download.fedora.us/fedora fedora/1/i386
os updates stable
```

4. Next, tell apt that you'd like your kernel upgraded when you do a dist-upgrade. To do this, you need to edit the main apt configuration file, /etc/apt/apt.conf. Within this file, find the line

```
Upgrade-Kernel "false";
```

and change it to true:

```
Upgrade-Kernel "true";
```

5. Next, install the fedora-release package found at http://download.fedora.redhat .com/pub/fedora/linux/core/1/i386/os/Fedora/RPMS/fedora-release-1- 3.i386.rpm (the URL should be one line, with no spaces). This package is an upgrade to the existing redhat-release package, so use the upgrade syntax of rpm (rpm -Uvh). This package includes the Fedora Core gpg key, which needs to be imported into your rpm system. After you upgrade to the fedora-release package, run the following command:

```
# /bin/rpm -import /usr/share/doc/fedora-release-
1/RPM-GPG-KEY-fedora
```

6. Now you're ready for the actual upgrade. You issue two commands: The first command updates apt's package information, and the second acts upon this package information to actually process the upgrade:

```
# /usr/bin/apt-get update
# /usr/bin/apt-get dist-upgrade
```

apt will check against its local package database and tell you which packages it will update, which packages will be replaced by a package with a different name, and which new packages will be added. It will also tell you what the size of your total download will be, and how much more disk space these packages will take once installed. Press the y key to proceed with the update.

Much like yum, apt will then download all the packages it needs, and proceed to install them. As apt installs the package, you will get progress indications on your screen. You will see the individual package progress indication, as well as the total task indication marked in percentage format:

```
210:kudzu
############################################ [ 43%]
```

This line tells us that the 210th package update, kudzu, is 100 percent complete with the installation, and this brings us up to 43 percent completion for the entire upgrade.

7. When the upgrade is complete, you will need to edit the /etc/grub.conf file. apt will not make the new kernel the default option. The default= stanza of the grub.conf file needs to be set to 0 for the first kernel listed. After that you can reboot, and enjoy your Fedora Core system.

Upgrading Using up2date: Not Recommended

A less common method of upgrading is with up2date. Since the up2date in Fedora Core can support yum or apt repositories, it can be used to upgrade your system using one of these two subsystems. Because of the added complexity of up2date on top of either yum or apt, I strongly recommend not using up2date to perform your upgrade, and instead using one of the three methods explained in the chapter.

Troubleshooting Upgrade Problems

Some issues may come up during your upgrade. The majority of problems that arise in upgrading a Linux release involves the third-party software. Since the Linux distribution can only really know about the software it provides, often third-party software can be ignored. However, when the third-party software replaces some distribution-provided software, problems can arise. The biggest example of this is Ximian Desktop software.

Updating a Ximian Desktop

Ximian desktop software is designed to be complete from Ximian. Because of this, it replaces many core components to GNOME that came with your Red Hat Linux system. This means that the predetermined dependency tree is no longer valid, and upgrades tend to break or ignore the entire GNOME tree, leaving you with a nonworking desktop environment. The following excerpt from the Fedora Core 1 release notes comments on this problem:

There have been issues observed when upgrading Red Hat Linux 7.<x>, 8.0, 9 and Fedora Core 1 systems running Ximian GNOME. The issue is caused by version overlap between the official Red Hat Linux RPMs (or the ones from the Fedora Project) and the Ximian RPMs. This configuration is not supported. You have several choices in resolving this issue:

1. You may remove Ximian GNOME from your system prior to upgrading to Fedora Core.

2. You may upgrade your system, and then immediately reinstall Ximian GNOME.

3. You may upgrade your system, and then immediately remove all remaining Ximian RPMs, replacing them with the corresponding Fedora Core RPMs.

You must resolve the version overlap using one of the above choices. Failure to do so will result in an unstable GNOME configuration.

The same strategy applies to most other third-party software.

Checking Third-Party Updates

The yum and apt upgrade process has a unique ability to handle third-party software issues. yum and apt can be configured to provide updates for that software, so your third-party software is updated along with your Red Hat base.

A quick way to determine which non-Red Hat packages are on your system is to run the following command:

```
# /bin/rpm -qa -queryformat "%{NAME}-%{VERSION}-
  %{RELEASE} Vendor: %{VENDOR}\ n"| grep -v "Red Hat, Inc."
```

This will query all your RPMs, with an output format of the name-version-release, followed by the vendor. You pipe this output into `grep`, which removes all entries containing Red Hat, Inc., leaving the non-Red Hat or third-party packages.

Breaking Graphics Drivers

Another issue that comes up quite often is that the graphical interface will not work after upgrading. Most often this is because the system was using third-party graphics drivers, like the NVIDIA 3D graphics module. These third-party graphics modules have to be built specifically for the kernel they will run on, but part of the distribution upgrade includes a new kernel. If you are using a third-party graphics module, consult the documentation for the driver on how to upgrade the driver for your new kernel.

How to Keep Your Current Red Hat Linux Systems Running

One challenge faced by many system administrators these days is what to do with legacy OS systems. At some point, known as the system *end of life*, a system may still run smoothly, but Red Hat no longer produces security or bug fix updates for the product.

Red Hat Linux systems have enjoyed a very lengthy support term, but that term is running short. Table 3-3 shows the recent Red Hat Linux releases, and their respective end of life.

Table 3-3: Red Hat Linux End-of-Life Dates

Red Hat Linux Release	End-of-Life Date
Red Hat Linux 7.1	December 31, 2003
Red Hat Linux 7.2	December 31, 2003
Red Hat Linux 7.3	December 31, 2003
Red Hat Linux 8.0	December 31, 2003
Red Hat Linux 9	April 30, 2004

Some systems will not be hurt by the drop in support, as they are used only internally, have no Internet access, and continue to run smoothly. Other systems, however, rely heavily on Red Hat support as they are public-facing, have heavy usage, and continue to need bug fixes for the software used.

The alternatives for a system administrator faced with this dilemma include upgrading the product to a more recent offering, leaving the system as is for as long as possible, or using a third-party updating service. As of this writing, there are two choices for third-party updates: the free and open Fedora Legacy Project, and the pay service provided by Progeny Linux Systems.

Fedora Legacy

The Fedora Legacy Project can be found at `www.fedoralegacy.org`. The following description is from the home page of the Project:

> The Fedora Legacy Project is a community-supported open source project. It is not a supported project of Red Hat, Inc. although Red Hat, Inc. does provide some support services for it.

> The goal of The Fedora Legacy Project is to work with the Linux community to provide security and critical bug fix errata packages for select End of Life Red Hat Linux and Fedora Core distributions. This will allow for a longer effective life for those releases.

Through a community effort, the Fedora Legacy Project keeps track of the software that is contained in certain end-of-life Red Hat products. Currently, the Fedora Legacy Project supports Red Hat Linux 7.2, 7.3, and 8.0. According to its website, the Project plans on supporting Red Hat Linux 9 when it goes end of life, as well as extending the life of the Fedora Core releases.

The Project does all of its development and communication through open media channels. Two public mailing lists are located at `www.redhat.com/mailman/listinfo/fedora-legacy-list/` and `www.redhat.com/archives/fedora-legacy-announce`. The Fedora Legacy List is for general discussions about the Fedora Legacy Project, as well as development discussions and test update announcements. The Fedora Legacy Announce List is a read-only (no posting by members is allowed) mailing list used to announce updates as they become available. The Project also has an IRC (Internet Relay Chat) channel where developers and end users can discuss issues and progress of package releases. Their channel is `#fedora-legacy` and it can be found on the Freenode IRC network (`www.freenode.org/`).

Currently, the Fedora Legacy Project supports package delivery methods of http, yum, and apt-get.

Progeny Linux Systems

Progeny Linux Systems provides a pay service called the Progeny Transition Service. The Progeny Transition Service offers software updates for Red Hat Linux 7.2, 7.3, and 8.0, with support for Red Hat Linux 9 scheduled to start early May 2004. The service is designed to provide a flexible migration path for Red Hat Linux systems.

Progeny's service fee is $5 per month, per system, or a flat fee of $2500 per month for unlimited machines. The minimal contract length is currently 6 months.

The Transition Service exists to help customers who are in the process of transitioning from their legacy Red Hat systems to a supported platform. Currently, the Progeny Transition

Service supports package delivery methods of http, and Novell's Ximian Red Carpet Enterprise version 2.0.

More information about Progeny Transition Service can be found on its website at http://transition.progeny.com/.

Summary

Keeping your Linux system updated is vital to the health and security of your system. You can obtain vendor-provided updates for your system, and even third-party-provided updates for end-of-life products. Fedora Core 1 includes yum and up2date as tools for keeping your system updated.

Upgrading to Fedora Core need not be a scary prospect. There are multiple ways to accomplish the task, and workarounds available for most problems. Backing up your data prior to upgrading your system is absolutely critical. Loosing your data once will solidify this concept, but you'll be happier if you accept it on faith, rather than through sad experience.

Preventing Problems

Securing and Automating Desktop and Server Installs

This chapter is targeted at IT administrators who are responsible for maintaining and installing large numbers of PCs. While Linux on the desktop is becoming more and more popular nowadays, without serious methods for standardizing, securing, and automating the install process, the interoperability of the desktop itself is only half the issue at hand.

This chapter builds upon the installation-related skills learned in Chapter 2 to help you secure your standardized desktop, workstation, and server OS installs. The *kickstart* technology covered here will enable you to create standardized desktop and server loads, customize those standard loads, and then roll them out to machines over the network. This client/server *kickstart* automated provisioning system comes with all Fedora Core– and Red Hat–based systems.

This type of OS install technology, when combined with OS hardening skills we cover in this chapter, is exactly what it takes to be able to roll out, or *provision*, Linux systems in the enterprise environment. This level of provisioning automation has been built into Red Hat–based systems for years and is one of the many features that really helps to decrease a Linux shop's Total Cost of Ownership (TCO), while increasing your bosses Return on Investment (ROI) (that is, justification for your salary).

We start off with a nice leisurely overview of the kickstart technology, and then get into how to customize your template machine loads. We review some best practices for locking down and securing your desktop and server template machines, go through the steps for creating your own kickstart provisioning server, and explain how to *run* a kickstart network install via boot floppy or CD. We wrap up with a couple of common kickstart problems (and their solutions).

A Kickstart Overview

Kickstarting a machine refers to the client/server method by which you can set up a centralized server with the OS Install CD content on it and offer this data out to the network (either via FTP, HTTP, or NFS services), and use this to automate your client OS loads. On the client side, you use special boot floppy or CD media to get a new PC up and then do either a manual interactive or fully automated desktop or server load.

Kickstart is Red Hat's own client/server technology. It lets you do local or network-based OS installs with as little as a network connection and a boot floppy. Kickstart builds upon older networking service technologies along with Red Hat's own client program, Anaconda. All these, combined with either a syslinux boot media or a PXE network boot environment, make up the complete kickstart automated provisioning system.

Note   Syslinux is a mini-Linux OS boot environment that can get a machine up and running with a basic network connection. Red Hat–based systems use it along with the Anaconda client side program to perform an OS load, either from CD, the hard drive, or over the network. For more information on syslinux or isolinux, go to http://syslinux.zytor.com/.

PXE Booting

PXE, short for *Pre-Boot Execution Environment* and pronounced "pixie," is a client-side boot specification by Intel that is usually implemented by network card hardware, and uses the network server-side DHCP/BOOTP protocols. If you have a network card that features PXE booting and a BIOS that can support booting from PXE, then you have the ability to "network boot" a blank machine (assuming you've set up a DHCP/BOOTP boot server). From there you can perform network-based installs, hardware testing, or cluster provisioning, without even inserting so much as a floppy or a CD. PXE is not recommended for a production LAN as accidental PXE-first booting on a production machine could prove catastrophic if a new OS is installed over a user's or administrator's production machine. For more information on PXE check these sites: www.linux-mag.com/2002-10/netbooting_01.html and ftp://download.intel.com/labs/manage/wfm/download/pxespec.pdf.

Starting Your Kickstart Templates

The nice thing about kickstart is that if you've ever installed Red Hat on a machine, you've created a kickstart config file without even knowing it. This file contains all the options that you entered during the install. After any Fedora Core- or Red Hat-based install, you should see your new kickstart config file (called anaconda-ks.cfg) in the root user's home directory /root/:

```
# ls -la /root/an*
-rw-r--r--    1 root root 1877 Dec 16 12:12 /root/anaconda-ks.cfg
```

You can also use Red Hat's GUI config tool to create a kickstart config file from scratch (see the *Using the Red Hat Kickstart Configuration Tool* section later in this chapter for details).

Looking Inside Your ks.cfg File

A kickstart or ks.cfg file is divided into four main parts:

✦ *The Install Command Area*—This portion of the file has the configuration information and commands, such as the new system's settings, the install media source (CD, network, or hard drive based), the new system's firewall settings, root password, authentication configuration, new install versus upgrade, and so on. This area also contains information such as whether the drive is to be wiped clean before starting the install, what partition types and sizes are to be set up, whether the system will use the MBR for booting, and if you're setting up drive/partition level options like software RAID or LVM.

✦ *The New System Packages Area*—This portion of the file lists all the RPM packages or metapackages (groups of packages) that are to be installed.

✦ *The Pre-Install Script*—This portion contains shell or programming commands that you want to run *before* the install begins.

✦ *The Post-Install Script*—This portion contains the shell or programming commands that run *after* the basic install, but before the end of the install or the reboot.

In short, this file has all the installation settings covered in Chapter 2. In fact, if you did an install on your machine, you should now have your own /root/anaconda-ks.cfg file that will enable you to install the same configuration settings on other machines. This anaconda-generated file is, essentially, your first kickstart template file. The next step is to back up your anaconda-ks.cfg file so that you can easily identify the original file and so that it won't be overwritten later:

```
#  cd /root
#  cp -a anaconda-ks.cfg ks-my-first-install.cfg
```

Tip

You can name these kickstart config files anything you want, but when you create boot disks later that will use them, by default anaconda looks for the file name ks.cfg on the media that you point it to. If you are running several different kickstart config files, it is wise to break away from the ks.cfg standard naming and use something such as ks-workstation-date.cfg so that you'll know exactly what file you're about to apply to a given system.

Take a look at the following /root/anaconda-ks.cfg config file generated when I did a server load from CD. My added comments appear in boldface italics (#-*The Install Command Area*):

```
# Kickstart file automatically generated by anaconda.
#-The Install Command Area
#-----------------------------------------
Install
cdrom                                    #- <--- The install source
lang en_US.UTF-8
langsupport --default en_US.UTF-8 en_US.UTF-8

keyboard us
mouse alpsps/2 --device psaux --emulthree
xconfig --card "S3 ProSavage KM133" --videoram 31680 --hsync 1.5-48.5 -
vsync 40-70 --resolution 1024x768 --depth 16 --startxonboot --
defaultdesktop gnome                     #- <--- xconfig all one line...
network --device eth0 --bootproto dhcp #- <--- Network setup
rootpw --iscrypted $1$td8M3NHj$1S.OkU.Pz.rGT2VzZpRND/
firewall --enabled --port=http:tcp --port=ssh:tcp
authconfig --enableshadow --enablemd5
```

```
timezone America/Winnipeg
bootloader --location=mbr --append hdc=ide-scsi rhgb
# The following is the partition information you requested
# Note that any partitions you deleted are not expressed
# here so unless you clear all partitions first, this is
# not guaranteed to work
#clearpart --linux --drives=had
#part /boot --fstype ext3 --size=100 --ondisk=had
#part / --fstype ext3 --size=1024 --grow -asprimary
#part swap --size=514 -asprimary
```

#-*Notice above that even if you do a fresh install, wipe all the*
#-*existing partitions and create new partitions, that this area gets*
#-*commended out in your anaconda-ks.cfg file. This is for safety*
#-*reasons. If someone tests their new ks.cfg file and doesn't quite*
#-*understand what they're doing, this will save them from nuking*
#-*their own system. DO NOT FORGET TO UNCOMMENT THESE IN*
#- *YOUR FINAL TEST INSTALL*

#-*New System Packages Area*
```
#-------------------------------------------
%packages
@ kde-software-development    #- These are all meta packages
@ office                      #- or logical groupings of packages
@ kde-desktop
@ network-server
@ web-server
@ engineering-and-scientific
@ x-software-development
@ mail-server
@ dns-server
@ server-cfg
@ dialup
@ sound-and-video
@ sql-server
@ editors
@ admin-tools
@ system-tools
@ authoring-and-publishing
@ base-x
@ gnome-desktop
@ gnome-software-development
@ graphics
@ ftp-server
@ kernel-development
@ smb-server
@ development-tools
@ ruby
@ printing
@ games
@ text-internet
@ graphical-internet
```

```
vnc-server            #-These are the individual RPM
squirrelmail          #- packages that were added on
postfix               #- through the GUI installer when I
tsclient              #- set up this server load.
elinks
vim-X11
xpdf
ethereal-gnome
xmms-skins
dhcp
mailman
xcdroast
shapecfg
redhat-config-boot
tftp-server
koffice
gtkam-gimp
grip
nmap-frontend
kdepim
kdegraphics
rdesktop
gnomemeeting
kernel-pcmcia-cs
mysql-server
grub
abiword
spamassassin
fsh
kernel
talk-server
kdemultimedia
php-mysql
amanda-server
ncftp
vnc
amanda-client
imap
quanta
telnet-server
redhat-switch-mail

#-Pre Install Script
#-----------------------t
%pre
echo Pre-Install bash commands go here...

#-Post Install Script
#------------------------
%post
echo Post-Install bash commands go here...
echo
```

Tip

Sometimes manually adding RPMs to the Packages section will lead to dependency issues and can cause your automatic install to fail from dependency errors. To handle this and automatically install any required subdependency packages, you can add the `--resolvedeps` switch to the packages header like this:

```
%packages --resolvedeps
```

For more information on this topic, see Chapter 9 of Red Hat's online RH-EL3 Administration Guide documentation at `www.redhat.com/docs/manuals/enterprise/RHEL-3-Manual/sysadmin-guide/ch-kickstart2.html`.

Note

Notice this file has no mention of the terms *server* or *workstation*, as in the original interactive Fedora Core installer. This is because these terms are just abstractions of the metapackages and RPMs or that define "groupings of groupings" of RPMs. The listing of packages in the config file example is the standard Server load, with a number of metapackages and RPMs added. These metapackages are all grouped logically and defined in the base comps XML file located on CD 1 in `Fedora/base/comps.xml`. You can see all of these metapackage names with the following command (typed as one line) while Fedora Core CD 1 is mounted:

```
$ cat /mnt/cdrom/Fedora/base/comps.xml | grep \ <id
| grep -v '\ -support'
```

In these metapackages and groupings you see groups such as `games` and `office` as well as our groups of groups `server` and `workstation-common`.

Network Enabling the ks.cfg File

Now that you have an idea of what a kickstart config file looks like, the next step is to make this config file usable as a part of a network install boot disk.

Note

At Rackspace Managed Hosting, one "Geek Rites of Passage" for all new Linux system administrators is to load their own workstation without using any CDs. This is done by downloading a Red Hat boot disk image from the one-line Red Hat mirror content `images` directory, using `dd` to write it out to a floppy, and then performing a CD-less network-based install from our Red Hat mirror server. Many people do not realize that they can install most Linux distros totally over the Internet or a LAN with nothing more than a network boot floppy or other network-aware boot environment (such as a PXE NIC/LAN setup). For more information on using `dd` to write out floppy disk images, see the *Creating Customized Boot Floppies* section.

Here are the lines in the `ks.cfg` file that we need to change to make the install pull the CD files from the network:

```
install
cdrom
lang en_US.UTF-8
langsupport --default en_US.UTF-8 en_US.UTF-8
keyboard us
```

```
   .
   .
   .
network --device eth0 --bootproto dhcp
rootpw --iscrypted $1$td8M3NHj$1S.OkU.Pz.rGT2VzZpRND/
```

The following block of code shows the changes required to have the install look to a network-based ftp kickstart server:

```
# TWW: 2004-02-22, Network install of the Fedora CD Media
# files from my FTP server...
 install
 url --url ftp://ftp.example.com/pub/fedora/core/1/i386/os/
lang en_US.UTF-8
langsupport --default en_US.UTF-8 en_US.UTF-8
keyboard us
   .
   .
   .
network --device eth0 --bootproto dhcp
rootpw --iscrypted $1$td8M3NHj$1S.OkU.Pz.rGT2VzZpRND/
```

Notice that first we've changed the type of install from a CD-ROM-based to a URL or network install. Also notice that we've defined the URL from which the new machine is to get its install files. (We have not yet set up that FTP file share, but will do so in the *Creating a Kickstart Provisioning Server* section later in this chapter.)

Tip   If you want to do your own network install of Fedora Core Linux from the Internet with nothing but a floppy and a PC, just go out to a Fedora mirror site, download the `bootdisk.img` and `drvnet.img` (or just the `bootdisk.iso` CD image), copy them to the correct media (more on this in the *Creating Your Kickstart Provisioning Boot Media* section), and boot off that media. You simply follow the prompts to do an FTP, HTTP, or NFS-based install, and point the install to one of the mirror sites, including the full path to the directory above the `Fedora` directory. For example, the full path to the `Fedora` directory (case matters, and all on one line) is

```
ftp://mirrors.kernel.org/fedora/core/1/i386/os/Fedora/
```

Then point your manual floppy/CD network install to

```
ftp://mirrors.kernel.org/fedora/core/1/i386/os
```

Whatever directory path you give it, it will expect to find the `Fedora` directory inside it. The same goes for Red Hat wanting the directory that houses the `RedHat` directory.

Using the Red Hat Kickstart Configuration Tool

The other "easy way" of creating a kickstart template file is via the Red Hat kickstart configuration GUI tool: redhat-config-kickstart. This tool is nice in that it gives you a GUI front end to that `comps.xml` file. Just take a peek inside that file and you'll want some form of abstraction. Trust me.

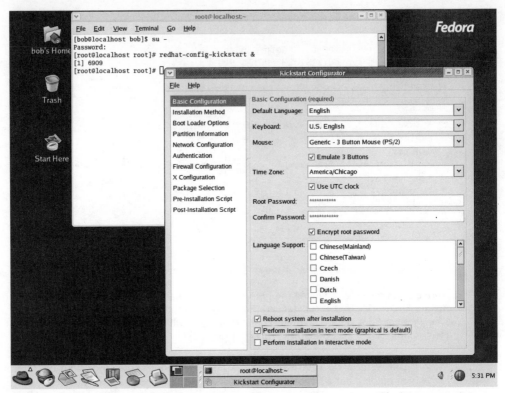

Figure 4-1: The redhat-config-kickstart GUI config tool makes a `ks.cfg` file for automating Fedora Core or Red Hat Enterprise network-based OS installs.

You can start Red Hat's kickstart configuration tool either from the command line (as shown in Figure 4-1) or by the clicking on Red Hat ⇨ System Tools ⇨ Kickstart.

Note   You do not have to be root to run the config file generation tool. It just is not in the $PATH of nonroot users, so Figure 4-1 shows how to start it after becoming root with `su -`. I also could have run it as user `bob` by simply running it by its absolute path of `/usr/sbin/redhat-config-kickstart`, or via the desktop menu Red Hat ⇨ System Tools ⇨ Kickstart.

Although redhat-config-kickstart tool looks like the solution to all the headaches of manually playing with raw `ks.cfg` files, don't be fooled. This GUI utility has its shortcomings. First, it's not that stable and has problems reading existing `ks.cfg` files. GUI tools are nice to look at and occasionally handy for whipping up something quickly, but be careful.

Caution   Some Red Hat GUI tools do not work well, have problems reading existing config files, or in the worst cases (as with the apache config tool) can even *overwrite your existing config file*. Just be careful when using them and back up your original flat files before trying them out.

With this caveat noted, this tool is very convenient for throwing together a base `ks.cfg` file without having to do a full install on a box. After using the tool to get started, you can open the new `ks.cfg` file in your favorite text editor and further refine and tweak it.

Although learning to use the tool is fairly easy, a complete breakdown of its usage is available online at *Red Hat's EL3 Admin Guide* documentation, Chapter 10, at `www.redhat.com/docs/ manuals/enterprise/RHEL-3-Manual/sysadmin-guide/ch-redhat-config-kickstart .html`.

Saving Your ks files

Now that you have the base kickstart template file(s) set up and network ready, take a moment to name them accurately and organize them for easy retrieval. I've used my first template and the config tool to create a few specific OS loads (for example, desktops, workstations, and servers) for use throughout my company. Typically a directory of these `ks.cfg` files should be neatly organized to look something like this:

```
ks-everything.cfg
ks-IT-desktop_2004-02-16.cfg
ks-IT-desktop_2004-02-20.cfg
ks-my-first-install_2004-02-21.cfg
ks-server-laptop-install_2004-02-22.cfg
ks-workstation_2004-02-19.cfg
ks-workstation_2004-02-20.cfg
```

Tip   Besides naming your files with descriptive names and date stamps, you should also consider keeping an internal comment-based change log so that you can track down problems to specific changes made to your `ks.cfg` file on specific dates.

The next section shows you how to lock down your desktop and server loads by modifying these `ks.cfg` files to include some common "lock down best practices" settings. This will empower you to secure your OS loads by guaranteeing that all machines that you provision with this system will have your exact configuration settings.

Locking Down Desktops and Servers

This section covers some example settings you might want to add to your template workstation or server loads to lock them down, secure them, or just customize or standardize them for your enterprise environment.

Anything that you could normally run or do on a client PC or a new server install from the command line can be put into your `ks.cfg`'s postinstall script section to be automated. To begin, you'll need to think through the kind of standardized settings your enterprise PC and server installs will require.

Identifying Your Enterprise Desktop Needs

Just pointing some of your client PCs to different DNS servers, giving them all the same internal home page, bookmarks, or company directory can be invaluable. And how about creating standard command aliases or desktop icons for common company tasks, or "back door" administrative accounts, or a help desk VNC remote desktop setup? Wouldn't you like your people to have standardized corporate NFS/SMB drive mappings, printer settings, and antivirus package configurations? Not to mention things like desktop backups and system health warnings. These are just a few of the things a customized installation template can provide.

Most experienced IT administrators already know the importance of building a customized OS install template. Many inexperienced IT guys learn this the hard way: by months of fighting with users over the phone, countless visits to the cube farms, manual matching, reinstalls, and troubleshooting sessions. A smart set-up design can help you avoid wasted hours and frayed tempers.

Identifying Your Enterprise Server Needs

This is an area where you really want to sink some thought: Would you like all of your servers to have nightly cron jobs to download and apply the latest security patches? Does a root-kit or intrusion security check and e-mail you anything out of the norm? Send you an e-mail if the machine is rebooted? Tar up and backup, to a single place on the network, a set of important config files, logs, or database files? What about setting up trusted SSH keys in every new server that goes online so that you can log into any new server, even if the root password has changed? These are all things that can be put into the %postscript area of your `ks.cfg` file.

Planning and defining each of your enterprise server issues is really the key. It's also essential to discuss these plans with all the system administrators in your company to make sure everyone understands the benefits of a standardized kickstart file and to generate ideas for useful %postscript options.

Every company's needs are different. You need to sit down, hash out, and plan for your departmental and organizational needs. Now with all that out of the way, let's take a look at what you can do to make a standard install of Fedora Core Linux (or most any Linux), a bit more tight and secure.

Locking Down Your Template Installs

In this section are some good rules of thumb for locking down and securing the common services that you have running on your machines. What you use here depends on your security needs. You might find it useful to refer to the iptable/firewalling configurations, discussed in Chapter 11, to set up and implement some basic iptable automation for all of your server loads. Just follow along and you'll quickly get an idea of what's possible.

Note　If you have not yet done a basic install of your server template machine, you should do one before proceeding. The commands that we are going to use in our %postscripting section will need to be run and tested as if from the actual install machine itself. As such, you will need to have a test machine to run these commands on to verify proper operation before implementing them in your own `ks.cfg` file. To assemble a reliable set of %postscripting commands, you will need to run the various test commands, take notes, and copy and paste your good commands into what will end up being the final %postinstall script section within your `ks.cfg` file.

The main install changes that you want to examine right off for your servers and perhaps for some desktop systems, include the following:

✦ Shutting off unneeded services

✦ Locking down networking/IPv4 settings

✦ Patching automation

✦ System "Health checks"

✦ Basic intrusion detection or root-kit checks

✦ On-disk hardware testing packages

The following subsections cover each of these items.

Shutting Off Unneeded Services

Before you can lock down services, you should first see what your default runlevel is. On most Red Hat/Fedora Core–based Linux systems it will either be a default runlevel of 3 (for console/text logins) or 5 (for X11 GUI display manager logins). Reboot your template server and type the following:

```
# cat /etc/inittab | grep    ^id:
id:5:initdefault:
#
# runlevel
N 5
```

If you're on a Red Hat/Fedora machine and both results are 5, you are running a X11 GUI-based login machine. If you prefer a text login only server, edit /etc/inittab and change the line you see above to an initdefault of 3, reboot, and check it again. Runlevel 3 should be most servers' default runlevel if a run-time GUI is not desired. In the examples here, I'm operating on a server load installed on my laptop, so runlevel 5 will be the default.

Tip
You want to have a good reason before running a server in runlevel 5 with X11 GUI running, not only is this a security issue but it also eats up system resources, there are serious performance issues with running a server with X windows in place. Just think about some 3-D screen savers and the processing power they eat up. Do you really want your web server or mail server that's under attack from the latest virus having to tread water while competing for system memory and CPU resources with the latest 3-D "The Matrix" screen saver? I think not.

The following chkconfig listing shows the services I have running in my runlevel 5:

```
# chkconfig --list|grep 5:on|sort
acpid        0:off   1:off   2:off   3:on   4:on   5:on   6:off
anacron      0:off   1:off   2:on    3:on   4:on   5:on   6:off
apmd         0:off   1:off   2:on    3:on   4:on   5:on   6:off
atd          0:off   1:off   2:off   3:on   4:on   5:on   6:off
autofs       0:off   1:off   2:off   3:on   4:on   5:on   6:off
crond        0:off   1:off   2:on    3:on   4:on   5:on   6:off
cups         0:off   1:off   2:on    3:on   4:on   5:on   6:off
gpm          0:off   1:off   2:on    3:on   4:on   5:on   6:off
httpd        0:off   1:off   2:on    3:on   4:on   5:on   6:off
iptables     0:off   1:off   2:on    3:on   4:on   5:on   6:off
irqbalance   0:off   1:off   2:off   3:on   4:on   5:on   6:off
isdn         0:off   1:off   2:on    3:on   4:on   5:on   6:off
kudzu        0:off   1:off   2:off   3:on   4:on   5:on   6:off
messagebus   0:off   1:off   2:off   3:on   4:on   5:on   6:off
```

```
microcode_ctl  0:off    1:off    2:on    3:on    4:on    5:on    6:off
named          0:off    1:off    2:on    3:on    4:on    5:on    6:off
netfs          0:off    1:off    2:off   3:on    4:on    5:on    6:off
network        0:off    1:off    2:on    3:on    4:on    5:on    6:off
nfslock        0:off    1:off    2:off   3:on    4:on    5:on    6:off
pcmcia         0:off    1:off    2:on    3:on    4:on    5:on    6:off
random         0:off    1:off    2:on    3:on    4:on    5:on    6:off
rawdevices     0:off    1:off    2:off   3:on    4:on    5:on    6:off
rhnsd          0:off    1:off    2:off   3:on    4:on    5:on    6:off
sendmail       0:off    1:off    2:on    3:on    4:on    5:on    6:off
smartd         0:off    1:off    2:on    3:on    4:on    5:on    6:off
spamassassin   0:off    1:off    2:on    3:on    4:on    5:on    6:off
sshd           0:off    1:off    2:on    3:on    4:on    5:on    6:off
syslog         0:off    1:off    2:on    3:on    4:on    5:on    6:off
touchpad       0:off    1:off    2:off   3:on    4:off   5:on    6:off
vsftpd         0:off    1:off    2:on    3:on    4:on    5:on    6:off
xfs            0:off    1:off    2:on    3:on    4:on    5:on    6:off
xinetd         0:off    1:off    2:on    3:on    4:on    5:on    6:off
```

That's a lot of services configured to be running. Also, don't forget about all the xinetd spawned daemons. These subdaemons will either be configured to be on or off at the same runlevel that xinetd is configured to be on:

```
#  export LC_ALL=C
#  chkconfig --list| grep [a-z]: | grep on$| sort
      cups-lpd:            on
      finger:             on
      imap:               on
      imaps:              on
      pop3s:              on
      sgi_fam:            on
```

If any of the aforementioned services are unfamiliar, take note of them. We'll tell you how to look up and determine what unfamiliar services are, so that you can decide on whether to shut them down or not.

You should also check which services are bound to the network IP addresses, with the netstat command:

```
# netstat -at
Active Internet connections (servers and established)
Proto Recv-Q Send-Q Local Address          Foreign Address        State
tcp       0      0 *:imaps                 *:*                    LISTEN
tcp       0      0 *:pop3s                 *:*                    LISTEN
tcp       0      0 *:printer               *:*                    LISTEN
tcp       0      0 *:pop3                  *:*                    LISTEN
tcp       0      0 localhost.localdoma:783 *:*                    LISTEN
tcp       0      0 *:imap                  *:*                    LISTEN
tcp       0      0 *:finger                *:*                    LISTEN
tcp       0      0 *:http                  *:*                    LISTEN
tcp       0      0 *:ftp                   *:*                    LISTEN
tcp       0      0 dav.mydomain.com:domain *:*                    LISTEN
tcp       0      0 mydomain.com:domain     *:*                    LISTEN
```

```
tcp        0    0 10.10.10.1:domain     *:*                      LISTEN
tcp        0    0 192.168.128.25:domain *:*                      LISTEN
tcp        0    0 localhost.locald:domain *:*                    LISTEN
tcp        0    0 *:ssh                 *:*                      LISTEN
tcp        0    0 localhost.localdoma:ipp *:*                    LISTEN
tcp        0    0 *:smtp                *:*                      LISTEN
tcp        0    0 localhost.localdom:rndc *:*                    LISTEN
tcp        0    0 *:https               *:*                      LISTEN
tcp        0    0 localhost.localdoma:ipp localhost.localdo:32963 FIN_WAIT2
tcp        1    0 192.168.128.25:32926  216.239.39.104:http      CLOSE_WAIT
tcp        1    0 192.168.128.25:32925  216.239.57.99:http       CLOSE_WAIT
tcp        1    0 localhost.localdo:32963 localhost.localdoma:ipp CLOSE_WAIT
tcp        1    0 localhost.localdo:32921 localhost.localdoma:ipp CLOSE_WAIT
```

In this netstat, you see quite a few protocols listening on IP address 0.0.0.0, or in nonnetworking talk, *all* IPs. Do you want all of these services exposed to the outside? Again, take notes on these template machine settings.

First, you want to turn off the services that you don't want running in your default runlevel, or for good measure, runlevels 2 to 5. For example, browsing though the first chkconfig listing above, I know that the services autofs, cups, isdn, kudzu, and nfslock don't need to be running. Configure them to be off for all usable runlevels (2, 3, 4, and 5) with the chkconfig *service* off command, and then stop the ones that are currently running by calling the daemon init script directly with the stop option; do this for each service that you don't want running:

```
#  chkconfig autofs off ; /etc/init.d/autofs stop
Stopping automount:              [ OK ]
#  chkconfig cups off ; /etc/init.d/cups stop
Stopping cups:                   [ OK ]
.

.
#  chkconfig nfslock off ; /etc/init.d/nfslock stop
Stopping NFS statd:              [FAILED]
```

Don't worry about FAILED messages. This is usually because of an interrelated service dependency or an issue that a reboot will clear up. Do another netstat -at if you're not sure whether you just locked down those services.

And for xinetd subdaemons, if you don't want cups-lpd, finger, or imap running on your server load by default either, switching xinetd services to off will stop them immediately:

```
#  chkconfig cups-lpd off
#  chkconfig finger off
#  chkconfig imap off
```

Now do a netstat listing again with netstat -at and see what services are now bound to your IPs. Then, do another chkconfig -list | grep 5:on listing and *now* look as to what's configured to come up at boot time. Better?

Tip   If you're not sure what certain services do and you want a quick run down of each, Red Hat– and Fedora Core–based systems offer a quick, easy-to-use ncurses TUI (or text-based GUI) interface tool called ntsysv. After running ntsysv, it has a concise F1 help description for every service installed on your system. Invoke it as root by running ntsysv, or use the new, handsome, full GUI version redhat-config-services. It gives you a very good description of each service on your machine. You can read up and then decide whether to turn off each service or leave it running. WARNING: If you're not sure about a given service, ask someone or leave it on until you learn more.

So the chkconfig service off ; /etc/init.d/service stop commands that you just ran to lock down the services on this template server did a good job. Now copy/paste them into a text file called /root/post-script.txt or the like for eventual inclusion in your ks.cfg file later. Your file should look something like the following:

```
# Shut off all the services we don't want running....
chkconfig autofs off ; /etc/init.d/autofs stop
chkconfig cups off ; /etc/init.d/cups stop
chkconfig isdn off ; /etc/init.d/isdn stop
chkconfig kudzu off ; /etc/init.d/kudzu stop
chkconfig nfslock off ; /etc/init.d/nfslock stop
chkconfig cups-lpd off
chkconfig finger off
chkconfig imap off
```

Now that you have a basic starting place for your ks.cfg file's %post config, let's continue to see what you can do to tighten your kickstart-based OS install.

Locking Down Networking/Ip Stack Settings

Professionals who know Linux love it when it comes to networking because you have control over the networking and TCP/IP stack more so than any other production operating system. You interact with networking and the IPv4 settings in a number of ways (such as with iptables, as you'll see in Chapter 11), but when dealing with the real-time kernel settings, you're usually reading and writing the settings to some kernel variable under the the Procfs, aka the /proc virtual filesystem. There are a lot of settings for the IPv4 networking system under /proc. Most of these /proc parameters can be controlled very nicely with the sysctl system via the /etc/sysctl.conf file. This file is run every time the system boots, and is the more modern and safer way of working with /proc changes (as compared to the old school method of using post-boot echo *variable*> /proc/sys/... commands in the rc.local file). If you need any kernel run-time parameters changed, do it here when possible. Many times when people need a kernel recompiled to make some adjustment to the kernel runtime parameters, for things like running Oracle, memory hungry apps, or specialized networking apps, sysctl is what they really need (since it will remain active even after a kernel upgrade or the like).

Note In the old days, administrators used to control the kernel settings either with a kernel recompile or via /proc directly by echoing changes out to specific settings within proc from the rc.local startup file, as in this snippet:

```
# stops SYN flood attacks
echo 1 > /proc/sys/net/ipv4/tcp_syncookies
```

This is old school, rather dirty, and not really safe since most administrators did this when the /etc/rc.d/rc.local file was run, which is very late in the boot process. This creates time-related vulnerabilities, and in some cases (such as Oracle) simply cannot be done. Instead of echoing values like this out to /proc, simply poke such values into the /etc/sysctl.conf file. Read the man sysctl.conf page for more information.

To help secure your TCP/IP stack on a standard Linux mahcine, you will want to add the following lines to your /etc/sysctl.conf file:

```
##TWW: 2004-02-22
# stop syn-flood attacks
net.ipv4.tcp_syncookies = 1

# Throws off people trying to fingerprint your OS by its TTL (def=64)
net.ipv4.ip_default_ttl = 61
# stops the routing table from being modified by packets non-sourc routed
net.ipv4.conf.all.accept_redirects = 0

# same as above but stops your system doing the same to others
net.ipv4.conf.all.send_redirects = 0
```

You can add this to your script by storing these settings on a local FTP server (that the kickstart will have access to), and in the %post config pull them down from your ftp.example.com FTP server (for example) and append it on the end of the existing /etc/sysctl.conf:

```
# Get all of our sysctl/networking adjustments
wget ftp://ftp.example.com/pub/installs/sysctl-append
cat sysctl-append >> /etc/sysctl.conf
```

So with this in your %post config script, you will append the contents of your standard sysctl-append file to the end of your new install's /etc/sysctl.conf file, thus enabling these settings every time one of these systems is booted—a very nice way to ensure all of your systems are just that much more secure.

Additional System Lock Downs

Here are some common security measures that some system administrators like to see in place on their servers. These are basically a collection of shell-based commands that will help lock down and secure various aspects of the system.

```
# restricts those not in the root group from being able to su to root
chmod 4750 /bin/su

# restricts the mount/umount commands to root group only users
chmod 4750 /bin/mount
chmod 4750 /bin/umount

#Install "scponly" scp replacement for bash and add to /etc/shells
rpm -ivh ftp://ftp.example.com/pub/installs/scponly-3.8-1.i586.rpm
echo /usr/bin/scponly >>/etc/shells

#make scponly the default user shell
wget ftp://ftp.example.com/pub/installs/useradd
mv -f useradd /etc/default/useradd
```

And finally, here are some details we would like to add on all servers that get put online with our kickstart file:

```
#Send an email whenever this box is rebooted
echo "echo |  mail -s\ "Server \ $HOSTNAME Rebooted\ " \
pager@mail.example.com">>/etc/rc.d/rc.local
#Document which kickstart file this is:
echo ks-server-install_2004-02-22.cfg > /etc/ks-release
```

Note that the Rebooted line will work with either the trailing \ on the first line or as a single unwrapped line without the trailing \.

These two lines are very nice. The first will send you an e-mail whenever one of the servers that it's installed on is rebooted, and the second will allow you to track which kickstart created a given server.

You may want to add other lock down measures, such as these:

✦ Adding SSH-key based authentication (Chapter 18)

✦ iptable/firewall service restrictions by network (Chapter 11)

✦ On-disk hardware testers such as memtest86 (`www.memtest86.com`), smartctl (`http://smartmontools.sourceforge.net`), or cpuburnin (`http://users.bigpond .net.au/cpuburn/`)

You can add these in your %postscript and test them out.

The only real limit to what you can do with the `%post` config scripts in an enterprise environment is how general you want your `ks.cfg` files to be (that is, how many or few you wish to maintain), and how much time you have to spend on fine-tuning them.

Tip   If you want good support for getting great lock-down information from other departments, make their system administrators and professionals a part of the effort. Show them what is possible with package adds, lock downs, security settings, and so on—and let them "own" their own little section of the script that deals with their work (security, FTP/Web admin, DNS admins, backup folks, and so forth). Not only will you get better acceptance of this methodology and be including others in setting de facto policy, but you'll get some really great scripts out of it!

The Final %postscript

Frankly, you can spend years tweaking this type of script. Let's take a look at what we have after all the changes thus far. I have also added some sections that are "works in progress." Some of these sections are commented out but left in so that you can see how they work:

```
%post
#########Setup##########
exec < /dev/tty6 > /dev/tty6 2>/dev/tty6 #Set up chvt to handle VTtoggles
chvt 6                                   #put this in all post-scripts
mkdir /tmp/install                       #Set up temp file space
cd /tmp/install
#######iptable-ssh from MY LAN######
# May have to do this in the "first boot" after install
#/etc/init.d/iptables restart
```

```
#iptables -I RH-Firewall-1-INPUT 7 -s 10.1.1.0/24 -p \
#tcp --dport 22 -j ACCEPT
#iptables-save >/etc/sysconfig/iptables
##########Services Stuff##########
# Shut off all the services we don't want running....
chkconfig autofs off ; /etc/init.d/autofs stop
chkconfig cups off ; /etc/init.d/cups stop
chkconfig isdn off ; /etc/init.d/isdn stop
chkconfig kudzu off ; /etc/init.d/kudzu stop
chkconfig nfslock off ; /etc/init.d/nfslock stop
chkconfig cups-lpd off                    #These are xinetd based
chkconfig finger off
chkconfig imap off
##########Networking###########
# Get all of our sysctl/networking adjustments
service network start                     #Turn on the network
wget ftp://ftp.example.com/pub/installs/sysctl-append
cat sysctl-append >> /etc/sysctl.conf
##########System Stuff##########
# Only root group has access to su
chmod 4750 /bin/su
# Only root group users have mount/umount
chmod 4750 /bin/mount
chmod 4750 /bin/umount
# Install "scponly" scp replacement for bash
rpm -ivh ftp://ftp.example.com/pub/installs/scponly-3.8-1.i586.rpm
# And add it to /etc/shells
echo /usr/bin/scponly >>/etc/shells
# Make scponly the default user shell
wget ftp://ftp.example.com/pub/installs/useradd
mv -f useradd /etc/default/useradd
#########Intrustion Detection########
## Need to get latest chkrootkit and put here....
## Get from http://www.chkrootkit.org/ and
#wget ftp://ftp.pangeia.com.br/pub/seg/pac/chkrootkit.tar.gz
# Untar it:
#tar xzvf chkrootkit.tar.gz
# Compile it:
#cd chkrootkit-*/
#make sense
#cd .. ; mv chkrootkit-* /root/
# Clean up
#/bin/rm -rf chkrootk*
# Can also set up automation scan & updates via cron
# Also see chapter 10 on how to "hide" chkrootkit for
# better post-hack trustworthiness of the binary.
########AutoPatching/Up2date##########
# uncomment when we're ready to use with registration
#up2date-nox -uf
##########Final Custom Config#######
# Send an email whenever this box is rebooted
echo "echo | mail -s\ "Server \ $HOSTNAME Rebooted\ " \
```

```
pager@mail.example.com">>/etc/rc.d/rc.local
#Document which kickstart file this is:
echo ks-server-install_2004-02-22.cfg > /etc/ks-release
##########CLEAN UP#############
cd /root
/bin/rm -rf /tmp/install
echo | mail -s"Done With Kickstart on $HOST" admin@example.com
chvt 1                                    #Tear down the fancy chvt
```

Note Installing things like chkrootkit at install time is rather cool, but ultimately not very useful. This is because once a box is cracked (a.k.a. hacked), you cannot trust anything on the box. Many of the newer rootkits out there can change the way the kernel works and modify system memory (infecting seemingly secure parts of the system) systemically. The chkrootkit install in this kickstart %postsection is just a demonstration to just let you see what's possible from within this environment (on the fly downloading, decompressing, and compiling and installation of a package). For more information on the modern issues of crackers and the threats of rootkits, see this article: http://neworder.box.sk/newsread.php?newsid=4182.

That's it. Save the changes to the `%post` config area of your `ks-server.cfg` file to do some testing in the next section.

Creating a Kickstart Provisioning Server

You're going to love this part. All you have to do to create a kickstart server is to set up an FTP, HTTP, or NFS server and dump the CDs on it in an easy-to-reach place. It can even be password protected if you want.

All the footwork is really done on the client side with our boot media, anaconda, and our `ks.cfg` files.

Tip Some administrators who like to centrally administer their kickstart files and who don't want a lot of outdated kickstart floppies or the like out there floating around, put their actual production `ks.cfg` files out on the network in a centralized place. This way when they make an update to the centralized `ks.cfg` file(s), all new installs make use of them, regardless of what old boot disks are out there.

The first step to setting up your new kickstart content server is to put the install content of the three Fedora Core CDs in place on the FTP server.

1. Sit down at your FTP server with the Fedora Core install CDs in hand.

2. Insert Fedora Core CD 1 and run the following commands:

```
# mount /mnt/cdrom/
# cp -af /mnt/cdrom/* /var/ftp/pub/
# eject
```

3. Insert Fedora Core CD 2 and run these commands:

```
# mount /mnt/cdrom/
# cp -af /mnt/cdrom/Fedora/ /var/ftp/pub/
# eject
```

Insert Fedora Core CD 3 and run the same commands as with CD 2.

Note Depending on your distro, you may not need to issue the `mount` commands. Some newer Linux distros have automounting services configured to do this for you.

4. Clean up all the TBL files in the FTP area:

```
# find /var/ftp/pub/ -name "*.TBL" -exec rm {} \;
```

5. Make sure that your FTP daemon is on and configured:

```
# /etc/init.d/vsftpd start ; chkconfig vsftpd on
Starting vsftpd for vsftpd:                    [ OK ]
#chkconfig --list vsftpd
vsftpd      0:off  1:off   2:on  3:on  4:on 5:on 6:off
```

Congratulations, you've just set up a Fedora Core Linux Kickstart Provisioning Server! Setting up Red Hat distro kickstart servers such as RH 9 or Red Hat Enterprise Linux; these are identical to Fedora except that they use the directory name `RedHat` instead of `Fedora`.

This can also be done via username-protected FTP space or even via login-protected httpd/web share.

Centralizing and Standardizing Your Kickstart Files

Now that you have the CD content in place, I recommend also setting up your `ks.cfg` files for your server, workstation, laptop loads, and so on out on a centralized web share with standard link names that point to the latest version (you'll see). Some place that anyone can get to (unless you have security concerns, and then it can be password protected). This will enable you to literally install a desktop from around the world over the Internet if the FTP file share and web share of `ks.cfg` files are available, all with nothing more than a network connection and a boot floppy. Very powerful. Very nice.

To make web-based file shares where our own (non-CD) kickstart-related files will go, simply make a directory on the web server called `installs` (we're using `ssh` remotely to do this for us) and then copy (`scp`) the `ks.cfg` files over to your web server's default website under your `installs` directory:

```
# ssh root@www.example.com mkdir /var/www/html/installs
root@www.example.com's password:
# scp ks-files/ks-*.cfg root@www.example.com:/var/www/html/installs/
root@www.example.com's password:
ks-everything.cfg                              100% 1812     67.2KB/s   00:00
ks-IT-desktop_2004-02-16.cfg                   100% 1446     98.0KB/s   00:00
ks-IT-desktop_2004-02-20.cfg                   100% 1446      1.7MB/s   00:00
ks-my-first-install_2004-02-21.cfg             100% 1877     89.0KB/s   00:00
ks-server-laptop-install_2004-02-22.cfg        100% 1877      1.9MB/s   00:00
ks-workstation_2004-02-19.cfg                  100% 1446      1.5MB/s   00:00
ks-workstation_2004-02-20.cfg                  100% 1446      1.5MB/s   00:00
```

Note In the kickstart example in this chapter we are using a centralized `ks.cfg` file that is accessed via HTTP. Once you load your `ks.cfg` file (either locally from disk or remotely)

and get the kickstart up, you see (as somewhat seen in our `ks.cfg` file) how you can access data, scripts, and packages located on other data shares including HTTP, NFS, and FTP. This is done just to illustrate the various ways in which you can load your data over the network. So if you're going to set up your own kickstart server, you can mix and match data stores of NFS, FTP, or HTTP throughout the install process, or keep them in one unified share such as HTTP or NFS. It's up to you.

And then log in to the web server and set up standard symlink pointers from standard names that you reference from the client side of the kickstart, to point to the specific file names that you change, update, and have date stamps on the centralized web server:

```
# ssh root@www.example.com
root@www.example.com's password:
Last login: Thu Feb 19 23:17:12 2004
# cd /var/www/html/installs/
#
# ls
ks-everything.cfg                        ks-server-laptop-install_2004-02-22.cfg
ks-IT-desktop_2004-02-16.cfg             ks-workstation_2004-02-19.cfg
ks-IT-desktop_2004-02-20.cfg             ks-workstation_2004-02-20.cfg
ks-my-first-install_2004-02-21.cfg
```

Set up your symlink pointers:

```
# ln -s ks-server-laptop-install_2004-02-22.cfg ks-server.cfg
# ln -s ks-workstation_2004-02-20.cfg ks-workstation.cfg
# ln -s ks-IT-desktop_2004-02-20.cfg ks-desktop.cfg
# ls -la | tr -s " "| cut -f9,10,11 -d" "
.
..
ks-desktop.cfg -> ks-IT-desktop_2004-02-20.cfg
ks-everything.cfg
ks-IT-desktop_2004-02-16.cfg
ks-IT-desktop_2004-02-20.cfg
ks-my-first-install_2004-02-21.cfg
ks-server.cfg -> ks-server-laptop-install_2004-02-22.cfg
ks-server-laptop-install_2004-02-22.cfg
ks-workstation_2004-02-19.cfg
ks-workstation_2004-02-20.cfg
ks-workstation.cfg -> ks-workstation_2004-02-20.cfg
# exit
```

The `ls` command was to keep the output clean and understandable. The point here is how the standard names that you are going to reference from your kickstart clients will be standardized file names, which are simply pointers to the actual newest version of each particular `ks.cfg` file.

Now your client site boot media will be able to point to standard `ks.cfg` file names like

```
http://www.example.com/installs/ks-server.cfg
```

or

```
http://www.example.com/installs/ks-workstation.cfg
```

while keeping some form of sanity and organization on the back side of things. Next comes the fun part: creating and testing the client-side boot media.

Creating Your Kickstart Provisioning Boot Media

You've got the kickstart server set up. You've modified the various ks.cfg files and have ks-server.cfg file and a ks-workstation.cfg files ready to be used remotely. Now let's take a moment and talk about Red Hat's (and now Fedora Core's) standards for client side, kickstart install boot media.

Caution

Many people who set up production kickstart servers put the ks.cfg files on the boot media itself. In practice, especially the IT environment, this is begging for trouble. With this setup, every time you make an update to a ks.cfg file, you have to contact everyone in the company and get them to download your latest and greatest boot floppy or boot CD and discard or erase their old boot disks with the old ks.cfg files. In short, it doesn't work, and those old boot floppies just keep popping up and messing things up for everyone. Just take a tip from those who have gone before you and centralize your ks.cfg files—pointing to standardized web reference names (or links) from your modified and automated boot media. The result is that by doing it this way, your "boot media version" is now irrelevant. The only better solution is either a homegrown integrated PXE-LAN environment (diskless kickstarts) OS provisioning system or Red Hat's own Satellite/Provisioning server, which huge provisioning shops like Rackspace might run. For more information on the Red Hat servers, see www.redhat.com/software/rhn/table/#architecture

Finding Red Hat Boot Images

Red Hat boot floppies used to be divided into local media boot floppy images called boot.img and network-capable boot images called bootnet.img. These can still be seen in the older (nonenterprise) sections of Red Hat mirror sites such as the one we maintain at Rackspace:

```
ftp://mirror.rackspace.com/redhat/linux/7.3/en/os/i386/images/
```

This system was nice, but with all the motherboard chip sets, IDE controllers, and network card drivers, Red Hat quickly ran out of room on that bootnet.img floppy image.

To remedy this, Red Hat now provides only one boot floppy image, called bootdisk.img. It allows for basic local HD- and CD-based installs to IDE drives. For network installs or installs that require network drivers (FTP, HTTP, NFS installs), SCSI/RAID or PCMICA mass storage drivers (that is, any third party drivers), bootdisk.img needs to load the drivers (after booting from bootdisk.img) from either the drvnet.img, drvblock.img, or pcmciadd.img driver disk, respectively. This process can be a nuisance, so Red Hat also has a bootable CD image that has all of these drivers built in. Figure 4-2 shows the boot screen from the bootdisk.img or the boot.iso (CD).

These boot media images are available on all Fedora Core FTP mirror sites as well as on Fedora Core CD 1. See Table 4-1 for a description of what each image does.

To get a listing of Fedora Core mirror sites where you can download these boot images, go to http://fedora.redhat.com/download/mirrors.html.

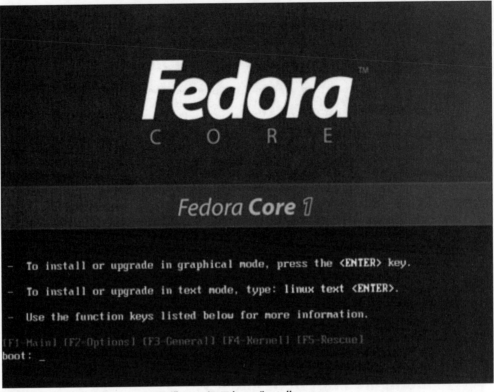

Figure 4-2: The Fedora Core CD/floppy/PXE boot/install screen.

Table 4-1: Fedora Core Boot Images on CD and Mirror Sites

Media Files	Description
Bootdisk.img	Required boot floppy image for Fedora Core installs from CD or hard drive media. Also base boot for network and block device (SCSI/RAID) installs (1.44M).
Drvblock.img	Supplemental block device drivers such as storage controllers, SCSI, and RAID controllers (1.44M).
Drvnet.img	Supplemental network device drivers such as NIC (network interface card) drivers (1.44M).
Pcmciadd.img	Supplemental PCMCIA/PC-Card driver disk (1.44M)
Pxeboot/	The directory of files to put on your PXE/DHCP server to allow pure network-based boot and installs (~3–4M)
Boot.iso	A standalone CD image that includes all the boot and driver info from bootdisk.img, the drvblock.img, drvnet.img, and the pcmpciadd.img floppy images. Good for doing machine boots for single media network installs.

Considering Network Install Options

There are three general boot options for performing a network install: floppy disks, CDs, and PXE.

✦ *Stock or custom boot floppy network installs* : This type of installation uses the bootdisk.img floppy image, along with one to three standard driver disks. These driver disks enable the install time environment to get to network or media that has other install-related files (such as kickstart config files). Within such floppy-based installations you have two alternatives:

- Stock: Use the stock bootdisk.img boot floppy image and whichever of the three driver disks you might require (block device driver, network driver, and PCMCIA driver disk images). This method can require manually swapping floppies at least once, so this makes for a poor automated install process. You also have to make your clients manually point the boot/install process to a centralized network share of your kickstart config file(s) where all of your install parameters are defined. This method is very prone to typos and not very user friendly.

- Slightly Customized: This method uses the same one to four driver floppies as with the Stock method, but you slightly modify the boot disk to have your boot config file automatically point to the correct network location for the kickstart config file(s). Of the two main forms of floppy installs, this tends to be the more popular since it is more automated.

 Note There is a third, less common method that can totally automate the entire install process all from a single boot floppy (with network and other drivers built-in), but it is technically very complex and beyond the scope of this chapter. This is a method by which you can make your own custom, automated, single, hybrid boot/driver floppy with all the drivers that you need. This single boot/install/driver floppy has your own custom initrd (initial RAM disk) file needed to automate everything from a single boot disk. If you don't know what an initrd file is, then you probably don't want to even think about this option. If you're still interested more information on this useful subject can be found at http://linuxcourse.rutgers.edu/bootdisk.html.

The fact is we are more and more moving away from floppies as a common media, especially for specialized boot environments like kickstart. Some newer laptops no longer come with floppy drives. Keep in mind, however, that if you prefer using floppies, the first of these alternatives is simpler for you (creating the floppies), but more difficult and error prone for the end user doing the install. The second method is probably the way most people should do floppy-based network installs, as it is much easier for the end user, still requires a bit of floppy swapping by the user, but only slight customization on your behalf. Details on the second option are covered in the *Creating Customized Boot Floppies* section later in the chapter.

Note It should also be noted that while it is considered a technically bad management practice (in an enterprise at least) to put your ks.cfg file(s) on the floppy itself, this is still an option available to you. If you decide to do this, the boot option to point anaconda to the floppy for the ks.cfg file from the boot: prompt is linux ks=floppy.

✦ *Stock or Custom Boot CD* : Use the boot.iso CD image, and either have your clients manually point to a centralized HTTP share of your ks.cfg files or make your own slightly customized CD image that totally automates this. Either way, you have a single media network install solution. These procedures are covered in the *Making a Network Install Boot CD* section.

✦ *LAN PXE boot solution* : This solution is available only if all of your people have a PXE-capable network card and have the card and machines BIOS set up for PXE network booting. Since most IT administrators do not have access (or clearance) to set up a full PXE boot environment, and since this configuration would also have to be duplicated across all company LANs (since PXE/DHCP/bootp is a LAN broadcast only solution), this solution falls outside the scope of this book. If interested in this option, see `www.redhat.com/docs/manuals/enterprise/RHEL-3-Manual/sysadmin-guide/ch-pxe.html`.

Given all this, the boot CD seems to be the easiest and more forward-compatible network install option for doing Red Hat Enterprise or Fedora Core kickstart/anaconda installs. Since all CDs and machines are pretty much bootable nowadays, it's usually easier to either use a stock boot.iso boot CD and point it manually to your network-based `ks.cfg` file(s) or to modify the `boot.iso` image for automatic kickstarts for fire-and-forget installs. Rebuilding the floppy image with a single disk hybrid OS/kernel/initrd setup is beyond the scope of this chapter, but we give a link to more information on doing this in one of the aforementioned notes. Let's start with the older and more unruly to manage multifloppies method, and then we'll turn to the more elegant modern CDs method.

Creating Customized Boot Floppies

If you want to do your network-based OS install using the three floppy images, first copy the `bootdisk.img`, `drvnet.img`, and `drvblock.img`, from the CD 1 (in `Fedora/images/`) or from a mirror site. Then follow these steps:

1. Write your floppy images out to three blank/formatted disks using `dd`:

   ```
   # dd if=bootdisk.img of=/dev/fd0
   ```

   ```
   # dd if=drvnet.img of=/dev/fd0
   ```

   ```
   # dd if=drvblock.img of=/dev/fd0
   ```

Note　The drvblock floppy is needed only if you're installing to or from mass media storage such as SCSI, RAID, or specialized storage hardware. It's not bad to have, but usually not required on most PCs.

2. Insert and mount the bootdisk floppy:

   ```
   #  mount /dev/fd0 /mnt/floppy/
   #  cd /mnt/floppy/
   #  ls
   boot.msg       initrd.img     options.msg    rescue.msg     splash.lss    vmlinuz
   general.msg    ldlinux.sys    param.msg      snake.msg      syslinux.cfg
   ```

   Now with your new boot floppy mounted, you can start editing and customizing it to point to your kickstart files out on the network.

Tip　If you don't want to have to do this every time you want another identical boot disk, then after you work all the bugs out and tweak out your bootdisk just so, you can *loopback mount* the actual `img` file as a *loopback file system* (with the `-o loop` mount option):

   ```
   # mount -o loop,wr bootdisk.img /mnt/floppy/
   ```

cd into /mnt/floppy and edit away on your "phantom floppy" image. Then when you're done:

```
#  cd
#  umount /mnt/floppy
```

and from then on when you dd a copy of the img file to a disk you will have all of your changes! Try doing *that* on a stock Windows box!

3. After mounting your new bootdisk floppy, you need to make some space on the disk by deleting the .msg files:

```
# /bin/rm *.msg
```

Tip

Keep a few of these .msg files around. These would be handy later when you decide that you want an interactive user menu with directions and help options.

4. Now edit the syslinux.cfg file to look like this and add the bold bit (all on one line):

```
default linux
prompt 1
timeout 1
label linux
  kernel vmlinuz
  append initrd=initrd.img ramdisk_size=8192
         ks=http://example.com/installs/ks-server.cfg
         ksdevice=eth0 dd   <--- Note

label memtest86
  kernel memtest
  append -
```

Note

The trailing dd boot option in the isolinux.cfg file has nothing to do with the dd command that we used earlier. The dd boot option is what tells anaconda to ask for the drvnet and/or drvblock driver disks so that it can either get online or install SCSI or RAID card drivers—must in our case since we need the dvrnet disk's network card drivers to get online and our kickstart file! This required "floppy swapping" illustrates how floppy's time has come and gone, and we will see how using the single boot CD boot.iso is a much nicer and more modern option.

5. After you're done with your edits, cd back home and unmount the floppy:

```
# cd
# umount /mnt/floppy
```

Tip

You can keep the boot.msg if you want to have user messages and a time out with pointers to the various ks.cfg files that you have on your web server. It's up to you, but just watch the space on the floppy. You may have to do your editing off disk and then copy your final edits back over.

Also, if you use an editor like vi or vim (which most of you will), and you want to quickly do your edits in place (on the floppy), then invoke vi/vim like this: vi -n /mnt/floppy/syslinux.cfg. The -n will keep a temporary swap file from being created by vim (which can create really problems when trying to edit files when you have very little elbow room).

Finally, unlike most UNIX/Linux systems, these config files are standard (or nonstandard) MS-DOS CR/LF text files, so you can actually get away with using DOS/Windows type editors on them, such as notepad. The filesystem is also FAT(12) so it can be accessed from just about any OS without much of a problem.

Now take your new bootdisk and driver disks to a test machine and see how they work!

Floppies, Laptops, and Kernels

A couple things to know about laptops: If you expect to use the PCMCIA or PCCard slots during the install, you will also need the `pcmcia.img` floppy driver disk (unless you're using the CD boot media, which includes it). If you don't need the PCMCIA hardware during install time, don't worry about it. After the postboot OS downloads kicks in and begins to run, the same Fedora installer that installs from CD will be running, and will detect any supported hardware and install the correct drivers for your machine. `pcmcia.img` (as well as the other driver disks) is just an install time thing in case you need a PCMCIA network card, external CD-ROM, or SCSI/RAID driver support to gain access to the `ks.cfg` file and the remaining bootstrap image itself.

This being said, there have been some strange problems with Fedora Core's support of PCMCIA/PC-card controller technology as well as with some older network cards. If you are experiencing similar hardware problems, monitor the buzilla bug lists at `https://bugzilla` `.redhat.com/bugzilla/query.cgi?format=simple`.

After going to this URL, just search on the "Product: Fedora Core," "Version: <your version>", and "Component: kernel-pcmcia-cs" for an up-to-date status of these issues. It was still in a state of flux at the time of this writing.

On newer laptops, if you also experience problems with battery monitoring, PCMCIA/PCCard hardware, network service lockups, and other such *Laptop-isms*, try adding the `acpi=on` kernel boot option to your `grub.conf` kernel line (the one below is wrapped):

```
title Fedora Core (2.4.22-1.2129.nptl)
        root (hd0,1)
        kernel /vmlinuz-2.4.22-1.2129.nptl ro root=LABEL=/
            hdc=ide-scsi acpi=on
        initrd /initrd-2.4.22-1.2129.nptl.img
```

Adding the `acpi=on` will ensure that your laptop's ACPI functions will be enabled. As with Fedora Core (1 at least) this kernel option is compiled to be off by default. Additionally, if you have a built-in CDRW drive and you're having problems writing to it, you may also want to add the `hdX=ide-scsi` option (where X is the device letter of your CDRW drive). Hopefully, many of these issues will be fixed in newer versions of Fedora Core and by the next release of Enterprise Linux.

Making a Network Install Boot CD

Given the problems with floppy-based network kickstart installs, let's look at the CD option via the stock CD boot image `boot.iso` from our own CD 1's path `Fedora/images/boot.iso`.

Note   You can get this CD boot image `boot.iso` from one of the Fedora Core mirror sites if you don't have the Fedora stock install CDs handy.

We're going to cover a couple of different ways of installing from a CD—an easy (stock) way and a not-so-easy (custom) way. The easy way is, well, easier for the admin upfront, but it forces the clients (or installer person) to type in special pointers to point to your centralized `ks.cfg` file(s) out on the network. The second, not-so-easy, way is cool because it requires no intervention from the install person at all (other than inserting a CD), but it takes a lot more footwork on your part.

Creating a Boot CD the Easy Way

First mount CD 1 and copy the stock boot.iso file from the `Fedora/images/` directory:

```
#   cd /root
#   mkdir tmp ; cd tmp
#   cp -a /mnt/cdrom/images/boot.iso
```

Next, insert a blank CD-R into your burner. Since this is only a 3 to −4MB image file, I recommend using the small "business card" CD-Rs (more impressive too). Proceed to burn the `boot.iso` with the following command:

```
#   cdrecord dev=0,0 /root/tmp/boot.iso ; eject
```

See the man page for `cdrecord` and use `cdrecord -scanbus` to see your CDR/W drive id number, or if more convenient, iso files can also be burned by Windows-based CDR burning software such as Nero.

CD Burning Errors

If you try to burn your CD with `cdrecord` and get errors like this

```
# cdrecord dev=0,0,0
/var/ftp/pub/fedora/core/1/i386/os/images/boot.iso ; eject
Cdrecord-Clone 2.01a19 (i686-redhat-linux-gnu) Copyright (C)
1995-2003 Jrg Schilling
scsidev: '0,0,0'
scsibus: 0 target: 0 lun: 0
Linux sg driver version: 3.1.25
Error trying to open /dev/scd0 exclusively ... retrying in 1
second.
[...]
Error trying to open /dev/scd0 exclusively ... retrying in 1
second.
Error trying to open /dev/scd0 exclusively ... retrying in 1
second.
bailing out..
```

then something else may have control of your CD-R device. Sometimes processes such as `kscd` or

Continued

Continued

the like may have a hold on it. You can detect and kill such processes like this:

```
# ps auxw|grep [k]scd
tweeks 4187 0.0 4.1 24984 9272 ? S 15:09 0:00 kscd -session
117f00000100010721452290000042380008_1080711996_7
26640
# killall kscd
# ps auxw | grep [k]scd
```

Now your cdrecord session should work fine.

Next, try a test boot/install on a test client machine. When you get to the boot prompt, type

```
Boot: linux ks=http:// www.example.com/installs/ks-server.cfg ksdevice=eth0
```

substituting the http path where you've placed a copy of your ks-server.cfg file. (This is why it takes a bit more work on the client side. One typo by the client, and the install will fail to start.)

Creating a Boot CD the Not-So-Easy Way

You can make things easier for the person doing the client side of the install by creating your own boot.iso disk with the http:// pointer built in. To do this, you need to have the boot CD automatically have its ks= pointer pointing out to your web server's ks files. The following instructions show you how to do that:

1. Mount the boot.iso image to some mount point (such as /mnt/tmp or even /mnt/cdrom):

```
#  mount -o loop,rw /root/fedora-core-1-boot.iso /mnt/tmp
#  ls -la /mnt/tmp/isolinux
total 4257
drwxr-xr-x   2 root    root         2048 Nov 3 17:45 .
drwxr-xr-x   3 root    root         2048 Nov 3 17:45 ..
-r--r--r--   1 root    root         2048 Nov 3 17:45 boot.cat
-rw-r--r--   2 root    root          292 Nov 3 17:45 boot.msg
-rw-r--r--   2 root    root         1034 Nov 3 17:45 general.msg
-rw-r--r--   4 root    root      3012543 Nov 3 17:45 initrd.img
-r--r--r--   2 root    root         9428 Nov 3 17:45 isolinux.bin
-r-xr-xr-x   2 root    root          569 Nov 3 17:45 isolinux.cfg
-r--r--r--   2 root    root        84420 Nov 3 17:45 memtest
-rw-r--r--   2 root    root          788 Nov 3 17:45 options.msg
-rw-r--r--   2 root    root          872 Nov 3 17:45 param.msg
-rw-r--r--   2 root    root          490 Nov 3 17:45 rescue.msg
-rw-r--r--   2 root    root          549 Nov 3 17:45 snake.msg
-rw-r--r--   2 root    root         6773 Nov 3 17:45 splash.lss
-r--r--r--   1 root    root         2880 Nov 3 17:45 TRANS.TBL
-rw-r--r--   4 root    root      1228344 Nov 3 17:45 vmlinuz
```

2. Copy all the files to a "scratch area" for editing:

```
#  cd /root
#  mkdir boot-iso-files
#  cp -a /mnt/tmp/* boot-iso-files/
#  umount /mnt/tmp
#  cd boot-iso-files/
#  cd isolinux/
#  ls
boot.cat    initrd.img   memtest      rescue.msg TRANS.TBL
boot.msg    isolinux.bin options.msg snake.msg vmlinuz
general.msg isolinux.cfg param.msg    splash.lss
```

Note The `isolinux.bin`, `initrd.img`, and `vmlinuz` together are what boots the system here. The `inslinux.cfg` is like a `lilo.conf` file that you're going to edit to provide control over the automatic `ks=. . .` parameters.

3. Edit the `isolinux.cfg` file down to this and add the bold bit (all on one line):

```
default linux
prompt 1
timeout 300              <--- Timeout in seconds before it starts
label linux
  kernel vmlinuz
  append initrd=initrd.img ramdisk_size=8192
     ks=http://example.com/installs/ks-server.cfg
     ksdevice=eth0

label memtest86
  kernel memtest
  append -
```

Include and change the boot message files if you want.

Caution The append line and the two following lines should all be a single line. Allow it to simply wrap around the screen. Do not break the line.

Tip The `memtest86` you see listed is a built-in hardware memory tester, one of the best out there for Linux. These CDs are also very useful for doing memory burn in tests. Remember this the next time you have some suspected bad RAM you need checked out.

4. `cd` back one dir and make your new iso image to save out to `my-server-boot.iso` on your hard drive:

```
#  cd ..
#  ls
isolinux TRANS.TBL
#
# mkisofs -o ../my-server-boot.iso -V 'Fedora Core Server
Install' -b isolinux/isolinux.bin -c isolinux/boot.cat
```

```
-no-emul-boot -boot-load-size -boot-info-table
 -R -J -T .
```

5. Insert a blank CD-R disc and burn your new `boot.iso` image to CD:

```
# ls -lah      my-server-boot.iso
-rw-r--r--  1 root    root            4.3M Feb 23 10:00 my-server-boot.iso
# cdrecord dev=6,0 speed=6 my-server-boot.iso
```

When `cdrecord` finishes, you should be able to boot a test system from your new automated `boot.iso` disc. If your customized kickstart file is correctly located at `http://example.com/installs/ks-server.cfg`, as I had shared it out previously (or whatever URL/share *you* are using), then everything should autoinstall just fine with zero human intervention aside from inserting the CD and powering up.

> **Tip**   These instructions just covered the bare essentials. You might want to spend a little extra time and create a network boot and install CD that can allow various install time options of using a server load, a desktop load, or a workstation load via different `ks.cfg` files—all located out on your http server via standardized symlink names. Then you can use the built-in menus (in `isolinux.cfg`) on the `boot.iso` to give the install person some more options, while you still centrally control what happens with each one of those loads from the `ks.cfg` links and files you have stored online at `www.example.com/installs/`.

More Floppy and CD Customization Information

For more information on customizing your floppy and CD images, look at the following links:

✦ `http://linuxcourse.rutgers.edu/bootdisk.html`

✦ `www.linuxjournal.com/article.php?sid=6473`

✦ `http://birger.sh/computing/RedHat_9_customized_install_media_howto.html`

✦ `http://acd.ucar.edu/~fredrick/linux/linux-kickstart/`

Testing Your New Kickstart Media

Testing your kickstart boot media is fairly simple. Pop in the `bootdisk.img` floppy or `boot.iso` CD, verify that the machine BIOS is set to boot off that media, that your networking hardware is all connected, and that you're on a DHCP LAN (if you're doing nonstatic IP network loads), and power up.

Floppy Installs

Remember, if you're using the `bootdisk.img` and the network, you're going to have the driver disk in hand.

If you're using a stock `bootdisk.img`-based floppy, before you get any drivers loaded up you will still need to tell the program from where to get its `ks.cfg` file. In this example, we manually point it to the web share that we've created when it gives up the boot prompt:

```
boot: linux ks=http://  example.com/installs/ks-server.cfg ksdevice=eth0
```

You will then have to manually feed it the drvnet driver floppy so it can see the network and go to the `ks.cfg` file that you pointed it to.

If you're running a custom build (automated) floppy and configured your boot floppy correctly, it should default to the proper URL for the `ks.cfg` (even though you may not see it), load the syslinux boot environment, and then prompt you for your driver disk(s). At this time you'll need to start feeding it floppies for whatever hardware you need access to during the install (usually just the drvnet disk).

Regardless of the type of floppy install you're going with (manual or automatic), you will need to insert the `pcmcia.img` disk (if you have a PCMCIA-based network card) and/or your `drvnet.img` disk for network drivers. Also, if you are installing any block device or mass storage devices such as SCSI drives or RAID controllers or the like, you'll also want the `dvrblock.img` floppy handy.

After these drivers are all loaded and if you're running a customized/automated `bootdisk.img` floppy, the Anaconda installer should take off and start following your kickstart config file and scripts. No more intervention should be required.

Note If the automation aspect of the installer stops somewhere and it starts prompting you for questions that are supposed to be automated (such as the keyboard, mouse, partition layout, and so on), this indicates that there is a problem in your kickstart config file. It's probably a typo, or maybe you left something commented out that shouldn't be (the `clearpart` or `part` lines are common mistakes). Go back and check your install script line by line.

CD Installs

CD installs are a bit nicer if you ask me. If you've set up your own custom `boot.iso` CD with the preconfigured `ks.cfg` network pointers, then this is really a fire-and-forget operation. Just be sure not to walk away and forget about it if you have configured the kickstart to reboot when it's done. Doing so would put the machine into a perpetual install–reboot–install–reboot loop that will most likely get you a visit from your NOC (network operation center) wanting to know who's been DoSing the network and eating up the network bandwidth all day. This type of event usually lands one a colorful nickname with your cohorts as well.

If you are using a stock boot.iso-based CD image, you will still have to give only one piece of information at the initial `boot:` prompt:

```
boot: linux ks=http://example.com/installs/ks-server.cfg ksdevice=eth0
```

Tip If your install does stop, hang, or start asking you questions that should be automated, use the virtual terminals detailed in Table 2-3 to look at the various parts of the install mechanism. After the install has begun, CTRL+ALT+F2 will give you a root bash prompt so you can see the hard drive where the files are being installed, poke around the kernel modules, config files, and so on. Just be aware that this shell is a very sparse minimalist implementation and is for basic troubleshooting only—no man pages or advanced functionality. However, you can do things like FTP out, download packages, and affect changes on the system. Just be careful. ALT+F3 gets you the install log, ALT+F4 all kernel messaging, and ALT+F5 all partitioning and formatting information. These can really help you when tracking down problems (and some times fix them) during your first few install troubleshooting sessions. Above all, take your time and read the logs to help you troubleshoot problems in your `ks.cfg` file. It usually takes several attempts to come up with a perfect install script.

You are now armed with all the information that you need to kickstart your own desktop, workstation, server, or customized systems automatically and from any network enabled PC.

Troubleshooting Common Kickstart Problems

Kickstarting systems entail a ton of client-side, boot media, network-related, and server-related issues. It can be a real bear to track down kickstart provisioning issues even for experienced administrators, much less the newly initiated! Here are a few of the most common problems users face with kickstart, and some tips for resolving them.

✦ *How do I make a bootable floppy or bootable CD from the* `bootdisk.img` *or* `boot.iso` *file, respectively*? If you have downloaded the `bootdisk.img` and other files, follow the procedures here to create a bootable disk.

- To create a bootable floppy disk from Linux:

    1. insert a blank floppy

    2. type the following command:

        ```
        #  dd if=bootdisk.img of=/dev/fd0
        ```

- To create a bootable floppy disk from Windows:

    1. type the following line to get the rawrite command from the install CD 1 (where D: is your CD-ROM drive):

        ```
        C:\temp\>  copy D:\dosutils\raw*.*
        ```

    2. Insert a blank/formatted floppy and run the following command with your disk image file:

        ```
        C:\temp\>  rawrite -f bootdisk.img
        ```

    3. Reboot

    4. If it does not boot off the floppy, verify that your BIOS is set up to boot from the floppy first and hard drive second, and then reboot.

- To create a bootable CD from Linux with a blank CD-R in your burner, as root type

    ```
    #  cdrecord dev= 0 ,0 /root/boot.iso
    ```

    See the man page for `cdrecord` and use `cdrecord -scanbus` to see your CDR/W drive id number (the first zero in the preceding code).

- To create a bootable CD from Windows use your favorite burning software to burn the `boot.iso` file (type ISO-9660) to a blank CDR

✦ *The system locks up when some people try to connect to the FTP shares on the kickstart server.* This can be caused by firewalls, or especially iptables, interfering with the underlying FTP, HTTP, or NFS-based protocols. Try getting around this problem by using an HTTP/web file share instead of an FTP share, or just by quickly shutting off iptables on the client, and then the server (if this is feasible). If the problem clears up, then this was the cause. If you're running FTP and want to try using HTTP quickly instead, just put your CD install files (the Fedora or Red Hat directories from your CDs) into a web directory like `/var/www/html/kick-data` and reconfigure your `ks.cfg` file's `url -url` line accordingly:

```
.
install
url --url  http://example.com/kick-data/
lang en_US.UTF-8
.
.
```

Put the `ks.cfg` file back on the floppy or on your network share and try it again.

✦ *My kickstart gets to the same place every time and then just stops. It never starts actually installing files.* The problem could be a number of variables, from a typo in your `ks.cfg` file to problems with the network, DNS, your server, or firewalls. One great troubleshooting method is to use the virtual terminals to switch over and see what's going on. Remember to use (CTRL+)ALT+F2 to get to a bash prompt to poke around the system while it's being installed, ALT+F3 to view the actual install log, ALT+F4 to see all kernel messaging as it's happening (good to identify many errors), and ALT+F5 to see any partitioning and formatting information in real time. ALT+F7 will take you back to the GUI install screen (if GUI install mode is being used). If you are not able to change even virtual terminals, then you're not all the way through the network boot stage and you probably have a typo on your kickstart config file that is preventing it from coming all the way up (look specifically at your `url -url` and `network` lines).

✦ *My kickstart always dumps me out of the automated install and makes me enter the keyboard type, network settings, and media install source (CDROM, FTP, NFS, and so on)—just as if I were doing a completely manual install.* This is a clear indicator that you have a problem either in the `syslinux.cfg/isolinux.cfg` file not pointing to your `ks.cfg` file correctly (either locally or over the network), or there is a typo in your `ks.cfg` file. Check them all and follow the flow of pointers.

✦ *My kickstart floppy install just keeps asking me for driver disks, never loads my network card driver, and never allows me to even get a DHCP address to get on the network!* This is usually associated with unsupported hardware or hardware that is having problems being autodetected by the syslinux bootstrap environment. The problem is sometimes as simple as reseating your network card, or setting the machine's BIOS to reissue all of the PCI bus IRQs. Sometimes it will start working by simply moving a PCI NIC (and telling the BIOS to shuffle IRQs), because a PCI shared IRQ bug with your PCI/motherboard chipset and your cards. This latter problem seems to crop up more in systems with mass storage cards such as SCSI or RAID cards, but you might see this also with other types of cards such as sound cards, which have several IRQs. Try the hardware IRQ tricks first. If this does not clear things up, also try the `boot:` prompt kernel modifier variations of `acpi=on`, `pci=biosirq`, and `pci=noacpi`. If nothing works there, then it's time to hit Google, or visit `http://bugzilla.redhat.com/`.

✦ *My kickstart starts off just fine, and then half way through the install I get an error message saying something about unresolved dependencies.* This is usually because you manually added RPM packages to the `%packages` section of your `ks.cfg` file. If you're not sure to also install any packages that that package may need, then you can get this error. The proper thing to do is to check out the dependencies a given package has *before* adding it to your kickstart (check this via `rpm -q -requires <packagename>`). That being said, the quick fix is to add the `ks.cfg` option `%packages -resolvedeps` to the packages line, which will hunt through the XML and RPM dependency lists to discover everything you need to install a given package, get those packages and install them first, as well as any of *their* sub-dependencies! A *very* nice change from the old days of manually tracking this stuff down.

Kickstart Troubleshooting References

It's hard to find good information on kickstart installs if you don't even know what questions to ask. So Table 4-2 contains a few time-tried resources that will help round out some of the more detailed aspects and options of setting up a kickstart provisioning environment.

Table 4-2: Kickstart Troubleshooting References

Reference	*Location (addresses should be one single line)*
Red Hat EL3 System Administration Guide: Ch9, Kickstart Installations	`www.redhat.com/docs/manuals/enterprise/ RHEL-3-Manual/sysadmin-guide/ch- kickstart2.html`
Red Hat EL3 System Administration Guide: Ch10, Kickstart Configuration	`www.redhat.com/docs/manuals/enterprise/ RHEL-3-Manual/sysadmin-guide/ch-redhat- config-kickstart.html`
Red Hat EL3 Security Guide	`www.redhat.com/docs/manuals/enterprise/ RHEL-3-Manual/security-guide/`
Creating a boot disk for unattended kickstart installation of RH 9: Great technical info on creating your own customer-driver initrd for a single boot/install kickstart floppy.	`http://linuxcourse.rutgers.edu/bootdisk .html`

Summary

The ability to standardize and automate your enterprise OS installs is critical for doing business effectively. Red Hat/Fedora Core allows you to add value by allowing detailed customization of automated enterprise installs with open ended, open source tools such as syslinux/isolinux/anaconda and general networking protocols such as NFS, HTTP, and FTP that together form the backbone of kickstart-based technology.

By leveraging common protocols such as FTP, HTTP, NFS, kickstart allows you perform your own custom, stock, LAN, or even Internet-based OS installs from just about anywhere in the world. The key to making it work for you and keeping it manageable is in the departmental planning, work, and maintenance that goes into the `ks.cfg` files for your various OS install target platforms. Kickstart is just the tool by which you are able to execute these corporation-wide technical strategies.

✦   ✦   ✦

Preparing for Backups and Migration

◆ ◆ ◆ ◆

In This Chapter

Backup types, media and hardware

Backup tools and how to use them

Testing and doing restores

Server migrations

◆ ◆ ◆ ◆

Any system administrator who is serious about running servers in a production environment must have plans for backups and restores. Backups are often overlooked by less experienced IT managers, or are relegated to the new guy as a minor task.

I tell people that backups are a lot like insurance. You don't know how much you really need them until you need them. You can often tell experienced administrators from inexperienced ones when they're putting together productions systems. Those who are experienced (or have been burned in the past) will always ask about backups, backup types, media rotation, retention times, and doing test restores. Those who may not be as experienced may try to save money by including only limited backups, thinking RAID addresses backup-related issues, or even trimming this important aspect of the production server environment from the budget completely.

This chapter starts off with a general discussion of backup types and media, then gets into the included and more traditional backup tools. We explain how to use them, and how to test and actually do restores on a system. We discuss how to migrate data between systems (either old system to new system or data from backups to a reinstalled OS/server), and along the way we touch upon some common backup-related troubleshooting issues that system administrators see in the real world.

Backup Types

Backups can consist of tar-balling your data up and sticking it on another server, dumping a live filesystem to tape, or e-mailing yourself 562MB uuencoded tar files to be reassembled at home. Although none of these are really production quality forms of backup, the whole point of backups is being able to get your system back to its original operating condition after some catastrophic event.

Most production systems require a regular and strictly regimented backup schedule to a set of tapes. To be effective, your plan should include backing up regularly and often, and occasionally rotating sets of tapes off site for safekeeping in case of disaster.

Before you learn how to work with the software tools to get the job done, you need to understand the basics of various types of backups (levels), backup methodology, media, and various related technologies. Then you can start making intelligent decisions about what backups tools to use and how to use them most effectively.

The Myth of RAID Backups

RAID stands for Redundant Array of Inexpensive/Independent Disks. It's a set of hardware and/or software configuration(s) that grants you higher storage hardware availability (from failed disks), storage capacity, and/or gets you storage speed—nothing more. Some people are under the misconception that RAID can function as a backup for their system. This is simply not true.

RAID gets you *hardware availability* with respect to hardware failures (that is, it keeps things running after one of your hard drives die). Backups get you *data availability* with respect to *time*. RAID will NOT save your assets if you accidentally `rm -rf /home` (don't ever type that!), or if you accidentally `rpm -Upgrade` to the latest kernel instead of `-i`nstalling it, nor will RAID help you get your data back if you get hacked, cracked, or rooted. When data is written to a RAID array, it gets written to ALL the disks. RAID *will* save you if one of your hard drives fails. That's all. Hardware availability with respect to, well, hardware!

Backups get you *data availability* for when your *data* fails (that is, `rm -rf *`, `rpm -i kern*`, or `h4x0r3d`). I've heard from many people who were baffled as to why they couldn't just recover their system from RAID. (These are likely the same unfortunate souls who thought that a firewall would protect them from the CodeRed or Nimda Internet Worms.) In short, if you want to protect your system from being down from blown drives, get RAID. If you want to protect your data and OS configuration from, well, yourself and others, get backups.

You may have heard of some newer forms of pseudo-RAID/backup-ish type technologies such as snapshots, LVM, and off line RAID-1 that do give some measure of "data availability" or backup type of functionality. But these are not very common, are beyond the scope of this chapter, and should not be confused with regular RAID-1 or RAID-5. Plus, these solutions do not get you all the security and flexibility of off-site rotated backup tapes.

Types of Backups

What are commonly referred to as *types* of backups should really be called *levels* of backups. What level of backup you want dictates how many files make it to tape (or your backup media of choice). The following sections describe the three main types of backups: full backup, incremental backup, and differential backup.

Full Backup

A *full backup* is simply backing up every file in the system or target directories, regardless of the previous backup time or changes since the last backup. A full backup is what most nonadministrators think of when they think of backups; however, this is not what you should do every time you want to run backups of your system. The time it requires and amount of tapes it needs makes this solution something you don't want to do every time backups are needed, but it *is* still required once in a while to achieve a good overall *backup strategy*.

If you have a corporate file server, for example, running full backups of it every night of the year just is not feasible—not to mention all of your other systems in the corporation. Let's say you have a 300GB RAID-5 corporate file server and you want to back this up every night to your local, measly little four 12/24GB tape drives. If you get a 70% compression rate (yielding

~20GB/tape), this would take you around 15 tapes per night at a cost of around $60/night with a standard 90 data day retention time—over $5,400 for 3 months of tape. And that's just one of your servers. You may have only spent half that much the server itself. The bad thing is over 90 percent of the data on all those tapes is all the same. This is not an efficient method to use in a production environment.

Another issue with full backups is the time required. If each of your four little 12/24GB tape drives chugs along at 35MB/min transfer rate (real world), the effective transfer rate is 140MB/min (assuming that you have your four tape drives on separate SCSI busses running full speed, with a constant *data stream*). All things being equal, your *daily* 300GB file server full backup should take you around 36 hours of continuous backing up, or around *1.5 days*! (And this is assuming that you're there for the full backup, swapping tapes when prompted, and making runs to Taco Bell between tapes.) As you can see, this is not feasible in most real world environments. But more than this, it's wasteful and will turn you into a gray, bitter, old adminstrator who mumbles to himself in the hallway. Don't do it.

But do you really need full backups every night? After all, how much of your data really changes every day? From experience, I can tell you that that the delta (or amount of file change) on our example would generally be less than 1 percent. So in the real world, you could probably just get away backing up the delta of no more than 3GB of data per night (you could get a whole week on one tape!). This leads us to consider other alternatives—incremental and differential backups.

Incremental Backup

Incremental backups are more frugal than full backups. Simply put, incremental backups record everything that's changed since the last backup. To do a restore, you will need the most recent full backup tape(s), plus the tapes of each incremental backup since the full. So with incrementals, you start with a full backup, and then build on that with each incremental only backing up what's changed from night to night. This translates to less data to back up per night, hence less tape used. In fact, you can probably squeeze more than one day's backup per tape if you're careful. However, when implementing an incremental backup system, if you have to do a full restore on Friday, you need the tapes from Thursday, Wednesday, Tuesday, Monday, and all the full tapes from Saturday. Figure 5-1 shows what a daily incremental-based backup looks like.

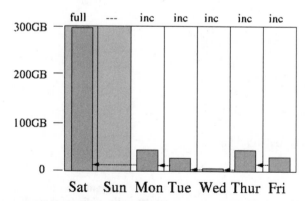

Figure 5-1: Example of using full and incremental backups together.

Note If you don't have people working weekends and can afford to skip backups on Sunday, consider keeping this "the day of rest" (for the tape drives anyway). It gives you an emergency time slot to do large unexpected backups, restores, or run into "full backup overflow" from Saturday if need be so that you don't eat into Monday morning when people start coming in. Nothing slows down live file server access more than running a remote backup of it while people are trying to get to it and use it.

Since more tapes are required to do a full and current restore from any given day with this scheme, (today's tape plus each tape back to and including the full backup) this can make for serious trouble if you can't locate and retrieve all of the tapes required. Even so, an incremental-based backup system *can* be used in a production environment; it's just a nightmare to restore from and increases restore failure risks. It can effectively allow you to get the job done, especially if your department is in a financial pinch and doesn't want to buy all those tapes for full. Just keep in mind: there is not "one best solution" here. The pros and cons of each backup scenario must be considered for your given situation. As we'll see a bit further down, *occasional* incrementals make for a good diverse backup strategy, they're just not ideal to rely on as your sole backup strategy.

Tip If you don't always have budget for new tapes, get them when you can. You'll need them the most when you're totally out. Trust me.

Differential Backups

While an incremental backup records whatever has changed since the last backup of *any* type, a *differential backup* only backs up what has changed since the last full backup. So if we first backup the 300GB file server with a full backup on Saturday, and then every night we backup using differentials, we will typically have something like in the graph shown in Figure 5-2.

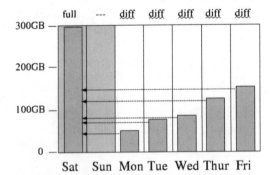

◄-- = new/changed files compared to

Figure 5-2: Example of using full and differential backups together.

Tip When scheduling backups with cron via `crontab -e`, many inexperienced administrators just schedule a time such as midnight or 1:00 A.M. for the backup job. Don't do this. Pick the hour you want your backups to start, and then add a random number of minutes from −12 to +12 to come up with your backup start time (for instance, 1:08 A.M.). Scheduling your backups like this will keep you from running into the classic "top of the hour" problem that less experienced administrators face when their system starts an even-hour database dump, runs backups, fires off a massive tar ball download, and starts scanning the system for file alterations all at once. All this activity starting at the exact same second is bad and can take down an otherwise stable server. Also, note the system's own standard mass cronjob times in `/etc/crontab` and avoid those times as well.

Figure 5-2 shows a full backup on Saturday, with differential backups beginning on Monday. Each day you back up what has changed since the full backup on Saturday (differentials). The great thing about this is that to do a full restore of your system, all you need is the previous night's differential tape, as well as the last full backup set (from Saturday in this case). The major disadvantage of this scenario is that you are still backing up data that has been backed up multiple times (on weeknights), and so you still really use more tape space (or tapes) than the absolute minimum required to get the job done.

Which Backup Strategy Should You Use?

So incremental backups are great in that they use less tape, but you need ALL of them plus the full backup tapes to do a restore. Differentials are great because you only need the latest tape, plus the full backup tape to do a restore. But man, that's a lot of wasted tape.

Wouldn't it be nice if you could use less tape *and* not need so many tapes to be able to do a current restore? You can, using both backup concepts together with *backup levels* in what's called the *Tower of Hanoi* backup strategy.

The Classic Elegance of Level-Based Backups

Some of the more expensive backup suites today have tried to make backups easier and prettier. They wrap a GUI around the backup engine, abstract you from what's really going on at the file/schedule level, and paste slick marketing terminology throughout the tech manual, mixing up or inverting terms like differential and incremental, and even inventing their own terms such as *occasional incremental* or *true differential*. Such muddying of terminology, marketing spin, and sales-speak only add to the confusion when you're planning your company's data recovery strategy. Rather than relying on these commercial suites, consider an established system used by serious UNIX administrators: *backup levels*.

Backup levels are a simple system of numbers from 0 to 9 that allow you to describe and arrange exactly what, how, and when you want your files put to tape. Level 0 is your full backup and levels 1 to 9 are "levels of incrementals" that back up the data changed since the next lower backup level used. See the bird's eye view in Table 5-1.

The idea here is that a backup level of 1 to 9 will backup everything that has changed since the next lower level that it can find. For example, a backup of level 3 will backup everything that has changed since the last level 2 backup. If there was no level 2 backup done, then it backs up to the last level 1; if no level 1, then level 0. Look at Figure 5-3 to see how you could use backup levels to provide a pure incremental backup strategy.

This level-based backup schedule looks just like the Figure 5-1 *incremental* backup configuration, right?

Table 5-1: Backup Level

Backup Level	Description
Level 0	A full backup; backs up all files.
Level 1	The first incremental level; gets all files that have changed since the last level 0 backup. It acts like a differential by getting everything that has changed since the level 0/full backup.
Levels 2–9	Backs up whatever files have changed since the next *lower* level backup. Can work as an incremental if used sequentially, or as a differential if all the same number is used. Can also be "mixed" to create hybrid backup strategies.

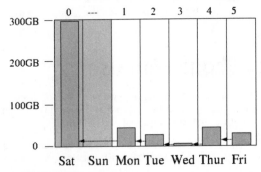

◄-- = new/changed files compared to

Figure 5-3: Using sequential levels to achieve incremental backups.

Now, knowing how these levels work, imagine what you would get if you ran the following level-based backup schedule:

```
S  S  M  T  W  T  F
0  -  2  2  2  2  2
```

Since a backup level seeks the file changes since the next level lower than itself, a 0 2 2 2 2 2 backup schedule would behave like a pure *differential* backup, backing up all changes since the last full backup every night.

So, with numerical backup levels, we can control how much data actually goes to tape. Let's mix and match to see if we can get the most effective and efficient blend: full, incrementals, and differentials.

The Power of TOH

The classic "best scenario" for balancing the most efficient use of tape, data assurance, and file redundancy over time is referred to as the *Tower of Hanoi* (TOH) backup schedule. A formal description of the full TOH schedule can be found at www.pcmag.com/article2/ 0,1759,1155464,00.asp.

Implementing a full TOH schedule can be a real pain with a basic command-line tool like dump and no advanced index/tape pool tracking software. However, if you're on a budget and don't want to use the fancier backup suites that we discuss later, consider the simplified and modified TOH tape rotation schedule that we show here. It does nicely for a production server environment, using nothing but the included dump and restore backup utilities. The TOH schedule proposed here will keep your data safe, secure, and will keep you from having to run full/level 0 or level 1 backups on weekdays (which would slow your system(s) and possibly network access). I am representing our modified TOH schedule here in a 3-week cycle, which looks something like this (this schedule assumes an early morning start time, such as 1:34 A.M.):

Sat	Su	M	T	W	T	F
0_C	-	3	2	5	4	7
1_R	-	3	2	5	4	7
1_R	-	3	2	5	4	7 -> **start over**

The idea here is that you start off the 3-week cycle with a level-0 (full) backup, making a dated Copy of this first level-0 for later. The rest of the first week is followed by the modified TOH schedule. On the second Saturday, you perform a level-1 and date it, which gets everything back to the original level-0. At this point you are able to safely do a full restore with nothing more than your current level-1 and last Saturday's level-0. Next you Rotate the first week's tape set (with the dated copy of your level-0) off-site for safe keeping in a fire safe for disaster recovery. For the rest of the second week, follow the 1, 3, 2, 5, 4, 7 schedule. The third Saturday you repeat the previous Saturday's tasks—complete level-1, date it, and rotate out the second week of tapes for off-site storage. You could now do a full restore to date with your second level-1 and the original level-0. Continue with the TOH schedule through the end of the third week, bringing back the first week's tapes (minus the copy of the level-0) to do it all over again.

Tip

I recommend rotating tape sets out like this and when bringing them back for reuse, keeping Saturday's 0-1-1 tapes all at the remote storage site. This allows you to go back to any week of the year and fetch files from that week's Saturday with no more than a copy of the level-0 that they kept, or the level-0 plus level-1. This method will take only around 70 tapes per year and will give you an unlimited archive ability. At the end of each year you can even reabsorb all the archive tapes for reuse except for a level-0 for each quarter.

While this is not a pure TOH implementation (it's much more simple), this modified TOH backup strategy has several advantages:

✦ *Less restore work and less to go wrong*—If you need to do a restore on Friday of the first week, for example, then you only need tapes 0, 2, 4, and last night's 7—instead of 0, 1, 2, 3, 4, and 5 as would be required if doing a pure incremental (0 to 5 as in Figure 5-3).

✦ *Less tape waste*—You're not copying the same files onto the tape night after night as with the differentials or nightly full backups. Less waste of tape and backup time means saved money and added capacity for growth.

✦ *Off site rotation*—Into the second week of the schedule, simply keep the original level-0 tape, and rotate a copy of tape 0 along with Monday–Friday tapes off-site to a fire safe or vault for disaster recovery. You can still perform a full restore with the original level-0 and the first Saturday's level-1 (and the 3, 2, 5. . . moving forward).

✦ *Data security*—Files that have changed since the level 0 make it to tape at least twice in this scheme.

Note After each level-0 backup, you need to make a "dated clone" of your level-0 tape to go with your off-site rotation tape set, keeping the original onsite for restores. This will guarantee that anyone needing to do a full recovery from the off-site tape set will be able to do so with your safe, clearly labeled and dated 0, (1), 2, 4, 7 off-site tapes.

The main disadvantage of a TOH/levels-based backup strategy is that it usually takes more than one night's tape(s) to do a full restore. And that's about it really.

If you walk into most enterprise environments, you'll find that even if they're running some high end GUI based backup suite, this type of backup strategy is what the little software man behind the GUI curtain is actually doing.

You can take a closer look at how to implement this form of backup strategy in the *Backup Tools and How to Use Them* section.

Tip A 4- or 8-mm tape on a helical scanning backup drive can be used a couple of hundred times (for in-depth info, see www.datman.com/tbul/dmtb_035.htm), but after this you need to replace the tape with a new one before it starts encountering errors. Any time you introduce a new tape to your facility, you need some system to tell when it came into use and thus when it needs to be replaced. Most higher end backup suites do this for you automatically, but a simple manual tape-aging system that I've found useful is color-coded circle stickers from any office supply stores. Each color represents a given month. When you put a tape into commission, write the year in the color dot so you'll know how long you've been using it (only put the dot on the front edge of the tape, never on the flat body). Starting out, to help determine your usage frequency, put a tick mark on the circle every time you back up to it. After a few months you'll know how many uses/months your tapes get for your given backup strategy, so you can figure out how long it takes for tape in your backup schedule to "expire." After this, you can just put a color dot and year on all new tapes and know (ahead of time) when to dispose of them and get new tapes.

Backup Media Types and Hardware

You can find a huge array of modern tape drives and media types to choose from. Not one media is best for all applications; you need the right tool for the right job. For example, while a CD-RW might be fine for backing up your mom's My Documents folder, a few binaries, and config files on your server, it is really not considered to be a production-quality backup solution. A DVD+/−RW is fine for offloading your MP3 collection to archive or maybe even cloning your boot partition for doing emergency boot recoveries, but these forms of backup are limited and can be inherently expensive and too fragile for long-term use. They're not really suited for continual server backups, unless you're doing something special such as boot images or random access configuration file archiving. CD and DVD+/−RWs can be considered in some low-end backup scenarios, but are not considered a safe or viable solution for single production server or multiserver backup arrangements.

Some people prefer using hard disk drive based storage for either disk-to-disk cloning, or archiving, or nightly full backups. While this practice may be okay in the mind of new sys-admins, it really is not practicing safe backups. Unless something like external or hot swap drives are used, the media is not easily removable/storable; it usually stays in the machine spun up and running. This means that problems such as electrical damage, fire, or flooding can all render both source and backup drives inoperable. Even if you use some form of external or removable media, if you were to try to employ a large scale removable hard drive backup and rotation scenario, you would quickly find it to be very cost prohibitive and dangerous with the fragile nature of hard drives. In fact, if you need rotated and secure copies of data, this is actually one of the most expensive ways of backing up large volumes of data over time—and also clumsily awkward and frustrating to implement. The only way drive-based backups tend to be done today is via external *SAN* (storage area network), which we'll talk about later, but SAN is not really considered to be a classic disk-to-disk solution.

Some determinedly creative administrators create a hybrid disk *and* tape backup solution that can have all the benefit of on line or "drag-n-drop" access (via the backup disk), while using a local or remote tape solution to backup the backup disk for tape rotation and off-site storage purposes. This offers a nice functional compromise, as the backup drive does not have "open file" issues that more traditional live backups have. This type of backup can be easily scripted, and you can even do prebackup database dumps or "hot copies" (such as using mysqlhotcopy) to static files on the backup drive before the backup drive-to-tape portion of the script runs, thus backing up the database also.

So what type of backup media do you need? This varies a lot based on your data size, type of data, pocketbook, and the scale of your operation. Let's take a look at a few of the various common business models out there and see which fits you best and based on that and other variables, which resulting media type you should consider.

SmalltoMedium Backups

Single or multitape drive backups are commonly used for small to medium server configurations. This is generally effective for a system of four to six servers; beyond that, you should consider using a tape library or mass robotic tape changer type arrangement. The up-front costs of implementing small, medium, or large tape backup arrangements tend to be higher than that of other less traditional forms of backup (such as DVD+/−R or disk-to-disk); however, tapes are used because they end up costing less per GB and are more robust than other "neat idea" solutions like disk-to-disk or CD/DVDs. When it comes down to it, the cost of tapes over the long haul is cheaper and they are easier to handle, rotate, and move. They also give you greater flexibility when growing into a large-scale backup, rotation, and off-site storage arrangement than do most other forms of backup. Table 5-2 compares the advantages and disadvantages of various tape drive and media types for small-, medium-, and large-scale backups.

Price per giga byte of the media is probably the most important figure to look at when starting production-grade backups. However, keep in mind that newer more expensive tape prices (such as AIT-3 and LTO) often come down quickly 2 to 3 years after introduction. Plan ahead.

The rightmost column in Table 5-2 includes the price of the drive. This figure is not a linear comparison but just a ballpark figure to show much your first 10TB of backups on this drive and media will cost you. You really need to account for your giga bytes/month needs and project it over the course or a year to get a useful comparison for your scenario.

Table 5-2: Backup Media Type Comparison

Media	Drive Price	Media Price	Capacity Nat/Comp.	$/GB	$/10TB
CD-RW	$50	$0.45	0.700GB	$0.64	$6,450

Pro: Good for small workstation/personal data

Con: Expensive and cumbersome for large/servers, fragile (scratches). Recent studies also indicate media degradation in as little as 18 months

DVD-RW	$100	$1.50	4.7GB	$0.39	$4,000

Pro: Good for server config backups, DBs, and recovery data and boot tools

Con: Still expensive, easy to outgrow, fragile (scratches)

Hard Disk	$150	N/a	150GB	$1.00	$10,000

Pro: Good for "instant recoveries," live/instant random access. Fast

Con: Very expensive and awkward for archiving/rotation, easy to outgrow

DDS3 Tape	$400	$4	12/24GB	$0.20	$2,400

Pro: Cheap drive and price/GB, good for small jobs, easy to find media

Con: Outdated, limited growth potential, slow backup/restore speed

DDS4	$500	$8	20/40GB	$0.24	$2,900

Pro: Cheaper drive and media. Good current solution for small or multiple small servers, fairly common media

Con: Represents last drive in "end of life" technology. 2–4 years remaining maximum

AIT-1 Tape	$700	$40	35/70GB	$0.67	$7,400

Pro: Cheaper end of AIT drives, good for secondary and small-medium servers

Con: Comparative ROI of media over time is low because of low capacity

AIT-2	$1,100	$45	50/100GB	$0.53	$6,400

Pro: Good middle road tape with growth potential. Good for changers

Con: Media still expensive/GB, in decline of acceptance

AIT-3	$3,000	$50	100/200GB	$0.29	$5,900

Pro: Higher end of AIT drives, great for growth servers and changers, good tape/capacity ROI

Con: Expensive initial cost of drive somewhat prohibitive

LTO-1 Tape	$2,800	$35	100/200GB	$0.21	$4,900

Pro: Great cost/GB, good for for mid-high end servers, and for streaming

Con: Newer tech, hard to find media, not good for start/stop

LTO-2 Tape	$3,800	$75	200/400GB	$0.22	$6,000

Pro: Fair costs, good future growth direction for changers, and for streaming

Con: Expensive drive, newer tech, hard to find media, not good for start/stop

Note *Streaming* means that when you're taking a backup, you feed the tape drive an uninterrupted stream of data. If the tape drive is much faster than the data it is being fed, then the tape will have to slow, stop, reverse (while buffering the now incoming data), pick up where it left off, and start going again. This causes unneeded wear and tear on the drive and tape, and depending on your scenario, can greatly slow your backup process. Fast tape LTO and DLT tape drives are a good fit for streaming backups, while helical scan tape drives such as DDS, AIT, or Mammoth are better for start/stop or nonstreaming scenarios.

More information on various Linux-compatible tape drive tests and specs can be found at the Linux Tape Device Certification Program site: www.linuxtapecert.org/drives.php.

Medium- to Large-Scale Backup Solutions

It's ironic that as the computing industry has gone from a centralized (mainframe) environment to a distributed one (PCs and servers) over the past 30 years, backups have moved the opposite direction. Even 10 years ago, each new server usually came bundled with its own tape backup drive. Now, doing backups to a local tape drive on every server is considered wasteful. Even from a purely administrative perspective, backup administrators would rather have centralized backup control and tape management over multiple remote systems. Innovations in the networking arena in the past 10 years have made this natural shift toward remote centralized backups possible.

Some medium to large corporations find that implementing network backups is a good way of minimizing tape drive costs and the complexity of tracking dozens of tape pools. In a nutshell, this process is handled by each machine running a network-backup client program that talks to a centralized backup server. This backup server is in turn hooked up to a single large robotic tape library (that is, a bunch of tapes, tape drives, and one or more robotic arms in a big cabinet). In this arrangement, your many servers all talk to the single centralized backup server daemon that is controlled, scheduled, and monitored centrally. This is often implemented with either DDS3/4 4-mm tape (on the low end) or AIT/Mammoth/LTO tape and drives (at the high end). This type of setup can be configured with tapes and all for under $20,000. Another larger enterprise backup solution is a *Backup SAN* (Storage Area Network) or what's sometimes called *LAN-Free Backup*. In the same way that a LAN allows distributed access to *computing resources*, a SAN allows for distributed access to *storage resources*. SAN is a more pricey arrangement by which all the production servers or machines to be backed up use a common (but "off-LAN") pool of high-speed *fibre channel* or *iSCSI* (Internet SCSI that runs over a second dedicated TCP/IP backup network) attached tape storage that forms a *Backup SAN* (see Figure 5-4). This is nice as it gives you centralized backup management, without the normal network/LAN congestion and timing issues you have when backing up over the corporate LAN. A tape backup SAN is segmented up for each of the production servers or machines. Each of these machines on this SAN has a Fibre Channel HBA (or dedicated high-speed NIC with iSCSI) and the backup client software installed and configured. The backup server sees all of the tape SAN client machines and schedules and directs the backup clients on the machines to the tape SAN for back up locally. The tape backup library's large streaming set of parallel tape drives and/or tape changer and library makes quick work of getting the data to tape, indexed, and accounted for. This type of arrangement (streaming or continuous writing of data) makes good use of high speed, linear tape technologies such as DLT (Digital Linear Tape) or LTO (Linear Tape Open standard, a.k.a. "Ultrim") because the high speeds needed for nonstop streaming is guaranteed by the throughput of the SAN to backup system. This is a higher end solution and can be pulled together for more on the scale of $80 to 120k on the low end to several million dollars on the high end.

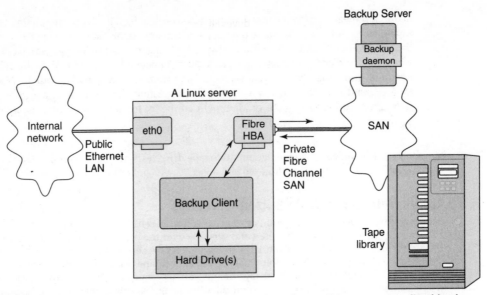

Figure 5-4: A Linux server/machine running a backup client talking to a centralized backup SAN via high-speed fibre channel.

Other Backup Hardware Tips

Here are several words of wisdom regarding hardware-related backup issues, so you can use the pain and suffering of others in your pursuit of backup Zen.

SCSI or IDE Tape Drives?

Most serious administrators use SCSI tape drives. Nowadays, even higher end tape drives such as the AIT drives are coming with an optional cost-saving IDE/ATAPI interface. With blazing fast ATA-UDMA speeds being what they are these days, IDE/ATAPI tape drives are looking less vile than they once were, especially since ATA with UDMA is not burdening the system with Processor taxing Input/Output mode (PIO) based data movement any longer. However, running ATAPI on Linux is still not an ideal setup. Sometimes ATAPI drives work, but they often fail or lock up. It's been my observation that administrators who choose ATAPI tape drives for backup tend to care more about the price of their system more than they do the quality of their backups. That being said, if you enjoy living on the edge and want ATAPI tape drive based backups anyway, just be sure to disable `ide-tape` kernel driver support (`rmmod ide-tape`) and use SCSI emulation instead (`insmod scsi_mod; insmod ide-scsi; insmod st`). This will change your tape device from `/dev/ht0` to `/dev/st0`. And be sure to make these changes permanent in your `/etc/modules.conf` file. Good luck.

Tip   If you're going to risk it and run IDE/ATAPI interface tape drives, at least don't put them on the primary ATA interface with your system drive. Either put it by itself (or with a CD-ROM) on the secondary interface (cable) or get yourself a separate PCI ATA hard drive card for $20 and put it on that. You don't want your tape drive on the same controller as your production OS and data drives. Doing so will simply slow down your entire system.

Caution
Feeling lucky with IDE/ATAPI tape drives? If you want to try these, the ATAPI AIT drives are fairly popular. Just do not use the low-end IDE/ATAPI (or even SCSI) versions of Travan- or QIC-based tape drives for production quality backups. These drives have caused many problems in the production backup arena and using them is begging for trouble. Besides lack of error feedback and high bit error rates, they require regular tape retensioning (via commands like `mt -f /dev/st0 reten`) and will plague you with frequent backup failures, or even worse, no "failures"—just bad backups! And did I mention that the average Travan tape costs $30 to 40 as compared to a DDS3/4 tape price of $4 to 8?

Dedicated Backup Interface

If you're running SCSI-based tape drives, be sure to put the SCSI tape drive on its own SCSI bus. I don't mean just external, or on the narrow external connector of a wide channel, I mean have more than one SCSI bus—usually another dedicated SCSI card or separate SCSI bus on a multichannel SCSI controller. You definitely don't want to put a SCSI tape drive (or other slow r/w devices) on the same SCSI bus as your high-speed SCSI or RAID devices. Doing so will just slow down your whole system, especially during backups. Just get yourself a cheap little SCSI card that will work with your drive and use that. Be sure to get a narrow card if you have a narrow tape drive, or a wide card if you have a wide tape drive. Some server-grade motherboards actually have a secondary SCSI bus built in just for this purpose. Some newer SCSI tape drives even run high-speed SCSI LVD or UltraXXX. Be sure to check this out on the drive and card specs before making the purchase. Almost any decent (or even older) SCSI card will work with the Linux kernel now days, at least for tape backups.

Tape Drive Error Flash Codes

Be sure to get a good tape drive that has some type of "LED flash codes" or "error codes" so that you can notice problems just by looking at the tape drive. Problems such as incorrect tape type, dirty/cleaning required, and other r/w errors are most often detected and fixed when a drive communicates them directly to the backup administrator or tape rotation staff via direct visual cues or LED error codes. Many times when your tape drives are remote from the backup software, your backup software may not report on such errors correctly, or the guy changing the tapes may just leave a problem drive alone if it keeps spitting a tape out or the drive just locks up on him. These types of critical errors are best reported directly from the drive itself and error flash codes seem to be the best way to communicate them.

Tape Drive Cleaning

Oh, don't forget to keep your tape drive clean and failure-free! When you buy backup tapes, spend $60 or more and get yourself a ten-pack of high-quality cleaning tapes too. They're a must in a production backup environment. Always keep at least two on hand for your specific tape drive. Consult your tape drive manual for further cleaning and maintenance details.

Set up a policy-based system so that after every X number of backups you load a cleaning tape and let the drive take care of itself. Follow your specific tape drives recommended cleaning schedule.

One more caution: Don't lend your cleaning tapes out! If you lend it to someone in another department, you never know where it has been or what it has cleaned when you get it back. You don't want an 8-mm cleaning tape back that just cleaned some guy's coffee-soaked Hi8 CamCorder coming back to your department to clean your server tape drives! Keep a couple extra on hand to just *give* to people who want to borrow one of your production cleaning tapes.

Backup Strategies

Before you decide how you want to backup your system(s), you need to ask yourself some basic questions: "What can I not afford to lose?" "How much money could it cost my company if this data was irretrievable?" "How long do I need to keep my data?" Only after considering questions like these can you start to look at your company's business and business data intelligently to address things such as the following:

✦ Data to be backed up

✦ Retention times

✦ Tape rotation and off-site storage policy

✦ Processes and policies surrounding backups

All of this is essential to ensure that the unspeakable partial or complete data loss never happens to you.

The following sections get directly into the technical details of what is generally important to backup on a Linux system, and what to do about things like databases, log files, e-mail, and other system content that is always in a state of flux or changing.

What to Back Up?

Your backup strategy needs to focus on what you want to back up, or in some cases, what *not* to back up.

As you can see in Table 5-3, some parts of the OS hard drive are important to back up, others are less important to backup on a regular basis, while still other directories don't need backup at all.

If you have any valuable system configuration data, be sure to back up /etc/. This is the most common area for system-wide configuration data. Don't forget it.

Other directories you don't really need to back up unless you're doing a full backup. These include /opt/ (for third party and FHS based applications), /usr/local, /bin/, /boot/, /dev/, and the other directories in the last section of Table 5-3.

Note　Some people do not back up /lost+found/ because this is where corrupted files end up being stored. However, in some gradual disk crash scenarios where you're slowing losing hard drive blocks over time, this type of directory could be useful for getting back those lost and partially corrupted files. Don't just discount it without considering such issues.

For some directories you just do not want to back up, ever; of these, the two big ones that come to mind are /proc/ and /mnt/. /proc/ is a special directory that does nothing more than give the kernel a place to mount itself so that user space apps can "talk" to it, look at, and in some cases change running kernel parameters on the fly. If you boot from a Linux boot floppy and take a look in your system's /proc/ directory on the hard drive, there's nothing in there. And if you try to back it up, you may run into problems.

Table 5-3: Backing Up System Directories

Definite, frequent backups required

/etc/	System-wide OS/software/daemon config files
/home/	User home directory space
/var/	System variable files; logs, mail/printer queue, and so on
/root/	Root's "home" directory
/var/www/	web file system (servers only) on newer Linux
/var/ftp/	FTP file system (servers only) on newer Linux

Backup rarely or never

/mnt/	File system mount points (floppy, CD-ROM, NFS, and so on)
/proc/	Kernel/OS dynamically created information

Backup less frequently or only if a full OS backup is desired

/bin/	OS essential binaries
/boot/	Boot files, kernel files, and so on
/dev/	OS device files (hard drive, floppy, serial, and so on)
/lib/	OS shared library (program) files, pam, and kernel modules
/lost+found/	Corrupt and unlinked file storage directory for / filesystem
/opt/	Third-party and FHS compliant software (such as Open Office)
/sbin/	OS binaries (usually only run by root or system)
/tmp/	Application, OS, and user temp file space
/usr/	Distro installed/OS, binaries, docs, source, shared, X11, and so on

The /mnt/ directory is kind of special. While the subdirectory names in this directory can be important, most of the important (system-wide ones) should be referenced in the /etc/fstab file and should be able to be restored fairly easily.

Caution   If you know what you're doing with your specific backup suite, then you *can* back up the /mnt/ directory and its top-level directories, if you're careful. However, if you're not careful and you have things like CD-ROMs, floppies, NFS, and SAMBA/Windows drive mappings to this directory, you could quickly find yourself backing up your own removable media and the corporate file server! Just watch it with this directory.

Backing Up the Entire Operating System

Why wouldn't you want to backup the whole OS on a server? The UNIX-/Linux-based file systems are clearly divided by function. So when doing a recovery, many people assume that they'll be doing an OS reinstall anyway—so they don't bother backing up the parts of the OS that never change after an install is complete. This stance varies depending on what you define as critical for your environment. If you lose the main and only drive in a server, do you think you'll just be getting a new drive, reinstalling, reconfiguring fresh, and then restoring the data? Or do you want to restore everything (including the OS) from tape? Most administrators don't bother with OS backups of their servers. They get the users, application configurations, and just apply those to a fresh OS install.

When might you want to backup the entire OS? If you have a highly specialized OS nonserver or workstation install with many customized user application and OS settings (such as a developer workstation or remote desktop terminal server) you probably want to get the whole OS and all of its installed and configured apps.

When might you want *not* to backup everything? A likely example would be on a single-purpose server such as a user home-dir fileserver, vanilla web server, BIND/DNS server, or the like. These types of application configurations can usually be quickly brought back up by an OS reinstall, then using up2date (for RPM systems) or apt-get (for Debian systems) to bring the system up to a fully patched state, and finally putting the backed up data back in place from tape.

For example, after a reinstall a BIND DNS server would simply need its DNS zone files put back into place in either /var/named/ or /var/named/chroot/var/named/ (for chroot'd systems) along with the main named config file /etc/named.conf. Restart the named service and you're back up and running. It's kind of a waste to back up the rest of the OS (several GB) every week when it is not really warranted.

Most home/desktop systems only require backup of user data in /home/ and /etc/ (configuration data), and possible /var/ if you store e-mail, web, and/or ftp data there. In such cases only /home/ should probably get backed up, since home Linux users tend to do a lot of OS switching anyway. In fact, one very convenient thing I have found is to just keep your /home/ filesystem on its own dedicated drive. This way when you go to reinstall a new Linux distribution on your system, you just unplug the /home/ drive, install the OS on your main drive, and then plug in and mount the old /home/ drive back into place. Be sure you get the new /home/username/ directories' content copied over into the old home drive. Many desktop apps and environments need their newer config directories in place and will balk if you try to forcefeed them the older counterpart's config directories and settings.

Other Important System Config Files

Even if you do a total system backup, there are some important configurational aspects of your system that you should backup, such as your hard drive's partition layout, your important /etc/ configuration files, and so on.

To make your Linux system back up its partition table(s) to a flat text file, you can use the following commands:

```
# mkdir /etc/config-data ; chmod 700 /etc/config-data ;
  chown root.root/etc/ config-data
# fdisk -l/dev/hda > /etc/config-data/hda-fdisk.txt
# dd if=/dev/hda of=/etc/config-data/hda-part-boot.img bs=512 count=1
1+0 records in
1+0 records out
# fdisk -l /dev/hdc > /etc/config-data/hdc-fdisk.txt
# dd if=/dev/hdc of=/etc/config-data/hdc-part-boot.img bs=512 count=1
1+0 records in
1+0 records out
```

The first command sets up a /etc/config-data/ directory and root-restricted permissions. The next fdisk line grabs the human-readable partition table config from drive /dev/hda (IDE primary-master) and dumps it out to the flat text file /etc/config-data/hda-fdisk.txt. The third line then backs up the actual partition table and MBR out to the file /etc/config-data/ hda-part-boot.img. Likewise, the last two command lines do the same for the IDE secondary-master or hdc.

Doing this will ensure that you have backups of your drive partition layouts as well as your actual master boot record (MBR), which can be used in case someone ever corrupts and renders your system unbootable. And since you always backup /etc/ to tape, you should have these archived safely.

Backing Up Databases

Backing up a database (or any other file that is in a state of change) is like photocopying a sheet of paper. If you wiggle it while copying it, then you get a corrupted copy. If you want a good backup of a database (or other such "wiggling" file), you need to choose one of the following options:

✦ *Backup directly with a backup agent*—This is a special piece of backup software (usually added on in the form of a commercial backup module) that "talks" to both the database and to the backup software. The backup software starts copying the database and when the agent senses a change in the database, it finds out what that change was and communicates it back to the backup suite and so the uncorrupted change can be accounted for in the final backup. The database backup agents are not always available for all database systems or backup suites or may cost several hundred dollars, plus their use varies from vendor to vendor.

✦ *Stop, copy, and back up*—You stop the database or service, quickly copy the related file(s) somewhere else, and then restart the service and get your backup. This technique is appropriate for backing up files like mySQL/database, sendmail, and syslog.

✦ To use this method, see the *Shutting off services* section later in this chapter. Shutting off services is great for getting everything related to that service on tape. However, if you're on a production server, you may not be able to shut off mission-critical services such as web and databases.

✦ *Freeze, copy, and back up*—This method is generally more difficult, but you can usually lock your databases using simple script-driven programs like mysqldump or mysqlhotcopy (more on these later). This method uses the same concept as the previous technique, but you don't stop the services; you just use these tools to "freeze" them (read-only) while you quickly copy them out, and then unfreeze them when you're done with your copy. See the rest of this section for more information on how this is done with MySQL.

The Backup Agent method may not always be available to you, depending on what type of database and backup suite you're using. Some Linux databases are starting to get third-party commercial backup agents that will talk to the database and the backup system to effectively back up a live, or *hot*, database. (A MySQL backup agent for ARCserve is available at www3.ca .com/Solutions/ProductOption.asp?ID=4691.) However, MySQL comes with a couple of utilities to help you use the Freeze and Copy method.

For the Freeze, Copy, and Backup database backup method, there are various options depending on what database you are using. Because MySQL is the most popular open source database, let's take a look at that. MySQL is good in that there are a few tools with which to get the job done. The first, older program is called mysqldump. It does not get binary log files (required in some cases), and it dumps to flat .sql files (which can take up more room than the actual data base files). If neither of these issues bothers you, then this mini-app might be just what the doctor ordered. mysqldump's general shell usage looks like this:

```
# mysqldump --opt --all-databases --user=root >
  /root/all-databases_$( date +%Y-%m-%d).sql
```

This will freeze and copy all of the databases out to a time-stamped flat file under /root/.

In newer MySQL database Freeze and Copy option is another included tool called mysqlhotcopy. This does a table level or all-database read-only lock effectively, clones everything in the mysql data directory (/var/lib/mysql/ for most RPM-based systems) out to a directory of your liking, and then unlocks the databases when done. This is what the shell usage looks like:

```
#  mysqlhotcopy --user=root --allowold --regexp=".*" /root/mysql-backup
```

Your regular system backups will now get the static database files in /root/mysql-backup/ and you'll be good to go.

mysqlhotcopy is great if you're running MyISAM storage engine table types. But if you're running innodb table tapes, you really do need to shut down the whole service and do a cp -a /var/lib/mysql/*/root/mysql-backup/, otherwise you will not get your innodb database content. If you're not sure which engine/table type you're running, then you're probably running the default MyISAM type and you have nothing to worry about.

For more info, do a mysqlhotcopy --h or perldoc /usr/bin/mysqlhotcopy.

Note   As of the Fedora Core RPM of mysql-3.23.58-4, there is a known bug with Red Hat's copy of mysqlhotcopy that creates an error when trying to use the program. As this book goes to press, there seems to be a patch file for this on bugzilla that should be released in MySQL 3.23.58-8 along with Fedora Core 2. See Red Hat bugzilla and mysql for the latest info on this: https://bugzilla.redhat.com/bugzilla/show_bug.cgi?id= 112693.

Setting Up Tape Drive Devices

Commands from dump, restore, mt, and tar will all want to see the device file called /dev/ tape in place to backup and restore from. For example, mt rewind and mt -f /dev/st0 rewind should do the same thing if you have a symlink set up from /dev/tape to /dev/st0. But with some of these commands, if no device file is given /dev/tape is the default, so you should have this link set up. If you don't and you are using a SCSI tape drive (/dev/st0) set that up now, using the following commands:

```
# ln -s /dev/st0 /dev/tape
# ls -la /dev/tape lrwxrwxrwx 1root root 8 Mar 14 15:17 /dev/tape->/dev/st0
```

Note   When working with tape devices, you have two device names (besides /dev/tape) that signify two different tape drive behaviors. The device name /dev/st0 will be your first auto-rewinding SCSI tape device, and the device /dev/nst0 will be the same device but it will not auto-rewind at the end of a backup. This is significant in that multiple backups to `st0` will overwrite each other (what most backup software expects). `Nst0` will not overwrite, but will continue to append backups to the end of the previous backup. In this chapter, we will be assuming that `/dev/tape` is always pointing to `/dev/st0` and rewinding after each backup.

Shutting Off Services

As previously mentioned, you don't want to back up a system with a bunch of actively changing files on it. You get around this by shutting down these services or using the Stop and Copy method.

One of the most orderly ways of doing this is via runlevel 4. In most Linux distributions, runlevel 3 is the command line or *headless* mode in which you might run a web or e-mail server; you don't need a GUI/X11 display (as you would on a desktop). Desktops and workstations, on the other hand, need to run in a default runlevel of 5 (at least for Red Hat-based systems).

Using Runlevel 4

If you want good system backups, you will probably want to turn off your "disk chatty" services in runlevel 4, and then use this runlevel as your *system backup runlevel* to run your backups.

Here's a list of some services that you might want to shut down on a server for backups:

- ✦ sendmail
- ✦ mysqld
- ✦ apache
- ✦ vsftpd
- ✦ syslog
- ✦ lpd or CUPS (printing services)
- ✦ rhnsd (Red Hat Network daemon)
- ✦ autofs
- ✦ sshd (to keep others off, but only if you're feeling confident in your backup's stability)
- ✦ xinetd

You can quickly get a listing of your services running in runlevel 4 with the following command:

```
# chkconfig --list | grep -e 4:on -e on$
```

This will show you everything running in runlevel 4 plus the services running under xinetd. These problem services can be configured to be off in runlevel 4 individually with the command syntax:

```
# chkconfig --level 4 syslog off
# chkconfig --level 4 sendmail off
# chkconfig --level 4 xinetd off
# chkconfig --level 4 mysqld off
...
```

Then runlevel 4 will be ready to be used as a backup runlevel that you toggle to just before backups, and back out of when they're complete.

Tip

If you're not sure which services are which, or what each one in /etc/init.d/ actually does, then on Red Hat Fedora systems you can simple run the command ntsysv from the command line and flip through all the service names, hitting F1 for the ones that you would like a description of.

The command runlevel will tell you what runlevel you are currently in, and the init 4 command will put you in whatever runlevel you want to go to (runlevel 4 in this usage).

Caution

Changing run levels affects the entire system. If you shut off most things (including ssh or networking) in runlevel 4, this can have drastic effects on other users and other services. Only change runlevels and services on a production server when you're mindfully thinking of who and what you may affect. If unsure, just do a chkconfig —list |grep —e 4:on to see who and what you may affect on that runlevel. It is common for people to remotely change runlevels and by doing so effectively locking themselves off of the server. After an "oops!" like that, usually only a visit to the physical console can reestablish connectivity.

After you have your services all figured out and shut off in runlevel 4, a simple script such as this one will be able to back up the majority of your system, using tar, to a local tape drive:

```
#!/bin/bash

## Do a MySQL-HOT-COPY to /root/mysql-bak
mysqlhotcopy --user=root --allowold --regexp=".*" /root/mysql-backup

## Rewind tape
mt rewind

## Change Run Levels to 4, backup, back to 3
init 4
sleep 10
tar -czf /dev/tape /bin /boot /dev /etc /home /lib /lost+found
  /opt /root /sbin /tmp /usr /var > /dev/null 2>&1
echo -Backups complete...
## Eject tape...
mt eject
sleep 5
init 3
echo -Done
```

This script is more an example of using runlevels with backups than it is a hardened backup tool. Even though you can backup your system with tar, it's not something that I would recommend doing for all of your production servers. Lets take a look at some of the other options out there.

Backup Tools and How to Use Them

This section covers the basic backup tools that come with most all Linux distributions, explains how they work, and discusses the pros and cons of each.

Tar or Star

Tar is short for Tape ARchive and it's been around a very long time. The GNU version of tar that comes on all Linux systems is a feature-laden miracle worker that most praise for its convenience and rich feature set, and a few curse for its non-POSIX compatibility. Star (pronounced "ess-tar") is pretty much like tar, but much faster for doing local streaming to tape as well as more POSIX-compliant. It also handles file attributes like creation time, access time, and modification time, which makes it a bit more powerful than plain old tar.

Tar and related backup utilities hit the system through the filesystem, just as a user would access files. As a result, it can be a bit slower than some other form of raw device backup such as dump, cat, or dd (depending on the usage).

Tar functions very well as a general-purpose file system/directory archiving tool, as well as doing network-based backups in conjunction with things like ssh. However, in and of itself it does not support "level backups" and so must be used creatively with other tools to create a full TOH or level 0 to 9 backup script.

Tar is also nice in that it comes bundled with gzip compression compatibility built in; however, this needs to be used with caution on live filesystems. If a file system changes underneath the tar/gzip session, this can break the compression stream and break the tar session all together. We'll examine ways to get around this later.

Dump/Restore

Dump and restore are actually two different programs that are included in the dump package. Dump is one of the more popular OS-included, production level, filesystem-based backup utility packages out there. Dump, used in conjunction with other backup programs or by itself, is used across most all UNIX systems to do full system backups with level 0 to 9/differential/incremental support.

Dump talks to the raw block devices that underlie your filesystems, and as such is never supposed to be used on a live, mounted r/w, nonstatic, filesystem. That being said, many people choose to do this anyway. Red Hat and even Linus Torvolds warns against using it like this (see warnings about using dump at `http://dump.sourceforge.net/isdumpdeprecated.html`, along with info on how to use it safely). However, even with such authoritative foreboding, you can still safely use it and get great results if you do so carefully, and prepare the system with a little admin sleight of hand.

Besides having a default "batch mode" for scripting, both dump and restore's other features include an interactive command line interface. Restore's interface allows one to browse back into the backup dump file—cd'ing through directories, adding files to your restore list, and then restoring them with the interactive `extract` command. Dump/restore also handles multivolume (tape) support, post-/pretape scripting (for changers), file/device/stdout output, and much more.

Major issues to watch out for with dump are (as previously mentioned) copying live and changing filesystems (active logs, e-mail, databases, and so on), as well as dump and restore binary compatibility issues. Dump and restore are tied at the hip. Never try to do a dump with one version and a restore with another. This will often fail. Be sure you know what versions of dump you have on all of your systems and make sure that you have the corresponding version of restore. In fact, I recommend getting a copy of your dump/restore binaries off your backups system for safekeeping, so that if the restore you're using doesn't seem to be reading the data off the tape, you'll have another copy to fall back on. Red Hat Fedora is currently coming with dump/restore version 0.4b34. You can see this with the following commands:

```
# which dump restore
/sbin/dump
/sbin/restore
# rpm -q dump
dump-0.4b34-1
# dump 2>&1 | grep ^dump
dump 0.4b34 (using libext2fs 1.34 of 25-Jul-2003)
# restore 2>&1 | grep ^restore
restore 0.4b34 (using libext2fs 1.34 of 25-Jul-2003)
```

Be sure that you have both binaries on your system, that they're the same version on all of your servers that you're doing dumps and restores on, and that there are no other dump/restore binaries anywhere in your system path, like this:

```
# locate bin/dump | grep dump$
/sbin/dump
# locate bin/restore | grep restore$
/sbin/restore
```

Note Most backup-related packages, including dump, expect to use a standard device file or symlink to be set up to point to the tape drive. The link name expected is /dev/tape. If you do not have it, then you will have to manually point the system to the tape device /dev/st0 (for example). To fix this, create a symlink with the ln --s command like this:

```
# ln -s /dev/st0 /dev/tape
# ls -la /dev/tape
lrwxrwxrwx 1root root 8 Mar 14 15:17 /dev/tape->/dev/st0
```

Amanda Client/Server

Short for Advanced Maryland Automatic Network Disk Archiver, Amanda is a pretty slick and polished automated, production client/server backup package that's free and comes installed on many Linux systems out of the box, including Red Hat/Fedora systems.

Amanda is a suite of command-line tools that brings together the best backup commodity tools such as dump/restore, tar, ssh, and production quality backup concepts such as parallel client dumps, a caching "holding disk" for caching client dumps to disk while tape busy, and many other advanced features.

Note Amanda is a very advanced backup suite, and replaces much of the manual level-x and TOH work shown in this chapter, but it also demands a more complex setup configuration. See Table 5-4 at the end of this chapter for more information on setting up the client/server configuration for Amanda.

The server config files are located in /etc/amanda/, where each backup set is defined in its own subdirectory.

The daemon is configured on the centralized backup server, and the service turned on like this:

```
# chkconfig --list | grep amanda
      amandaidx: off
      amanda: on
# chkconfig amanda on
# chkconfig --list amanda
amanda            on
```

Note As you can see from the grep, it's on, but there are no runlevels visible. This means that it is actually a subservice (on Fedora anyway) of the xinetd service.

One the best walkthroughs in setting up and using this comprehensive client/server backup package is located at `http://backupcentral.com/amanda.html`.

Other Useful Tools

One of the most useful tools you'll find out there for implementing great backup feats of wonder is the find command. It epitomizes the UNIX philosophy of many small tools that do one thing well. For example, it can be used to find all files on your file server that have not been accessed in over a year, and move them off the system and back them up to tape:

```
# find /mnt/fileserver/ -atime +365 -exec mv-and-backup.sh {} \ ;
```

Or, how about finding, backing up, and deleting all files on a hard drive that are owned by an ex-employee?

```
# find / -user bob -exec backup-n-rm.sh {} \ ;
```

Note These examples are using an imaginary backup script. In this example, you could substitute the script for the command "`tar -czvf /dev/tape {}; rm -rf {}`" or the like.

If you want to master UNIX or Linux, find is one of those commands that can greatly assist you, while making you appear all-powerful to those who are less inclined to use a non-GUI interface.

The command mt is another tool you'll need to understand to do backups well. It stands for magnetic tape, and it allows you to send commands to and talk to the tape drive. The thing to remember is that it expects to talk to the tape device `/dev/tape`. If that device is not in place, then it will not work without pointing it elsewhere. Be sure you have that set up. It should look something like this:

```
# ls -la /dev/tape
 lrwxrwxrwx 1root root 8 Mar 14 15:17 /dev/tape->/dev/st0
```

If you do not have this symlink set up, please refer back to the *Dump/Restore* section for details on how to fix this. After this is set up, you can issue simple tape drive control commands such as rewind, erase, and status:

```
# mt status
SCSI 2 tape drive:
File number=0, block number=0, partition=0.
Tape block size 512 bytes. Density code 0x13 (DDS (61000 bpi)).
Soft error count since last status=0
General status bits on (41010000):
 BOT ONLINE IM_REP_EN
```

If you're working with tape changer libraries (with robot arm changers and the like), you'll need to familiarize yourself with the mtx package. This is the software that allows you to talk directly to the tape changer and tape drive using standardized commands.

Backup Examples

You've got the theory of backups under your belt, and you know some of the tools. Now let's get down to it and start giving some examples of useful methods in which to perform various types of backups.

Using Tar Locally

You may have seen this done, but here is how to tar up all the user's home directories in the /home directory:

```
# tar -czvf home-dir-userdirs.tgz /home
```

The flags (czvf) stand for create, z compress, verbose, and output file. Then the two (or more) options the command takes are the target tgz file (including the file extension) and then the director(ies) to be tar-balled into the target file.

Want something more creative? How about combining the find tool with tar. Use them together to find all new files on the hard drive that belong to the user tweeks and are less than 30 days old, and put them in backup archive:

```
# find / -user tweeks -ctime -30 -exec tar Azvf /home/BACKUPS/
  tweeks-new- files.tgz {}\ ;
```

Or use tar to back up all the standard OS and user files and directories on a system to tape locally:

```
# tar czvf /dev/tape /bin /boot /dev /etc /home /lib /lost+found
    /opt /root /sbin /tmp /usr /var
```

That will back up everything to the tape. One nice command, no unneeded fancy backup software to get in the way.

Caution

This last tar command is not guaranteed to backup active and changing files. You still must shut off important services and stop writing to key files that you want backed up. The undefined system runlevel of 4 is perfect for shutting down active disk writing services and doing backups. Look back to the *Shutting Off Services"* section to see how this is accomplished.

Scripting Tar with Runlevel 4

Using the customized runlevel 4 Stop and Back up method (not a Freeze and Copy; that was for the database), we can now apply a simple backup script such as this one to go to runlevel 4, run a set of full tar backups, and e-mail us the results.

```
#!/bin/bash
## backup-rl-4.sh
## A simple script that switches to runlevel 4, tars up the dirs
## to tape, emails the results, and changes back to the previous runlevel.
```

```
## Use the COMPRESS and BACKUPDIRS variables below to change how it runs.
## Tape device or symlink expected is /dev/tape.

######### User Variables ############
RLBAK="4"
##COMPRESS=""                     # compression off=""
COMPRESS="z"                      # compression on="z"
BACKUPDIRS="/bin /boot /dev /etc /home /lib /lost+found /opt /root
  /sbin /tmp /usr /var "
## All dirs "/bin /boot /dev /etc /home /lib /lost+found /opt /root
  /sbin /tmp /usr /var"
MYEMAIL="admin@example.com"
TAPE=/dev/tape


########## Do not change ##########
RL="$(runlevel | cut -f2 -d" ")"
RLORIG="$RL"
CURDIR=$(pwd)

## Do a MySQL-HOT-COPY to /root/mysql-bak
######################################
echo -Performing a MySQL Hot Copy to /root/mysql-backup
mysqlhotcopy --user=root --allowold --regexp=".*" /root/mysql-backup
echo -MySQL hotcopy complete...

## Change Run Levels and Log Activity
######################################
echo
echo -Current runlevel is $RLORIG
logger -t BACKUP "Runlevel 4 tar backup script was run..."
echo -Changing run levels to $RLBAK for backups
logger -t BACKUP "Changing run levels to $RLBAK for backups"
init "$RLBAK"
sleep 10
echo -Now in runlevel $(runlevel | cut -f2 -d" "), starting backups
logger -t BACKUP "Now in runlel $(runlevel | cut -f2 -d" "), starting backups"
echo "   -preparing to backup directories $BACKUPDIRS to tape"
logger it BACKUP "      -preparing to backup directories $BACKUPDIRS to tape"

## Do the needful
######################################
echo "   -rewinding tape"
mt rewind
echo     -tarring content to tape
tar -c$COMPRESS -f $TAPE $BACKUPDIRS > /dev/null 2>&1
ERROR=$?
if [ $ERROR -ne 0 ] ; then
  #logger -t BACKUP "Failure in backup script couldn't run tar" $ERROR
  echo "tar errored out this " $ERROR | mail -s "BACKUP FAIL: tar
    could not run" $MYEMAIL
  exit " -FAILURE doing tar" $ERROR
fi
```

```
## Cleanup...
####################################
echo -Backups complete...
logger -t BACKUP "Backups complete..."
echo $BACKUPDIRS | mail -s "BACKUP GOOD: directories listed below" $MYEMAIL
echo -Ejecting tape...
mt eject
echo
echo -Returning to runlevel $RLORIG
logger -t BACKUP "Returning to runlevel $RLORIG"
init $RLORIG
echo
sleep 5

echo    Now back in runlevel $RL
echo -Done
```

Note   If you are going to use this type of script, be sure that you are not shutting off syslog if you use the logger logging function to record backup status to the system log.

This is a good example of a backup script that works for performing simple, full system backups. It will get mysql using `mysqlhotcopy` and everything else (assuming that you have shut such services off in runlevel 4). There are tons of good backup scripts out there for you to choose from—most of them in shell or perl scripts for free. You can find many good backup scripts at `http://linux-backup.net`.

Tar can handle incremental backups. However, if you want to do level-based incremental/differential or TOH backups using this script, then you need to do this with dump (see the *Using Dump* section later in this chapter).

Note   For more information on tar, see the man tar page, or check out `http://linux-backup.net/full_inc.gwif.html`.

Using Tar Remotely

A very nice tar trick I like to show is how to use tar (and other such tools) remotely. Most sysadmins are very familiar with ssh (or its older insecure cousin, rsh), but not all have ever used it to transport standard output (or stdout) from a Linux server, over the network to a backup server. This is particularly useful for systems without tape drives.

```
# tar cvf - /home /var /etc | ssh root@10.1.1.10 "cat
>/mnt/backup/remoteserver1_$(date +%Y-%m-%d).tar"
```

Tip   Some geek types like to use tar/ssh to go directly to a remote tape device, but I would recommend against using tar/ssh this way. I've seen this cause backup stability problems. I would instead recommend using *remote tarring* by tarring up your data to what's called a remote holding disk on the remote tape backup machine (as we discussed earlier). After all of your remote servers have pushed their data up to individual holding disk directories on the tape backup server, just have the backup server back up all your remote content from disk to tape. You'll get much better performance *and* better system predictability.

Using Dump

Dump is probably one of the more fun backup packages. However, you need to be mindful that it is not backing up the file system *through the file system* as you and other programs see it, but *at the block device level*. But what makes dump even more sensitive than tar and other such tools to disk content changes is that dump looks at the block device before the backup begins and at all the inodes that it needs to back up. If many of those inodes change before it gets them to tape, these excessive errors can cause dump to abort its backup all together.

This means that before you actually perform a backup, you should definitely use runlevel 4 or a similar method to shut down disk-chatty services, lock and copy your databases (or just shut them off completely), and quiet anything else on the system before using dump to back up to tape. If you do all of this (and are running a supported file system (such as ext2/ext3), then you shouldn't have any problems with dump.

Here's the basic usage for a local dump session doing a level-0 (full) backup to tape by the hard drive device name /dev/hda1:

```
# dump -0uf /dev/tape /dev/hda1
```

This will back up the first file system (/boot) on the first hard drive to tape (on this particular system). It's fairly fast and will create few (if any) errors if you've sufficiently quieted your system.

Note   Notice the u option. This is important as it allows you to keep track of the backup dates and levels automatically in the /etc/dumpdates file.

If you have three file systems on your server, /boot, /, and /home (for example), then you do not want to rewind the tape after each backup. This would be bad in that it would only yield the last partition you backed up on the tape. So if you have three partitions on a given disk, you need to use the /dev/nst0 device for at least the first two partitions and then the /dev/st0 or /dev/tape for the last backup on that given tape. These are the three commands that you might want to execute for the first level-0 backup:

```
dump -0uf /dev/nst0 /dev/dha1
dump -0uf /dev/nst0 /dev/dha2
dump -0uf /dev/st0 /dev/dha3
```

You might call this your Saturday backup. If you are using the TOH backup plan, what do you think your Monday backup would look like? Probably something like this:

```
dump -3uf /dev/nst0 /dev/dha1
dump -3uf /dev/nst0 /dev/dha2
dump -3uf /dev/st0 /dev/dha3
```

If you want to get fancy and also give each day's tape its own dump label, this might help things a bit if tapes get mixed up:

```
dump -3u -L "L3_2004-03-04_Mon" -f /dev/nst0 /dev/dha1
...
```

Based on this general usage, we can create a total system backup script. Using some fancy shell script conditionals and the date command, you can autodetect the correct date in our 3-week TOH backup schedule, use the correct related runlevel, and with tools like mysqlhotcopy can build a simple backup script that can pretty much take care of your whole system. Here's a simple example script that employs everything that we've discussed thus far:

```
#!/bin/bash
# Name:    dump-disks.sh
# Version: v2004-04-26 by tweeks
# Takes:   /dev/dev1 [/dev/dev2] [/dev/dev3]
# Does:    Does modified Tower of Hanoi tape backup on three week rotation
# Details: Looks at day of the week and day of the month and implements a
#          modified TOH dump of /dev/dev1 [/dev/dev2] [/dev/dev3] as per:
#          S  S  M  T  W  T  F
#          0  -  3  2  5  4  7
#          1  -  3  2  5  4  7
#          1  -  3  2  5  4  7
# Output:  log to /tmp/backuplog.txt emailed to $MYEMAIL
# Returns: "1" on Sunday error

######## User Variables ###########
RLBAK="4"
MYEMAIL="backups@example.com"
TAPEDEV=/dev/nst0        # use the "n" device for no rewind (e.g. /dev/nst0)
MYSQL=/etc/init.d/mysqld
########## Do not change ##########

RL="$(runlevel | cut -f2 -d" ")"
RLORIG="$RL"
CURDIR="$(pwd)"
LEVEL=""
DEV1="$1"
DEV2="$2"
DEV3="$3"


## Detect Day of Week/Month
##################################
# Thanks to Henry Pugsley/Rackspace
dow=`date "+%a"` # Day of Week
dom=`date "+%d"` # Day of Month
#disks="/dev/hda1 /dev/hda2 /dev/hda3"
if [ $dow == "Sat" ] && [ $dom -lt 7 ] ; then LEVEL=0
elif [ $dow == "Sun" ] ; then echo "Not on Sunday" && exit 1
elif [ $dow == "Sat" ] ; then LEVEL=1
elif [ $dow == "Mon" ] ; then LEVEL=3
elif [ $dow == "Tue" ] ; then LEVEL=2
elif [ $dow == "Wed" ] ; then LEVEL=5
elif [ $dow == "Thu" ] ; then LEVEL=4
elif [ $dow == "Fri" ] ; then LEVEL=7
fi


## Command Line Error Check/Usage
```

```
##################################
if [ "$DEV1" = "" ] ; then
  echo
  echo ERROR
  echo "Usage: dump-disks /dev/dev1 [/dev/dev2] [/dev/dev3]"
  echo "Modified TOH backups run Mon-Sat. Will abort on Sundays..."
  exit
fi


#### sanity check ####
echo -----IS THIS RIGHT?------
echo dump-disks.sh about to run like this:
echo     Backup Level=$LEVEL, Backup Devices= $DEV1 , $DEV2 , $DEV3
echo
echo Backup will be:
echo dump -$LEVEL -auL "L$LEVEL_$(date +%Y-%m-%d)" -f $DEV1 $DEV2 $DEV3
echo -----CTRL-C TO STOP------
sleep 10
echo


## Set up logfile: /tmp/backuplog.txt
#######################################
echo dump-disk.sh run on $(date +%Y-%m-%d_%H:%M) by $USERNAME
>/tmp/backuplog.txt
echo "                    o-------------------------------o"
 >>/tmp/backuplog.txt


## Do a MySQL-HOT-COPY to /root/mysql-bak
#######################################
echo -Performing a MySQL Hot Copy to /root/mysql-backup
echo -Performing a MySQL Hot Copy to /root/mysql-backup>>/tmp/backuplog.txt
mkdir -p /root/mysql-backup
# ensure mysql is actually running...
$MYSQL start
mysqlhotcopy --user=root --allowold --regexp=".*" /root/mysql-backup
 >>/tmp/backuplog.txt 2>&1
$MYSQL stop
echo -MySQL hotcopy complete...>>/tmp/backuplog.txt
echo "                  o-------------------------------o"
 >>/tmp/backuplog.txt


## Change Run Levels and Log Activity
#######################################
echo
echo -Current runlevel is $RLORIG
echo -Changing run levels to $RLBAK for backups
init "$RLBAK"
sleep 10
echo -Now in runlel $(runlevel | cut -f2 -d" "), starting backups
echo "-preparing to L-$LEVEL dump Devices=$DEV1, $DEV2, $DEV3 to tape"
echo "-preparing to L-$LEVEL dump Devices=$DEV1, $DEV2, $DEV3 to tape"
 >>/tmp/backuplog.txt
```

```
## Do the needful
####################################
echo "   -rewinding tape"
mt -f $TAPEDEV rewind
# ----------------
if [ "$DEV1" != "" ] ; then
   echo -dump of $DEV1...
   dump -$LEVEL -auL "L$LEVEL_$(date +%Y-%m-%d)" -f $TAPEDEV $DEV1
 >>/tmp/backuplog.txt 2>&1
   echo "                        o-------------------------------o"
 >>/tmp/backuplog.txt
fi
# ----------------
if [ "$DEV2" != "" ] ; then
   echo -dump of $DEV2...
   dump -$LEVEL -auL "L$LEVEL_$(date +%Y-%m-%d)" -f $TAPEDEV $DEV2

 >>/tmp/backuplog.txt 2>&1
   echo "                        o-------------------------------o"
 >>/tmp/backuplog.txt
fi
# ----------------
if [ "$DEV3" != "" ] ; then
   echo -dump of $DEV3...
   dump -$LEVEL -auL "L$LEVEL_$(date +%Y-%m-%d)" -f $TAPEDEV $DEV3
 >>/tmp/backuplog.txt 2>&1
   echo "                          o-------------------------------o"
 >>/tmp/backuplog.txt
fi


## Cleanup...
####################################
echo -Backups complete...
echo -Ejecting tape...
mt -f $TAPEDEV rewind
echo
echo -Returning to runlevel $RLORIG
init $RLORIG
echo
sleep 5
echo Now back in runlevel $RL
echo -Done >>/tmp/backuplog.txt
echo -Done
if [ "$LEVEL" = "0" ] ; then
   echo | mail -s"Following Backup was Level=0 dump. Make a copy."
 $MYEMAIL
fi
cat /tmp/backuplog.txt | mail -s "$(date +%a) Dump status" $MYEMAIL
```

The command line usage for backing up to three partitions with this script looks like this:

```
# dump-disks.sh /dev/hda1 /dev/hda2 /dev/hda3
```

And this will give us a modified TOH backup based on the day of the week and the calendar date. Additionally, the first Saturday of the month will always get a level-0 dump and the script will even send us an e-mail reminder to tell us to clone our level-0 tape! This is a configuration that we can fire and forget, and it will be completely automated (except for the insertion of the tapes).

The nice thing about this date smart script configuration is that now we can easily automate this into a daily cronjob and it will know what to do. This is all you need in root's cronjob (by editing with `contab -e` as root):

```
########## Smart Three Week TOH Backup Script ###########
34 1 * * *        /root/bin/dump-disks.sh /dev/hda1 /dev/hda2 /dev/hda3
```

And that's it. The smart TOH dump script will now run every morning at 1:34 A.M., and will even autoabort on Sundays (see the script for how this works).

As you can see, with the backup tools provided in most Linux distributions, it doesn't take that much to get an intelligent, hands off, backup configuration set up that makes good use of backup levels, tape usage, and easy recovery strategies. You just need to sit down and plan these things out a bit, and automate things with scripts whenever possible.

If the aforementioned backup script is still a little to "in the rough" for your tastes, you definitely owe it to yourself to check out Amanda at `http://backupcentral.com/amanda.html` and `www.amanda.org`. Newer backup suites such as Amanda even go beyond backup levels and the TOH as automate things by simply asking you questions about number of tapes, retention times, and data sets. Very nice indeed!

Using Dump Remotely

Although it is not often done, you can run dump remotely over ssh. You do this with a special usage of dd on the machine with the tape drive on it. The stream is pushed over ssh, into dd on the tape machine, and get put directly to tape. The usage looks like this:

```
# dump -f - /dev/hda2 | ssh root@backupserver.example.com dd \
 obs=10k of=/dev/st0
```

Pretty neat! You can also use a pull method from the tape/backup server, like this:

```
# ssh -n root@desktop.example.com dump f - /dev/hda2 | dd \
 obs=10k of=/dev/nst0
```

These can be very convenient if you can't be in more than one place at a time.

Testing and Doing Restores

Never restore files back into their original location! Doing so is wrong and can crash your system even worse than a regular crash. If you use tar or dump, always create a special `RESTORE` directory wherein you put your restored files in. Then as you need to place system or data files back into place, just use `cp -a` to copy them from place to place.

Also, when restoring system files, you must be in single-user mode. You may have to remount your root partition in r/w mode; however, this is a must for a stable full restore.

Restoring from Tar

Tar is very straightforward. If done from a file, it looks like this:

```
# pwd
/root/RESTORE
# ls
home.tgz
#  tar xzvf home.tgz
home/bob/
home/bob/.kde/
home/bob/.kde/Autostart/
[...]
home/bob/.htpasswd-BAJ
home/bob/.Xauthority
# cd ./home
# pwd
/root/RESTORE/home
```

We put the backup tar-ball into /root/RESTORE/, untarred it, and cd'd into /root/RESTORE/home/ before we starting doing file copying around the system.

Un-tarring from tape usage is pretty much the same, but you should do so to a clearly marked RESTORE directory of some type. Here's an example of rewinding the tape with mt, then restoring some files for a user's (bob) tape. The operation shows how you can have tar e**X**tract with compre**Z**sion **V**erbosely (xzv) from the file /dev/tape, into the directory /home/bob/RESTORE/:

```
# mt -f /dev/tape rewind
# tar xzvf /dev/tape /home/bob/RESTORE/
```

It's that simple.

Restoring from Dump

For system-wide restores, the same words of wisdom regarding the RESTORE directory apply here. The idea is to restore files into a temporary holding place that is clear in its purpose, but not viewable by the world. This is why we're putting the RESTORE directory in /root/ in this case:

```
# cd /root/RESTORE/
```

The usage of the dump package's restore command is rather strange. It's a real time, interactive restore where you are in the restore shell, interacting with the backup file in real time. The idea is that you look around the inside of the backup file, pass the restore package parameters, and have it add the files to your restore (or extraction list). Then when you're ready to restore, you just type **extract** and the files pop out of the dump archive and into your current directory with a new relative path from your current location.

It's easier to show than to describe:

```
# mt rewind
# restore -i -s1 -f /dev/tape
```

This `restore` command we tell to go into interactive mode (`-i`) and to source (`-s`) the first file on the tape. This source file number is simply the sequential order of the data files on the tape. If we had three backed up partitions on the system of `/dev/hda2` `/dev/hda3` and `/dev/hda6`, they were laid down to tape in that order, and we wanted to restore from the second partition file on tape, we would tell `restore` to source `-s2` this time.

Now that we're in the restore environment looking at the dump archive in real time, we can browse it as if it were a live file system:

```
restore > ls
.:
System.map                      lost+found/
System.map-2.4.18-24.7.x        message
System.map-2.4.18-26.7.x        module-info
System.map-2.4.18-27.7.x        module-info-2.4.18-24.7.x
System.map-2.4.18-27.7.xsmp     module-info-2.4.18-26.7.x
System.map-2.4.18-3smp          module-info-2.4.18-27.7.x
boot.b                          module-info-2.4.18-27.7.xsmp
chain.b                         module-info-2.4.18-3smp
config-2.4.18-24.7.x            os2_d.b
config-2.4.18-26.7.x            vmlinux-2.4.18-24.7.x
config-2.4.18-27.7.x            vmlinux-2.4.18-26.7.x
config-2.4.18-27.7.xsmp         vmlinux-2.4.18-27.7.x
config-2.4.18-3smp              vmlinux-2.4.18-27.7.xsmp
grub/                           vmlinux-2.4.18-3smp
initrd-2.4.18-24.7.x.img        vmlinuz
initrd-2.4.18-26.7.x.img        vmlinuz-2.4.18-24.7.x
initrd-2.4.18-27.7.x.img        vmlinuz-2.4.18-26.7.x
initrd-2.4.18-27.7.xsmp.img     vmlinuz-2.4.18-27.7.x
initrd-2.4.18-3smp.img          vmlinuz-2.4.18-27.7.xsmp
kernel.h                        vmlinuz-2.4.18-3smp

restore > cd grub/
restore > ls
./grub:
device.map              jfs_stage1_5            stage1
e2fs_stage1_5           menu.lst                stage2
fat_stage1_5            minix_stage1_5          tnt_whitemount.xpm.gz
ffs_stage1_5            reiserfs_stage1_5       vstafs_stage1_5
grub.conf               splash.xpm.gz           xfs_stage1_5
```

After we find what we're looking for (`grub.conf` in this case), we add it to our archive extraction list, add any other files or directories that we might want, and then we extract them.

```
restore >  add grub.conf
restore >  extract
You have not read any volumes yet.
Unless you know which volume your file(s) are on you should start
with the last volume and work towards the first.
Specify next volume # (none if no more volumes):  1
set owner/mode for '.'? [yn]  y
restore >  quit
```

Now we're out of the interactive restore session and back in our shell:

```
# pwd
/root/RESTORE
# ls -la
total 1204
drwxr-xr-x    3 root      root          4096 Mar 15 04:00 .
drwxr-xr-x   29 root      root          4096 Mar 15 04:00 ..
drwxr-xr-x    2 root      root          4096 Apr 10 2003 grub
# cd grub/
# ls
grub.conf
#ls -la
total 12
drwxr-xr-x    2 root      root          4096 Apr 26 06:29 .
drwxr-xr-x    3 root      root          4096 Apr 26 06:29 ..
-rw-r--r--    1 root      root           884 Mar 21 23:13 grub.conf
# pwd
/root/RESTORE/grub
#
```

That's about all there is to restore. Just remember that you need to add all of the files that you want while in the restore shell before you run the extract command. Also, remember that it will create a relative set of directories to contain the file(s) that you added for extraction. This is another reason that we use a RESTORE directory; it's safer. We wouldn't want to happen to be in the / directory and extract backup files over top live operating OS files. That would be a bad thing.

Restoring MySQL Databases

To restore a backed up database from a mysqldump-created .sql file requires only a one line command:

```
# mysql < all-databases_2004-03-15.sql
```

Just make sure that your database is running when you issue this mysql client command. If the mysql client cannot talk to the mysql server database, it will not be able to recreate all the tables and data.

To restore a backed-up database from mysqlhotcopy cloned files (or restored files from tape), use the following command:

```
# /bin/rm -rf /root/mysql-backup/*old
```

This makes sure that any old copies of databases are wiped out. Then shut off the mysqld service, copy the files back, and turn the service back on like this:

```
# /etc/init.d/mysqld stop
Stopping MySQL:                                    [ OK ]
# cp -af /root/mysql-backup/* /var/lib/mysql/
# /etc/init.d/mysqld start
Starting MySQL:                                    [ OK ]
```

The database is now restored and operational.

Server Migrations

Sometimes you just need to back up everything, reinstall a new or different OS, and restore all your data onto the new server load. This can be done, but it's tricky when you're not going right back into the exact same environment. Here are some things to watch for if you find yourself in this situation.

Disk-to-Disk Magic

If you're being pressed into a massive server upgrade, don't risk it all with the dangers of an *in place* upgrade. I've done in place upgrades on other people's systems just to see if they really work. Sometimes they do and some times not. But at the other end of the spectrum, why bother moving all the existing server data to tape when you're just going to have to move it all right back into place? Tape is slow; so there is no need to do it that way. If you're able to get a couple extra hard drives lined up, there's a much easier way.

First, get yourself a couple of extra drives. One of the new drives will be your new OS drive— the one you're going to install a fresh new OS on. The second drive is going to be your insurance. Take your second drive and clone your original old OS/data drive with imaging software such as Symantec Ghost or Drive Image Pro (this is assuming an X86 environment, but Ghost can also clone non-x86 filesystems). Either Ghost or DIP will allow you to make a block-level copy of your old drive to your temporary migration drive. Now take that original old data/OS drive, clearly label and date it, and put it in a safe place for at least 6 months, just in case.

Now take your ghosted drive and install it in your new system under somewhere obvious like `/mnt/old-drive/`, mounted read only. It should look something like this in your `/etc/fstab` file:

```
/dev/hda3     /               ext3    defaults      1 1
/dev/hda2     /boot           ext3    defaults      1 2
/dev/hdc6     /mnt/old-drive  ext2    defaults,ro   0 0
```

After you have the drive mounted, begin migrating your data carefully and slowly. If you don't want to overwrite new server configuration data and files with your old stuff, DO NOT just blindly copy of large chunks of data such as `/home` directories, websites, users, and config files. Many times, new software package (such as apache 2's `httpd.conf` file) is not compatible with its older cousins. The same goes for even some user content. Be sure to inspect `/home/username` directories before just blindly copying them over. You should usually to spend a few minutes on each one before letting loose with your `cp -a /mnt/backup/home /home`. In fact, sometimes before starting to move over the larger chunks, I just go ahead and back up the new stuff just in case (if I have the space):

```
# cp -a /home /home-BAK
```

If you don't feel so comfortable with doing a lot of this on the command line, you can use a GUI environment such as KDE, GNOME, or even a cool shell tool such as Midnight Commander (or `mc` on the command line).

Software Issues

The software and server daemons on the source and target servers make up a major part of the server migration checklist. In short, you need to do your homework and make sure that the content and web programs you are moving do not have application version reliance that could make things difficult for you later (such as perl versus mod_perl, php versions, and so on). From a bird's-eye view, some of the technical issues that you need to check on the new server before the move begins include the following:

✦ OS install and supported libraries (for example, Linux and glib versions)

✦ Versions of apache (or other web server service used)

✦ Version of Sendmail (or mail service used)

✦ Apache modules, Perl, and CGI engines installed and configured

✦ BIND /DNS software (formatting of zone files)

✦ Same or greater patch levels (old versus new) for network visible services

✦ Same or greater hardware configuration

✦ Same security/access rights (TCP-Wrappers, ACLs, and so on)

✦ Any software or configuration dependencies on your IP address

✦ Any commercial packages that register their key based on IP, FQDN, or server name

✦ Roughly the same OS and filesystem UID/GID (user/group) permissions

This last point is usually one of the trickier ones. You need to examine your old /etc (now on /mnt/old-disk/etc/) and start looking for differences with users (/etc/passwd and /etc/shadows) and groups (/etc/group). Then recreate the users on the new system with the same UID/GIDs if possible.

Caution   No matter how tempting it is, DO NOT just copy over the old /etc/passwd on top of the new one. There are often many services that will conflict between the old and new systems. You may want to copy over one or two user lines that have UID and GIDs of 500 or higher. After you get a feel for this, you may be able to step this up a bit. If the old and new OS versions are close enough, and you can verify that the system crypt/hash functions are the same (that is, the passwords are encrypted using the same algorithm), you may be able to copy/paste parts of the old /etc/passwd, shadow, and groups files over to the new system. Just be careful to match up up user and group ids (UID/GIDs). Sometimes you may actually be able to keep the system and user passwords intact! Just remember NOT to copy entire /etc config files over the new install's config files.

Here's an example and breakdown of what the user accounts in /etc/passwd look like, and which column does what:

```
bsmith:x:503:503:Bob Smith:/home/bsmith:/bin/bash
  ~~~    ~~  ~~  ~~~      ~~~~~        ~~~~
  user   UID GID  username home dir    login shell
```

The file system and movement of data can be the hardest parts of a migration, because every file in the system maps to a specific user/UID and group/GID (not to mention special file links, security settings, and so on). Simply tar'ing or zipping-up and moving all the files from the source server over to the target server and then manually trying to match everything up can be a daunting job—even for a professional. Even though cp -a will preserve user/group IDs perfectly, your new OS install will often have slightly different directory, group, and security settings that you will have to keep battling, sometimes months after the migration is complete.

Web/Apache Gotchas

Here are a few of the things to watch out for with regards to apache migrations:

✦ Comparing the old and new `httpd.conf` configurations and modules of your two servers (assuming UNIX/apache)

✦ Verifying that system automation scripts, that may, for example, restart the web server, use the correct start/stop commands and paths

✦ Checking the paths of logs that are written and read (if you're doing any log analysis reporting)

✦ Checking all user and system crontab files, moving them over, and verifying each absolute path reference

✦ Apache 1.3 versus 2.0 module incompatibilities

One big web migration issue that is often overlooked is checking to make sure that your SSL engines (underlying SSL server programs) on your old and new servers are the same or at least certificate-compatible. If they are not, you could be looking at either regenerating and repurchasing all of your SSL certificates (which could take up to 2 weeks per certificate, and hundreds of dollars each), or installing a different SSL engine on the new server.

Also, if you're bringing new SSL sites to your server that has existing SSL certificates that they've paid for, you will need both the SSL key and certificate for each site. Otherwise, the certificate is useless. I also recommend getting the cert request if it is still available. This can sometimes save the site owner money if the cert needs to be recreated.

Security

This too is a big category, so I'll just mention the basics of what you'll want to check out and compare on the new target server. This includes the following:

✦ TCP-Wrappers or IP based ACL (access) controls

✦ IP-Chain/IP-Table configurations

✦ FTP access rules

✦ Mail/SMTP/SMTP-Auth settings and relaying rules

✦ Mail/POP-locks and access rules

✦ Firewall ports, IP rules

✦ DNS zone transfer lock-downs/allows

Usually security ends up taking a back seat to getting everything moved over and working in the migration priorities. While this might end up being your de facto strategy, just don't forget to follow up with your server's security settings or you may end up experiencing a not so pleasant reminder in the form of hacked users accounts and/or compromised systems.

Backup-Related Resources

Table 5-4 provides a list of resources for more information on backups.

Table 5-4: Backup-Related Resources

Resource	Location (addresses should be one single line)
Backup resource#1	`www.address.com/stuff`
Red Hat EL3 backup tools and examples	`www.redhat.com/docs/manuals/enterprise/RHEL-3-Manual/admin-guide/s1-disaster-rhlspec.html`
Data Media Pocket Guide (Sony)	`http://www.cbtsoft.fi/cbtware/docs/Sony_DataMediaPocketGuide.pdf`
	Good reference, albeit vendor-biased, for comparing many forms of backup media.
Linux-backup	`http://linux-backup.net/`
	Great collection backup scripts, articles, and related information. All free.
AMANDA client/server	`http://amanda.org`
	`http://backupcentral.com/amanda.html`
	The more advanced AMANDA client/server backup suite that performs dynamic level-x backups given a fixed number of tapes in a backup set. Very nice for production environment backups.

Summary

Running production-grade backups takes a lot of planning, pricing, and consideration of policies on things like data retention and tape rotation issues. Doing it well in a large enterprise often draws on technical coordination among departments and server administrators, especially if you're running centralized backups.

There are a number of useful tools that come with Red Hat, Fedora Core, and most other Linux distributions. Using them effectively not only with the OS but also with your applications such as databases (such as MySQL) is critical for getting backups that you can rely on. In addition, knowing what to backup, what not to, and how to restore is also important in ensuring that there are no technical glitches along the way.

Just remember, with backups you must always be thinking at least 6 months to a year ahead. Plan for new tapes, server growth, tape pools, and rotations. With careful planning, you'll be ready when they come to you to get the full restore of that critical system, and then it will all be worthwhile.

✦   ✦   ✦

Troubleshooting Basic Features

Troubleshooting Tools

To this point in the book, we have focused on procedures and tips for getting your Fedora or other Red Hat Linux distribution installed and ready to deploy—sort of the "ounce of prevention" approach to troubleshooting. For the rest of the book, the focus is on learning the skills to troubleshoot running Linux systems.

You will be able to get up to speed much faster if you bring some Linux skills to the table. The first section of this chapter quickly goes over some skills you need to troubleshoot Linux (the shell, ways of gaining root access, and so on), but if you are fairly new to Linux you should refer to some basic Linux text for more help in learning the general skills you need.

Note   *Red Hat Linux Bible: Fedora and Enterprise Edition* should help provide the foundation of knowledge you need to move on to some of the more advanced troubleshooting techniques described in this book.

While you might want to jump right to a chapter on a particular feature you want to troubleshoot, there are some tools that are useful across a variety of Linux features. For example, tools such as `modprobe`, `lsmod`, and `modinfo` are useful for working with modules when your hardware needs to be manually configured. Tools such as `ssh` and `screen` can help you connect to computers on the network, regardless of the particular feature you are troubleshooting on the remote machine. Those and other helpful Linux troubleshooting tools are described in this chapter.

Getting Around with the Shell

The next few pages cover the basic tools and concepts that a Linux system administrator and troubleshooter needs, to get around the shell command-line interpreter—or just *shell* for short. If you are a Linux pro, you can probably skip ahead to some of the less common administration tools.

Knowing your way around the shell, for typing commands and traversing the file system, will make it possible for you to do most of the tasks laid out in the rest of this book. There are a few tricks you can use to get to and work with Linux through shell interfaces. I go through some ways of starting up, switching to, and working with shells in this section.

Using Fancy Shell Tricks

To troubleshoot a Linux system, you won't be able to stay with the graphical interfaces. Being able to get to a shell command-line interface, or more likely several interfaces at once, is a critical component of Linux system administration.

On a Linux system that has no graphical interface (or boots to runlevel 3), the shell is all you will have to start with. Login from your text-based login screen and the next thing you will see is a shell prompt. From a graphical user interface (GUI) desktop, however, there are lots of different ways of accessing shells and tricks for using shells efficiently.

Ways to Get to a Shell

The most common way to get to a shell from any Linux desktop is to open a terminal emulator window. Back in the old UNIX days, before graphical interfaces (or Linux) even existed, a character-based terminal was the only way to access UNIX-like systems. A terminal emulator, as the name implies, emulates one of those old character terminals when you open a terminal emulator window on the desktop. As an alternative, you can open a virtual terminal to get to a shell.

Terminal Windows

In Fedora Linux, a terminal emulator running on the desktop is simply referred to as a Terminal window. Unlike early editions of Red Hat Linux, Fedora and other recent Red Hat Linux systems don't have an icon on the desktop or panel for opening a Terminal window. However, there are still lots of ways to get to one.

Here are a few ways to open the default Terminal window from a KDE (konsole) or GNOME (gnome-terminal) desktop:

✦ **Ctrl+t**—From the KDE desktop, click anywhere on the desktop background, then press Ctrl+t.

✦ **Desktop menu**—Right-click on the GNOME desktop background to see the desktop menu. Then select Open Terminal.

✦ **Red Hat menu**—Click on the Red Hat menu, then select System Tools ⇨ Terminal.

Figure 6-1 shows two Terminal windows. The top one is the Konsole window (`konsole` command) and the lower one is the GNOME Terminal window (`gnome-terminal` command).

Each of the Terminal windows shown currently has two shell interfaces open. On the Konsole window, the small terminal icons each represent a different shell, while the GNOME Terminal window has a tab representing each shell. The prompt in each window shows the user you are logged in (as root), the name of your local computer (shuttle, in this case), and the name of the current directory (`/root` and `/tmp`, respectively).

There are other terminal windows that are less commonly used. The `xterm` command launches the classic X terminal emulator window. The KDE kterm terminal window offers additional multilingual support. Both xterm and kterm allow many options for changing colors, fonts, and other attributes. However, those features are not selectable from menus on the window, as they are with Konsole and GNOME Terminal windows.

Tips on using Terminal windows are described a bit later. Besides the default bash shell, there are other different shells available (which are also described a bit later in this chapter).

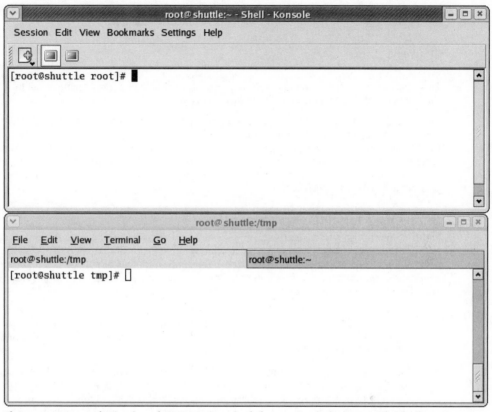

Figure 6-1: Konsole (top) and GNOME Terminal (bottom) windows provide shell access on a Linux desktop.

Virtual Terminals

Another way to get to a shell from Linux is by using virtual terminals. When you first boot Linux, six virtual terminals are started, offering you six text-based login screens. If you start Linux in graphical mode (the default runlevel 5), it will typically use a seventh virtual terminal.

You can switch to different virtual terminals from any Linux desktop, using the Ctrl+Alt+function key sequences or one of several virtual-terminal-switching commands (such as chvt or switchto). The number of the virtual terminal corresponds to the function key you use to switch, such as Ctrl+Alt+F1 (virtual terminal 1), Ctrl+Alt+F2 (virtual terminal 2), Ctrl+Alt+F3 (virtual terminal 3), and so on. From any nongraphical virtual terminals (1 to 6), you can drop the Ctrl key. For example, you could use Alt+F7 to get back to your X desktop.

Note Use the Alt key from the left side of the keyboard.

To use either the `chvt` or `switchto` commands to change to another virtual terminal, follow the command with the number of the virtual terminal. For example:

```
# chvt 3
```

This changes to virtual terminal 3. The `chvt` and `switchto` commands are most useful at times when some application may have taken over your function keys.

The programs run in virtual terminals need not be purely text based. Programs that have been implemented using the new curses (ncurses) library routines can offer menu-driven interfaces that run in virtual terminals and Terminal windows. You can use Tab and arrow keys to move around and make selections. Examples include `redhat-config-printer-tui` and `redhat-config-network-tui` (the tui stands for text user interface) to see text-based interfaces for printers and network interfaces.

Tuning up a Terminal Window

In this chapter, I'm focusing on the gnome-terminal and konsole terminal emulation windows because these are the two default Terminal windows used with GNOME and KDE desktop environments, respectively. Of course, once a Terminal window is open, you can just type the commands you want and not fuss about it. However, here are a few tips that might make using your Terminal window more pleasant:

✦ **Multiple shells**—You can have multiple shells running in the same Terminal window. Figure 6-1 shows a Konsole window with terminal icons representing multiple shells and a GNOME Terminal window with a tab displayed for each open shell.

Multiple shells in one Terminal window can provide a convenient way to keep track of a lot of programs running at the same time. You might want separate shells open to compile software, read a man page, tail a log file, and edit a text document, for example. Here's how to open multiple shells in GNOME and KDE Terminal windows:

- **GNOME**—With the GNOME Terminal window selected, press Shift+Ctrl+t to open a shell in a new tab. Click the tab you want, to go back and forth between the tabs. Press Shift+Ctrl+n to open a new Terminal window.

> **Note**   There are also keyboard shortcuts to move among tabs in the GNOME Terminal window. Use the Alt key plus a number to go to a particular tab (such as Alt+1, Alt+2, or Alt+3 to go to tabs 1, 2, or 3, respectively). To step through tabs, press Ctrl+PageUp to go to the previous tab or Ctrl+PageDown to go to the next tab.

- **KDE**—In the KDE Konsole Terminal window, click the plus sign (+) icon in the menu bar. A new terminal icon appears, representing the new shell. Click the different icons to go between these shells.

✦ **Scrolling settings**—If you have ever had an output that you wanted to read scroll past you on the screen, you might be interested in the Scrollback feature. For the GNOME Terminal window, you can edit your profile (click Edit ➭ Current Profile, then select the Scrolling tab) to set the number of lines of output that you can scroll back in the Terminal window. The more lines that are saved for scrollback, the more memory in kilobytes is needed to store that information. Setting the scrollback value in lines or kilobytes will automatically change the amount of the other value (the more lines you save, the more memory is required).

In the Konsole window, you can search back through all scrolled output, to find the text you are looking for. Click Edit ➪ Find in History and type the text you are looking for into the search box.

✦ **Changing font size**—If you are having trouble reading some text, you can change the font size in the Terminal window. In the GNOME Terminal, press Shift+Ctrl++ to zoom in to a larger font or Ctrl+− (Ctrl and a minus sign) to zoom out to a smaller font. In Konsole, click Settings ➪ Font, then select the font size you want (Normal, Tiny, Small, Medium, Large, or Huge). Or, in Konsole, choose Custom to select a particular font style and size.

✦ **Changing colors**—You can change the default black text on white background in both Konsole and GNOME Terminal windows. In Konsole, click Settings—Schema, then choose a color combination. In GNOME Terminal, click Edit ➪ Current Profile, then select the Colors tab. By default, GNOME Terminal will use colors for the Terminal window, based on the current system color scheme. As an alternative, you can select from among several built-in schemes or create your own.

When it comes to performance, a single GNOME Terminal will consume more memory than a single Konsole Terminal. However, the GNOME Terminal will use the same process for each new window and increase memory usage only slightly, while each new Konsole window starts a new process and consumes the same amount of memory again.

To improve performance of GNOME Terminal, reduce the scrollback buffer. Not only do large scrollback buffers consume memory, but a process that is doing a lot of text scrolling in a Terminal window (such as a kernel build or listing a large file) can greatly harm overall performance. Listing a large text file to the screen on a virtual terminal (no X or Terminal window overhead) might take only one-tenth the amount of time to complete. On an xterm, text scrolling will be done in about half the time of that required on a Konsole or GNOME Terminal window.

Features that drain performance in the GNOME Terminal window include using background images or transparent backgrounds (see the Effects tab on the GNOME Terminal Current Profile window). A plain, solid-colored background will yield best performance.

Choosing and Using a Shell

While bash is the default shell used in Fedora Linux, it is not the only one available. There are more than a half dozen different types of shells included with Fedora. Each shell includes some different features and different configuration files. Shells that come with Fedora and most Red Hat Linux systems include the following:

✦ **ash**—The ash shell is a copy of the Bourne shell (sh) that was part of the Berkeley UNIX distribution. While ash includes many features that are in the sh shell, it is more lightweight than sh.

✦ **bash**—The bash shell is the default shell used with Fedora and most Linux systems. It was originally created to be compatible with the Bourne shell (sh), but has since added features from C shell (csh) and Korn shell (ksh), as well as some features of its own. Bash configuration files include $HOME/.bashrc (for each user) and /etc/bashrc (for all users).

✦ **ksh**—The Korn shell (ksh) was created at AT&T and became the command predecessor to the Bourne shell (sh). In Linux, the pdksh shell (which is linked to ksh) is the open source version of ksh. When ksh is started as a login shell, shell settings are read from the user's `$HOME/.profile`, as well as from the system `/etc/profile` file.

✦ **csh**—The C shell (csh) was the default shell commonly used with Berkeley UNIX systems (including early UNIX versions from Sun Microsystems). The tcsh shell is the open source version of csh that comes with most Linux systems (although you can call it from csh as well). Configuration settings for the C shell are stored in `$HOME/.tcshrc` (for each user) and `/etc/csh.cshrc` and `/etc/csh.login` files (system wide).

✦ **sh**—The Bourne shell (sh) was the standard shell used in early UNIX systems. In Linux, the `sh` command actually runs the bash command in sh compatibility mode.

> The sh-compatibility mode in bash is not completely compatible with sh. If you request a bash feature that is not in sh, the feature will not fail (as it would in sh) if bash is able to provide it. Also, some sh features, such as how braces are handled, are done differently in bash. Start sh with the +B option if you need to use the Linux sh in a way that is completely compatible with the traditional sh shell.

✦ **zsh**—The Z shell (zsh) is similar to the Korn shell, with many enhancements added. Extra features in zsh include spelling correction, programmable command completion, autoloading of shell functions, loadable modules, and an FTP client, to name a few. To add setting to be used by zsh, you can use several files in the user's home directory (`.zshrc.zwc`, `.zshrc`, `.zshenv`, `.zproflie`, `.zlogin`, and `.zlogout`) and in `/etc` (`zshenv`, `zprofile`, `zshrc`, `zlogin`, and `zlogout`).

When you add a user in Fedora Linux, bash is assigned as the default shell. You can change the default shell for a particular user, by running `usermod` with the `-s` option. For example:

```
# usermod -s /bin/tcsh jjones
```

This example changes the default shell (the one that starts when you open a Terminal window or virtual terminal) to `/bin/tcsh` for the user `jjones`. When you first add a user, you can also indicate that the user be assigned a particular default shell. The following example adds a user named `tsmith` and assigns the ash shell to this user.

```
# useradd -s /bin/ash tsmith
```

To change the default shell (for example, to csh) for all users that you add in the future, type the following.

```
# useradd -D -s /bin/csh
```

Because bash is the default shell (and used by most people with Linux), for a quick review of how to tune your shell to suit the way you work, I focus on the bash shell.

Tuning a Bash Shell

Each time a bash shell starts up, it reads several configuration files. If there are any options you want to add to bash, you can add them to one of those files. In order, it reads the following files and directories (assuming they exist):

✦ `/etc/bashrc`—System-wide bash configuration file, read by shells started by anyone on the system. This file sets the default umask to 022, so files created from the shell have 644 permissions and directories have 755 permissions). It also sets the terminal to an

appropriate value (such as xterm or linux) and the command-line prompt (to
[user@host curr_dir], showing the user name, host name, and current directory).
You can override any of these values in your personal .bashrc file.

✦ /etc/profile.d—This directory contains files that set configuration information for
different applications that are needed for each type of shell you run. For example, the
colorls.csh and colorls.sh define the colors in which different objects appear when
you type an ls from the screen. You can add your own files, or modify existing files if you
don't like the way certain features are handled.

✦ $HOME/.bashrc—Each home directory can contain its own .bashrc file (notice the
leading dot in the filename). The file is the best place to put any personal settings you
want to use for your shell environment.

Here are some examples of the kinds of settings you might want to add to your personal
.bashrc, **system-wide** /etc/bashrc, **or application-specific** /etc/profile.d/ **file.**

```
set -o vi
set -o notify
alias rm="rm -i"
alias c="tput clear"
alias la="ls -Al"
export D="/home/chris/documentation/book1"
```

Each of the commands just shown is an example of the type of command you can add to a
shell configuration file (permanent) or type directly into the shell (temporary). The first two
set commands assign the vi command to be used to edit your command lines and history
(emacs is the default) and cause the shell to notify you immediately when a background job
completes (the default is to tell you at the next command prompt).

The alias commands rm, c, and la set what happens when those commands are run. The rm
-i causes you to be prompted before removing each file, tput clear clears your screen, and
ls -Al prints a long listing of files, including dot (.) files. The export example is simply used
here to set a long path name to a single variable. You could then type cd $D to go to the
/home/chris/documentation/book1 directory or the command vi $D/index.html to edit
the index.html file from that directory.

There are many other options you might want to set to configure your shell. I recommend that
you refer to the bash man page for details on built-in commands and options you can use.

Useful Shell Commands

Again, if you are not familiar with a shell from Linux, you should really get an introductory
Linux book to learn the basic commands to use. Those commands should include cat, chgrp,
chmod, chown, cd, ls, pwd, mv, rm, cp, mkdir, rmdir, ln, touch, less, and probably a few
dozen others, as suits the job you need to do with Linux.

Here are a few commands that you as a system administrator engaged in troubleshooting
Linux will find invaluable.

Finding and Sorting through Files

With most configuration and log files still stored as plain text in Linux, the ability to search,
sort, and list information from these files is a critical skill for Linux troubleshooters. The sort,
grep, tail, head, and find commands are valuable tools for troubleshooting text files in Linux.

The sort command can be used to sort lines of text in alphabetical order. For example, to alphabetically sort the users on your system, you could type the following.

```
# sort /etc/passwd | less
```

You can also sort by fields in a file, by identifying the field separator and the field you want to sort by. In the following example, the /etc/passwd file is sorted by the contents of the third field (the UID field).

```
# sort -t :--key=3 /etc/passwd | less
```

The grep command is a handy troubleshooting tool because it provides a very powerful means of searching through a large number of text files for particular text. For example, let's say that I just removed a computer from the network named duck and want to find all of my configuration files that have a reference to it. The following command suppresses error messages (-s) and recursively (-r) checks all the files beneath the /etc directory for the string duck.

```
# grep -s -r duck /etc
```

Options that I commonly use with grep include -i (ignore case), -n (list the line number on which the term occurs), and -w (list only if term appears as a separate word). I also commonly use regular expressions to more precisely define what I am looking for. For example, ^duck or duck$ would find only those lines in which the word duck appears at the beginning or end of a line, respectively.

A period is another handy character for indicating to match on any character. For example, let's say that you have done such a good job troubleshooting your Linux systems that you have time to do a crossword puzzle. Here's how you could search the dictionary for a five-letter word beginning with l and ending with ty:

```
# grep ^l..ty$ /usr/share/dict/words
lofty
lusty
```

A lot of times when you are looking at log files or, for that matter, any file that is getting new information all the time, you might want to watch information being added to that file in real time. The tail command is a great way to do that. I often use the tail command when I am troubleshooting a particular feature (with debugging turned on) and want to watch log messages as they progress. Here's an example:

```
# tail -f /var/log/messages
```

Without the -f option, the default of the tail command is to just list the last ten lines of the selected file. With the -f, this command waits for more lines to be written to the file and lists them as they arrive. Conversely, if you want to see only the first ten lines of a file, you can use the head command.

```
# head /var/log/messages
```

The find command is useful for finding files by their name, rather than by content. After finding the files you want, based on the parameters you choose, you can also act on the files you find, by executing (-exec) another command on the find command line. Here are some examples.

```
# find /var/log -exec grep "ip_forward" '{}' \ ; -print
```

The previous example finds all files in the /var/log directory and its subdirectories. Next, the command line searches (grep) the files that are found for the string "ip_forward" and lists the results. If you are troubleshooting disk space problems, you can use find to look for files over a particular size. For example:

```
# find /home -size +1024000k -exec du -h '{}' \ ; -print
1.1G /home/chris/movie1.avi
1.3G /home/chris/movie2.avi
```

In the previous example, find searches the /home directory for files over 1,024,000KB. Then it executes the du -h command. This allows you to see any files that are over about 1GB and print that information in a human-readable output. By following this format you can also substitute any command you want for the du -h to act on the files found. For example, you could remove (rm), move (mv), or change permissions (chmod) of the files found.

There are many other useful options you could use with the find command. To check for a certain type of file, use -type followed by f (file), d (directory), l (symbolic link), b (block special device), c (character special device), or s (socket). The -xdev prevents the find command from searching directories on other file systems (which is useful if you have NFS files systems or CDs mounted, which you don't want to search).

Finding the State of the System

If you are coming on to troubleshoot a system that you didn't set up, it's a good idea to do just a few quick checks to find out basic information about the system. Here are a few commands you can run.

The uname command can tell you the name of your kernel (Linux), name of your computer, the kernel release it is running, the date the kernel was created, the processor type and hardware platform on the computer, and the name of the computer operating system:

```
# uname -a
Linux shuttle.linuxtoys.com 2.4.22-1.2115.nptl #1 Wed Oct 29
    15:42:51 EST 2003 i686 i686 i386 GNU/Linux
```

To see the amount of disk space available on all your mounted partition, type the df -h command as follows.

```
# df -h
Filesystem      Size  Used  Avail  Use%  Mounted on
/dev/hda6        59G   52G   4.1G   93%  /
/dev/hda1        99M  6.3M    88M    7%  /boot
/dev/hda2       9.7G  7.4G   1.8G   81%  /mnt/backup
/dev/hda5       4.9G  1.2G   3.5G   25%  /mnt/isos
none            252M     0   252M    0%  /dev/shm
```

To see all the partitions available on all the hard disks (including those that are not currently mounted), use the fdisk -l command.

```
# fdisk -l

Disk /dev/hda: 80.0 GB, 80026361856 bytes
255 heads, 63 sectors/track, 9729 cylinders
Units = cylinders of 16065 * 512 = 8225280 bytes
```

```
Device    Boot   Start    End     Blocks   Id  System
/dev/hda1   *       1      13      104391   83  Linux
/dev/hda2          14    1288    10241437+  83  Linux
/dev/hda3        1289    1364     610470    82  Linux swap
/dev/hda4        1365    9729   67191862+    f  Win95 Ext'd (LBA)
/dev/hda5        1365    2001    5116671    83  7Linux
/dev/hda6        2002    9729   62075128+   83  Linux
```

To tell if the computer was booted into graphical mode (runlevel 5), text mode (runlevel 3), or some other run level, type the runlevel command. This example shows that the previous state was N (none) and the current state is 5 (graphical). Since there was no previous run level, the computer most likely booted to runlevel 5.

```
# runlevel
N 5
```

To take a quick check of your hardware, run the lspci command. This will show you what PCI hardware is installed on your computer.

```
# lspci
00:00.0 Host bridge: Intel Corp. 82845G/GL [Brookdale-G]
     Chipset Host Bridge (rev 03)
00:01.0 PCI bridge: Intel Corp. 82845G/GL [Brookdale-G]
     Chipset AGP Bridge (rev 03)
00:1d.0 USB Controller: Intel Corp. 82801DB USB (Hub #1)
     (rev 02)
00:1d.1 USB Controller: Intel Corp. 82801DB USB (Hub #2)
     (rev 02)
00:1d.2 USB Controller: Intel Corp. 82801DB USB (Hub #3)
     (rev 02)
00:1d.7 USB Controller: Intel Corp. 82801DB USB2 (rev 02)
00:1e.0 PCI bridge: Intel Corp. 82801BA/CA/DB/EB PCI Bridge
     (rev 82)
00:1f.0 ISA bridge: Intel Corp. 82801DB LPC Interface
     Controller (rev 02)
00:1f.1 IDE interface: Intel Corp. 82801DB Ultra ATA Storage
     Controller (rev 02)
00:1f.3 SMBus: Intel Corp. 82801DB/DBM SMBus Controller
     (rev 02)
00:1f.5 Multimedia audio controller: Intel Corp. 82801DB
     AC'97 Audio Controller (rev 02)
01:00.0 VGA compatible controller: nVidia Corporation NV34
     [GeForce FX 5200] (rev a1)
02:06.0 Ethernet controller: Realtek Semiconductor Co., Ltd.
     RTL-8139/8139C/8139C+ (rev 10)
02:07.0 FireWire (IEEE 1394): VIA Technologies, Inc. IEEE
     1394 Host Controller (rev 46)
02:08.0 Multimedia video controller: Brooktree Corporation
     Bt878 Video Capture (rev 11)
02:08.1 Multimedia controller: Brooktree Corporation Bt878
     Audio Capture (rev 11)
```

As an alternative, you can use the `dmesg` command. Besides showing your PCI devices, `dmesg` also shows information about other hardware and drivers as they are detected and accessed by the kernel.

```
# dmesg | less
Linux version 2.4.22-1.2115.nptl
(bhcompile@daffy.perf.redhat.com) (gcc version 3.2.3 20030422
(Red Hat Linux 3.2.3-6)) #1 Wed Oct 29 15:42:51 EST 2003
BIOS-provided physical RAM map:
BIOS-e820: 0000000000000000 - 000000000009fc00 (usable)
BIOS-e820: 000000000009fc00 - 00000000000a0000 (reserved)
BIOS-e820: 00000000000f0000 - 0000000000100000 (reserved)
    .
    .
    .

PCI: PCI BIOS revision 2.10 entry at 0xfb5d0, last bus=2
PCI: Using configuration type 1
PCI: Probing PCI hardware
PCI: Probing PCI hardware (bus 00)
PCI: Ignoring BAR0-3 of IDE controller 00:1f.1
Transparent bridge - Intel Corp. 82801BA/CA/DB/EB PCI Bridge
PCI: Using IRQ router PIIX/ICH [8086/24c0] at 00:1f.0
PCI: Found IRQ 11 for device 00:1f.1
PCI: Sharing IRQ 11 with 00:1d.2
PCI: Sharing IRQ 11 with 02:06.0
    .
    .
    .
```

A recommended technique for debugging problems with hardware detection is to direct the output of `dmesg` to a file (`dmesg > boot.msg`), so that the contents of this file can be e-mailed or posted to someone who can help you figure out the problem.

Finding out about Yourself

You can find out about your current user environment, using some of the following commands.

Using the `set` command (piped to `less`), you can step through the environment variables set for shell environment.

```
# set | less
BASH=/bin/bash
BASH_ENV=/root/.bashrc
BASH_VERSION='2.05b.0(1)-release'
COLORS=/etc/DIR-COLORS.xterm
COLORTERM=gnome-terminal
COLUMNS=110
DISPLAY=:0.0
HISTFILE=/root/.bash_history
HISTFILESIZE=1000
HISTSIZE=1000
HOME=/root
HOSTNAME=shuttle.linuxtoys.com
```

The previous code example shows only a small part of the output from the set command. Here you can see information about your bash shell, definitions of how colors are used in terminal windows, the width of your Terminal window (in columns), and your X display number (0.0). It also shows information about your command-line history, your home directory, and host name.

You can type the groups command to see what groups you are in.

```
# groups
chris wheel
```

You can use the who command to find out about your current session. The output of who am i shows your username, the terminal where you are logged in (a terminal window in this case), the date and time the terminal session started, and (if applicable) the display screen you are currently on (:0.0).

```
# who am i
chris   pts/2 Mar   19 14:30 (:0.0)
```

To see more information about your user and group accounts, type the id command.

```
# id
uid=500(chris) gid=500(chris) groups=500(chris)
```

Find out about Others on Your Computer

If you are troubleshooting a computer that has multiple users with login accounts, you might want to list information about those users. Here are some suggestions on how to do that.

With the lastlog command you can see when a person last logged into the computer and the terminal device they used to login on. Many of the users should be listed as Never logged in because they are administrative logins that don't have valid shell accounts. So a login date listed for lp or bin accounts would probably indicate a break-in.

```
# lastlog | less
Username         Port    From          Latest
root             pts/3   duck Sun Mar 21 21:24:22 -0800 2004
bin                                    **Never logged in**
daemon                                 **Never logged in**
adm                                    **Never logged in**
lp                                     **Never logged in**
sync                                   **Never logged in**
chris            tty4         Fri Mar 19 15:41:46 -0800 2004
robby            :0           Fri Jan 23 22:15:03 -0800 2004
two              tty1         Thu Jan 22 16:24:26 -0800 2004
```

Using the finger command, you can see who is logged in and actively working at the moment. Notice that jimh has been inactive for 2 days. There are two root logins that have been inactive for over 3 and 6 hours respectively. The other two root logins are currently active. (You can run the pinky command to get similar output.)

```
# finger
Login    Name      Tty    Idle   Login Time    Office Office Phone
jimh     Jim Hall  tty4    2d     Mar 19 15:41
root     root      tty2   3:36    Mar 19 14:29
root     root      *:0            Mar 18 12:10
root     root      pts/2          Mar 19 14:30 (:0.0)
root     root      pts/3  6:38    Mar 21 21:24 (duck)
```

Again, there are hundreds of commands you will want to use over time. I recommend getting a basic text on Linux or UNIX use and administration, to get more information on how to use the shell and shell commands.

Obtaining Root Privilege

The root user is the primary user account used for Linux system administration. Despite file ownership and group assignment, the root user always has the ability to change, add, or delete any file or directory on a Linux system (provided that the device itself is not a read-only device).

Troubleshooting and administering any standard Linux or UNIX systems begins with the root user. While regular user accounts may be able to display information about your system and even modify selected features, the root user is expected (in fact, is the only user allowed) to do most system-wide configuration changes to a Linux system. This section goes through ways of accessing and sharing root privilege in Linux.

Getting Root Access from the Shell

Troubleshooting system-wide features almost always means acting as root user. The most common ways to obtain root privilege from a shell are as follows:

✦ **Login as root**—Whether you login to a computer over the network using ssh (described later in this chapter) or from a login prompt, you can simply login with root as the username and, when prompted, the root user's password. By default, the prompt will end in a pound sign (#) and all subsequent commands run from the login will be run as the root user.

✦ **su (new shell)**—By using the su command while you are logged in as another user, you can effectively become the root user for all subsequent commands from the current shell. It is most common to run the su command followed by a dash (-) as shown here.

```
$ su -
Password:
#
```

The dash causes the su command to open a new shell for the root user, as a login shell. So all configuration files read during an initial login (such as the /etc/profile file) are read before starting the new shell you just opened with su.

If you forget to use the dash after the su command, the most common failure you will experience is that your shell will not find common administrative commands that are in /sbin, /usr/sbin, and /usr/local/sbin directories. This is because the /etc/profile file is not examined to include these directories in the root user's PATH. The common annoyance you will experience is that you are changed to the /root directory as your current directory, so you might need to return to the directory you were in if you want to do some work there.

Note

The su command, though commonly used to become the root user, can be used to change to any user that has a valid shell account on your system. (You can't su to a user that has /sbin/nologin or /bin/false as its default shell.)

✦ **su (single command)**—If you just want to execute a single command as root user, you can use su with the -c option. Simply follow the su command with -c and the command you want to run (along with any arguments), and then provide the root password when prompted. For example, if you want to create a directory in a location that is restricted to root-only access while you are logged in as another user, you could run the following.

```
$ su - -c "mkdir /root/tmp"
Password:
```

In this case, the -c tells the su command to run the command in quotes as the root user. After entering the root password you have full root privilege to create, in this case, a directory that requires root privilege to do so. As soon as the command completes, you return to your original shell (which was presumably owned by a non-root user).

✦ **sudo**—As an alternative to logging in as root or using su to get to root, you can configure the /etc/sudoers file to allow selected users to have limited (or unlimited) root access on your Linux system via the sudo command. To change the /etc/sudoers file, run the following command.

```
#visudo
```

The visudo command locks the /etc/sudoers command while you edit it with the vi command. The following are some ways of configuring the sudoers files, most of which are based on entries that you can activate from within the default sudoers file itself.

```
# User privileges
root        ALL=(ALL) ALL
sandy       ALL=/usr/bin/lprm, /usr/sbin/lpc

# Group privileges
%wheel      ALL=(ALL) ALL
%wheel      ALL=(ALL) NOPASSWD: ALL
%users      ALL=/sbin/mount /mnt/cdrom,/sbin/umount /mnt/cdrom
%users      localhost=/sbin/shutdown -h now
```

The privilege specification for the root user allows root to have complete access to the Linux system as it relates to the sudo command (ALL). The second line shows the user sandy being given the privilege to remove printer jobs (lprm) and control printers (lpc). This indicates how you can give one person the privilege to do a certain task (such as manage printers), without giving the person full control of the Linux system.

The first wheel line gives complete access to all users in the wheel group (as listed in the /etc/group file). To gain that access, users in the wheel group have to use the sudo command and (when prompted) enter their own password (not the root user password). The second wheel line gives users in the wheel group the same access as the previous line, except that they can do so without entering a password.

The two %users lines shown in the example represent what functions those who belong to the users group can do that are typically restricted to root user privilege. Presumably you would add all regular user accounts (by default, UID 500 and higher) to the users line in the /etc/group file. In the first case, these users would be able to mount a CD (/sbin/mount /mnt/cdrom) and unmount a CD (/sbin/umount /mnt/cdrom). In the second case, anyone in the users group on the localhost will be able to shutdown the computer (using the /sbin/shutdown -h now command).

Caution   As a Linux troubleshooter, on a multiuser system it may be tempting to provide limited administrative capability to other people on that system. However, be warned that some commands (such as the vi editor) include features that let the user escape to a shell. That will effectively give the user full access to your system and undermine the intention of providing limited access to the user.

Getting Root Access from the GUI

A nice feature of the Red Hat graphical administrative tools that come with Fedora and other Red Hat systems is that they can be run from any user's desktop. If a regular user launches an administrative window, either from the main menu or by running a redhat-config-* command, the user is prompted for the root password before being allowed to continue.

Figure 6-2 shows an example of the Query window prompting for the root password before allowing the user to access the Network Configuration window.

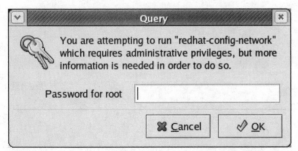

Figure 6-2: Before you can run GUI administration tools, you are prompted to enter the root password.

After you have entered the root password, look at the panel at the bottom of the desktop. A pair of keys should appear, indicating that you continue to be authorized to run applications that require a root password. Click on those keys to choose to keep that authorization, or forget about it.

Examining System Processes

When some software or hardware seems to be broken in Linux, there are some standard tools you can use to monitor what is happening with your system. Temporarily slow performance can be monitored using tools such as top, to see what the processes are doing at the moment.

If an application isn't completing properly, you can trace the system calls it is making, by using the strace command.

Tracking Processes with Top

If system performance takes a quicknosedive, top is a good way to check out what is going on. The top command shows the running processes on your system and allows you to sort these processes based across several parameters. Its graphical counterpart in the GNOME environment, called gtop, lets you easily sort information by clicking on columns in the gtop window.

The top command doesn't require a GUI, which makes it convenient for running from a virtual terminal or after logging in over a network using ssh from a Terminal window. To start top from a shell, simply type:

```
# top
```

A list of running processes appears, displaying activity in real time. When you start top, processes are listed in order of current CPU usage (from most to least). By default, the screen is updated every 5 seconds to show the new order of CPU usages by your processes. Press the space bar to update information immediately. Figure 6-3 shows an example of an active top window in Fedora.

```
08:27:59  up 3 days, 20:18,  6 users,  load average: 0.33, 0.15, 0.05
101 processes: 98 sleeping, 1 running, 2 zombie, 0 stopped
CPU states:  cpu    user    nice  system    irq  softirq  iowait    idle
           total   0.0%    0.0%    0.0%   0.0%    0.0%    0.0%    0.0%
Mem:   514560k av,  496736k used,   17824k free,      0k shrd,  262504k buff
       313232k active,              144500k inactive
Swap:  610460k av,   84328k used,  526132k free                  96252k cached

  PID USER     PRI  NI  SIZE  RSS SHARE STAT %CPU %MEM   TIME CPU COMMAND
 4094 root      15   0  201M  37M 15864 S    38.1  7.4  1176m  0 X
11383 root      15   0 12624  12M  9512 S     2.3  2.4   0:03  0 rhythmbox
 4237 root      15   0 12044 9180  6416 S     1.3  1.7   0:19  0 gnome-terminal
 4227 root      15   0  6224 5804  4892 S     0.7  1.1   0:21  0 metacity
 4456 root      15   0  6892 6224  5268 S     0.7  1.2   0:08  0 wnck-applet
    1 root      16   0   408  380   356 S     0.0  0.0   0:03  0 init
    2 root      15   0     0    0     0 SW    0.0  0.0   0:00  0 keventd
    3 root      15   0     0    0     0 SW    0.0  0.0   0:00  0 kapmd
    4 root      34  19     0    0     0 SWN   0.0  0.0   0:00  0 ksoftirqd/0
    6 root      25   0     0    0     0 SW    0.0  0.0   0:00  0 bdflush
    5 root      16   0     0    0     0 SW    0.0  0.0   0:16  0 kswapd
    7 root      15   0     0    0     0 SW    0.0  0.0   0:00  0 kupdated
    8 root      20   0     0    0     0 SW    0.0  0.0   0:00  0 mdrecoveryd
```

Figure 6-3: Use top to sort processes by CPU, memory, or other system usage.

To get a feel for the information you are seeing on the top screen, you can try sorting the data in different ways. With top running and the Terminal window it's running in selected, sort the processes in the top window in the following ways:

N Display processes numerically, by process ID

A Display processes by age, with the newest processes being displayed first

P Display processes by CPU usage (highest to lowest)

M Display processes by resident memory usage (highest to lowest)

T Display processes by total CPU time each process has consumed

Sorting this data in various ways can help you uncover problems on your system. Here are a few things you can do with top:

✦ **Check for memory usage**—Press the M key to sort the top output by memory usage. Look under the RSS line to see the actual amount of physical memory being used by each process (such as 40M for 40 megabytes). Under the %MEM column, you can see the percentage of total physical memory the process consumes. Shared memory used by the process is listed under the SHARE column.

The Mem: line in the upper section of the top screen shows the total memory available on the system, along with how much is used and how much is free. It also shows shared memory and memory used for buffers. Swap information shows the total size of your swap area, along with how much of it is free or currently being used.

A large amount of swapping will cause a performance drag. Adding more RAM will improve performance in such situations.

✦ **Check for memory leaks**—If an application has a memory leak (the memory it is consuming continues to grow over time), sorting by resident memory usage will point up processes that have grown out of whack with their memory use. Performance hits tend to really occur in cases where the growing process has caused frequent hits on swap space.

To check whether your system is frequently relying on swap space, try the free command.

```
# free -m
             total used free shared buffers cached
Mem:          502      389  112        0       42    213
-/+ buffers/cache:     133  369
Swap:         596        0  596
```

In this example you can see that no swap space is being used, so if there is a memory leak, it probably isn't adversely affecting the system.

In some cases, processes that may appear to be experiencing memory leaks may not be leaking at all. An example is the gnome-terminal process (which is associated with a Terminal window). Over time, the gnome-terminal process may consume larger amounts of memory. This comes from the fact that each time you open a new gnome-terminal window, the new window relies on the old gnome-terminal process, but simply causes a small increase in the process' memory use.

✦ **Watch only selected processes**—If you want to monitor only a few processes, you can enter the PID for the commands you want to watch on the top command line (up to 20 processes). Here is an example of top being used to monitor three different processes with PIDs of 4043, 4584, and 4353.

```
# top -p4043 -p4584 -p4353
```

✦ **Check general processor activity**—There are a lot of things you can check regarding the general status of the CPU. The first line on the top screen shows the current time, followed by the uptime (how long the system has been running) and the load average. The three load average numbers represent the average number of processes ready to run in the previous 1, 5, and 15 minutes.

From the second line on the top screen, you can see the total number of processes currently running (since the screen was last refreshed). You can also see the number of processes that are sleeping (waiting for something to happen), running, or stopped. Zombie processes, which are also listed on this line, are actually processes that are dead but remain in the process table because their parent processes have not checked their exit status.

High load averages might indicate that the CPU is the bottleneck for slow performance. Press P to sort by processor usage to see which processes are making the most demands on the processor (as indicated by the %CPU column). Try some processor-intensive applications, such as 3D-graphics or video or audio compression to check out how much the processor can handle.

Sleeping and zombie processes are not drawing on the CPU. While some people find zombie processes disconcerting to have around, when exited their resources are released, so they store only a small amount of data (the exit status and process ID of the now defunct process). To see which of your processes are zombies, list the current processes (ps ax) and look for a process with a Z in the STAT line.

✦ **Give processes more priority**—If you are using top as the root user, you can increase or decrease the priority of a running process (referred to as re-nicing the process). Press the r key, then type the PID of the process you want to re-nice. Next, enter the priority number you want to use. Priorities you can enter as root user range from 19 (lowest priority) to –20 (highest priority).

Caution

Re-nicing can be dangerous. It can cause some processes to hog the CPU beyond where you would intend, while causing others to be shut out from the CPU. Use this feature at your own risk.

✦ **Kill processes**—While you are on the top window, you can kill (or at least try to kill) any process you like. Press the k key and enter the PID of the process you want to kill. You are asked for the signal to use. By default, it will use the –15 signal (SIGTERM). Sometimes to kill a process, you might need to use –9 (SIGKILL) instead. (SIGKILL cannot be ignored and will kill the process without cleaning up.)

You can simplify the information you see in the top window in several ways. Press the i key to get rid of idle processes and just see the processes that are currently demanding attention from the processor. Normally, top just shows however many processes will fit on the screen. Press the t key to toggle some of the display summary information on and off.

Tracing down Failed Commands with strace

Sometimes you run a command and it just hangs or fails outright with no indication of what went wrong. To find out what exactly is going on with the command, you can run the command using strace.

With the strace command, you can watch the system calls being made through the entire run of the command. I most often use strace to see where a command is getting configuration information from and what devices it's trying to open. As each call is made, a listing of that call is sent to standard error. Here's an example.

```
# strace /bin/ping anyhost.linuxtoys.net 2>/tmp/ping_out
```

Here I try to ping a host computer on the network. By running the ping with the strace command and directing standard error (2>) to the /tmp/ping_out file, a ton of processing messages are sent to the ping_out file. Just to get a quick idea of where ping is going to get its information from, I look for all the occurrences of open to see what files it is opening. Here's the result.

```
# grep ^open /tmp/ping.out
open("/etc/ld.so.cache", O_RDONLY)      = 3
open("/lib/libresolv.so.2", O_RDONLY)   = 3
open("/lib/tls/libc.so.6", O_RDONLY)    = 3
open("/etc/resolv.conf", O_RDONLY)      = 4
open("/etc/nsswitch.conf", O_RDONLY)    = 4
open("/etc/ld.so.cache", O_RDONLY)      = 4
open("/lib/libnss_files.so.2", O_RDONLY)  = 4
open("/etc/host.conf", O_RDONLY)        = 4
open("/etc/hosts", O_RDONLY)            = 4
open("/etc/ld.so.cache", O_RDONLY)      = 4
open("/lib/libnss_dns.so.2", O_RDONLY)  = 4
```

Besides opening the libraries, the ping command opened several configuration files to look for IP address information. I could see that it opened the resolv.conf, nsswitch.conf and host.conf files to find out where it should look to resolve names to IP addresses. Locally, it checked the hosts file for addresses.

From this output, I would be able to tell if any configuration files ping wanted could not be found or opened. Failed opens usually appear with a -1 return value and a No such file or directory message. Besides opens, you can also look for system calls such as lstat (which check the existence of a file), read (to see calls that read information from files), and signal symbols and strings (to see processes being interrupted).

There are many options to strace that you can read about on the strace man page. You can trace child processes (-f) and print relative timestamps (-r). You can also have it trace only certain system calls. For example to just trace open system calls in the previous example, you could type:

```
# strace -e trace=open /bin/ping anyhost.linuxtoys.net
```

Because GUI administration tools sometimes fail mysteriously, I will often run an strace on them to find out what is wrong. Launching some redhat-config-* commands with strace from a Terminal window will show where Red Hat is saving and accessing the information it is using with the tool.

Going into Rescue Mode

It is possible for something to go wrong, which could cause your system to be unable to boot from the Linux partition on your hard disk. Your master boot record may have become corrupted or your /boot partition may have, for some reason, become inaccessible.

The following procedure describes how to go into rescue mode, using the Fedora boot CD (CD #1 of the installation set). The procedure should work the same for any recent Red Hat Linux system.

1. Insert the Fedora installation CD #1 into the disk drive.

2. Reboot your computer. Your computer should begin booting the installation process for the CD and you should see the boot: prompt.

3. At the boot prompt, type the following.

   ```
   boot: linux rescue
   ```

Note If you need other `boot` options (such as `nodma` or `vga=`) to get Linux working properly, you can add these after Linux rescue.

You are asked to choose a language.

4. Scroll down to select your language and press Enter. You are asked to choose your keyboard type.

5. Scroll down to choose your keyboard type and press Enter. You are asked if you want to start the network interfaces on your computer.

6. Choose Yes to start the network interfaces on your computer. If you choose Yes, be ready with configuration information (IP address, netmask, or choose DHCP if that service is available).

Note The network may not be necessary if you are simply fixing your master boot record. However, if the Linux operating system on your hard disk turns out to be unbootable, the network connection can provide a convenient way to copy critical files off of your computer.

At this point, rescue mode looks for your Fedora or other Red Hat Linux system and tries to mount it on the `/mnt/sysimage` directory.

7. If rescue mode finds your Linux system on hard disk, you can:

   • Continue, to have it mount your Linux partition from hard disk on `/mnt/sysimage`

   • Read-only, to have the file system mounted read-only (to let you copy and use, but not change files)

   • Skip, to not try to mount your Linux partition

   I recommend you select Continue in most cases, so you can get to and possibly change your Linux partition.

8. If your Linux partition was mounted successfully, you will be told so. Press OK. You will see a shell prompt.

9. Type `ls /mnt/sysimage`. You should see the same directories you would normally see from your system's root directory (/).

10. To change it so that `/mnt/sysimage` becomes your root directory, type the following:

    ```
    # chroot /mnt/sysimage
    ```

Now, your system should appear just as it does for a normal reboot. What you do next depends on what went wrong. Here are some possibilities:

✦ You want to reinstall your master boot record. If you are using GRUB as your boot loader and you want the MBR to go on the first IDE hard disk on your computer, type the following:

```
# grub-install /dev/hda
```

✦ Copy files off. If the system seems to be unbootable, use any commands you are used to for backing up or copying files from the system.

If you have corrected the problem, you should be able to remove the boot CD from the drive and reboot your computer from hard disk.

Detecting and Configuring Hardware

Fedora and Red Hat Linux systems use the kudzu utility to automatically detect when hardware is physically added and removed from your computer, and then configure that hardware as best it can. For most popular hardware, kudzu works quite well. Other times, however, you might need to add the drivers or modules you need to use the hardware yourself.

Using Kudzu to Detect Hardware

Most people never run kudzu manually at all. When you reboot your computer after adding a new network card, storage device, modem, or other piece of hardware, kudzu runs automatically and asks how you would like to configure that hardware. What kudzu does is:

✦ Probes your computer hardware (devices connected to the PCI bus, serial ports, parallel ports, usb ports, pcmcia slots, SCSI connections, and so on).

✦ Compares the hardware it detects against the system's current hardware listed in the /etc/sysconfig/hwconf file.

✦ Prompts you to configure or remove hardware, based on the differences in the two hardware lists.

✦ Updates the /etc/sysconfig/hwconf file to reflect the new hardware configuration.

In many cases, kudzu will find the right modules needed by the hardware and configure your system to load them automatically each time your system boots. If you want to use kudzu without rebooting, you should first shut down your graphical desktop interface. You can do that by changing to runlevel 3 (init 3). Then, as root user, simply type kudzu.

Configuring Hardware Modules

If kudzu can't configure your hardware drivers, or if you want to configure the drivers differently, you can use tools from the modutils package to load the modules you need to get your hardware working.

Using modules, instead of having drivers for every possible piece of hardware built into the kernel, allows the kernel to contain a minimal set of drivers. When hardware is added and removed, associated modules can be loaded and unloaded with only a small amount of overhead.

The following is a brief overview of utilities in the modutils package for loading, unloading, and listing information about modules.

Checking Loaded Modules

To see what modules are currently loaded on your system, you can use the lsmod command. Here's an example.

```
# lsmod | less
Module               Size  Used by    Not tainted
parport_pc          18468  1 (autoclean)
lp                   8356  0 (autoclean)
parport             36800  1 (autoclean) [parport_pc lp]
autofs              12052  0 (autoclean) (unused)
pcmcia_core         55232  0
via-rhine           14672  1
mii                  3992  0 [via-rhine]
floppy              56348  0 (autoclean)
sg                  34796  0 (autoclean)
sr_mod              17016  0 (autoclean)
ide-scsi            11856  0
scsi_mod           109384  3 [sg sr_mod ide-scsi]
ide_cd              34176  0
cdrom               34048  0 [sr_mod ide-cd]
keybdev              2624  0 (unused)
mousedev             5204  0 (unused)
hid                 23652  0 (unused)
input                5824  0 [keybdev mousedev hid]
ehci_hcd            19784  0 (unused)
usb_uhci            25740  0 (unused)
usbcore             77984  1 [hid ehci-hcd usb-uhci]
ext3                70532  3
jbd                 50796  3 [ext3]
```

The information for each module includes the module name, the module size (in bytes), and the number of modules using that module. Information in the last column is either unused (if the module is loaded but not being used), autoclean (if the module can be autocleaned using rmmod-a), or the names of modules that depend on this module.

If you are interested in what any of the modules are, you can use the modinfo command. Here is an example.

```
# modinfo parport_pc
filename:    /lib/modules/2.4.22-
             1.2140.nptl/kernel/drivers/parport/parport_pc.o
description: "PC-style parallel port driver"
author:      "Phil Blundell, Tim Waugh, others"
license:     "GPL"
parm:        io int array (min = 1, max = 16), description
             "Base I/O address (SPP regs)"
parm:        io-hi int array (min = 1, max = 16), description
             "Base I/O address (ECR)"
```

```
parm:          irq string array (min = 1, max = 16),
               description "IRQ line"
parm:          dma string array (min = 1, max = 16),
               description "DMA channel"
```

Here you can see that the module is a "PC-style parallel port driver". You can also see parameters that can be passed to the module (parm:). Other options to modinfo let you display partial listings of the information just shown. For example, modinfo -p *module* lets you just view parameters used by the module.

Loading Modules

To manually load a module (that was either not detected or improperly detected), you can use the modprobe command.

> **Note**   The insmod command can also be used to load modules in Linux. However, insmod loads only the requested module and does not load modules on which the one you want depends. Module dependencies queried by modprobe before loading a module are contained in the /lib/modules/*/modules.dep file.

Supported modules that come with Fedora and other Red Hat Linux systems are typically stored in /lib/modules/*/kernel directory (where you replace the asterisk with the name of your current kernel). There are modules listed as unsupported by Red Hat that are contained in the /lib/modules/*/unsupported directory.

Before just randomly loading the modules, you should know which modules are needed by the hardware you want to use. If you have the kernel-source package installed, you can read descriptions of many of the modules in the /usr/src/linux-*/Documentation directory for your kernel.

To load a module that is included in a Red Hat distribution using the modprobe command, you can simply type modprobe and the module name. For example:

```
# modprobe appletalk
```

The modprobe command will first look in the /etc/modules.conf for anything required of this module. Then it will look in the /lib/modules/*/modules.dep file and load any modules listed as being needed by the one you want. Then it will load the module itself. If there are options you want to pass to the modules, you can also do that when you run modprobe. For example:

```
# modprobe pwc size=cif fps=10
```

The pwc module is used for several different models of Philips Webcams. The options shown here specify the resolution of the image (cif is 352 × 288) and the number of frames per second being used (in this case, 10). I found the descriptions of these particular parameters in the /usr/src/linux-*/Documentation/usb/philips.txt file.

If you are getting third-party modules, you should be careful that:

✦ You know and trust the source of that module.

✦ You know whether you are using a tainted module. A tainted module is one that is not distributed under the GPL or other acceptable license. Some vendors distribute modules in binary-only format. Because the Linux community cannot fix problems that might occur with these modules, kernel developers will not respond to problems that occur with these tainted kernels. There are times when you must use a binary-only module to use the hardware at all. (I personally use binary-only modules for my NVIDIA video card and my Webcam.)

To continue with my Philips Webcam example, there is a pwcx decompressor module available to use with the pwc core driver as a plug-in. Although this module will allow larger images and higher frame rates, it is a binary-only module and is considered tainted. If you decide that you want to load this module anyway (which you do at your own risk), you need to force installation of that module. To temporarily try the module (with the module downloaded and unzipped to the current directory), type the following:

```
# insmod --force ./pwcx.o
Warning: kernel-module version mismatch
         ./pwcx.o was compiled for kernel version 2.4.23
         while this kernel is version 2.4.18-14
Warning: loading ./pwcx.o will taint the kernel:
non-GPL license - Proprietary. See
http://www.smcc.demon.nl/webcam/tainting.html
   See http://www.tux.org/lkml/#export-tainted for information
         about tainted modules
Warning: loading ./pwcx.o will taint the kernel: forced load
Module pwcx loaded, with warnings
```

As you can see, there are warnings about tainting the kernel, but it loads the module anyway. Follow the links shown in these warnings to see some good descriptions of the issue.

The behavior of modprobe can be modified by adding entries to the /etc/modules.conf file. Some of the more interesting things you can do within this file include setting commands to be run before, after, or instead of loading the requested module. Here are a few examples of entries added to the modules.conf file that make the modules perform better.

```
post-install sound-slot-0 /bin/aumix-minimal -f /etc/.aumixrc -L \
        >/dev/null 2>&1 || :
post-install pwc /sbin/insmod --force / moddir/pwcx.o >/dev/null 2>&1 || :
```

Here are two entries that are run after the modules they are associated with are installed. The first entry runs the aumix-minimal command after the sound-slot-0 modules (representing the first sound card) are loaded. The command reads in the values in the /etc/.aumixrc file to set initial levels for the sound card. The second line continues the example with the pwcx driver. After the pwc module is loaded, the insmod command forces the pwcx.o module to be loaded. (You would replace moddir with the full path to the pwcx.o file.)

Using Network Troubleshooting Tools

If you are responsible for troubleshooting multiple machines, you need efficient ways of connecting to those machines over a network and watching the communications that goes on between them. Tools for connecting to remote computers and troubleshooting them are quite plentiful in Linux. Some of the most basic tools you need are those that let you do remote login (such as ssh), watch network traffic (such as ethereal), and those that let you open sessions and reconnect to them later (such as screen).

Remote Login and Execution with ssh

The ssh command is the preferred command for doing remote logins between Linux and UNIX systems. Unlike older login commands (such as telnet and rlogin), ssh creates a secure, encrypted connection between the two communicating parties. In its most simple form, you can just use ssh with the host name you want to communicate with as an argument.

```
# ssh myhost.linuxtoys.net
root@myhost.linuxtoys.net's password: ******
Last login: Tue Jun 15 01:21:46 2004 from abc.linuxtoys.net
[root@myhhost root]#
```

After entering the root password (represented here by stars, although you won't see anything), you should see a shell prompt. From here, you can just use the shell as though it were your local shell. A few tips about using ssh if you are new to it:

✦ The first time you ssh to a machine, if you have not configured host authentication, ssh will remind you of that, to give you the opportunity to reject the ssh session. If you accept the connection, the RSA key fingerprint it gets from the remote machine will be used at each subsequent connection to that machine.

New Feature

The RSA key fingerprint is stored in your $HOME/.ssh/known_hosts file. It is possible that you may fail to connect to a remote host with ssh because the remote host changed something about its network configuration (different IP address or NIC card). You will have to remove the entry for that host from the known_hosts file to be able to ssh to the machine again.

✦ Both the login prompt and the title bar of the Terminal window (if you are using the default Terminal window in GNOME) will show the user you are logged in as, the remote host name, and the current directory. Make sure you remember where you are. If you forget that you are working in a remote shell, you could mistakenly reconfigure or reboot a remote server and really make a bunch of people mad.

✦ One of the coolest features of ssh that is enabled by default on Red Hat distributions is X11 forwarding. During your ssh session, if you launch an X application from the remote host, instead of ssh trying to open that application on a desktop of the machine where the application was launched, it will open on your local desktop.

✦ The X11 forwarding feature is done on the ssh client machine in the /etc/ssh/ssh_config file by the line ForwardX11 yes at the end of the file. If you are hooked on GUI administration tools, this feature lets you launch them remotely from server machines that may not even have an X server running.

The ssh command can also be used for remote execution. If you just want to execute a command and return to the local shell, without having to login to the remote system, you can do that on a single ssh command line. Here is an example:

```
# ssh myhost.linuxtoys.net date
root@myhost.linuxtoys.net's password: ******
Tue Jun 15 03:11:18 CST 2004
#
```

As you can see, after entering the password for root on myhost.linuxtoys.net, the date command ran on the remote host. The output (the current date and time) was displayed on the local shell, the connection was closed, and the local shell prompt was returned.

To debug your ssh connection, you can add the -v option to the command line. This causes a bunch of debugging messages to be output to your screen (standard error). Using this verbose output can help you debug problems you might be having in authenticating to the remote computer or getting local configuration requests to work (such as X11 forwarding).

Monitoring the LAN with Ethereal

Ethereal is a graphical utility that lets you capture and analyze network protocol data from any of the network interfaces configured on your computer. You can watch every packet that is broadcast as it is delivered live, or capture and store the data to analyze later.

You typically start ethereal without options (type ethereal or launch it from the Red Hat menu by clicking Internet ⇨ More Internet Applications ⇨ ethereal). From the Ethereal window, click Capture ⇨ Start, then select the capture options you want, which includes at least the interface you want to listen on. Click OK to start gathering data and click Stop on the Capture window to stop gathering data.

There are lots of ways to configure Ethereal to capture as much or as little data as you want. You can set capture limits to a certain number of packets, kilobytes of data, or seconds. You can wait for your capture to complete before displaying the data or update the list of packets on the screen in real time.

Figure 6-4 shows an example of the Ethereal window, with capture options in the foreground.

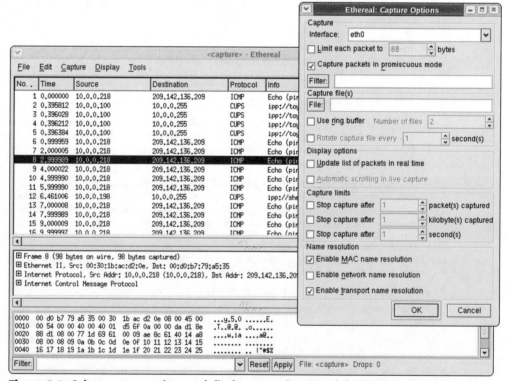

Figure 6-4: Select capture options and display network protocol data in the Ethereal window.

On networks with any significant amount of traffic at all, you will probably want to do some filtering of the packets you collect. You can filter on many different fields and save the output to a file. You can also import capture files from many different network protocol analyzers, including snoop, atmsnoop, Surveyer, LANalyzer, Sniffer, Microsoft Network Monitor, and many more.

Keeping a Session Active with Screen

If you want to be able to login to a remote computer and leave an active session going so that you can come back to it later, you can use the screen utility. Using screen, you can detach from an active login session, then login to that computer again at another time from possibly another location and have it resume exactly where you left off.

I got this tip for using screen from Charles Mauch of the Tacoma Linux Users Group. Here's what you do:

1. Login to a remote computer using ssh.

2. Open a session with screen by simply typing:

   ```
   # screen
   ```

   You should now have one screen open with a shell started and ready to do your work. Change to a directory and do something like run a long make process.

3. To open a second screen, press Ctrl+a, c (hold the Ctrl key, press a and then c). Start another ongoing activity, such as an IRC chat session.

4. To get back to the first screen, press Ctrl+a, 0 (as in the number zero). Then go back to the second screen by pressing Ctrl+a, 1.

5. Now, to detach from this screen session press Ctrl+a, d. The [detatched] message indicates that you are now detached from your screen session.

6. At this point, you can log out from the remote computer completely.

7. When you are ready to resume your screen session, login to the machine again.

8. To resume your active screen sessions, type screen-r.

9. At this point, you can again bounce between the different screens (Ctrl+a, 0 and Ctrl+a, 1) and detach and resume from the session as you please.

Screen gives you the freedom to start a long compile or stay connected to a remote session of some sort, which you might not be able to do if you knew you were going to have to disconnect before the activity is completed. As a Linux troubleshooter, you can leave a sticky debugging problem and know that you can get back right where you were (with your current directory, command-line history, and running commands) exactly where you left them.

Trying Network Troubleshooting Basics

If you are having difficulty communicating from one system to another, here are a few basic commands that most troubleshooters will use first from a Linux system:

1. Run ping. Running a ping command will tell you immediately if a remote system is up and running. The time shown on each output line of ping will indicate how long a packet takes to make a round trip.

2. Some servers block the port that ping talks to since it can be used for denial of service attacks. In those cases, you can try using the telnet command to connect directly to a

particular port that you know is accepting requests. For example, if the remote computer is a mail server, you can try using telnet to connect to the simple mail transfer protocol (SMTP) port 25. For example:

```
# telnet toys.linuxtoys.net 25
Trying 10.0.0.1...
Connected to toys.linuxtoys.net (10.0.0.1),
Escape character is ']'
220 toys.linuxtoys.net ESMTP Postfix
~.
```

In this example, we connected to the SMTP port (25) on toys.linuxtoys.net. We saw that we connected to the service from the line 220 toys.linuxtoys.net ESMTP Postfix. Once we knew the server was up, we could just disconnect by typing ~. on a line by itself.

3. If those and other network commands seem to just hang, it may be that your network connection is not active. You can try starting or restarting the network by typing:

```
#  service network restart
Shutting down interface eth0:   [ OK ]
Bringing up interface eth0:     [ OK ]
```

If your Ethernet interface (eth0) doesn't come up, check for a disconnected cable, possibly a bad Ethernet card, or a misconfigured network interface. Also, check the link lights on both ends of the link.

4. If you can get on your network, but can't get on the Internet (or other remote network), try to ping the router or machine acting as your gateway to Internet. Then try to ping an address past that gateway.

5. If you can get out on the network, but you can't reach a particular host computer, try running a traceroute.

```
# traceroute linuxtoys.net
```

This will give you an idea of where your connection is not going through.

6. If you are getting on to the network, but are not getting a response from a computer that you know is up, try watching network traffic with ethereal or tcpdump.

In most cases, running the simple set of commands will give you a sense of where your connection to the network stands.

Summary

To begin Linux troubleshooting, you should be familiar with a few basic tools. Mastering the shell and various shell tools is a must for a serious Linux troubleshooter. Choosing and tuning the shell of your choice will make your work more efficient.

Knowing basic commands for finding and sorting files, checking the state of your system, and monitoring users will make it easier to watch over your computer's resources. Learning ways to obtain and use root privilege is necessary to get to critical configuration tasks.

While there are many tools for monitoring your Linux system to prevent or react to trouble, some tools are particularly valuable. The top command lets you display and manage running processes. Features like kudzu, modprobe, modinfo, and lsmod help you configure your computer's hardware. The `strace` command can let you watch every system call a command makes to track down problems it might be having.

There are some commands that almost every Linux administrator uses to troubleshoot network connections. The `ssh` command is now the most common way to do remote login among Linux systems. Ethereal and tcpdump can let you watch and analyze network traffic. With screen, you can keep sessions active, even if you have to disconnect from them for a while. Commands like `ping`, `telnet` and `traceroute` can tell you if a remote machine is alive and track down failed network connections.

✦　　✦　　✦

X Troubleshooting: Video, Mouse, and Keyboard

A dysfunctional video card can stop new Linux users in their tracks. Getting video card, monitor, and desktop settings tuned just right can take some doing, even for an experienced system administrator. Without a working graphical user interface, a desktop system can end up stuck in command line mode.

This chapter will help you get your video card, monitor, display, mouse, and keyboard all working happily together. It also points you toward resources where you can get further help if you need it.

Beginning with X (Video, Mouse, and Keyboard)

All graphical user interface (GUI) activity in Fedora is based on the X Window System (www.x.org/X11.html)—often simply referred to as X. Likewise, most other Linux and UNIX systems are based on X. The open-source version of X that is included with all versions of Red Hat Linux and Fedora Core 1 is XFree86 (www.xfree86.org). As of Fedora Core 2, the X Window system is being taken directly from the X.org source code.

An interesting aspect of X is that the programs you use (X clients) don't have to run on the same computer as the X display (X server). This presents some very powerful possibilities, such as using low-end computers as displays while actual applications may actually be launched from more powerful computers on the network. (Some people are confused about the fact that the X server runs on the local display and the clients can run from remote displays, and pop up on the local display.)

A casual user will not even deal with any of the X configuration files directly, since the setup of those files is typically done during installation (where the video card can be automatically probed and configured) or using tools such as the Display Settings window (redhat-config-xfree86 command). If all goes well with those tools, the user can simply:

✦ *Boot to the GUI*—During Fedora Core installation, if you successfully configured X, the default run level will be set to 5. This causes the computer to boot to a graphical login screen, so that X is running for each login session.

✦ *Run startx*—If X was not configured, the computer will probably boot to run level 3. Runlevel 3 is a text-only mode. You may have to run the redhat-config-xfree86 or XFree86 commands to configure your video card and monitor. To start the GUI after running those commands, you can run the startx command.

X by itself is not very usable. Run the X command from a text log in and you get a plain gray screen with an "X" as your mouse pointer. There are no menus, windows, colors, panels or anything else you need to use a desktop. There are not even any controls to exit from X (press Ctrl+Alt+F1 to switch back to a virtual terminal and kill the X process).

You need to add a desktop environment, or at least a window manager, to be able to work with an X desktop. After X starts, by default you will see the GNOME desktop in Fedora and Red Hat Linux. GNOME provides the desktop environment: menus, panels, window borders, icons, and definitions of things such as how your keyboard and mouse behave. There are many window managers available for X, but Fedora Core lets you choose among the following:

✦ *GNOME*—The GNOME desktop environment (www.gnome.com) is installed by default with most installation types of Fedora Core. On the surface, GNOME includes components to manage windows, set preferences through a Control Center, launch applications and applets from panels, and manage sessions and files. Underneath, there are libraries for creating applications that can take advantage of GNOME desktop features.

✦ *KDE*—The KDE desktop environment (www.kde.org) provides more applications than its GNOME counterpart. In general, the KDE environment requires more RAM and CPU power than GNOME does to run effectively. However, KDE is also richer in features.

✦ *TWM*—If you want a very simple display manager, without the overhead of panels, menus and everything else that comes with a full-blown desktop environment, you can bypass a full-blown desktop environment and set the window manager to TWM. The TWM desktop manager will run when you start X, with only a simple left-click menu to start applications.

Note   Run the switchdesk command from the desktop to pop up a window that lets you select a different desktop environment or window manager. Restart X (by exiting the desktop and restarting it with the startx command) to use the new desktop.

If Fedora Core was able to detect and configure your desktop environment in such a way that you are happy with your desktop (video, mouse, and keyboard) when it starts up, then you might well be done with this chapter. However, if your desktop, mouse, or keyboard does not start up correctly or require further tuning, read on.

Configuring Video, Mouse, and Keyboard

Your video card, monitor, mouse, and keyboard may be automatically detected and configured during Fedora Core installation. If they are not, there are a few things you can do to make sure they get properly configured. The following sections describe some techniques for getting a stubborn video card working, either during Fedora Core installation or later after the system boots up in text mode.

For even more stubborn configurations, try the *Video Troubleshooting Tips* and *Tips for Particular Video Cards* sections.

Configuring Video, Keyboard, Mouse during Installation

One of the first things Fedora Core does after you launch its Anaconda installer is try to probe for your display-related hardware. After you launch the install process, you should see the following messages:

```
Probing for video card:      video card found
Probing for monitor type:    monitor found
Probing for mouse type:      mouse found
Attempting to start native X server
Waiting for X server to start...log located in /tmp/X.log
1...2...3...4...5.... X Server started successfully.
```

If the X server doesn't start, you have a few choices, depending on how it fails:

✦ If you don't even get far enough to see these messages, you may have problems other than your video card. Refer to Chapter 2 for information on troubleshooting installation.

✦ If your video card is not detected and X doesn't start, you might need to run the installation in text mode. To start installation in text mode, type the following from the first installation boot screen:

```
linux text
```

Continue through the install procedure in text mode. You will have the opportunity to configure your keyboard and mouse, but not your video card and monitor. After installation, your computer will boot Fedora Core to text mode (init 3). You can then go to the section on configuring your video card after installation.

If your video card was detected during installation, you can probably run the install in graphical mode. During that procedure you have the opportunity to configure the following features:

✦ **Keyboard**—Different languages and countries use different keyboard layouts, which can also include special characters not available in other languages. The installation process lets you choose from more than 50 different keyboard configurations.

✦ *Mouse*—You select your mouse configuration based on the way the mouse is connected to your computer. Select USB, PS/2, Bus, or Serial. With a serial mouse, you need to identify which serial port the mouse is connected to (for COM1 use /dev/ttyS0; COM2 use /dev/ttyS1; and so on).

✦ *Monitor*—A list of known monitors and their manufacturers is displayed. When possible, choose the exact model/manufacturer of the monitor you have. Otherwise, you can choose a generic CRT or LCD setting, based on the screen resolution you want to use. Or, you can select Unprobed Monitor and choose the horizontal and vertical sync rates based on documentation that comes with the monitor.

After installation is completed, if your computer boots to a graphical boot screen (after completing the first boot procedure), you can log in and see if the desktop is acceptable to you. However, even if you were able to graphically install, your video card may not have been detected properly. Continue to the next section to check the video card settings and configure it further.

Configuring Video Card after Installation

The Display Setting window is the interface that Red Hat, Inc., recommends for configuring video cards in Fedora Core. It's a good idea to run this window (either by typing `redhat-config-xfree86` or clicking on the Red Hat menu ➪ System Settings ➪ Display). Figure 7-1 shows a shot of the Display Settings window.

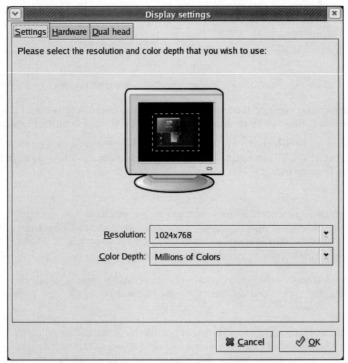

Figure 7-1: Choose basic settings for your video card and monitor.

There are three tabs on the Display Settings window: Settings, Hardware, and Dual Head. The settings you configure in this window will end up in the configuration file used when the X server starts up (`/etc/X11/XF86Config`).

Note If the Display Settings window fails to run (because it is unable to probe and identify your video hardware), go to the *Video Troubleshooting Tips* section for other ideas on how to proceed.

Changing Settings

Basic choices on the Settings tab include the screen resolution and color depth. Acceptable resolutions and color depth for your video card should be available from those boxes. You can switch among acceptable resolutions on the fly later from the Screen Resolution window (from the Red Hat menu, click Preferences ⇨ Screen Resolution).

Changing Monitor Type and Video Card

You can modify more critical settings by clicking on the Hardware tab and selecting Monitor Type or Video Card. You should be able to see the monitor model and video card settings that were configured during Fedora Core installation. If you can't find your exact models of monitor or video card, try the following:

✦ *Monitor Type*—There are Generic CRT and Generic LCD display settings you can choose if your monitor's manufacturer and/or model are not listed. It is often best to choose a generic model rather than select a monitor from the same manufacturer that seems similar.

✦ *Video Card*—If your video card is not listed, you might try VESA driver (generic) for most desktop systems. I've tried that on several systems, using an 800×600 resolution, just to get the GUI going. You can search for a better driver later if you like. Many laptop computers will use NeoMagic drivers. For further information on selecting the right driver for your video card, refer to the *Tips for Particular Video Cards* section later in this chapter.

Setting Up Dual Head

By adding another video card to your computer, you can operate your display on two monitors at the same time. With this feature, you can either have the two displays operate as two different desktops or as one virtual desktop, where your desktop area simply expands across the two screens.

From the Display Settings window, select the Dual Head tab. Then click on the Use Dual Head check box. After that, from the information that is un-grayed, configure your second video card as you would your first one, by selecting monitor, video card, resolution, and color depth. Then you can select whether the two screens act as individual desktops or spanning desktops.

Configuring the Keyboard after Installation

To reconfigure your keyboard after installation (presumably because you want to use a different keyboard arrangement for a different language), open the Keyboard window (from the Red Hat menu, click System Settings ⇨ Keyboard).

Select the keyboard type you want to use. When you click OK, the new keyboard layout immediately takes effect (the system updates the XFConfig file with a new XkbLayout value).

Configuring the Mouse after Installation

Run the redhat-config-mouse command to reconfigure your mouse (if your mouse isn't working or if you changed to a different mouse). Since you are probably not getting around on the desktop if your mouse isn't working, the redhat-config-mouse command will start in text mode if no GUI is detected. There are generic settings if you can't find the specific model of your mouse on the list.

Digging into the X Server and XF86Config File

The major components for working with X are the X server (a process that runs in the background, overseeing the GUI) and the XF86Config file. While GUI tools are nice in most cases, if the GUI isn't working at all or if it needs tuning that isn't addressed through a GUI tool; you might need to roll up your sleeves and dig into what the X server and its configuration files are doing.

Note   If you are just looking to change the look and feel of your desktop, select Preferences from the Red Hat menu. From there, you can select Background, Keyboard Shortcuts, Menus and Toolbars, Screen Resolution, Screensaver, Theme or Windows to modify how your desktop looks and behaves.

Understanding the X Server

In Fedora Core, you typically start the X server in one of the two ways: by booting the system to a graphical login screen (which starts X automatically from system runlevel 5) or booting to a text-based login screen and starting X by running the startx command. In either case, there are several major files that the X server keys off of as it's configured in Fedora Core:

✦ *XF86Config*—This is the system-wide configuration file (located in the /etc/X11 directory) that tells the X server the keyboard, mouse, video driver, and other critical information it needs to run properly. This file is used regardless of which user logs into the system from the computer's monitor.

✦ *desktop*—The /etc/sysconfig/desktop file defines the default desktop environment started by X (once X itself starts successfully). By default, the value is GNOME, to start the GNOME desktop environment, but you can change it to KDE to start that desktop environment instead (assuming KDE is installed). Here's how the contents of the desktop file looks by default:

```
DESKTOP="GNOME"
```

Users who have not specifically selected a desktop environment will get the GNOME desktop when they log in. Changing the line to DESKTOP="KDE" (as root user) changes the system-wide default to KDE.

✦ *$HOME/.Xclients-default*—Users can select their own desktop environment to override the default. To do that, they can simply type the switchdesk command with one of the following options: KDE, GNOME, or TWM. The command to switch to KDE would be as follows:

```
$ switchdesk KDE
```

The result is that the .Xclients-default file in the user's home directory will be set to execute the KDE environment (exec startkde), and the users will see the selected desktop each time they log in.

Tip   The TWM option starts the TWM window manager (/usr/X11R6/bin/twm). TWM is great if you just want a basic X environment that loads quickly. You don't get the fancy panels, icons, or workspaces. However, you do get an efficient environment if you just want to launch a simple X application and have it perform with little overhead. Once in TWM, click the left mouse button to get to the menu. If you are experienced with window managers, you can probably figure it out from there.

Besides the TWM window manager, Fedora Core also includes the Motif window manager (/usr/X11R6/bin/mwm). If you install other window manager packages, such as WindowMaker, you can launch any of them from the .Xclients-default file as well. (It doesn't work from switchdesk.)

The X server itself is actually called X (run from /usr/X11R6/bin/X). In previous versions of XFree86, there were multiple X servers available for use. Now there is just a single X server (a link to XFree86 in the same directory) that relies on having multiple modules loaded to provide the features needed by the video card. (Ways of adding modules are described in the *Module Configuration* section.)

You can add options to run with the X server itself. The X command is taken from the /etc/X11/xdm/Xservers file. The default line for the X server (/usr/X11R6/bin/X) that runs on the local system (local), on the first screen (:0) appears as follows in the Xservers file:

```
:0 local /usr/X11R6/bin/X
```

You can add X options to the end of this line to have those options take effect when X is launched. (See different troubleshooting sections later in this chapter for suggestions of options you might want to use with the X server.)

Note

To view options available for your X server, type manXFree86.

Remember that X is a network-ready display server. That means that connections to display applications on the desktop can come from the local computer or (given proper permission) another machine over the network. By default, the X server listens on TCP port 6000 for display :0 (6001 for :1; 6002 for :2, and so on).

Understanding the XF86Config File

When X is launched, it starts up using information contained in the /etc/X11/XF86Config file. In most cases, you will have a single group of settings that bring together one set of screen, mouse, and keyboard definitions. Settings can be adapted, however, to handle multiple video cards and monitors.

The XF86Config file begins with a ServerLayout section that identifies the primary screen, mouse, and keyboard used by the server. Here's an example of a ServerLayout for a single-head (one monitor) configuration created by the Display Settings window (redhat-config-xfree86 command).

```
Section "ServerLayout"
        Identifier      "single head configuration"
        Screen      0   "Screen0" 0 0
        InputDevice     "Mouse0" "CorePointer"
        InputDevice     "Keyboard0" "CoreKeyboard"
        InputDevice     "DevInputMice" "AlwaysCore"
EndSection
```

Other sections describe different aspects of the X server components. Read on to see the kind of information you can expect to find in the XF86Config file.

Caution

Be careful if you decide to edit this file manually. Always make a backup copy. Also, keep in mind that entering bad or poorly formed data into this file can possibly keep the X server from working at all and may make the file unusable by GUI tools, such as the Display Settings window.

Screen Configuration

Most PCs with a single video card and a single monitor have their screen identified as screen 0.0. If you have multiple video cards, you will have multiple screens that can each have its own set of options configured in the XF86Config file. So, in the ServerLayout section near the top of the file, you should see the following line identifying the screen:

```
Screen          0    "Screen0"   0   0
```

Later in the XF86Config file, there is a Screen section where the attributes of that screen are defined. Associated with Screen0 is the video card device (Videocard0) and the monitor (Monitor0). There can be multiple Display subsections that can set multiple screen resolutions (Modes) for different color depths (Depth). Here's how a Screen section might appear:

```
Section "Screen"
        Identifier    "Screen0"
        Device        "Videocard0"
        Monitor       "Monitor0"
        DefaultDepth    24
        Subsection "Display"
                Depth    16
                Modes      "1024x768" "800x600" "640x480"
        EndSubSection
        Subsection "Display"
                Depth    24
                Modes      "1024x768" "800x600" "640x480"
        EndSubSection
    EndSection
```

In this example, the screen will allow 16- and 24-bit color depths. For each of those depths, screen resolutions of 1024×768, 800×600, and 640×480 can be used.

Note

When you launch an X application, it is sent to the screen based on the value of the DISPLAY variable (type echo $DISPLAY to see that value). Because X lets you run applications on one computer and display them on another, screen addresses can contain host names or IP addresses to point to a display on another computer. For example, the first display on the first screen for a computer named mybox.example.com would be mybox.example.com:0.0.

Mouse Configuration

In the basic ServerLayout section, a single CorePointer must be identified to the X server. This is typically set to the first mouse definition as follows:

```
InputDevice          "Mouse0" "CorePointer"
```

Later that Mouse0 device is defined. For example, here's an InputDevice section defining the options for Mouse0:

```
Section "InputDevice"
        Identifier      "Mouse0"
        Driver          "mouse"
        Option          "Protocol" "IMPS/2"
        Option          "Device" "/dev/psaux"
        Option          "ZAxisMapping" "4 5"
EndSection
```

In this case, the Protocol used for the mouse is IMPS/2 (IntelliMouse PS/2 protocol). That protocol works with many wheel mice. The protocol could be PS/2 if there is no wheel on the mouse, usb if it is a USB mouse, or Auto, to detect a serial mouse automatically.

The mouse itself is connected to the PS/2 port for the mouse (/dev/psaux) in this example. A serial mouse could use /dev/ttyS0 (for the COM1 port). The ZAxisMapping option is used to set wheel motion for a wheel mouse. (See the "Mouse Troubleshooting Tips" section for information on setting up a left-handed mouse and a multi-wheel mouse.)

Keyboard Configuration

With Keyboard0 as the keyboard identifier, an InputDevice section may look like the following:

```
Section "InputDevice"
        Identifier      "Keyboard0"
        Driver          "keyboard"
        Option          "XkbLayout" "us"
EndSection
```

This section sets Keyboard0 to use the keyboard driver. The keyboard layout is the English, United States (us) layout, as set by the XkbLayout option. Chances are, that would be the primary option you would want to change for your keyboard if you are using Linux for a different language/keyboard layout. However, there are several other options you could put in an InputDevice section for your keyboard device. Here are a few examples:

```
Option "AutoRepeat" 500 30
Option "XkbRules" xfree86
Option "XkbModel" pc101
```

The Option values just shown represent the default values for AutoRepeat, XkbRules, and XKbModel. Autorepeat sets the first value as the delay time before a key that is held down starts repeating (500 milliseconds, as shown here) and the second value defines the number of times the key is repeated per second (30 times is the default here). For XkbRules, you could change xfree86 to xfree98 for Japanese PC-98 platforms. For many keyboards outside the United States, you could change XkbModel from pc101 to pc102. Likewise, a U.S. Microsoft Natural Keyboard can have the XkbModel set to microsoft.

To see descriptions of these and other options you can set for the keyboard driver, type man keyboard.

Monitor Configuration

The Monitor section identifies the attributes of the physical monitor (or monitors) you are using. When possible, this should identify a particular vendor's monitor, to get the best

possible chance of matching your monitor's attributes. The following example shows a
`Monitor` section that is configured for a generic 1024 × 768 display:

```
Section "Monitor"
        Identifier      "Monitor0"
        VendorName      "Monitor Vendor"
        ModelName       "Monitor 1024x768"
        HorizSync       31.5 - 57.0
        VertRefresh     50.0 - 70.0
        Option          "dpms"
EndSection
```

Key elements in this example are the `HorizSync`, which sets the horizontal sync rate to
between 31.5 and 57.0 and `VertRefresh`, which sets the vertical refresh rate to between 50.0
and 70.0. The `dpms` option turns on the Display Power Management Signaling extension. This
extension allows X screen savers to blank out screens after a selected amount of time or in
low-power situations. It also supports standby and suspend modes.

Module Configuration

When the X server starts up it always loads the bitmap font module, and then looks to the
`Module` section of the `XF86Config` file to see which other modules to load. In particular, the
`Module` section is for loading font modules and extension modules. After those modules are
loaded, specific modules from `InputDevice` and `Device` sections are loaded (such as the
mouse, keyboard, and other driver options set).

The set of modules in the `Module` section is different for different video card configurations.
Here's an example of a `Module` section:

```
Section "Module"
        Load "dbe"
        Load "extmod"
        Load "fbdevhw"      /
        Load "glx"
        Load "record"
        Load "dri"
        Load "freetype"
        Load "type1"
EndSection
```

In general, you shouldn't mess with the modules configured for you automatically when your
card is first probed and the `XF86Config` file is created. However, here is information about
some of the modules that might interest you:

✦ *dbe*—Implements double-buffering to improve rendering of animation. The result should
be flicker-free animation. Don't remove this module. Type `man DBE` to read more about it.

✦ *extmod*—Loads some miscellaneous extensions needed to make common features work
properly. Don't remove this module.

✦ *fbdevhw*—Loads the Linux framebuffer module used to let X communicate with the
framebuffer device in Linux (typically `/dev/fb0`). Type `man fbdev` or `man fbdevhw` to
read about options for this module.

✦ *glx*—Adds the GLX extension to your X server. This extension essentially connects
together the DRI 3D library and X. Running the `glxgears` command tells you if the DRI

extension is loaded on your X server, gives you information about the GLX module, and shows the frames per second at which your X server can display the gears (for the size window you are using).

```
# glxgears -info
```

✦ *record*—Adds the record extension to capture events that are associated with recording and playing back user actions in X. Do not remove this module.

✦ *dri*—Loads the Direct Rendering Interface (DRI) to provide hardware accelerated 3D graphics. See the DRI section later in this chapter for details.

As noted earlier, the bitmap module is loaded automatically when the X server starts to handle bitmap fonts (.bdf, .pcf, and .snf fonts). The preceding example shows `freetype` and `type1` modules loaded to handle fonts as well. The following list describes those and other font modules that can be loaded into X:

✦ *freetype*—Loads the module that can handle TrueType (.ttf and .ttc fonts), OpenType fonts (.otf and .otc), and Type 1 fonts (.pfa and .pbf).

✦ *type1*—An alternate backend to load .pfa and .pfb Type 1 fonts.

✦ *xtt*—An alternate backend for loading TrueType fonts (.ttf and .ttc).

✦ *speedo*—Loads the module to handle bitstream Speedo fonts (.spd).

Besides the modules mentioned here, there are a variety of other modules you can have loaded for special purposes as well. Libraries for these modules are contained in the `/usr/X11R6/lib/modules` directory.

Video Configuration

The `Device` section that identifies the driver to use with your video card is one of the most critical pieces of information in your `XF86Config` file. The `Screen` section (described in the *Screen Configuration* section earlier in the chapter) points to the device identifier (`Videocard0` or `Card0`) that is associated with your video card. Here's an example:

```
Section "Device"
        Identifier   "Videocard0"
        Driver       "savage"
        VendorName   "Videocard vendor"
        BoardName    "S3 ProSavage KM133"
EndSection
```

Every video driver also has a set of available options. See the *Tips for Particular Video Cards* section for a procedure on adding and modifying options for the selected video driver.

Setting and Tuning Your Video Driver

While it is important to know the manufacturer and model number of your video card when you set out to troubleshoot it, the key item you need to know to get the X driver working is the video chipset being used on the card. The XFree86 project organizes its support information based on these chipsets.

Note   Information on the latest XFree86 version can be found at `www.xfree86.org/current`. Follow the Driver Status link to look up information on your particular card. Fedora Core 1 includes XFree86 version 4.3.0-42. The troubleshooting issues described in this section are based on that version. If you upgrade to a later version of XFree86, some of the information in this section may not apply.

While XFree86 version 3.3.6 had several different X servers available (with the one you were using linked to `/usr/X11R6/bin/X`), in version 4.3.0 there is only one X server (linked to `XFree86`), which loads the appropriate driver modules when X starts up.

If you have gone through the basic X setup procedures at the beginning of this chapter, you should have a working GUI. (If that is not the case, go to the *Video Troubleshooting Tips* section for further direction.) The following sections step through procedures for determining which video driver to use and tuning and testing your card.

Determining Your Video Card Driver

Follow this procedure to determine which chipset is used with your video card and to look for ways of tuning that card:

1. With the X desktop running, start the Hardware Browser from the Red Hat menu by clicking System Tools ➪ Hardware Browser (or by typing `hwbrowser` from a Terminal window).

2. Click Video Cards in the left column. Information about your video card should appear on the right side of the window. Note the manufacturer and driver that are displayed for the card.

3. Open a Web browser and go to the Driver Status for XFree86 page for the current release of XFree86 (`www.xfree86.org/current/Status.html`).

4. Select the manufacturer's chipset for your card. Driver information for cards made from that chipset is displayed.

5. Look to see whether your card is shown as supported for the current release of XFree86. If it is, note which driver should be used for that chipset.

Note   Check the Fedora Core Release Notes for a list of video cards for which support was added to Fedora after the latest XFree86 release. By default, opening your Web browser in Fedora will show those Release Notes from this address in your file system: `file://user/share/doc/HTML/index.html`. In particular, the radeon driver has been updated to provide support for many new ATI video cards.

6. Check your `/etc/X11/XF86Config` file to make sure that the proper video driver is being used. It should have been autodetected and added to this file for you. For example, for my S3 ProSavage KM133 video card, the `Device` section for `Videocard0` shows `savage` as the driver.

7. Once you have determined your driver, there are a few ways you can look up the options available for that driver:

    Check the XF86Config man page—Type `man XF86Config` or go to `www.xfree86` `.org/current/XF86Config.5.html`. The `Device` Section part of the page lists options that can be used with many X video card drivers. Because most of these options should be autodetected, in most cases you will only use them to override the defaults.

Check the driver's man page—Each driver has its own specific man page that lists options specific to that driver. From the XFree86 Documentation page (www.xfree86.org/current), select Section 4 under the Manual Pages heading. Then choose your specific driver from the list. Options that are specific to that driver are listed there.

8. Check the /var/log/XFree86.0.log file (the 0 in the file name represents the first video card on your computer). This is a critical file for tuning and debugging your video card! As your X server starts up, details of what it is doing are sent to this file. By looking through this file, you can see what modules are being loaded and which options are being set.

There are hundreds of lines in this file, so I've whittled it down to a handful of lines related to the video driver for my particular video card (in this case, an S1 ProSavage8 KM266 video device):

```
(II) LoadModule: "savage"
(II) Loading /usr/X11R6/lib/modules/drivers/savage_drv.o
(II) Module savage: vendor="The XFree86 Project"
     compiled for 4.3.0, module version = 1.1.27
     Module class: XFree86 Video Driver
     ABI class: XFree86 Video Driver, version 0.6
(II) SAVAGE: driver (version 1.1.27mh) for S3 Savage
     chipsets: Savage4,
Savage3D, Savage3D-MV, Savage2000, Savage/MX-MV, Savage/MX,
Savage/IX-MV, Savage/IX, ProSavage PM133, ProSavage KM133,
Twister PN133, Twister KN133, SuperSavage/MX 128,
SuperSavage/MX 64,
SuperSavage/MX 64C, SuperSavage/IX 128, SuperSavage/IX 128,
SuperSavage/IX 64, SuperSavage/IX 64, SuperSavage/IXC 64,
SuperSavage/IXC 64, ProSavage DDR, ProSavage DDR-K
```

Because the driver is set to "savage" in the XF86Config file, the savage driver is loaded from the directory shown. Note the module version (you'll need this if you go to a mailing list to ask questions about X). Following that is a list of Savage chipsets that the driver supports:

```
(II) Primary Device is: PCI 01:00:0
(--) Chipset ProSavage found
(**) SAVAGE(0): Depth 16, (--) framebuffer bpp 16
(==) SAVAGE(0): RGB weight 565
(==) SAVAGE(0): Default visual is TrueColor
(**) SAVAGE(0): Option "HWCursor" "false"
(**) SAVAGE(0): Using SW cursor
(--) SAVAGE(0): Chip: id 8d04, "ProSavage DDR-K"
(--) SAVAGE(0): Engine: "ProSavage"
(II) SAVAGE(0): Monitor0: Using hsync range of 31.50-57.00kHz
(II) SAVAGE(0): Monitor0: Using vrefresh range 50.00-70.00Hz
(II) SAVAGE(0): Not using default mode "1152x768" (width too
     large for virtual size)(--) SAVAGE(0): Found 13 modes at
```

```
          this depth:
          [13c] 1400 X 1050, 60Hz, 75Hz
          [122] 1600 X 1200, 60Hz
(--) SAVAGE(0): Virtual size is 1024x768 (pitch 1024)
(**) SAVAGE(0): *Default mode "1024x768": 75.0 MHz, 56.5 kHz,
          70.1 Hz
(II) SAVAGE(0): Modeline "1024x768" 75.00 1024 1048 1184
          1328 768 771 777 806 -hsync -vsync
(**) SAVAGE(0): *Default mode "800x600": 40.0 MHz, 37.9 kHz,
          60.3 Hz
(==) SAVAGE(0): DPI set to (75, 75)
```

The actual chipset found on the device (PCI 01:00:0) was the ProSavage chipset. At this point, X goes about further identifying the driver (id 8d04, ProSavage DDR-K with ProSavage Engine) and setting the options used for the chipset. Some of the options set here are based on default values, while others can be explicitly set in the XF86Config file.

The next section describes how to change options to help debug or improve performance of your video card.

Tuning and Testing Your Video Card

To tune and test the basic operation of your video card, follow this procedure. It will let you change options for your driver, quickly turn the X server on and off, and then run some performance tests to see how well each of the options you use performs.

1. Close any applications that are open on your desktop.

2. As root user from a Terminal window, shut down the GUI by typing:

   # init 3

3. If the desktop is still active, from the Red Hat menu click Log Out and log out of your current session. If you see a login prompt, log in as root user. Otherwise, obtain root privilege (su -) and just continue to work at the shell.

4. Change your default desktop (if you like) to a simple X plus TWM window manager. This will make it quicker to test your changes. Type the following:

   # switchdesk TWM

5. Make a backup copy of your XF86Config file as follows:

   # cd /etc/X11
   # cp XF86Config XF86Config.bkup

6. Using your favorite character-based text editor (typically vi or emacs), open the XF86Config file.

Note   Most UNIX and Linux experts use vi or emacs as text editors. The joe editor is a bit easier to use, if you don't know vi or emacs. Type joe filename to start. Then press Ctrl+K, H to see the help screen as you work. Use the Ctrl key, followed by a letter in the Help screen to move around, change, save, and exit the file. If you get stuck, press Ctrl+C to get out.

7. Make changes to your XF86Config file, based on suggestions in the *Understanding the XF86Config File* section of this chapter.

8. Type `startx` to start up the X desktop. Hopefully, X comes up on a blank desktop with the TWM window manager running.

9. Click on the desktop and open an Xterm window (Terminal window).

10. Next, you can run some performance tests to see how the changes you made impact your basic X server performance. You can use the `x11perf` command with various options to check (and recheck) the performance of your X server in different activities. Here's an example:

```
# x11perf -repeat 3 -reps 10 -subs 10 100 -circulate
x11perf - X11 performance program, version 1.5
The XFree86 Project, Inc server version 40300000 on :0.0
from toys.example.com
Sat Jan 24 22:00:51 2004
Sync time adjustment is 0.0000 msecs.
 100 reps @ 0.0282 msec ( 35400.0/sec): Circulate window (10 kids)
 100 reps @ 0.0276 msec ( 36300.0/sec): Circulate window (10 kids)
 100 reps @ 0.0283 msec ( 35300.0/sec): Circulate window (10 kids)
 300 trep @ 0.0280 msec ( 35700.0/sec): Circulate window (10 kids)
1000 reps @ 0.0336 msec ( 29700.0/sec): Circulate window (100 kids)
1000 reps @ 0.0333 msec ( 30000.0/sec): Circulate window (100 kids)
1000 reps @ 0.0334 msec ( 29900.0/sec): Circulate window (100 kids)
3000 trep @ 0.0335 msec ( 29900.0/sec): Circulate window (100 kids)
```

The `x11perf` command in this example circulates a set of windows from the lowest to the top. Here, the `circulate` action is repeated three times, first with a group of ten windows circulated ten times (100 repetitions). Then it is repeated with a group of 100 windows, again circulated ten times (1000 times each). At the end of each group the total number of repetitions and average amount of time it took to complete the set of actions are displayed.

There are many other activities you can run to test the performance of your X server. Here are some examples:

```
# x11perf -repeat 2 -reps 1000 -ftext
# x11perf -repeat 2 -reps 500 -copywinwin500
# x11perf -repeat 2 -reps 800 -scroll500
# x11perf -repeat 2 -reps 10 -subs 10 100 -destroy
# x11perf -repeat 2 -reps 10 -subs 10 100 -resize
```

With each of these command lines, you can set how many times the action is repeated before noting the time and how many repetitions make up each action. The `subs` option can be used when you want to set how many subwindows are used in the action (when appropriate).

There are dozens of options available with `x11perf` that can be used to test the performance of your X server. Available options are listed on the x11perf man page. The options shown in the examples above are:

- Send 1000 80-character lines of text to the display (`-ftext`).

- Copy a 500 × 500-pixel square from one window to another (`-copywinwin500`).

- Vertically scroll a 500 × 500-pixel box 800 times.

- Destroy a set of windows ten times, first with 10 subwindows, and then with 100 (-destroy).

- Repeatedly resize sets of 10 windows, followed by sets of 100 windows (-resize).

Run each of those commands separately from a command line. Or, better yet, put them into a shell script and direct the output to a file. Save the output to a file.

11. Run glxgears (as described earlier in this chapter) to test the performance of 3D OpenGL too.

12. Try different options in your XF86Config file. Then repeat the previous few steps (restart the server, re-run the performance tools, and compare the results). Again, read through the troubleshooting tips sections to help you find ways of changing options on your X server.

13. When you are done, you can change your desktop environment back to GNOME or KDE. You can also return your system to runlevel 5, so you will see a graphical login. Here's how:

```
# switchdesk GNOME
# init 5
```

Refining Video Settings with xvidtune

Using the xvidtune command, you can refine some of the settings on your video display, and then save those settings to use them permanently. Here's the procedure for using xvidtune:

1. From a Terminal window on the display you want to adjust, type:

```
# xvidtune
Vendor: Monitor Vendor, Model: LCD Panel 1024x768
Num hsync: 1, Num vsync: 1
hsync range 0: 31.50 - 48.50
vsync range 0: 40.00 - 70.00
```

Information about your monitor, screen resolution, and horizontal and vertical sync ranges are displayed. Then the xvidtune window opens, as shown in Figure 7-2.

Note

A window will appear at this point, warning you that xvidtune can damage your monitor and/or video card. While this is unlikely, you should keep in mind that you use this utility at your own risk.

2. Select the Auto button, so that any resizing of the screen (up, down, right, left, wider, narrower, shorter, or taller) occurs in real time.

3. Change the display vertically by clicking Up, Down, Shorter, and Taller buttons.

4. Change the display horizontally by clicking Left, Right, Wider, and Narrower buttons.

5. Click the Show button. A line will appear that shows the line to put in your XF86Config file. Here's an example:

```
"1024x768" 65.00 1024 1048 1184 1344 768 771 777 806 -hsync -vsync
```

6. You can make the settings permanent by copying and pasting the line shown into a Modes line in your XF86Config file.

7. Click Quit to quit the window when you are done.

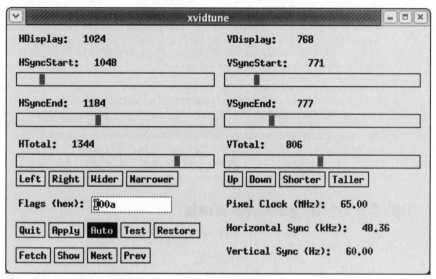

Figure 7-2: Adjust video settings with xvidtune.

Video Troubleshooting Tips

Here are some general tips (followed by sections with sets of specific tips) to help you out when you are troubleshooting your video card:

✦ *How to start troubleshooting a video card*—The primary way to troubleshoot your video card when it either isn't working at all or isn't working well is to try starting the server and see what messages it displays. These messages are stored in the /var/log/XFree86.0.log file.

✦ Another way to begin troubleshooting X is to have X only probe your display hardware and display some messages, without actually starting the server. You can do this by typing: X-probeonly

✦ *Find driver-specific options*—For each of the X video drivers supported in Fedora Core, you can check the driver's man page for specific options you can use with the driver. If you run the XFree86-configure command to create an initial XF86Config file, that command adds a large number of options to the configuration file for the video driver, with those options commented out. You can simply start uncommenting and adapting the options to try them out with your video driver.

Another place you can look for driver-specific options is in the /usr/share/hwdata /Cards file. Video cards are identified in that file by name and chipset used in the card.

✦ *Find current state of X server*—Run xdpyinfo|less to see information about the running X server. In particular, you can see the color depth, dimensions (in pixels), and dots per inch. You can also see what extensions are in use (such as DRI for hardware acceleration).

✦ *Use VESA when in doubt*—Most video hardware for the PC available today is supported under XFree86. However, not every new card will be properly detected in Linux. For most desktop systems, if you can't determine which video driver to use, most hardware that isn't supported exactly can use the VESA driver. To use the VESA driver identify "vesa" on the Driver line of the XF86Config file or select VESA from the Display Settings Window when you configure your video card.

✦ *Improve performance with a low-memory video card*—If you reduce the screen size and color depth you can dramatically improve performance. This is particularly true for video cards with less than 16MB of memory where you are trying to run 3D applications.

✦ *My video card stopped working when I upgraded XFree86*—Support for some older video hardware was lost when XFree86 went from version 3.3.6 to version 4 (currently 4.3.0 in Fedora Core 1). Find out how driver support changed between 3.3.6 and 4.3.0 on the Driver Status Page (www.xffree86.org/current/Status.html).

Tips for Getting DRI to Work

Direct Rendering Infrastructure (DRI) allows you to do 3D hardware acceleration on selected video cards. To see if DRI is enabled on your display, type the following:

```
#  glxinfo | grep direct
direct rendering: Yes
```

The Yes shows that DRI is on. If it says No instead, you should check that your video card is on the list of cards supported by DRI (visit the DRI website at dri.sourceforge.net/doc/dri_driver_features.phtml). If DRI should be supported, but appears to be disabled, make sure the following lines appear in your XF86Config file:

```
Section "DRI"
            Mode 0666
```

One limitation of DRI is that it does not run in resolutions greater than 1024 × 768. Trying to run X in a higher resolution on a card that supports DRI, then backing down (using Ctrl+Alt+F1) may cause your X server to crash. The reason is that the higher resolution will consume lots of your video RAM, and not release it when you switch to the lower resolution. When DRI goes to get the memory that it needs, the X server crashes.

If you have trouble getting or keeping the X server running with DRI enabled, try setting a low resolution for the X server (maybe 640 × 480 with 16-bit color depth). If this works, try increasing the resolution (up to 1024 × 7668) and color depth (up to 32 bits) as long as the X server continues to run. If the server doesn't run at the lower resolution, you might have to disable DRI for your card.

Tips for Particular Video Cards (Chipsets)

The following are some tips that may help you through some problems that are specific to certain video cards and chipsets. For configuration information that applies to all video cards, see the XF86Config and XFree86 man pages.

3dfx Chipsets

Even though the maker of 3dfx products, 3dfx Interactive, Inc., is out of business, there are still a lot of video cards around that use 3dfx chipsets. Although the cards are officially unsupported, many Voodoo cards that use 3dfx chips are so inexpensive that you might want to give them a try. Here are a few tips to help you with your 3dfx cards:

✦ *Identify chipset*—To physically identify a 3dfx chipset, try this site: `www.plasma-online.de/english/identify/picture/3dfx.html`.

✦ *Video driver*—Use the tdfx video driver for Voodoo Banshee, Voodoo3, Voodoo4, and Voodoo5 cards (type `man tdfx`).

✦ *Hardware acceleration*—DRI is supported on these cards to do hardware acceleration. However, you cannot use resolutions higher than 1024 × 768 at 16-bit color depth.

If you run into problems with a 3dfx card, try the `voodoofiles.com` website. They have a 3dfx forum where you can get help with your Voodoo 3, 4, 5, Banshee, or other 3dfx cards.

Intel i810 Chipsets

The i810 video chipsets are used on Intel 810 motherboards (i810, i810-dc100, i810e, and i815). For pixel depths up to 24 bits, hardware accelerated 2D drawing is supported. High-resolution video modes are supported up to 1600 × 1200.

The driver name is i810. Since XFree86 version 4.3.0, this graphics chipset has included 2D, 3D (using DRI), and XVideo support. Here are a few tips:

✦ *Video driver*—Use the i810 video driver (type `man i810`).

✦ *Hardware acceleration*—DRI is supported on these cards to do hardware acceleration. However, you cannot use resolutions higher than 1024 × 768 at 16-bit color depth for i810 and i815 chipsets. Later chipsets allow depths up to 24 bits.

✦ *Increasing video RAM*—The i810 graphics chipsets use a unified memory architecture in which they can use system RAM for video memory. By default, 8MB of system RAM is assigned for graphics. You can increase this number using the VideoRam option in the `Device` section of `XF86Config` file for the i810 driver. Here's an example of what that line might look like to use 16MB of RAM for graphics:

```
Section "Device"
        Identifier "Intel 810"
        Driver "i810
        VideoRam 16384
        VendorName "Intel 810"
EndSection
```

NVIDIA Chipsets

Although a driver for NVIDIA cards is included with XFree86 (the nv driver), it only supports 2D acceleration. That includes support for PCI and AGP video cards that include the following chips: RIVA 128, RIVA TNT, RIVA TNT2, GeForce 256-Quadro, GeForce2-Quadro2, GeForce3-Quadro DCC, nForce-nForce2, GeForce4-Quadro4, and GeForce FX-Quadro FX.

To get 3D acceleration on NVIDIA boards, you need to install NVIDIA's own proprietary binary X drivers. Go to the NVIDIA website (`www.nvidia.com`) and click on the Download Drivers link. From there, follow the link to Linux Drivers to download and install the NVIDIA driver.

Note   It is possible that the redhat-config-xfree86 window will not recognize the proprietary NVIDIA driver. You may need to run `XFree86-configure` to create your `XF86Config` file.

ATI Chipsets

The ATI Rage 128-based video cards use the r128 driver, while the ATI Radeon-based video cards use the radeon driver. Although your X server should autodetect this information, you can specify the following values in the `Devices` section for the driver:

✦ *VideoRam*—Specify in kilobytes how much RAM is available on the card.

✦ *ChipID*—Identify the PCI device ID (run the `lspci` command to get this ID).

✦ *IOBase*—Identify the physical address of the MMIO register.

✦ *MemBase*—Identify the physical address of the linear framebuffer.

Many options are available to use with the r128 and radeon drivers. Type `man r128` or `man radeon` to view available options for the drivers.

Tips to Fix Video Crashes

✦ *Broken XF86Config file*—It is possible that you, or some tool you used, may have trashed your `/etc/X11/XF86Config` file. If you are unable to fix the file manually so X can start, you can delete `XF86Config` (actually, make a copy first, and then delete it). Run `redhat-config-xfree86` again to get, hopefully, a sane `XF86Config` file to start with. If that doesn't work, try typing this:

```
# XFree86 -configure
# XFree86 -xf86config /root/XF86Config.new
```

If the X server starts properly using the `XF86Config.new` file you just created, you can copy the file to its permanent location and restart X when you are ready.

```
# cp /root/XF86Config.new /etc/X11/XF86Config
```

✦ *There's nothing I can do to get this card to work!*—If the card is not listed as supported, and you can't get it to go, consider buying a new card. There are good, brand-new video cards starting at about $30 that will work well, and some screaming great ones starting at around $100. Xfree86.org recommends S3-based boards and ATI-based boards. I have had good luck with NVIDIA cards, but you need their proprietary drivers to get them to work well.

The Driver Status for XFree86 page (`www.xfree86.org/current/Status.html`) is a good place to start. Beware, however, that even some boards that are listed as supported may become unsupported if the manufacturer decides to change the chipset on the board without changing its name or model number.

Mouse Troubleshooting Tips

The X server in Fedora Core supports several different mouse types, depending on how the mouse is connected to the computer: serial, PS/2, bus, and USB mouse types. Two-button, three-button and wheel mouse types are supported. Selecting the appropriate mouse type/connection using the Mouse Configuration window usually does a good job configuring the mouse.

Here are some cases where you might want to go beyond what you can do through the Mouse Configuration (`redhat-config-mouse`) window:

✦ *Accessibility*—There are accessibility features that let you adjust how your mouse works. To see the accessibility options available for your mouse, from the Red Hat menu click Preferences ⇨ Accessibility. Then click on the Enable Keyboard Accessibility Features box and choose the Mouse Keys tab. From there, you can adjust maximum pointer speed, the time to accelerate to maximum speed, and the delay between keypress and pointer movement.

✦ *Remapping mouse buttons*—You can remap any of the mouse buttons or wheels using the `xmodmap` command. For example, the following command switches a mouse from a right-handed to a left-handed mouse:

```
# xmodmap -e "pointer = 3 2 1 4 5"
```

This command switches the functions of the first and third buttons on a three-button mouse. The 4 and 5 positions define how scrolling is done on a wheel mouse. You can switch the directions that the wheels scroll by switching the numbers 4 and 5. You can also map the actions of multiple wheels on pointing devices that have more than one wheel. (See the `xmodmap` man page for details.)

Video Troubleshooting Reference

Table 7-1 provides a reference for finding and troubleshooting the X Window System video to work in Linux.

Table 7-1: Video Troubleshooting References

General X Information	
XFree86 project	`www.xfree86.org`—The XFree86 Project is the primary source for information on the open-source version of the X Window System running in Fedora Core
XFree86 documentation	`www.xfree86.org/4.3.0`
XFree86 support	`www.xfree86.org/support.html`
XFree86 mailing lists	`www.xfree86.org/lists.html`
XFree86 driver information	Various README files in the `/usr/X11R6/lib/X11/doc` directory of Fedora Core

Continued

Table 7-1: *(continued)*

General X Information	
/usr/X11R6bin/XF86Config	Primary configuration file for the X (XFree86) server
Current mouse driver information	`www.xfree86.org/current/mouse.html`
Mouse driver man page (serial mouse)	Type `man mouse`

X Performance Commands	
glxinfo	Displays information about OpenGL rendering in the X server. Use this to check if DRI has been enabled to do hardware acceleration
glxgears	Displays three spinning gears and shows how many frames per second your X server can display the gears spinning
xvidtune	Tunes the height and width of your display, and then saves those settings to your `XF96Config` file
x11perf	Runs performance tests (based on parameters you choose), and then reports how quickly the X server can complete those tests

Summary

Most modern video cards that come with personal computers today will work with the X window system (XFree86) that comes with Fedora Core. In those cases where Fedora can't properly probe and configure a video card automatically, you can use the tips in this chapter to track down and fix your video card.

This chapter described ways of configuring, troubleshooting, and tuning performance for video cards in Fedora. It also provided pointers to many other resources that are available to help you if you run into trouble with your video card.

Software Package Troubleshooting

RPM Package Management (RPM) provides the framework in which software is installed, updated, and uninstalled in Fedora Core and Red Hat Enterprise Linux systems. Many other Linux distributions are based on the RPM system, including SUSE, Mandrake, and others. RPM command line and GUI tools can provide the means to query, verify, and otherwise manage the software on your computer.

This chapter describes the basic tools you need to manage software packages in RPM format in Fedora and other Red Hat Linux systems. It also helps you verify and query RPM packages before you install them and troubleshoot problems you may encounter, such as resolving package dependencies and fixing broken RPM databases.

Introduction to RPM

For those who need to set up and maintain Linux systems, software management is a critical issue. You need to strike a balance between having the most up-to-date versions of the software you want and the stability that you need for the systems you maintain. You also need to make sure that your software is both compatible (doesn't break other software) and secure (hasn't been compromised).

By using RPM tools that come with all Red Hat software distributions, you can learn skills for managing and securing your software packages. The primary tools for managing RPM packages in Fedora Core and Red Hat Enterprise Linux include the following:

✦ rpm *command*—This offers options for querying, verifying, installing, upgrading, and removing packages. There are also various options for working with the RPM database.

✦ *Package Management window*—The Package Management window provides a graphical means of viewing, adding, and removing packages that are part of the Linux distribution. Packages are grouped together and dependencies are taken into account when you try to add or delete packages. To get to the Package Management window, from the Red Hat menu, click System Settings ⇨ Add/Remove Applications.

As a bonus, the skills you'll learn while working with these tools will apply to many different RPM-based Linux distributions.

In this chapter, I focus primarily on using the `rpm` command to manage and query the software packages on your Linux systems. Because rpm is such a useful tool, its uses are also described in a few other places in this book:

✦ *Installing, updating, and upgrading*—Chapters 1 and 2 cover the basics of installing Linux, then doing subsequent software updates and upgrades. Whether these packages are grabbed from an installation CD or from yum or apt software repositories, for the most part you should end up with all or most of your software installed from RPM packages. Some useful rpm examples are included in these chapters.

✦ *Detecting intrusions*—Chapter 10 describes how to use RPM to see if someone has tampered with the software on your Linux system, based on the contents of your RPM database.

Assuming that you have already installed your basic Linux operating system, this chapter will give you examples of lots of different ways you can manipulate those packages and the RPM database that stores information about them.

Installing, Upgrading, and Deleting Packages

The basic ways of using the `rpm` command to install, upgrade, and delete packages are covered in many introductory books on Fedora and Red Hat Linux (such as the *Red Hat Linux Bible*). By way of review, and for troubleshooters who are new to Linux, here are a few basic ways to use the `rpm` command.

Note   If the package you want is in a yum or apt repository, I recommend you use the appropriate yum or apt tools to install the package. See Chapter 3 for descriptions of yum and apt.

The most common way to install a new package or upgrade an existing package is by using the `-U` option of `rpm`. With the file you want to install in the current directory, type the following:

```
# rpm -Uhv packagename-1.1.1.i386.rpm
```

If the package (represented by *packagename-1.1.1.i386.rpm*) is not yet installed, this command will install it. If it is a later version of an already installed package, the command will also install it (actually, upgrade it). The `-h` option prints hash marks (for positive feedback as the package installs) and `-v` gives verbose output (add multiple v's to see even more verbose output, such as `-Uhvvv`).

Note   Instead of `-U` you can use the `-i` option to install a package. If it is a package that is not yet installed on your computer, it should install just fine. If the package (or an earlier version) is already installed, the install will fail and you will have to use `-U` to install it. For installing kernel packages, always use the `-i` option.

A great option when you are upgrading a whole lot of packages on an existing system is the freshen (`-f`) option. Let's say that you download a directory of packages with security updates, but you only want to install new versions of packages that are already installed. With that directory as the current directory, you could type the following:

```
# rpm -Fvh *.rpm
```

Packages that are already installed on your computer, but for which there are later versions in the current directory are installed. All other packages in the directory are not installed. (Keep in mind that packages not installed are skipped silently.)

To delete an installed package, use the -e (erase) option to rpm. For example,

```
# rpm -e Wnn6-SDK-devel
```

Again, the deletion of the package is done silently. So if you want positive feedback, add one or more -v options (for example, rpm -evvv).

There are a lot of options to the rpm command that you can use during basic package installs, upgrades, freshens, and deletions. Again, I'd recommend the *Red Hat Linux Bible* or the rpm man page for details about rpm options. Here are a few options you can use with basic install, upgrade, freshen, and delete options:

✦ *Saving space*—You can save some space by excluding certain files from being installed from a package. In particular, --excludedocs excludes any files marked as documentation from being installed and --excludepath *PATH* excludes any files in the specified path from being installed.

✦ *Verbose*—Add a single -v option to make the output more verbose. Add multiple -v options (-vv, -vvv, and so on) to see lots of debugging output.

✦ *Install it anyway*—There are several reasons that a package installation may fail, almost all of which can be overridden. On a production machine, you should probably fix the problem before continuing (as in, fix the dependency).

✦ However, on a noncritical computer where you just want to check out a package, you can skip dependency checking (--nodeps), not verify any digests (-nodigests), and not verify signatures (--nosignature). You can even skip checking for sufficient disk space (--ignoresize) and install despite having binaries intended for a different computer architecture (--ignorearch).

Caution Dependency, digest, signature, and architecture checks are all put in to make sure that you are installing software that is safe and correct for your environment. Overriding these safeguards can be dangerous. Do so at your own risk.

✦ *Watch progress*—There are several options for watching the progress of a package installation. You can print 50 hash marks (#) as rpm unpacks a package archive using the -h option. Likewise, you can tell rpm to print the percentage at which the file was unpacked with the -percent option.

✦ *Test it*—Before you go ahead and do a real install or uninstall of a package, you can test it using the --test option. I recommend you add one or more -v options to get as much information as possible before running the install or uninstall for real.

Now that you have had a quick review of the basics, the rest of this chapter is devoted to learning how to prevent and track down problems with software packages.

Checking Software Packages

Before you install RPM packages, you may want to run some checks to answer a few questions about those packages. For security purposes, you can make sure that the package was properly signed. You can also find out what dependencies the package has and information about what the package contains. The following sections explore these topics.

Checking Software Package Signatures

Whether you do it to a pile of RPM packages on your hard disk or to packages downloaded from an apt or yum repository, checking the signature of the packages you plan to install on your Linux system is a good idea. Using the `rpm` command, you can import public keys that are then used to verify the contents of your RPM packages.

The Fedora Core distribution comes with several GNU Privacy Guard (GPG) keys that it uses to verify the packages you install that come directly from the Fedora project. Many software repositories that let you download RPM packages outside of any official Red Hat or Fedora distribution will have their own GPG keys, which you can use to verify that their packages have not been tampered with.

 Cross-Reference For more information on the GNU Privacy Guard project, visit the project's home page at `www.gnupg.org`.

Checking Fedora/Red Hat Public Keys

If you install Fedora Core from the three install CDs, you can find the PGP public key signatures from Red Hat, Inc., in the top-level directory of each CD. After the install, the keys are stored in the `/usr/share/doc/fedora-release-1` directory (for Fedora Core systems) or the `/usr/share/doc/redhat-release-*` (for Red Hat Linux systems). Files containing the two keys that are installed and used automatically on Fedora Core systems include the following:

✦ RPM-GPG-KEY—This file contains the PGP public key used by Red Hat, Inc., to build its own software packages.

✦ RPM-GPG-KEY-fedora—This file contains the PGP public key used to sign packages that are specific to the Fedora Project.

The two keys stored in these files are installed in the RPM database during Fedora Core installation so they can be used to check that the packages have been properly signed.

Viewing Installed GPG Keys

GPG keys are stored in your RPM database and can be manipulated using some of the same options you would use to work with regular RPM packages. To see the keys installed in your computer, type the following:

```
# rpm -qa gpg-pubkey*
gpg-pubkey-4f2a6fd2-3f9d9d3b
gpg-pubkey-db42a60e-37ea5438
```

The `gpg-pubkey-db42a60e-37ea5438` represents the Red Hat, Inc., public key used to sign its packages. The `gpg-pubkey-4f2a6fd2-3f9d9d3b` represents the Fedora Core public key. To get information about any public key, you can use the `rpm` command as you would from any RPM package. For example, to see who owns the first public key type

```
# rpm -qi gpg-pubkey-4f2a6fd2-3f9d9d3b | less
Name        : gpg-pubkey         Relocations: (not relocateable)
Version     : 4f2a6fd2              Vendor: (none)
Release     : 3f9d9d3b          Build Date: Thu 05 Feb 2004 09:44:00 PM PST
Install Date: Thu 05 Feb 2004 09:44:00 PM PST Build Host: localhost
Group       : Public Keys        Source RPM: (none)
```

```
Size         : 0                    License: pubkey
Signature    : (none)
Summary      : gpg(Fedora Project <fedora@redhat.com>)
Description :
-----BEGIN PGP PUBLIC KEY BLOCK-----
Version: rpm-4.2.1 (beecrypt-3.0.0)

mQGiBD+dnTsRBACwnlz4AhctOLlVBAsq+RaU82nb5P3bD1YJJpsAce1Ckd2sBUOJD11NUCqH
.
.
.
-----END PGP PUBLIC KEY BLOCK-----
```

From this output, you can see how the key's name is divided into version and release numbers. In the Summary line, the key is identified as gpg for the Fedora Project. I pipe the output through less here (|less) so that you can page through the text. Press the space bar to page through and type **q** to quit at the end. I pipe output to less in several examples throughout the chapter.

Importing GPG Keys

If, for some reason, either of the keys (Fedora or Red Hat) is not installed, you can import each to your RPM database as follows:

```
# cd /usr/share/doc/fedora-release-*
# rpm --import RPM-GPG-KEY-fedora
# rpm --import RPM-GPG-KEY
```

When you install new or updated RPM packages from Fedora Project or Red Hat, Inc., the keys are automatically checked and you are notified if they don't match any package you try to install. If you ever want to remove a GPG key, you can do so using the -e option of rpm. This is the same command you would use to remove any regular RPM package as well. For example, the following would remove the Fedora public key:

```
# rpm -e gpg-pubkey-4f2a6fd2-3f9d9d3b
```

Checking Third-Party Public Keys

By adding packages to your Fedora or Red Hat Enterprise Linux systems that are not released as part of those distributions, you are assuming more risk for the quality and security of those packages. Getting and using GPG keys to check the signatures on packages you get from third-party software repositories can verify that they haven't been altered since they were created and help insure that the packages come from an identifiable place.

As described in Chapter 3, tools such as yum and apt can be used to download and install RPM packages from the Internet. Getting GPG keys from a download site before you use the software it offers is one way to help check that the software hasn't been compromised. The following procedure describes how to get and import GPG keys to check software you get from the freshrpms.net software repository (a well-known software repository for Fedora and Red Hat Linux software):

1. Get the freshrpms.net public key by typing the following (if the key file has moved, you might need to go to freshrpms.net and poke around for it):

```
#wget http://freshrpms.net/packages/RPM-GPG-KEY.txt
```

2. With the `RPM-GPG-KEY.txt` file in your current directory, type the following to import the `freshrpms.net` public key into your RPM database:

```
#rpm --import RPM-GPG-KEY.txt
```

3. Check information for the public key you imported (the next command reflects the public key name currently being used with freshrpms packages).

```
#rpm -qi gpg-pubkey-e42d547b |less
```

The output should list Matthias Saou in the `Summary`.

At this point, you should be able to download packages from the `freshrpms.net` site (either from your web browser or using a download/install tool such as yum) without getting complaints about not having a key to validate them. You can repeat this procedure for any software repository you want to use.

Troubleshooting Software Package Signatures

To check a package before you install it, you can use the `checksig` option to `rpm`. Because an RPM package can contain multiple digests and signatures, the `checksig` option will check each digest and signature to make sure it is correct.

For example, let's say that you copied the `fedora-logos` RPM package into the current directory. You could check the signature on that package as follows:

```
# rpm --checksig fedora-logos-1.1.20-noarch.rpm
fedora-logos-1.1.20-noarch.rpm: (sha1) dsa sha1 md5 gpg OK
```

This output shows that the package uses the Secure Hash Algorithm, version 1 (sha1) header digest, which acts as a fingerprint of the contents of the RPM. It uses a DSA header signature and includes md5 digest and GPG signature. You can tell that this package is all right (was properly created with the given key) by noting the following:

✦ Each digest and signature is shown in lower case.

✦ There is the word OK at the end (as opposed to NOT OK).

If you want to see more information about the signature checking, you can add a `-v` or `-vv` option. Here is an example:

```
# rpm --checksig -vv fedora-logos-1.1.20-1.noarch.rpm
D: Expected size:      263841 = lead(96)+sigs(344)+pad(0)+data(263401)
D:   Actual size:      263841
D: opening db environment /var/lib/rpm/Packages joinenv
D: read h#   1624 Header sanity check: OK
D: ========== DSA pubkey id b44269d04f2a6fd2
fedora-logos-1.1.20-1.noarch.rpm:
    Header V3 DSA signature: OK, key ID 4f2a6fd2
    Header SHA1 digest: OK (b712be20fa0b6d3bf89f6a3d0c91f86efce24f0e)
    MD5 digest: OK (94d9d20ce0265cb1f36d5fb8fa0dfc30)
    V3 DSA signature: OK, key ID 4f2a6fd2
```

The output shows that the number of characters expected in the file (263,841) was actually found. You can see that the command connected to the RPM database environment (`/var/lib/rpm/Packages joinenv`). The header passed a sanity check (`OK`), and the DSA public key with id number b44269d04f2a6fd2 was found. After this each signature and digest was checked (DSA signature, SHA1 digest, MD5 digest, and DSA signature) and found to be correct (OK).

If the package checks out, and you trust the keys you are using, you can probably go ahead and safely install the package.

The following examples illustrate some cases where the package did not check out:

✦ *Missing key*—If for some reason, the public key associated with the signed package was not installed in your database, you might see the following error message:

```
fedora-logos-1.1.20-1.noarch.rpm: (SHA1) DSA sha1 md5
    (GPG) NOT OK (MISSING KEYS: GPG#4f2a6fd2)
```

In this case, the key 4f2a6fd2 (for Fedora Project packages) is missing. Note that a missing key causes the SHA1, DSA, and GPG notations to display in upper case (indicating a failure). However, the fact that sh1 and md5 are in lower case indicates that the package itself is not corrupted, because the SH1 and MD5 digests were consistent with the contents of the package. Chances are if you install the proper key, the package will pass the check.

✦ *Corrupted RPM*—If the contents of an RPM file have been badly corrupted, all digest and signature indications might appear in upper case or the package might not even be recognized as an RPM file. The following messages reflect these two results:

```
fedora-logos-1.1.20-1.noarch.rpm:(SHA1) DSA SHA1 MD5 GPG NOT OK
error: fedora-logos-1.1.20-1.noarch.rpm: not an rpm package
```

You won't be able to install this package even if you wanted to. Get a new copy of the package.

✦ *Modified RPM content*—It is possible that the content of an RPM file has been changed, but the headers appear to be valid. In that case, even though the dsa and sh1 appear to be all right, the MD5 and GPG will appear as BAD. Here's what verbose output looks like (rpm --checksig -vv) in that case:

```
fedora-logos-1.1.20-1.noarch.rpm:
    Header V3 DSA signature: OK, key ID 4f2a6fd2
    Header SHA1 digest: OK (b712be20fa0b6d3bf89f6a3d0c91f86efce24f0e)
    MD5 digest: BAD Expected(94d9d20ce0265cb1f36d5fb8fa0dfc30) !=
(835891bb30ca96d73dc4bce78ddb36d7)
V3 DSA signature: BAD, key ID 4f2a6fd2
```

In this case, you should not use the RPM since it was probably tampered with.

Checking Software Package Dependencies

Most RPM packages include built-in information about other components (such as libraries) that they require to work. If you try to install or upgrade a package, and components the package depends on are not already installed, package installation fails (by default). Likewise, if you try to remove a package on which other installed packages depend, it will also fail.

If you install a package from Fedora or Red Hat Linux installation CDs (or if you are installing from a well-maintained yum or apt repository), dependency checks are done automatically when you try to add or remove packages. When you install using yum or apt programs, they ask you if you want to install any dependent package(s) as well. If you say yes, yum or apt will go ahead and install the dependent package(s). Problem solved.

Note   Installing RPMs from a software repository using yum or apt is always preferred over installing individual packages from an FTP or HTTP server. Yum and apt can insure dependencies are met in a way that can't be done by downloading packages individually.

This is a troubleshooting book; however, you might be interested in dealing with those times when there is not a package already installed to fulfill the requirements. In that case you can do the following:

✦ *Skip dependencies*—The rpm command allows you to skip dependency checking using the --nodeps option. While this will get the package installed, it will most likely leave you with a package that doesn't work.

✦ *Look for the needed RPM package*—You might need to do some digging around to find the package that contains the components you need. Then you can install the package that contains the required component so the package you want can be installed.

To find out what dependencies are not being met, you can just try to install or upgrade the package you want. The missing dependent components will be listed by default and the install will fail. Alternatively, you can ask to explicitly list the dependencies of the package. Once you know what is missing, you can do the following:

• Search installed RPM packages for the component.

• Search the full database of RPM packages that are on the full CD set representing Fedora Core, Red Hat Linux 9, or other operating system. (See the *Using the RPM Universal Database* sidebar for more information.)

• Check the FTP or HTTP directory where you got the initial package, search the rpmfind.net site for the package you need, or just search the Internet.

Using the RPM Universal Database

Each Red Hat Linux distribution (Fedora, Red Hat Linux 9, and Red Hat Enterprise Linux) includes a package containing a database of information that describes all the RPMs in that distribution. In Red Hat Linux install the rpmdb-redhat package; in Fedora install rpmdb-fedora package.

The entire database of RPM information is in the /usr/lib/rpmdb/i386-redhat-linux/ redhat directory. You can query that database for dependencies using the rpm --redhat provides and rpm --redhatrequires command. When searching for how to resolve dependencies for a package you want to install, this "universal" database is a good place to look.

The following procedure takes you through the process of checking a package for dependencies, finding the package needed to fulfill the dependencies, and then getting and installing that package.

1. Get an RPM package you want to install. For this example, I downloaded the xmame-0.78.1-2.fr.i386 package for Fedora Core 1:

ftp.freshrpms.net/pub/freshrpms/ayo/fedora/linux/1/i386/RPMS.freshrpms/

2. Run a test install on the package to see the dependency checking (among other things):

```
# rpm --test -Uhvv xmame-0.78.1-2.fr.i386
D: ============== xmame-0.78.1-2.fr.i386.rpm
D: Requires: /bin/sh                               YES (db files)
D: Requires: /usr/bin/tclsh                        YES (db files)
D: Requires: libc.so.6                             YES (db provides)
D: Requires: libc.so.6(GLIBC_2.0)                  YES (db provides)
D: Requires: libc.so.6(GLIBC_2.1)                  YES (db provides)
D: Requires: libc.so.6(GLIBC_2.3)                  YES (db provides)
D: Requires: libz.so.1                             YES (db provides)
D: Requires: rpmlib(CompressedFileNames) <= 3.0.4-1 YES (rpmlib provides)
D: Requires: rpmlib(PayloadFilesHavePrefix) <= 4.0-1 YES (rpmlib provides)
D: Requires: xmame-bin = 0.78.1                    NO
D: package xmame-0.78.1-2.fr has unsatisfied Requires: xmame-bin = 0.78.1
error: Failed dependencies:
        xmame-bin = 0.78.1 is needed by xmame-0.78.1-2.fr
```

As you can see from the output (which I edited down to include just required items), most of the required components needed by the xmame package are already provided by the packages that are already installed. The sh and tclsh files are there, as are several libc libraries and rpmlib features. What is missing is xmame-bin.

3. You can see if any installed package has the component you need using the query option –whatprovides. (Of course, we already know the component is not in an installed package, since the dependency failed. But we'll just go through the motions anyway.)

```
#rpm -q --whatprovides xmame-bin
no package provides xmame-bin
```

4. Next, you can search the universal RPM database, which contains all the RPM packages in the entire Fedora Core or Red Hat Enterprise Linux CD set. This will tell us if the component is in any package from your CD set, whether or not the package is installed.

```
#rpm --redhatprovides xmame-bin
no package provides xmame-bin
```

5. Next, I suggest opening the FTP site where you got the package in an FTP client and seeing if the package needed is there. In my case, I went to the freshrpms.net directory that contained the xmamb package and downloaded the xmame-x11 package to the current directory. I then checked to see what the package provided:

```
#rpm -q --provides -p xmame-x11-078.1-2.fr.i386.rpm
xmame-bin = 0.78.1
xmame-SDL = 0.78.1-2.fr
```

This package seems to provide the xmame-bin component we need. So we can go ahead and try installing it. If this installs without a problem, we can install our original xmame package. Although in this case it worked, if you could not find a package to meet the dependency in the FTP directory of the original package, continue with the rest of this procedure.

Note   Instead of using the name of the package in the current directory to check for the needed component, you could have provided the full URL to the package in the FTP or HTTP directory. It makes you type a long URL, but adds an extra download step.

6. If the package is still not found, try searching the `rpmfind.net` site. Go to `www.rpmfind.net` and search for the needed component. All RPM files that are found that include your search term are displayed. Click on one that is listed for Red Hat Linux 9 or other appropriate distribution.

7. If you still have not found the component, as a last resort go to `www.google.com` or other search engine and simply search the Internet for the component.

There may be some cases where you can't match the dependency exactly. For example, the package you want to install may be looking for an exact version of the component and you might only have access to a later version. The later version may well work. In that case, you might want to try the `--nodeps` option to force the package to install. Here are some of the types of dependent components you may run into:

✦ *Package*—An exact package may be required. In that case, the dependency may specify only the package name or package name and version number. The requirement may also be that the package be less than, greater than, or equal to a certain version.

✦ *Component*—A particular library or binary file may be required. Where that component comes from may not matter, as long as it is provided by some RPM package. In this example, an exact version of xmame-bin was required (xmame-bin = 0.78.1). This represents an `xmame` binary that can be available from several different RPM files. As long as one is installed, the dependency check will pass.

Cross-Checking Software Package Contents

After your software packages are installed, the RPM database remains an excellent resource for cross-checking original information about a package against the actual installed components on your hard disk. In other words, you can tell if someone has been fooling around with your software.

Chapter 10 is a more complete reference to techniques for verifying if any of your software has been tampered with, including ways of using the `rpm` command to verify that someone hasn't planted a trojan horse in an executable. A simple way of checking a whole RPM package for files that have been tampered with is the `rpm -V` command. For example, to check the entire samba package, you could type

```
# rpm -V samba
```

Any files in the samba package that have been changed since they were installed will appear after the command. The next procedure can be used for checking whether a single file has been tampered with.

1. For the file or command you want to check, find out what package it is from. In this example, I'm checking the startup script for the Samba service:

```
#rpm -qf /etc/rc.d/init.d/smb
samba-3.0.0-15
```

2. List the files (`-ql`) contained in the samba software package (from the RPM database of installed software) and dump (`--dump`) data out about each file. Then sort out (`grep`) everything except the smb script.

```
#rpm -ql --dump samba | grep /etc/rc.d/init.d/smb
/etc/rc.d/init.d/smb 1928 1064589271
99d3f786f9dc199fe0221cce496c5795 0100755 root root 1 0 0 X
```

Interesting information associated with the dump includes the following:

- The original number of characters in the file (1928).

- The md5sum digest that reflects the contents of the smb file (99d3f786f9dc199fe0221cce496c5795).

- Permission associated with the file (0755).

- Ownership of the file (root **owner and** root **group**).

3. Next, check the actual file to see if the contents have been changed. Type the following:

```
#ls -l /etc/rc.d/init.d/smb
-rwxr-xr-x 1 root root 1928 Sep 26 08:14 /etc/rc.d/init.d/smb
#md5sum /etc/rc.d/init.d/smb
99d3f786f9dc199fe0221cce496c5795 /etc/rc.d/init.d/smb
```

The long list of the file (ls -l) shows that there are 1928 characters in the file, the owner and group are both root, and file permissions are 0775 (-rwxr-xr-x). All of that matches the dump output shown earlier. Likewise, the md5sum output (99d3f... c5795) also matches the dump output for the file.

In this case, information about the installed smb script seemed to match the information about the original script stored in the RPM database. If you believe that the RPM database might have been tampered with as well, you could check against the actual samba RPM file from the CD or other trusted source. For example, with the samba RPM in the current directory, I could type

```
# rpm -ql --dump -p samba-3.0.0-15.i386.rpm | grep /etc/rc.d/init.d/smb
```

Hopefully, you would get the same results as you got from the similar command line you ran against the RPM database.

Cross-Reference For more information on using the rpm command to verify the contents of a command, library or configuration file, refer to Chapter 10.

Checking Software Package Scripts

Many RPM packages include scripts that run when the package is installed or uninstalled. In particular, when you are upgrading from one version of a package to another and something messes up, you might want to see what those scripts did to your system.

The rpm command has a means of listing the contents of

✦ scripts in an RPM package that run during the install or uninstall process and

✦ trigger scripts that are kicked off when certain conditions are met.

The following sections describe how to list scripts and trigger scripts in an RPM file.

Check for Scripts

Use the --scripts query option to the rpm command to see scripts that are run before and after installs and uninstalls of a package are done. Here is an example:

```
# rpm -q --scripts samba
postinstall scriptlet (using /bin/sh):
```

```
/sbin/chkconfig --add smb
preuninstall scriptlet (using /bin/sh):
if [ $1 = 0 ] ; then
    /sbin/chkconfig --del smb
    rm -rf /var/log/samba/* /var/cache/samba/*
    /sbin/service smb stop >/dev/null 2>&1
fi
exit 0
postuninstall scriptlet (using /bin/sh):
if [ "$1" -ge "1" ]; then
    /etc/rc.d/init.d/smb condrestart >/dev/null 2>&1
fi
```

This example shows the scripts that are included in the samba package. After the samba package is installed (postinstall), the chkconfig command is called to turn on the samba service (--add smb). Before the package is uninstalled (preuninstall), the samba service is removed from starting again (chkconfig --del smb) and all log files (/var/log/samba/*) and cache files (/var/cache/samba/*) are removed.

After the package is uninstalled (postuninstall), if the package still exists on the system, the service is restarted. (This is done in cases where you are removing an old version of the package and the new version has been installed and needs to be restarted.)

Scripts that have some level of complexity include those for packages that use the alternatives system and therefore may or may not be activated by default (including sendmail, postfix, and cups). Special scripts that are only used in particular conditions are referred to as trigger scripts.

Check for Trigger Scripts

Some packages have trigger scripts that are kicked off during installation if certain conditions are met. These are particularly useful in upgrades where the software packager wants different installation actions to take place, depending on the current package release you are upgrading from. Here's an example of how to display the trigger scripts included in the sendmail package:

```
# rpm -q --triggers sendmail
triggerpostun scriptlet (using /bin/sh) -- sendmail<8.10.0
/sbin/chkconfig --add sendmail
triggerpostun scriptlet (using /bin/sh) -- sendmail<8.11.6-11
/usr/sbin/alternatives --auto mta
```

Here you can see that upgrades from pre-8.10.0 versions of sendmail add the sendmail services to be turned on when the computer boots (chkconfig --add sendmail). Pre-8.11.6-11 sendmail versions have the alternatives command set the mail transfer agent (mta) to auto state (which makes the highest priority mail services used as the mta). By default, sendmail is chosen over postfix.

There have been some reports of trigger scripts breaking services. So if a service that was recently upgraded, such as sendmail or initscripts, is broken, you can check for triggers to see if there are trigger scripts that could have caused a problem.

Querying Software Packages

With the rpm query feature, you can display many details about the form and content of the RPM packages in your Linux system. You can then output that information in any way that is useful to you. Querying can be done on individual packages or over the entire RPM database.

Querying Local or Remote Packages

For each of the following query options, if you give the RPM package's base name, rpm will query the database for information about that installed package. If you want to query a package that is not installed, you must use the -p option followed by the package name (in the current directory), the full path to the package name, or a URL to the package. For example, to see the description for a mozilla package in my current directory, I could type

```
# rpm -qi -p mozilla-1.4.1-17.i386.rpm
```

A package may also be contained on a website (HTTP) or FTP server. Here is an example of the rpm command being used to list the contents of an RPM on a remote FTP site. The following example displays all files contained in the apt package from the ftp.freshrpms.net shown (the entire command should be on one line):

```
# rpm -ql -p ftp://ftp.freshrpms.net/pub/freshrpms/fedora/linux/1/apt/apt-
  0.5.1cnc3-0.1.fr.i386.rpm
```

The -p option provides a good way to check out packages on remote systems before you install them. If a username and password are required, they can be added to the command line. In this example, the user is tina and the password is my44hat as follows:

```
# rpm -ql -p ftp://tina:my44hat@ftp.example.net/pub/any.rpm
```

Querying Individual Packages

You can find out a lot of information for any rpm package installed on your system. Here are a few examples:

✦ *All files in a package*—Use the -ql option to display all the files in a package. In the following example, we query a package that is installed on the computer:

```
#rpm -ql samba | less
/etc/logrotate.d/samba
/etc/pam.d/samba
/etc/rc.d/init.d/smb
/etc/samba/smbusers
```

Here you can page through all the files contained in the samba package.

✦ *Documentation in a package*—Instead of listing all the files (-ql), you can list only documentation files contained in a package using the -qd option. For example,

```
#rpm -qd bind-utils
/usr/share/man/man1/dig.1.gz
/usr/share/man/man1/host.1.gz
/usr/share/man/man5/resolver.5.gz
/usr/share/man/man8/nslookup.8.gz
/usr/share/man/man8/nsupdate.8.gz
```

This shows that the bind-utils package contains documentation in the form of five man pages (for example, type man dig to see the first one). Besides man pages, packages often include documentation that comes in Texinfo format (type info) and files in /usr/share/doc for the package.

✦ *Configuration files in a package*—You can list configuration files associated with a package with the `-qc` option. Most packages will keep their configuration files in `/etc` (or a subdirectory of `/etc`).

```
#rpm -qc samba
/etc/logrotate.d/samba
/etc/pam.d/samba
/etc/rc.d/init.d/smb
/etc/samba/smbusers
/etc/sysconfig/samba
```

Sometimes the `-qc` option will turn up files in locations outside of `/etc` that you might want to reconfigure. For example, the httpd package lists files in the `/var/www/error` directory you could change if you want different information displayed by your Apache web server for different error conditions.

✦ *Changelog for a package*—To see changelog entries made to an RPM package, you can use the `--changelog` query option. If the software developer has been verbose about his updates, this information can help you understand what has been done to the package lately. For example,

```
# rpm -q --changelog XFree86 | less
* Mon Oct 20 2003 Mike A. Harris <mharris@redhat.com> 4.3.0-42

- This release is the long awaited answer to the meaning of life, the
  universe and everything.
- Added XFree86-4.3.0-redhat-exec-shield-GNU-stack.patch to make the
  complete XFree86 build including Mesa et al. exec-shield friendly
  (arjanv, mharris)
- Updated to new XFree86-4.3.0-Mesa-SSE-fixes-from-MesaCVS-v2.patch which
  should fix compatibility problems between DRI and 2.6.x kernels which
:
```

✦ *Description of a package*—A formatted set of information about a package can be displayed using the `-qi` option. Here's an example:

```
# rpm -qi XFree86
Name        : XFree86           Relocations: (not relocateable)
Version     : 4.3.0                   Vendor: Red Hat, Inc.
Release     : 42                  Build Date: Fri 24 Oct 2003 03:19:36 PM PDT
Install Date: Tue 11 Nov 2003 04:26:51 PM PST Build Host: porky.redhat.com
Group       : User Interface/X    Source RPM: XFree86-4.3.0-42.src.rpm
Size        : 64230711               License: XFree86
Signature   : DSA/SHA1, Tue 28 Oct 2003 04:20:58 PM PST, Key ID
              b44269d04f2a6fd2
Packager    : Red Hat, Inc. <http://bugzilla.redhat.com/bugzilla>
URL         : http://www.xfree86.org
Summary     : The basic fonts, programs and docs for an X workstation.
Description :
XFree86 is an open source implementation of the X Window System. It
provides the basic low level functionality which full fledged
graphical user interfaces (GUIs) such as GNOME and KDE are designed upon.
```

✦ *Name of a package*—Say that you are looking for a package that has the characters "bind" in it, but you can't remember the package's exact name. The `-qa` option lets you list all packages, from which you can then search for the string of characters that interests you. Here's an example:

```
# rpm -qa *bind*
bind-utils-9.2.2.P3-9
kdebindings-devel-3.1.4-1
redhat-config-bind-2.0.0-18
bind-chroot-9.2.2.P3-9
bind-devel-9.2.2.P3-9
kdebindings-3.1.4-1
ypbind-1.12-3
bind-9.2.2.P3-9
```

Querying Multiple Packages

The content of an RPM package consists of a header, signatures, and the actual files that you are installing from the RPM. Each piece of information in the header is marked with a tag. When you query an RPM package, you are inquiring about the content of one or more of these tags.

The rpm command lets you query the RPM database for tags that you request and then displays the resulting information in a format that you choose. This section provides some useful examples of the rpm query feature for finding and displaying information for multiple RPM files.

You can start out by listing all the query tags that may be available in RPMs on your computer. You do that as follows:

```
# rpm --querytags | less
```

This example lets you page through the list of tags. I counted 139 tags available on my Fedora Core 1 system. Any of the tags that interest you can be put in an rpm query command so that information from those tags can be displayed in the format you choose. Here are some examples:

✦ To display the name and summary information for every package beginning with the string XFree86, you could type the following:

```
# rpm -qp --queryformat "%{NAME} *** %{SUMMARY} \ n" XFree86*
XFree86-base-fonts *** The collection of XFree86 base fonts
XFree86-tools *** Various tools for XFree86
XFree86-ISO8859-14-100dpi-fonts *** ISO8859-14-100dpi-fonts
XFree86-font-utils *** Utilities required for installing fonts
```

✦ To list the name of every package along with the web address (URL) to the package's website, you could type the following rpm command. This command is piped to the less command, which lets you page through the output.

```
# rpm -qp --queryformat "%{NAME} >>> %{URL} \ n" | less
libattr >>> http://acl.bestbits.at/
mktemp >>> http://www.mktemp.org
less >>> http://www.greenwoodsoftware.com/less/
shadow-utils >>> http://shadow.pld.org.pl/
pam >>> http://www.us.kernel.org/pub/linux/libs/pam/index.html
rmt >>> http://dump.sourceforge.net
zip >>> http://www.info-zip.org/pub/infozip/Zip.html
```

```
logwatch >>> http://www.logwatch.org/
bind-utils >>> http://www.isc.org/products/BIND/
libxml2-python >>> http://xmlsoft.org/
```

✦ In the following example, the installed RPM database is queried, then the output is in the form of P: followed by the package name, then S: followed by the summary line for the package. Finally, the output is piped to the grep command, which displays only those lines that contain the term image.

```
# rpm -qp --queryformat "P: %{NAME} S: %{SUMMARY} \ n" | grep -i image
P: desktop-backgrounds-extra S: Desktop background images.
P: SDL_image-devel S: Development files for the SDL image loading library.
P: gimp S: the GNU Image Manipulation Program.
```

Verifying Software Packages

Because your RPM database knows all about the packages and files you have installed on your system, you can use that information to compare the original executable commands, configuration files, and other package components against those items as they exist on your hard disk. To do that, you can use the -V option to RPM.

The basic format of the rpm command with the verify option is

```
# rpm -V package-name
```

Replace package.rpm with the package you want to verify. The output from that command will show you any files on your hard disk that are different in any way from how they were originally installed. Here is an example of running the rpm-V command on the initscripts package:

```
# rpm -V initscripts
prelink: /bin/ipcalc: prelinked file size differs
S.?....T   /bin/ipcalc
S.5....T c /etc/inittab
S.5....T c /etc/rc.d/init.d/functions
```

The component (file or command) that was shown not to match the original is shown on the right. On the left are indications of what is wrong. The first message, prelink: /bin/ipcalc: prelinked file size differs indicates that the ipcalc command is somehow corrupted. The ? indicates that it is too damaged to be trusted.

The two other files shown (inittab and functions) illustrate two configuration files that have been modified (in my case, they were properly modified). Each of the lines starts with eight characters (either dots or some alphanumeric character). When a dot appears in the location, it means the item it represents passes the test. A letter or a question mark indicates that the test doesn't pass. Table 8-1 illustrates what each of the eight slots to start each line represent.

From the output shown in Table 8-1, you can see for inittab and functions that the file size differs (S), the MD5 sum differs (5), and the time stamp on the file (T) differs as well. For configuration files, changes to the file size, MD5 sum, and time stamps are not unusual. What is unusual is if an executable file has been changed, because that could indicate that someone is trying to replace a real program with one that might be doing some mischief.

To see more details with the output shown, you can add -v or -vv options. This will show each item being checked.

Table 8-1: Output from RPM Verify

S	The original file size differs from the current file size (indicating that someone has changed the content). This might reflect normal changes to configuration files.
M	The permission mode is different. Included in the permission mode are the read/write/execute values, as well as the file type.
5	The md5sum value, generated from the original contents of the file, is different than it was for the original. This indicates that someone has changed the content of the file.
D	For a device file, the major and/or minor number are mismatched.
L	The readLink path is mismatched.
U	The user ownership is different than it was on the original.
G	The group ownership is different than it was on the original.
T	The time stamp on the file is different than it was on the original.

Cross-Reference   For more information on using rpm with the -V option, refer to Chapter 10. Chapter 10 describes how the verify option of rpm can be used as part of a larger scheme for protecting the security of your Linux system.

Repairing a Broken RPM Database

On occasions, the RPM database can break. The result is that when you try to install a package, remove a package, or query the database, your request might just hang.

The problem of corrupted RPM databases seemed to be much worse in Red Hat Linux 8 than it is in Fedora Core 1 or Red Hat Enterprise Linux. However, if your RPM database is showing signs of hanging processes that talk to it, here are a few steps you can go through that should help correct your broken RPM database:

✦ Remove the current RPM database by typing

```
# rm -f /var/lib/rpm/__ db.*
```

✦ Rebuild the database by typing (use the -vv or just -v depending on how much you like to watch output scroll by)

```
# rpm -vv --rebuilddb
```

This step can take a while to complete.

Troubleshooting Software Package Tips

Following are a bunch of extraneous troubleshooting tips that you might find useful when you are working with RPM packages:

✦ *Check installed packages over 5 days*—Once each day, a list of all installed RPM packages is created and copied to the /var/log/rpmpkgs file. You can refer to that list to see the full package name for each RPM package. The most recent 5 days of package are contained in the /var/log directory: rpmpkgs, rpmpkgs.1, rpmpkgs.2, rpmpkgs.3, and rpmpkgs.4. You can compare these files to see if any packages have been added, removed, or upgraded in the past 5 days.

✦ *Find packages most recently installed*—Some software on your Linux system isn't working properly and you want to see if any software that has been added or upgraded recently might be the problem. Use the --last option to list your RPM packages in the order they were installed (starting from the most recent):

```
# rpm -qa --last | less
gpg-pubkey-4f2a6fd2-3f9d9d3b      Fri 06 Feb 2004 10:02:09 PM PST
gpg-pubkey-e42d547b-3960bdf1      Fri 06 Feb 2004 12:49:58 AM PST
acroread-5.06-4                   Wed 04 Feb 2004 11:40:25 AM PST
mozilla-js-debugger-1.4.1-18      Mon 26 Jan 2004 11:33:50 PM PST
mozilla-dom-inspector-1.4.1-18    Mon 26 Jan 2004 11:33:43 PM PST
```

From this example, you can se that I installed two GPG public keys on Friday. Before that I installed the Adobe Acrobat reader and upgraded a bunch of mozilla packages. I could then page through the entire 1500 or so packages on by system, in the order they were installed.

✦ *Find what package a file is in*—Locating what package a file, command, or library comes from can help you track down documentation or other components related to that item. The -f query option to rpm lets list the package associated with any file. For example,

```
#rpm -qf /etc/alternatives
chkconfig-1.3.9-1
```

You see that the alternatives feature is included in the chkconfig package, which includes components to change system services.

✦ *Change an RPM to a Cpio archive*—Convert an RPM package to cpio format by using the rpm2cpio command. Cpio is a standard utility for creating software archives and extracting files from those archives. By converting a package to cpio, you can essentially use the resulting cpio archive to copy the original contents of an RPM package to any Linux or UNIX system, or to extract a single file from an RPM package.

Software Package Troubleshooting Reference

Table 8-2 provides a reference for finding and troubleshooting RPM packages.

Table 8-2: RPM Package Troubleshooting References

General RPM information	
RPM project	www.rpm.org
RPM documentation	Maximum RPM (.ps format): www.rpm.org/local/maximum-rpm.ps.gz
RPM HOWTO	www.rpm.org/support/RPM-HOWTO.html
RPM mailing lists	RPM.org mailing list: www.rpm.org/mailing_list/ Usenet newsgroup: linux.redhat.rpm

RPM documentation in Fedora	`/usr/share/doc/rpm-*`
	Man pages: rpm, rpm2cpio, rpmbuild, rpmcache, rpmgraph, gendiff, and rpmdeps
RPM configuration and log files	
`/etc/rpm` **directory**	Files that set the locations for RPM components. Generally there's no need to touch these files.
`/var/lib/rpm`	Location of the database of RPM packages that are currently installed.
`/usr/lib/rpmdb/i386-redhat-linux`	Location of the database of total RPM packages that are available on the full Fedora or Red Hat Linux distribution (when installed).
`/var/log/rpmpkgs`	List of all RPM packages on the current system.
RPM commands	
`rpm`	Basic command for adding, removing, upgrading, and querying RPM packages.
`redhat-config-packages`	Launches the GUI tool to add and remove software packages.
`rpm2cpio`	Converts an RPM package into a cpio archive file.

Summary

Software in Fedora and other Red Hat Linux systems are packaged in RPM format. To install, upgrade, and delete those packages, you can use the `rpm` command.

Besides adding and removing software, the `rpm` command can be used for a variety of other duties, such as querying the RPM database or verifying the validity of the contents of an RPM package. The `rpm` command can also be used as a security tool to check installed software against software in the original RPM package, to make sure it hasn't been tampered with.

File System, Disk, and Power Troubleshooting

Journaling file systems, excellent hardware probing, and sensible shutdown procedures have gone a long way toward taking the adventure out of managing your hard disks and the file systems that are stored on them in Linux. There are times, however, when something goes wrong or you want to do more than just sit back and let Linux run the show alone.

You might not be happy just sticking with the defaults when there are some performance gains to be had. Or you might want to get that extra bit of life out of your laptop's battery by better controlling when idle disks are spun down or when nonessential services are turned off. This chapter will help you look for trouble (and opportunities) when it comes to tuning and working with your hard disks, file systems, and battery power.

Starting with Linux File Systems

Much of what was once done manually to set up file systems in Linux can now be done automatically when you install most major Linux distributions. During installation, your hard disks are probed and configured based on:

◆ *Hard disk type*—Linux determines the type of hard disk you are using and tries to set appropriate parameters for operation (data transfer modes, read or write-caching, 16- or 32-bit I/O support, and so on). Linux usually chooses workable hard disk settings, but allows you to change those settings if you like. (Ways of checking and changing hard disk settings are described in the *Checking and Tuning Your Hard Disk* section later in this chapter.)

◆ *Partitioning*—The Linux installation process can automatically divide your hard disk into appropriate partitions or give you the opportunity to divide your hard disk yourself. During installation, Fedora and other Red Hat Linux systems offer Disk Druid to partition your disk. After your computer is installed, you can use tools such as fdisk to add, delete, and modify partitions.

✦ *File system types*—Each disk partition is assigned a file system type and is structured in such a way that Linux can access the files, directories, devices, and other components that make up the file system. The ext3 file system is the default for Fedora and other Red Hat Linux systems, while Windows systems typically contain FAT, VFAT, or NTFS file systems. There are also a handful of specialty file systems you can use, such as iso9660 (the standard for CD-ROM file systems).

Instead of stepping through how to partition your disk and assign file systems during installation, we will go through different methods of troubleshooting problems that can arise later with your disks and file systems. Assuming that you are starting with an installed Fedora or Red Hat Linux system and you want to fix some problems with it, we're going to start by taking a look at what you have installed on your system.

Checking Partitions and File Systems

To see what partitions and file systems are configured on your computer, with Linux running perform the following steps from a Terminal window:

1. Run the fdisk command to list information about your hard disk partitions, as follows:

```
#fdisk -l
Disk /dev/hda: 6505 MB, 6505712640 bytes
255 heads, 63 sectors/track, 790 cylinders
Units = cylinders of 16065 * 512 = 8225280 bytes

   Device Boot    Start     End    Blocks   Id   System
/dev/hda1    *        1      13    104391   83   Linux
/dev/hda2            14     766  6048472+   83   Linux
/dev/hda3           767     790    192780   82   Linux swap
```

This example shows a relatively small (6505MB or about 6GB) IDE hard disk (/dev/hda). That disk is partitioned into three parts: /dev/hda1 is an ext3 file system (Id 83) that starts at cylinder 1 and ends at cylinder 13 (104,391 blocks). The asterisk shows that it is a bootable file system. The next partition (/dev/hda2) is a much larger ext3 partition (6,048,472 blocks). The final partition is a swap partition (Id 82) that consists of 192,780 blocks.

Your fdisk output will almost surely be of a different size. Here are some other ways that it might vary:

• *Disk name*—The type of hard disk you have will be reflected in the disk device names you see. The hda stands for the first (1) IDE hard disk (hd). Other IDE hard disks would be named hdb, hdc, and so on. SCSI disks are named /dev/sda, /dev/sdb, and so on. A RAID device would look something like this when displayed from fdisk:

```
   Device  Boot    Start   End    Blocks    Id   System
/dev/hda1    *        1     13    104391    fd   Linux raid autodetect
```

• *File system types*—In most cases, you will see ext3 (Id 83) and swap (82) file systems assigned to partitions. If you have a system where you can dual boot with Windows, you might also see HPFS/NTFS (Id 7), WIN95 FAT32 (Id b), FAT, or DOS 16-bit (Id 6). To see a complete list of available file system types, you can type the l option within fdisk as follows:

```
#  fdisk /dev/hda
Command (m for help): 1
   0 Empty            1c Hidden Win95 FA    70 DiskSecure Mult   bb Boot Wizard hid
   1 FAT12            1e Hidden Win95 FA    75 PC/IX             be Solaris boot
   2 XENIX root       24 NEC DOS            80 Old Minix         c1 DRDOS/sec (FAT-
   3 XENIX usr        39 Plan 9             81 Minix / old Lin   c4 DRDOS/sec (FAT-
   4 FAT16 <32M       3c PartitionMagic     82 Linux swap        c6 DRDOS/sec (FAT-
   5 Extended         40 Venix 80286        83 Linux             c7 Syrinx
   6 FAT16            41 PPC PReP Boot       84 OS/2 hidden C:    da Non-FS data
   7 HPFS/NTFS        42 SFS                85 Linux extended    db CP/M / CTOS / .
   8 AIX              4d QNX4.x             86 NTFS volume set   de Dell Utility
   9 AIX bootabl      4e QNX4.x 2nd part    87 NTFS volume set   df BootIt
   a OS/2 Boota       4f QNX4.x 3rd part    8e Linux LVM         e1 DOS access
   b Win95 FAT32      50 OnTrack DM          93 Amoeba            e3 DOS R/O
   c Win95 FAT32      51 OnTrack DM6 Aux    94 Amoeba BBT        e4 SpeedStor
   e Win95 FAT16      52 CP/M               9f BSD/OS            eb BeOS fs
   f Win95 Ext'd      53 OnTrack DM6 Aux    a0 IBM Thinkpad hi   ee EFI GPT
  10 OPUS             54 OnTrackDM6          a5 FreeBSD           ef EFI (FAT-12/16/
  11 Hidden FAT1      55 EZ-Drive           a6 OpenBSD           f0 Linux/PA-RISC b
  12 Compaq diag      56 Golden Bow         a7 NeXTSTEP          f1 SpeedStor
  14 HiddenFAT16      5c Priam Edisk        a8 Darwin UFS        f4 SpeedStor
  16 HiddenFAT16      61 SpeedStor          a9 NetBSD            f2 DOS secondary
  17 HiddenHPFS/      63 GNU HURD or Sys    ab Darwin boot       fd Linux raid auto
  18 AST SmartS1      64 Novell Netware     b7 BSDI fs           fe LANstep
  1b HiddenWin95      65 Novell Netware     b8 BSDI swap         ff BBT
Command (m for help):  q
```

After you exit from fdisk, you can try listing the file systems that are in use or currently available on the system by typing `cat/proc/filesystems`. Note that this doesn't necessarily mean that a file system of that type is currently mounted. Also, many other file system types may be available as loadable modules. You can find some of those file system type modules in the directories in Fedora: `/lib/modules/*/kernel/fs` and `/lib/modules/*/unsupported/fs`.

2. Check the size of each partition and how it is mounted on the file system with the `df` command:

```
# df -h
Filesystem       Size   Used Avail Use% Mounted on
/dev/hda2        5.7G   3.3G  2.2G  61% /
/dev/hda1         99M   6.6M   88M   8% /boot
none              30M      0   30M   0% /dev/shm
```

Notice here that the `/dev/hda2` partition is mounted at the root of the file system (/). The `/dev/hda1` partition is mounted on `/boot`. The swap partition is represented by the `/dev/shm` device. It is possible that some partitions listed from fdisk are not shown by `df`. That's because partitions are only mounted if they are configured to mount automatically at boot time, configured to mount when inserted (such as with a CD), or if they were mounted manually later. For example, if you installed Fedora on a hard disk that contains a Windows partition (so you can dual boot), the Windows partition will not automatically be mounted in Fedora.

3. To see what partitions are being mounted automatically at boot time, display the contents of the `/etc/fstab` file:

```
# cat /etc/fstab
LABEL=/       /              ext3    defaults          1 1
LABEL=/boot   /boot          ext3    defaults          1 2
none          /dev/pts       devpts  gid=5,mode=620    0 0
none          /dev/shm       tmpfs   defaults          0 0
none          /proc          proc    defaults          0 0
/dev/hda3     swap           swap    defaults          0 0
/dev/cdrom    /mnt/cdrom     udf,iso9660 noauto,owner,kudzu,ro 0 0
/dev/hdc4     /mnt/zip       auto    noauto,owner,kudzu 0 0
/dev/fd0      /mnt/floppy    auto    noauto,owner,kudzu 0 0
```

There are three kinds of file systems you can see in this listing of the /etc/fstab file:

- *Automatically mounted file systems*—The / and /boot partitions are automatically mounted by default when the system boots. That's because by default, all ext3 file systems listed in this file are mounted at boot time (as are any file systems that are not listed as noauto). 1 in the fifth field indicates that a file system needs to be dumped. The number 1 in the sixth field indicates that a file system check should be done on the root file system (/) first. 2 in the sixth field for the /boot file system indicates that it should be checked after the root file system.

- *Pseudofile systems*—The pts, shm, and proc file systems are actually pseudofile systems (that is, they do not represent real disk partitions).

- *Manually mounted file systems*—With a noauto option listed in the fourth field, the devices listed are not automatically mounted at boot time. The noauto option is useful for removable media, such as the CD-ROM, Zip, and floppy disk drives shown in the example.

- Having an entry in the /etc/fstab file makes it possible for the mount command to mount the removable medium later with simply the device name (mount /dev/cdrom) or mount point (mount /mnt/cdrom) as an argument. The rest of the options are taken from the fstab entry.

4. If you are using the GNOME desktop (which is the default), by default CD and DVD media are automatically mounted when you insert one of those disks into a drive. To see, and possibly change, this behavior, click Preferences ➪ CD Properties from the Red Hat menu. Figure 9-1 shows an example of the window that appears.

As you can see from the top check box, by default a data CD will be mounted (on /mnt/cdrom) if you don't change this preference. This feature (referred to as magicdev) can also otherwise react to the content of the CD or DVD by playing an audio CD or movie DVD or by opening a blank CD so you can write on it (that is a nice feature of nautilus, by the way).

Another way you can have disks and partitions mounted automatically is with the automount feature. With automount, by changing to a mount point (or subdirectory) of a medium that is configured to automount, the device will be automatically mounted. That way, the medium is only mounted when it is needed.

Fedora and Red Hat Linux systems offer two different packages for implementing automount. The Autofs automounter (autofs package) is configured in the /etc/auto.master and /etc/auto.misc files. It is started by default from the autofs runlevel script. The BSD automounter (am-utils package) is configured in the /etc/amd.conf file and started with the amd runlevel script. Type man autofs or man amd for further information.

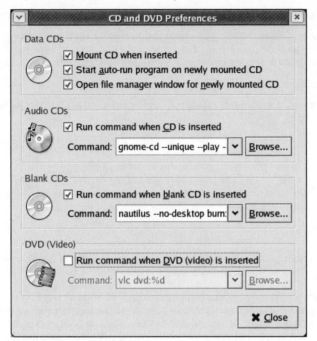

Figure 9-1: Set whether CDs are automatically mounted upon insertion.

Now that you have some idea of how the file systems and partitions are set up on your computer, let's go through some related troubleshooting issues that may come up.

Troubleshooting Partitions and File Systems

Here are some tips for troubleshooting the partitions and file systems on your hard disks.

Computer Won't Boot (No Boot Screen)

If you don't get a GRUB boot screen when you try to boot from hard disk (and are expecting one), it could be that the master boot record is corrupted. You can reload the master boot record by booting from a rescue CD (assuming Linux is installed on the first IDE hard drive). Here's how:

1. Reboot your computer with the first CD in the installation set for Fedora or Red Hat Linux in the CD drive.

2. When you see the boot prompt, type:

   ```
   # linux rescue
   ```

3. Add information about your language and keyboard as requested.

4. Choose whether or not to start the network interfaces (you probably don't need to in this case). The rescue process will now look for your Linux installation.

5. If the rescue mode finds your Linux installation on your hard disk, select OK to continue.

6. After the computer enters rescue mode, you should see a regular shell prompt (#). Assuming rescue mode mounted your hard disk under /mnt/sysimage, type the following to change your root directory to that of your Linux installation:

```
# chroot /mnt/sysimage
```

7. To install a new master boot record from the grub.conf configuration on your hard disk, type the following:

```
# /sbin/grub-install /dev/hda
Installation finished. No error reported.
This is the contents of the device map /boot/grub/device.map.
Check if this is correct. If any of the lines are incorrect,
fix it and re-run the script 'grub-install.'
# this device map was generated by anaconda
(fd0)   /dev/fd0
(hd0)   /dev/hda
```

Remove the CD and reboot your computer. You should see your original GRUB screen and be able to select which partition and/or kernel to boot.

If you had deleted a partition and simply reinstalling grub to the MBR doesn't work, you may need to do some more work. It's possible that your boot partition is no longer valid, so the boot loader is not able to find your /boot/grub/grub.conf file. Start by booting a rescue CD and running the grub command. Assuming you are booting from the MBR on your first IDE hard disk, type the following (with the first text followed by the tab key):

```
grub> root (hd0, <tab>
 Possible partitions are:
 Partition num: 0, Filesystem type is ext2fs, partition type 0x83
 Partition num: 1, Filesystem type is ext2fs, partition type 0x83
 Partition num: 2, Filesystem type unknown, partition type 0x82
```

After you press the Tab key, you will see a list of partitions on the first IDE hard disk. Look for the first one that shows up as ext2fs (ext3 file systems appear here as ext2fs). If the first ext2fs that shows up in the list is partition number 0, enter that into your grub command line by typing:

```
grub> root (hd0,0)
```

To make sure that you assigned the proper partition as your boot partition, try typing the following:

```
grub> cat /grub/grub.conf
```

If this lists the contents of your grub.conf file, you have assigned the correct partition as your boot partition.

Recovering a Deleted File

You deleted a file (or a set of files) by mistake and you want it back. Is it possible to get it back? Unfortunately, the answer is probably not. Unlike the earlier ext2, the ext3 file system erases pointers to the deleted file's inode.

If you are using an ext2 file system, however, you might be able to use the `debugfs` command to find and restore your lost file. With ext2, the blocks are simply marked as being unused, so if the space hasn't been reused yet, the file you need might still be there.

Let's say you deleted a file from your home directory (`/home/chris/myfile.txt`) and you want it back. If you have a separate `/home` partition (say, for example, `/dev/hda5`), you can have anyone using the computer log off for a moment, and then do the following:

1. Determine the partition containing the file you want to recover. Typing `df -h` or `mount` will show your currently mounted partitions.

2. Unmount the directory containing the file you want to recover. (If the file is on the root partition, you should shut down the computer and go into rescue mode, as described in Chapter 6.) Here's how to unmount the `/home` partition (if `/home` were on `/dev/hda5`, you could use that instead of /home):

   ```
   # umount /home
   ```

   If the directory fails to unmount, see the Can't Unmount a Directory section later in this chapter.

3. Run the `debugfs` command on the home partition. Then from the `debugfs` prompt, list the deleted files from the directory you are interested in:

   ```
   # debugfs /dev/hda5
   debugfs 1.35-WIP (07-Dec-2003)
   debugfs: ls -ld /home/chris
   ```

   Look for the inode number for the file you want to undelete. With an ext3 file system, the entry will look something like this and you will not be able to recover it:

   ```
   <      0>      0 (1)      0     0     0      myfile.txt
   ```

   However, if you see the number greater than zero surrounded by less than and greater than signs, you might be able to recover the file. That is the inode number for the file. For example, if you were to try this on an ext2 file system and if the inode is shown as <115>, you could copy it from the /home/chris directory from the unmounted home partition by typing:

   ```
   debugfs: dump <115> /tmp/myfile_dumped.txt
   ```

4. Remount the file system (`mount /home`) and you are back in business with your recovered file safely in the `/tmp` directory. Copy it where you want it to go permanently and you are ready to go.

Can't Unmount a Directory

You try to unmount a directory or device representing a partition and you see a message similar to the following:

```
unmount: /whatever: device is busy
```

The most common reason for an unmount to fail is that some process is holding a file or directory open on the partition. In particular, if a directory in the partition is the current directory for any shell, that will cause the device to be busy. To solve the problem, you can often simply close the shell or change the directory so that the current directory is on another partition.

On a multiuser system that has a lot of users logging in and out, it may not be as easy to find out who is making the partition busy. You can try using `ps aux` to see what is running and kill any run-away process. Or you can go into single-user mode, if it is critical to unmount the directory now. If you can bear to wait a bit, try a lazy unmount:

```
# umount -l /whatever
```

The lazy unmount detaches the file system from the hierarchy. However, it waits until the file system is no longer busy to clean up all references to the file system.

Don't Know what Kind of a File System Is on a Device

You can find out what file system type is on a device using the `blkid` command. For example, to check the first partition on the first IDE hard disk, type:

```
# blkid /dev/hda1
/dev/hda1: LABEL="/boot" UUID="69477377-81c2-4846-bd3e-
ad5fe8c2caee" SEC_TYPE="ext3" TYPE="ext2"
```

Checking a File System

If a file system was not cleanly unmounted (for example, when someone kicks out the power cord) or if the time has been reached for a scheduled file system check, an fsck process will run and check (and correct) the file system when you boot the computer. You can check a file system yourself, without rebooting the system, however, if you like. To do that, first unmount the file system.

Note   If you are checking the root file system, you should boot from a rescue disk. You should not do an fsck on a mounted file system, and you cannot unmount the root file system on a running Linux system. You could mount the root file system (/) read-only (add `ro` to the mount entry in `/etc/fstab` and reboot) and run `fsck` on it.

Running fsck

Once the file system is unmounted, run fsck. For example, if you are checking the /boot partition, type the following after it is unmounted:

```
# fsck /boot
fsck 1.34 (25-Jul-2003)
/boot: clean, 42/26104 files, 11632/104388 blocks
```

Checking for Bad Blocks

To see if there are bad blocks on the file system, run the `badblocks` command as follows:

```
# badblocks -v /dev/hda1
Checking blocks 0 to 104391
Checking for bad blocks (read-only test): done
Pass completed, 0 bad blocks found.
```

Repairing a Damaged ext3 File System

You can force a more thorough check of an ext3 file system using the `-f` option. To see more details about the output, use the `-v` option as well:

```
# e2fsck -fyv /dev/hda1
e2fsck 1.34 (25-Jul-2003)
fsck 1.34 (25-Jul-2003)
Pass 1: Checking inodes, blocks, and sizes
Pass 2: Checking directory structure
Pass 3: Checking directory connectivity
Pass 4: Checking reference counts
Pass 5: Checking group summary information
42 inodes used (0%)
        1 non-contiguous inode (2.4%)
          # of inodes with ind/dind/tind blocks: 10/4/0
   11632 blocks used (11%)
        0 bad blocks
        0 large files

25 regular files
        3 directories
        0 character device files
        0 block device files
        0 fifos
        0 links
        5 symbolic links (5 fast symbolic links)
        0 sockets
--------
        33 files
```

This shows a forced, thorough check being done of a small file system. The -y option indicates that if any errors are encountered, and e2fsck would normally ask if you wanted to try to correct each error, it should instead just correct them all without asking for each one individually.

Creating, Modifying, and Deleting File Systems

The fdisk command and related commands such as sfdisk and cfdisk are used to display, modify, delete, and add disk partitions. Once added, file systems can be assigned to the partitions and those file systems can be mounted and used by Linux.

Caution   On a critical system, an inexperienced user shouldn't use fdisk other than for listing the partitions on your system (the -l option). If you do want to use fdisk to change, delete, or add partitions, be aware that a small mistake can completely destroy your data or make it inaccessible. If you are just learning, try this on a machine you don't require. Regardless of your experience, you should make sure that any critical data is backed up.

In this example, I had left about 1GB of free space on my hard disk that I wanted to create into a partition that is mounted on the /mnt/backup directories (so I could use it to make backup copies of my document files). Here is what I did to start the fdisk session, and create the new partition:

```
# fdisk /dev/hda
Command (m for help): n
Command action
   l   logical (5 or over)
   p   primary partition (1-4)
```

```
p
Selected partition 3
First sector (75987450-78165359, default 75987450): <Enter>
Using default value 75987450
Last sector or +size or +sizeM or +sizeK
    (75987450-78165359, default 78165359): <Enter>
Using default value 78165359
Command (m for help): w
```

In the previous example, I created a primary partition (partition 3 was available) and just took the defaults. That allowed me to use the rest of the available disk space for the new partition.

After that, I made the partition into an ext2 file system. Here is an example of creating an ext2 file system on the /dev/hda3 partition:

```
# mkfs -t ext2 /dev/hda3
mke2fs 1.34 (25-Jul-2003)
Filesystem label=
OS type: Linux
Block size=4096 (log=2)
Fragment size=4096 (log=2)
135648 inodes, 271096 blocks
13554 blocks (5.00%) reserved for the super user
First data block=0
9 block groups
32768 blocks per group, 32768 fragments per group
15072 inodes per group
Superblock backups stored on blocks:
        32768, 98304, 163840, 229376
Writing inode tables: done
Writing superblocks and filesystem accounting information: done
This filesystem will be automatically checked every 32 mounts or
180 days, whichever comes first. Use tune2fs -c or -i to override.
```

Next I added a label to the partition, based on its mount point:

```
# e2label /dev/hda3 /mnt/backup
```

If I want to make it into a journaling file system (ext3) now, I can do that using the tune2fs command. This action will take about 33MB of disk space to create the journal file needed by ext3. Here's an example:

```
# tune2fs -j /dev/hda3
tune2fs 1.34 (25-Jul-2003)
Creating journal inode: done
This filesystem will be automatically checked every 32 mounts
or 180 days, whichever comes first.
Use tune2fs -c or -i to override
```

After that, I created an entry in the /etc/fstab file, so the partition would be automatically mounted each time Linux started (if I hadn't added the journal, the file system type would be ext2 instead of ext3):

```
LABEL=/mnt/backup    /mnt/backup    ext3    defaults 1 2
```

After that I can mount the file system immediately by typing:

```
# mount /mnt/backup
```

At this point, the new partition will be mounted on the /mnt/backup directory each time the system boots.

Checking and Tuning Your Hard Disk

To get the best performance out of your hard disk, you sometimes have to do a bit of tuning. Although Linux will properly detect and configure most hard disks so they will work, sometimes the default settings will be either too conservative (so you get slow performance) or too aggressive (not as likely, but can result in errors).

This section describes how to display information about your hard disk. It then describes different ways of tuning disk options and benchmarking the results of those changes.

Getting Information about Your Disk

You can find out information about your hard disk using hdparm, fdisk, and other commands. To find out some general information, you could start out with hdparm simply followed by the name of the disk device. For example, you would identify the first IDE (ATA) hard disk using /dev/hda in the following command line:

```
# hdparm /dev/hda
/dev/hda:
   multcount    = 16 (on)
   IO_support   = 1 (32-bit)
   unmaskirq    = 1 (on)
   using-dma    = 1 (on)
   keepsettings = 0 (off)
   readonly     = 0 (off)
   readahead    = 8 (on)
   geometry     = 4865/255/63, sectors = 78165360, start = 0
```

The output shows some basic information about your hard disk. You can also list most of these items separately using options described below:

✦ *multcount*—With multcount set to a number other than 0, IDE block mode is enabled. This allows multiple sectors to be transferred with each I/O interrupt (2, 4, 8, 16, or 32 sectors). Type hdparm-m /dev/hda to list just this line.

✦ *IO support*—IO support set to 1 indicates that the hard disk supports 32-bit data transfers across the bus (usually PCI) to the interface card. From the interface card to the hard drive, data actually only uses a 16-bit connection over the ribbon cable. To take advantage of the 32-bit bus, however, data is packaged together in two 16-bit groups before it is sent to RAM or the CPU. Type hdparm-c /dev/hda to list just this line.

✦ *unmaskirq*—The unmaskirq setting of 1 turns on the ability of the disk's driver to unmask other interrupts while processing a disk interrupt (to improve performance). Type hdparm-u /dev/hda to list just this line.

✦ *using dma*—Describes whether or not DMA is on for the hard drive (1 is on; 0 is off). If the hard drive supports DMA, having DMA on can improve performance substantially. It should improve I/O throughput without increasing CPU use.

✦ *keepsettings*—Shows whether or not DMA (`-d`), multcount (`-m`), and unmaskirq (`-u`) settings are kept after a soft reset. This is typically off, so that a reset will change settings back to a sane state in case of bad `-dmu` settings. Type `hdparm-k/dev/hda` to list just this line.

✦ *readonly*—Tells whether or not the hard disk device is set for read-only. If read-only is on (1), no write operations are allowed to the disk. Type `hdparm-r/dev/hda` to list just this line.

✦ *readahead*—This setting describes whether read-ahead seeks are on and, if so, how many sectors are read ahead. During large sequential reads, performance can improve by reading ahead some number of sectors, in anticipation that they will be needed by the operation requesting the data. The default eight sectors causes the file system to read ahead 4kb of data. Type `hdparm-a/dev/hda` to list just this line.

✦ *geometry*—Displays information about the disk's geometry. From the output just shown, you can see that the hard disk has 4,865 cylinders, 255 tracks, and 63 sectors per tracks. The total number of addressable sectors is 78,165,360. The starting offset of the device is 0. Type `hdparm-g/dev/hda` to list just this line.

To display detailed identification information about your hard drive, you can use the `hdparm -i` command. The information displayed by `hdparm-i` was detected from the hard drive when you booted the computer. Here is an example:

```
# hdparm -i /dev/hda
/dev/hda:

Model=WDC WD400JB-00ENA0, FwRev=05.03E05, SerialNo=WD-WCAD13418938
Config={HardSect NotMFM HdSw>15uSec SpinMotCtl Fixed DTR>5Mbs FmtGapReq}
RawCHS=16383/16/63, TrkSize=57600, SectSize=600, ECCbytes=40
BuffType=DualPortCache, BuffSize=8192kB, MaxMultSect=16, MultSect=16
CurCHS=4047/16/255, CurSects=16511760, LBA=yes, LBAsects=78165360
IORDY=on/off, tPIO={min:120,w/IORDY:120}, tDMA={min:120,rec:120}
PIO modes:  pio0 pio1 pio2 pio3 pio4
DMA modes:  mdma0 mdma1 mdma2
UDMA modes: udma0 udma1 udma2 udma3 udma4 *udma5
AdvancedPM=no WriteCache=enabled
Drive conforms to: device does not report version:

 * signifies the current active mode
```

The model of this hard drive is a Western Digital WD400JB Caviar 40GB hard drive. If you ever need to contact technical support team about the drive, you can see the firmware revision (FwRev) and serial number (SerialNO) for the drive from this output. Because your settings can change after Linux starts running, you can see current hard drive settings using the `-I` option as follows:

```
# hdparm -I /dev/hda
/dev/hda:
ATA device, with non-removable media
  Model Number:       WDC WD400JB-00ENA0
```

```
   Serial Number:        WD-WCAD13418938☐
   Firmware Revision:    05.03E05
Standards:
   Supported: 5 4 3 2
   Likely used: 6
Configuration:
   Logical       max    current
   cylinders     16383  4047
   heads         16     16
   sectors/track 63     255
   --
   CHS current addressable sectors: 16511760
   LBA    user addressable sectors: 78165360
   device size with M = 1024*1024:      38166 MBytes
   device size with M = 1000*1000:      40020 MBytes (40 GB)
Capabilities:
   LBA, IORDY(can be disabled)
   bytes avail on r/w long: 40 Queue depth: 1
      .
      .
      .
```

The information just shown was obtained directly from the current drive. So if you have done **any disk tuning since the system booted, this output (rather than output from `-i`) should be used.** Near the end of this output is the `Commands/features` section. This section shows features that are supported by the drive. If the feature is supported, an asterisk appears in the `Enabled` column. Here's an example of the commands/features output from `hdparm -I` for a Western Digital WD800JB 80 GB hard drive:

```
Commands/features:
   Enabled Supported:
      *    READ BUFFER cmd
      *    WRITE BUFFER cmd
      *    Host Protected Area feature set
      *    Look-ahead
      *    Write cache
      *    Power Management feature set
           Security Mode feature set
      *    SMART feature set
      *    FLUSH CACHE EXT command
      *    Mandatory FLUSH CACHE command
      *    Device Configuration Overlay feature set
      *    48-bit Address feature set
           Automatic Acoustic Management feature set
           SET MAX security extension
      *    DOWNLOAD MICROCODE cmd
      *    SMART self-test
      *    SMART error logging
```

Many of the features described in the next section are listed in this section. As you turn these features on and off, you'll notice the asterisk in the Enabled column going on and off when you re-run `hdparm-I`.

Changing Hard Disk Settings

The hdparm utility is one of the key tools for setting parameters for tuning your hard disk. Before we talk about changing disk settings with hdparm, however, take a look at the first comment in the configuration file (/etc/sysconfig/harddisks) that comes with the hdparm utility:

```
WARNING!!!
The kernel will autodetect the correct settings for most
drives. Overriding these settings with hdparm can cause data
corruption and/or data loss.
```

I think it's a great idea to practice and learn about some of the more potentially destructive features of hdparm on a test computer—or at least on a computer before it is deployed in your business. With that said, however, there are times when you might want to override some conservative defaults to improve the performance of your hard disk.

This section describes some ways of using hdparm to check and tune your disks. It also describes ways of benchmarking your system to check whether the options have improved or affected your disk performance.

Benchmarking Your Changes

A common practice is to check the performance of your hard disk before and after you make changes to it. This gives you some idea of the effect of your changes. Common tools for testing your hard disk performance (as well as the general act of reading and writing data on your system) are the hdparm-Tt and time commands. I also describe the bonnie utility for testing performance, which is not part of Fedora or other Red Hat Linux distributions.

Timing Reads

Using hdparm, you can time cache reads (-T) and device reads (-t).

  ✦ *-T option*—This option essentially checks the how quickly data can be passed between the processor, memory, and disk cache.

  ✦ *-t option*—This option reads continuously from the hard disk without reading previously cached data. This gives an indication of the speed at which Linux can read sequential data from the disk.

Here's an example of hdparm-Tt:

```
# hdparm -Tt /dev/hda
/dev/hda:
Timing buffer-cache reads: 1476 MB in 2.00 seconds = 740.00 MB/sec
Timing buffered disk reads: 164 MB in 3.01 seconds = 35.18 MB/sec
```

The output just shown is from a Western Digital Caviar 80MB hard drive (WDC WD800JB). The first line of output shows the number of MB of data (1,476MB) that can be read from cache in about 2 seconds, without touching the hard disk at all. The second line shows the number of MB of data (164MB) that can be read from the hard disk directly in about 3 seconds.

By way of comparison, I ran the same command on a Quantum Bigfoot CY6480A 6GB hard drive:

```
# hdparm -Tt /dev/hda
/dev/hda:
Timing buffer-cache reads: 128 MB in 2.01 seconds = 63.56 MB/sec
Timing buffered disk reads: 20 MB in 3.31 seconds =  6.04 MB/sec
```

You can see that the reads are considerably slower from this circa 1996 hard drive (not a bad command to try if you are looking to buy a used computer).

Here are a few tips for benchmarking with `hdparm-Tt` to get the best results:

✦ Have as few processes as possible active when you do the benchmark. (You can run the `top` command to see active processes. Type P (which is the default) to sort by CPU usage. Then you can kill any very active processes that you don't need.)

Caution

Don't just randomly go killing processes, even processes that are consuming a lot of CPU time. A better idea might be to go into single-user mode, since that should provide you with a system with very little activity.

✦ Run it a few times, to be sure a momentary hiccup doesn't skew your results.

✦ Have some free memory available. (If you are using `top`, press M to sort by memory usage and kill any process that is not required to free some memory.)

Timing Writes

To test options that change how writing is done to a disk (such as write-caching), you can simply time a large write operation with the options on or off. Here is an example where I used the time command to see how long it would take to copy a large file (in this case, a 637MB iso image) from one partition to another:

```
# time cp severn-i386-disc1.iso /root
real    0m34.295s
user    0m0.110s
sys     0m7.860s
```

Note

Because the I/O speed depends to some extent on the location of the data on the platter, you will probably get different results from running the exact same command several times. By running it a few times, however, you can get an idea of the average amount of time the command takes.

The example just shown copies the iso image from the current directory to the /root directory. The time command shows that the operation took 34.295 seconds in real time. The user and sys lines show the amount of CPU time that was consumed by user-space calls and from kernel-space calls, respectively. Next, I turned off the write-caching feature (`hdparm -W0`), removed the iso file from /root, and ran the command again:

```
# time cp severn-i386-disc1.iso /root
real    1m59.077s
user    0m0.60s
sys     0m8.900s
```

You can see that the copy took about four times as long (1 minute, 59.077 seconds) to complete. So, if you are willing to risk possible data loss in case power goes out, you can see that the `time` command shows significant improvement in completing a large copy operation with write-caching on in this case. (Of course, if you are that worried about data loss due to power going out, you should get a UPS.)

Instead of a plain copy, you can use the `dd` command to take a bit more control over the writes you test. With `dd`, you can precisely specify the block size and the number of blocks being copied. Using /dev/zero as the input file, you can copy as many "\0" characters to the output file as you like. Here's an example:

```
# time dd if=/dev/zero of=/tmp/my-file bs=8k count=65536
65536+0  records in
65536+0  records out
real     1m7.649s
user     0m0.030s
sys      0m3.780s
```

This created a 513MB /tmp/my_file. I can adjust the blocksize from 8k or the count from 65536 to test the disk performance based on different amounts and sizes of data.

Checking Reads, Writes, and CPU with Bonnie

Bonnie is a nice tool for checking performance of your hard disk, CPU, and other components in ways that emulate how the system is actually used. Using bonnie, you can check the actual system calls that are being made by the kernel to different devices as well as library calls to the basic libc library. The following are the types of performance activities you can check with bonnie:

✦ *Programs that read and write single characters*—Bonnie can test writes of single characters (putc call) and (getc call) to hard disks. The potential bottleneck for these operations is the time it takes to make libc library calls on your computer.

✦ *Programs that read and write blocks of data*—Bonnie can test writes (write call) and reads (read call) of blocks of data. Because performance of these activities may reflect buffering (that is, data that is in memory but not being currently read or written to hard disk), you might want to add some options to insure that you are testing disk performance and not just buffering. With the -y option to bonnie, buffered data is synced to hard disk after each write.

✦ *Database applications*—Bonnie can test activities that are similar to the way applications access data in a database. The block in/out rewrite test that bonnie does interacts with data on a hard disk by reading some data, changing several bytes, writing the data back to disk, and rereading the data. This is a kind of overall test of how well your system might handle database access.

✦ *Busy system*—By requesting more data than the system can handle (using the lseek call), bonnie can emulate how an overloaded system will perform. This tests how fast the hardware is at randomly accessing data from the hard disk.

The Bonnie project (www.textuality.com/bonnie) contains descriptions of bonnie and links where you can get the software (it's not included in any Red Hat distribution). I found a SuSE RPM version at www.garloff.de/kurt/linux/bonnie, which had a few nice enhancements. You can build from the source RPM you get there or use the SuSE i386 binary (which seems to work fine on Fedora and other Red Hat systems). You can also get that package from rpmfind.net (until they change the release number) by typing the following (all on one line):

```
# wget rpmfind.net/linux/SuSE-Linux/i386/8.2/suse/i586/bonnie-1.4-
124.i586.rpm
```

It is a good idea to run bonnie with amount of data larger than the default (100MB by default). Likewise, for a better test of hard disk performance, adding the -y option will work the disk harder by syncing all writes to disk. I ran the following bonnie command with write-caching on (hdparm-W1/dev/hda) or you could drop -y if write-cashing is off:

```
# bonnie -s 300 -y
Bonnie 1.4: File './Bonnie.18177', size: 314572800, volumes: 1
Writing with putc()...        done: 20386 kB/s 89.0 %CPU
Rewriting...                  done: 15913 kB/s 25.1 %CPU
Writing intelligently...      done: 34819 kB/s 31.8 %CPU
Reading with getc()...        done: 20819 kB/s 95.6 %CPU
Reading intelligently...      done: 36583 kB/s 31.3 %CPU
Seeker 1...Seeker 2...Seeker 3...start 'em...done...done...done...
          ---Sequential Output (sync)----- ---Sequential Input- -Rnd Seek-
          -Per Char- --Block--- -Rewrite-- -Per Char- --Block--- -04k (03)
Machine MB K/sec %CPU K/sec %CPU K/sec %CPU K/sec %CPU K/sec %CPU /sec %CPU
toy 1* 300 20386 89.0 34819 31.8 15913 25.1 20819 95.6 36583 31.3 257.2 1.7
```

With the command just shown, 300MB of data (`-s 300`) is used for each operation and all writes are synced to disk (`-y`). Assuming a system with little or no extra activity, the CPU numbers above show cases where character-at-a-time writes (`putc`) and reads (`getc`) proceed about as fast as the processor can handle (89.0% and 95.6%, respectively). The hard disk, rather than the CPU, is the bottleneck for block writing and reading (31.8% and 31.3%, respectively), as well as rewriting (25.1%).

After that, I turned off write cache (`hdparm-W0/dev/hda`) and ran bonnie again.

```
# bonnie -s 300 -y
Bonnie 1.4: File './Bonnie.18151', size: 314572800, volumes: 1
Writing with putc()...        done: 5950 kB/s 26.0 %CPU
Rewriting...                  done: 5070 kB/s 8.0 %CPU
Writing intelligently...      done: 6179 kB/s 5.6 %CPU
Reading with getc()...        done: 20820 kB/s 96.0 %CPU
Reading intelligently...      done: 33795 kB/s 29.7 %CPU
Seeker 1...Seeker 2...Seeker 3...start 'em...done...done...done...
---Sequential Output (sync)----- ---Sequential Input- -Rnd Seek-
          -Per Char- --Block--- -Rewrite-- -Per Char- --Block--- -04k (03)
Machine MB K/sec %CPU K/sec %CPU K/sec %CPU K/sec %CPU K/sec %CPU /sec %CPU
toy 1* 300 5950 26.0 6179 5.6 5070 8.0 20820 96.0 33795 29.7 226.2 1.8
```

As you might guess, writing to disk in particular slowed down quite a lot. Writing operations were three to five times faster with write cache enabled. For more information on options to use with `bonnie`, see the bonnie man page or the bonnie README file (in `/usr/share/doc/packages/bonnie`).

Enabling Disk Write-Back and Read-Ahead Caches

You can improve overall write performance to disks by enabling disk write-back caches. Likewise, tuning the disk to do read-ahead caches can improve disk read performance when large amounts of sequential data are requested from the hard disk.

Turning on Write-Back Cache

With the write-back option on, a write operation can appear to be done after data is written to cache, but before it is actually moved to the hard disk. The driver can move on to get more data, and delays that come from slow seek times and disk revolutions can be made up over time.

Risks to enabling write-back caches include:

✦ *Power failures*—If someone kicks out the power cord or if there is a power surge, it is possible that data the driver has been told was written to hard disk is not yet written on the physical hard disk. This can lead to data corruption.

✦ *Data flushed out of order*—It's possible that a second data block can be flushed to disk before the first block arrives, which might also cause data corruption.

✦ *Data might become inconsistent*—In instances where data must always be consistent, write-back caching should be turned off. In RAID systems where write stripes can span multiple disks, it is more likely for inconsistencies to arise if write-back caching is on.

Most modern hard drives have write cashing enabled by default. In fact, in many cases, the driver will not let you disable it. However, with some older hard drives, you can risk data corruption by turning this feature on. In fact, the hdparm command labels this feature as DANGEROUS.

If this feature is not already on (and you have assessed the risk of data loss as acceptable), you can turn on write-caching using the following command:

```
# hdparm -W1 /dev/hda
/dev/hda:
 setting drive write-caching to 1 (on)
```

When I used the time command to time a large file copy (see the *Timing Writes* section), there was significant real-time improvements (about four times faster) with write-caching on (-W1).

Turning on Read-Ahead Cache

With the read-ahead cache option turned on (which is the case by default in most cases), the hard disk's driver will read ahead a specified amount of data with the assumption that the read action will need more data. If the feature is turned on, you should see the following near the end of hdparm -I output:

```
Commands/features:
   Enabled Supported:
     *     Look-ahead
```

You use the -A option to turn on (1) or off (0) the read-ahead feature. The following shows the feature being turned on:

```
# hdparm -A1 /dev/hda
/dev/hda:
 setting drive read-lookahead to 1 (on)
```

With read-ahead on, you can try different values to set how far ahead data should be read. You do that with the -a option. For example, to set the read-ahead value to eight sectors (4KB) you would type

```
# hdparm -a8 /dev/hda
/dev/hda:
 setting fs readahead to 8
 readahead    = 8 (on)
```

With a slow, older hard disk, it can help to have a higher read-ahead value (to a point). The following examples show how read performance differed when I changed the read-ahead values with my old Quantum Bigfoot hard drive (described earlier).

Note Notice that changing the read-ahead value doesn't have any impact on the buffer-cache test. That's because the buffer-cache reads test only gets data from cache and doesn't touch the hard disk.

The following shows read performance with read ahead turned off (-A0). I had similar results when I set read ahead to 8 (-a8).

```
# hdparm -a8 /dev/hda
# hdparm -Tt /dev/hda
/dev/hda:
 Timing buffer-cache reads:    128 MB in 2.00 seconds = 63.98 MB/sec
 Timing buffered disk reads:    10 MB in 3.60 seconds =  2.77 MB/sec
```

The next example shows how performance improved with read ahead set to 128 (I had similar results on setting it to 256):

```
# hdparm -a128 /dev/hda
# hdparm -Tt /dev/hda
/dev/hda:
 Timing buffer-cache reads: 128 MB in 2.01 seconds = 63.69 MB/sec
 Timing buffered disk reads: 22 MB in 3.24 seconds =  6.79 MB/sec
```

Setting read ahead to 64 resulted in improved performance, although not quite as much as setting it to 128 or 256:

```
# hdparm -a64 /dev/hda
# hdparm -Tt /dev/hda
/dev/hda:
 Timing buffer-cache reads:    128 MB in 2.01 seconds = 63.56 MB/sec
 Timing buffered disk reads:    20 MB in 3.25 seconds =  6.16 MB/sec
```

Turning on DMA

Hard disks typically support several different modes for transferring data. direct memory Access (DMA) is enabled on most hard disks today by default. In most cases, DMA will be turned on and the best possible DMA mode will be enabled. Older disks that don't operate in DMA mode can operate in the slower PIO mode. Here are descriptions of popular transfer modes for IDE/ATA hard disks:

✦ *Programmed I/O (PIO)*—This is a fairly safe transfer mode, but requires a lot of CPU overhead and results in slower data transfers. Available modes include pio0, pio1, pio2, pio3, and pio4.

✦ *Multiword DMA (MDMA)*—Multiword DMA allows the hard disk to communicate directly with system memory, bypassing the CPU. It does this using a feature called bus mastering, which lets the hard disk device control the PCI bus. Available modes include mdma0, mdma1, and mdma2.

✦ *Ultra DMA (UDMA)*—UDMA refers to certain DMA modes that operate at a much higher rate of speed than multiword DMA rates. Available UDMA modes include udma2 (ATA/33), udma4 (ATA/66), udma5 (ATA/100), and udma6 (ATA/133).

Caution   Use caution when you are changing DMA settings. Linux will let you switch to an un-supported DMA mode using `hdparm`, which could result in data corruption. Be sure to back up any important data before trying different DMA modes.

To enable UDMA, your computer's BIOS must support DMA and the I/O controller and the hard drive itself must be capable of UDMA transfers. For modes greater than udma2, your hard disk must be connected with a 40-pin, 80-conductor cable. The hard disk should report which DMA modes it supports. Here's an example of the portion of `hdparm-i` output that describes supported DMA modes:

```
#  hdparm -i /dev/hda
    .
    .
    .
PIO modes:   pio0 pio1 pio2 pio3 pio4
DMA modes:   mdma0 mdma1 mdma2
UDMA modes: udma0 udma1 udma2 udma3 udma4 *udma5
```

The asterisk next to udma5 shows that it is the mode that was activated during boot time. To see the current setting (in case you changed it), use the `hdparm -I` option. To turn on DMA mode, you can use the `hdparm-d` option and to switch DMA modes you use the `-X` option. For example, to turn on DMA and set the current mode to mdma2 for the first IDE hard disk, you could type the following:

```
#  hdparm -d1 -X34 /dev/hda
/dev/hda:
 setting using_dma to 1 (on)
 setting xfermode to 34 (multiword DMA mode2)
 using_dma        = 1 (on)
```

Table 9-1 shows the different `-X` values you could use to set different DMA and PIO modes.

Table 9-1: DMA and PIO Transfer Modes

Mode	Option to hdparm	Theoretical Maximum Transfer Rate
pio0	-X08	3.3MB per second
pio1	-X09	5.2MB per second
pio2	-X10	8.3MB per second
pio3	-X11	11.1MB per second
pio4	-X12	16.7MB per second
mdma0	-X32	4.2MB per second
mdma1	-X33	13.3MB per second
mdma0	-X34	16.6MB per second
udma0	-X64	16.7MB per second

Mode	Option to hdparm	Theoretical Maximum Transfer Rate
udma1	-X65	25MB per second
udma2	-X66	33.3MB per second
udma3	-X67	44.4MB per second
udma4	-X68	66.7MB per second
udma5	-X69	100MB per second

Again, most times Linux will probe the best available DMA settings for your hard drive and configure it correctly. You can change them as just described, however, if you feel that the settings were either too conservative or too aggressive. After you change these modes, try running some benchmarks described earlier to choose the mode that is working best.

Trying Other Disk Tuning Options

Here are a few other parameters you can tune with hdparm:

✦ *Block mode transfers*—Turn on multisector I/O mode (also called IDE Block Mode) to allow the driver to transfer more than one sector for each I/O interrupt. The -m0 option turns off this feature. A number other than zero sets the amount of data transferred in each interrupt to that number (-m2, -m4, -m8, or -m16). This is often set to 16 for 16 sector transfers. (See the MaxMultSect setting from the hdparm-i output to see the maximum number you can set multcount to.)

✦ Hard disks with smaller drive buffers may perform better with smaller sector counts. This includes some WD Caviar drives. The following is an example of this option being set to 16:

```
# hdparm -m16 /dev/hda
/dev/hda:
 setting multcount to 16
 multcount    = (on)
```

✦ *Keep settings over reset*—You got your disk tuned just the way you want it. So you want to preserve all your settings as long as your machine stays up. The problem is that once the drive is reset, your drive goes back to all the default options. To override that behavior, you can use the hdparm options -k1 (to preserve -dma options) or -K1 (to preserve -APSWXZ options).

Note

The -K1 option only preserves settings over a reset of the disk drive controller. To make the changes permanent across a computer reboot, see the *Making hdparm Changes Permanent* section.

✦ *Set options quietly*—When you set options in a configuration file or any other time that you don't want any output, you can add the -q option in front of each option. For example, hdparm-qd1-qX69/dev/hda will suppress output when turning on DMA support and udma5 mode.

Making hdparm Changes Permanent

Once you find hdparm settings you like, you can make them permanent in Fedora and other Red Hat Linux systems by adding them to the /etc/sysconfig/harddisks file. That way, the settings are used each time you boot your computer. You can set some options by simply uncommenting appropriate lines from the hard disk file. For example:

```
USE_DMA=1
MULTIPLE_IO=16
EIDE_32BIT=3
LOOKAHEAD=1
```

By uncommenting those lines (removing the "#" character) you can turn on DMA, enable I/O transfer in multiple sectors (16 as set here), enable 32-bit I/O support, and turn on the read-ahead feature, respectively. As an alternative, you can add hdparm parameters directly to the EXTRA_PARAMS line at the end of this file. For example:

```
EXTRA_PARAMS="-d1 -X67"
```

In this example, DMA is turned on (-d1) and the mode is set to udma3 (-X67).

Managing Power Settings for Laptops

Laptop computers need to be able to efficiently manage battery power to be effective tools. Besides settings used for manipulation in your laptop's BIOS, there are several utilities that come with Fedora Core and other Linux systems that can be used to monitor power use on your laptop and respond to power events that occur, such as:

✦ *Low battery power*—The computer can send warnings, display low-battery icons, or even suspend hardware activity.

✦ *Inactivity*—If there has been no activity on the computer for a set amount of time, you can extend battery life by spinning down disks and turning off services (such as audio and network services).

By detecting whether your laptop is running on AC power or battery, your computer can go into different levels of power savings for each of those states. Tools for managing and troubleshooting power problems on laptop computers in Fedora include:

✦ *Advanced Power Management (APM)*—The APM software in Fedora consists of the apmd daemon (which monitors battery use) and several utilities for displaying and reacting to battery activity. These features are contained in the apmd software package.

✦ *Advanced Configuration and Power Interface (ACPI)*—The acpid event daemon monitors power management events and allows you to set up rules to react to those events. Those rules can do things such as turn off hardware components or power down the system. ACPI is meant to replace APM power management with more generic tools. At the moment, however, ACPI has not yet lived up to its potential.

✦ *hdparm command*—The hdparm command can be used to turn power management features on and off. There are options to do things such as spin down your hard drive or put it in a standby state.

With ACPI, the operating system and not the BIOS is responsible for handling power management. Although ACPI will allow greater power and flexibility in managing power issues,

APM currently has more user-level features built around it. With ACPI, you currently have to tell it yourself what power events to look for and how to respond to those events.

Note   If you want to have a visual representation of your battery power on your GNOME desktop, you can add a Battery Charge Monitor applet to your panel. Right-click on the panel, select Add to Panel ➪ Utility ➪ Battery Charge Monitor. By default, the applet will change colors from green (charged) to yellow (40%), orange (25%), and red (15%) to show battery levels. Figure 9-2 shows the Battery Charge Monitor icon for a computer currently running on AC power.

Figure 9-2: Watch your battery charge from an icon in the GNOME panel.

Managing Power with APM

APM is configured in Fedora to detect certain power events and respond to them. It does this by running a daemon process (/usr/sbin/apmd) that listens for events, and in turn responds to those events, based on settings in a configuration file that comes with the service (/etc/sysconfig/apmd).

To configure APM to run (which it already may be, but it won't hurt to do it again), type the following:

```
# chkconfig apmd on
# service apmd restart
```

Note   Both apmd and acpid should not be trying to control power services at the same time. So, turn off the service you don't want by changing on and restart to off and stop for that service (you'd turn off acpid in this case).

If APM starts successfully, you should see messages in the /var/log/messages file that show the service starting and listing the current battery charge. By default, the apmd daemon runs based on settings in the /etc/sysconfig/apmd file. You can list the running process to see what options apmd is running by default:

```
# ps ax | grep apmd
/usr/sbin/apmd -p 10 -w 5 -W -P /etc/sysconfig/apm-scripts/apmscript
```

Based on these settings, here is how the apmd daemon behaves in Fedora Core:

✦ *Logs battery power changes*—If the battery power changes by 10% or more, a message is sent to the system log file (/var/log/messages by default). This based on the -p 10 option.

✦ *Logs low battery*—When the battery power falls below 5% and is not being charged, a warning message is sent to the system log file. This is based on the -w 5 option.

✦ *Warns users*—If battery power falls below the value set by the -w option, a warning message is sent to all users currently logged into the computer (using the wall command). This is based on the -W option.

✦ *Uses apmscript to respond to events*—When power events occur, apmd forwards those events to a script that is set up to respond to those events. As shown in the command line above, the script that is run is the /etc/sysconfig/apm-scripts/apmscript shell script (based on that file being used as an option to -P).

Besides the low-battery and power change settings just described, most of the responses to power events are handled within the apmscript file just mentioned. I recommend you review the contents of that file if you are interested in seeing what power management is being done on your computer.

If you want to add your own responses to power events in Fedora Core, you can create your own script. By default, the existing apmscript points to the file /etc/sysconfig/apm-scripts/apmcontinue. The apmscript file currently handles the following events:

✦ *suspend*—If your computer goes into a suspend or standby state, the apmscript file stops all sound programs, suspends operation of all hard drives, stops any NFS connections, shuts down network connections, and turns off pcmcia card services.

✦ *resume*—In resume state, apmscript tries to restore everything that was stopped during the suspend actions.

✦ *change power*—If the power source changes, the script changes the laptop to operate with better performance on AC power and more efficient battery use if the laptop is running off the battery.

✦ *change battery*—If the power of battery is low, this event gives apm the opportunity to stop services and go into an extreme powersaving mode.

✦ *start*—When the computer starts up, apmscript doesn't do anything special except checking whether you have any events you entered yourself to be run at startup in the apmcontinue file.

✦ *stop*—Likewise, when the computer shuts down, apmscript just checks whether you have any events you entered yourself to be run at shutdown time in the apmcontinue file.

All other events are directed to the apmcontinue file (which doesn't exist by default), giving you the opportunity to respond to those events any way you choose. Here you have the option to create a /etc/sysconfig/apm-scripts/apmcontinue script that can be set up to respond to events in the same way as the apmscript file does.

If you want to just poke around or make any real-time changes to your APM service, you can use the apm command. With no options, the apm command reports whether power is plugged in and the status of your battery charging:

```
# apm
AC on-line, battery charging: 100%
```

You can also put your laptop in suspend mode (apm-s) or standby mode (apm-S). If you are running on AC power, you can tell the laptop to ignore any suspend and standby events generated by APM (apm-i).

Managing Power with ACPI

Like APM, ACPI operates by having a daemon listen for power events, and then pass those events to a program that can respond to them. In this case, the `acpid` daemon runs by starting the acpid service as follows:

```
# chkconfig acpid on
# service acpid restart
```

Note   Again, remember to turn off the power management service you don't want. In this case, turn off apmd (`chkconfig apmd off` **and** `service apmd stop`).

ACPI will only work on Linux systems that have ACPI enabled in the kernel. You may have to enable ACPI by force by adding `ACPI=force` as a boot option. You also need to enable ACPI in the BIOS. If ACPI is working, you should see a `/proc/acpi/event` file that contains ACPI events.

The `acpid` daemon monitors each event it receives from `/proc/acpi/events` and tries to match it against entries in files in the `/etc/acpi/events` directory. By default, only one file exists: `sample.conf`. The contents of that file show a simple form of an ACPI event and action:

```
# This is a sample ACPID configuration
event=button/power.*
action=/sbin/shutdown -h now
```

In this example, when a `button/power.*` event is received, the `shutdown` command is run immediately (`-h now`). To configure your own actions to ACPI events, you can add your own files (owned by the root user) to the `/etc/acpi/events` directory that contains entries in the same format. (Type `man acpid` to see the exact format of these configuration files.) When the event you listed occurs, any command you listed on the `action=` line is run as root user.

To find the names of events, type `cat/proc/acpi/event`. To track acpid activities, you should view the contents of the `/var/log/acpid` file. Try changing power states a few times (unplug, plug in again, press suspend, and so on) and see how each of these events are logged into the log file.

Changing Power Settings with hdparm

If you are using a laptop computer, there are options to `hdparm` you can use to control power consumption. Some of these options allow you to take immediate actions (such as putting a hard drive into sleep mode), while others set actions to occur after a certain period of time (such as spinning down the hard disk after a period of inactivity).

To see the IDE power mode status for your computer, type:

```
# hdparm -C /dev/hda
/dev/hda:
drive state is: active/idle
```

This shows the power mode set for normal operation. If the drive doesn't support this feature, the drive state is listed as unknown.

One of the most widely used ways of gaining power savings is to set the spindown mode (`-S`) to a low value. Some believe that even the minimum of a spindown after 5 seconds of idle time can improve overall battery life without drastically affecting performance. Spindown is set in 5-second increments using the -S option of hdparm and you can set the value from 0 (off) to 240 (20 minutes). So, for example, the following value of 3 tells the disk drive to go into standby mode (spindown) after 15 seconds:

```
# hdparm -S3 /dev/hda
/dev/hda:
setting standby to 3 (15 seconds)
```

Note

You can also set the disk to spindown at increments higher than 20 minutes. Values of -S from 241 to 251 each signify 30-minute increments, so 241 sets the spindown value to 30 minutes, while 251 sets it to 5.5 hours.

You can send a hard disk immediately into standby mode using the -y option as follows:

```
# hdparm -y /dev/hda
/dev/hda:
issuing standby command
```

Alternatively, you can enter sleep mode (the lowest power mode) using the -Y option:

```
# hdparm -Y /dev/hda
/dev/hda:
issuing sleep command
```

The next time the hard drive is needed, Linux will automatically reset to start the disk drive again.

Disk, File System, and Power Troubleshooting References

Table 9-2 provides some references for troubleshooting your hard disks, file systems, and power management features.

Table 9-2: Troubleshooting References

File System Troubleshooting

NTFS File system in LInux	http://linux-ntfs.sourceforge.net/rpm/index.html
File systems HOWTO	www.tldp.org/HOWTO/FIlesystems-HOWTO.html
The Software-RAID HOWTO	www.tldp.org/HOWTO/Software-RAID-HOWTO.html
Linux System Administrator's Guide, Chapter 6. Using Disks and Other Storage Media	www.tldp.org/LDP/sag/html/c973.html
Large Disk HOWTO	www.tldp.org/HOWTO/Large-Disk-HOWTO.html
Linux Partition HOWTO	www.tldp.org/HOWTO/Partition/index.html

Table 9-2: *(continued)*

Disk Performance Troubleshooting

Benchmarking disk I/O (bonnie)	`www.tux.org/bench/Disk-IO/bonnie.tar.gz`
PC Guide to Hard Disk Drives	`www.pcguide.com/ref/hdd` (Hard drive general reference)

Power Management Troubleshooting

Advanced Configuration and Power Interface (ACPI) HOWTO	`www.tldp.org/HOWTO/ACPI-HOWTO/`
ACPI Specifications	`www.acpi.info`
ACPI Project	Home page: `http://acpi.sourceforge.net` Documentation: `http://acpi.sourceforge.net/documentation` Mailing list: `http://lists.sourceforge.net/lists/listinfo/acpi-devel`
TuxMobil: Power Management with Linux	`http://tuxmobil.org/apm_linux.html` Good overview of Linux power management. The whole site is a great general resource for Linux laptop computers, including information on power management issues.

Summary

In the past few years, the ability of Linux to detect and configure hard disks has greatly improved. In most cases, you don't have to do anything to have Linux properly probe your hard disk during installation, choose good settings (transfer rates, read/write-caching, and so on), and even select and create usable partitioning.

However, if something goes wrong with your disk or file systems, it's nice to be able to understand what is going on and possibly even fix up a few things. Using tools such as hdparm, you can tune your hard disk behavior. With utilities such as fdisk and mkfs, you can create and modify your own partitions and file systems. With a little bit of care (and, hopefully, the security of good data backups), you can tune your disks and file systems to peak efficiency.

✦   ✦   ✦

Troubleshooting the Network

Detecting and Responding to Intrusions

In years past, the term *intrusion detection* had a general meaning: the methods by which an administrator learned about system intrusions, or about attempts to intrude, on a given system. As in most technological areas, intrusion detection has evolved and specialized. The security industry has grown to include a number of disciplines and subspecialties, each with its own cadre of professionals.

Why worry about intrusion detection if you have a good firewall? Just remember: no lock is unpickable. Firewalls have holes so that services can run (web, mail, and so on). Where there's a hole, there's a way. Furthermore, most security experts will tell you that security is not a destination, but a journey. Even if you have outstanding security policies in place, rock-hard firewalls, and a completely trustworthy user and administrator base, you still need to watch your system like a hawk to make sure that everything remains safe.

In this chapter, we explain the basic concepts of intrusion detection and response. We also show you how to use common Linux tools and shell scripts to maintain the security of your system, keep a watchful (and automated) eye on your system, and offer some solutions to common intrusion detection problems.

Intrusion Detection and Response: An Overview

Modern intrusion detection covers a wide range of systems, functions, and tools. Some of these tools simply detect, log, or report intrusion attempts. Others respond to such attempts proactively. It's easiest to understand security as a multilayered issue. Firewalls and *network intrusion detection systems* (NIDS) make up the outer shells of a comprehensive security solution. In this chapter, we take a host-centric view of security, and thus view these external forms of intrusion detection as the outer layer of defense.

Once past these outer layers, you'll find other security tools for the inner layers. These host-level ID tools, or HIDS, monitor local user, file, and log activity. Some HIDS are host-network-based, but many are not

network-based at all. These programs watch for signs of user escalation violations, deviations of regular activity from baseline comparisons, and log or file monitoring, among other functions.

Network-based intrusion detection tools watch for attack precursors (scans), attempts, and related network signatures. Generally, these tools are referred to as *intrusion detection systems*, or IDS. There are many subcategories of IDS, such as *network-node-based IDS* (NNIDS) and *network-based IDS* (NIDS), as well as *host-based IDS* (HIDS). In addition to these, you'll also find passive and reactive xIDS systems. Reactive systems can be tied into firewalls and are called *intrusion prevention systems*, or IPS. Learn more about these security tools at www.securityfocus.com/infocus/1733.

Even though it's common to think that the greatest threat to a system is external, remember that valid local user accounts should also be considered untrusted or potentially hostile. System attacks that succeed usually install a *rootkit* of some sort, software that compromises your system and leaves a *back door* daemon installed and running. Thus, to add to your layers of security, you should also consider local file-system-level forms of intrusion detection in the form of *file alteration* and *system baseline scan* comparisons, as well as system to watch for signs of *trojans*, *worms*, and new, related cracking tools. These defense tools can include both native and third-party tools or suites. Examples of these would include cracking and rootkit detection tools, automated systems that keep an eye on local user access, accounts, user and system files, and common security auditing tools (which can be maliciously used to serve the cracker's needs).

This chapter is, by necessity, a mere introduction to the basics of host-based intrusion detection for Linux systems. We show you the basics of *file alteration monitoring*, a useful aspect of host-based intrusion detection, as well as offer pointers to other tools that may be useful in your installation. However, if you are responsible for security, take advantage of the many other books and resources on these topics. Don't take our word for it—do your own homework. You'll find a list of references and resources at the end of this chapter.

Intrusion Detection Tools

Many Linux distributions include stock operating system tools that make file alteration monitoring easy and reliable if properly configured. In this section, we introduce some security functionality built into Red Hat and Fedora Core Linux, as well as additional common file alteration monitoring tools that you can download and install. If you want to purchase a commercial alternative, you can certainly do so; however, equally effective tools are available at no charge and as part of your regular installation. There's no excuse. Additionally, home-brewed security tools are sometimes seen as *more secure* than commercial OTS (of the shelf) solutions, as there is no known program for the intruder or his tools to detect as *being installed*.

Red Hat Package Manager

You probably think of RPM, or the Red Hat Package Manager, as an easy way to install and track software packages. Did you know that it also tracks individual file size, stock permission, user, group, and time settings, and even each file's MD5sum, or personal "fingerprint"? Using all this install-time information, you can check for all sorts of changes on your system. As you will see, all this information makes RPM an effective security tool in and of itself.

With RPM, you can are able to track every file on your system that was installed via RPM. With a bit of creative scripting and automation, you can even use RPM to watch all your files for changes over time. This is called *file alteration* or *file integrity monitoring*, and it is a critical aspect of host-based intrusion detection. Such monitoring shows you local intrusions in a way that network-based tools can't.

Learn more about RPM's file attribute tracking capabilities by issuing the command man rpm. Search down to the QUERY OPTIONS section, as well as the mnemonic keyword for much more detail on RPM *file alteration* tracking.

File System Tools

You can use other native Linux file system tools to detect cracker presence on your system. After a successful break-in, crackers like to use the command-line tool chattr (change attribute) to lock in their cracked changes at the ext2/3 file system level. However, you can use the counterpart of this tool, lsattr (list attribute), to sniff out the infiltrators and detect files that they have replaced and locked.

If you're using the Debian Linux distribution, consider using the debsums program. Just like RPM on Red Hat or SuSE Linux, debsums tracks MD5sums and other file attributes. Not all Debian packages use debsums yet, but an increasing number are being released with this capability.

An MD5sum or *digest* is a mathematical *checksum*, or "fingerprint," that can be generated for any given file. One way of creating an MD5sum is with the md5sum command-line tool. When the md5sum command is run against a file, it reads in the entire file and generates a 32-hexadecimal character label that is statistically unique to that file. If even one bit of data in the file changes, the MD5sum will be completely different the next time the digest is generated. This is a robust method for tracking the validity of files on your system, and is used in most commercial grade file alteration suites.

Watching Your System

Other basic Linux tools can help you keep an eye on your system and let you know what's going on, whether through e-mail or in real time. If you prefer to get regularly scheduled information through e-mail, consider logwatch. This program scans the various log files on your machine and sends a daily report (usually depending on log rotation frequency) of important system activity, ranging from e-mail access attempts to SSH login attempts on your system.

The logwatch automated monitoring service is configured by default on Red-Hat- and Fedora-Core-based systems. Do a man logwatch or locate logwatch on other systems to see if you have it installed and configured.

If you'd rather get your information in real time from the console, consider the Red Hat System Logs tool. To run this program, issue the following command.

```
redhat-logviewer
```

The tool will open, as shown in Figure 10-1. You can use the System Logs tool to look through the various log files, filter them for keywords, or even scan installed RPM packages to quickly see what version of a given package or packages you have installed.

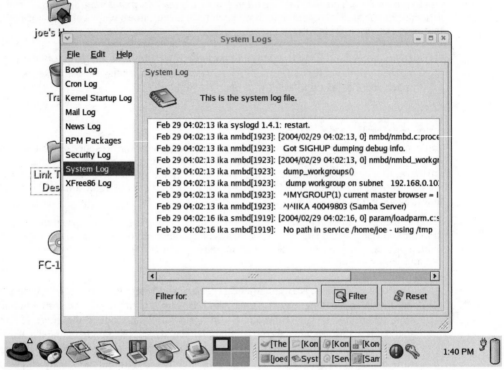

Figure 10-1: The Red Hat System Logs tool simplifies log file monitoring.

On non-Red-Hat-based systems, the various log files are usually located in /var/log/, and these files can each be parsed or searched with your favorite tools for any of the information discussed above.

Third-Party Tools

If you're ready to move beyond the basic tools included with your Linux distribution, check out some of the third-party software solutions. There are a number of excellent IDS and host-based security suites for Linux, most of which are open source, and are free. Just because they aren't installed shouldn't keep you from giving them a try.

One of the most popular and powerful IDS for Linux is Snort. This tool does real-time traffic analysis and packet logging, as well as full-blown intrusion detection. It can detect a wide range of attack, probe, or scan types. Snort can even identify buffer overflows, port scans, CGI attacks, SMB probes, OS fingerprint attempts, and stays current with all the latest signatures that the cracker community is using. Once Snort notices an intrusion attempt, it can log the attack, fire off a script, or spawn another program to rebuff it.

Tip   Learn more about Snort at `www.snort.org/about.html`.

If you need to monitor kernel system calls, check out SNARE. It's a client application and kernel module combination, which work together to set up a monitoring tool that's truly operating system-wide. Any time a system call is made, whether for a simple file permission change or a file deletion, SNARE will log the information. Note that if you're installing SNARE on a Red-Hat-based machine, you'll probably need to recompile the kernel.

Tip   Find more information on SNARE at `http://snare.sourceforge.net`.

Finally, many Linux administrators rely on Portsentry. This is a small package that can be easily integrated into your iptables- or netfilter-based firewall. Portsentry is a port scan detector and blocking tool, and does a great job of identifying would-be crackers who are rattling your doors and windows for vulnerable services. Even though it's small, it's very responsive and a critical defense mechanism to many high profile Internet sites.

Tip   Portsentry is distributed as part of the sentrytools package, found at `http://sourceforge.net/projects/sentrytools/`.

Verifying Your Files with RPM

In order for any file alteration tracking method to work, you must have a baseline snapshot of your system so that you can compare the potentially compromised files to the intact versions. In this section, we show you how to do host-based file integrity checks with RPM. Later in this chapter, we'll show you how to use it to create a system-wide security baseline, and how to automate file alteration scanning, using RPM so that it becomes a regular part of your security routine.

Note   If you want to use RPM's file alteration tracking capabilities as part of a truly secure installation, you should consider moving your system's RPM database and some basic system tools off the hard drive and onto write-protected removable media. These tools include many of the programs in `/bin`, `/sbin`, `/lib`, and `/var/lib/rpm`, as well as RPM's binaries and some statically compiled tools like `/sbin/sash` or `/bin/ash.static`. The truly savvy cracker might be able to compromise RPM itself, making it meaningless as a security tool.

Using RPM for Maintenance

RPM is much like a scientific calculator. While it's got a huge array of functions and features, most people just use it to manage packages and installations, just like most people use scientific calculators to figure percentages and do long division. However, if you poke around RPM a bit, you'll find a number of ways to simplify package maintenance, track files and package versioning, and even utilize methods for bolstering system security.

You probably already use RPM for basic package management. For example, you can use the query mode to track package versions, with the following command

```
# rpm -q sendmail
sendmail-8.12.10-1.1.1
```

RPM will show you all the packages on your system that have a given string in their name.

```
# rpm -qa | grep mail
mailx-8.1.1-31.1
fetchmail-6.2.0-8
sendmail-cf-8.12.10-1.1.1
mailman-2.1.2-2
mailcap-2.1.14-1.1
sendmail-8.12.10-1.1.1
sendmail-doc-8.12.10-1.1.1
redhat-switch-mail-0.5.21-1
mozilla-mail-1.4.1-18
squirrelmail-1.4.0-1
procmail-3.22-11
```

You can even use RPM to figure out what package a deleted or missing file belonged to, so that you can reinstall or repair the damage.

```
# rm /bin/ping
rm: remove regular file '/bin/ping'?  Y
# ping localhost
-bash: ping: command not found
# rpm -qf /bin/ping
iputils-20020927-9.1
```

By querying the RPM system for the missing file (with -qf), you can see what package the file belonged to, and which package would need to be reinstalled to fix the system. Assuming that you have already downloaded the package to be installed, here's how to use RPM to upgrade (reinstall), verbosely (with hashes), the package iputils.

```
# rpm -Uvh iputils-20020927-9.1.i386.rpm
Preparing...                ########################### [100%]
        package iputils-20020927-9.1 is already installed
```

Because the system thinks that the package is already installed, you may need to force it to reinstall (we'll also do the install from a remote copy of the package located on an FTP server).

```
# rpm -Uvh --force ftp://example.com/pub/RPMS/iputils-20020927-
  9.1.i386.rpm
Retrieving ftp://example.com/pub/RPMS/iputils-20020927-
9.1.i386.rpm
Preparing...    ################################# [100%]
   1:iputils    ################################# [100%]
```

The problem should be fixed. Use the following command to check it.

```
#  ping -c 1 localhost
PING localhost.localdomain (127.0.0.1) 56(84) bytes of data.
64 bytes from localhost.localdomain (127.0.0.1): icmp_seq=0
 ttl=64 time=0.113 ms
```

```
--- localhost.localdomain ping statistics ---
1 packets transmitted, 1 received, 0% packet loss, time 0ms
rtt min/avg/max/mdev = 0.113/0.113/0.113/0.000 ms, pipe 2
```

The example shows the usefulness of this functionality; however, most newer administrators never even use RPM to *this* level. If this basic functionality is surprising to you, just think about how much else you're missing out on.

How can you use RPM to track changes to critical system files? Let's revisit the example just shown.

```
# rm /bin/ping
rm: remove regular file '/bin/ping'?  Y
# rpm -V iputils
missing    /bin/ping
```

Here, we've used the --V switch, for *verify*. This option tells RPM to go through a listing of all of the files that were originally installed by the package being referenced, and compare all the file attributes (size, date, MD5sum, and so on) to those that now exist. Any differences are listed. If nothing is output from the command, then nothing has changed since the package install time.

This verify option can also be used against all packages installed on the system (and all their files), to see what files are missing or changed.

```
# rpm -Va | grep missing
missing    /usr/src/linux-2.4.22-1.2129.nptl/arch/i386/math-emu/.depend
missing    /bin/ping
```

RPM compares the existing file listings to the RPM database of files that were installed and should be present. Anything that's different is listed. In the example, we're missing a file called .depend, as well as our deleted ping.

Note   Always send the output of such RPM verifies into grep to filter it down. Otherwise, the output will flood your console, since many files on the system get modified in one way or another after they're installed (for example, config files, user files, logs, and the like). You usually want to use grep like this to return only the things that you're interested in.

The RPM database is rebuilt each time a new package is installed. Every database entry contains a list of the files that should be included in each package and what these files should look like. Very useful.

Caution   Using the -V or verify option is disk—and processor—intensive. Only run this command on a machine under light load, or run it during nonprime times. For example, the rpm -Va | grep missing command shown above took nearly 15 minutes to run on a 1.6 GHz system, and drove the system load over 1.2 at times. This is not a tool for the heavily used production system.

Using RPM to Check Security

Yes, knowing whether a file is missing is helpful. What if a file still exists, but has changed? If a cracker has gotten into your system and replaced a critical system file with a version that includes a *trojan* or *back door* in place, you need to know about it. Use the verify all option again, but this time, limit the output to files that have the string bin/ in their path, like this.

```
# rpm -Va | grep 'bin\/'
.M......  /usr/bin/smbmnt
S.5....T  /bin/netstat
S.5....T  /bin/ls
S.5....T  /usr/bin/passwd
missing   /bin/ping
S.?....T  /bin/login
S.5....T  /bin/ps
```

This output shows that someone has modified several of the system files with `bin/` in their path. The 5 mnemonic indicates that the MD5sum, or fingerprint, of the file has changed. A question mark shows that RPM could not calculate the MD5sum of the file for some reason. If you have one or more critical system files with a modified fingerprint, it's likely that you've been cracked.

Tip   Commonly attacked files on Linux systems to watch out for include `/bin/ls`, `/usr/bin/passwd`, `/bin/login`, `/bin/netstat`, `/bin/ps.`, `/sbin/ifconfig`, and `/usr/bin/chattr`, just to name a few.

Caution   Once a system has been compromised, you can no longer trust anything, not even unmodified files. The only solution is to get the system off-line, get all nonexecutable content off the system, and reformat and reinstall fresh.

RPM stores a number of attributes about every file on the system for which it's responsible. These attributes are represented by the following mnemonics:

✦ S: File size

✦ M: Modes (includes permissions and file type)

✦ 5: MD5sum

✦ D: Device major/minor numbers

✦ L: readLink(2) paths

✦ U: User ownership

✦ G: Group ownership

✦ T: Timestamp

You can use RPM to check for differences between the install time and the existing file system using any of these attributes.

Caution   If you're going to use RPM as a security tool, commit to it. Avoid mixing RPM package management with other forms, such as `pkg`, `tarball`, source code files, or converted Debian packages. Everything needs to be installed through RPM so that you can count on the RPM database when you need accurate information.

Once you've checked the existing files against the RPM's MD5sum information in it's database, you may need to look at the files a bit more closely. A compromised system sometimes includes other tracks or evidence. Collecting such information is referred to as *intrusion forensics*.

Other evidence you may detect on a compromised system may include special file attributes that shouldn't be on a normal Linux system, hidden within the ext2 and ext3 file system itself. One of these of these cracker-utilized file system attributes is the immutable control bit. On a compromised system, you might see settings in the /bin directory, from the output of the *list attribute* or lsattr command, that look like this.

```
# lsattr/bin/* /sbin/* /usr/bin/* /usr/sbin/*| grep "i--"
----i-------- /bin/login
----i-------- /bin/netstat
----i-------- /bin/ps
----i-------- /sbin/insmod
----i-------- /sbin/kallsyms
----i-------- /sbin/ksyms
----i-------- /sbin/lsmod
----i-------- /sbin/modprobe
----i-------- /sbin/rmmod
----i-------- /usr/sbin/sshd
```

Unless you've set these files to be immutable yourself, this is another good indicator that your system has been cracked. These immutable bits keep even the root user from deleting, moving, changing, or even reinstalling the files. The ultimate fix, as previously mentioned, is a complete reinstall. However, the way in which you "un-set" these bits is with the chattr command, like this.

```
# chattr -i /bin/login
# lsattr /bin/login
------------- /bin/login
```

Now this file, at least, appears to be back to normal. Just remember, we really can't trust our own eyes on this system as even the kernel could be faking us out and we would never know it. This type of fix is really more of a band-aid to give you a stopgap measure on a production system (to get it as patched up as you can) until you can migrate all the content off and reformat the system.

Creating a Security Baseline

In order to get useful information about your system, you need to compare the existing reality against a known standard, or baseline. While the RPM database has a recording of all packages as they were when installed, many things get modified by administrators and users after that point. It's important to get a production system up and running (but not yet live), and create a secure operational baseline against which you can regularly measure against as a security check. It is best to create this baseline as soon as you get your operating system installed, configured, and ready to go online. Be sure to make the baseline before you connect this machine to the Internet. It's no good to baseline a machine that's already compromised.

Making an RPM Baseline

In this section, we show you how to create a system baseline with RPM. We'll store the baseline in a directory called /root/stuff/—don't call it anything obvious like /root/security/original.baseline unless you *want* the crackers to find it. The first step is to build an RPM change-snapshot of the system (what's been changed since install time—MD5sum differences), and store that in a baseline file.

```
# rpm -Va | grep ^..[5?]'>/root/stuff/RPMV_$(date +%Y-%m-%d)
```

This command invokes a full system verify, producing a list of files that have the MD5sum state of 5 (changed), or ? (unknown/cannot check), and saves it to the filename with a date stamp in the name. In about 15 minutes on a reasonably fast machine, you should have a file with a name similar to RPMV_2004-01-30. The contents of the file will look like this.

```
S.5....T c /etc/pam.d/system-auth
S.5....T c /etc/ldap.conf
S.5..... c /etc/rndc.key
S.5....T c /etc/sysconfig/named
S.5....T c /etc/xinetd.d/ktalk
S.5....T c /etc/ssh/sshd_config
S.5....T c /etc/yum.conf
S.5....T c /etc/sysconfig/redhat-config-securitylevel
S.5....T c /etc/xinetd.d/telnet
S.5....T c /etc/xinetd.d/amanda
S.5....T c /etc/krb.conf
S.5....T c /etc/sysconfig/pcmcia
S.5....T c /etc/auto.master
S.5....T c /etc/aliases
S.5....T c /etc/mail/sendmail.cf
S.5....T c /etc/mail/sendmail.mc
S.5....T c /etc/mail/statistics
SM5....T c /etc/mail/submit.cf
S.5....T c /etc/httpd/conf/httpd.conf
```

All these files have changed since the time they were first installed and their original MD5sum fingerprint was recorded. Note that these are mostly configuration files (the lower case c next to the T); if you're making the baseline as part of the installation process, it's obvious that you probably changed these things yourself. This file is now the template against which you will run the diff command to check system file integrity in the future.

Note If you're storing other security tools on write-protected media like a floppy disk, this file should probably go there as well. However, later in this chapter we show you how to store baseline files on a special hidden area of the system.

Next, append this single line to the end of the RPMV file you just created.

```
----TESTING bin/ for MD5SUM Changes, Nothing ^ ^ Above^ ^  Means System Is
Secure----
```

This line is used as a trigger during the diff comparison of the baseline and the daily scan. It will prove that the daily scan is working. If anything shows up in the daily report displayed above this line, then you know you've got some type of suspicious change on your system to check out further. Now that we have a baseline file established, let's turn to another tool. We'll come back to RPM in a minute.

Adding chkrootkit Scans

It's a good idea to get multiple sources of input when you're scanning your system for signs of intrusion. The chkrootkit package is an excellent addition to RPM baseline comparison checks. This intrusion detection tool is a set of automated reporting programs run through a single shell script that can be updated with the latest rootkit signatures to detect all the latest cracker exploits. Think of it as a "cracker virus scanner."

Tip　Obviously, if a cracker sees chkrootkit on your system, he'll probably delete it. From this point on, we begin to hide security tools in a secret spot on the disk, where crackers are unlikely or unable to look.

First, download the latest version of the program (this link is from www.chkrootkit.org).

```
# wget ftp://ftp.pangeia.com.br/pub/seg/pac/chkrootkit.tar.gz
```

Untar it:

```
# tar xzvf chkrootkit.tar.gz ; /bin/rm chkrootkit.tar.gz
```

Then, compile it.

```
# cd chkrootkit-0.43/
# make sense
gcc -DHAVE_LASTLOG_H -o chklastlog chklastlog.c
gcc -DHAVE_LASTLOG_H -o chkwtmp chkwtmp.c
gcc -DHAVE_LASTLOG_H -o ifpromisc ifpromisc.c
gcc -o chkproc chkproc.c
gcc -o chkdirs chkdirs.c
gcc -o check_wtmpx check_wtmpx.c
gcc -static -o strings-static strings.c
#
```

Now it's time to create the hiding place. These next commands make a *soft partition* of 150MB. You can think of a soft partition as a "floppy image file," used to store data without a hard location on the drive.

```
Use the dd command to create the boundaries of the soft partition:# dd
 if=/dev/zero of=/home/bob/Desktop/chk-file bs=150M count=1
```

Then, format the partition.

```
# mke2fs /home/bob/Desktop/chk-file
mke2fs 1.34 (25-Jul-2003)
/home/bob/Desktop/chk-file is not a block special device.
Proceed anyway? (y,n) y
Filesystem label=
OS type: Linux
Block size=1024 (log=0)
Fragment size=1024 (log=0)
...
```

Make a mount point for the new *soft* partition and mount it as a loop device file system.

```
# mkdir /mnt/tmp
# mount -o loop /home/bob/Desktop/chk-file /mnt/floppy/
```

See what we just created?

```
# df -h
Filesystem                    Size Used Avail Use% Mounted on
/dev/hda3                     18G 7.5G 9.5G  44% /
/dev/hda2                     99M 12M   83M  13% /boot
none                          109M 0    109M  0% /dev/shm
/home/bob/Desktop/chk-file    146M 1.2M 137M  1% /mnt/tmp
```

Now you can hide the chkrootkit scanning tool in the new partition.

```
# cd ..
# mv chkrootkit-0.43/ /mnt/tmp/
# ls -la /mnt/tmp/
total 12
drwxr-xr-x   3 root   root   4096 Feb 29 22:59 .
drwxr-xr-x   8 root   root   4096 Feb 29 22:58 ..
drwxr-xr-x   2 1000   1000   4096 Feb 29 22:52 chkrootkit-0.43
```

This should work just fine. To be sure, test it.

```
#   cd /mnt/tmp/chkrootkit-0.43/
#   ./chkrootkit | grep INFECTED
#
```

Just as planned. If the scan had found evidence of some back door or cracker rootkit on your box, you would have seen an `INFECTED` flag pop up from that last command. Go ahead and try running it without the `grep` filter to see what the output normally looks like, and what files on your system get scanned.

Now we have a second cool scanning tool that we can bring up (by mounting its soft partition on the fly), quickly scan the system with for cracker tools or signs of intrusion, and then unmount again when done. By hiding the program in the soft partition, we can't see it by stupid script kiddie scripts. Leave the soft partition mounted for now, because we're going to develop and hide our RPM baseline comparison scanner system in that soft partition file as well.

Note   Write-protected removable media is still the best thing to use for this type of project. Something like a floppy, USB flash disk, or the like will give you better security even still. The former is probably more common; the latter probably better overall. Some added level of physical security and assurance can also be found by bringing a USB bus to the inside of your server case (via either motherboard USB connectors or USB card), and just leaving the solid-state flash disk permanently hooked up inside the locked server's case. This would ensure that your new intrusion detection tool kit isn't tampered with, removed, or stolen.

Automating System Scanning and Notification

At this point, you've created some basic security tools and built a secret place to store them. Now, you need to bring it all together and build a single coherent system-scanning mechanism customized for your machine. This mechanism should be automated so that you get the results of a daily check-up without having to remember to run it. In this section, we build a script that will tie all these host-based intrusion detection elements together.

As you begin to build your scanning tool, you need to decide how you want your system to be monitored. In general, we recommend the following daily tasks:

+ Run an RPM verify and compare it against the RPM baseline you created

+ Scan for ext2/3 immutable attribute file settings (created with `chattr +i`), using the `lsattr` program

+ Run `chkrootkit` to see if any known tools have compromised your system

+ Scan system logs for unusual entries

+ Have the program place the output of all these operations into a file for daily system-scan results, and e-mail this scan summary to you

With these actions, all system scans are output into a single location. You can then set it up so that the results are e-mailed to you daily. If there's a problem, chances are that you'll detect it with one of these tools. In the worst case, you won't get your daily report, indicating that the crack has sufficiently crippled the system to stop all cron jobs. In either case, you'll know something is wrong.

To begin this process, make sure that your soft partition is still mounted. We're going to group all the necessary programs and command-line tools in this hidden location.

First, make two subdirectories in the soft partition.

```
# mkdir /mnt/tmp/bin
# mkdir /mnt/tmp/logs
```

Next, copy the packages that the script will need in order to function.

```
# cp -a /bin/ls /bin/echo /bin/cat /bin/mail /bin/rpm
 /usr/bin/lsattr /usr/bin/diff /bin/grep /mnt/tmp/bin/
```

Note This is not a full complement of programs, as you are not adding the required libraries or using a static compilation. If you set this partition up as a part of your regular security protocol, be sure you have everything necessary for the programs to run properly, including a static shell. Another popular addition to this stash of tools is a statically compiled shell such as BusyBox (see www.busybox.net).

Finally, move the RPM baseline file you created earlier.

```
# mv RPMV_2004-02-29 /mnt/tmp/logs/RPMV_2004-02-29_golden
```

A Simple Scanning Script

Now that everything's in place, you can create the shell script that will run all the programs and get the output you want. This sample script runs under the bash shell; if you prefer another shell, we assume that you've already got the skills to duplicate these functions in that environment. Create a script similar to this one, and place it somewhere unexpected on your disk with an inconspicuous name.

```
#!/bin/bash
MYMAIL=bob@example.com
```

```
PATH=/mnt/tmp
DATE="$(date +%Y-%m-%d)"

### Setup System ####
mount -o loop /home/bob/Desktop/chk-file $PATH
# Report usage of mount point into system-scan file
df -h | grep mnt\ /tmp > $PATH/logs/system-scan_$DATE
curdir=$(pwd)

#### 1) Daily RPM Verify -->"system-scan_[date]"
$PATH/bin/echo -----DIFFERENCES IN RPM-DB AS OF $DATE----- \
>>$PATH/logs/system-scan_$DATE

$PATH/bin/rpm -Va | grep '^..[5?]'>$PATH/logs/RPMV_$DATE
#compare current to our "golden" baseline file
$PATH/bin/diff $PATH/logs/RPMV_$DATE
$PATH/logs/RPMV_2004-02-\
29_golden| $PATH/bin/grep "bin\ /">>$PATH/logs/system-scan_$DATE

$PATH/bin/echo ^^^^^END RPM DIFFERENCES^^^^^ >>$PATH/logs/system-scan\
_$DATE
$PATH/bin/echo >>$PATH/logs/system-scan_$DATE

### 2) Quickly check for any immutable bit hacks -->"system-scan_[date]"
$PATH/bin/echo >>$PATH/logs/system-scan_$DATE
$PATH/bin/echo ------IMMUTABLE CHECK-------- >>$PATH/logs/system-scan\
_$DATE
$PATH/bin/lsattr /bin/* /sbin/* /usr/bin/* /usr/sbin/* | grep 'i--'>>$PATH/\
logs/system-scan_$DATE
$PATH/bin/echo ^^^^^END IMMUTABLE CHECK ^^^^^>>$PATH/logs/system-\
scan_$DATE

### 3) Root Kit Scan -->"system-scan_[date]"
$PATH/bin/echo >>$PATH/logs/system-scan_$DATE
$PATH/bin/echo ------CHKROOTKIT -------- >>$PATH/logs/system-\
scan_$DATE

cd $PATH/chkrootkit-0.43/
./chkrootkit -q | grep INFECTED >>$PATH/logs/system-scan_$DATE
cd $curdir
$PATH/bin/echo ^^^^^END CHKROOTKIT ^^^^^>>$PATH/logs/system-\
scan_$DATE

### 4) Daily Log Scan&Grep -->"system-scan_[date]"
$PATH/bin/echo-----LOG-SCAN----->>$PATH/logs/system-scan_$DATE
$PATH/bin/echo --POSSIBLE BREAK IN ATTEMPT>>$PATH/logs/system-scan_$DATE
$PATH/bin/cat /var/log/messages | grep POSSIBLE >>$PATH/logs/system\
-scan_$DATE
$PATH/bin/echo >>$PATH/logs/system-scan_$DATE
$PATH/bin/echo --SYN SCAN>>$PATH/logs/system-scan_$DATE
$PATH/bin/cat /var/log/messages | grep SYN >>$PATH/logs/system-\
scan_$DATE
```

```
$PATH/bin/echo >>$PATH/logs/system-scan_$DATE
$PATH/bin/echo --portsen>>$PATH/logs/system-scan_$DATE
$PATH/bin/cat /var/log/messages | grep portsen>>$PATH/logs/system-\
scan_$DATE
$PATH/bin/echo >>$PATH/logs/system-scan_$DATE
$PATH/bin/echo --LOGIN>>$PATH/logs/system-scan_$DATE
$PATH/bin/cat /var/log/messages | grep LOGIN>>$PATH/logs/system-\
scan_$DATE
$PATH/bin/echo >>$PATH/logs/system-scan_$DATE
$PATH/bin/echo --SSHD>>$PATH/logs/system-scan_$DATE
$PATH/bin/cat /var/log/messages | grep sshd>>$PATH/logs/system-\
scan_$DATE
$PATH/bin/echo >>$PATH/logs/system-scan_$DATE
$PATH/bin/echo ^^^^^END LOG-SCAN^^^^^>>$PATH/logs/system-\
scan_$DATE
$PATH/bin/echo >>$PATH/logs/system-scan_$DATE
$PATH/bin/echo --DONE-->>/mnt/tmp/logs/system-scan_$DATE

### 5) Mail out the "system-scan_[date]" file to MYMAIL
$PATH/bin/cat $PATH/logs/system-scan_$DATE | $PATH/bin/mail \
    -s"System Scan for $DATE" $MYMAIL

cd $CURDIR
umount $PATH
###Remove All Comments Once You Get It Fully Customized
```

Set permissions with the command `chmod 750` *filename* so that it will run.

This is a straightforward and basic script using only command-line functions. Of course, you can build much more complex scripts with their own logic, real-time monitoring triggers, and various e-mail messages. However, this script will do the simple dirty work that's necessary.

Note

Section 4 of this script is used to look for SSH logins, port scans, SYN flood attacks, and the like in your system log file put there from the Portsentry portscan detection package. Portsenty is a useful package that watches your system for pre-attack-type traffic such as port scans, stealth scans (both TCP and UDP based), Denial of Service attacks, and so on. You can even have Portsentry block would-be attackers, and even launch counterstrikes (really not recommended). If you want to implement this function, install Portsentry. See the *Intrusion Detection Resources* section for more information on this valuable package and where to get it.

Running the Script

Test your script a few times to be sure it works, before you start to rely on it. Before running it, set up your system to register some positive signs of cracker activity so you'll be sure to see what it looks like. Do this by modifying a system binary in /bin/ (back it up first), putting a test rootkit binary on your system (carefully), or setting an immutable bit on a file, such as /bin/ls or /bin/ps. If you decide to install and run Portsentry, have an administrator portscan you from another network to verify that it sees the scan and blocks it (with iptables in most Linux installs). After you do some of this, test your script.

When you get the output from your test session, you will see something that looks like this if the box has been compromised.

```
146M 1.2M 137M 1% /mnt/tmp
-----DIFFERENCES IN RPM-DB AS OF 2004-03-01-----
> .M......   /usr/bin/smbmnt
> S.5....T   /bin/netstat
> S.5....T   /bin/ls
> S.5....T   /usr/bin/passwd
> S.5....T   /bin/login
> S.5....T   /bin/ps
----TESTING bin/ for MD5SUM Changes, Nothing ^^Above^^ Means
System Is Secure----
^^^^^END RPM DIFFERENCES^^^^^

------IMMUTABLE CHECK--------
----i-------- /bin/ls
^^^^^END IMMUTABLE CHECK ^^^^^

------CHKROOTKIT --------
Checking 'ls'... INFECTED
^^^^^END CHKROOTKIT ^^^^^

-----LOG-SCAN-----
--POSSIBLE BREAK IN ATTEMPT
--SYN SCAN
--portsen
--LOGIN
--SSHD
Mar  1 03:31:02 localhost sshd: sshd -TERM succeeded
Mar  1 13:42:30 office101-89 sshd: succeeded
^^^^^END LOG-SCAN^^^^^
--DONE---
```

As you can see, the script found a number of file integrity violations on critical system files. In addition, the /bin/ls system binary now has an immutable bit set, and possibly has also been infected with a rootkit. Any of these three violations would give you reason to start digging through history files. If this were for real, with hits on all three, this box would definitely be considered compromised.

Compare the output of the compromised box above to this, which is the output from a clean machine.

```
146M  1.2M  137M   1% /mnt/tmp
-----DIFFERENCES IN RPM-DB AS OF 2004-03-01-----
----TESTING bin/ for MD5SUM Changes, Nothing ^^Above^^ Means
System Is Secure----
^^^^^END RPM DIFFERENCES^^^^^

------IMMUTABLE CHECK--------
^^^^^END IMMUTABLE CHECK ^^^^^

------CHKROOTKIT --------
^^^^^END CHKROOTKIT ^^^^^
```

```
-----LOG-SCAN-----
--POSSIBLE BREAK IN ATTEMPT
--SYN SCAN
--portsen
--LOGIN
--SSHD
Mar 1 14:38:023 localhost sshd: sshd -TERM succeeded
Mar 1 16:42:30 office101-89 sshd: succeeded
^^^^^END LOG-SCAN^^^^^
--DONE---
```

A script like this is an essential part of ensuring that your security measures are working. If you keep your server patched and locked down, and you implement the *foundational security policies* as described in the troubleshooting section of this chapter, and in the *Internet Server Security* article listed in the resources, then you may never have to see the "unhappy" version of the script's output.

Automating the Script

Once you've verified that the script works, it's time to automate the daily scan. This could be as simple as adding an entry to root's `crontab` file with a bit of camouflage.

```
# crontab -e
01 1 * * *   /some/dummy/script.sh
02 2 * * *   /some/out/oftheway/dir/sys-cleanup.sh
03 3 * * *   /some/other/dummyscript.sh
```

A stealthier option is to attach the script to another automated system, like `logrotate`.

```
/var/log/messages /var/log/secure /var/log/maillog
/var/log/spooler /var/log/boot.log /var/log/cron {
    prerotate
        /some/out/oftheway/dir/sys-cleanup.sh
    endscript
    sharedscripts
    postrotate
        /bin/kill -HUP `cat /var/run/syslogd.pid 2>
            /dev/null`2> /dev/null || true
    endscript
}
```

However, `cron` is easily killed by an invader. Using `cron`, or anything spawned by `cron`, is probably not the best idea. Consider using the `at` scheduler to put the script on a timer, and running it from some other system shell script or from `/etc/inittab` as a daemon instead.

> **Tip**
>
> Do a `man at` to learn more about how to use this often-overlooked scheduling tool.

Intrusion Troubleshooting

Tracking down a cracker or cracker tools on a live system is a very scary but exciting thing. It's somewhat like strolling through a really good haunted house: pounding heart, adrenaline, tunnel vision, the whole nine yards, especially when you know the deviant is actually on the box with you.

Try not to give your moves away to the opponent. I tell our other administrators at Rackspace, "Don't lose your head. Think clearly and slowly. What will you need later in the way of evidence? Log files? User .bash_history files? Output from netstat? Copies of trojan binaries?" Think it through, collect what you need and get off the box. Here are some tips below for what to do in these situations.

I think I've Been Cracked!

Does something on your system just not seem right? Worried that your machine's integrity has been compromised? Here are a few things to look for:

✦ Commonly modified files include ls, find, w, who, last, netstat, login, ps, top, lsattr, and chattr. Check these files for MD5sum changes with RPM or debsum.

✦ If running ext2/3 file systems, any files with the -i, or immutable, bit set, as in:

```
# lsattr /bin/* /sbin/* /usr/bin/* /usr/sbin/*|grep "i--"
----i-------- /bin/login
----i-------- /bin/netstat
----i-------- /bin/ps
```

✦ Strange filenames or directory names with spaces where none should be, as in ../, or other attempts to make the file appear hidden.

✦ Strange files or directories in places where they do not belong, like /var/spool, /tmp, or /dev. In particular, do an ls -la | more and look for non link(l), char(c), or block(b) files types (the left-most character from ls) in the /dev/ directory.

✦ Odd, slangy filenames like r00t, b0nez, or war3z in home and system directories.

✦ Modified boot files like /etc/inittab, /etc/rc.d/rc.local, or /etc/rc.d/rc.sysinit.

✦ Unfamiliar or unusual user names in /etc/passwd or /etc/shadow.

✦ Spikes in your system's outgoing bandwidth usage (serving warez or porn files or participating in denial of service (DoS) attacks).

✦ Commands you never entered in /root/.bash_history.

Watch for false positives, or items that make you think you've been compromised when you really haven't. Automated updates, system cron jobs, slow machine performance, poor programming (such as memory leaks), or unusual port connections are not always indicative of a system attack. Look for evidence and proof, not just unthinking reaction.

If you have definitely been cracked, see the next section for more information.

What Should I Do if I've Been Compromised?

What you need to do in this situation depends on what your machine does. If it's a production server and you can't shut it down, carefully get as much information as you can about the intrusion, without making yourself known. Don't immediately start shutting off services and locking things down. If you're compromised, the time to be secure is over. Now you need to be stealthly, thoughtful, and cool-handed before shutting the system down.

You need filenames, history and log files, and any rootkit packages, source code, or compiled code left behind by the invader. Don't do anything too system-intensive that gives away your presence, though, such as using `dd` to clone the drive. If there's a live cracker on the system, he could get nervous or have some fun by wiping logs and binaries while you're watching. Copy all of your evidence and forensic data to some place not so obvious, like `/root/tmp/stuff/` or the like.

To get the forensic data and evidence off the system and to somewhere safe, use `tar` and `scp` to transfer all of the data that you've collected (using `nice` so as to not draw too much attention to your actions) off to another safer machine like this.

```
# nice -15 tar cz0 /root/tmp/stuff/| ssh \
    root@example.com "cat > /root/my-hacked-tarball.tgz"
```

Caution

If you suspect that this might involve any type of prosecution or that legal counsel or the authorities may become involved, be very careful as you collect the forensic data. It is wise to have two people collect and witness the data gathering. It's also a good idea to make two complete images of the drive and to not change or even touch the master drive from this point forward. cClone drives like this later, off-line with tools such as Symantec's Ghost in image mode `-ir`. Remember that you're recording and handling evidence that can be used in court, and you're working within "the crime scene" as it were. Use appropriate caution.

If you suspect that the cracker is after you specifically, is intending harm to you and your system, or you're witnessing data destruction in action, then pull the plug (yes the AC wall plug). Most modern journaling file systems, like those used under Linux, can handle the abrupt or ungraceful power-down, and normal shutdown or reboot scripts could contain dangerous self-destruct `dd` scripts or the like. After you've powered off, hook up another identical hard drive, reboot with a DOS boot floppy, and make a drive image to one or preferably two other backup drives (again using Ghost with the `-ir` switch). Remove the original drive, label and date it, and lock it away. Remember: evidence. The copy drive can now be hooked to another workstation to be `fsck`'d and analyzed, or you can boot the system off a forensic boot media such as *Knoppix STD* (Security Tools Distribution `www.knoppix-std.org`). Then you can safely `fsck` (like scandisk) the cloned drive and perform your forensic research off-line.

Trust No One

No matter how safe you think you have made the machine, a compromised system can never be trusted again. Treat every standard system file as the enemy. If you have a hidden set of system tools in a soft partition or on removable media, use them to look at your cloned drives. Never

Continued

Continued

boot off the compromised system drive again unless you have good reason. Format the drive and install a fresh copy of the operating system, mount the old drive (or a copy of the old drive) as read-only under a location such as /mnt/hacked/, and migrate over the static content files only. **Never** migrate over executables, scripts, or third-party applications from the compromised drive.

Never move system files in /bin, /lib, or /etc when you are cleaning up an attack. Move only the users that you know about in /home, and only static verified content from /var/ftp and /var/www. Don't move CGI, PHP, or Perl scripts or executables, or web content with extensions other than .html. In particular, don't copy web applications that you've installed such as Vbulletin or PHPNuke. Download the latest versions and install from scratch. These are common targets for back doors. At Rackspace, we've seen quick and dirty content migrations, moved over to another machine, simply reinfect the new fresh install and even notify the cracker that the back doors are back on line and ready for business.

If you didn't have system tools on removable media before you got cracked the first time, make that a priority. You should have a statically compiled shell like sash, ash.static, or even BusyBox, as well as common /bin/ tools, RPM, and supporting shared libraries (usually in /lib/). You might want a copy of your RPM database as well, and of course your handy copy of chkrootkit. Make the disk read-only and keep it in a secure location, or readily mountable.

Note Many compromised systems aren't actually cracked by a live person on the other end of the connection. Rather, they're hit by an automated Internet worm with a scanning exploit (a crowbar executable that leverages a known security vulnerability) and a rootkit. Automated scanning worms are responsible for the bulk of hacked boxes. Although such compromised machines may not have a live person on them, the machine is still tainted and must be wiped and reloaded, even if it's not the work of someone intent on harassing you personally. In most cases, where there's a cracker involved directly on your box, it's someone who just wants to use your box to transfer warez (illegal files), porn, or send spam—or just a kid taking the Internet equivalent of a joyride. Though it's still serious, it's not necessarily time to call the cops. In fact the FBI typically won't even talk to you unless there is proof of at least $5,000 in damages on the line.

My ISP Is Threatening Me

If your system is compromised and your upstream provider notices it before you do, you may get an unsettling e-mail or call. Many providers will give you 24 hours notice to get your files off the drive before they unplug the machine, wipe it, and reload it from scratch. Despite the way it may feel, your ISP is not threatening you. They have to protect their own investments, keep their network safe for others, and prevent their machines from becoming remote scanning tools for all your cracker's pals. Think of it as a type of Internet quarantine.

There are a couple of solutions to this situation. Remember, you're working against the clock. Pick something and do it, rather than wasting time wondering what's the best thing to do. (You do back up your account regularly, right? You can always restore from that file.)

First, consider moving all of your nondynamic content to a new location, including web files, e-mail, and FTP-able data. Scan this content with the chkrootkit tool, and watch for extensions like `.pl`, `.cgi`, `.php`, `.sh`, and other indicators of executable files. Do not move binary executables. If you're moving data from a file server, watch out for Windows executable extensions like `.pif`, `.exe`, `.com`, and so forth.

Use the find command to find these files.

```
# find ./ -iregex ".*\ .sh$" -o -iregex ".*\ .exe$"
./runme.exe
./root-me.sh
```

If you have various types of executables (as in this example), you can move them to a holding place or quarantine like this.

```
# find ./ -iregex ".*\ .sh$" -exec mv {} /tmp/EXECUTABLES/ \;
```

The most common way of migrating data directly from a hacked drive to a freshly reinstalled new drive is to move the hacked master drive aside to a secondary bus (for example, an IDE secondary slave). Then reload the operating system on a new drive, and then mount the hacked data as read-only under `/mnt/hacked/` (for example) with the command `mount -o ro /dev/hdc2 /mnt/hacked`.

> **Note**   Some administrators believe that they can "resecure" a compromised machine. Though I've known this to be done in extreme cases, there is almost always a back door somewhere that even the most eagle-eyed administrator will miss. Once a system is compromised, you simply can't trust anything on the system at all. You're going to have to wipe and reinstall before you can breathe easily.

I Thought I Was Covered! What Happened?

Even the most apparently secure system, with a working N/HIDS installation and a strong firewall, may be compromised. How can this be? Administrators who throw money and off the shelf "security solutions," and yet still become targets of successful attacks, are usually outraged and bewildered at this turn of events.

For example, lousy server administrators with big expensive firewalls got as mad as hell when the infamous Nimda and Code Red Internet worms drilled right through their firewalls. How could such a thing happen? Well, if a firewall in front of a web server running IIS must, by definition, have port 80 (http) open to the world to serve web traffic, and if that administrator doesn't keep the daemon behind that firewall (IIS) fully patched and secure, then the firewall is literally useless to protect him from his own poor patching practices, and from the worms that look for such vulnerable systems.

Here's the cold hard truth: security measures of every type are built on assumptions of underlying security—an assumed *security foundation* if you will. In order for add-on security systems such as NIDS and firewalls to work, your systems need to be based on common *foundational security steps* and policies, including these basic tenets:

> ✦ **Passwords**: You have, and enforce, a strong password policy.
>
> ✦ **Patches**: You apply all critical security patches (as soon as they have been tested in production).
>
> ✦ **Services**: You have shut down or secured as many daemons as possible to decrease your network profile, or attractiveness to would-be crackers or deviants.

✦ **Scanning and Reporting**: You are running an active host-based intrusion detection system that regularly monitors network activity and portscans, log file red flags, file alteration, and other internal systems—and then *reports* on such data.

Only when you have your own house in order can you begin to install additional solutions, like firewalls or other monitoring and mitigation systems confidently. Why build up a massive outer defensive wall to protect a house of cards? If you don't patch the holes and lock the doors, someone will get in no matter how scary the outer alarm system looks. Good security isn't contained in a single silver bullet or commercial product—it results from incrementally applied common sense measures over time.

Tip

Stay secure. If you know you're not good with routine checks and updates, automate your patching with tools like up2date/RHN/yum for Red Hat Linux and Fedora Core, apt-get for Debian, or whichever automatic update tools your Linux distribution offers.

It's best to install critical patches only after you've verified that they won't crash your production systems. But if you don't have the time or manpower to manually check your major production patches, then when they are available "turn on" these automated patching systems and let the servers keep themselves up to date. It's easier to fix a crashed daemon than to clean up a hacked server.

Remember, critical security patches are released in response to known vulnerabilities, exploits, and common bugs. Not keeping such patches relatively up to date is like flirting with disaster.

In the Open Source world, vulnerabilities are usually discovered and patches released before exploits exist (unlike in the closed source realm). When a patch is offered, this is usually, on average, from 1to 3 weeks before a mainstream exploit based on that vulnerability is seen *in the wild*. That being said, if you bank on this statistic, you may come up short. I have seen a blow worm grow up into its final worm form in as little as 3 days and spread across the net like wildfire. So the real hot time for action is between 24 and 48 hours of vulnerability identification and patch release. This is the time in which you need to examine your own systems and get them tested for the patch(es) and fixed up.

Intrusion Detection Resources

Table 10-1 provides a few resources for intrusion detection information.

Table 10-1: Intrusion Detection Resources

Resource	Location
The Security Quick-Start HOWTO for Red Hat Linux	www.ibiblio.org/pub/Linux/docs/HOWTO/other-formats/pdf/Security-Quickstart-Redhat-HOWTO.pdf
Chkrootkit	www.chkrootkit.org
The Coroner's Toolkit	www.fish.com/tct/
Building a Security Audit Toolkit	www.netadmintools.com/art279.html

Resource	Location
Host Hardening and Intrusion Detection—The Open Source Way	`www.unixreview.com/documents/s=7459/uni1030462740022/`
Internet Server Security: The Best Things in Life Are Free, But There's No Silver Bullet	`www.datacenterhub.com/features/1205_Rackspace_Weeks.shtm`
Intrusion Detection, Take 2	`www.nwc.com/1023/1023f1.html`
SANS Intrusion Detection FAQ	`www.sans.org/resources/idfaq/ipe.php`
Security Focus	`www.securityfocus.com/`
CERT Coordination Center	`www.cert.org/`
Security mail lists	`http://seclists.org`
Security tools	`www.insecure.org/tools.html`

Summary

You can watch your systems by systematically scanning them with some stock and some add-on packages that are all readily available and free (as in liberty *and* beer). With the automated and watchful assistance of built-in baseline tools such as RPM and MD5 fingerprints, lsattr, and logwatch, combined with add-on freebies such as chkrootkit, Portsentry, and other related tools, you can do a good job of keeping things in check. Some of these tools watch for outer preemptive signs of attack, while others watch the inside of your system and flag you when something's gone wrong. Having balance here is important.

To keep from getting hacked, you should employ *foundational security elements* to make your house of cards into a buttressed fortress, impervious to such attacks. This takes incrementally applied security steps such as strong passwords, up-to-date system-wide patches, auditing and minimizing of network-facing services, as well as the scanning and reporting intrusion detection practices that we've focused on in the bulk of the chapter. Without all of these elements, measures such as NATed firewalls and fancy NIDS systems may be a house built on sand.

When systems do get hacked, there are things that should be done in a specific fashion, depending on your particular system configuration. If you have a bit of time, forensic data should be collected, archived off site, data saved, and the system reloaded. If there is active destruction, you may need to actually pull the plug, clone the drive for evidence, and work on salvaging data from the clone. Regardless, such systems can no longer be trusted, and must be taken down one way or another. Make sure you don't reinfect yourself in the data migration process.

If you follow the rules for building your systems upon a strong and secure foundation, keep an eye on them by monitoring various aspects of their inner workings, and don't trust in single-vendor, shrink-wrapped security products that promise the sky, you should never have to worry about collecting evidence of an intruder or doing mass data migrations, with your boss screaming in your ear.

✦　　✦　　✦

Firewall Troubleshooting

Most people are familiar with the term *firewall* and realize that it is a device or system that keeps unwanted people and data out of computer systems or networks. However, the word means slightly different things to different people. This can lead to difficulty when discussing the concept.

If you ask home users whether they have a firewall, they will probably think first of a software program installed on their home computers, like BlackICE Defender or ZoneAlarm, referred to as *personal firewalls*. At most they might have a Linksys dedicated router/firewall. These utilities range in price from $50 to 100. Ask a small office network administrator about firewall, and the person will probably think of something like the NETGEAR or NetScreen router/firewall, or a stronger, dedicated router/firewall system running software like SmoothWall or Astaro Linux. These are often referred to as small office/home office (SOHO) firewalls and cost anywhere from $100 to a few hundred dollars. Meanwhile, if an enterprise security specialist is asked what firewall means, he or she will think more of the heavy-duty enterprise network firewall systems such as a Cisco PIX, Check Point, or SunScreen, costing hundreds to thousands of dollars.

The enterprise-level firewalls include heavy-duty network authentication, DMZ (demilitarized zone) functionality, and even intrusion prevention, antispam, and antivirus technology. As firewall technology improves, however, many of these features filter down to the smaller, cheaper firewall systems. For example, many SOHO and personal firewalls now offer Virtual Private Network support, Denial of Service protection, and stateful packet inspection (SPI). Now even Linux software firewall distros such as Astaro are including cutting-edge enterprise type functionality that only the big players had before.

Note　*Stateful packet inspection*, or SPI, is the method used by most modern firewalls to determine whether incoming traffic is related to an existing protocol connection state, and thus if such incoming traffic is *related* and permitted through or *new/unrelated* and rejected by the firewall. The state is determined by the packet-level inspection of several protocol-centric variables as compared to previous incoming/related packet variables that are stored in a *state table* maintained by the firewall, which tracks said protocol-sensitive states (such as with FTP and NFS).

In this chapter, we explain the basic firewall functionality included with most Linux distributions, and really drill into some of the specifics of Red Hat and Fedora Core based systems. We'll show you how to set up a firewall and configure both a single stand-alone server type system and a network firewall, and describe the various security concerns you face with each. Most Linux distributions provide all the technology you'll need to set up an efficient and controllable firewall, but you might also want to install a third-party administrative firewall tool to make firewall rule set administration a bit easier. We introduce a few such packages later in the chapter.

Firewall Theory

In the most general sense, firewalls look at incoming data packets, examine their source or destination addresses and ports, and make decisions about those packets based on a set of configured rules. Before you can set up a firewall, you must create these rules. To do so, you need to determine which services (or ports) on your network are required in or through your network, and should be left open, and which services or ports should be locked down.

In this section of the chapter, we describe the various ports and port ranges found on a standard Linux machine. If you have some port knowledge, consider reading this section anyway—port terminology and standard ranges have changed in the last few years and your basic understanding may be somewhat outdated.

Ports and the IP Stack

Every IP address has 65,535 *ports* associated with it. Ports are used to associate a network connection with a service and protocol running on a machine attached to a TCP/IP-based network. Ports are often described as windows or doors in an office building: if you want to see Person A, you open the door to Person A's office. In the same way, if you want to get a web page from a particular server with the http protocol, you request services through port 80 on that server.

In the past few years, port assignments on UNIX-based operating systems have changed from their original locations. Here is a list of current Red Hat–based Linux port assignments:

✦ Ports 0–1,023: The *Well-Known* or *Reserved* ports are standardized and controlled by IANA, the Internet Assigned Numbers Authority. These ports are generally used for standard incoming system and protocol interactions.

✦ Ports 1,024–49,151: The *Registered* ports are also used for incoming services, but are not regulated as strictly as the first 1,024 ports (remember, under UNIX, 0 counts as a number). These ports are controlled by community standards, not by dictated rules.

✦ Ports 32,768–61,000: These *Ephemeral* or *Dynamic* port assignments are specific to the Linux 2.4 kernel, but can very by distro. They are used by outgoing client requests and programs to establish connections with other servers. On some systems, Ephemeral ports range up to 65,535. You can see this kernel setting on your Linux 2.4 kernel by looking at the kernel's proc filesystem:

```
# cat /proc/sys/net/ipv4/ip_local_port_range
32768    61000
```

Ephemeral ports used to be defined as 1,024–4,999 on Linux and other platforms, but in recent years they have shifted upward for several performance, standardization, and security reasons.

You may have noticed the overlap of ports from 32,768 to 49,151. This is not particularly critical to the average Linux administrator, and is a legacy issue that is documented in RFC's and in IANA's own internal documentation. It does not affect regular Linux use in any significant way. The more of these Dynamic or Ephemeral ports that you open for use, the more simultaneous outgoing connections your server can make. This keeps busy servers from fighting over limited outgoing server resources, and on such servers the additional ~24k outgoing ports can speed things up a bit (when talking about max outgoing connections per second such as a large mail server).

Note   IANA is the regulatory group that controls IP address allocations, top-level domains, port assignments below 1,024, and other Internet-related public standards. The IANA port list (www.iana.org/assignments/port-numbers) shows both the regulated *Reserved* or *Well-Known ports*, as well as a list of industry common *Registered ports*.

Port Assignments

To see the human-readable service names that your server associates with port numbers, look the /etc/services file. This file lists the most commonly used ports and the protocols or programs associated with each one. For example, this command's output lists the TCP ports associated with several common Internet protocols:

```
$ cat /etc/services | grep -e ^http -e ^ftp -e ^ssh|grep tcp
ftp-data    20/tcp
ftp         21/tcp
ssh         22/tcp                         # SSH Remote Login Protocol
http        80/tcp    www www-http  # WorldWideWeb HTTP
https       443/tcp                        # MCom
```

If you'd like to see the daemons that are currently bound to your various IP addresses by a specific service name, instead of simply the number or the port, issue this command and use grep to look at the one service that you're interested in:

```
$  netstat -at|grep "http "
 tcp        0        0 *:http       *:*          LISTEN
```

Leave off the grep to see all such bindings.

TCP/IP Packet Structures

With a basic understanding of port allocation under your belt, take a closer look at TCP and IP packet structures.

When on a TCP/IP-based network, each packet you send out has either a TCP packet wrapped or encapsulated in an IP datagram, or a UDP packet wrapped in an IP datagram. The former is a TCP/IP packet and the latter is called a UDP/IP datagram. You look at the information contained in a TCP/IP packet (in most of our examples in this chapter) to determine where the packet came from, where it's going, and what protocols are being used or requested. This is the very nitty-gritty nature of TCP/IP firewalling. But before we can get much further into this discussion, we need to take a quick peek inside these data structures to speak intelligently about how we're using this information.

These TCP and IP structures can be used in various ways to trigger on and control the different types of traffic that flow across your network or into/out of your server.

Note   If you plan to take full advantage of these packet-level mechanisms, you'll want to use the iptables form of Linux firewalling rules as opposed to the older, less powerful TCP wrappers—which is really more of a service/host ACL than a real firewall control system.

TCP and IP structures are defined by RFC 793 and RFC 791. The basic layout for TCP looks like this:

```
TCP Header:
    0                   1                   2                   3
    0 1 2 3 4 5 6 7 8 9 0 1 2 3 4 5 6 7 8 9 0 1 2 3 4 5 6 7 8 9 0 1
   +-+-+-+-+-+-+-+-+-+-+-+-+-+-+-+-+-+-+-+-+-+-+-+-+-+-+-+-+-+-+-+-+
   |          Source Port          |       Destination Port        |
   +-+-+-+-+-+-+-+-+-+-+-+-+-+-+-+-+-+-+-+-+-+-+-+-+-+-+-+-+-+-+-+-+
   |                        Sequence Number                        |
   +-+-+-+-+-+-+-+-+-+-+-+-+-+-+-+-+-+-+-+-+-+-+-+-+-+-+-+-+-+-+-+-+
   |                     Acknowledgment Number                     |
   +-+-+-+-+-+-+-+-+-+-+-+-+-+-+-+-+-+-+-+-+-+-+-+-+-+-+-+-+-+-+-+-+
   | Data  |           |U|A|P|R|S|F|                               |
   | Offset| Reserved  |R|C|S|S|Y|I|            Window             |
   |       |           |G|K|H|T|N|N|                               |
   +-+-+-+-+-+-+-+-+-+-+-+-+-+-+-+-+-+-+-+-+-+-+-+-+-+-+-+-+-+-+-+-+
   |           Checksum            |         Urgent Pointer        |
   +-+-+-+-+-+-+-+-+-+-+-+-+-+-+-+-+-+-+-+-+-+-+-+-+-+-+-+-+-+-+-+-+
   |                    Options                    |    Padding    |
   +-+-+-+-+-+-+-+-+-+-+-+-+-+-+-+-+-+-+-+-+-+-+-+-+-+-+-+-+-+-+-+-+
   |                             data                              |
   +-+-+-+-+-+-+-+-+-+-+-+-+-+-+-+-+-+-+-+-+-+-+-+-+-+-+-+-+-+-+-+-+
```

Reading from left to right you will see the packets that actually get transmitted across the wire.

Although there is a great deal of information in this TCP packet diagram, the easiest elements to identify and use from a firewalling perspective are probably the TCP packet's source and destination ports. In short, this identifies what protocols are being used or requested. Also, when setting up firewall rules and allowing or denying access to services (remember, services = ports), you might want to use the *sequence number* to track session-based protocols. This idea of session and protocol tracking is the basis for SPI or session tracking for bidirectional transfer protocols like FTP or NFS. Doing session tracking is pretty much automatic in iptables after you enable it, but we'll still cover this later.

Tip   Although this chapter does not cover data pattern and string matching, you might be interested in this subject if you're doing things like intrusion detection or packet filtering. If you want to learn more on those topics, check these sites:

✦ http://articles.linuxguru.net/view/120

✦ www.linuxsecurity.com/feature_stories/feature_story-148.html

✦ www.securityfocus.com/infocus/1531

In the IP structure, as shown following, you'll also want to be able to trigger on the IP *source* and *destination addresses* (who it's coming from and who it's going to). Triggering on and allowing or denying access based on these addresses (as well as the attributes we already covered) is, in essence, what firewalling is all about.

Let's take a closer look at the *IP datagram* structure and see what useful information firewall administrators would use from this low-level protocol. The IP datagram looks like this

```
IP Datagram:
      0                   1                   2                   3
      0 1 2 3 4 5 6 7 8 9 0 1 2 3 4 5 6 7 8 9 0 1 2 3 4 5 6 7 8 9 0 1
     +-+-+-+-+-+-+-+-+-+-+-+-+-+-+-+-+-+-+-+-+-+-+-+-+-+-+-+-+-+-+-+-+
     | Version|  IHL  |Type of Service |          Total Length         |
     +-+-+-+-+-+-+-+-+-+-+-+-+-+-+-+-+-+-+-+-+-+-+-+-+-+-+-+-+-+-+-+-+
     |          Identification        | Flags|      Fragment Offset   |
     +-+-+-+-+-+-+-+-+-+-+-+-+-+-+-+-+-+-+-+-+-+-+-+-+-+-+-+-+-+-+-+-+
     |   Time to Live |    Protocol  |          Header Checksum        |
     +-+-+-+-+-+-+-+-+-+-+-+-+-+-+-+-+-+-+-+-+-+-+-+-+-+-+-+-+-+-+-+-+
     |                        Source Address                          |
     +-+-+-+-+-+-+-+-+-+-+-+-+-+-+-+-+-+-+-+-+-+-+-+-+-+-+-+-+-+-+-+-+
     |                      Destination Address                       |
     +-+-+-+-+-+-+-+-+-+-+-+-+-+-+-+-+-+-+-+-+-+-+-+-+-+-+-+-+-+-+-+-+
     |                          Options               |    Padding    |
     +-+-+-+-+-+-+-+-+-+-+-+-+-+-+-+-+-+-+-+-+-+-+-+-+-+-+-+-+-+-+-+-+
```

The main aspects of the IP datagram interesting to the firewall administrator are *source* and *destination addresses* and the *protocol*. These elements are important for both TCP wrappers and iptables-based firewalls. However, some of the other fields are useful when setting up a dual-homed firewall with NAT and masquerading, such as TTL (as described in the following section).

Firewalls in Action

No matter how complex the firewall is, in its most simple form, a firewall allows and disallows access to specific services based on host addresses, networks, or other such trigger criteria. The services, ports, and daemon names (for Red Hat/Fedora Core systems) that most Linux sys-admins are concerned about are shown in Table 11-1.

Table 11-1: Services and Daemons

Service Name	Port	Description	Red Hat/Fedora Daemon Name
Ftp	21	VS-FTP	Vsftpd
Ssh	22	OpenSSH/sftp/scp	Sshd
Http	80	Apache/Web	Httpd
Sunrpc	111	RPC/NFS related service	Portmap
Https	443	Apache/web SSL	Httpd
Smtp	25	Sendmail/SMTP mail	Sendmail
Domain	53	BIND DNS	Named
Ipp	631	CUPS	Cupsd
Nfs	2049	Network file system	nfs
Mysql	3306	MySQL database	mysqld

You'll need to know these service names and ports whether you're controlling access to them on a single stand-alone server firewall or protecting an entire network of these services as a NAT router firewall setup would do.

Lets take a look at when you might want to just use basic service access control on a single server with TCP wrappers.

Full Firewall or Trusted Access Control?

If the services that you want to allow or disallow access to are running on a server connected to a trusted network or LAN, you can use either TCP wrappers or iptables to set up your local server-side service access control (*personal firewall*). That said, TCP wrappers is really not considered to be a true hardened firewall grade form of access control because incoming data is allowed past the networking stack into what's called *user space*. This is where many Internet worms and attacks are launched to strike, and this in turn means that you can still be cracked if your TCP wrappers-based system is attacked with a known TCP wrappers exploit. Armed with this knowledge, if you have a single server on an untrusted network or directly on the Internet and you wish to run a serious single host-based firewall configuration, iptables should be your only real choice for a real firewall.

If you're already on a secure network and you just want to allow/disallow services to various IP addresses, hosts, or networks within your network, then TCP wrappers might be easier for you to use.

Caution   While TCP wrappers is fine for doing basic allow/deny access to services on a trusted network or LAN, it should not be used in the wild, on an untrusted network, or on the Internet without some form of real firewall in front of it (such as iptables or a full-blown network firewall).

Figure 11-1 shows a basic single-homed or *stand-alone* firewall. Note the single computer with its single network connection. This would typically be the configuration of a server running its own iptables-based firewall or TCP wrappers service control, already behind a network-wide corporate firewall, for example.

Dual-homed firewalls (Figure 11-2) are designed to protect an entire network of PCs or servers, and sometimes act as NAT-based routers for your LAN (more on this later). See Figure 11-2 for an example of a dual-homed firewall or network firewall configuration.

Note   In addition to single-homed and dual-homed firewalls, you may also run across *tri-homed* firewalls. These firewalls incorporate a DMZ, or demilitarized zone, which is a semiprotected network outside the protected internal network. Tri-homed firewalls are beyond the scope of this book, but you can learn more by consulting RFC 2647 or doing a Google web search on firewall and DMZ.

As you read more about firewalls, you will come across the terms *trusted* and *untrusted* *interfaces*. These terms are used in relation to network and security boundaries. A dual-homed (or two network card) firewall is usually placed between a trusted and an untrusted network, and so the two interfaces on the firewall that physically connect to these networks get their names accordingly. If you have a trusted network interface (for example, eth0) and an untrusted network interface (such as eth1), you need to use iptables (along with *ip forwarding*) to control network access through your firewall from one interface to the other. (You can see the interfaces and the networks they're connected to in Figure 11-2.)

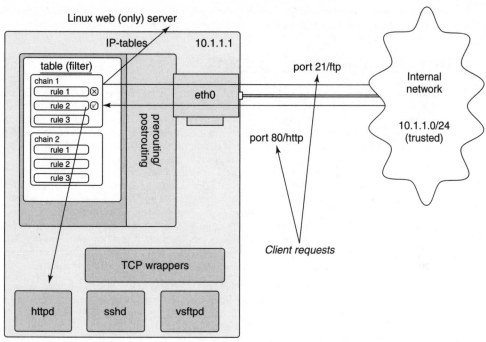

Figure 11-1: A single-homed *stand-alone* server can use an iptables-based firewall config or TCP wrappers to control incoming service requests, but not all services can be controlled with TCP wrappers by default.

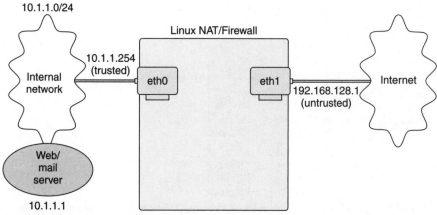

Figure 11-2: Dual-homed or *network* firewalls are designed to protect entire networks of machines, not services running on the same server. These firewalls should only be using iptables.

Now that some of the basics on firewall theory are out of the way, the next section focuses on the differences between TCP wrappers and iptables, and when and how to use each.

Linux Firewall Mechanisms

Most Linux distributions, including Fedora Core, provide two forms of service access control: TCP wrappers and iptables. I use the term *access control* and not firewalling because TCP wrappers should really not be referred to as a firewall *per se*. The older TCP wrappers offers centralized daemon host access control in one nice and easy to edit file. It can be configured to monitor incoming requests for a range of daemons, works in tandem with xinetd, and changes to it are instantly applied. TCP wrappers is somewhat insecure if used on an untrusted network, is not very powerful, and so should only really be used on trusted networks or where very specific requirements demand it. iptables is the newer Linux form of true firewalling. Its technology is generally referred to as *netfilter,* as it exists on several OS platforms. iptables itself is a packet/kernel-level, system-wide, *user space* control system that allows control of the real-time network filter rule sets in the running kernel. These rules allow for multinetwork SPI, control, modification, and redirection. It is much more powerful than TCP wrappers, but can also be more complex to use. It can be used on trusted or untrusted networks and so makes a perfect multihome, multinetwork firewall/router solution.

Figure 11-3 shows how iptables and TCP wrappers (on top of various daemon configuration files for access control security) together form various levels of service access control, or what is often loosely referred to as firewalling. The various levels of security shown in this figure are illustrated in the order that incoming network client requests encounter them.

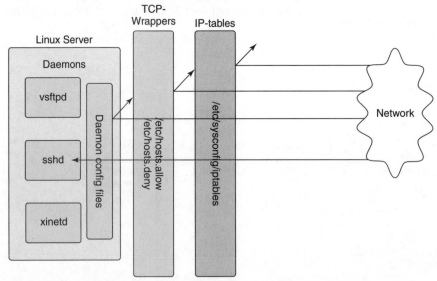

Figure 11-3: Incoming client requests pass through levels of security on a system. iptables is the most secure outer level of defense or access control.

As the network client requests come in through the network card, they encounter the iptables portion of the kernel. In Red Hat and Fedora Core systems, this config is controlled from the

/etc/sysconfig/iptables file. If the clients pass these tables of filters and rule-chains, they then pass through to the TCP wrappers level of the system, assuming that the requested daemon is compiled with TCP wrapper's libwrap support. If the service or daemon has libwrap support compiled in, and thus can even be controlled by TCP wrappers, TCP wrappers then allows the client requests to pass or blocks them per the allow/deny files. The final layer of network client restriction is sometimes configurable by the daemon via the daemon's own internal configuration file (for example, Apache = httpd.conf and FTP = vsftpd.conf). These last two levels of TCP wrappers and daemon level config file service security are not considered true firewall quality forms of network protection, but are usually just used as a convenient way for an administrator to allow or deny daemon-level access on a trusted network. Although many administrators sometimes use wrappers and deamon config allow/deny settings on untrusted networks (such as the Internet), such configurations are not recommended. These older and less secure forms of access control only form a quick and easy service/host access system for trusted networks and should really not be considered a real firewall.

TCP Wrappers

As previously stated, TCP wrappers does not actually function as a firewall. Instead, it is a simple and effective application-level daemon wrapper. TCP wrappers is a set of libraries that xinet.d and other daemons are compiled against. Among other things, it lets you form simple service/host-based access control lists (ACLs) based rule sets that control which hosts or networks are allowed to access your various daemons. Daemons that are compiled against the libwrap library like this can then be controlled through the host access control files /etc/hosts.allow and /etc/hosts.deny.

Several, but not all, of the network daemons in Fedora Core and other Linux distributions are already compiled against libwrap. To determine which of your daemons have libwrap support, locate them with the following command:

```
# egrep libwrap /sbin/* /usr/sbin/*| sort
Binary file /usr/sbin/in.tftpd matches
Binary file /usr/sbin/mailstats matches
Binary file /usr/sbin/makemap matches
Binary file /usr/sbin/praliases matches
Binary file /usr/sbin/rpc.rquotad matches
Binary file /usr/sbin/sendmail.sendmail matches
Binary file /usr/sbin/smrsh matches
Binary file /usr/sbin/snmpd matches
Binary file /usr/sbin/snmptrapd matches
Binary file /usr/sbin/sshd matches
Binary file /usr/sbin/stunnel matches
Binary file /usr/sbin/vsftpd matches
Binary file /usr/sbin/xinetd matches
```

Because they have libwrap support, these daemons should be able to be controlled through the /etc/hosts.allow and /etc/hosts.deny files.

Is TCP wrappers the appropriate service solution for you? If you're running a services-based server (from which services are being offered) on a trusted network, and all of your running daemons use libwrap, and you're already protected by a full-blown internetwork firewall, then TCP wrappers *can* be a quick and simple way for you to control which machines and networks have access to services on your server. If you need more security on your services-based server, more feature-rich or complex firewalling rules like session tracking, or stateful inspection, *or* you're running a network firewall in a multiple network card (multi-home) NAT configuration, then you definitely need the strength of iptables.

Remember, if you're just running a basic FTP or sendmail mail relay server or the like, then TCP wrappers can be used *if* you're on a trusted network. But a true firewall cannot, nor can it be used to limit access *through* a network firewall.

iptables

iptables is essentially the fourth generation of a packet filter system for the Linux kernel called *netfilter*. Packet filtering was originally released on BSD via ipfw and was integrated into the Linux kernel in version 2.0. When the 2.2 version of the Linux kernel was released, packet filtering was controlled by a user-space tool, *ipchains*. With the 2.4 and newer kernels, we have the modern iptables tool and related kernel modules that offer complete control over almost every piece of network data that comes into or leaves our networks.

To summarize, iptables is a stateful packet network control, filtering, modification, and redirection system that is one of the more advanced and readily available implementations of netfilter available today. Plus, it's free. Unfortunately, iptables can be somewhat difficult to learn for the uninitiated, or for those who do not have a firm grip on the packet-level operations of networking protocols, especially so if you want to control iptables manually via flat configuration files or scripts rather than via a graphical tool. Some people find it easier to use such graphical control tools to *do stuff*, then look at the iptable config output, and learn the inner workings of iptables this way, while others prefer to just dive right into the command line syntax. In this chapter we mainly use the command line approach, but feel free to download one of the graphic tools discussed later and check out the GUI approach.

At its most basic level, a packet filter is a program that scans network traffic as it flows through the system and then makes decisions about each packet. Based on the filters or rule tables that the administrator configures, iptables can DROP (discard) or ACCEPT a given packet. In addition, iptables offers more sophisticated tools like Network Address Translation, masquerading, and the ability to forward packets to other machines or networks. This is why Linux and iptables is such a perfect fit for high-powered firewall configurations, and why we're starting to see this combination secretly appear in several commercial and SOHO firewall products such as the SnapGear PCI635 (www.cyberguard.com/snapgear/pci635.html), the ProWall (www.protectix.com/prowallspecs.html), and others. It's powerful, small, and cheap.

Third-Party Firewall Solutions

If simply using raw iptables isn't functionally enough for you, you can add other Open Source firewall GUI tool solutions atop the system to increase your Linux firewall's flexibility and ease of use. You can either go the enterprise route and pay for full-featured commercial firewall distros/tools and get enterprise-level support contracts (such as with some CD bootable firewall distros). However, if you're looking for a free or noncommercial solution, you can download free, Open Source "bolt-on" firewall GUI tools that will transform your raw, hand-crafted iptables rule creation into a to sleek, web-based, secure, iptable-firewall enterprise network/router firewall appliance.

For the latter, there are a number of streamlined commercial-grade, but free iptables configuration graphical tools available at little or no cost, such as SmoothWall Express or Guarddog. These packages are called *firewall tools* and run on top of your Linux/iptables installation. We introduce some of these programs, including CD-bootable firewalls, later in the chapter

TCP Wrappers: Securing Local Services

As we explained, TCP wrappers is a good choice for a single-homed/stand-alone server on a secure network where you want to limit host/network access to just a couple of services. Many application server administrators use the TCP wrappers /etc/hosts.allow and /etc/hosts.deny files to control daemon access from one easy-to-view area, then use iptables for more advanced state-based, filter, and packet-level service control (of course, you can use iptables for all of this if you prefer.)

Tip

If you control client access with TCP wrappers, keep as much of your client control data in the /etc/hosts.allow and /etc/hosts.deny files as you can, rather than spreading it across both TCP wrappers and iptables. This will help prevent you from defining conflicting rules across the two mechanisms and potentially save your hours of chasing down ghosts when troubleshooting service-related issues.

Table 11-2 shows common services and daemons, with notes that are critical when configuring your services in /etc/hosts.allow and /etc/hosts.deny. The first column shows the service name, while the daemon name is the actual binary daemon name that you use in the /etc/hosts.allow and /etc/hosts.deny file. Many of these services are controlled by the xinetd master daemon. You can see which services are xinetd-based with this command:

```
# chkconfig --list| grep -v 0:
xinetd based services:
        chargen-udp:    off
        rsync:   off
        chargen:        off
...
```

The xinetd daemon itself can be viewed with the following command:

```
# chkconfig --list xinetd
xinetd      0:off   1:off   2:on    3:on    4:on    5:on    6:off
```

Table 11-2: Common Services' and Deaemon's Usage of libwrap

Service	Port	Description	Daemon	Notes
FTP	21	VS-FTP	Vsftpd	Libwrap support. Stand-alone daemon, no xinetd.
SSH	22	OpenSSH/sftp/scp	sshd	Libwrap support. Stand-alone daemon, no xinetd.
HTTP	80	Apache/web (HyperText Transport Protocol)	httpd	No libwrap support. Use iptables or daemon's own allow/deny features. Stand-alone daemon, no xinetd.
POP3	110	Post Office Protocol V3	ipop3d	Libwrap support. xinetd based.

Continued

Table 11-2: *(continued)*

Service	Port	Description	Daemon	Notes
IMAP	143	IMAP2 mail Daemon	`imapd`	Libwrap support. xinetd based.
SunRPC	111	RPC/NFS related service	`portmap`	Special case or multi-port protocol. Stand-alone daemon, no xinetd.
HTTPS	443	Apache/web SSL	`httpd`	NO libwrap support. Use iptables' or daemon's own allow/deny features. Stand-alone daemon, no xinetd .
SMTP	25	Sendmail/SMTP mail	`sendmail`	Libwrap support. Stand-alone daemon, no xinetd.
Domain	53	BIND DNS	`named`	NO libwrap support. Use iptables or daemon's own allow/deny features. Stand-alone daemon, no xinetd.
CUPS-LPD	515	CUPS/LPD Compat. Port	`cups-lpd`	Libwrap support. xinetd based.
IPP	631	CUPS Printing	`cupsd`	Only runs bound to localhost (127.0.0.1). Stand-alone daemon, no xinetd.
IMAPS	993	IMAP over SSL	`imapd`	Libwrap support. xinetd based.
POP3S	995	POP3 over SSL	`Ipop3d`	Libwrap support. xinetd based.
NFS	2049	Network ile System	`Nfs`	Libwrap support. Special case or multi-port protocol. Requires portmap/SunRPC service. Stand-alone daemon(s), no xinetd.
MySQL	3306	MySQL database	`mysqld`	No libwrap support. Use iptables or daemon's own allow/deny features.

Note   Table 11-2 is really only accurate for newer Red Hat– and Fedora Core–based systems. Older systems or non-Red Hat–based distributions will need to compile their own list of such services. See the "Compiling a Daemon List for non-Red Hat Distributions" sidebar for instructions on how to do this.

The services in Table 11-2 are common services that most administrators offer on their Internet or intranet servers. Services not compiled with `libwrap` support need to have network access controlled from either their own configuration files, as with Apache's `/etc/httpd/conf/httpd.conf`, or through iptables. The latter option is the most secure.

Note   The terms libwrap and TCP wrappers are often used synonymously. The first is the library, and the second is the name of the package. Likewise, you may hear the terms `/etc/hosts.allow` or `/etc/hosts.deny` used interchangeably with the term `host_access`. Here the first two are the files used, and the latter is what these files are functionally referred to as in the man page for the files.

Note that NFS atop `portmap` is a special case. NFS is actually not a single daemon, but several daemons tied together to the network daemon called `portmap` that offers the Remote Procedure Call or SunRPC service. In this way, NFS can be controlled through `/etc/hosts.deny` by blocking access to the `portmap` daemon, which in turn identifies and allows NFS services to run. However, remember that TCP wrappers still allows clients to hit the userspace service (libwrap and a daemon), so it is inherently less secure. If you want a truly hardened and secure NFS implementation on the Internet, use iptables and not TCP wrappers.

Compiling a Daemon List for Non-Red Hat Distributions

If you're not on a Red Hat– or Fedora Core–based system and can't rely on Table 11-2 to determine your services use of `libwrap` or `hosts_acces`, you can compile your own complete list of daemons controllable through your `hosts_access` files, as well as all your `xinetd` subdaemons, and save the output as a single text file for future reference. First, get the list of stand-alone binaries in `/usr/sbin` with the following command:

```
# strings -f /usr/sbin/* /sbin/* | grep hosts_access | cut -
f1 -d:| sort -u > wrapper-daemons.txt
```

We're using strings on the single line command above instead of `egrep`, as we did previously, because it creates cleaner output and is the way Red Hat recommends doing this check.

Next, get the list of `xinetd`-controlled subservices with this command:

```
# chkconfig -list | grep -v [0-z]:[\!o] | cut -f1 -d:|
sort | cut -f2| grep -v ^xin >> wrapper-daemons.txt
```

The output from both commands will be saved in the file `wrapper-daemons.txt`. For related port numbers, see the file `/etc/services` for the human-readable ports for each service.

Remember that the first step to securing a server, whether you use TCP wrappers or iptables, is to shut down all the services you don't need. Cutting down the number of running services decreases your *network security profile,* that is, how big of a target your server appears to be. See Chapter 4 for more information.

The host_access Files

The behavior of TCP wrappers `hosts_access` controls is controlled by the values stored in `/etc/hosts.allow` and `/etc/hosts.deny`. In this section, we show you the default versions of these files and offer some tips on configuring them appropriately.

The default `/etc/hosts.allow` file is quite basic:

```
# cat /etc/hosts.allow
#
# hosts.allow     This file describes the names of the hosts
#                 which are allowed to use the local INET
#                 services, as decided by the '/usr/sbin/tcpd'
#                 server.
#
```

Same is the default /etc/hosts.deny file:

```
# cat /etc/hosts.deny
#
# hosts.deny    This file describes the names of the hosts
#               which are *not* allowed to use the local INET
#               services, as decided by the '/usr/sbin/tcpd'
#               server.
#
# The portmap line is redundant, but it is left to remind you
# that the new secure portmap uses hosts.deny and hosts.allow.
# In particular you should know that NFS uses portmap!
```

The basic idea behind TCP wrappers is that the hosts.allow file contains hosts that are allowed to access services on your machine, while hosts.deny contains hosts that are denied entry. Specifically, any service request that does not match a service : host pairing value contained in either file, or which is not denied by a wildcard in the deny file (or is not compiled against libwrap at all), is allowed by default. If a librwrap service : host match is made in the hosts.allow file, then the service is let in. If a librwrap service : host match is made in the hosts.deny file, then the service is not allowed.

Let's see how this is used in the real world. Assume that you want to set up and control resources on a multiservice server in your department. You want to run an extranet web server (internal resources such as webmail on the Internet to only select clients) to only remote office clients in the IP space 172.16.1.*, and also want to have some limited internal e-mail SMTP/POP and SSH/sFTP access on the server. The users of this system need to get their e-mail via POP3 from an internal LAN with IP addresses in the 10.*.*.* range, as well as from dial-up and wireless networks in the 192.168.1.* range. However, only administrators should be able to SSH into the server from the internal administrative LAN (10.1.1.*). You can set these parameters with TCP wrappers. Unfortunately, Apache access is controllable only through iptables or its own daemon config file; we'll deal with this and SMTP later with iptables. Let's just do the SSH/sFTP and POP3 part with TCP wrappers. See the following table:

Service	Allowed Network(s)	How to control access
SSH/sFTP	10.1.1.*	TCP wrappers or iptables
SMTP	10.*.*.*/192.168.1.*	TCP wrappers or iptables
POP3	10.*.*.*/192.168.1.*	TCP wrappers or iptables
HTTP	172.16.1.*	Only iptables (or httpd.conf)

We'll show how SSH and POP3 are done with wrappers/hosts_access and do the rest with iptables.

Note   Under Fedora Core, sendmail/SMTP is fully SMTP-Auth enabled, meaning that to relay mail through your server users provide both username and password before sending mail. However, the default SMPT-Auth does not encrypt the password information or the mail itself. To have encrypted mail sessions, you need to enable additional measures such as TLS(SSL) and POP3S or IMAPS. For more information on enabling SMTP-Auth w/TLS, see www.falkotimme.com/howtos/sendmail_smtp_auth_tls/index.php.

The line formatting of the /etc/hosts.allow and /etc/hosts.deny files are the same. The only difference is in how they impact daemon client–host requests. Entries in both files are written in three comma-delimited columns, as in

```
daemon_list :  hosts_list [ :  spawn ( shell-command) ]
```

The daemon's name goes in the first column, then the hosts allowed or denied access (designated by host name, IP address(es), or network(s)), and finally an optional shell script or program that runs when a request triggers a daemon:host match.

To serve the needs of the server in our example, you might construct an /etc/hosts.allow file that looks like this:

```
...
# TWW: Added 2004-01-30 (always date and comment)
# httpd flows through or is controlled by iptables
# sshd only from 10.1.1.x network, and pop3s from all of 10. + admin LAN
sshd: 10.1.1.                    #ssh allowed from local admin LAN
ipop3d, sendmail: 192.168.1. , 10. , .example.com  #pop3s allowed from
here...
...
```

Notice that the daemon name for the service is listed, not just ssh or pop3. This is key if you expect it to work.

Caution

All requests that match the daemon and host pairings in the allow file will be allowed into the server. If there is no match in this file, then the request is matched against the /etc/hosts.deny file. If there is no match in this file also, then the service is allowed by default. This illustrates why you need to remember to populate that /etc/hosts.deny file with some type of catch-deny entry, otherwise the entries above are ineffectual.

This configuration allows our admin SSH sessions from the 10.1.1.* network, and allows SMTP and POP traffic from the 192.168.1.* network, the entire 10.*.*.* network, and any IPs that resolve back to the domain *.example.com. TCP wrappers can use domain names here as it offers an autoreverse-lookup feature that should resolve any IP address that has a reverse IP to name DNS record.

Note

The daemon_list and client_list are columns separated by colons, and the lists of daemons or hosts within each column are separated by commas. If you want to allow sshd and ipop3d connections from both the 10.*.*.* and 192.168.1.* networks, simply add the following line:

```
sshd, ipop3d : 192.168.1. , 10.
```

Once you've configured /etc/hosts.allow for the connections you want to allow, it's time to block the requests you don't want. If you leave /etc/hosts.deny with no entries, all requests not explicitly matched in /etc/hosts.allow will flow through the deny file and be allowed to connect. This makes the whole point moot, so be sure to configure /etc/hosts.deny. You can do this simply, as in this example:

```
...
#TWW: Block Everything else...
ALL:ALL
```

Note that the ALL daemon listing only matches daemons compiled against `libwrap` and TCP wrappers. `Apache/httpd` does not check the `allow` and `deny` files, so it must be blocked at the outer iptables layer or in the daemon's own configuration file. The `ALL:ALL` entry in `/etc/hosts.deny` will block all service requests not explicitly permitted in `/etc/hosts.allow`, but will *not* control requests from blacklisted hosts for non-TCP wrappers compatible daemons.

Caution

Whenever making dangerous entries in `/etc/hosts.deny`, such as sshd:ALL or ALL:ALL, you must verify that the entries in `/etc/hosts.allow` are valid. If you make a mistake in `/etc/hosts.allow`, you could lock down all access to the server! A typo as simple as `ssh:...` instead of `sshd:...`, combined with an ALL:ALL entry in the `deny` file, would bar all logins no matter from whom.

TCP Wrappers Troubleshooting Tips

TCP wrappers is fairly straightforward. Even so, there are some things that might trip you up if you don't pay careful attention while you're working with the `hosts_access` files. Here are a few tips to keep you on the right path:

✦ When troubleshooting TCP wrappers problems, either flush or turn off iptables-based firewalling entirely. Wrappers and iptables are layers of security, and you can make yourself crazy trying to fix the problem in one layer when it's actually happening in the other service. The `/etc/init.d/iptables stop` command is your friend.

✦ In the same vein, if you're troubleshooting iptables, check `/etc/hosts.deny` to be sure that you don't have an unexpected `ALL:ALL` or a block that's triggering your iptables problem.

✦ Always keep a spare shell or terminal window open while working on your `allow` and `deny` files remotely! Changes in TCP wrappers affect only new client connections. If you manage to lock yourself out, you can use the open shell to get back into the file and fix the error. Just don't reboot until you're really sure it's fixed!

✦ If you choose not to use `ALL:ALL` entries in your `deny` file, you can use line-item entries with EXCEPTions like this one:

```
ipop3d, sendmail:          ALL EXCEPT 192.168.1.
```

✦ Just be sure to first *verify* your denies by inverting the logic, as in

```
ipop3d, sendmail:          ALL EXCEPT !192.168.1.
```

✦ This flips the `deny`, letting the request work from every location except the one you specify. With this, you can verify that there are no typos in the daemon name or client listing and that the wrapper is working as expected. When you're satisfied, remove the ! (UNIX negation symbol) and save the file.

✦ Even though they're helpful in line-item entries, you can't use ! and EXCEPT with ALL. The ALL daemon setting is a special case that overrides all other deny rules, and can only be overridden itself by a positive daemon:client match in the `allow` file.

✦ Some administrators like to add one or two *white-list* IP addresses to their `deny` files so that there is always a back door into the system even if they make errors elsewhere in `/etc/hosts`. Do this with a single entry in `/etc/hosts.deny` that looks like this:

```
ALL: ALL EXCEPT 192.168.1.3
```

✦ Even if you don't get a daemon name or IP address right in the `allow` file, you will always be able to get in from the `EXCEPT IP`. Just remember that the `deny` file adopts the most secure entry method. If you use this trick, you'll need to configure all allows in `/etc/hosts.allow` and let all denials flow through to the `deny` file.

Detect and Respond to Port Scans

You can use an older feature of TCP wrappers to monitor port activity. This feature causes a shell script or process to spawn when an allow or deny rule is matched. The following sample `/etc/hosts.deny` file line shows how to set this up:

```
portmap: ALL : spawn (/usr/bin/logger -t WRAPPER_DENY sunrpc host %a)
```

This will create `/var/log/messages` entries like this:

```
Feb 5 22:58:10 localhost WRAPPER_DENY: sunrpc hit from host
192.168.128.25
Feb 5 22:58:10 localhost WRAPPER_DENY: sunrpc hit from host
example.com
Feb 5 22:58:10 localhost WRAPPER_DENY: sunrpc hit from host
www.example.com
Feb 5 22:58:10 localhost portmap[2009]: connect from 192.168.128.25 to
getport(mountd): request from unauthorized host
Feb 5 22:58:10 localhost WRAPPER_DENY: sunrpc hit from host
192.168.128.25
Feb 5 22:58:10 localhost WRAPPER_DENY: sunrpc hit from host
example.com
Feb 5 22:58:10 localhost WRAPPER_DENY: sunrpc hit from host
www.example.com
Feb 5 22:58:10 localhost portmap[2016]: connect from
192.168.128.25 to
getport(mountd): request from unauthorized host
```

The script called here is actually the syslog client program that adds an entry to the system log with a date and time stamp and the entry `WRAPPER DENY: sunrpc from host <source IP/host>`.

However, this method will not log stealth scans and other nonconnecting types of port scanning. Most intrusion-detection professionals agree that there are newer and better ways to monitor port scans and report them and even automate the whole port monitoring job. See Chapter 10 for more information on `portsentry` and some of the powerful automation and detection options that it offers, especially when coupled with iptables.

iptables and the Single Server

If you decide that you need more features, or that TCP wrappers can't handle all the services you want to restrict, iptables is probably the best solution for you. In this section, we show you how to configure iptables for a stand-alone server. Later in the chapter, you'll learn how to set up iptables for a full-blown, dual-homed network firewall.

iptables Configuration Tools

Under Red Hat Linux and related distributions, such as Fedora Core, iptables is controlled at boot time by the /etc/sysconfig/iptables file. If you turned on firewalling at installation, this file is created by default. To ensure that your firewall rules are persistent across reboots, all changes to iptables need to be saved back to this file. There are several ways to do this: You can edit this file by hand and restart iptables to make your changes live, make live run time changes with the iptables command directly and then use /etc/init.d/iptables save to save your changes back out to /etc/sysconfig/iptables, or for very basic changes, you can use the Red Hat security level graphical administration tool. To open the tool, click the Red Hat icon in the toolbar and select System Settings ⟿ Security Level, or issue the command redhat-config-securitylevel at a command prompt. The GUI tool will appear, as shown in Figure 11-4. If you're not running X windows, use the ncurses (text-user interface) version redhat-config-securitylevel-tui.

Figure 11-4: Red Hat Linux offers a graphical tool to configure iptables.

Caution

You must run this tool as root. Because the operating system can hold on to the root password for up to 5 minutes, be sure that you click the Forget Authorization button when you are finished with iptables configuration. If you plan to leave the machine before 5 minutes are up, log out of everything and lock it down. Firewalls can't enforce physical security.

The graphical interface is a basic tool that lets you enable/disable firewall (iptable) settings, and if enabled, customize the iptables for trusted network interfaces, services, and custom ports.

Caution

When you use this tool, it totally overwrites all existing configurations in /etc/sysconfig/iptables. If you tell it to disable the firewall, it *deletes* the file all together! Use the tool only if you have not already configured iptables by hand, or if you want to erase your previous settings and start over with a default iptables configuration.

Be sure to back up your iptables configuration files on a regular basis. You can do this with a simple command:

```
# cp -a /etc/sysconfig/iptables
/etc/sysconfig/iptables-$(date +%Y-%m-%d)_BAK
```

This command saves a date-stamped version of the configuration file. Back up the file every time you want to make changes to the configuration. If you make a mistake, it will be easy to restore settings that work.

The graphical security tool is a good way to get started with iptables configuration. It creates a basic /etc/sysconfig/iptables file, and lets you get a simple—but operational—stand-alone server firewall configuration in place quickly. You can then poke around the /etc/sysconfig/iptables file it creates and get a feel for how iptables works. If you want to disable any of the settings created by the tool, simply go into the file and comment out the lines that you don't want to use, and restart iptables. For example, in this /etc/sysconfig/iptables file we have commented out a default line that, combined with the last two lines of the file, would normally keep the server from answering ICMP/pings (or answering with a Destination Unreachable message):

```
...
-A INPUT -j RH-Firewall-1-INPUT
-A FORWARD -j RH-Firewall-1-INPUT
-A RH-Firewall-1-INPUT -i lo -j ACCEPT
#-A RH-Firewall-1-INPUT -p icmp --icmp-type any -j ACCEPT
-A RH-Firewall-1-INPUT -p 50 -j ACCEPT
-A RH-Firewall-1-INPUT -p 51 -j ACCEPT
...
-A RH-Firewall-1-INPUT -j REJECT --reject-with icmp-host-prohibited
COMMIT
```

As you can see, rule ordering is very important here. Once you've made your changes, whether by hand, restart iptables so that the manual changes to the file will take effect:

```
#  /etc/init.d/iptables restart
Flushing firewall rules:                        [ OK ]
Setting chains to policy ACCEPT: filter         [ OK ]
Unloading iptables modules:                     [ OK ]
Applying iptables firewall rules:               [ OK ]
```

Caution   Try not to work on iptables remotely if at all possible. If you must, be sure that you have a back door or other safeguard in place. Inevitably, the one time you forget this will be the one time you lock yourself out.

Configuring a Stand-Alone Server

Remember the server that we configured in the *TCP Wrappers* section? Only some of its services could be managed with wrappers. In this section, we will secure the Apache and sendmail services with iptables.

Note   Stand-alone server iptable configurations, or *personal firewalls,* are usually more simple to create than are network firewall configurations. With stand-alone server configurations, you're usually only concerned with service/packet filtering, rather than multiinterface NAT rules used in multihomed *network* firewall configurations.

Before you begin making firewall rule changes, however, do a baseline port scan. You can compare the before and after scans to see how well your iptables configurations worked.

First, turn off iptables with this command:

```
# service iptables stop
```

Next, go to a different Linux box on your network and use the nmap program. nmap is a free portscanner; if it is not already installed on your network, you can download it from www.insecure.org/nmap/. Issue the command nmap *x.x.x.x*, where *x.x.x.x* is the IP address of the server you're creating iptable entries on. You will need to issue this command as root. The output will look like this:

```
Starting nmap V. 2.54BETA31 ( www.insecure.org/nmap/ )
Interesting ports on mydomain.com (10.1.1.1):
(The 1542 ports scanned but not shown below are in state: closed)
Port       State       Service
21/tcp     open        ftp
22/tcp     open        ssh
25/tcp     open        smtp
53/tcp     open        domain
79/tcp     open        finger
80/tcp     open        http
110/tcp    open        pop-3
143/tcp    open        imap2
443/tcp    open        https
515/tcp    open        printer
993/tcp    open        imaps
995/tcp    open        pop3s
Nmap run completed -- 1 IP address (1 host up) scanned in 0 seconds
```

Use the nmap usage nmap -vv x.x.x.x if you want a more verbose description.

Save this information or redirect it out to a file by appending >first-scan.txt to the command; after your stand-alone firewall configuration is up and running scan the system again to compare the effect your settings had.

Tip

If you only need to control access to services on a trusted network, then TCP wrappers may be sufficient to allow and disallow networks or groups of IP addresses to your system. From a security perspective, however, TCP wrappers allows attackers to "touch" your networking stack and, ultimately, some aspects of the services running on it, whether they're blocked with wrappers or not. If vulnerability, buffer overflows, and IP stack access are of concern to you, then look toward iptables and its kernel-level protection rather than the application/daemon level of control offered by TCP wrappers.

The iptables Command

Many security experts will argue that iptables is best managed from the command line if you have the time and expertise that it requires. The iptables command has a number of options that allow you to access the iptables subsystem in a variety of ways. Before you begin to issue iptables commands, however, make sure that the kernel modules are loaded:

```
# lsmod | grep ^ip
ipt_REJECT    4216    1    (autoclean)
```

```
ipt_state      1080   3  (autoclean)
ip_conntrack   27752  1  (autoclean) [ipt_state]
iptable_filter 2444   1  (autoclean)
ip_tables      14560  3 [ipt_REJECT    ipt_state iptable_filter]
```

This output shows that the base kernel module ip_tables is running, and that several related modules are loaded on top of it. This is roughly the default state on a Fedora Core system. If you see output similar to this, you can check the status of the iptables service with the following command:

```
#  /etc/init.d/iptables status
Table: filter
Chain INPUT (policy ACCEPT)
target prot opt source          destination
RH-Firewall-1-INPUT all -- anywhere            anywhere

Chain FORWARD (policy ACCEPT)
target  prot opt source         destination
RH-Firewall-1-INPUT all -- anywhere            anywhere

Chain OUTPUT (policy ACCEPT)
target prot opt source          destination

Chain RH-Firewall-1-INPUT (2 references)
target prot opt source          destination
ACCEPT all -- anywhere           anywhere
ACCEPT icmp-- anywhere           anywhere  icmp any
ACCEPT ipv6-crypt-- anywhere        anywhere
ACCEPT ipv6-auth-- anywhere         anywhere
ACCEPT all -- anywhere           anywhere          state RELATED,ESTABLISHED
ACCEPT tcp -- anywhere           anywhere          state NEW tcp dpt:http
ACCEPT tcp -- anywhere           anywhere          state NEW tcp dpt:ssh
REJECT all -- anywhere           anywhere          reject-with icmp-host-
prohibited
```

This output shows that iptables is running, that you are looking (by default) at the table named "filter," and that there are several chains of rules in the "filter" table.

In a nutshell, iptables contains three base tables (nat, mangle, and filter), each of which contains various chains of rules. Some functions (such as INPUT, OUTPUT, RH-Firewall-1-INPUT, intrusion, portsentry, and so on) contain an ordered set of access control rules called a *chain*. Each chain is named for the associated function. A chain of rules determines the ACCEPT or REJECT ordering and behavior toward a given packet flowing through the chain. Figure 11-5 illustrates this concept.

Note   The status of iptables can be determined in several ways, using one of these commands:

```
#  /etc/init.d/iptables status
```

```
#  service iptables status
```

```
#  iptables -L
```

In the last command, if you do not specify a table to display, the default table is "filter," though there are two other tables of chains called "nat" and "mangle." The nat table is what allows you to set up a multihome network firewall.

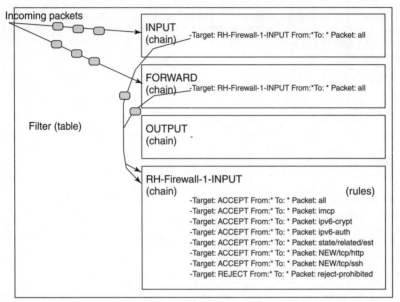

Figure 11-5: The most commonly used iptables for simple firewalls, called "filter." iptables is composed of multiple sets of tables of chains, and these chains have ordered sets of rules.

The "filter" table contains INPUT, FORWARD, and OUTPUT chains by default (as seen in Figure 11-5). In newer Red Hat Linux and Fedora Core systems, you will also see a custom chain in "filter" called RH-Firewall-1-INPUT. This custom chain is installed for you, and is configured at installation time based on the options you select. (Yours may appear slightly different from the one shown here depending on your installation selections.) Note that the INPUT and FORWARD chains pass control to the RH-Firewall-1-INPUT chain. Most of the ACCEPT and REJECT rules in this final chain control what is allowed into the server and what is not. For example, if you follow along Figure 11-5 or the previous iptable listing, in this particular setup it looks as if the first rule in the RH-Firewall-1-INPUT chain ACCEPTs "all" from "*" to "*". This is not for all interfaces on the server but actually just for the lo (localhost) loopback device (the server itself), but it is just not identified as such in this type of listing. The second rule in the RH-Firewall-1-INPUT chain ACCEPTs icmp (for example, ping) packets, followed by IPv6 encryption and authentication packets, incoming traffic state related to already established sessions, incoming NEW web (http) and ssh requests, in that order. Everything else is caught by the last REJECT rule in that chain and rejected. Remember, order is important when setting up chains of rules (or ACLs) like this.

/etc/sysconfig/iptables

Querying iptables for its table listing is a good way to see what's currently running in your firewall configuration. If someone has added a new rule from the command line, you'll see it in the output of `iptables -L`. However, you can also examine the `/etc/sysconfig/iptables` configuration file to view the "filter" table and its boot time chains. Here's the `/etc/sysconfig/iptables` configuration file that produced the rule set we listed above:

```
# cat /etc/sysconfig/iptables
# Firewall configuration written by redhat-config-securitylevel
# Manual customization of this file is not recommended.
*filter
:INPUT ACCEPT [0:0]
:FORWARD ACCEPT [0:0]
:OUTPUT ACCEPT [0:0]
:RH-Firewall-1-INPUT - [0:0]
-A INPUT -j RH-Firewall-1-INPUT
-A FORWARD -j RH-Firewall-1-INPUT
-A RH-Firewall-1-INPUT -i lo -j ACCEPT
-A RH-Firewall-1-INPUT -p icmp -icmp-type any -j ACCEPT
-A RH-Firewall-1-INPUT -p 50 -j ACCEPT
-A RH-Firewall-1-INPUT -p 51 -j ACCEPT
-A RH-Firewall-1-INPUT -m state --state ESTABLISHED,RELATED -j ACCEPT
-A RH-Firewall-1-INPUT -m state --state NEW -m tcp -p tcp --dport 80-j ACCEPT
-A RH-Firewall-1-INPUT -m state --state NEW -m tcp -p tcp --dport 22-j ACCEPT
-A RH-Firewall-1-INPUT -j REJECT --reject-with icmp-host-prohibited
COMMIT
```

Caution   As with most ACL systems, order rules in chains is critical. If the last `REJECT` line were higher in the file or another `-A` append command was issued after iptables was reloaded, the rules after or below the `REJECT` would never be used since the `REJECT` would effectively block any additions from ever being used. If you want to add rules to `/etc/sysconfig/iptables`, keep this in mind. If you like to add rules to your chains manually via the command line with the `iptables` command, options like `iptables -L line-number`, and the `-I` insert option can save you a lot of troubleshooting pain (instead of just using the regular `-A` append option). (More on this last method later.)

Stepping through the RH-Firewall-1-INPUT Chain

If you're having problems thus far, don't worry. In this section we'll step through each rule in our filter table here.

The settings in this example `RH-Firewall-1-INPUT` chain are fairly basic. The first entries are the rules that tell the `INPUT` and `FORWARD` chains to *jump* (`-j`), or send, their output on to the `RH-Firewall-1-INPUT` chain:

```
-A INPUT -j RH-Firewall-1-INPUT
-A FORWARD -j RH-Firewall-1-INPUT
```

These settings are actually not a part of the `RH-Firewall-1-INPUT` chain itself (they belong to the `INPUT` and `FORWARD` chains), but without them the `RH-Firewall-1-INPUT` chain would never be referenced since all incoming requests come through either the `INPUT` or the `FILTER` chain.

The first rule of the `RH-Firewall-1-INPUT` chain is actually

```
-A RH-Firewall-1-INPUT -i lo -j ACCEPT
```

This rule tells iptables to automatically `ACCEPT` all packets coming in from lo (the loopback device). Remember this line from the `iptables -L` output shown earlier?

```
ACCEPT all -- anywhere          anywhere
```

Although `all` from `anywhere` is allowed, the first rule in the `RH-Firewall-1-INPUT` chain shows that this actually happens only for the lo or the loopback or localhost interface (127.0.0.1), as defined by the `-i lo` component of the rule.

The next line of the chain contains the first all-interface rule:

```
-A RH-Firewall-1-INPUT -p icmp --icmp-type any -j ACCEPT
```

This line shows that the firewall is appending (the `-A` switch) a new rule to the chain and that the protocol type ICMP (`-p icmp`) will jump to the target `ACCEPT`. The location to which these requests jump is called the target, and it defines how this type of incoming data will be handled. Since ping uses ICMP (Internet Control Management Protocol), this rule says that the firewall will `ACCEPT` and react normally to ping requests, as well as other ICMP packet types.

If you've never used iptables before, or don't have a good feel for it, it is critical that you *get a feel for* how this all works. For those readers who aren't functionally familiar with iptables, let's stop for a moment and test some of what I've been showing you.

Hands-on Testing with iptables Rules

To test the aforementioned set-up with ICMP and just get a better feel for iptables usage and behavior, work through this minilab to familiarize yourself with iptables on a Red Hat Linux or Fedora Core systems.

If you're fine so far and you've done this kind of thing before, feel free to just skim through this section and move on to the *RH-Firewall-1-INPUT chain (continued)* section that follows.

In this exercise, you remove the ICMP `ACCEPT` rule, restart iptables, and see what happens, and then follow up with a few more modifications of our default ICMP rule. But first, just follow the following steps to get a feel for how you make changes to and do testing of iptables.

1. On your Fedora Core or Red Hat Linux server, which we'll call Machine 1, open `/etc/sysconfig/iptables` with your favorite text editor. Save a backup copy with the name `/etc/sysconfig/iptables-BAK`.

2. Comment out the line that controls ICMP requests:

   ```
   #-A RH-Firewall-1-INPUT -p icmp --icmp-type any -j ACCEPT
   ```

3. Save the file with the original name, `/etc/sysconfig/iptables`, and exit the text editor.

4. Go to another machine on the network and ping Machine 1:

   ```
   # ping 10.1.1.1
   PING 10.1.1.1 (10.1.1.1) 56(84) bytes of data.
   64 bytes from 10.1.1.1: icmp_seq=0 ttl=64 time=0.086 ms
   64 bytes from 10.1.1.1: icmp_seq=1 ttl=64 time=0.060 ms
   ...
   ```

   If you are pinging from a Windows box, be sure to issue the command as `ping -t` so that it will ping continuously. Otherwise, it will ping only five times before ending the command.

5. While the ping from the second machine is active, go back to Machine 1 and restart iptables. This will load your change into the active iptable system:

```
#  /etc/init.d/iptables restart
Flushing firewall rules:                        [ OK ]
Setting chains to policy ACCEPT: filter         [ OK ]
Unloading iptables modules:                     [ OK ]
Applying iptables firewall rules:               [ OK ]
```

6. Return to the second machine and notice what the ping process is now reporting:

```
64 bytes from 10.1.1.1: icmp_seq=0 ttl=64 time=0.086 ms
64 bytes from 10.1.1.1: icmp_seq=1 ttl=64 time=0.060 ms
...
From 10.1.1.1 icmp_seq=28 Dest Unreachable, Bad Code: 10
From 10.1.1.1 icmp_seq=29 Dest Unreachable, Bad Code: 10
From 10.1.1.1 icmp_seq=30 Dest Unreachable, Bad Code: 10
From 10.1.1.1 icmp_seq=31 Dest Unreachable, Bad Code: 10
```

7. Stop the ping on the second machine with Ctrl+C and return to Machine 1.

Does this give you a feel for how to work with iptables settings on a live server? Don't forget to remove the hashmark that you used to comment out the line in /etc/sysconfig/iptables, or you won't have ping service! Re-save the configuration file and restart iptables to get everything back to normal.

You may be wondering why, if the rule ACCEPTed ICMP traffic and we commented it out, the ICMP traffic would stop. After all, the target action, ACCEPT, should only happen if there is a match; removing the rule alone should not stop ICMP itself. So, what happened when we removed the rule? Look back at the bottom of the /etc/sysconfig/iptables file and remember how packets flow through chains. Can you find the REJECT rule that triggered the behavior?

Testing Other iptables Rule Variations

If you want to change the *jump* action, or *target behavior*, to actively DROP ICMP packets immediately rather than relying on a REJECT rule later in the file, try this rule instead of the default ICMP line:

```
-A CHAIN-NAME -p icmp --icmp-type any -j DROP
```

DROPping a packet is the most secure way to *not accept* traffic. To the machines on the outside, it looks like the packet just goes away.

You may configure this rule to affect only the networking interface eth1 with (if you have a second network card)

```
-A CHAIN-NAME -p icmp --icmp-type any -i eth1 -j DROP
```

What about stopping this type of traffic only from outside networks?

```
-A CHAIN-NAME -p icmp --icmp-type any -s ! 10.1.1.0/24 --j DROP
```

Target values can be set to ACCEPT, QUEUE, RETURN, or DROP. The target QUEUE is little used, but can pass a specified packet from the kernel into user program space. RETURN is another uncommon target that simply passes a packet back to the previous chain.

The DROP target is an excellent security solution as nothing at all is returned to the requesting client. From the client's perspective, it looks like the machine isn't there at all. The machine does not appear to be on the network, which can be very useful.

Note   What happened to REJECT? REJECT is what's called a *target extension*. A target extension is a target that has been added to the core iptables system, but which comes with most base distributions of iptables, like an add-on option, if you will. There are over a dozen of these target extensions; see the man page for iptables for more information on this subject.

However, depending on the type of reject message you want to return to the client, you may want to use REJECT instead of dropping the packet cold. There are several types of REJECT messages that send specific ICMP information. Search the iptables man page for "reject-with" to learn more.

Tip   When testing iptables configurations from another machine, always use REJECT before going to DROP. Only add DROP to harden a firewall rule after you're sure the rule is working properly, and something on the network isn't at fault.

RH-Firewall-1-INPUT Chain (continued)

Now that you are familiar with more of the inner workings and functionality of iptables in action, we can return to the RH-Firewall-1-INPUT chain.

We've seen the first couple of rules in this chain (accept lo and accept icmp); the next two rules in our RH-Firewall-1-INPUT chain are

```
-A RH-Firewall-1-INPUT -p 50 -j ACCEPT
-A RH-Firewall-1-INPUT -p 51 -j ACCEPT
```

to append the acceptance of IPv6-Crypt and IPv6-Auth protocols. These are the encryption and authentication protocols defined in /etc/protocols for initiative IPv6-based connections.

Next, the entry

```
-A RH-Firewall-1-INPUT -m state --state ESTABLISHED,RELATED -j ACCEPT
```

triggers *stateful inspection*. The -m, or MATCH, extension allows you to load specialized packet-matching modules for specific packet types and uses. The -m state component tells iptables to load the special state-tracking kernel module called state. (The actual module name is ipt_state, and it requires ipt_conntrack to run properly.)

With this stateful inspection and conntrack in place, iptables can use state tables to track which incoming and outgoing packets are associated with each other over time. In essence, the system will know that incoming packet X is associated with the existing two-way session Y using protocol Z; the *state* of the session is known and tracked over time. The aforementioned rule allows ESTABLISHED bidirectional continuing packets to come in if they are associated with a known connection, and RELATED for new packets if they are associated with a known connection, even if the session is on a different port or spread over multiple ports (such as NFS or FTP).

You can even enable custom kernel modules to track other special bidirectional multiport applications like active FTP, IRC, and SNMP. This type of stateful firewalling is what allows iptables to handle, for example, active (nonpassive) FTP sessions started from your machine's `ftp` client, connecting to another FTP server, and allowing that server to establish the data channel (port 20) back to your machine. Older firewalls that don't use stateful tracking have serious problems letting external boxes establish *anything* "back in" through not-so-intelligent firewall software, and as such require passive FTP connections.

Note

This level of application-aware state tracking comes from additional `iptable` kernel modules such as `ipt_state`, `ip_conntrack`, `ip_conntrack_ftp`, and so on. To learn more, issue the command `locate netfilter/ip_|grep modules/$(uname -r)\/.`

The next two rules from our `RH-Firewall-1-INPUT` chain are something new:

```
-A RH-Firewall-1-INPUT -m state --state NEW -m tcp -p tcp --dport 80 -j
  ACCEPT
-A RH-Firewall-1-INPUT -m state --state NEW -m tcp -p tcp --dport 22 -j
  ACCEPT
```

These are rule matches for client requests on ports 80 and 22. These two rules are *holes* that have been punched in the firewall to allow new sessions (anyone who wants to try), or clients with the state `NEW`, on these ports, which happen to allow us to serve HTTP and SSH respectively. These holes were probably punched at installation when we enabled WWW and SSH traffic in the firewall for the example server we've been building, or from running the `redhat-config-securitylevel` tool.

Tip

Keep in mind that when you poke a hole in a firewall for a protocol such as HTTP or SSH, you have just decreased your overall system security by exposing two of your daemons to the outside world. You have to do this to be able to serve content (without running some type of proxy service), but by doing so you're also assuming that both daemons are secured, correctly configured, and fully up to date with the latest security patches applied. This is the weak area of firewalls. For a firewall to do its job with service holes punched in it, you are assuming that it is allowing access to services that are fully secure and up to date. If this assumption is not correct, then a firewall, even a big expensive unit, will not keep you from getting cracked or hacked. To stay safe when opening holes for your services, follow the *foundational security elements* outlined in the paper "Internet Server Security" (`www.datacenterhub.com/features/1205_Rackspace_Weeks.shtm`).

The final rule is probably the most important from a security perspective:

```
 -A RH-Firewall-1-INPUT -j REJECT --reject-with icmp-host-prohibited
```

This `REJECT`-all rule ensures that if a packet has gotten this far without matching any `ACCEPT` rules, it will match and be rejected here. Such packets won't make it past iptables into any daemons or applications, not even TCP wrappers. This function is usually managed with either a `REJECT` or a `DROP` rule. In this case, we're being network-friendly and returning a message that says `icmp-host-prohibited`.

Caution

Note that in this chapter we have already set up allow/deny of SSH traffic in the TCP wrappers level. Remember NOT to make overlapping firewall application rules in both the TCP wrappers and iptables layers of the firewall system unless you have a very specific reason to do so. If you want to use both forms of service security, you must remove the last chain rule that `REJECT`s all packets, or stop using TCP wrappers (and then non-libwrap services may be able to get through). Whichever method you choose, be sure to leave yourself a note in both /etc/hosts.allow and /etc/hosts.deny, as well as at the bottom of /etc/sysconfig/iptables, so that you don't forget your overall firewall strategy.

Finally, you must be sure that this /etc/sysconfig/iptbales file-specific command ends your iptables config file:

```
COMMIT
```

Without this, there is no firewall.

After making any changes you need in /etc/sysconfig/iptables, save the file, and exit the text editor. Restart iptables with the /etc/init.d/iptables restart command.

Firewall State Triggers

You might wonder how we figured out the various state triggers to use in our rules, such as NEW, RELATED, and ESTABLISHED. Luckily, the match module itself can help you out. Once you've loaded the module into iptables from the command line, you can ask it for help at the command line. The module will append its own help file onto the regular iptables help output. For example, to get help on the match module named state, issue this command:

```
#  iptables -m state-help
iptables v1.2.8
Usage: iptables -[AD] chain rule-specification [options]
       iptables -[RI] chain rulenum rule-specification [options]
       iptables -D chain rulenum [options]
...
  --set-counters PKTS BYTES   set counter during insert/append
  --version   -V              print package version.


state v1.2.8 options:
  --state [INVALID | ESTABLISHED | NEW | RELATED][,...]
                     State(s) to match
```

In the next to last line, the module prints all the valid states that can be used in your firewall. Try this with other match modules—but, you may ask, how do I know what other match modules I've got? Issue these commands:

```
#  export LC_ALL=C
#  locate netfilter/ipt_|grep \/$(uname -r)\/.*[a-z].o$
```

There you go—enough iptables black magic to consume your time for the next year (and potentially double your salary in the process!).

Now that you've seen the rules in /etc/sysconfig/iptables and determined the settings for your basic firewall, we can return to the example server shown earlier in this chapter. Remember that we wanted to lock down the Apache web server so that only our 172.16.1.* remote office network can access these web resources. Do that by changing the port 80 web server line from

```
-A RH-Firewall-1-INPUT -m state --state NEW -m tcp -p
   tcp --dport 80 -j ACCEPT
```

to

```
-A RH-Firewall-1-INPUT -m state --state NEW -m tcp -p
   tcp -s 172.16.1.0/24 --dport 80 -j ACCEPT
```

This will only match all of our criteria when the source IP address is from the 172.16.1.*
network. Save the file, exit the editor, and restart iptables.

Tip   Your should always test such configurations before going live. If you need to test something like this, here are two useful tips: First, simply use a ! (logical not) symbol in front
of the IP range like this ! 172.16.1.0/24 while you're testing. Second, you can even
use the IP of another desktop PC combined with the ! test to verify it works before
changing the network address back.

Once the stand-alone server's iptables firewall is set up and restarted, you can rescan your
system with the nmap program to see how the new firewall looks from the outside. The scan
will take much longer this time, since you've locked down a whole range of ports. Go to
another Linux machine on your network and issue this command:

```
# nmap 192.168.128.25
Starting nmap V. 2.54BETA31 ( www.insecure.org/nmap/ )
Interesting ports on mydomain.com (192.168.128.25):
(The 1552 ports scanned but not shown below are in state: filtered)
Port       State      Service
22/tcp     open       ssh
80/tcp     open       http
Nmap run completed -- 1 IP address (1 host up) scanned in 680 seconds
```

This network profile looks a lot better than the first time we scanned the server. All those old
services are still running, but no one but the people we want can get to them now. The fewer
doors and windows you leave open to curious passersby, the more secure your house. Notice
how long this scan took, as well. Most script kiddies will get bored and move on long before a
scan this lengthy is complete.

Note   With this iptable configuration, not even our mail services (SMTP, POP3) or FTP service
previously configured with TCP wrappers will be able to get through. If you want TCP
wrappers to be able to control them, you may need to open up iptables to universally let
those ports through. Just be sure that you track which services you're controlling through
wrappers and which ones you're controlling through iptables, or future troubleshooting
will be very frustrating indeed.

iptables and Network Firewalls

In this section, we build on the last section's dive into iptables and use it to introduce
dual-homed *network firewalls*. Entire books have been written on the complexities of this
subject, so you'll find enough to get you going. We focus on the basic configuration of such
firewalls, as well as offer some help on troubleshooting existing installations.

When securing an entire network with iptables instead of just a single server, you need to
think in different terms. Whereas a firewall on a single server accepts and rejects packets for
applications on that machine, when you set up a network NAT-based firewall you are basically

configuring a type of security-based network router, which performs functions such as Network Address Translation, state tracking, and port/address forwarding. Some people even use Linux NAT firewalls to handle tasks like web/FTP proxying, bandwidth throttling, and Quality of Service (or QoS) controls.

Note Network Address Translation, or NAT, is the technology used on a network gateway, router, or firewall that allows it to translate network addresses and usually also track sessions between networks with SPI. Such devices in the commercial world are usually configured for the enterprise with routable IP ranges on the outside and nonroutable IP address ranges on the inside. This is a very secure arrangement, as nothing from the untrusted outside interface will be allowed through the firewall unless it has been requested by an IP on the inside or otherwise explicitly permitted via NAT by the firewall. Some people refer to this configuration as a type of *Transparent TCP Proxy Router*. See www.ipprimer.com/nat.cfm for more information on NAT theory.

Earlier in this chapter, we described iptables as the outer layer of network security, followed by TCP wrappers and then by individual daemon configuration files. In this dual-homed routing firewall configuration the layout is somewhat different. Figure 11-6 shows a simplified view of this concept. Note that this figure does not indicate actual packet flow, but simply illustrates an idea.

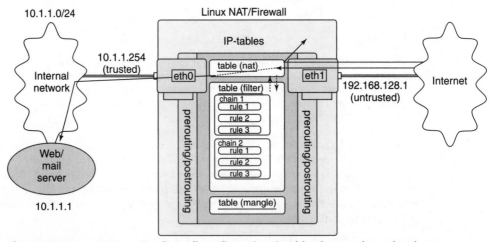

Figure 11-6: In a NAT routing firewall configuration, iptables forms a boundary between networks.

As you see in this figure, when configured as a NAT routing firewall, iptables forms a security boundary between internal and external networks. The firewall in this figure is set up so that all connections going through the firewall are translated between interfaces automatically. And since it is state based, it is session/protocol sensitive.

If you have the hardware for this configuration and are going to assemble it, be sure that you stop iptables, and delete the iptables file before continuing. You don't want any other settings interfering with what you're working on. Use these commands to stop iptables and list the filter table:

```
# /etc/init.d/iptables stop
Flushing firewall rules:                                    [ OK ]
Setting chains to policy ACCEPT: filter                     [ OK ]
Unloading iptables modules:                                 [ OK ]
# iptables -L
Chain INPUT (policy ACCEPT)
target     prot opt source                    destination

Chain FORWARD (policy ACCEPT)
target     prot opt source                    destination

Chain OUTPUT (policy ACCEPT)
target     prot opt source                    destination
```

If you want to check the NAT table before beginning work as well, issue this command:

```
# iptables -L -t nat
```

Caution

Even if you're working on a Red Hat or Fedora Core box, *never* use the Red Hat graphical firewall configuration tool (`redhat-config-securitylevel`) to build dual-homed systems. It is not intended for building hardened network NAT firewalls.

Building Firewall Rules

In the previous section, we showed you how to build the "filter" table using the packet flow from input and output chains into the default `RH-Firewall-1-INPUT` chain. In this section, as we begin to work with packets flowing from one network and being routed to another, it's easier to work with the "nat" table and its related chains.

Manually Entering and Saving Rules

Now that you've backed everything up, it's time to start adding your own rules to the existing configuration. In this example, we'll show you how to do it by hand so that you'll be able to follow along no matter what version of Linux you're using. At the end, we'll save the configuration so that it's usable on a Red Hat–based system; if you're using another Linux distribution, save your commands out to a file and use that new file as your iptables firewall startup script.

Note

Under Red Hat Linux and Fedora Core, when you manually enters iptable commands directly from the command line tool `iptables`, you need to then save them out to `/etc/sysconfig/iptables` with the `iptables-save` command:

```
# iptables-save > /etc/sysconfig/iptables
```

or

```
# /etc/init.d/iptables save
```

Be aware that your settings will look slightly different when they are saved through this method, but they'll be organized and separated in a logical manner, and you will lose any commenting that you previously had.

Setting up NAT/PAT

The "nat" table can be configured for SNAT (Source NAT), and DNAT (Destination NAT), packet modifying or mangling. This means that anything from a specified IP address can be *mangled* (rewritten) to appear as if it comes from another location using SNAT. Likewise, anything destined for a specified IP address can be mangled and sent to a different IP or port under DNAT. This concept is often called *port/IP mapping* or *Port Address Translation* (PAT).

 Tip If you aren't running a Red Hat–based Linux and you don't want to mess with manually configuring NAT/PAT, you might consider running a simple boot-time iptables setup script. There are a number of these firewall scripts available on the Internet. Some of the basic versions are designed for single-homed firewalls, like KISS, while others have advanced multihomed features. Advanced Policy Firewall, for example, offers dshield.org blocklist support, simple configuration, management scripts, and a very nice cross-distribution modular design. See the *Firewall Resources* section at the end of the chapter for more information.

The remainder of this section shows how to create a dual-home network firewall iptables config file that does the following:

1. Sets up Port Address Translation for web (80), SMTP (25), and "Ident" so that all web and incoming e-mail will get routed to our web/e-mail server (10.1.1.1).

2. Keeps internal LAN broadcast traffic (in 10.1.1.*) from being processed on the firewall or looping back in on itself.

3. Sets up internal LAN-based masquerading and forwarding for the "nat" table for internal traffic (eth0/10.1.1.* as in Figure 11-6) going out over eth1 (external Internet) so that it adopts the external IP address of the firewall (192.168.128.1).

4. Enables packet forwarding in iptables for eth0 (internal LAN) to be sent to the "nat" table so the last step works.

5. DROPs Syn, invalid, and unclean packets hitting the external or *unstrusted* (eth1) interface.

6. Sets up a default DROP policy (default rule) for any unmatched packets in the FORWARD chain.

7. Allows SSH access to the firewall itself from the internal LAN (for administrator access from inside).

8. Allows pings of the firewall.

9. DROPs everything else on the INPUT chain.

10. Applies some final security/logging settings.

11. And sets up IPv4 forwarding in the kernel so that this will all work.

You must be logged in as root to run the following commands. As you see each group of commands, simply type them in without the comments, in order, and only once. If you mess up use iptables-save or iptables -L to display your settings, starting over or inserting/deleting entries as needed.

We used the Debian Linux nat-fw-up firewall scripts as a reference while writing this chapter. You can see the whole script at www.thing.dyndns.org/debian/iptables.htm.

The first commands to enter in your chain will configure DNAT-based port mapping, or PAT. These commands send all incoming web, e-mail, and identification traffic requests to the web/e-mail server machine:

```
# iptables -A PREROUTING -t nat -p tcp -i eth1 --dport 80 -j DNAT --to
10.1.1.1
# iptables -A PREROUTING -t nat -p tcp -i eth1 --dport 25 -j DNAT --to
10.1.1.1
# iptables -A PREROUTING -t nat -p tcp -i eth1 --dport 113 -j DNAT --to
10.1.1.1
```

With these commands, you'll be working with the PREROUTING chain in the "nat" table. These rules will affect only traffic coming in from the external eth1 interface on ports 80 (http), 25 (smtp), and 113 (identification). All requests will be mangled and redirected to the web/e-mail server at 10.1.1.1 on the same ports. With these settings in place, any external user can hit the firewall's IP address and get web or e-mail services from an internal server.

Tip   You can do this with almost any service on any server that's on your internal network. You can even mangle requests to multiple internal IP addresses to do round-robin load balancing.

The next command is a safeguard that prevents internal traffic from looping back in on itself. With this command, anything coming from eth0, going through the nat/PREROUTING chain, and heading back to the 10.1.1.0 network will be dropped rather than rattling around in a loop:

```
# iptables -A PREROUTING -t nat -i eth0 -d 10.1.1.0/24 -j DROP
```

Next, set up the masquerading and forwarding rules that allow all internal network hosts to assume the identity of the firewall's external IP address. Issue the command

```
# iptables -t nat -A POSTROUTING -s 10.1.1.0/24 -o eth1 -j MASQUERADE
```

to set up the nat/POSTROUTING chain. Any internal IP addresses that are output to the eth1 interface will now be masqueraded as the external address.

Next, issue this command:

```
# iptables -A FORWARD -i eth0 -j ACCEPT
```

Traffic coming from the trusted internal network over the eth0 interface will be let out through nat/POSTROUTING to the untrusted external network.

Note   The FORWARD chain is a special type of chain. It passes packets outside the normal filtering, mangling, and local processing routines, and sends them directly to the "nat" table's postrouting chain. FORWARD effectively moves a packet past NAT to another interface.

The next set of commands will clean up known "dirty" packets that will inevitably hit the firewall:

```
# iptables -A FORWARD -p tcp ! --syn -m state --state NEW -j DROP
# iptables -A FORWARD -m state --state INVALID -j DROP
# iptables -A FORWARD -m unclean -j DROP
```

These commands keep the packets from passing the firewall, since they are not legitimate requests for services or data.

Now, issue the command that defines the DROP policy for the filter/FORWARD chain. This command sets the default FORWARD chain's DROP policy, which is a critical security element of a good firewall:

```
# iptables -P FORWARD DROP
```

The next step is to define general settings for expected traffic. The following commands will allow SSH connections (at this point, only for internal eth0 connections to the firewall itself), return ESTABLISHED/RELATED packets, and permit outgoing NEW connections from the local and trusted interfaces (lo and eth0):

```
# iptables -A INPUT -p tcp --syn --dport 22 -j ACCEPT
# iptables -A INPUT -m state --state ESTABLISHED,RELATED -j ACCEPT
# iptables -A INPUT -m state --state NEW -i ! eth1 -j ACCEPT
```

The final entry in the filter/INPUT chain is to allow pings and DROP everything else that has made it this far down the chain. You may or may not want to allow pings to your machine. If not, don't use the first of these commands:

```
# iptables -A INPUT -p icmp -s 0/0 --icmp-type echo-request -j ACCEPT
# iptables -P INPUT DROP
```

Apply Security Settings

Now that the basic operational rules have been set, it's time to apply some security settings. In this section, we'll configure logging and lock out intrusion attempts like Denial of Service attacks and port scans.

First, let's set up simple FORWARD chain logging based on matched FORWARD packet frequency (three/minute). For tracking down people who are scanning you, use the following commands:

```
# iptables -A FORWARD -m limit --limit 3/m -j LOG
# iptables -A FORWARD -j LOG
```

In order to stop DoS attacks, use these commands to block ping floods:

```
# iptables -A FORWARD -p tcp --syn -m limit -j ACCEPT
# iptables -A FORWARD -p tcp --tcp-flags SYN,ACK,FIN,RST RST -m limit
# iptables -A FORWARD -p icmp --icmp-type echo-request -m limit
```

Caution   Before you can use the FORWARD functions that you set up, you'll need to turn on IPv4 forwarding in the kernel. We describe this process in the *Troubleshooting iptables* section later in the chapter. If you don't turn this function on, none of these settings will work, and no data will flow through your firewall. This is one of the most often overlooked problems with new firewall setups.

You're almost done! Take a step back and look at the whole set of rules that you've created using the tool iptables-save:

```
# iptables-save
# Generated by iptables-save v1.2.8 on Sun Feb 15 14:19:40 2004
*filter
:INPUT DROP [0:0]
:FORWARD DROP [0:0]
:OUTPUT ACCEPT [42:5145]
```

```
:RH-Firewall-1-INPUT - [0:0]
-A INPUT -p tcp -m tcp --dport 22 --tcp-flags SYN,RST,ACK SYN -j ACCEPT
-A INPUT -m state --state RELATED,ESTABLISHED -j ACCEPT
-A INPUT -i ! eth1 -m state --state NEW -j ACCEPT
-A INPUT -p icmp -m icmp --icmp-type 8 -j ACCEPT
-A FORWARD -i eth0 -j ACCEPT
-A FORWARD -p tcp -m tcp ! --tcp-flags SYN,RST,ACK SYN -m state --state NEW -j DROP
-A FORWARD -m state --state INVALID -j DROP
-A FORWARD -m unclean -j DROP
-A FORWARD -m limit --limit 3/min -j LOG
-A FORWARD -p tcp -m tcp --tcp-flags SYN,RST,ACK SYN -m limit -limit
    3/hour -j ACCEPT
-A FORWARD -p tcp -m tcp --tcp-flags FIN,SYN,RST,ACK RST -m limit --limit
    3/hour
-A FORWARD -p icmp -m icmp --icmp-type 8 -m limit --limit 3/hour COMMIT
# Completed on Sun Feb 15 14:19:40 2004
# Generated by iptables-save v1.2.8 on Sun Feb 15 14:19:40 2004
*nat
:PREROUTING ACCEPT [0:0]
:POSTROUTING ACCEPT [8:460]
:OUTPUT ACCEPT [8:460]
-A PREROUTING -i eth1 -p tcp -m tcp --dport 80 -j DNAT
    --to-destination 10.1.1.1
-A PREROUTING -i eth1 -p tcp -m tcp --dport 25 -j DNAT
    --to-destination 10.1.1.1
-A PREROUTING -i eth1 -p tcp -m tcp --dport 113 -j DNAT
    --to-destination 10.1.1.1
-A PREROUTING -d 10.1.1.0/255.255.255.0 -i eth0 -j DROP
-A POSTROUTING -s 10.1.1.0/255.255.255.0 -o eth1 -j MASQUERADE
COMMIT
# Completed on Sun Feb 15 14:19:40 2004
```

Note   You may use the `iptables -L` **or** `/etc/init.d/iptables status` **commands to get information instead of using** `iptables-save` **as shown here, but these other forms do not show interface information. Use** `iptables-save` **to get output that looks like what you'd see in your** `/etc/sysconfig/iptables` **file.**

If this is accurate and you're ready to use it, you can save these configurations out to `/etc/sysconfig/iptables` with the command

```
# iptables-save > /etc/sysconfig/iptables
```

or

```
# /etc/init.d/iptables save
```

As long as you've set iptables to run in the appropriate runlevels, these changes will now persist when you reboot. Check the runlevels with the following command:

```
# chkconfig --list iptables
iptables     0:off   1:off   2:on   3:on   4:on   5:on   6:off
```

Tip   You aren't done working with your /etc/sysconfig/iptables file until you go in and add thorough comments to describe what you've done. If you don't leave comments, we bear no responsibility for the headache you'll suffer in 3 months when you try to untangle your configurations! Just remember to either use your /etc/sysconfig/iptables as your master working file, or keep a backup of your running iptables file, and any time you reissue an /etc/init.d/iptables save that you add your commenting back in. I recommend the former over the latter.

The Final Configuration

Once you have completed all the steps, this is what your /etc/sysconfig/iptables file should look like:

```
# cat /etc/sysconfig/iptables
# Generated by iptables-save v1.2.8 on Sun Feb 15 13:03:25 2004
#### MY CUSTOMIZED IPTABLE DUAL HOMED FIREWALL CONFIG ####
################################################################
## UPDATED 2004-02-15, TWW

*nat
:PREROUTING ACCEPT [1:245]
:POSTROUTING ACCEPT [2:127]
:OUTPUT ACCEPT [2:127]
########### PORT FORWARDING ##########
## Running PAT for out web/mail server (with a polite IDENT too)
-A PREROUTING -i eth1 -p tcp -m tcp --dport 80 -j DNAT
    --to-destination 10.1.1.1
-A PREROUTING -i eth1 -p tcp -m tcp --dport 25 -j DNAT
    --to-destination 10.1.1.1
-A PREROUTING -i eth1 -p tcp -m tcp --dport 113 -j DNAT
    --to-destination 10.1.1.1

######### LOOPBACK PROTECTION #########
## Don't allow internal traffic to loop back in on itself
-A PREROUTING -d 10.1.1.0/255.255.255.0 -i eth0 -j DROP
######### NAT/MASQ & TRUSTED OUT #########
## Setting up the POSTROUTING NAT/MASQUERADE
-A POSTROUTING -s 10.1.1.0/255.255.255.0 -o eth1 -j MASQUERADE
COMMIT

# Completed on Sun Feb 15 13:03:25 2004
# Generated by iptables-save v1.2.8 on Sun Feb 15 13:03:25 2004
*filter
:INPUT DROP [0:0]
:FORWARD DROP [0:0]
:OUTPUT ACCEPT [10:533]
:RH-Firewall-1-INPUT - [0:0]

################ ALLOW IN ##############
## Allowing SSH, return ESTABLISHED/RELATED, and outgoing NEW conns
-A INPUT -p tcp -m tcp --dport 22 --tcp-flags SYN,RST,ACK SYN -j ACCEPT
```

```
-A INPUT -m state --state RELATED,ESTABLISHED -j ACCEPT
-A INPUT -i ! eth1 -m state --state NEW -j ACCEPT

############### ICMP TRAFF ###############
## Allowing pings, but DROP any/everything else
-A INPUT -p icmp -m icmp --icmp-type 8 -j ACCEPT

## If coming from the trusted network, let it out...
-A FORWARD -i eth0 -j ACCEPT

############# DROP BAD STUFF #############
## Don't allow any nasty packets to be forwarded to the inside...
-A FORWARD -p tcp -m tcp ! --tcp-flags SYN,RST,ACK SYN -m state --state NEW
-j DROP
-A FORWARD -m state --state INVALID -j DROP
-A FORWARD -m unclean -j DROP

################ Logging ################
## Basic FORWARD logging based on frequency
-A FORWARD -m limit --limit 3/min -j LOG
################ DoS Attacks #############
## syn-flood protection
-A FORWARD -p tcp -m tcp --tcp-flags SYN,RST,ACK SYN -m limit
    --limit 3/hour -j ACCEPT
## stealth port scans
-A FORWARD -p tcp -m tcp --tcp-flags FIN,SYN,RST,ACK RST -m limit
    --limit 3/hour
## ping of death
-A FORWARD -p icmp -m icmp --icmp-type 8 -m limit--limit 3/hour
COMMIT
```

There you are. You've just created a really nice, iptable-based, network firewall configuration that you could legitimately use in a production environment or sell to a consulting client for several hundred dollars.

Know Thyself

Everyone who puts a firewall online should configure one by hand, at the command line level, at least once or twice. If you are relying on a graphical firewall tool, you need to know how it works in order to fix it when it breaks, and some graphical tools hide the actual settings under the guise of making it easier to use. Remember, security that you don't both fully understand *and* fully control is just an illusion. You can use GUI tools, as long as you're able to still get under the hood and see what's really going on.

Once you know how to do it by hand at the command line, and how to peek behind the curtain to check things out once in a while, you might find that a GUI tool makes your life easier from the management side. We describe some of these GUI tools in the next section.

 Caution   Whether you continue to work with iptables by hand or use a GUI, be aware of the people who know your firewalling strategies internally. The FBI has found that 80% of all *successful* system cracks/hacks come from people *within* the organization, although the vast majority of attempts are made by outsiders. This is because insiders know more about your internal systems than anyone on the outside, including your weak points. When it comes to security, you really can't trust anyone. Many organizations even go so far as to have internal checks and balances so that no single person has the passwords to everything on a secure system. If your data is precious, know who holds the keys and don't forget about internal defenses.

Graphical Firewall Tools

The vast majority of Linux firewalls are now based on iptables. If you've got the hang of iptables, and know how to "get under the hook" and check them at the command-line level, and now just want to streamline the management of your system(s) a bit, a graphical firewall administration tool may be in order. Such tools can be divided into two rough categories: full bootable or installation *firewall distributions*, which are complete systems, and *firewall tools*, which are simply graphical front ends for iptables itself on your existing system(s).

Firewall Distributions

The higher end firewall distributions tend to be commercial packages, with enterprise-type support packages. The advantage to paying for the full commercial suite is that you can often purchase support packages or higher end corporate server variants with various commercial SLAs (service level agreements) in place for when things go awry. If firewall administration is not your full-time job, such options might be quite beneficial, useful, and justifiable.

SmoothWall is a Linux-based firewall distribution that has become popular in the small business world, home offices, and medium-sized corporate installations. It's been around for quite some time and has kept up with Linux firewall innovations as they are implemented in the operating system. SmoothWall is modular, so you only have to install the features you will use. It offers VPN gateways, bandwidth management, and web content filtering, among other possibilities. On the noncommercial side, it can be had for free. Great for kicking the tires and testing! For the commercial version, it starts at around $330, and with the various add-on modules can go up to a few thousand dollars. Learn more about SmoothWall at www.smoothwall.org/ or www.smoothwall.net/.

Another good turnkey solution for corporate installations is the SUSE Firewall on CD, which is based on a bootable CD firewall distro. It is a well-rounded distribution with a host of caching and proxy services, as well as a web-based administrative tool. This package is liked because all config files are stored on floppy and upgrades come on replacement CDs that boot to RAM. So to upgrade to the latest version, you just eject the CD, insert the new one, and reboot! And if the system ever does get compromised from the inside, again, just reboot! You can even install a special VPN gateway version. Learn more at www.suse.de/en/business/products/ suse_business/firewall/index.html. Note that Novell, Inc., has recently bought the SUSE company, so the name, pricing, and nature of this product may change.

One of the newer contenders in this Open Source firewall space is Astaro Linux. It's a full install distro that is an all-in-one solution. It offers a great array of features, such as full firewall management, intrusion detection and protection, virus protection, spam protection, VPN gateway, proxy based URL filtering capabilities, and more. Pricing for this suite starts at about $350. For the latest pricing and numerous optional packages go to www.astaro.com.

Firewall Tools

If you don't need a full commercial firewall for your network, consider streamlining your firewall management by using a graphical tool to administer your iptables configuration. These tools range from simple X window GUI displays to full-fledged, firewall control systems. Choose the one that works best for the level of firewall information you need on a regular basis.

One of the newer and more powerful firewall administrative tools is KMYFirewall, which comes from the KDE project. It offers an intuitive graphical interface, is designed to work with multihome network firewalls, and gives the technical information and control over the user's system in a simple easy to follow format. Learn more and download packages from `http://kmyfirewall.sourceforge.net`.

Other front ends to iptables, such as Firestarter or Shorewall, are aimed more at personal firewalls-type control of iptables than for the full-blown network firewall. If you run a stand-alone personal firewall iptable config, you might want to check out `http://firestarter.sourceforge.net/` and `http://shorewall.net/`. These tools are a bit easier and quicker than working with iptables in a text editor and display firewall information in a way that may help you track down problems more rapidly.

Caution

Many graphical firewall tools are incompatible with each other or with existing firewall configurations on your Linux system. These programs usually do not read existing iptables configurations; in some cases, they require that you shut off your iptables set-up (such as the RH `/etc/sysconfig/iptables` and `RH-Firewall-1-INPUT`) altogether and keep it turned off with `chkconfig`. If you decide to use a graphical administrative tool for your firewall, pick one and stick with it, and don't switch back and forth between the tool and editing iptables manually.

Firewalls on CD

For those who need a simple firewall for a home network or small office, consider the free (as in beer) mini-firewall distributions on CD or floppy disk. These low- to no-cost firewalls are intended for consumer-level broadband and serve basic DHCP to the internal LAN. Some even have the option of running a tri-homed DMZ. The best thing about these little distributions is that they are usually customizable and run completely off external media.

For example, the FrazierWall firewall will e-mail you port scanning activity and firewall logs to a designated address, offers a web interface, and has a console interface as well. It runs from a single boot floppy and works just fine on a 486 machine with 16MB of RAM. FrazierWall is just one of several popular floppy and CD-based firewall distributions:

✦ FrazierWall: `www.frazierwall.com/`

✦ BBIagent: `www.bbiagent.com/en/index.html`

✦ CoyoteLinux: `www.coyotelinux.com/`

✦ FREESCO: `www.freesco.org/`

✦ LEAF: `http://leaf.sourceforge.net/`

✦ CD-Linux: `http://cd-linux.org/`

✦ Sentry Firewall CD: `www.sentryfirewall.com/`

Learn more about each of these, and other firewall options, at `http://xcssa.org/files/firewall-notes.html`.

Troubleshooting iptables

No matter how careful you are when you set up firewall rules and tables, it's likely that you'll run into a persistent problem that restarting iptables or rebooting doesn't fix. Here are some of the most frequent firewall troubles, along with hints to solve the problem quickly and efficiently.

Enabling Packet Forwarding

You may have done everything right in setting up an iptables-based dual-homed network firewall, even down to copying someone else's working /etc/sysconfig/iptables file and rebooting. This common problem doesn't seem logical and many people are just left wondering what's wrong.

Assuming there are no other networking issues at work, check to make sure that kernel support for IPv4 packet forwardng is enabled. You can check the status with the command

```
# sysctl -a | grep ip_forward
net.ipv4.ip_forward = 0
```

which is the same as this:

```
# cat /proc/sys/net/ipv4/ip_forward
0
```

To enable packet forwarding, open /etc/sysctl.conf in a text editor and make this change:

```
# Controls IP packet forwarding
net.ipv4.ip_forward = 1
```

Save the file, exit the text editor, and force sysctl to re-read /etc/sysctl and boot with the proper changes:

```
# sysctl -p
net.ipv4.ip_forward = 1
net.ipv4.conf.default.rp_filter = 1
kernel.sysrq = 0
kernel.core_uses_pid = 1
```

Try rebooting your firewall again. This allows packets to be forwarded in the kernel and traverse network interfaces. Even though iptables may be set up correctly, this can keep it all from working on a network firewall or multihome/router-based system.

This change will persist until you turn off packet forwarding (=0) through the same mechanism.

SSH Access Denied

If you set up iptables on a stand-alone workstation to allow SSH access but you cannot get in, something is obviously wrong, but what? Your problem may exist at one of several levels. You need to narrow the problem down to look at one part of the system at a time.

Fixing this is a process of elimination. First, turn off iptables:

```
# /etc/init.d/iptables stop
Flushing firewall rules:                                 [ OK ]
Setting chains to policy ACCEPT: mangle nat filter       [ OK ]
Unloading iptables modules:                              [ OK ]
```

Try logging in now. If you can get in, you've probably got a bad rule or a conflict in one of the "filter" table's chains. Check `RH-Firewall-1-INPUT` rules carefully and fix anything that's wrong.

If this doesn't work and you're running TCP wrappers as well, do you have an `ALL:ALL` entry in `/etc/hosts.deny`? Even if you have an appropriate entry in `/etc/hosts.allow`, a typo in the `allow` entry will let the `deny` file's `ALL:ALL` override the allow setting. Comment out the `ALL:ALL` and try again to test for this type of problem.

Still not working? It's probably not the firewall. Did you set up the SysV init scripts for sshd to be persistent (in your default run level) across reboots? Check to see if it's running and configured to "be up" in your default run level:

```
# /etc/init.d/sshd status
sshd (pid 3619) is running...
[root@localhost root]#  chkconfig --list sshd
sshd        0:off  1:off   2:on  3:on  4:on  5:on  6:off
```

Make the necessary changes and reboot the SSH daemon. You should also issue the command `netstat -ant|grep :22` to ensure that sshd binds to the proper port and IP. The default settings are stored in `/etc/sshd/sshd_config` and you can make changes there:

```
...
#Port 22
#Protocol 2,1
#ListenAddress 0.0.0.0
#ListenAddress ::
...
```

If all of these solutions still leave you hanging, watch your log files as you attempt to SSH in from another machine. The log messages should give you an idea of the problem:

```
# tail -f /var/log/messages
```

Conflict with ipchains

If you start iptables and get an error like this

```
# /etc/init.d/iptables start
ipchains and iptables can not be used together.    [WARNING]
```

your iptables rules or firewall won't work properly. In this case, someone has either manually loaded the older and now outdated ipchains kernel module or configured the system to load it automatically. This older `netfilter` module, not fully supported under Fedora Core, can be checked with the following command:

```
# lsmod | grep ^ip
ipchains              49516    0  (unused)
```

You need to remove ipchains from the kernel with this command:

```
# rmmod ipchains
```

Now, iptables should start without problems:

```
# /etc/init.d/iptables start
Applying iptables firewall rules:                 [ OK ]
```

To save dealing with this problem in the future, make sure that iptables is set to load automatically and ipchains is not:

```
# chkconfig --list | grep ^ip
iptables    0:off 1:off 2:on 3:on 4:on 5:on 6:off
```

No ipchains init script is configured. Good. Verify that ipchains is not being loaded in /etc/modules.conf or in your rc.local boot-time files:

```
# grep ipch /etc/modules.conf /etc/rc.d/rc.local
/etc/rc.d/rc.local:insmod ipchains
```

If you see output like this, ipchains is starting automatically. Edit the offending file, remove reference to ipchains, reboot, and run these tests again. You should see no reference to ipchains anywhere in the output and iptables should now start fine.

Denied Access Persists

You've added a rule to allow SSH connections into your workstation, but it won't connect. You've checked TCP wrappers files for typing errors, you've checked your "filter" table settings, and you've performed the sacred Dance of Firewall Strength, but nothing seems to work. All you get is this:

```
ssh: connect to address 10.1.1.1 port 22: No route to host
```

Everything else is working fine. What gives?

Remember that iptables is an Access Control List, and on ACLs, order matters. On a Red Hat or Fedora Core system, you might think you're covered if you just issue this command:

```
# iptables -A RH-Firewall-1-INPUT -p tcp --dport 22 -j ACCEPT
```

It's the right command, but it might not work because *order matters*. If you're appending a rule (with a -A) to an existing chain from the command line, be sure to list out the existing rules with the -line-numbers option:

```
# iptables -L --line-numbers
Chain INPUT (policy ACCEPT)
num target      prot opt source            destination
1   RH-Firewall-1-INPUT all --   anywhere            anywhere
...
Chain RH-Firewall-1-INPUT (2 references)
num target      prot opt source            destination
1   ACCEPT     all  --  anywhere          anywhere
2   ACCEPT     icmp --  anywhere          anywhere        icmp any
3   ACCEPT     ipv6-crypt--  anywhere        anywhere
4   ACCEPT     ipv6-auth--   anywhere        anywhere
5   ACCEPT     all  --  anywhere          anywhere
    state RELATED,ESTABLISHED
6   ACCEPT     tcp  --  anywhere     anywhere        state NEW tcp dpt:http
7   REJECT     icmp --  !pc          anywhere        icmp any reject-with
    icmp-port-unreachable
8   REJECT     all --  anywhere      anywhere        reject-with
    icmp-host-prohibited
9   ACCEPT     tcp  --  anywhere     anywhere        tcp dpt:ssh
```

Numerically insert (with the `-I` switch) your new "allow ssh" rule in the proper location (before the #7 or 8 `REJECT`), rather than append them. Be sure to use the chain name and the rule number location that you wish to insert to via the following syntax:

```
#iptables -I RH-Firewall-1-INPUT 7 -p tcp --dport 22 -j ACCEPT
```

Now the corrected chain listing should look like this:

```
#iptables -L --line-numbers
Chain INPUT (policy ACCEPT)
num  target      prot opt source              destination
1    RH-Firewall-1-INPUT  all --  anywhere            anywhere
...
Chain RH-Firewall-1-INPUT (2 references)
num  target      prot opt source              destination
1    ACCEPT      all  -- anywhere             anywhere
2    ACCEPT      icmp -- anywhere             anywhere            icmp any
3    ACCEPT      ipv6-crypt-- anywhere            anywhere
4    ACCEPT      ipv6-auth-- anywhere          anywhere
5    ACCEPT      all -- anywhere             anywhere
     state RELATED,ESTABLISHED
6    ACCEPT      tcp  -- anywhere           anywhere          state NEW tcp dpt:http
7    ACCEPT      tcp  -- anywhere           anywhere          tcp dpt:ssh
8    REJECT      icmp -- !pc                anywhere          icmp any reject-with
     icmp-port-unreachable
9    REJECT      all --anywhere             anywhere          reject-with
     icmp-host-prohibited
```

That should do it.

Firewall Resources

Firewalling and system/network security is a *huge* subject. Table 11-3 shows some of the more useful sites and information that you can use to quickly get up to speed on the various topics in this chapter, as well as keep an eye on the industry and the latest security vulnerabilities and exploits by joining the included security mail lists.

Table 11-3: Firewall Resources

TCP/IP resources	
Daryl's TCP/IP Primer	`www.ipprimer.com/section.cfm`
TCP: RFC793	`www.faqs.org/rfcs/rfc793.html`
IP: RFC791	`www.faqs.org/rfcs/rfc791.html`
Linux Firewall and Proxy Server HOWTO	`www.tldp.org/HOWTO/Firewall-HOWTO.html`

Continued

Table 11-3: *(continued)*

TCP wrapper resources	
Red Hat Enterprise Linux Reference Guide	`www.redhat.com/docs/manuals/enterprise/RHEL-3-Manual/ref-guide/ch-tcpwrappers.html`
Iptables resources	
Red Hat Enterprise Linux Reference Guide	`www.redhat.com/docs/manuals/enterprise/RHEL-3-Manual/ref-guide/ch-iptables.html`
IP tables/IP Masquerading	`http://mia.ece.uic.edu/~papers/WWW/iptables.html`
	`www.e-infomax.com/ipmasq/howto/m-html/ipmasq-HOWTO-m.html`
Packet Filtering HOWTO	`www.netfilter.org/documentation/HOWTO/packet-filtering-HOWTO.html`
Iptables quick HOWTO	`www.cse.msu.edu/~minutsil/iptables.html`
Linux 2.4 NAT HOWTO	`www.netfilter.org/documentation/HOWTO/NAT-HOWTO.html`
Netfilter Extensions HOWTO	`www.netfilter.org/documentation/HOWTO/netfilter-extensions-HOWTO.html`
Firewall resources	
Advanced policy firewall suite	`www.r-fx.org/apf.php`
iptables tables and chains	`www.yolinux.com/TUTORIALS/LinuxTutorialIptables NetworkGateway.html`
Internet firewall FAQ	`www.interhack.net/pubs/fwfaq/`
Other resources	
Red Hat Enterprise Linux Security Guide	`www.redhat.com/docs/manuals/enterprise/RHEL-3-Manual/security-guide/ch-server.html`
"Paranoid Penguin: Seven Top Security Tools"	`www.linuxjournal.com/article.php?sid=7235`
RFC 2647—Benchmarking Terminology for Firewall Performance	`www.faqs.org/rfcs/rfc2647.html`
Red Hat Linux 9 Firewalls	`www.redhat.com/docs/manuals/linux/RHL-9-Manual/custom-guide/s1-basic-firewall-gnomelokkit.html`
RFC 2647—Benchmarking Terminology for Firewall Performance	`www.faqs.org/rfcs/rfc2647.html`

Other resources	
Sentry Tools Project (includes `portsentry`)	`http://sourceforge.net/projects/sentrytools/`
Daryl's TCP/IP Primer, Network Address Translation (NAT)	`www.ipprimer.com/nat.cfm`
"Battling hackers," Jim DeBrosse	`www.crime-research.org/eng/news/2003/03/Mess1603.html`
Good security mail lists for sys-admins to join	**CERT:** `www.cert.org/contact_cert/certmaillist.html`
	SecurityFocus: `www.securityfocus.com/cgi-bin/forums.pl`
	NTBugTraq: `www.ntbugtraq.com`
	Xforce: `xforce.iss.net/maillists/index.php`

Summary

Anyone with a machine or network that interacts with the Internet should have a firewall in place. Firewalls block unwanted or unknown traffic while letting legitimate packets gain access to valid services or systems.

Under Linux, there are three ways of controlling service access by hosts or networks: iptables, TCP wrappers, or individual daemon config settings. The first is the only method that can both be considered a truly hardened method of limiting service access on an untrusted network (personal firewall) and be used in either a stand-alone server or a full-blown network firewall configuration. It can be difficult to master, but there are various GUI tools to assist you in this journey. The other two methods of service access control are good for trusted networks and setting up quick departmental restrictions to various services on stand-alone server installs, but technically cannot be classified as firewalling.

Just remember three important points:

✦ The more ports you open up in a firewall, the less secure your system is.

✦ To be truly effective, firewalls and external security systems must be built on top of systems that already have best practice *foundational security elements* in place.

✦ Security that you don't both fully understand *and* fully control is just an illusion.

Troubleshooting BIND9 and DNS

The Internet is a big place. Theoretically, there are roughly 4.3 billion available IP addresses, though this includes reserved IP addresses and nonroutable addresses. Still, the average human can't remember a hundred or so IP addresses, let alone more than four billion!

Luckily, the Domain Name Service is there to help. DNS resolves, or looks up assignments of, Internet names to IP addresses as well as IP addresses back to names. Names are far easier than numbers for the human mind to store and retrieve. Which is easier to remember, yahoo.com or 66.218.71.198? We suspect that you could list more than a hundred domain names without thinking too hard, whereas you'd be hard pressed to list 50 IP addresses (the sequential numbers in your own network don't count). In simple terms, DNS is basically a giant phonebook for the Internet, wherein you can use a name to get an address or vice versa.

Note

The new DNS administrator is often confused by the difference in terminology when talking about DNS servers from the server side and DNS servers from the client side. From the server side, BIND/DNS servers are referred to as *master* and *slave*. This indicates which server holds the master DNS records and which one retrieves its DNS records for DNS services. The terms *primary* and *secondary* only refer to how clients access the DNS servers (which may be backwards from the *master/slave* designations in some cases).

DNS History and Theory

In the early ARPANET years, all these machine names and addresses were kept in one master hosts file (/etc/hosts) at Stanford University. Every time a new machine or group of machines was added to the network, updates had to be sent out to all the other universities and military installations attached to the network. As you can imagine, this grew to quite a task! Think of all the potential problems with records synchronization and IP/name conflicts, not to mention the single-point-of-failure issue.

In 1984 RFC 1034 was released. This document described a new way in which machine *namespace* could be delegated, decentralized, and configured. The DNS utilizes a client/server configuration that allows any user to get to any *Fully Qualified Domain Name*, or FQDN, in a short amount of time. DNS brought almost total reliability and nearly infinite scalability to the growing Internet.

DNS Structure

DNS is divided into three parts: the namespace, the resolver, and the servers. To continue with the phonebook analogy, the *namespace* is the section of the phonebook that contains phone listings. The *resolver* is the program that asks for DNS information and, by extension, the user looking up the address. Finally, *DNS servers* are machines all over the Internet and provide DNS information: in this example, multiple copies of the phonebook. These three components create a functionally delegated system that resolves names to addresses and vice versa.

How does DNS work? It's easiest to imagine if you think of the Internet as a top-down tree (Figure 12-1). At the very top, there are 13 root name servers that are spread across the planet. All these name servers do is point requests to the next layer of machines, the *Top-Level Domain Servers*. Each of these servers then provides data to another level of servers, and so on. Much like your hard drive filesystem, domain namespace is small at the top level and increasingly complex the deeper you delve.

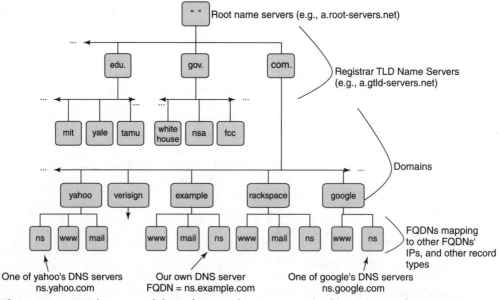

Figure 12-1: DNS is managed through a set of servers organized in an inverted tree structure.

Note

When the Internet was designed, there were seven *top-level domains*, now called the original gTLDs or Generic TLDs: com, gov, mil, org, edu, net, and int (used for international treaty organizations like NATO). These seven soon expanded to include state and country codes that now span the world.

The 13 root name servers at the top of the tree diagram are named `A.ROOT-SERVERS.NET.` through `M.ROOT-SERVERS.NET.` Notice the trailing dot in the machine names? This is critical for DNS service, as the terminating dot gives the DNS name an absolute reference point, much like a file on your hard drive is described by its full path name including drive and filename designation. Without the top level / how would you know where the file was located? Similarly, if a domain name does not have a terminating dot, your computer can't tell whether `www.yahoo.com` is really `www.yahoo.com.nike.com` or some other nested address. You might be able to figure it out, but your machine can't.

Between the 13 root name servers and the top-level domain (TLD) servers, you'll find name servers at the *Registrar* level. These registrar name servers control a set of TLD name servers. When you buy a domain name from a registrar, you must supply the IP addresses of two name servers managed by you or by your Internet provider. In doing so, control of your domain name is *delegated*, or handed down, from the registrar to your provider. When a search is done on your domain name, the last name server IP given is the one you or your provider controls.

Once the registrar delegates control to the name servers you provided, these become the *authoritative* name servers for your domain. Any client or user that does a DNS search on your domain name will now ultimately come to your name server to resolve fully qualified domain names in your namespace and match them to the actual IP addresses of your hosts. This is why it is critical to keep your primary and secondary DNS server listings up to date with the registrar who handles all your domain names. If the server information is incorrect, authority for the domain name has been delegated to the wrong machine.

Master and Slave DNS Servers

Every domain on the Internet relies on at least two name servers: a *primary* server and a *secondary* server (from the client perspective). These registrar designations usually refer ultimately to what are called *master* and *slave* DNS servers. As its name implies, the master server is the main name server for that domain. It holds the master copy of the domain files describing each domain for which it is authoritative. It's the master name server's job to store the latest copy of the *zone files*—files that contain all the pointers that connect machine names and aliases to IP addresses within your domain.

The slave server contains copies of the master zone files, which it downloads from the master server on a regular basis. These downloads are called *zone transfers*. You might also see tertiary, or third-level, name servers, though they are the exception rather than the rule.

Note   If you want to learn more about the functions of master and slave DNS servers, consult `www.tldp.org/HOWTO/DNS-HOWTO-5.html#ss5.6`.

While many web administrators set up master and slave DNS services on a single machine, this is rarely a good idea. If DNS service goes down on that machine or is blocked for some reason, then nobody outside the local network can see your name server. Thus, nobody can see the domains over which that server has authority. It's best to set up your slave DNS server on another network, or even with another provider altogether (unless your provider can offer you a multinetwork, multidata center DNS hosting solution).

Some hosting or network providers will split DNS hosting with you, running either master or slave DNS service on their system and letting you run the other component on your local server. This might save you from having to buy a second machine just to host half your DNS service.

DNS Caching

DNS caching is the function that makes the modern Internet usable. DNS caching is nothing more than a local machine holding onto the DNS information from external zones for a given amount of time. If it were not for DNS caching, most Internet traffic would be nothing but DNS queries for domain names and IP addresses.

Your local ISP, along with other ISPs and networks, usually provide some level of DNS caching to their internal network users.

The amount of time for which information is cached (aka the *TTL* or *Time to Live* value) is determined by the master zone file of a given domain, and set by the domain owner or DNS administrator. The TTL can be as short as a second or a few minutes, to 24 hours, to a week or more. Twenty-four hours is a typical setting. Caching name servers all around the world should honor these TTL values and treat cached information as "official" for that defined period before requesting the domain information from the authoritative server again.

For example, assume that you are the first person from your ISP to type `www.example.com` into your browser. Your browser contacts your ISP's DNS server to find the IP information for `www.example.com`. In turn, your ISP goes on your behalf to the root domain name server, then to the TLD and registrar servers, and finally to the authoritative name server for the requested domain with a request for the IP address associated with `www.example.com`. Once this chain of requests is complete, the IP information remains cached at your ISP's DNS server for the period of time defined in `www.example.com`'s master zone file's TTL setting.

When a DNS server need only consult its cache to find the requested IP information rather than pass the request to remote name servers, the query is called a *recursive query*. If you ask a DNS server to map a fully qualified domain name to an IP address but the server does not already have the information in its cache, it will go and get the information rather than simply saying "I don't know." Most DNS servers that do recursive queries also provide DNS caching, to lessen the load of individual requests.

Registering Domain Names

If you want to have your own presence on the Internet without being stuck under someone else's domain name, you need to get your own domain. Domain name registration is essentially an annual rental, as ultimate control over the domain remains with the registrar. While there are now many organizations that will manage domain name registration for you, most savvy users handle their own registration directly with a registrar. Some of the most popular US-based registrars include

✦ `http://register.com/`

✦ `www.godaddy.com/`

✦ http://networksolutions.com/

✦ www.gandi.net/

You'll usually pay between $7.50 and 35 a year, with a required 2-year initial registration, for a domain name in the original TLD. For the newer TLD like .biz and .info, you might pay much more. Individual countries also offer unique vanity TLD like .tv and .cc, and set their own prices. Some registrars will give you a price break if you pay for several years at once.

Be careful that you renew your domain name when the notice arrives in the mail, and that your renewal comes before the domain name expires. There is now a bustling business in domain name thievery, called *cyber-squatting*, which involves specialized software that watches for soon-to-expire domains. These squatters then buy your domain name out from under your neglectful eye and will resell it to you for a price. We think this is essentially blackmail, but note that the entire distasteful situation can be completely avoided if you pay attention or use your registrar's autorenewal plans.

Configuring a Master DNS Server

If you've chosen to run your own DNS servers on your local network and you use Linux, you will probably want to set up BIND (Berkeley Internet Name Domain) to manage your DNS records. This configuration is quite detail oriented, and the smallest error can cause the entire service to grind to a halt. Pay attention while you're working, and make sure that you enable whatever security tools will safeguard your site most effectively.

Installing BIND on a Linux or UNIX machine can be a bit confusing, especially on Red Hat–based systems. While the general service is called the *Domain Name Service*, the actual RPM package is called bind:

```
#  rpm -q bind
bind-9.2.2.P3-9
```

Even more confusing, the daemon is called neither bind nor DNS, but named! This can be very annoying, especially if you are an administrator who does not have regular responsibilities for DNS services but needs to troubleshoot an immediate crisis while your DNS guru is on vacation. Your immediate response might be

```
#  service bind restart
bind: unrecognized service
```

Obviously, this won't work. Instead, you need to issue this command:

```
#  service named restart
Stopping named:                                    [ OK ]
Starting named:                                    [ OK ]
```

Just another one of those UNIX idiosyncrasies that enhances job security.

Note   In this section, we assume that you have a domain name registered to you. If you don't have a domain name yet, see the *Registering Domain Names* sidebar earlier in this chapter.

BIND9 Directory Structure

Before you begin to configure BIND9 on your DNS server, take a moment to study the directory structure. BIND9 files live in the /bin directory:

```
/bin/
  /boot/
  /dev/
  /etc/named.conf
  /home/
  /initrd/
  /lib/
  /lost+found/
  /misc/
  /mnt/
  /mnt-usb/
  /opt/
  /proc/
  /root/
  /sbin/
  /tftpboot/
  /tmp/
  /usr/
  /var/named/
          localhost.zone
          example.com.zone
          named.ca
          named.local
          slaves/
  /var/named/chroot/
          localhost.zone
          example.com.zone
          named.ca
          named.local
          slaves/
```

If you are running BIND in chroot mode, all the files must be under /var/named/chroot/. If you are running in nonchrooted mode, all the files must be under /var/named.

The /bin/etc/named.conf file contains the configurations for the named daemon. If you choose to run BIND in chroot mode (the default, and most secure choice), as described later in the *BIND9 Security* section of this chapter, you will store zone files in the /var/named/ chroot subdirectory.

Caution   Read the *BIND9 Bug* sidebar later in this chapter to learn more about a serious security risk that may affect your installation. If you choose to run in chroot mode, you will need to copy some files into /var/named/chroot/ before you start the service.

/etc/named.conf

The /etc/named.conf file handles all configurations for the name daemon, or named. In order for DNS service to work properly, you will need to make a number of changes to this file. If DNS isn't working for some reason, chances are that it's an error in /etc/named.conf that is causing the problem.

Tip   The named daemon is pronounced "name-dee," not "named" (as in "My geeky sister *named* her dog Denethor"). This is one of those Secret Passwords of UNIX Competence, like knowing how to pronounce Linus Torvalds.

In this section, we show you a complete /etc/named.conf file, interspersed with comments and explanations. If you have a running installation of BIND9 already, look at your own /etc/named.conf to see what configurations have already been made.

Note   If you do not have an /etc/named.conf file and you're on a Red Hat–based system, then you must also install the caching-nameserver RPM package. This will create /etc/named.conf. Also be aware that if your BIND DNS server is running in chrooted mode, you may find the file under /var/named/chroot/etc/named.conf, which is installed by the related Red Hat package bind-chroot. On a Red Hat system, issue the command rpm -qa|grep -e ^bind -e nameserv to see the bind-related packages you have installed. On a non-Red Hat system that has been running for at least 24 hours, you can issue the command locate named.conf as root to help you find your named config file.

```
// generated by named-bootconf.pl

options {
        directory "/var/named";
```

The directory setting determines the directory where all zone files should be stored. If you store zone files in any other directory, DNS will break.

```
/*
    * If there is a firewall between you and nameservers you
    * want to talk to, you might need to uncomment the query-
    * source directive below. Previous versions of BIND
    * always asked questions using port 53, but BIND 8.1 uses
    * an unprivileged port by default.
       */
      // query-source address * port 53;
};
```

This block doesn't look like normal UNIX commenting. In /etc/named.conf, you will find three different comment methods:

✦ C style: /* comment inside here */

✦ C++ style: // to the end of line

✦ Unix style: # to the end of line

You can probably determine what is commentary and what is not, but it's good to be aware of the various notations.

```
//
// a caching only nameserver config
//
```

```
controls {
        inet 127.0.0.1 allow { localhost; } keys { rndckey;
};
};
```

The `controls` setting tells `named` how to run `rndc`, the BIND9 name server control utility.

The next sections contain the zone file definitions. Any line that says

```
file "somedomain.com.zone"
```

indicates that the zone file for this zone, or domain, is located at /var/named/*somedomain*
.com.zone. Be sure that whatever you have in /etc/named.conf points to the actual file
that you create. The name itself is irrelevant; it's the location and filename accuracy that
matters.

```
zone "." IN {
        type hint;
        file "named.ca";
};
```

The first line of the preceding section indicates that the section will define the root zone. The
third line identifies the file that contains the root of the zone.

```
zone "localhost" IN {            #<--Good to use as a template
        type master;             #<-- The master zone
        file "localhost.zone";   #<--The name of zone file located
        allow-update { none; }; #       In /var/named/
};
```

This section is an excellent template for actual zone settings later in the file. The first line
names the zone, the second line indicates that this is a master DNS server for that zone, and
the third line specifies the location of the zone file in /var/named. To add your own zones,
copy the preceding block in your named.conf file, paste it further down, and fill it in with your
own zone file information.

```
zone "example.com" IN {
        type master;
        file "example.com.zone";
        allow-update { none; };
};
```

Caution   Whenever copying blocks like this, be sure to include the all-important closing };
characters.

As you can see here, the administrator has simply replaced the template information with
actual zone information. Doing this through copy-and-paste is the safest way to be sure that
your zone entries are formatted properly.

The next two blocks of information define how BIND handles reverse lookups for your domain:

```
zone "0.0.127.in-addr.arpa" IN {
        type master;
        file "named.local";
```

```
        allow-update ( none; );
);
```

The first configuration file block controls reverse lookups for your loopback device's IP.

Note

Reverse lookups function like a phone book in reverse, to find a name associated with an IP address. The following entry, and its related zone file, is one that will allow anyone to nslookup the IP address 10.1.1.x. This zone will associate the IP back to a reverse (or PTR) name record.

```
zone "1.1.10.in-addr.arpa" IN (
        type master;
        file "1.1.10.in-addr.arpa.zone";
        allow-update ( none; );
);
```

Tip

Just as you copied down the 0.0.127 block as a template within the named.conf file, you can also copy the actual zone file it references named.local (usually in /var/named/) to use for a new reverse zone file called 1.1.10.in-addr.arpa.zone for the 10.1.1.x IP block.

If you actually own the IP block that you use (unlikely, since most of us rent IP addresses from upstream providers), you would use the aforementioned configuration file block. Those who own an IP block control the reverse lookup authority for that entire block.

```
include "/etc/rndc.key";
```

This final line contains a pointer to the Remote Name Daemon Controller configuration file, which sets up local and remote secure control for the BIND9 server. Unless you are prepared to research this key-based secure service thoroughly, it is recommended to not make any changes to this reference or the file it references.

Note

Good information on implementing RNDC/TSIG can be found at www.apnic.net/training/download/2004/20040115-in-dns/7-rndc-tsig.pdf.

Now that you've seen an /etc/named.conf file in action, you can begin to edit your own. When adding your own zone blocks and file references, we strongly recommend typing the filename for new zones into named.conf, then copying it to the clipboard, and saving the filename from your paste. One of the most common errors is a typo in a zone filename, either in the named.conf file or in the /var/named/ filename itself. For example, if you use the vi text editor, you might issue the command

```
# vi /var/named/paste-file-name-here
```

or just copy the named.local file as a template:

```
# cp /var/named/namd.local /var/named/paste-file-name-here
```

Caution   More DNS-related problems are caused by typing errors than anything else. The entries in `/etc/named.conf` and the zone filename must be identical or `named` will fail.

After you have finished adding zone references to `/etc/named.conf`, it's time to create the actual zone files. Remember that you must store these files in the location you defined in `/etc/named.conf`. For example, in the `/etc/named.conf` file, we set up a zone reference for `example.com`, which has its zone files stored at `/var/named/example.com.zone`.

The localhost Zone File

Before you begin creating zone files for actual domains, take a look at the `localhost` zone file. This defines information for your local machine, which uses the reserved IP address 127.0.0.1.

Note   There are two typographical conventions found in zone files. If a line has a space in its left-most column then that line's configuration adopts the domain name from the previous line. The @ symbol is used as a placeholder for the full domain or zone name defined in the `/etc/named.conf` file.

```
#  cat /var/named/localhost.zone
$TTL    86400
```

This line defines the default zone TTL, or the length of time for which zone information is authoritative. TTLs are written in seconds, so the value 86400 equals 1 day. Caching name servers use this value to ignore or refresh their cached information about a given domain name.

```
$ORIGIN localhost.
```

This line defines the domain name. The domain name must always end with a trailing dot. Later in `example.com`, this line would read `$ORIGIN example.com.` (note the trailing dot).

```
@       1D IN SOA       @ root (                    \
        42                      ; serial (d. adams)
        3H                      ; refresh
        15M                     ; retry
        1W                      ; expiry
        1D )                    ; minimum
```

This section creates the *Start of Authority Record*, or SOA. The SOA configures zone behavior and determines how the zone information may be pulled down by other name servers.

The serial number (42) found in the first indented line is used as a date stamp. It is written in the format `YYYYMMDD##`, where the ## is an actual number. Increment this number by one every time you make a change to the zone file (starting at 00 or 01). If you make a change to the zone file and do not increment this number, then caching name servers as well as your slave servers will ignore all following data and assume that their stored data is correct. For example, if today is January 16, 2008, and you are making the first change of the day, the serial number should be 20080011701. (Those of you who are Douglas Adams fans will be amused by the default placeholder for the serial number. It's set to 42 instead of the proper `YYYYMMDD##` date code.)

Tip You can learn more about Start of Authority records and their construction at `http://secu.zzu.edu.cn/book/NetWork/NetworkingBookshelf_2ndEd/tcp/appc_03.htm`.

```
                    1D IN NS              @
                    1D IN A               127.0.0.1
```

Finally, these lines define the *internet-type* (IN) name server (NS) record for the domain this zone file represents. Written in an expanded format, these lines could also be

```
localhost.       1D IN NS     localhost.
   ^^^           ^^ ^^ ^^        ^^^
the domain        TTL        NameServer
```

The name server for the domain `localhost.` (represented by the unseen space at the front of the line) is the server FQDN, `localhost.`; that is, you can find the IP address assigned to this name server at the name server called `localhost.`.

NS records declare the machines that provide DNS service for the zone in question. Even after the registrars have pointed requests to your DNS server, this is still required.

Because this zone file is authoritative for the `localhost` domain (in this case, because `localhost` is always locally authoritative), you will also see the A record defined:

```
                    1D IN A          127.0.0.1
```

which could be rewritten as

```
@                   1D IN A          127.0.0.1
```

or

```
localhost.          1D IN A          127.0.0.1
```

Note An A record always points a name to an IP address. An NS record always points to whoever should be doing DNS for this domain (which in the case of `localhost.` will always be you).

Name Service Tools

If your DNS client is set to query your own machine before it queries the DNS server for the network, then your own name server will respond with this information:

```
#  nslookup localhost
Server:         192.168.128.2
Address:        192.168.128.2#53

Name:   localhost
Address: 127.0.0.1
```

Note The `nslookup` command has been deprecated, and may be removed from future Red Hat releases. Consider using the `dig` or `host` programs instead. If you like using `nslookup`, run it with the silent option to prevent this message from appearing, as in `nslookup -sil`.

Note that in the preceding example nslookup did not actually query the name server running on the local machine. The Server and Address fields show that the resolver client went out and queried another DNS server running on IP 192.168.128.2. In order to query your own DNS server directly, you must supply the correct IP address. Issue the command like this:

```
#  nslookup -sil localhost 10.1.1.1
Server:          10.1.1.1
Address:         10.1.1.1#53

Name:   localhost
Address: 127.0.0.1
```

This is much better. Now you're querying against your own machine (assuming that you are 10.1.1.1), and the output is correct. Compare the output from nslookup to the information you receive from the newer tools host and dig:

```
#  host localhost 10.1.1.1
Using domain server:
Name: 10.1.1.1
Address: 10.1.1.1#53
Aliases:localhost has address 127.0.0.1
```

The usage and output from host is generally the same as that from nslookup. With the dig command, however, you'll see quite different information. dig takes slightly different syntax to query a name server other than the default, with *@nameserverIP* rather than the plain IP address:

```
# dig localhost @10.1.1.1

; <<>> DiG 9.2.2-P3 <<>> localhost @10.1.1.1
;; global options: printcmd
;; Got answer:
;; ->>HEADER<<- opcode: QUERY, status: NOERROR, id: 27676
;; flags: qr aa rd ra; QUERY: 1,  ANSWER: 1, AUTHORITY: 1, ADDITIONAL: 0

;; QUESTION SECTION:
;localhost.                    IN      A

;; ANSWER SECTION:
localhost.          86400    IN      A      127.0.0.1

;; AUTHORITY SECTION:
localhost.          86400    IN      NS     localhost.

;; Query time: 2 msec
;; SERVER: 10.1.1.1#53(10.1.1.1)
;; WHEN: Sat Jan 17 22:44:18 2004
;; MSG SIZE rcvd: 57
```

This is quite a bit more information than that from the other tools. The dig output contains data about the query itself and the various answers, as well as statistics about the queried domain, including its TTL and authoritative name server. With the information from the AUTHORITY section, you can use dig to "walk down the DNS tree" for a given domain.

For example, use dig to step down through the DNS tree for yahoo.com. In the first query, use dig to find the gTLD name server(s) for the .com TLD:

```
#  dig com
[...]
;; QUESTION SECTION:
;com.                            IN      A

;; AUTHORITY SECTION:
com.                   10737    IN      SOA     a.gtld-
servers.net. nstld.verisign-grs.com. 2004011701 1800 900
604800 86400
```

Next, query the gTLD server that you found in the first output for information about the yahoo.com domain:

```
#  dig yahoo.com @a.gtld-servers.net
[...]
;; QUESTION SECTION:
;yahoo.com.                      IN        A

;; AUTHORITY SECTION:
yahoo.com.             172800 IN        NS      ns1.yahoo.com.
yahoo.com.             172800 IN        NS      ns2.yahoo.com.
yahoo.com.             172800 IN        NS      ns3.yahoo.com.
yahoo.com.             172800 IN        NS      ns4.yahoo.com.
yahoo.com.             172800 IN        NS      ns5.yahoo.com.

;; ADDITIONAL SECTION:
ns1.yahoo.com.         172800 IN        A       66.218.71.63
ns2.yahoo.com.         172800 IN        A       66.163.169.170
ns3.yahoo.com.         172800 IN        A       217.12.4.104
ns4.yahoo.com.         172800 IN        A       63.250.206.138
ns5.yahoo.com.         172800 IN        A       216.109.116.17
```

Here you see a request to the world gTLD name servers serving the .com TLD for the IP address of yahoo.com. It gave back authoritative name servers and their IPs. In this output, you can see that there are a number of authoritative name servers for this domain.

Now you can ask one of those servers to answer your question about the yahoo.com domain directly:

```
# dig yahoo.com @66.218.71.63

; <<>> DiG 9.2.2-P3 <<>> yahoo.com @66.218.71.63
;; global options: printcmd
;; Got answer:
;; ->>HEADER<<- opcode: QUERY, status: NOERROR, id: 5356
;; flags: qr aa rd; QUERY: 1, ANSWER: 1, AUTHORITY: 5, ADDITIONAL: 5

;; QUESTION SECTION:
;yahoo.com.                      IN      A

;; ANSWER SECTION:
yahoo.com.             1800     IN      A     66.218.71.198

;; AUTHORITY SECTION:
yahoo.com.             172800   IN      NS    ns1.yahoo.com.
yahoo.com.             172800   IN      NS    ns2.yahoo.com.
```

There you have it: the authoritative IP address for the yahoo.com domain as defined by its own DNS server's zone file.

This is the work that your ISP or network provider's DNS server does when it performs *recursive requests* for their clients. Name servers that recurse, or search, for domains on behalf of their client's requests are usually also set up as *caching name servers*. Caching servers retain the information they gather for a set period of time, defined by the remote domain's TTL setting in its own zone file. In this way, by running your own DNS server, not only do you control the IP addresses that people get resolved to but also (with the TTL) how long they can hold onto this information. This helps to speed up DNS and keep DNS chatter on the Internet to a minimum.

Tip   Learn more about recursive DNS requests at www.intac.com/~cdp/cptd-faq/section2.html#iterrec.

Misconfigured Caching Name Services

Most Internet service providers (ISPs) run caching name services for their dial-up and broadband clients. In recent years, some ISPs have begun to configure their caching name servers so that they ignore the authoritative TTL values for all domains on which they have done recursive searches. Some of the biggest ISPs in the United States are guilty of this misconfiguration.

Why is this a problem? Consider a mail administrators at another domain who decides to move their mail and web servers to another machine. To prevent querying clients (and thus incoming e-mail) from being out of sync and going to the wrong place when they move their mail server, they lowers their TTL from 1 Day to 5 Minutes. If the client's ISP chooses to ignore this TTL change by hard-coding all its DNS caches to a longer TTL value, like 1 or 2 weeks, the ISP clients may get bounced e-mail or (for the web) web pages that fail to load until the cache refreshes! True, this hard-coding of the TTL is done because it reduces the DNS server load and bandwidth on the ISP side (and saves money by requiring fewer DNS servers), but it makes more work for the tech staff and for administrators at remote sites who don't even work for the offender. If you have the technical authority to do such a thing on your own DNS caching servers, don't. It's not an Internet friendly practice and causes problems for many people.

Creating Your Own Zone Files

Now that you have your DNS server running and doing recursive lookups, be sure that /etc/named.conf points to the correct zone file for your domain. Once the pointer is in place, you can create the authoritative zone file. In this section, we set up a file for the fictitious domain example.com.

As we warned earlier, don't type in the name of this file manually when you save it for the first time. Cut and paste from your /etc/named.conf to save yourself from later work due to fumbling fingers. In fact, save yourself a lot of typing by using a template taken from the localhost.zone file. Issue this command:

```
# cp -p /var/named/localhost.zone /var/named/example.com.zone
```

Be sure to paste the copied zone filename at the end of the line, where we have italicized our zone filename.

Open this new file in your favorite text editor. If your text editor has search and replace capabilities, use it to replace every occurrence of `localhost.` with `example.com.` (If you don't have search and replace in your editor, you'll have to do this by eye.) Be sure to include those trailing dots. Check the default settings and see if you need to change them at this time:

```
$TTL    86400
```

Is this TTL an appropriate length? 86400 seconds is 1 day. If you want caching name servers to hold your information longer, thus reducing load on your local machine, consider lengthening this setting:

```
$ORIGIN example.com.
```

Be sure that your domain name ends in a trailing dot.

```
@                    1D IN SOA    ns.example.com tom.yahoo.com.
(                    2004011700              ;
```

Remember to change the name server for this domain (`ns.example.com`) and the e-mail address (without the @ here is `tom.yahoo.com`). Also, change the serial number to the date format `YYYYMMDD##`. Increment the serial number by one each time you make any changes to this file from now on.

```
                     3H                 ; refresh
                     15M                ; retry
                     1W                 ; expiry
                     1D )               ; minimum

@                    1D IN NS     ns.example.com.
@                    1D IN NS     ns2.example.com.
ns                   1D IN A      10.1.1.1
ns2.example.com.                  1D IN A     192.168.128.1
```

Note The only reason that this sample zone file must have A records for its NS records is that the DNS servers for this domain exist inside the domain. That is, the DNS server `ns.example.com` exists inside the `example.com` domain, which is being defined by this file. If the name servers were outside this domain (for example, in `ns.mydns.com`), you would not use A records in this zone file since this zone file is not authoritative for the domain `mydns.com`.

Since our name servers are also in this domain, we need to include A records that point to a specified IP address for the servers. There is an entry for the master name server and one for each slave server.

Note In the aforementioned example, the record for `ns` could also be written as `ns.examaple.com.` or just as `ns<space>`, which expands out to the FQDN. Either of these work, but sometimes using just the last part of the hostname (`ns` in this case) is clearer and easier to read.

```
www          1D IN CNAME @        ;
ftp          1D IN CNAME @        ;
mail         1D IN CNAME @        ;
webdav       1D IN CNAME @        ;
@            1D IN A      10.1.1.1 ;
```

While A records point domain names to IP addresses (last line), CNAME records are aliases that point names to other names. These names must resolve to an A record (ultimately to a defined IP address).

Note   The e-mail address for this domain is tom@yahoo.com, and it can be found in the third line, expressed as tom.yahoo.com. This form is used because the @ symbol is used in zone files to represent the entire domain name. The standard syntax for e-mail addresses in zone files is user.domain.gtld.

Note that this zone file defines two name servers. The IPs you would use to define these servers are usually the primary and secondary servers that you provided when you registered your domain name. In this case, we used ns.example.com/10.1.1.1 and ns2.example.com/ 192.168.128.1. This is a bit more complex than the usual practice of most DNS administrators, who would use the equally functional method:

```
@          1D IN NS    ns
@          1D IN NS    ns2
ns         1D IN A     10.1.1.1
ns2        1D IN A     192.168.128.3
```

This usage requires less typing, and thus less room for human error. However, while you're learning to set up zone files, there is something to be said for writing everything out at least once to get a feel for doing it correctly.

The only other element of note is that all the *Canonical Name*, or CNAME, entries point to the same server, @. Remember that @ is shorthand for the example.com. domain. It is only in the final record where the example.com. name is pointed to the IP address 10.1.1.1 with an *Address Resource record*, or A record.

Defining Reverse Lookups

If you have control over your own IP space, as you would on a corporate LAN, you will need to be able to service reverse lookups. As we explained earlier, *reverse lookups* are queries that seek a domain name to match a known IP address, whereas *forward lookups* seek an IP address to match a known domain name. If you do forward lookups for your own IP space, then you need to do reverse lookups as well.

To set up reverse lookup resolution, open the /etc/named.conf file in your text editor of choice:

```
zone "1.1.10.in-addr.arpa" IN {
        type master;
        file "1.1.10.in-addr.arpa.zone";
        allow-update { none; };
        allow-transfer { 192.168.128.3; 127.0.0.1;
192.168.128.25; };
};
```

The zone file needs to have a name that means "/var/named/ for the IP block of 10.1.1.*", more precisely expressed as 10.1.1.0/24. This file is most easily created by copying the existing file /var/named/named.local to the new zone filename, and then editing it as necessary. For example, the `1.1.10.in-addr.arpa.zone` file named in the previous example might look like this if we started adding additional machines:

```
$TTL     86400
@        IN     SOA     ns.example.com. root.localhost. (
                               2004011600 ; Serial
                               28800      ; Refresh
                               14400      ; Retry
                               3600000    ; Expire
                               86400 )    ; Minimum

         IN     NS      ns.example.com.
         IN     NS      ns2.example.com.

1        IN     PTR     ns1.example.com.
2        IN     PTR     bob.example.com.
3        IN     PTR     ns2.example.com.
4        IN     PTR     4-1-1-10.example.com.
5        IN     PTR     5-1.1.10.example.com.
6        IN     PTR     6.1.10.example.com.
7        IN     PTR     staging-server.example.com.
...
254      IN     PTR     netmon.example.com.
```

The last block of records are *PTR*, or *reverse*, records. They simply point known IP addresses back to the associated domain name. Typically, only the owner of that IP network block is granted the authority to "do reverse" on a public IP address. In this situation, however, these are not public IP addresses. Rather, they are nonroutable from the 10.* class-A block. The only stipulation is that you must at least control the DNS servers on your network so that internal users look at the local DNS server for this block.

Note   Remember that the default DNS server setting for every PC on your network is typically pushed out to the client PCs by your own network's DHCP server. If you issue your own IP addresses on your network, you control what DNS server(s) they go to. Instructions for pointing your DHCP clients to your DNS servers are beyond the scope of this chapter.

To test your configuration, use the `host` command to resolve an IP (10.1.1.5 in this example) against your own name server:

```
#  host 10.1.1.5 10.1.1.1
Using domain server:
Name: 10.1.1.1
Address: 10.1.1.1#53
Aliases:

5.1.1.10.in-addr.arpa domain name pointer 10-1-1-5.example.com.
```

or

```
#  host 10.1.1.7 10.1.1.1
Using domain server:
Name: 10.1.1.1
```

```
Address: 10.1.1.1#53
Aliases:

7.1.1.10.in-addr.arpa domain name pointer staging-server.example.com.
```

Set-Up Tips

As long as you remember a few basic pieces of information, configuring your local DNS server and zone files will be no problem:

✦ The main configuration file `/etc/named.conf` (or if chrooted, `/var/named/chroot/etc/named.conf`) defines how the server runs and determines which zone files are loaded into memory.

✦ The domains, or zone files, are stored in the `/var/named/` directory. If you are running BIND9 in `chroot` mode, they are stored in `/var/named/chroot/var/named/`.

✦ Know the difference between A records, NS records, and CNAMEs.

✦ Terminate fully qualified domain names, or FQDNs, with a trailing dot. If not, your `www.example.com` will become `www.example.com.example.com`!

✦ If you make a change to the zone file, increment the serial number by one. If you exit without changing the serial number, the changes will not take effect on all external name servers.

✦ Whenever you make a zone addition or change, be sure to reload or restart the `named` daemon with the command `/etc/init.d/named restart` or `service named reload`.

Slave BIND9 DNS Servers

If you have made the commitment to hosting master DNS services locally, it is likely that you need to run a slave server as well. All but the most frugal administrators who are serious about staying online run a slave name server on a separate LAN, or at least on a separate machine from the master server. The slave server comes into play when your master server is bogged down, or completely offline. Clients will be directed by other name servers to the DNS server with the lowest latency time. This functions as a sort of natural load balancer.

Caution   You should run slave name servers on separate physical boxes, if not on separate networks altogether. System administrators who have a "damn the torpedoes" philosophy, or who are simply inexperienced, sometimes point the registrar toward two IP addresses on the same server. In many cases, this server also provides web and e-mail services. This "single-point-of-failure" design is unwise, but popular nonetheless among those who need a shoestring budget solution on a single machine. A better alternative involves hosting master DNS service locally and using one of your upstream provider's DNS servers as the slave server, or reverse, if your provider offers simple web tools to manage your domains and IPs.

The slave name server pulls its records from the master server on a regular basis. This basis is defined by the Start Of Authority (SOA) block in the master zone file as shown previously. In this section, we show you how to configure a slave name server and make sure that it synchronizes cleanly with the master name server for your domain.

Configuring the Slave Server

Slave name servers use the same file layouts as does the master name servers: /etc/named.conf and the zone files in /var/named/. Only the path of the zone files is defined in a slave's /etc/named.conf file. The zone files themselves are created by the named service itself when it pulls the zone information from the master name server.

Thus, a zone entry in a slave server's /etc/named.conf file will look much like an entry in the master server's /etc/named.conf. In this example, the slave server is configured to pull information from a master server at 10.1.1.1 and save start-up zone data to its disk:

```
zone "example.com" IN {
        type slave;
        file "example.com.zone";
        masters { 10.1.1.1; };
};
```

In order to ensure that the master name server knows that there are slave name servers, and that it will notify all slave name servers of zone changes, you must edit the master server's /etc/named.conf file to include the notify yes directive. You should also enable the allow-transfer directive, which permits the specified IP addresses (either slave name servers or internal administrative workstations) to pull down *zone transfers*. The following sample block shows slave transfer and notification enabled:

```
zone "example.com" IN {
        type master;
        file "example.com.zone";
        allow-update { none; };
        notify yes;
        allow-transfer { 192.168.128.3; };
};
```

If any zone changes are made on the master name server, a NOTIFY signal is sent to all slave name servers. The slave name servers will refresh their caches if the serial number on the master server's zone file is higher than the serial number on the file in the slave name server cache. This is why you must be sure to increment the serial number each time you change the master server's zone file.

When you make a change to the zone file and increment the serial number, you must reload the named service. Once the service is reloaded, you will see entries like these in the system log stored at /var/log/messages:

```
#  tail /var/log/messages
...

Jan 18 19:45:13 localhost named[5622]: loading configuration from
    '/etc/named.conf'
Jan 18 19:45:13 localhost named[5622]: no IPv6 interfaces found
Jan 18 19:45:13 localhost named[5622]: zone example.com/IN: loaded
    serial 2004011809
Jan 18 19:45:13 localhost named[5622]: zone example.com/IN: sending
notifies
    (serial 2004011809)
Jan 18 18:45:13 localhost named: named reload succeeded
Jan 18 19:45:14 localhost named[5622]: client 192.168.128.3#32934: transfer
    of 'example.com/IN': AXFR-style IXFR started
```

The output shows that the `named` daemon was reloaded and a change in `example.com`'s zone file was detected. A `NOTIFY` message and associated serial number were then sent to all relevant addresses stored in NS records. Once the `NOTIFY` is received, slave name servers check with the master server and complete a zone transfer for the affected domain.

> **Tip**
>
> Notification keeps your master and slave name servers in synchronization. You might want to implement this setting globally in the `options` section of the master name server's `/etc/named.conf` file, if it is not already set.

Zone Refresh Settings

If you use notification to maintain your DNS updates, you might think that zone refresh rates don't even need to be established. After all, the master name server tells the slave name servers when a change has been made, right? Unfortunately, in the real DNS world this is not always the case.

Imagine what would happen if you had master and slave name servers configured properly and running cleanly, until one day the administrator of the LAN hosting your slave name server decides to install a firewall to protect his network. All of a sudden, your master name server's `NOTIFY` signals are being bounced, and the slave name server on Mr. Security'sLAN is not getting any updates. If you had set up standardized zone refresh settings on the slave name server, you would have far less of a problem.

Zone refresh settings are configured in the Start Of Authority (SOA) block in the slave name server's `/etc/named.conf` file. The default SOA block configured for localhost looks like this:

```
@       1D IN SOA        @ tom.yahoo.com (
        20040117              ; serial  number for zone
        3H                    ; Refresh after 3 Hours
        15M                   ; Retry   after 15 Minutes
        1W                    ; Expire  after 1 Week
        1D )                  ; Negative TTL of 1 Day
```

In this example, we've added comments (in bold) that show what each setting does. These refresh settings affect the way in which the slave name server pulls down records and, when it cannot contact the master name server, how long the slave name server can continue to serve its data until the zone information must expire. Unless you are running a specialized BIND9 configuration (in which case you are probably not in need of this chapter), the default `Refresh`, `Retry`, and `Expire` values are usually sufficient. However, you might want to change the value of the `Negative TTL` field.

The `Negative TTL` field is fairly new in BIND configuration. It used to be called the `Minimum TTL`, but this is no longer the case. `Minimum TTL` functioned much like the zone-wide TTL at the top of each zone file:

```
$TTL    86400
```

`Negative TTL`, however, is the special *Time To Live* that caching name servers use when they provide *negative*, or false, responses. Such responses are issued when a name server receives a query for a domain name that does not have an associated zone or record. These negative responses can be cached and reissued without forcing the server to recheck the queried domain to see if anything exists yet. Just as caching DNS helps reduce the load on the Internet and on target DNS servers, so does this setting allows us to further reduce the load our DNS machine. If you do not have frequent requests for nonexistent domains, you are probably safe in leaving this set at the same value as the main TTL (by default, 1 day or 86,400 seconds).

Note   If you issue new DNS entries several times a day, you may need to change the `Negative TTL` value to a very low number. If you are adding new machines every day to an Internet-exposed network and want those new machines to be seen instantly, you will need to reduce the amount of time in which DNS servers claim that your new machines do not yet exist.

BIND9 Security

BIND9 offers a number of new security settings that you can use to lock down your DNS servers. Although we don't have the space to cover them here, if you run BIND9, you should take the time to get to know these features:

✦ Access control lists

✦ Transaction signatures

✦ RNDC and TSIG

✦ DNSSEC

✦ Split DNS

Tip   To learn more, consult the BIND9 Administrator Reference Manual at `www.nominum .com/content/documents/bind9arm.pdf`.

Whether or not you use these advanced security features, there are a few simple habits that will keep your DNS server secure. In this section, we describe two of these and show you how to keep DNS under control. In addition, use the security methods you have established for your other Internet services.

Lock Down Your Name Servers

The first thing you should do to enhance security on your DNS server is to lock it down. By doing this, you disallow zone transfers from anyone except your machines that have legitimate need for zone transfer data. By default, the zone definitions in `named.conf` look like this:

```
zone "example.com" IN {
        type master;
        file "example.com.zone";
        allow-update { none; };
};
```

This is a huge security risk if left as is. If not locked down, anyone can do *zone transfers* from your DNS server and see all of the machines that your DNS has records for. Consider the output of the following `dig` command, which requests a zone transfer with the `axfr` option:

```
#  dig example.com axfr @10.1.1.1

; <<>> DiG 9.2.2-P3 <<>> example.com axfr @10.1.1.1
;; global options:  printcmd
```

```
example.com.              86400    IN     SOA     example.com.
     tom.yahoo.com.example.com. 2004011823 10800 900 604800 86400
example.com.              86400    IN     A       10.1.1.1
example.com.              86400    IN     NS      ns.example.com.
example.com.              86400    IN     NS      ns2.example.com.
ftp.example.com.          86400    IN     CNAME   example.com.
mail.example.com.         86400    IN     CNAME   example.com.
ns.example.com.           86400    IN     A       10.1.1.1
ns2.example.com.          86400    IN     A       192.168.128.3
webdav.example.com.       86400    IN     CNAME   example.com.
www.example.com.          86400    IN     CNAME   example.com.
example.com.              86400    IN     SOA     example.com.
     tom.yahoo.com.example.com. 2004011823 10800 900 604800 86400
;; Query time: 3 msec
;; SERVER: 10.1.1.1#53(10.1.1.1)
;; WHEN: Sun Jan 18 22:31:32 2004
;; XFR size: 12 records
```

If you were of a malicious mind, wouldn't that be useful information? Because you're a dutiful administrator, though, that output should frighten you. Luckily, it's easy to lock this down. Simply add the `allow-transfer` directive to your `named.conf` zone block, as in

```
zone "example.com" IN {
    type master;
    file "example.com.zone";
    allow-update { none; };
    allow-transfer { 192.168.128.3; 127.0.0.1; 192.168.128.25; 10.1.1.1; };
};
```

Now, `named` will prevent zone transfers from any IP addresses other than those specified in `allow-transfer`. If someone tries to snoop your DNS data now, that person will get this error message:

```
#  dig example.com axfr @10.1.1.1

; <<>> DiG 9.2.2-P3 <<>> example.com axfr @10.1.1.1
;; global options: printcmd
; Transfer failed.
```

Be sure to take care of this on all running DNS servers, including secondary, and tertiary servers (that is, all slave servers) if you are running them. Without this setting, you leave yourself open to would-be crackers. Anyone can fully enumerate all the hosts in your domain, or even all the hosts on your network, with DHCP unless you close this hole.

Tip   You can also fix this problem by setting the `allow-transfer` option globally to `{!0.0.0.0; }`, which will disallow zone transfers from all IPs on the Internet by default. Then you can simply allow them on a zone-per-zone basis as needed.

Running BIND9 in chroot Mode

If you want to enhance the security of your DNS server, consider running BIND9 in `chroot` mode. This ensures that if crackers get into your system, they will be trapped in the application's `chroot` **directory** (`/var/named/chroot`) and won't be able to get out into the rest of the filesystem where they could do real damage. It's a good option for those who are particularly nervous about external intrusion.

By default, Fedora Core Linux has started installing BIND9 to run in `chroot` mode. However, there are some concerns that you should know about before you decide to keep BIND9 in this mode. In particular, see the *BIND9 Bug* sidebar in this chapter. You can tell whether your system is running in `chroot` mode or normal mode with the `ps` command, as in

```
# ps auxw| grep [n]amed
named   7288  0.0  1.1 36796 2484 ?   S    00:36   0:00
/usr/sbin/named -u named -t /var/named/chroot
```

This output shows that you're in `chroot` mode. If you were running in normal mode, the output would look like this:

```
# ps auxw| grep [n]amed
named   7427  1.0  1.1  36348 2468 ?   S    01:13   0:00
/usr/sbin/named -u named
```

On Fedora Core, BIND's `chroot` mode is controlled by the file `/etc/sysconfig/named`. If you open this file in a text editor, you'll see a line beginning with `ROOTDIR`. This line determines whether BIND9 runs in `chroot` or normal mode. In `chroot` mode (the default), the line looks like this:

```
ROOTDIR=/var/named/chroot
```

To change BIND9 to normal mode, change the line to this:

```
ROOTDIR=/
```

If you decide to leave your system in `chroot` mode, be sure that you have a file at `/var/named/chroot/etc/named.conf` and that the file has content. You should also have these files to start with:

```
/var/named/chroot/var/named/
/var/named/chroot/var/named/named.ca
/var/named/chroot/var/named/named.local
/var/named/chroot/var/named/localhost.zone
```

The BIND9 Bug

At the time we wrote this book, there was an open bug in the BIND9/`named` implementation on Fedora Core. Normally, when running in `chroot` mode, the file `/var/named/chroot/etc/named.conf` contains the configuration file for `chroot`'d BIND9. Because of the bug, this file may be empty, which keeps DNS from running at all in `chroot` mode unless you apply the fix. There are two workarounds to solve this problem.

The easy way to fix this bug is to run BIND9/`named` in normal root mode, changing the `ROOTDIR` variable as described in the *Running BIND9 in chroot Mode* section of this chapter.

Continued

Continued

If you want to run in `chroot` mode and take advantage of its more secure environment, you will have to do a bit of extra work and copy the `/etc/named.conf` file into the `/var/named/chroot/etc/` directory. Do so with this command:

```
# cp -p /etc/named.conf /var/named/chroot/etc cp: overwrite
'/var/named/chroot/etc/named.conf'? Y
```

The same problem exists with the zone files stored in `/var/named`. You must copy these as well:

```
# cp -p /var/named/*.* /var/named/chroot/var/named
cp: overwrite '/var/named/chroot/var/named/localhost.zone'? Y
cp: overwrite '/var/named/chroot/var/named/named.ca'? Y
cp: overwrite '/var/named/chroot/var/named/named.local'? Y
```

This problem may be fixed by the time you read this book, but it's a good reminder that you should be careful when choosing an operating system for a production environment. You can always track bugs and patches at `http://bugzilla.redhat.com`.

Troubleshooting BIND9 and DNS Issues

If you have problems the first few times you set up DNS, you are not alone. Most people run into trouble at some point, until they've worked enough with DNS to figure out where problems are likely to hide. In this section, we show you some of the most common DNS-related problems and offer some tips on getting your service running again.

Caution

If you use the Red Hat GUI configuration tool `redhat-config-bind`, you may run into serious trouble. This tool overwrites your regular files and can make it difficult to diagnose problems. In addition, once you commit to working with the GUI tool, you **cannot** return to DNS configuration at the command line. (Think of it like switching to synthetic oil in your car.) Other GUI tools may hide crucial data in nonstandard locations or might even fail to parse all the options available in the service. We strongly recommend that you work with BIND9 and DNS services at the command line with a text editor.

Luckily, most DNS problems can be resolved with regular command line programs. Traditionally, the `nslookup` program has been the primary troubleshooting choice, but the newer program `dig` has quickly supplanted it. The output from `dig` provides a great deal of information that can help you fix your DNS server issues quickly and accurately.

For example, you can use `dig` to "walk" the DNS tree for a given domain, as demonstrated earlier in this chapter. You can also use `dig` to complete entire zone transfers from a specified name server, which is a very useful tool (or security check). To do so, issue this command:

```
# dig example.com axfr @10.1.1.1

; <<>> DiG 9.2.2-P3 <<>> example.com axfr @10.1.1.1
;; global options: printcmd
example.com.          86400    IN      SOA     example.com.
    tom.yahoo.com.example.com. 2004011824 10800 900 604800 86400
example.com.          86400    IN      A       10.1.1.1
```

```
example.com.          86400    IN    NS      ns.example.com.
example.com.          86400    IN    NS      ns2.example.com.
ftp.example.com.      86400    IN    CNAME   example.com.
mail.example.com.     86400    IN    CNAME   example.com.
ns.example.com.       86400    IN    A       10.1.1.1
ns2.example.com.      86400    IN    A       192.168.128.3
webdav.example.com.   86400    IN    CNAME   example.com.
www.example.com.      86400    IN    CNAME   example.com.
example.com.          86400    IN    SOA     example.com.
    tom.yahoo.com.example.com. 2004011824 10800 900 604800 86400
;; Query time: 3 msec
;; SERVER: 10.1.1.1#53(10.1.1.1)
;; WHEN: Mon Jan 19 01:21:40 2004
;; XFR size: 12 records
```

While this is useful if you are the administrator of example.com, think how much trouble this could cause if someone else was able to suck down all your unsecured reverse DNS records. Handing over a complete zone record, which contains every IP address on the network is not high on our list of Secure Administrative Policies.

Finding DNS problems can be a bit tricky. You need to think about the tools you use, the settings in /etc/named.conf versus settings in zone files or slave server settings, the zone transfer settings you've chosen, and what you're resolving against. Not to mention things like iptables and firewalling rules!

The entries in the /var/log/messages log file can be very helpful in narrowing down possible solutions. The remainder of this section offers solutions to common DNS service problems.

The Slave Name Server Is Not Updating Itself

One common DNS problem involves slave name servers. If you change the master example .com.zone file and restart the service, but the slave name server does not also update itself, external DNS requests might fail or receive the wrong information. To solve this question, think about how the master server works.

When a zone file is changed and named restarts, the daemon sends a NOTIFY command that should trigger the slave server to restart itself as well. To see whether your named did this, check your log files:

```
#  tail /var/log/messages
...
Jan 19 02:33:47 localhost named[7665]: zone example.com/IN: loaded serial
    2004011825
Jan 19 02:33:47 localhost named[7665]: zone localhost/IN: loaded serial 42
Jan 19 02:33:47 localhost named[7665]: running
Jan 19 02:33:47 localhost named[7665]: zone example.com/IN: sending
notifies (serial 2004011825)
```

If the NOTIFY command was executed properly, the next line in the log should have been

```
Jan 19 02:20:58 localhost named[7528]: client 192.168.128.3#33301: transfer
    of 'example.com/IN': AXFR -style IXFR started
```

Since this line did not display, the slave server at 192.168.128.3 did not perform a zone transfer. Thus, there's a problem. Perhaps the slave server can't find the master server or there is another configuration error. Use `dig` to trace the existing configuration:

```
#  dig ns2.example.com @10.1.1.1
...
;; ANSWER SECTION:
ns2.example.com.       86400 IN   A     192.168.128.3

;; AUTHORITY SECTION:
example.com.           86400 IN   NS    ns.example.com.
example.com.           86400 IN   NS    ns2.example.com.example.com.
```

The A record is fine, but note the oddness in the NS records. Why is there a double domain error here? Open your zone file, and you'll see the problem:

```
2004011825    ;
                           3H              ; refresh
                           15M             ; retry
                           1W              ; expiry
                           1D )            ; minimum
  @            1D IN NS    ns.example.com.
               1D IN NS    ns2.example.com
```

There it is, on the last line: rather, there it *isn't*. Remember that you need to supply a trailing dot for every domain name. Since this entry doesn't have a trailing dot, the NS record is broken and your slave server can't update. Simply add the dot, save the file, and restart the service again.

Using whois Effectively

With the explosion of domain name registrars across the world, the simple `whois` command isn't as immediately helpful as it used to be. For general use, `whois` is used with this syntax:

```
#  whois domain-name
```

as in

```
#  whois wiley.com
Domain Name: WILEY.COM
    Registrar: REGISTER.COM, INC.
    Whois Server: whois.register.com
    Referral URL: http://www.register.com
    Name Server: JWS-EDCP.WILEY.COM
    Name Server: NS1.WILEYPUB.COM
    Status: ACTIVE
    Updated Date: 21-nov-2003
    Creation Date: 12-oct-1994
    Expiration Date: 11-oct-2011
```

However, simple `whois` is reliable only for domain names in the .com, .net, and .edu TLD. To get a more accurate report of domain ownership, issue `whois` against a specific name server. the following code block shows the command issued with three widely used `whois` servers:

```
#  whois domain-name@whois.internic.net
```

```
#  whois domain-name@whois.register.com
#  whois domain-name@whois.geektools.com
```

If you can't get the result you need from one of these servers, and you're looking for a site in a different TLD, find the whois server for that domain's registrar of record. If you query that whois server, you should get the information you seek.

A New Alias or Address Record Won't Load

If your DNS server is up and running, everything may seem to be fine. However, if you add a new alias or address record at a later point, you may find that it won't load, no matter how many times you reload the zone files. Everything may seem to be in order, but clearly there is a problem. Bryan Bailey, a Rackspace Linux support sysadmin and RHCE, suggests the following approach.

Zone files are quite prone to user error. Think about the unusual syntax of entries in this file. You must use this syntax exactly when you add a new record, or the record will not load. As in the previous example, the trailing dot is the most common zone file omission.

The zone file shown here contains a CNAME record that will not load because it has a missing dot:

```
$TTL 38400
foo.com.     IN     SOA     ns.foo.com. hostmaster.foo.com.(
                    2003123166
                    10800
                    3600
                    604800
                    38400  )

foo.com.          IN      NS      ns.foo.com.
foo.com.          IN      A       192.168.0.1
www               IN      CNAME   foo.com.
mail              IN      CNAME   foo.com.
pop3              IN      CNAME   foo.com.
smtp              IN      CNAME   foo.com.
ftp               IN      CNAME   foo.com.
mysubdomain       IN      CNAME   foo.com
```

While named will reload the zone file without error, the added entry will never resolve. Instead, this entry will create the FQDN mysubdomain.foo.com.foo.com.

To fix this problem, just open the file in a text editor and add the dot to the final entry. Save the file, exit, and restart the service. Try to make a habit of checking the last line in every zone record to ensure that the trailing dot is there. For some reason, it's the final line that always seems to be the culprit.

Note   Always remember to increment the serial number in the zone file, whether you are adding a new record or fixing a problem. Compare this corrected version of the zone file to the problematic version shown previously:

```
$TTL 38400
foo.com.    IN   SOA    ns.foo.com.
hostmaster.foo.com.(
```

```
                    2003123167
                       10800
                       3600
                       604800
                       38400 )

    foo.com.        IN      NS      ns.foo.com.
    foo.com.        IN      A       192.168.0.1
    www             IN      CNAME   foo.com.
    mail            IN      CNAME   foo.com.
    pop3            IN      CNAME   foo.com.
    smtp            IN      CNAME   foo.com.
    ftp             IN      CNAME   foo.com.
    mysubdomain     IN      CNAME   foo.com.
```

Note that the serial number has been incremented by one, and the final trailing dot added. The zone file should now work properly.

Automated DNS Zone File Troubleshooting

Allen Rouse, a Rackspace Linux support sysadmin who does a lot of DNS troubleshooting, offers the following tip for easy automation.

Problems like the missing trailing dot example as well as malformed PTR records, bad SOAs, and many other zone file abnormalities and typos can be a real pain to track down. Rackspace sysadmins often use a special tool to automatically scan for and detect these zone file problems after making a zone file change but before restarting the customer's name server (to keep it from crashing on a bad zone file).

Try the DNS administrator tool dlint (www.domtools.com/dns/dlint.shtml). It's worth its weight in gold for the busy DNS administrator.

Troubleshooting Tools

Sometimes administrators can't solve a DNS problem simply because they don't know where to find the right tool. There are a number of useful DNS troubleshooting tools on the web. If you can't find the answer on one of these sites, you should at least be able to find links to other resources that might solve your problem:

✦ Traceroute tools: www.traceroute.org

✦ Various web tools: http://geektools.com/

✦ InterNic Whois: www.internic.net/whois.html

✦ Graphical traceroute: www.visualroute.com/server.html

DNS and BIND Resources

Because DNS has been around in a stable form for so long, there are a number of good DNS- and BIND-related resources available to the inexperienced administrator. Table 12-1 provides some useful sites for more information on DNS, domain names, and BIND.

Table 12-1: DNS and BIND Resources

Domain naming services	
HOWTO	`www.tldp.org/HOWTO/DNS-HOWTO.html`
Overview	`www.dns.net/dnsrd/docs/whatis.html`
General references	`www.dns.net/dnsrd/`
Domain names	
RFC 1034	`ftp://ftp.is.co.za/rfc/rfc1034.txt`
Top-level domains	`www.iana.org/gtld/gtld/htm`
Country codes	`www.iana.org/cctld/cctld-whois.htm`
Berkeley Internet Naming Daemon (BIND9)	

Red Hat Linux Customization Guide	`www.redhat.com/docs/manuals/linux/`
	`RHL-9-Manual/custom-guide/`
	`ch-bindconf.html`

Red Hat Enterprise Linux 3: Reference Guide	`www.redhat.com/docs/manuals/enterprise/`
	`RHEL-3-Manual/ref-guide/`
	`ch-bind.html`

Common mistakes	`www.redhat.com/docs/manuals/enterprise/`
	`RHEL-3-Manual/ref-guide/`
	`s1-bind-mistakes.html`

BIND9 FAQ	`www.isc.org/products/BIND/FAQ.html`
DNS and BIND (4th edition, O'Reilly & Associates)	`www.oreilly.com/catalog/dns4/index.html`
Administrator's manual	`www.nominum.com/content/documents/` `bind9arm.pdf`

Summary

Many large networks choose to run DNS services in-house. Others choose to allow their upstream providers to handle DNS issues. If you decide to run DNS locally, you will need to make careful configurations to the appropriate files. Although it can be time consuming to set up DNS service accurately, once it is configured properly there is little that needs to be done by the administrator.

✦   ✦   ✦

Modem Troubleshooting

✦ ✦ ✦ ✦

In This Chapter

Finding modem resources

Choosing a modem

Probing your modem

Setting up your modem in the GUI

Setting up your modem with minicom

Modem troubleshooting tips

✦ ✦ ✦ ✦

Although modems have been around for a long time, unsupported modems and modem with improper configurations can cause them to underperform or just flat-out fail. Add the fact that many common modems (referred to as winmodems) either don't work in Linux at all or need special drivers, and just getting a modem to work can be difficult.

Once you have a working modem, the next trick is to get it to communicate by dialing out to the service provider. This chapter describes how to get a modem working in Fedora, and then troubleshoot your dial-up connection to the Internet.

Because dealing with winmodems is one of the most common issues related to modem problems in Linux, refer to the "Using winmodems" sidebar to see descriptions of winmodems and linmodems.

Using winmodems

Winmodems are controller-less modems. They are missing essential parts needed in a modem, which are emulated by software in Windows operating systems. You can get some winmodems to work in Linux with special drivers. But, if you have a choice, don't choose to use a winmodem in Linux.

Although Winmodem is a trademark of 3COM Corp., winmodem is used to describe a class of these modems. To tell if your modem is a winmodem, there are a few things you can do. The modem probably is a winmodem if:

✦ It says on the box that a Windows operating system (Win95, 98, and so forth) is required, or the title of the modem says it is "for Windows."

✦ The modem is listed on the box as controller-less or as a Host Controller (HCF) modem from Rockwell.

✦ You bought the modem recently and it was really cheap (under $20).

Continued

Continued

✦ It is an internal modem, especially in a laptop. (See the *Using* USB Modems section for a list of supported internal PCI modems.)

Refer to Table 13-2 at the end of the chapter for a list of sites containing drivers that support certain types of winmodems. Remember that you can't always tell if a modem is a winmodem from the brand name. The key information you want is the chipset used on the modem (see the section *Checking Your Chipset for Linux Support* in this chapter). From that you can determine if there is a driver available for you to try.

Choosing a Modem

If you don't have a modem or are contemplating buying a new one, your safest bet is to choose an external serial modem. Every external serial modem I have used works fine from the get-go. USB modems can be a bit harder to get going, but basically work well. A few internal PCI modems are great, namely those that include a supported chipset.

The official word from Red Hat, Inc. (`www.redhat.com/software/rhl9_hcl.html`) on modem support as of Red Hat Linux 9 was:

100% Hayes-compatible internal and external serial modems with hardware UART. NOTE: Winmodems, host-based, HCF-, HSP-, HSF-, controller-less, host-controlled, and soft modems are NOT supported.

While officially this is true, there are ways to get some winmodems working in Fedora and Red Hat Linux if you care to take the trouble.

Note   If you already have a modem and you just want to give it a shot, go ahead. As you go through this chapter, I will describe how to determine the kind of modem you have and whether or not it is supported in Linux.

Using PCI Modems

A common way to distinguish between PCI modems you can use with Linux is distinguishing between controller-less and controller-based modems. Controller-less modems are referred to as *winmodems*. Winmodems that have drivers that allow them to work in Linux are sometimes referred to as *Linmodems*. While there are no officially supported Linmodems in Fedora or Red Hat Linux, there are drivers available you can try. (See the "Using winmodems" sidebar for further details.)

If you are going to purchase an internal PCI modem (one that plugs directly into a PCI slot on your computer), make sure that the modem:

✦ *Is controller-based*—In other words, all the basic modem functionality takes place within the modem and not in the operating system. The box or online description for the modem should note it as a controller-based modem.

✦ *Contains a supported chipset*—Linux modem drivers are written based on the type of communications chips inside the modem. Because the same chips can be used in different modems (and because, on occasion, the same modem name will include different chipsets), determining the chipset will tell you if the modem has a supported Linux driver.

Chipsets for controller-based PCI modems (in other words, not winmodems) include the following:

✦ *Lucent Venus chipset*—Includes the Zoom 2920 and Actiontec PCI56012 modems (as well as several MultiTech modems)

✦ *USR/TI Kermit chipset*—Includes the 3COM/US Robotics 3CP5610 family of modems (models 5610A, 5613 and 5609) and OEM models 2976, 2977, and 3258

✦ *TOPIC TP560i chipset*—Well Communications (FM-56PCI-TP, GVC MD0321) and the Archtek Smartlink 5634PCV

The modems just mentioned are generally more expensive than their controller-less counterparts. Because winmodems are cheap and plentiful, some people are willing to try to get a winmodem working before they go out and buy a real modem.

Checking Your Chipset for Linux Support

If you are not sure what kind of modem you have, examine the chipset on the card before you install it. Using that information, you can check out these websites for information on Linux modem support:

✦ *Winmodems are not modems* (`http://start.at/modem`)—To see if your PCI modem has a supported chipset, click Home Site, and then click the Chipset Database link. The site also contains a wealth of information on winmodems, other modem types (USB, ISA, and so on), and general modem operations.

✦ *A Linmodems support page* (`linmodems.technion.ac.il`)—Although it doesn't contain as large a database of supported modems as the previous site, the content here is very current (there are even references to Fedora).

Note

If you know at this point that you have a winmodem, before proceeding you should be sure that there is a Linux driver available for the winmodem. If there is none, you need to go and get a different modem. If you have a laptop computer, you might want to dig a bit deeper and check out linux-on-laptops.com to research how others who own your model laptop have dealt with their modems for Linux.

Installing the Modem

The next step for a PCI modem is to install it and check it out, using the following instructions.

1. *Physically install the modem*—Follow the manufacturer's instructions for installing the modem. Make sure that you have:

   ✦ Firmly seated the modem in the PCI slot

   ✦ Replaced the screw holding the modem to the case (if appropriate)

   ✦ Plugged the line jack on the modem to your telephone wall jack

2. *Boot Linux*—During the boot process, the kudzu utility checks the `/etc/sysconfig/hwconf` file to look for any hardware that has been added or removed since the computer was shut down.

   In this case, kudzu should find the new modem installed in one of your PCI slots and offer to let you configure it. Figure 13-1 shows an example of a kudzu screen where a supported Multitech modem is detected; in Figure 13-2 a nonsupported winmodem is detected:

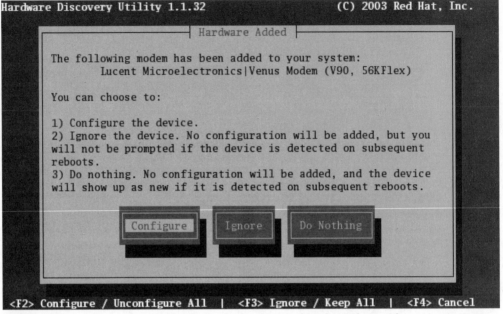

Figure 13-1: During boot-up, kudzu finds a supported Multitech modem with a 4Lucent Venus chipset.

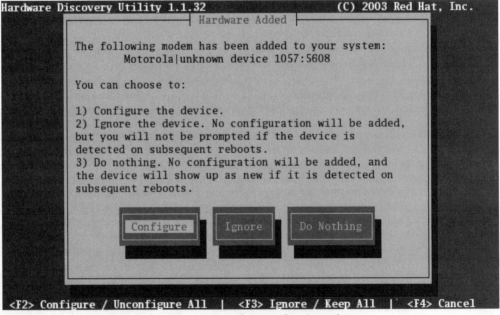

Figure 13-2: Here kudzu finds a nonsupported Motorola winmodem.

Note   If you are booting to runlevel 5 (the default state), a graphical screen is shown during startup. You need to click Show Details to be able to see the kudzu screen when it appears.

In Figure 13-1, you can see that a modem containing the supported Lucent Venus chipset was detected. In Figure 13-2, kudzu can tell that the device is a modem from Motorola, but it does not have a driver to support the device. In both cases, you are prompted for a response.

3. *Configure Modem in Kudzu*—From the kudzu screen, click Configure. Kudzu will try to add your modem to the local /etc/sysconfig/hwconf file (which contains information defining all the hardware on your computer).

Note   You can run kudzu from the command line by simply typing kudzu as root user. However, you might want to turn off the GUI (go to runlevel 3) to run kudzu because it probes the video card as well and can scramble your GUI.

Checking the Modem

At this point, if the modem was properly detected you should be able to list information about that modem. Here's how:

1. *List PCI devices*—Once the computer starts up, type the following to list all the PCI devices connected to your computer (presumably including the modem you installed).

```
# /sbin/lspci -vv | less
```

Page through the output (use the space bar) to view the hardware connected to your PCI slots. Here's an example of output for a PCI modem:

```
00:09.0 Communication controller: Lucent Microelectronics.
        Venus Modem (V90, 56KFlex)
    Subsystem: Lucent Microelectronics: Unknown device 5656
    Control: I/O+ Mem+ BusMaster+ SpecCycle- MemWINV-
      VGASnoop- ParErr- Stepping- SERR- FastB2B-
    Status: Cap+ 66Mhz- UDF- FastB2B+ ParErr-
      DEVSEL=medium>TAbort- <TAbort- <MAbort- >SERR- <PERR-
    Latency: 0 (63000ns min, 3500ns max)
    Interrupt: pin A routed to IRQ 10
```

In this case, the modem is a MultiTech MT5634ZPX-PCI. Key information is that it is a PCI modem that includes the Lucent Venus chipset. (That is one of a handful of chipsets you can find on internal PCI modems that are controller-based.)

The lspci output from the winmodem I tested gave less information about the modem:

```
00:09.0 Communication controller: Motorola:
        Unknown device 5608
    Subsystem: Motorola: Unknown device 0000
    Flags: bus master, medium devsel, latency 32, IRQ 10
    I/O ports at ec00 [size=256]
    Memory at dffff000 (32-bit, non-prefetchable) [size=4K]
    Capabilities: [40] Power Management version 2
```

This winmodem contained the Motorola 62412-51 chip, which I had to determine by physically looking at the card. By checking the Chipset Database at the `http://start.at/modem` site and selecting the Motorola SM56 PCI link, I could see that there was support for that Motorola chip through Red Hat Linux 7.1, but that modems with that chipset were not supported for later systems.

2. *Run scanModem*—To get more information about your PCI modem, download the scanmodem utility and run it. This utility gives you information about any PCI modems it finds (winmodems or not) and will give you any Fedora-specific information it has about modem drivers.

   a. Change to the directory in which you want to save the scanmodem utility and type the following:

      `# wget http://linmodems.technion.ac.il/packages/scanModem.gz`

   b. Unzip the utility by typing **gunzip scanModem.gz**

   c. Run the utility by typing **sh scanModem**

   d. Read the `ModemData.txt` file (for information specific to Fedora and your modem), `ModemData.txt.2` (for general scanModem information), and `ModemDriverCompiling.txt` (to compile your own winmodem driver).

3. *Continue*—Where you go from here depends on whether or not you have a controller-based or controller-less modem:

   • *Winmodem*—If you have a winmodem and are still determined to try to get it working, refer to the "Using Winmodems" sidebar and Table 13-2 for further information. They will help you understand what you need to do to get your winmodem working (if that's possible).

   • *Controller-based PCI modem*—With a supported controller-based PCI modem, Linux should automatically know to use the serial.o driver to provide a serial interface to the modem. Therefore, to Linux, the modem is configured to be used via a standard serial port (`/dev/ttyS0`, `/dev/ttyS1`, and so forth).

The next step is to make sure that Linux can find your modem and communicate with it. For that, skip ahead to the *Probing and Trying your Modem* section, given later in this chapter.

Using USB Modems

Because some new computers have limited PCI slots and often don't even have serial ports, USB modems are becoming more popular for those who still need dial-up. If you are choosing a USB modem for Linux, you should make sure that:

   ✦ It is *not* a controller-less modem (yes, there are USB winmodems).

   ✦ It *does* conform to the USB Communication Device Class Abstract Control Model (CDC ACM) specification.

In Linux, USB modems that comply with the CDC ACM should work with the acm driver. According to documentation that comes with that driver, USB modems known to work with the driver include:

   ✦ 3Com USB OfficeConnect 56k

✦ 3Com USB Voice FaxModem Pro

✦ 3Com USB Sportster

✦ Multitech USB Multimodem 56k

✦ Zoom 2986L FaxModem USB

✦ Compaq 56k FaxModem

✦ ELSA Microlink 56k

When Linux detects a supported USB modem, it creates the devices needed to access the modem. For the first USB modem, the /dev/ttyACM0 and /dev/cuacm0 devices can be used to access the modem. The second USB modem is accessible through /dev/ttyACM1 and /dev/cuacm1, and so on.

Note   The device name beginning with /dev/cu ... is a throwback from the first uucp (UNIX-to-UNIX copy) programs used with early UNIX systems. The cu stood for Call UNIX, and device names beginning with cu were used to access serial ports connected to modems that dialed other computers.

Using Serial Modems

With new, external serial modems starting at about $40 (and even cheaper if you get a used one), this might be the best way to go if you are getting a dial-up modem for Linux. To set up an external serial modem in Linux, simply follow these steps:

1. Follow the manufacturer's instructions to install the modem (typically, just plug in the modem to a serial port on your computer, the power cord to an electrical outlet, and the line to a telephone jack.)

2. Either reboot the computer or run the kudzu command from a shell (as root user) to configure the modem.

Next, go ahead to the *Probing and Trying Your Modem* section.

Probing and Trying Your Modem

Once a modem is physically installed, you can use the wvdialconf command to see if it can detect any modems on your computer. Then you can run wvdial to make sure that you can connect to the Internet Service Provider.

1. *Run wvdialconf*—The wvdialconf command checks devices that it expects might be connected to a modem, probes the modem (if it finds one) for information, and creates a configuration file of basic settings for the modem. Here's an example:

   ```
   # wvdialconf /etc/wvdial.conf.new
   ```

   Here's what the output looked like when I attached a serial modem to the second serial port (/dev/ttyS1, also referred to as COM2):

   ```
   ttyS1<*1>: ATQ0 V1 E1 -- OK
   ttyS1<*1>: ATQ0 V1 E1 Z -- OK
   ttyS1<*1>: ATQ0 V1 E1 S0=0 -- OK
   ```

```
ttyS1<*1>: ATQ0 V1 E1 S0=0 &C1 -- OK
ttyS1<*1>: ATQ0 V1 E1 S0=0 &C1 &D2 -- OK
ttyS1<*1>: ATQ0 V1 E1 S0=0 &C1 &D2 +FCLASS=0 -- OK
ttyS1<*1>: Modem Identifier: ATI -- 288
ttyS1<*1>: Speed 4800: AT -- OK
ttyS1<*1>: Speed 9600: AT -- OK
ttyS1<*1>: Speed 19200: AT -- OK
ttyS1<*1>: Speed 38400: AT -- OK
ttyS1<*1>: Speed 57600: AT -- OK
ttyS1<*1>: Speed 115200: AT -- OK
ttyS1<*1>: Max speed is 115200; that should be safe.
ttyS1<*1>: ATQ0 V1 E1 S0=0 &C1 &D2 +FCLASS=0 -- OK

Found a modem on /dev/ttyS1.
Modem configuration written to /etc/wvdial.conf.new
ttyS1<Info>: Speed 115200; init "ATQ0 V1 E1 S0=0
    &C1 &D2 +FCLASS=0
```

The output shows a modem was detected on /dev/ttyS1 (COM2 port) of your computer. The result of the output was written (in this case) to the /etc/wvdial.conf.new file.

2. *Edit wvdial.conf.new file*—View the contents of the wvdial.conf.new file you just created. Here is an example:

```
[Dialer Defaults]
Modem = /dev/ttyS1
Baud = 115200
Init1 = ATZ
Init2 = ATQ0 V1 E1 S0=0 &C1 &D2 +FCLASS=0
ISDN = 0
Modem Type = Analog Modem
; Phone = <Target Phone Number>
; Username = <Your Login Name>
; Password = <Your Password>
```

Remove the semicolons from the last three lines and replace the words in italics with the phone number of your ISP, username, and password, respectively.

3. *Copy to wvdial.conf*—Once you are satisfied with the file, copy it to the permanent /etc/wvdial.conf file:

```
# cp /etc/wvdial.conf.new /etc/wvdial.conf
```

4. *Try to dial the ISP*—To see if your modem is working and ready to create a PPP connection to your ISP, simply type the following command:

```
# wvdial
--> WvDial: Internet dialer version 1.53
--> Initializing modem.
--> Sending: ATZ
ATZ
OK
--> Sending: ATQ0 V1 E1 S0=0 &C1 &D2 +FCLASS=0
ATQ0 V1 E1 S0=0 &C1 &D2 +FCLASS=0
```

```
OK
--> Modem initialized.
--> Sending: ATDT5557846
--> Waiting for carrier.
ATDT5557846
CONNECT 115200
--> Carrier detected. Waiting for prompt.
login:
login:
--> Looks like a login prompt.
--> Sending: jwjones
jwjones
Password:
--> Looks like a password prompt.
--> Sending: (password)
choice: PPP session from (10.206.160.10) to
10.206.171.70 beginning....~[7f]} # @!}!}!} }4}
"}&} } } } }%}&S}/mH}'}"}(}".[~
--> PPP negotiation detected.
--> Starting pppd at Thu Dec 11 02:49:23 2003
--> pid of pppd: 23585
```

From this output you can see that wvdial successfully initialized the modem, dialed the phone number, sent the login and password (as prompted), and started a PPP session. The ISP gave your modem (client side) the address 10.206.160.10 and its modem (server side) the address 10.206.171.70.

If the wvdial session connected, you should be able to type /sbin/ifconfig and see a ppp0 interface running. If it did not work, check the *Modem Troubleshooting Tips* section at the end of this chapter.

Setting Up Your Modem through the GUI

Once you have a working modem in Linux, you can go right to the Red Hat Network Configuration window and step through the procedure for setting up a modem connection. If you can't get your dial-up connection to work, use minicom and some log files to troubleshoot the problems as described here:

The basic steps from a Fedora desktop to configure a dial-up modem are as follows:

1. Click System Settings ⇨ Network from the Red Hat menu.

2. Click New from the Network Configuration window.

3. Select Modem connection and step through the procedure. To complete the procedure, you need at least the phone number to dial the ISP, provider name, login name, and password. (Name the provider ppp0 to overcome a bug in the current release.)

4. Select File ⇨ Save.

5. With the new modem entry selected (probably named ppp0), select Activate to dial your ISP.

If everything is working properly, you should be able to communicate to your ISP (and beyond). If the communications fails, you can start by poking around in the following places:

✦ */etc/wvdial.conf*—Because the Red Hat Network Configuration window uses wvdial on the back-end to do the actual modem initialization and dialing, you can see the settings the window created in the wvdial.conf file. Consider trying different settings, as described in the *Setting Up Your Modem with minicom* section that follows, and then adding settings you like to the Init3 value in the wvdial.conf file.

✦ */var/log/redhat-config-network*—This log file gives you a detailed view of everything the Network Configuration window does. You can see exactly which values are being saved for the interface you added and which configuration files they are being saved in.

✦ */var/log/messages*—When you try to activate the dial-up connection, you can see messages detailing the initialization process (step-by-step) in this log file. These messages reflect the activities of the wvdial command (to dial the ISP) and pppd daemon (to initiate the PPP connection once the remote modem has picked up).

Note   I suggest you tail a log file when you start up a service (such as dial-up) to see messages in real-time. For example, as root user type tail-f/var/log/messages to watch the dial-up process from a Terminal window when you activate the modem from the Network Configuration window.

To try to get your modem settings to work, or to simply tune up those settings to work more efficiently, it helps to understand the AT command set.

Setting Up Your Modem with minicom

The protocol that a computer uses to communicate with standard Hayes-compatible modems is referred to as the AT command set. The AT command set lets you communicate directly to the modem for troubleshooting. If you were not able to get a dial-out connection going as described earlier with the wvdial command or Network Configuration window, you can try using minicom.

The minicom command provides an interface for communicating with devices that are connected to serial ports. Minicom is a Linux-equivalent to the HyperTerminal utility that you may be familiar with in Microsoft operating systems.

With minicom, you can send AT commands directly to your modem to get information about its features and current state. You can also dial out directly, test communications, and change settings.

The procedure in the following section illustrates a session where we use minicom to communicate directly to the modem. Using minicom, you can display and change settings on the modem by issuing commands. For the most part, we are interested in working with:

✦ *AT commands*—These include a standard set of commands used to operate most modems today. Each AT command starts with a letter, except for some that can be preceded by an ampersand (&) or a pound sign (#).

✦ *S registers*—Each "S" register contains a piece of information that can be stored and used on the modem. Some modems can contain over 300 S registers, which can be incompatible with S registers on other modems. The first 11 S registers are standard among most modems.

At this point, I assume that you have installed and configured a modem as described in the *Choosing a Modem* section earlier in this chapter and that you know the serial device (such as /dev/ttyS0) used to communicate with that modem. Refer to Table 13-1 for other minicom functions you can use.

Table 13-1: Using minicom Commands to Test Your Modem

General Functions

Letter	Description
C	Clears the screen
M	Initializes the modem
L	Captures your minicom session to a file. Type a file name to save it to, when prompted. Repeat Ctrl+A+L to close the capture session
J	Jumps to a command shell (then type fg to return to minicom)
P	Displays communications parameters (speed, parity, data, and stopbits)
Z	Shows the help screen
O	Configures settings for minicom (filenames and paths; file transfer protocols; serial port setup; modem and dialing; screen and keyboard; and save setup)
B	Scrolls the screen back
X	Exits and resets the modem
Q	Quits without resetting the modem

Dialing Functions

D	Accesses a dialing directory, where you can save a list of numbers to dial out
H	Hangs up the phone
F	Sends the modem a break signal
I	Initializes the modem

To begin a function in minicom, press Ctrl+A, and then type the appropriate letter.

Starting minicom

Use the following procedure to start minicom.

1. **Start Minicom**—From any Terminal window, type the following as root user:

```
# minicom -s
```

The minicom interface opens to the [configuration] menu.

Note

By default, all users have access to run minicom, based on the permission set in the `/etc/minicom.users` file. If, however, users are unable to access a modem through minicom, they should check the permissions of the modem's serial device. (For example, typing `chmod 755/dev/ttyS0` as the root user gives everyone access to the modem on the COM1 port.)

2. **Choose port settings**—Use the down arrow key to highlight Serial Port Setup, and then press Enter. At the top of the box that appears, you should see Serial Device, followed by the name of the serial device (such as `/dev/ttyS1`), and other information as shown below:

```
A -    Serial Device        : /dev/ttyS0
B - Lockfile Location        : /var/lock
C -    Callin Program        :
D -  Callout Program         :
E -     Bps/Par/Bits         : 38400 8N1
F - Hardware Flow Control     : Yes
G - Software Flow Control     : No
       Change which settings?
```

3. **Set serial device**—If the serial device listed does not represent the one connected to your modem, press A and type the name of your serial device. Examples of device names include:

   • */dev/ttyS0*—For the first serial port (also called COM1).

   • */dev/ttyS1*—For the second serial port (also called COM2)

   • */dev/ttyACM0*—For the first serial interface to a USB modem.

   After typing the device name, press Enter.

4. *Change line speed*—Change the Bps/Par/Bits lines to read 115200 8N1, if it doesn't already say that. (Press E, and then press I to select 115200 BPS as the speed at which your computer communicates to the modem. Then press Enter to return.) Press Enter to return to the [configuration] menu.

5. *Save settings*—Highlight `Save setup as df1` and press Enter. A message will say Configuration Saved. This saves configuration settings to the `/etc/minirc.dfl` file.

6. *Exit*—Highlight Exit and Press Enter. (You may need to restart minicom for the new settings to take effect. Press Ctrl+A, and then X to quit minicom. Then type minicom to restart it.)

Displaying and Changing Modem Settings

With minicom running and communicating with your modem, you should see something like the following:

```
Welcome to minicom 2.00.0
OPTIONS: History Buffer, F-key Macros, Search History Buffer, I18n
Compiled on Sep 12 2003, 17:27:02
Press CTRL-A Z For help on special keys
AT S7=45 S0=0 L1 V1 X4 &c1 E1 Q0
OK
```

This shows that minicom started successfully, and when it sent an AT command to initialize the modem, the modem received it and responded with OK. If you don't see OK, you are not communicating to the modem. In this example, several items were set during initialization:

✦ The number of seconds to wait for a carrier is set to 45 (S7 = 45)

✦ Auto-answering is disabled (S0 = 0)

✦ Speaker is set to low volume (L1)

✦ Result codes are in long form (V1)

✦ All messages are sent (X4)

✦ Receive line signal detect is set to follow the carrier's state (&c1)

✦ Command echo is enabled (E1)

✦ Result codes are sent to the DTE (Q0)

At this point, try some AT commands to get to know your modem better. The letters and numbers that follow the AT change or display the selected values.

1. *Show profiles*—To show the settings on the modem, type the following:

    AT&V

    The information you see will be specific to your modem. It is possible that you will see an active profile and one or more other stored profiles. With different profiles, you can have groups of settings for different situations.

    Refer to any of the AT command set links shown in Table 13-2 for information on what any of the AT commands means.

2. *Load profile*—Use the ATZ command to load a profile.

    ```
    ATZ     Load the default profile
    ATZn    Replace n with 0, 1, 2 to load the selected profile
    ```

3. *Change settings*—Type AT, followed by any number of commands or register settings. Refer to Table 13-2 for links to sites that contain descriptions of the AT command set. Remember, you can add multiple commands and registers on the same line. Here are a few examples:

    ```
    ATL3      Sets speaker volume to high
    ATM2      Sets speaker to always on
    AT&D2     Sets modem to hang up if the computer drops DTR
    AT&DOS12=5 Sets maximum time between the end of the
              escape sequence and sending OK (in 1/50th second)
    ATS6=10   Sets time to wait for a dial tone to 10 seconds.
    ```

4. *Save the settings*—To save settings to the current profile, type **AT&W**.

5. *Try dialing out*—You can use the DT command to try dial out from within minicom. Here is an example:

    ```
    ATDT5551212
    ```

    If you get a dial tone, or are not able to dial out and connect to the remote modem, you may find that you need to pause or wait for secondary tones during the dial-up procedure. Here are characters you can add after the DT (for tone dialing) or DP (for pulse dialing):

✦ W—Wait for a dial tone. You could use this, for example, if you need to dial 9 to get an outside line before dialing (`ATDT9W5551212`).

✦ —Wait for 5 seconds of silence.

✦ ,—Wait for 2 seconds before proceeding (you can add multiple commas to add multiple 2-second pauses).

✦ Sn—Replace n with an entry number of a phone number stored in the dial directory.

✦ L—Redial the previous number dialed.

Once you have gotten working settings and the ability to dial-up and connect to the remote modem, be sure to pass those settings back to the Network Configuration window (or `/etc/wvdial.conf` file) so they are set each time you dial out. The next section describes how to add the settings you come up with for your modem so that they are made permanent and used each time your modem connection starts up.

Making Modem Settings Permanent

Once you know the settings you like, you can add them to the Init3 line in the `wvdial.conf` file, as described earlier. For example, here's how the Init lines might look in the `wvdial.conf` file:

```
Init1 = ATZ
Init3 = ATM1L2S11=50
```

After the Init1 line loads the default profile (ATZ), I change the Init3 line. These values set the speaker to be on until a carrier is detected (M1), set the speaker volume to medium (L2), and also set the dialing tones to go as fast as possible to speed up dialing (set the S11 register to 50 milliseconds). (To add the options in the Network Configuration window, I edited the ppp0 interface name, chose the Advanced tab, and added `ATM1L2S11=50` to the Modem Initialization String box.)

Modem Troubleshooting Tips

Here are some problems you might run into when you try to use a modem in Linux, along with some suggestions on what you can do about those problems.

✦ *Dead modem*—For a PCI modem, check that the card is seated properly. For a serial modem, check that it is plugged into a serial port, that the phone line is connected (line, not phone port) and also that the electricity is plugged in. If one does not find the modem at all, it could indicate a hardware problem or an unsupported modem.

✦ *Not detected*—If you have multiple modems, wvconfig might not have detected the right one (it stops after it finds the first modem). Disable the modem you don't want to use and rerun wvvdialconf.

✦ *Modem performs slowly*—If there is a slow response when you type commands to the modem, there may be more than one device trying to use the same IRQ number. If you have an internal, nonworking modem and you attach an external modem, they both may be trying to use the same IRQ. To see what IRQs are assigned to each serial port, for example, you could type:

```
# setserial -g /dev/ttyS?
/dev/ttyS0, UART: 16550A, Port: 0x03f8, IRQ:4
/dev/ttyS1, UART: 16550A, Port: 0x02f8, IRQ:3
```

This will query `ttyS0`, `ttyS1`, and so on to `ttyS9` and display the device name, port type, hardware I/O port, and IRQ number for each. To solve the problem, you can disable or reassign the IRQ for the nonworking modem (or other device) that is trying to use your modem's IRQ.

✦ *Not logging in*—Double-check the phone number, username, and password. Make sure there are no typos in your username and password. Watch the `/var/log/messages` file to see where the login fails.

✦ *Not getting a dial tone*—Make sure your modem is connected to a telephone jack.

✦ *Modem keeps disconnecting*—If you have calls waiting on your phone, incoming calls could cause your dial-up connection to drop.

Finding Modem Troubleshooting Resources

Table 13-2 provides a reference for finding and troubleshooting modems to work in Linux.

Table 13-2: Linux Modem Reference Table

Description	Location
Information on Modems Supported in Linux	
Winmodems are not modems; Linux information page	`http://start.at/modem`
A Linmodem support page	`http://linmodems.technion.ac.il`
Linux Winmodem Support	`www.linmodems.org`
Linux on Laptops (Search laptops by model to view modem support)	`www.linux-on-laptops.com`
Linmodems discussion forum	Send e-mail to: `discuss@linuxmodems.org`. Mailer should show your reply address. Leave subject and text fields empty. View discussion forum by thread here: `http://linmodems.technion.ac.il/ archive-third/threads.html`
Sites Claiming to Get winmodems Working in Linux (Including Some Fedora or Earlier Red Hat distros)	
LTmodem Drivers for Linux (For Lucent Apollo-ISA and Mars-PCI chipsets)	`www.heby.de/ltmodem` `www.sfu.ca/~cth/ltmodem/dists/redhat`

Continued

Table 13-2: *(continued)*

Description	Location
ACP Modem Driver for Linux (For IBM ThinkPad 600, 600E, and 700 with Mwave chipset)	`www-124.ibm.com/acpmodem`
PCTEL modem for Linux (for Via, Asus, CM8x, Sis, PCT, and AMR modems. Includes patch for Fedora)	`http://linmodems.technion.ac.il/pctel-linux`
SmartLink (for HAMR5600, SmartRiser56; SmartPCI56; SmartUSB56; others under AC'97/MC97 controllers)	`ftp.smlink.com/linux/unsupported/`
Linuxant—Linux drivers for Conexant chipsets (RPMs up to Red Hat 9 available for HCF and HSF softmodems)	`www.linuxant.com/drivers`
Troubleshooting Modems	
AT command set (available from many sites; here are a few)	`www.modemhelp.net/basicatcommand.shtml`
	`http://nemesis.lonestar.org/reference/telecom/modems`
	`www.modem.com/general/extendat.html`
	`http://supportmech.virtualave.net/at-command.htm`
AT command set "S" registers	`www.dataip.co.uk/Reference/ATSRegisters.php`
Redhat PPP List (forum for discussing setting up dial-up networking)	`www.redhat.com/mailman/listinfo/redhat-ppp-list`

Summary

Start with a modem that is supported in Linux (that is, not a winmodem) and you will have a good chance of getting that modem to dial out and connect to a remote modem. With a supported modem in hand, the Network Configuration window can make it simple to set up a dial-up connection. If that doesn't work, there are log files you can monitor and commands such as minicom you can run to try different modem settings.

✦　　　✦　　　✦

Troubleshooting Internal Services

Printer Troubleshooting

No matter what else you do with your computer, you probably need to print. Printing is one of the most basic services offered on a computer system, no matter what operating system you choose to run. However, printing under UNIX has historically been somewhat difficult. Though standard page descriptor languages like PostScript and PCL have made it easier to get printers working under Linux, still there are challenges for the administrator.

In this chapter, we take you through the basic steps of printer configuration under Fedora Core and Red Hat Linux, using both command-line and graphical interfaces. We also offer some troubleshooting help, and show you how to tune your printers for the highest performance. With the information presented here, you should be able to get your printer up and running in no time at all.

CUPS: The Common UNIX Printing System

Print services under Fedora Core and Red Hat Linux, as well as under most other modern Linux and UNIX distributions, are provided by Common UNIX Printing System software, or CUPS. There are a number of command-line and graphical tools available to configure and troubleshoot CUPS, no matter which operating system you're using. In particular, CUPS allows administrators to manage their printers through a handy web interface.

Note

The LPRng printing facility that was in previous versions of Red Hat Linux is not included in Fedora Core. However, you can get RPMs for LPRng from any mirror site that carries Red Hat Linux 9 software. Note that the LPRng standard is being deprecated and will probably disappear from most distributions in the near future.

The CUPS package contains the commands, configuration files, and administrative tools used to manage printing in Fedora Core. It is automatically included in every Fedora Core installation choice except Custom, where you must choose the individual packages you want to install. When the package is installed, it turns on the cupsd daemon by default.

The cupsd daemon is the scheduler that manages CUPS printing. It is started by the cups init script, which is turned on by default by the /etc/init.d/cups script, which runs at boot. The daemon runs in the background and waits for requests to spool print jobs or provide information about printing status.

Tip   cupsd supports the Internet Printing Protocol, or IPP.

You can configure cupsd settings through the Printer configuration window (Figure 14-1) when you edit a printer definition. To open the Printer configuration tool, issue the command redhat-config-printer under Red Hat Linux, or system-config-printer under Fedora Core 2. From the Red Hat menu, you can select System Settings ⇨ Printing. Settings made with these tools are stored in the /etc/cups/cuspd.conf file.

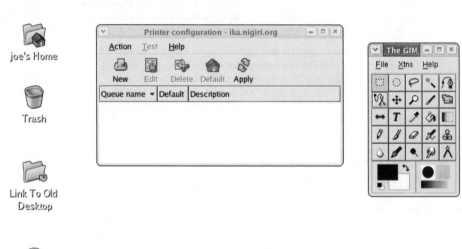

Figure 14-1: Use the Printer Configuration window to define the printers you can use.

The foomatic software package contains printer drivers and driver descriptions used by CUPS and other printing services. The options you set on these drivers determine how the drivers behave, and how print jobs are managed on each individual printer that is attached to your network. The foomatic package contains three main components:

✦ The foomatic database contains tables that describe how to execute the driver you select.

✦ The PostScript Printer Description (PPD) file contains printer-specific information that defines the features and options supported by the printer you define.

✦ The foomatic backend filter determines how the print job is executed, using the PPD file and any options specified by the user sending the job.

Note A PostScript Printer Description file (PPD) contains information that describes the features supported by a particular printer. The printer manufacturer typically creates a separate PPD file for every printer it builds. To improve the quality of printing on your network, you may need to visit the printer manufacturer's website and download the appropriate PPD file. Using the proper PPD file can significantly expand the range of features available for you to configure.

To learn more about the drivers included in the foomatic package and how to use them, visit www.linuxprinting.org. On this site, you'll find a great deal of information on managing print jobs under Linux, including help for Red Hat installations. You may also find patches or updated drivers for your printers here.

The foomatic database does not execute the appropriate driver itself. Rather, the drivers are executed by one of several different execution styles, including GhostScript, Uniprint, and Filter. GhostScript is used for most of the foomatic drivers. Uniprint drivers are actually GhostScript drivers that run from a different file than the one from the one the regular drivers. Finally, Filter drivers are non-GhostScript drivers that are run through GhostScript.

To see which drivers are available for use with the version of GhostScript on your Fedora Core box, issue the following command:

```
# gv -h
```

The output will show you the available device drivers:

```
GNU Ghostscript 7.07 (2003-05-17)
      .
      .
      .
Input formats: PostScript PostScriptLevel1 PostScriptLevel2 PDF
Default output device: x11
Available devices:
 AP21xx DJ630 DJ6xx DJ6xxP DJ8xx DJ9xx DJ9xxVIP alc2000 alc8500 ap3250
 appledmp atx23 atx24 atx38 bbox bit bitcmyk bitrgb bj10e bj10v bj10vh
 bj200 bjc600 bjc800 bjc880j bmp16 bmp16m bmp256 bmp32b bmpa16 bmpa16m
 bmpa256 bmpa32b bmpamono bmpasep1 bmpasep8 bmpgray bmpmono bmpsep1
 bmpsep8 ccr cdeskjet cdj1600 cdj500 cdj550 cdj670 cdj850 cdj880 cdj890
 cdjcolor cdjmono cfax cgm24 cgm8 cgmmono cljet5 cljet5c cljet5pr coslw2p
 coslwxl cp50 cups declj250 deskjet dfaxhigh dfaxlow dj505j djet500
 djet500c dl2100 dmprt dnj650c epl2050 epl2050p epl5800 eps9high eps9mid
 epson epsonc epswrite escp escpage faxg3 faxg32d faxg4 fmlbp fmpr fs600
 gdi hl1250 hl7x0 ibmpro ijs imagen inferno iwhi iwlo iwlq jetp3852 jj100
 jpeg jpeggray la50 la70 la75 la75plus laserjet lbp310 lbp320 lbp8 lex2050
 lex3200 lex5700 lex7000 lips2p lips4 lips4v lj250 lj3100sw lj4dith
 lj4dithp lj5gray lj5mono ljet2p ljet3 ljet3d ljet4 ljet4d ljet4pjl
 ljetplus ln03 lp2000 lp2563 lp8000 lq850 lx5000 lxm3200 lxm5700m m8510
 mag16 mag256 md1xMono md2k md50Eco md50Mono md5k mgr4 mgr8 mgrgray2
 mgrgray4 mgrgray8 mgrmono miff24 mj500c mj6000c mj700v2c mj8000c ml600
```

```
necp6 npdl nullpage oce9050 oki182 okiibm omni paintjet pbm pbmraw pcl3
pcx16 pcx24b pcx256 pcxcmyk pcxgray pcxmono pdfwrite pgm pgmraw pgnm
pgnmraw photoex picty180 pj pjetxl pjxl pjxl300 pkm pkmraw pksm pksmraw
plan9bm png16 png16m png256 pngalpha pnggray pngmono pnm pnmraw ppm
ppmraw pr1000 pr1000_4 pr150 pr201 psgray psmono psrgb pswrite pxlcolor
pxlmono r4081 sgirgb sj48 st800 stcolor stp sunhmono t4693d2 t4693d4
t4693d8 tek4696 tiff12nc tiff24nc tiffcrle tiffg3 tiffg32d tiffg4 tifflzw
tiffpack uniprint x11 x11alpha x11cmyk x11cmyk2 x11cmyk4 x11cmyk8
x11gray2 x11gray4 x11mono x11rg16x x11rg32x xes
```

As you can see, GhostScript supports quite a few print drivers, and you can download a
number more if they are required by your local printers.

Getting the Right Printer

Almost every modern printer is supported under CUPS, using one of the print drivers in the
foomatic database. To get a printer that will work for you under your particular Linux
installation, check the distribution's website to find a list of supported hardware. While most
printers from major manufacturers work under most Linux distributions, there are notable
exceptions. For example, the widely available Hewlett-Packard entry-level color laser jet
printer 1500L does not run under CUPS, since it uses a proprietary Page Description Language,
or PDL.

If you can find no information about your printer and the Linux distribution you run, check for
a generic driver based on the type of PDL that your printer supports. Here, the information on
www.linuxprinting.org may be of great help. Generic drivers may not permit you to use or
configure some features specific to your printer, but that is still better than not being able to
print at all.

Note
In general you can't go wrong with a PostScript printer. However, there are generic types
of drivers available, which work with many different PCL printers as well.

Understanding Page Description Languages

In the earliest days of printers, each printer had its own individual driver, and each application
that sent print jobs had its own way of sending that data. Understandably, this was a complex
and annoying situation for administrators. To solve this problem, programmers developed
Page Description Languages, or PDLs. These languages let printers and applications share a
common method of exchanging information, and removed a great deal of the mystery in print
management.

Two page description languages dominate the market:

✦ *PostScript*—Created by Adobe. This was the most common PDL used on UNIX (and now
   Linux) systems. This may have been true because UNIX tended to run on high-end
   workstations in environments that supported the more expensive printers.

✦ *Print Control Language* (*PCL*)—Created by Hewlett-Packard. Popular versions of PCL are
   PCL 3, 4, 5, 5c, 5e, and 6.

In cases where there are no specific drivers for your printer, you can select from the list of generic printer drivers available with CUPS in Fedora Core. As long as you know the PDL that your printer uses, you will be able to select an appropriate generic driver. These drivers include the following:

✦ *Postscript*—The generic Postscript driver that is used with CUPS should work with all PostScript printers, although this driver does not enable features particular to an individual PostScript printer.

✦ *PCL*—There are a variety of drivers recommended for different PCL versions:

  • PCL 3 Printer: `pcl3` (recommended), also `hpdj`

  • PCL 4 Printer: `laserjet` (recommended), also `gimp-print`, `gimp-print-ijs`, `ljet2p`, and `ljetplus` **drivers**

  • PCL 5 Printer: `ljet3` (recommended), also `ljet3d`

  • PCL 5c Printer: `hpijs` (recommended), also `cljet5`, `gimp-print`, `gimp-print-ijs`, `ljet4`, `ljet4d`

  • PCL 5e Printer: `hpijs` (recommended), also `gimp-print`, `gimp-print-ijs`, `hpijs-rss`, `ljet4`, `ljet4d`

  • PCL 6/PCL XL Printer: `pxlmono` (recommended), also `gimp-print`, `gimp-print-ijs`, `hpijs`, `hpijs-rss`, `lj5gray`, `ljet4`, `ljet4d`

Though it is convenient to use generic drivers, it is not always the best idea. When possible, you should use a driver that is specific to your particular printer model. You will have access to the particular features of the printer that way.

Finding Details on Print Drivers

If you want to know more about a particular driver or printer, there are a few ways to access additional information:

✦ Check the Printer Configuration window (Figure 14-1). Double-click an existing printer, select the Printer Driver tab, and select Printer/Driver Notes to read more about the printer (Figure 14-2).

✦ If you want to know more about the current driver options set for your printer, select the Driver Options tab from the Edit a Print Queue window (Figure 14-3).

✦ Search the LinuxPrinting.org database at `www.linuxprinting.org/printer_list.cgi`. Select a printer by manufacturer or manufacturer/model. You'll find interesting notes including a recommended driver and links to further information.

Where to Get Help Choosing a Printer

If you haven't bought a printer for your Linux machine yet, you will save a lot of time and headache by doing a bit of homework ahead of time. Consult the Suggested Printers for Free Software Users page at `www.linuxprinting.org/suggested.html`. Even though most printers are compatible with Linux, it often seems like the one that's on sale at the local big-box office store is never compatible. A quick check before you run out the door may keep you from standing in the return line a few hours later.

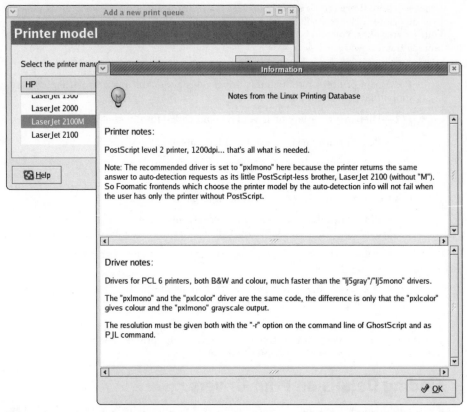

Figure 14-2: Learn about the printers on your system on the Printer/Driver Notes screen.

Setting Up a Printer under Fedora Core

In this section, we walk you through printer setup under Fedora Core. You can connect a printer directly to the Fedora Core machine through a parallel, serial, or USB port. You could also connect a printer across a network over another type of print spooler or through another operating system, such as HPJetDirect, UNIX using Line Printer Daemon (LPD), NetWare using NCP, CUPS using IPP, or Windows using SMB. If you're installing a local printer, you might choose to share it with other users across the network.

Setting Up a Printer during Installation

If you have a local printer that connects to your machine through the parallel, serial, or USB port and you have not yet installed Fedora Core Linux, make sure that the printer is connected when you begin installation. The kudzu utility may identify and configure your printer automatically if it is plugged in during the installation process.

Tip   This works best with relatively new and widely available printers. During one Fedora Core installation during the writing of this book, we connected an old DeskJet 722C printer to the parallel port. It was properly detected and configured during Fedora installation.

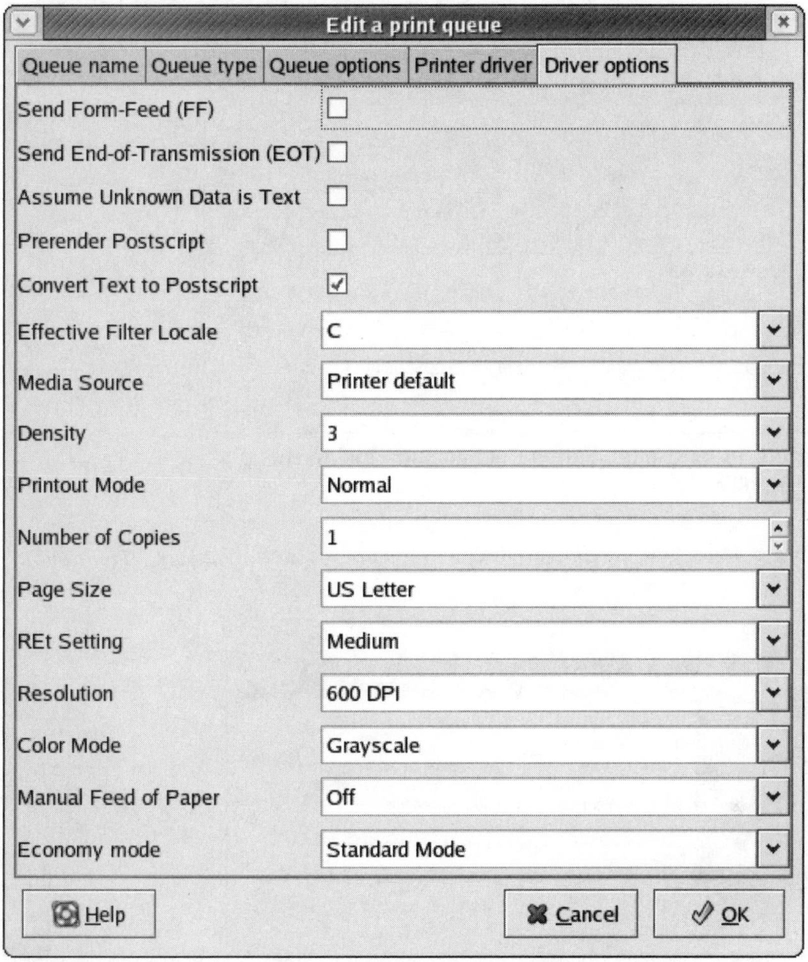

Figure 14-3: View current driver options from the Driver Options tab.

Even if kudzu identifies and configures your printer during installation, you should check the Printer Configuration tool once the system restarts. Use Printer Configuration to make sure that the printer was installed properly. If there are special functions available for your printer, you can configure them at this point.

Using Red Hat's Printer Configuration Tool

If you have already installed Fedora Core or Red Hat Linux on your machine and now want to add a printer to the system, the process is slightly more involved. One of the easiest ways to install a printer on a Red-Hat-based system is to use the Printer Configuration tool. Follow these steps:

1. From the Red Hat menu, select System Settings ➪ Printing or issue the command `redhat-config-printer`. Supply the root password when prompted.

2. The main Printer Configuration window appears (Figure 14-4).

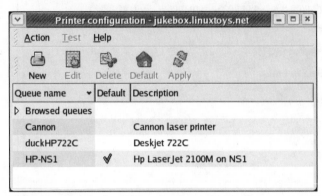

Figure 14-4: Use the Printer Configuration tool to set up a new printer.

3. Click the New button. The Add A New Print Queue window appears (Figure 14-5).

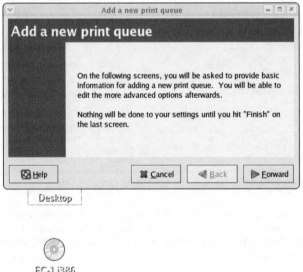

Figure 14-5: Begin the printer configuration wizard in the Add A New Print Queue window.

4. Click the Forward button. The Queue Type window appears. In this window, enter a name and description for the printer. The name is required; the description is optional, but quite helpful if you have multiple printers on this network.

5. Click Forward. In the next window, you must enter a queue type (Figure 14-6). Choose from several different types of queues describing local and several types of network connections. In this example, we chose a Networked CUPS queue. When you have made your selection, the screen changes so that you can enter the name or IP address of the print server, and the path to the queue (Figure 14-7).

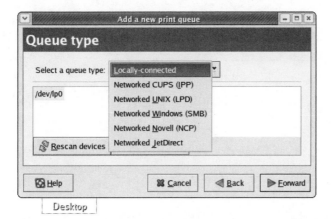

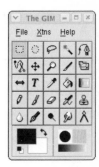

FC-1 i386

Figure 14-6: Select the appropriate queue type for this printer.

6. Click Forward. A new Printer Configuration window appears, the Printer Model screen. Here, you can select the make and model of your printer. Use the drop-down box to select the make, and that manufacturer's models will appear in the following frame (Figure 14-8). Select the appropriate model.

7. Click Forward. The final screen appears, containing the information you entered previously. If anything here is not correct, use the Back button to step back through the sequence and change the information. If the information is correct, click Finish.

Note

You will be prompted to print a test page. This is usually a good idea, but if you don't want to at this point, you can always print one later using the main window's Test menu.

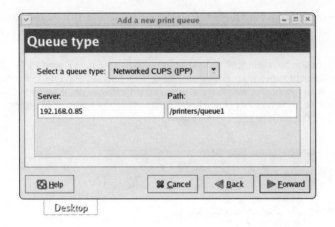

Figure 14-7: Once you've selected a queue type, provide specific information about your print server.

8. At this point, the printer should appear in the listing in the main Printer Configuration window (Figure 14-9). Assuming the test page printed successfully, the printer is configured and ready for use.

Adding a Printer Using the CUPS Web Configuration Tool

If you prefer to use a web tool, you can configure a printer with the CUPS web configuration tool. This is particularly useful if you are at a remote machine on the network. The CUPS daemon runs a small web server that listens on port 631, so be sure that you have configured that port appropriately if you want to use this service. If you have blocked this port while configuring a firewall with iptables, you will need to unblock it before using this tool.

To use the CUPS tool, follow these steps:

1. Open a web browser, and type `http://localhost:631` into the location bar. If you are working remotely, replace `localhost` with the correct IP address. The CUPS configuration main page loads (Figure 14-10).

2. Click Do Administration Tasks. The Administration page loads.

3. Click Add Printer. The Add New Printer page loads (Figure 14-11). On this page, add the name, location (IP or DNS name), and an optional description of the printer.

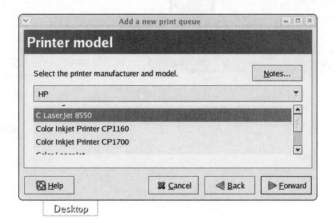

FC-1 i386

Figure 14-8: Identify your particular printer in the drop-down menu.

4. Click Continue. The Device page loads. On this page, use the drop-down box to choose the type of device that the printer is attached to. In this case, we selected Internet Printing Protocol (ipp) (Figure 14-12).

5. Click Continue. On the next page, you must add the URI for the printer. Several examples are shown. Enter the URI that describes the location and queue, as shown in Figure 14-13.

6. Click Continue. On the next page, select the make of your printer.

7. Click Continue. On the next page, select the model of your printer and the appropriate driver.

8. Click Continue. You should see a message that the printer has been added successfully.

9. Click Printers in the navigation bar. In the list that appears, you should see the new printer listed (Figure 14-14). You can now print a test page, using the button under the printer's icon. If the test page prints successfully, the printer is ready to go.

In general, Red Hat recommends using the Printer Configuration tool. However, the CUPS interface is good for configuring additional printer connections using Internet Printing Protocol (http and ipp) and for managing printer classes.

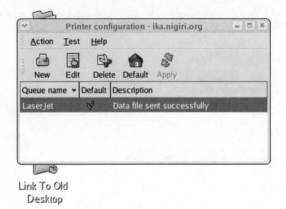

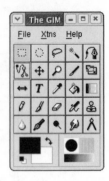

Figure 14-9: Once the printer appears in the main Printer Configuration window, it is ready to go.

There are a few things to keep in mind while using the CUPS web-based printer interface:

✦ You need the root password to do CUPS administration.

✦ To allow remote administrative access, you must change these lines in the /etc/cups/ cupsd.conf file:

```
<Location /admin>
AuthType Basic
AuthClass System
Order Deny,Allow
Deny From All
Allow From 127.0.0.1
</Location>
```

✦ You can add more Allow From lines to let other hosts (names or IP addresses) have access to CUPS administration on your server.

Note   In general, it's best to choose one printing administration interface and stick with it. Sometime hand-editing configuration files or using an alternate graphical user interface (GUI) tool can make the new entries unreadable by other GUI tools.

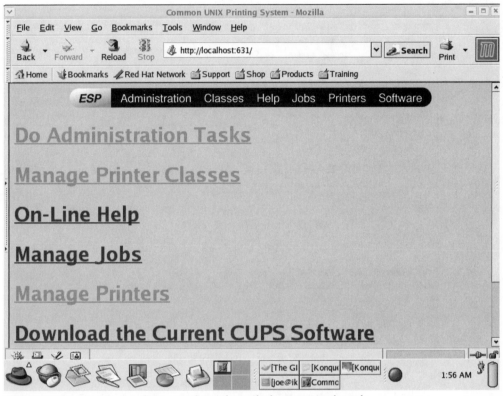

Figure 14-10: You can configure a printer through the CUPS web tool.

Sharing a Printer under Fedora Core

When you set up a printer using the Printer Configuration window, by default only people with accounts on the local computer can print to it. To share the printer with other users and computer on your network from CUPS, you must identify which computers, interfaces, or networks you will allow to print on your printer. Here's how:

1. In the Printer Configuration window, click on the printer you want to share.

2. Select Action ➪ Sharing. The Sharing properties window appears.

3. On the Queue tab, click This Queue Is Available to Other Computers. This allows access to the printer by all hosts that try to print to it (hence, the All Hosts entry that appears in the Allowed Hosts box).

4. Select All Hosts and click Edit. The Edit Allowed Hosts window that appears lets you leave All Hosts selected, or choose to limit the hosts that can have access to the printer.

5. Click Save.

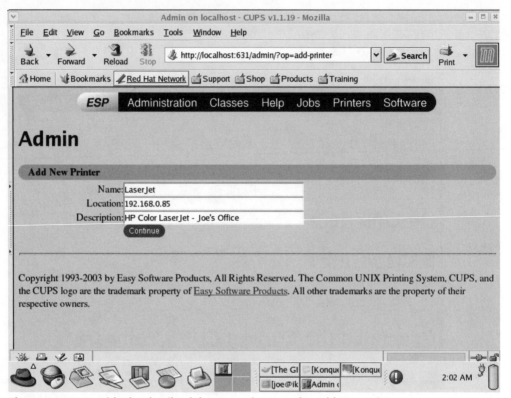

Figure 14-11: Provide the details of the new printer on the Add New Printer page.

You can limit the hosts that are allowed to access your shared printer in the following ways:

✦ Network devices—Select this, then choose the network devices on your computer that outside users can use to gain access to your shared printer. The interface could be an Ethernet interface (eth0), dial-up (ppp0), or other network interface.

✦ Network address—Identify network addresses by entering an IP address, followed by a CIDR network identifier or a netmask.

✦ Single IP address—Enter a single IP address.

After you have identified how the printer is being shared, information about who can share the printer (along with other information about printer options) is added to the /etc/cups/ cupsd.conf file. The cupsd daemon reads this information to decide whether or not to allow access to the printer when requests come to it. The following code shows the printer access lines for a printer named HP-NS1:

```
<Location /printers/HP-NS1>
Order Deny,Allow
AuthType None
Allow from All
</Location>
```

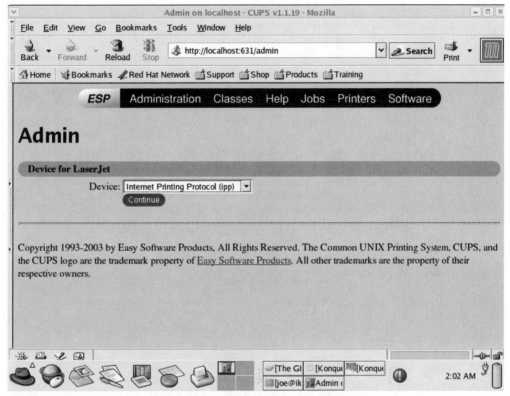

Figure 14-12: Choose the appropriate protocol used by your printer.

If there were no remote access available to the printer, the last `Allow from All` line would be removed.

Here are some other examples of access lines. The following example allows access from any requests that come in through the eth0 interface:

```
Allow from @IF(eth0)
```

The next line allows access to address 10 on network number 10.0.0. using the 255.255.255.0 netmask:

```
Allow from 10.0.0.10/255.255.255.255
```

Instead of entering 255.255.255.0, you could have entered the CIDR notation of 32 (which would immediately be translated into 255.255.255.0).

Going Beyond Setup

The printer may be working fine and dandy right now. If that's the case, go grab a cup of coffee and move on to another chapter. If you're having a problem, it's probably one of two things:

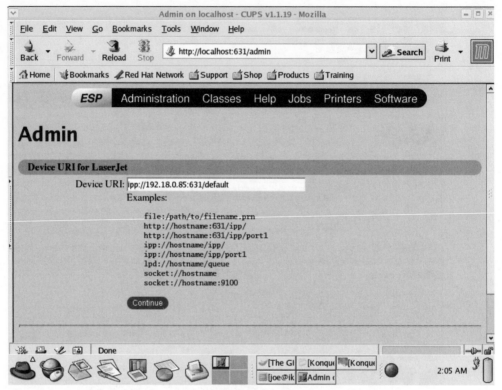

Figure 14-13: Define the printer with a URI that describes its specifications.

✦ *The printer is not responding*—The printer isn't working at all, or it can't be accessed by remote users.

✦ *The printer needs tuning*—The printer needs some tuning to work with different paper sizes, banners, margins, resolutions, or other features.

Troubleshooting the Basic Printer Setup

Whether you are configuring a local printer or a network printer, the first thing you want to do is make sure that the printer is connected properly and working on its local system. Assuming the printer you are configuring is physically connected to your Fedora Core computer, go through these steps to check your setup:

1. Is the hardware connected? Do you have the proper power supply and cables for the printer? Are the printer cartridges properly installed and of the right type?

2. Did you configure the printer as described in the previous section? Preferably, you had the printer plugged in during Fedora installation. Check the Printer Configuration tool to see if the printer is visible. (If the printer is not visible, return to *Using Red Hat's Printer Configuration Tool* section earlier in this chapter and set up the printer manually.)

3. From the Printer Configuration tool, click Test and print a test page. Select the appropriate page for the problem you are experiencing:

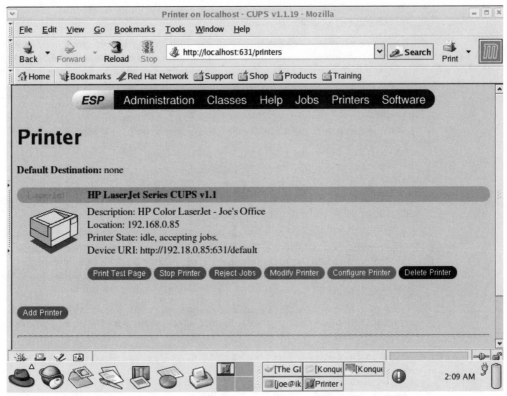

Figure 14-14: If the printer appears in the list, it has been configured properly.

- *General printing*—Select CUPS Test Page to see color wheel, 1 degree radial lines, and information about imageable area (page size and so on) and interpreter (PostScript, PCL).

- *Images*—Select JPEG test. This option prints a set of JPEG test images, grayscale, and primary color boxes.

- *Postscript*—Select US Letter PostScript test page. This lets you see if margins are lining up correctly and shows different colors (for color printers).

- *Plain text*—Select ASCII text test page.

Note

If the test page doesn't print correctly, click No. Printer error log information is then displayed. This information is stored in the file /var/log/cups/error_log.

Troubleshooting Remote Printer Access

If you have configured your printer to print from a remote client and nothing shows up, there are several ways to track down the problem:

✦ *Print locally*—Before you try debugging your remote printing connection, make sure that you can print a document from the local host.

✦ *Check printer name*—Check that the name of your printer was properly configured on the client computer. You may need to enter a fully qualified domain name of the printer, if that is required in your case. Here is an example of a full CUPS IPP name for a printer:

```
ipp://jukebox.linuxtoys.net:631/printers/HP-722C
```

If you check this printer in the Printer Configuration tool on another Fedora Core or Red Hat Linux computer, the information on the Queue Type page would be the following:

```
Queue type: Networked CUPS (IPP)
Server:     jukebox.linuxtoys.net:631
Path:       /printers/HP-722C
```

✦ *Check allowed hosts*—Make sure that you have allowed access to this printer for either all hosts or selected host computers.

✦ *Check browsing settings*—The cupsd daemon has the ability to broadcast the availability of the printers you configure on the network. This feature allows other computers to "browse" for available printers on the network, making it easier to configure connections to them. When you share a printer, using the interface pointed to in the previous step, browsing is turned on and broadcast to the selected hosts.

Here's an example of the Browsing lines in the /etc/cups/cupsd.conf file for a CUPS server that is sharing all its printers to computers on network 10.0.0. and broadcasting that fact to them:

```
Browsing On
BrowseProtocols cups
BrowseOrder Deny,Allow
BrowseAllow from @LOCAL
BrowseAddress 10.0.0.255
```

Here you can see that the Browsing feature is turned on, and that CUPS-style browsing is being used. BrowseOrder says to deny access to the service unless it is explicitly allowed. With BrowseAllow from @LOCAL set, Browsing is allowed on all your Ethernet (eth0, eth1, and so on) and other non-point-to-point interfaces and printer availability is broadcast on these network interfaces.

Note   The Browsing setting can be turned on and off through the Printer configuration window by selecting the printer you want to share and clicking on the Action ⇨ Sharing menu item. Click This Queue Is Available to Other Computers to turn on the service and then choose which hosts to allow (or just leave all hosts on).

✦ *Check your firewall*—If your Fedora Core system has a firewall installed, before anyone can print on your printer from outside the local host, you need to open port 631.

✦ *Check CUPS daemon*—Make sure that your printer service is running. You can simply type ps ax | grep cupsd to see if a cupsd daemon is running, or you can restart the service by typing service cups restart.

✦ *Run network traffic analyzer*—The Ethereal window can watch and capture live data from your LAN. To open Ethereal, select Internet ⇨ More Internet Applications ⇨

Ethereal from the Red Hat menu. Because IPP broadcasts the availability of its printers on the network, you can use Ethereal to see which printers are available.

In the Ethereal window, click Capture ⇨ Start. Select the interface to watch (such as eth0) and click OK. A pop-up window shows captured frames from the network. Click Stop after you have had a sampling. Packet data appears in the main Ethereal window.

Click on the Protocol column to sort packets by protocol. Look for packets with the CUPS protocol (scroll down if necessary). Here is an example showing several packet headers displaying the availability of printers:

```
1 0.000000 10.0.0.100 CUPS ipp:/a.linuxtoys.net:631/printers/HP1
(idle)
2 1.000513 10.0.0.198 CUPS ipp:/jb.linuxtoys.net:631/printers/JB1
(idle)
```

Here you can see that two printers have broadcast their availability on the LAN.

Tuning Up Your Printer

It is possible that you may be able to print, but are still unhappy with some of the settings on your printer. The color may not be quite right or the margins might be too large or too small, or there may be extra features specific to your printer that you want to access. To help you understand your printer better, we will walk you through the process of reviewing printer settings for Linux. We used two models as examples: a basic PostScript printer (HP LaserJet 2100M) and a low-end locally connected printer (HP DeskJet 722C).

1. *Check the notes*—If you added the printer using the Printer Configuration window, you can see the information about the selected driver from that window. From the Printer Configuration window:

   A. Double-click on the printer name. The Edit a Print Queue window appears.

   B. Select the Printer Driver tab.

   C. Click Printer Driver Notes to see information about the selected driver.

      • For the 2100M, the `pxlmono` driver was selected. The text says that the driver is faster than the `lj5gray` or `lj5mono` drivers. If we care to, we can try out these drivers.

      • For the 722C, the `pnm2ppa` driver was selected. These notes tell us that the printer supported by this driver is a *host-based* printer. This means that a special driver was needed, since much of the processing typically done in the printer is being done in the operating system. Because this is a special type of driver, no other options are listed for this printer.

2. *Check driver options*—Click the Driver Options tab. While the standard Postscript driver has only five or six settings, by selecting specific drivers for our 2100M and 722C printers, we have many more options to choose from.

      • The 722C has special settings, such as options for Color mode (color cartridges for photos, both cartridges for text with images, or grayscale with black cartridge only), bidirectional printing, and GhostScript Rendering Format.

- By selecting 2100M instead of the standard Postscript driver, we can select special options supported by this printer, including printout mode (normal, draft, or high quality), page size (US Letter, US Legal, A3, A4, and others), resolution (from 300 to 1200 dpi), and manual feed (on or off).

3. *Check printing database*—Go to www.linuxprinting.org/printer_list.cgi and search for your printer or driver. From this page, you can read a description of the printer's driver and go to links that provide further information. One nice feature is that you can view the PPD file. Because that file is in plain text, you can read the settings being used to define the printer options. For our two example printers, the PPD files tell us several things:

   - With the LaserJet 2100M, besides the px1mono driver that is recommended, the page lists several other drivers we could use with this printer. It also gives a link to download different PPD files to try with the printer.

   - For the Deskjet 722C, this page provides a link to the driver's project and home pages: http://sourceforge.net/projects/pnm2ppa and http://pnm2ppa.sourceforge.net. This site has some great guides for using the pnm2ppa drivers.

You can change any of the options in the Edit a Print Queue window. These options are then stored in the /etc/cups/lpoptions file. You can view the options set in this file for each of your printers. Change these options with the lpoptions command. However, keep in mind that any changes you make by editing the lpoptions file or running the lpoptions command will be overwritten if you make changes to the printer information again through the Printer Configuration tool.

Here's an example of how to change printer options with the lpoptions command:

```
# lpoptions -p printer1 -o page-bottom=80
```

This command sets the page-bottom option to 80 points for the printer named printer1.

If you'd like to change other features for your printer, you can do so in the Printer Configuration tool. From the Printer Configuration window, click on the printer and select Edit. There are several options you might want to explore:

✦ *Add banners*—You can add banners at the beginning or end of a print job. Click the Queue Options tab and choose one of six predefined banner pages. A standard banner tells you the JobID, filename title, and username.

✦ *Adjust margins*—Change top, bottom, left, or right margins. Click the Queue Options tab. Change any margin from the default point size (usually 36 points, which equals 1/2 inch).

✦ *Choose a different printer driver*—Some printers have multiple drivers available. To see if yours does, click the Printer Driver tab. Click the down arrow in the Available Drivers box to see if multiple drivers are available.

Note Click the Printer Driver tab and select Printer/Driver Notes. The page that appears contains notes from the Linux Printing Database.

✦ *Enable special features*—By selecting the Driver Options tab, you can enable features that are specific to the printer driver you are using. For example, with the standard

Postscript printer driver, you can set nonstandard page sizes, do double-sided printing, or change to a higher print resolution, if these features are supported.

Top Troubleshooting Tips

Though they are often easy to resolve, printer problems cause a lot of headaches. People generally need their print jobs NOW, and frustration can be high if the system isn't working properly. In this section, we share some of the most common printing problems and solutions.

Printing Clients Expect LPD and not CUPS

If you have a legacy print client that cannot use IPP, but needs LPD to print documents or get printer status, you can start the `cups-lpd` service. To turn on `cups-lpd`, type the following from the command line as root:

```
# chkconfig cups-lpd on
```

Printer Breaks Down with Jobs in the Queue

If your printer stops working but it still has print jobs, you can move these jobs to another printer. To move a particular print job to a new printer, use the `lpmove` command. Here's an example:

```
# lpmove 703 printer1
```

This moves the print job number 703 to the `printer1` print queue. If `printer1` is ready to print, the print job will immediately begin printing on it. Repeat this for each print job you want to move.

One Guy is Hogging the Printer

You can limit the amount of printing that one person can do for a set period of time, so that no one person can dominate the printer. Here is an example of how to set job limits:

```
# lpadmin -p p1 -o job-quota-period=86400 -o job-page-limit=50
```

Here the job-quota-period is set to 86,400 seconds (or 1 day) and the number of pages a person is allowed to print on that day is 50. You can also limit the number of kilobytes of data that can be printed in the selected time period using the `job-k-limit` option.

Nobody Can Print Outside the Local LAN

Polling doesn't work well across multiple subnetworks. You can explicitly configure CUPS to relay the broadcast of printer information outside the local LAN using the `BrowseRelay` directive. With your users on subnet1 and print server on subnet2, here is how you could configure a computer with interfaces on both subnetworks to relay to share broadcast printer information between the two subnets. Assuming that the computer wants to relay broadcast data from the CUPS printers from subnet 10.0.1 to 10.0.2, you could add the following lines to the `/etc/cups/cupsd.conf` on the computer on subnet1:

```
BrowseRelay 10.0.1 10.0.2.255
```

No-GUI Printer Administration

You don't need a GUI to administer CUPS printing in Fedora Core. In fact, some administrators don't even put GUIs on their servers. Even though many consider graphical administration interfaces to be more intuitive, some hard-core administrators will tell you that GUIs are for wimps. This section describes tools you can use to configure, tune, and troubleshoot printers from the command line.

Note   If you make changes to printer configuration files directly from the command line, you risk having these values overwritten the next time you use a GUI tool to edit that file. In general, you should use one interface and stick with it if possible.

Table 14-1 shows a list of commands and configuration files that you can use to administer printing from a command-line shell.

Table 14-1: Linux Printer Commands and Files

User Printing Commands

lpr	Command to send print jobs (documents) to a printer:
	lpr file—Sends to the default printer
	lpr -P printer1 file—Sends file to printer1
	man cupsd | lpr—Pipes cupsd man page to printer
lpoptions	As a regular user, list or change options that apply to your print jobs for selected printer. Options are stored in your $HOME/.lpoptions file:
	lpoptions -p printer1—Shows options for named printer
	lpoptions -o cpi=12 -p printer1—Changes cpi (characters per inch) value to 12 on printer1
lpq	List documents that are in the queue to be printed:
	lpq -P printer1—Shows if printer 1 is ready to print and has print jobs waiting
	lpq a—Shows queued jobs on all printers
lprm	Remove any of your own print jobs from the queue:
	lprm—Cancels the current print job on default printer
	lprm—-P printer1—Cancels all print jobs for user on printer1
	lprm 74 -P printer1—Cancels print job #74 on printer1 (Use lpq to see print job numbers)
lpstat	Show status of printers. You can add a printer name after each of the following examples to list just for that printer:
	lpstat -a—Lists available printers and tells how long they have been accepting requests
	lpstat -d—Shows default printer destination

`lpstat -o`—Shows all jobs queued to be printed

`lpstat -p`—Shows whether or not printers are enabled

`lpstat -s`—Shows summary of all printer status

Administrative Printing Commands

`cupsconfig`	Open CUPS graphical administrative interface (equivalent to typing `http://localhost:631` in a web browser window)
`cupstestppd`	Test a ppd file before you install it: `cupstestppd` *filename.ppd*
`disable`	Temporarily disable a printer. Jobs can still be queued, but will not be sent to the printer until re-enabled: `disable` *printer1*
`/usr/bin/enable`	Re-enable a printer that is disabled (use full path, so as not to conflict with enable shell built-in): `/usr/bin/enable` *printer1*
`lpoptions`	Change options for a selected printer and set them as system defaults. Options are stored in the `/etc/cups/lpoptions` file
`reject`	Reject attempt to send documents to a printer queue (use `lpstat -a` to check this status):
	`reject printer1`—Rejects jobs sent to printer1
`accept`	Begin again to accept jobs to selected printer (use `lpstat -a` to check this status):
	`accept printer1`—Accepts jobs sent to printer1
`cupsaddsmb`	Configure a printer client for Samba. See Chapter 15 for details about this command and general Samba printer sharing.
`lpadmin`	Configure print queues
`lpinfo`	List CUPS devices and drivers:
	`lpinfo -v`—Lists devices to which printers can be connected (serial, parallel, usb, and so on)
	`lpinfo -m`—Lists all printer drivers available

Printer Configuration and Log Files

`/var/log/cups/error_log`	See the activities of the `cupsd` daemon. Good place to look to see what values are being sent to the `cupsd` daemon if you are debugging printing problems
`/var/log/messages`	General Linux message file. Contains information about starting and stopping the CUPS service
`/var/log/cups/access_log`	Lets you view messages describing when print jobs were sent and who sent them

Note In Table 14-1, I assume that you are running administrative commands as the root user. In a few cases, commands are duplicated in user and administrative sections. In these cases, running the command as root will impact the whole system (that is, it will change options for all users). These same commands run by regular users will effect only that user's printing options and jobs.

Adding a Printer with lpadmin

If you plan to skip the GUI interfaces, you need to use the `lpadmin` command to add a printer. Here's an example:

```
# lpadmin -p printer1 -v parallel:/dev/lp0 -m deskjet.ppd
```

In this example, we added a printer named `printer1` that is connected to the first parallel port on the computer (`/dev/lp0`). The PPD file used for this printer is `deskjet.ppd`. You can find PPD files in the `/usr/share/cups/model/` directory.

To delete the printer at a later time, use the `-x` option:

```
# lpadmin -x printer1

Adding a printer class with lpadmin
```

To keep one printer from getting too backed up, you can create printer classes. By adding several printers together in a class, print jobs can be distributed across a group of computers. Here is an example:

```
# lpadmin -p printer1 -c myclass
# lpadmin -p printer2 -c myclass
```

The first command creates the printer class named `myclass` and adds `printer1` to that class. The second command adds the printer named `printer2` to that class. To see all the members of that class, issue the command

```
# lpstat -s
system default destination: printer1
members of class myclass:

        printer1
        printer2
```

Then, to send a print job so that the job goes to one of the printers in the class, you could simply use the class name instead of the printer name, as in

```
# lpr -P myclass file1.ps
```

Printer Resources

There are a number of websites and documents included with your Fedora Core installation that can help you with printer problems. Table 14-2 provides a starting set of references for finding and troubleshooting printers to work in Linux.

Table 14-2: Linux Printer Reference Table

Printing General Information

Description	Location
Linux printing	www.linuxprinting.org—First place to go for information on printing in Linux. Includes searchable driver and printer databases, overviews of CUPS and foomatic, tutorials, and links to other resources.
CUPS documentation that comes with Fedora	http://localhost:631/documentation.html—For troubleshooting, the Administration Manual contains some good information.
CUPS home page	www.cups.org—Go to this site for CUPS documentation, newsgroup information, and news. Click the support link to find ways of getting more help.
Forums	www.linuxprinting.org/forums.cgi—There are more than 50 forums for discussing printer problems based on printer manufacturer. The most active linuxprinting forums include linuxprinting.general, macosx.general, foomatic.devel, canon.general, epson.general, hp.general, and lexmark.general.
The Printing HOWTO	www.tldp.org/HOWTO/Printing-HOWTO—Provides information on how to print in Linux and other UNIX-like systems.

Printing Driver Information (Generic)

Description	Location
Ghostscript	www.ghostscript.com—GhostScript covers a group of software that can interpret PostScript input and convert it to a variety of different formats. GhostScript is generally used as a front end for printers that don't support PostScript, and can be used to interpret PDF files as well. To get documentation, go to www.ghostscript.com/doc/index.htm or check the local Fedora Core file system (/usr/local/share/doc/ghostscript*).
OMNI printer drivers	http://sourceforge.net/projects/omniprint—The Omni drivers support over 400 printers in a pluggable form.
Gimp-Print Printer Drivers	http://gimp-print.sourceforge.net—Describes gimp-print drivers that support many Epson Stylus, HP DeskJet and LaserJet printers, Cannon BJC printers, and Lexmark printers.
Postscript (use with Postscript printers when no specific driver is available)	www.linuxprinting.org/show_driver.cgi?driver=Postscript.
Raw	No driver is used. Printing output is passed directly to the printer.

Printer Driver Information (Examples of Information for a Few Specific Drivers)

Description	Location
Open source sites for HP Printer Drivers	http://http://hpinkjet.sf.net—Resource for all open source HP inkjet drivers.

Continued

Table 14-2: *(continued)*

Printing General Information (Examples of Information for a Few Specific Drivers)

Description	Location
`pxlmono`: **Driver for color and black and white PCL 6 printers. Over 100 printers are supported with this driver, including the HP LaserJet 2100M used in examples in this chapter.**	`www.linuxprinting.org/show_driver.cgi?driver=pxlmono`—**Describes** `pxlmono` **driver.**
`pnm2ppa`: **Driver for HP DeskJet 710C, 712C, 720C, 722C, 820Cse, 820Cxi, 1000Cse, or 1000Cxi printers (PostScript Level 2)**	`http://sourceforge.net/projects/pnm2ppa`—**Find tools and documentation related to this filter.** `/usr/share/doc/pnm2ppa*`—**Try COLOR.html, CALIBRATION.html, and INSTALL.REDHAT.html.** **Commands:** `calibrate_ppa`, `detect_ppa`, `pnm2ppa`, `pbm2ppa`, **and** `pbmtpg`. **This driver was used in the example troubleshooting shown in this chapter for the HP DeskJet 722C printer.**

Troubleshooting Printers

Description	Location
Information about how to go about troubleshooting CUPS	`www.cups.org/cups-help.html`—**Describes how to troubleshoot and get help from CUPS experts.**
CUPS printing newsgroups	`www.cups.org/newsgroups.php` From this page you can search news groups using keywords, or select from different CUPS newsgroups. For general questions, view the cups.general newgroup. Go here to subscribe to a newsgroup: lists.easysw.com/mailman/listinfo.

Summary

Whether you choose to enable printing through Red Hat/Fedora Core tools or through the distribution-independent CUPS, print services under Linux are easier to administer than ever before. As long as you purchase a printer that uses an available driver, you should be able to configure the printer to handle simple print jobs. With most modern printers, you should also be able to utilize additional features such as color selection, print direction, and paper size. Though printing is still regarded as somewhat of a headache among UNIX administrators, the various tools found under Linux will ease your printing-related workload.

✦   ✦   ✦

Samba Troubleshooting

I t is a rare network that consists of machines running a single operating system. Most administrators find themselves working in mixed, or heterogeneous, computing environments with networks that include Windows, Mac OS, Linux, and other UNIX-based operating systems. Although this might seem like a giant headache, recent years have brought methods that make heterogeneous network administration less problematic than in the past.

The Server Message Block protocol, or SMB, is now the most common way in which to share files and printers among computers on a secure network, regardless of their native operating systems. Under Linux, the SMB implementation of choice is called Samba. Samba is actually a set of applications and protocols that allows Linux machines to act as SMB clients or servers when interacting with Windows systems.

 Tip Because Mac OS X is also based on a system derived from UNIX, some of the same network services you use on Linux systems (such as Samba, NFS, and others) are also available on Mac OS X. So the skills you learn setting up a Samba server in Linux can be brought over to the Mac as well.

While Samba is very popular and most administrators are familiar with at least its basic features, it can be a challenge to get it working on any given network with its own peculiarities. In this chapter, we show you how to configure Samba on a Linux machine. Then we describe a number of common problems and offer simple ways to troubleshoot these situations.

Understanding Samba

Microsoft Windows uses the Server Message Block protocol to manage file and printer sharing across Windows-based networks. In order to integrate Windows machines into Linux or UNIX-based networks, the Linux machines must be able to communicate SMB to the Windows machines. Samba is the UNIX/Linux implementation of this protocol.

From the Windows user perspective, Samba is nearly transparent. When users click the Network Neighborhood or My Network Places icons on their desktop, they will see Samba shares represented just as they already see Windows machines on the network. This is an excellent way to keep important files on a central machine with tight security, while still allowing local users to access the data without having it stored on multiple insecure desktops.

Although there are other file and printer sharing facilities available in various Linux distributions, Samba is the most popular option. There are several reasons for its popularity:

✦ Windows is still the most popular desktop operating system in most businesses and organizations.

✦ In mixed computing environments, SMB is the most common protocol for sharing files and printers.

✦ Samba, as opposed to other Windows servers, lets you run SMB protocols on more powerful computers for file and printer sharing (Linux scales up from PCs to supercomputers).

✦ Samba allows your Linux machine to act as both an SMB server and a client, so that it can share its directories and printers with other Windows machines as well as pull those services from the Windows computers.

✦ Samba can help your organization transition from proprietary Windows systems to Linux or UNIX.

In many environments, IT departments are reasonably content with Windows on desktop workstations. While the IT techies themselves may prefer UNIX-based software such as Linux, most people understand that most popular business software are usually available only for Windows.

When it comes to the servers and workhorse machines, however, many IT departments are moving away from Windows-based server software for a variety of reasons. Whatever the criteria for that choice, Samba makes it easy to administer a mixed-OS environment. Files can be shared across the network between servers and workstations, with little concern for the operating system on either end of the connection.

Samba Users

Anyone using Samba services must have a Samba user account. Samba requires an associated user account for access to files, directories, or printers. When users attempt to access a Samba *share*, or shared resource, they must provide a username and password so that the server can authenticate user access.

A Samba administrator can open access to any user by assigning one of the following values to a particular share when configuring that share in the /etc/samba/smb.conf configuration file:

```
guest ok = yes
guest only = yes
```

The guest ok option allows you to assign varying permissions to the share, based on the user's profile. Individual known users may have different levels of access. The guest ok option defines a generic set of permissions based on those assigned to the guest user. If you choose the guest only option, only guest accounts are allowed to log into the share and there is only one set of associated permissions.

By default in Linux, the guest Samba user is assigned to the Linux user account called `nobody`. The default permissions given to `nobody` when a share is given guest access include:

✦ May print to local printers

✦ May access any files or directories with world readable and writable permissions

✦ May not log directly into the Linux machine

If you prefer to reserve the `nobody` account for other purposes, you can create another guest account for Samba. First, add a user with a generic name, such as sambaguest, with the `useradd` command. After you have added this user to the system and assigned the appropriate permissions, you can assign the Samba guest account to the new user:

```
guest account = sambaguest
```

Samba Shares

To fit seamlessly into the Windows environment, SMB shares are identified using the Universal Naming Convention (UNC). On a client Windows machine, that name will typically appear in the form

```
\\computer\share
```

where `computer` is the computer's NetBIOS name and `share` is the name of the shared resource.

Share names on the Linux machine must be constructed differently. Since backslashes are used as an escape character on the Linux command line, you cannot issue share names as shown above. Instead, you must issue the command with additional backslashes that escape the backslash character. For example, to use the `smbmount` command to mount a share identified as \\toys\Musicbox on the local /var/mytemp directory, you might issue the command

```
# smbmount "\\\\toys\\Musicbox" /var/mytemp
```

Some Linux software used to access SMB shares can use forward slashes instead of backslashes. For example, in Nautilus File Manager (which you can open by opening the Home icon on the desktop), you could access the \\ toys\Musicbox share by typing the following into the Location box:

```
smb://toys/Musicbox
```

Tip

On a Windows machine connected over a Samba network, frequently used shares can be mapped to letter drives.

Basic Samba Setup

Samba is included with the Server installation option under Fedora Core and Red Hat Linux. It is usually included with server installation packages under other Linux distributions. The Samba package includes both the Samba server and the `smbclient` client. Once you have determined that the Samba packages exist on your system and have been installed properly, there are several ways to configure Samba for your network.

Samba Configuration Tool

On a Red Hat Linux or Fedora Core system, click the Red Hat icon and select System Settings ⇨ Server Settings ⇨ Samba. The Samba configuration tool appears (Figure 15-1).

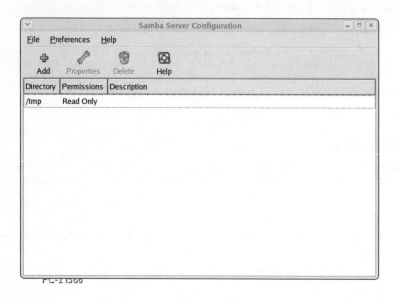

Figure 15-1: Use the Samba configuration tool for a quick start under Red Hat Linux or Fedora Core.

With this tool, you can define server settings including workgroups, descriptions, authentication modes, authentication servers, guest accounts, and whether or not to use encrypted passwords. You can also identify Samba users, and then identify which directories to share and who can share them.

This tool is easy to use and manages all the major components of a Samba configuration. However, you must be logged into the local machine in order to use it. If you need to manage Samba shares and configurations remotely, consider the SWAT Web tool described later in this chapter. You could also use X-based tools remotely if you have SSH configured to permit X forwarding.

Command-Line Configuration

As with most UNIX-based services, you can configure the Samba service by editing its configuration file, smb.conf. This file is usually kept in /etc/samba/smb.conf, though you may need to search for it if Samba installed it in a different directory on your system. Once the file is edited and saved, you can start the `smb` service.

The `smb.conf` file contains a number of sections:

✦ `[global]`—The section that contains global parameters.

✦ `[homes]`—The section used to share Linux user directories stored in `\home`.

✦ `[printers]`—The section used to share all printers in the local Linux printing file `/etc/printcap`.

Note that the `homes` and `printers` sections are actually share definitions, not unique section types.

`smb.conf` also contains a number of local sections. Each of these sections defines the parameters for a specific share—a given directory or printer that can be used across the network. Though you can name these share definitions anything you want, the `global`, `homes`, and `printers` sections must retain their original names.

Unlike a lot of service configuration files, `smb.conf` is easy to use. It is well-commented and the various options are named clearly. Here, we show a simple `smb.conf` example (with comments removed). This example describes a computer that is sharing its music directory and all its printers with anyone on its LAN.

```
[global]
workgroup = CSTREET
server string = Samba Server
log file = /var/log/samba/%m.log
max log size = 50
security = USER
load printers = Yes

[Musicbox]
    comment = My music collection
    path = /usr/local/share/music
    guest ok = Yes

[printers]
    comment = All Printers
    path = /var/spool/samba
    browseable = No
    guest ok = Yes
    printable = Yes
```

Note that in this file, the `[global]` section identifies the workgroup, sets a comment string identifying the server, sets the security level to SHARE, and loads all the printers named in `/etc/printcap`. The following sections share the `/usr/local/share/music` directory (for any user in read-only mode, such as a guest user) and define how all printers are shared on the Samba server.

Once you have saved the configuration file and exited the text editor, start (or restart) the Samba service with the following command:

```
# service smb start
Starting smb:                                      [ OK ]
```

> **Note** If smb fails to start, run the `testparm` command. It will tell you if anything is wrong with your `smb.conf` file.

At this point you can go to a Network Neighborhood or My Network Places window on a Windows client machine, and see the shared directory and shared printers available from the Samba server.

SWAT

The Samba Web Administration Tool, or SWAT, is available on most Linux systems that include the most recent Samba packages. One advantage of SWAT is that you can use it remotely to edit configurations or permissions (see the related sidebar, "Using SWAT Remotely"). To use this web-based Samba configuration tool, issue these commands as the root user:

```
# chkconfig swat on
# service xinetd restart
```

Then, from a web browser on the local system, type `http://localhost:901`. The SWAT tool appears in the browser, as in Figure 15-2.

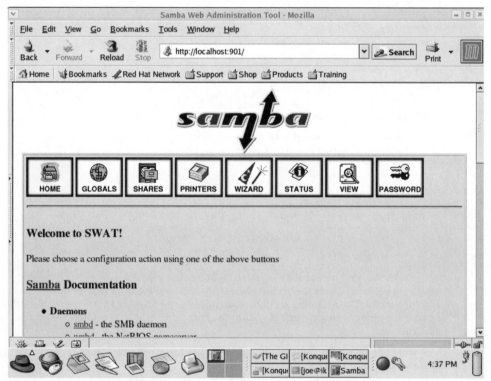

Figure 15-2: Use SWAT to work with Samba through your web browser.

You can view the current `smb.conf` file in SWAT by clicking the View button in the top button bar. As you work with SWAT, use the View button periodically to see how the options you select are reflected in the actual `smb.conf` file.

To add a new share through SWAT, follow these steps:

1. Click the Shares button. The Shares window appears (Figure 15-3).

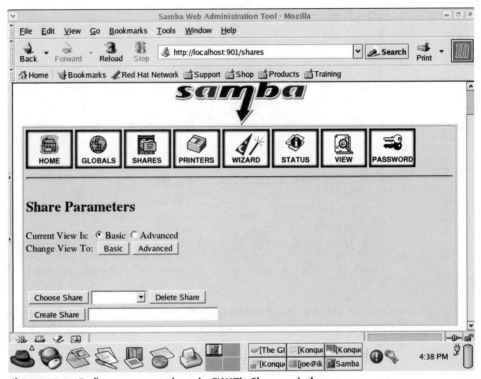

Figure 15-3: Define your new share in SWAT's Shares window.

2. In the Create Share box, enter the complete path name of the directory to be shared.

3. Click the Create Share button. The Share Parameters page appears (Figure 15-4).

4. Select the options you want to apply to the new share. These options affect the security and browsability settings of the share, and are described on the `smb.conf` manual page. You can also see a description of each parameter by clicking the Help link directly below its name.

5. Click the Commit Changes button to create the new share.

6. Verify the new share by clicking the View button and looking for the new section in `smb.conf`.

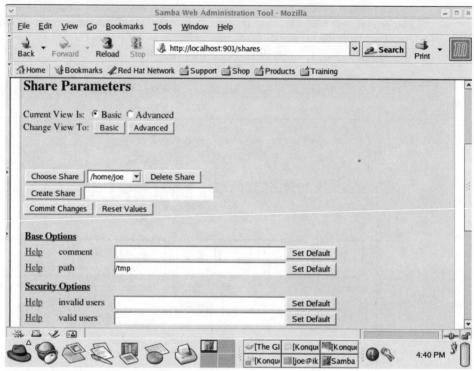

Figure 15-4: On the Share Parameters page, define the permissions for the new share.

Tip

You can add printers in the same way, using the Printers button on the main SWAT page.

You can also use SWAT to check the status of the three Samba server processes, smbd, nmbd, and winbindd. To do so, click the Status button. You can start, stop, or restart services from this tool as well. Note that winbindd is an optional daemon not required for basic sharing.

Using SWAT Remotely

By default, SWAT is configured to be available only on the `localhost` machine (127.0.0.1). If you want to use SWAT to administer a remote machine, you must edit the file `/etc/xinetd.d/swat`. The default `/etc/xinetd.d/swat` file looks like this:

```
# default: off
# description: SWAT is the Samba Web Admin Tool. Use swat \
#            to configure your Samba server. To use SWAT, \
```

```
#          connect to port 901 with your favorite web browser.
service swat
{
        disable = no
        port             = 901
        socket_type      = stream
        wait             = no
        only_from        = 127.0.0.1
        user             = root
        server           = /usr/sbin/swat
        log_on_failure   += USERID

}
```

In order to make SWAT available to a remote machine, you must edit the `only_from` line to include the IP address of the machine from which you plan to issue administrative commands. For example, if Samba is running on a machine with the IP address 192.168.0.55 and you want to administer it from a machine with the IP address 192.168.0.22, you would change the `only_from` line to read

```
only_from = 127.0.0.1 192.168.0.22
```

After you restart `xinetd`, the machine can be administered either locally or from 192.168.0.22 by typing `http://192.168.0.55:901` into a browser.

Be careful with this feature. Any time you open `xinet` services up to remote access, you lower the overall system security. However, it's useful to have remote access to Samba services, so this is a security decision that you'll need to make based on local guidelines and need.

Tip   If you just need a simple Samba configuration and you don't want to pore over `smb.conf` to figure out what you need, click the Wizard button in SWAT. You'll see the Wizard page (Figure 15-5), which will guide you through the process. Once you set parameters on this page and click the Commit button, `smb.conf` will be changed to reflect your selections.

Configuration Resources

If you need more help as you configure your Samba server, there are several ways to get additional information:

✦ *SWAT help*—As you go through the SWAT administration tool to configure globals, shares, and printers, a Help link next to each option will take you to a description of that option.

✦ *SWAT current configuration*—Click the View icon in SWAT to see the current version of the `smb.conf` file. Click the Full View button to see all the global defaults that are in place.

✦ `smb.conf` *man page*—Type `man smb.conf` to see details about each setting in the `smb.conf` file.

✦ `/etc/samba/smb.conf` *file*—The comments in the `smb.conf` file itself will help you fill out the entries correctly.

✦ `/usr/share/doc/samba-`*directory*—Contains a wealth of documentation about Samba.

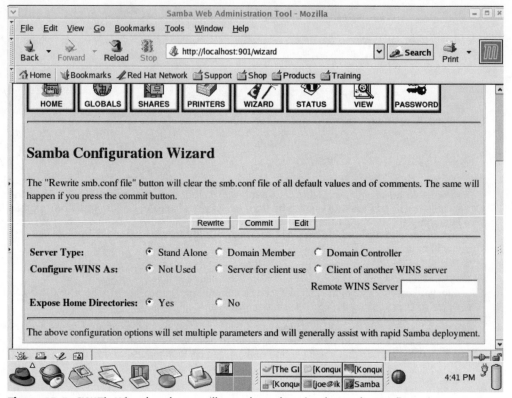

Figure 15-5: SWAT's Wizard tool can walk you through a simple Samba configuration.

Using Samba

Once Samba is configured and the service is running properly, there is very little you need to do to keep it going. However, Samba can provide you with a great deal of useful information about user behavior on your network. If you want to check out what's going on with Samba from your local system, there are a few different tools you can use. Some tools let you see how others are using the shared files and printers from your Linux system, while others let you view and access files and printers being shared by other computers.

See Who Is Connected

To see the users who are currently connected to the Samba server and what they are doing, issue the following command:

```
# smbstatus
Samba version 3.0.2-7.FC1
PID        Username   Group      Machine
-----------------------------------------------------------
Service        pid    machine    Connected at
```

```
----------------------------------------------------------
Musicbox      9399    maple      Thu Jan 29 00:30:21 2004
IPC$          9399    maple      Wed Jan 28 20:05:10 2004
```

Check an IP Address

If you can't remember the IP address of a computer attached to your network, but you do remember the machine name, use the Samba `net` command to get the IP number:

```
# net lookup host1
10.0.0.1
```

Check Available Shares

Use the `smbclient` command to see the status of shares from other computers on your network. `smbclient` will report all shared directories and printers, including those attached to Windows or Linux client machines. Here is a sample output from the `smbclient` command:

```
# smbclient -L fileserver

Sharename       Type      Comment
---------       ----      -------
homes           Disk
Musicbox        Disk      My music collection
IPC$            IPC       IPC Service (Toys samba server)
ADMIN$          IPC       IPC Service (Toys samba server)
lp0             Printer   Created by redhat-config-printer
chris           Disk      Home directory of chris


Server                    Comment
---------                 -------


Workgroup                 Master
---------                 -------

CSTREET                   DUCK
```

The output shows that shared directories include `homes`, `Musicbox`, and `chris`. The printer `lp0` is also being shared. The master browser for the `CSTREET` workgroup is `DUCK`.

If you like, you can actually connect to and work with the share from Linux using the `smbclient` command. Using the example above, assume that you want to connect to the `Musicbox` share. The following example shows a session started to a share using the `smbclient` command:

```
# smbclient \\\\ fileserver \\ Musicbox passW3d
smb: \> help
?         altname    archive     blocksize    cancel
cd        chmod      chown       del          dir
du        exit       get         help         history
lcd       link       lowercase   ls           mask
md        mget       mkdir       more         mput
newer     open       print       printmode    prompt
put       pwd        q           queue        quit
```

```
rd         recurse    reget      rename     reput
rm         rmdir      setmode    symlink    tar
tarmode   translate   !
smb: \ > cd Bob
smb: \ Bob \ > ls
  .                                   D        0  Mon Feb 2 13:16:44 2004
  ..                                  D        0  Mon Feb 2 12:13:18 2004
  01-Tangled_Up_In_Blue.ogg                 7867809  Mon Feb 2 12:11:07 2004
  02-Simple_Twist_Of_Fate.ogg               6344707  Mon Feb 2 12:11:13 2004
  03-You_re_A_Big_Girl_Now.ogg              6421634  Mon Feb 2 12:11:19 2004
     62014  blocks of size 524288. 44544 blocks available
smb:  \ Bob \> quit
```

You can put the password on the smbclient command line, as shown in the first line of the code block by the passW3d element, or be prompted for it. However, if you type the password on the command line, it can be retrieved through the .bash_history file. It's better to use the prompt. Type help to see available commands. Once connected, you can use smbclient like an FTP interface. Use cd to change directories, ls to list, and get, mget, put, and mput to get and put files. Type quit when you are done.

Samba Troubleshooting Tips

Though Samba is quite simple to run, administrators should be aware of a few common problems. In this section, we describe some configurations you might want to make to your Samba installation. We pay particular attention to Samba security.

Tip
If you need more help on a problem not covered here, check the files in the /usr/share/doc/samba* directory. You can also look through the Samba mailing list archives at http://lists.samba.org/archive/samba.

Preventing Outside Access to Samba

SMB and Samba were not made for file and printer sharing outside the LAN environment. If you suspect that someone is gaining access from outside of your private network to your Samba service, here is a checklist of things you can do:

✦ *Block perimeter firewalls*—Every network feature that is intended for use on a private LAN should always begin with a strong firewall configuration on the perimeter of that LAN. Perimeter firewalls (those with connections to the outside world) should block ports 137, 138, 139, and 445 to external interfaces. However, computers on your LAN that you want to have Samba access should make those ports accessible.

Computers with external as well as internal connections to your private network can have different ports blocked or open on different interfaces.

In a home or small office situation, where a Samba server acts as a router, as well as a file/printer server, you can use iptables with the -i option to selectively allow or block access to a particular interface. For example, to identify an interface in a rule definition for the first Ethernet card, you would add -i eth0 to the options you give to the iptables command.

✦ *Block interfaces*—Within Samba, you can define the interfaces it will use for browsing, name registration, and related NetBIOS communications. By default, Samba listens on all network interfaces available on the computer. You can identify interfaces by interface name (eth0), IP address with netmask (192.168.0.10/255.255.255.0), or CIDR-style IP address (192.168.0.10/24) in the smb.conf file. Here's an example:

```
interfaces = eth0
```

✦ *Block host access*—You can block host access to the Samba service on your server in the /etc/samba/smb.conf file. Typically, the best way to do this is to allow access only to selected computer or group network addresses and deny all others. Here is an example:

```
host allow = 127.0.0.1 192.168.10.0/24
host deny = 0.0.0.0/0
```

This example allows connection to the Samba service from the local host or any computers on the 192.168.10 network (presumably your local LAN). Access from all other hosts is denied.

✦ *Block users and groups*—As with blocking hosts, the best way to block unwanted users is to allow only selected users to have access to your Samba service. To do that, add a list of valid users or groups to your smb.conf file. For example:

```
valid users = mary, jim, bill, sarah, @marketing @sales
```

In this example, clients who successfully log in with the names mary, jim, bill, or sarah are allowed access. Likewise, users from the groups marketing and sales can also have access.

Other types of security are best described in terms of the security mode you are using.

Troubleshooting Security Modes

The security mode you choose will have the most dramatic effect on who can connect to your shared directories and printers, as well as how you otherwise configure your Samba server. The following sections describe each mode, and mention some of the different challenges you may face depending on the security level you choose.

Share Level Security

The share security level, which was once the default level used with Samba, is no longer encouraged. It may be useful in cases where an older Windows client needs to connect, but you can't get it to provide the proper type of username and password. However, the more secure alternative is to upgrade the client, and not leave your Samba installation vulnerable.

User Level Security

Modern Samba security is managed in user level. When a client tries to connect to a Samba server, the client sends username, password, and name of the client machine. Given the permissions set for that user, he or she will be able to mount any shares the server allows him to.

There are different subtypes of user authentication in Samba—domain, ADS, and server modes—as, well as plain user mode with a username/password pair.

Domain Security Mode

With domain security, a domain member can sign on once to a primary Domain Controller's Security Account Manager (SAM) database. The client machine, rather than an individual user, is authenticated in this scheme. Thus, it is not the best solution for a Samba installation that must have individual verification, but it is useful for group workstations or relatively open networks.

If the Samba server is participating in an NT4 domain, which authenticates both the user and the machine, it can be set to act as a member server to provide members with a number of services:

✦ A central location to authenticate for access to all member machines in the domain

✦ Associated file ownership and access

✦ Ability to use network logins

✦ Ability to access network applications, based on the rights of the authenticated user

The Domain Controller server maintains Machine Trust Account information (referred to as a *secret*) that a client machine uses to authenticate. Note that NT4 domains do not use Domain Controllers, but rather Primary Domain Controllers.

> **Note**
>
> Not all Windows operating systems support Machine Trust Account information. Windows 95, Windows 98, Windows ME, and Windows XP Home cannot be full domain members. Windows NT, Windows 2000, and Windows XP Professional can be full domain members. In general, the business versions of Windows are more secure than the individual versions.

Use the `smb.conf` file to set various options for domain mode security.

ADS Mode Security

ADS mode takes advantage of Microsoft's Active Directory Service. In this mode, the Samba server can join an ADS domain and take advantage of Kerberos user authentication rather than NT-compatible authentication methods. If you choose to use ADS mode, you must specify values for the realm and security options in `smb.conf`, as in

```
realm = local.Kerberos.REALM
security = ADS
```

Server Security Mode

With this security mode, the Samba server tries to use another SMB server, previously designated as a password server, to authenticate users. This server is specified in `smb.conf` with the `password server` option. This option takes the NetBIOS name of the password server machine.

> **Caution**
>
> Samba no longer recommends use of server security mode (user level security), for a number of reasons. For example, there is no way to ensure that the password server requested is the one that is ultimately used. Even if the proper password server is used, a given session may remain open for much longer than necessary. There are too many security compromises with this security mode for the modern safety-conscious installation.

Troubleshooting [homes] Directory Sharing

The special [homes] section offers special opportunities (and problems) related to shared home directories. Here are some problems you may encounter and potential ways around them.

✦ *Too much user access*—Users who are allowed access to certain shared directories may get access to directories that they are not intended to share. Once users log in to a Samba server, they have the permissions of a Linux user. If users leave access to their /home directories open so other users can view or change their files in Linux, permissions are open from Samba as well.

The solution is to make sure that user Linux file and directory permissions are set to provide the Samba access you intend. For example, home directories should usually be closed to access by anyone but the owner of that directory (which they are by default). Guest users should not have access to the [homes] share. To solve the problem of unwanted access to home directories, add a users list to the global section of the smb.conf file:

```
valid users = %S
```

Then add the following line to the [homes] section:

```
only user = %S
```

Users can close permission to their own home directories while they are logged into Linux by typing chmod 700 $HOME.

✦ *Different home directory path*—You may put your home directories somewhere other than /home. In that case, you can add a path option to the [homes] share. For example, to direct Samba that you store your home directories in /var/people (such as /var/people/sarah, /var/people/mike, and so on), you could add this line to smb.conf in the [homes] section:

```
path = /var/people/%S
```

Troubleshooting Printer Sharing

When you use the [printers] section to share all the printers listed in the Samba server's /etc/printcap file, you may encounter some of the following common problems:

✦ *Can't see printers from client*—Make sure the printable = yes option is set. Otherwise, Samba won't load the printers from the /etc/printcap file.

✦ *Don't want to share all printers*—If you would rather share a limited number, but not all, of the printers in your /etc/printcap file, you can copy the printers you want to share to a different file. Then, for example, if you wanted to share printers listed in the /etc/prcap2 file, you could add the following to your [printers] section:

```
printcap name = /etc/prcap2
```

✦ *Printer settings are wrong*—In most cases, you should set printer options (such as duplex, paper size, and so on) in the printer settings tool of the Windows clients. To try to have Samba generate Device Mode, you can add the line

```
default devmode = yes
```

This should be tested before putting it into service, however, since it can cause the client print spooler to crash.

Name Service Problems in Samba

One of the biggest tricks in Samba is getting names to address resolution to work properly. On a single LAN with a WINS server, you are likely to experience fewer problems than you would if you are trying to configure workgroups that cross multiple subnets or are simply broadcasting availability of services without a central place for resolving names.

How Samba Resolves names

Having a Samba name server is a good idea. Without one, Samba will just broadcast to ask who has the address for a client requesting service. If there are conflicting names on the network, this could cause problems. Here is how a Samba machine gets the IP addresses for the NetBIOS names it encounters:

1. *Local NetBIOS hosts* (`lmhosts`)—First, Samba checks the /etc/samba/lmhosts file. You can use this file to map a particular NetBIOS name to an IP address. For example, to map MYPC to address 192.168.0.5, you would add this line:

   ```
   192.168.0.5   MYPC
   ```

2. *TCP/IP hosts lookup* (`host`)—Next, Samba uses the mechanism used to resolve any IP address on your system to find the IP address for the NetBIOS name it is looking for. The search uses the contents of the /etc/nsswitch.conf and /etc/host.conf files. By default, this will cause the /etc/hosts file to be checked, followed by NIS and DNS lookups.

3. *WINS server* (`wins`)—You should specify a WINS server to resolve NetBIOS addresses whenever possible. You can do that using the wins server option. If no WINS server is identified, Samba will skip this step.

4. *Broadcast* (`bcast`)—If the name is still not found, Samba will broadcast for the IP address of the computer it is trying to contact on any defined interfaces. (By default, it will use all known network interfaces, unless restricted by the interfaces parameter.)

You can change the order in which names and addresses are resolved using the name resolve order option. The following global option in the smb.conf file would cause the WINS server to be used before the default TCP/IP host lookup, but after any local names are resolved from the lmhosts file:

```
name resolve order = lmhosts wins host bcast
```

How Windows Clients Resolve Names

With no special configuration, most Windows SMB servers/clients just broadcast their NetBIOS names on the network using UDP broadcast packets. So in the default configuration, Windows file and printer sharing is restricted to the local LAN since broadcast messages will not, by default, cross subnet boundaries. There are two ways around this problem if you do not want to run a WINS server:

✦ `lmhosts`—Add addresses to the Windows client's lmhosts file to identify the names and IP addresses of all computers it wants to communicate with outside of the local subnet.

✦ *Remote announce*—A Samba client can force an announcement of itself on a remote network, using the `remote announce` option. That causes the Samba server to be put on the browse list of Windows clients on a remote network.

It is always more reliable, however, to assign a WINS server for SMB/Samba file and printer sharing. The WINS server can then route information about the Windows peer outside of the local LAN.

NetBIOS Tips

By default, TCP/IP names are used as NetBIOS names for Samba servers. If you want to identify your Samba server by a different NetBIOS name, use the `netbios` name option in `smb.conf`. You might need to do this if you have a particularly long host name. For example, to change the Samba server's NetBIOS name to TRICKSY, you could add the following line:

```
netbios name = TRICKSY
```

No Server Access

Some of the most common problems have simple solutions. If a client cannot connect to a server across the network, it might be something as simple as the server having stopped functioning or the client being configured improperly. There are different solutions for clients and servers under Linux and Windows.

Windows Server, Linux Client

Here are some things to check if you can't see a shared Windows folder from Linux:

✦ *File and Print Sharing*—On the Windows machine, right-click on a folder. If no Sharing option appears on the menu, you probably need to turn on File and Print Sharing for the computer. From Windows, check that File and Print Sharing are turned on (from Control Panel ➪ Network ➪ File and Print Sharing, then select to give others access to your files and let others share your printers).

✦ *Sharing*—If the Sharing option appears when you right-click, select it. Then turn on Share As and select the appropriate options for sharing the folder.

Samba Server, Windows Client

If you cannot connect to the Samba server from a Windows machine, consider some of these common reasons why you may not be able to connect:

✦ *Is Samba running?*—Make sure that Samba is running:

```
# ps ax |grep smb
31406 ?        S      0:00 smbd -D
```

If it's not, start it with the command `service smb start`, and set it to turn on automatically when your server starts up with the `chkconfig smb on` command.

✦ *Firewall*—If you enabled the firewall feature on the Samba server when you installed Linux, you are probably blocking access to ports needed to provide the Samba service. Turn off your firewall temporarily by issuing the command `iptables -F`. If your client can connect, turn the firewall back on with `service iptables restart`. Then fix your firewall to allow connections on ports 137, 138, and 139 from the clients on your LAN to which you want to allow access.

Windows 98 Clients

Windows 98 clients may generate a particular sort of Samba error. If you open Network Neighborhood from a Windows 98 client and a pop-up window asks for a password to make this connection to *Resource*:*server**IPC$*, no password will work. The problem is that, instead of asking for a login name and password, Windows 98 automatically supplies your current Windows username and password in encrypted form to the Samba server. When that fails, Samba asks for another password. There are several possible solutions to this common problem:

✦ Make sure that the same account name and password on the Windows 98 client is configured on the Samba server if you are using user level security.

✦ If you prefer, you can map the Windows username to the Linux username by editing the /etc/samba/smbusers file. For example, to map Windows user chris to Linux user chrisn, add this line to /etc/samba/smbusers:

```
chrisn = chris
```

✦ If the username and password are correct, but connections are still failing, check whether you are allowing encrypted passwords in the Samba server. Alternatively, you can change registry entries to enable plain text passwords.

Tip   Registry settings for various versions of Windows can be found in the /usr/share/doc/ samba*/docs/Registry/ file.

Performance Problems

In most cases, Samba tends to be a minimal user of system resources. If you notice that Samba is causing performance problems on your server machines, you may want to tweak your installation so that it runs faster and more smoothly. There are two options in smb.conf that are of particular help in improving server performance:

✦ *Auto disconnect*—If there are a lot of inactive connections to your Samba server, it can be a drag on performance. To disconnect after a certain number of minutes of dead time, you could set the deadtime parameter. For example, to disconnect a share from a client after an hour of inactivity, set this global option in the smb.conf file:

```
deadtime = 60
```

✦ *Limit connections*—You can use the max connections option to limit how many connections are allowed to a particular service. For example, you could add the following to a share section in smb.conf to limit the maximum number of connection to 20:

```
max connections = 20
```

Troubleshooting File Permission Problems

Samba assigns Linux file and directory permissions when someone tries to add, modify, or delete files and directories through SMB. You can change that behavior somewhat using some of the following settings in the smb.conf file:

✦ *Restrict directories*—If users are able to get into a directory structure that you would rather keep them out of, you can use the `dont descend` option to restrict access to any point below a selected point in the file system. (This feature can be a bit flaky, so use standard Linux file permissions to restrict access in most cases.) Here's an example:

```
dont descend = /proc,/dev
```

✦ *Unexpected permissions for DOS users*—You can change Samba's behavior from Linux to DOS-like when it comes to the rights to modify file and directory permissions. To do that, add the following to the global section:

```
dos filemode = yes
```

✦ *Problems changing file times from DOS*—Check the `dos filetime resolution` and `dos filetimes` options.

✦ *Following symbolic links*—By default, Samba will follow symbolic links that are in shares. To turn off that behavior, add the following line to a share definition:

```
follow symlinks = no
```

✦ *Forcing file/directory creation modes*—You can force the file permissions used when someone creates a file or directory in a Samba share. Use the `force create mode` and `force directory mode` parameters. These parameters are used in conjunction with the `create mask` and `directory mask` options.

Samba Resources

Samba is a particularly well-documented service. You will find a great deal of Samba information on the web, as well as in various files installed by default with the Samba package. Table 15-1 provides links to helpful sites and files, as well as a list of useful utilities and diagnostic commands that you can use with your Samba installation.

Tip   Most of the commands shown in Table 15-1 have man pages that explain the command in further detail and describe optional flags.

Table 15-1: Samba Resources

General Samba Information	
Samba project	`www.samba.org`
Samba documentation	`http://us1.samba.org/samba/docs`
Samba support	`http://us1.samba.org/samba/support`
Samba mailing lists	`http://us1.samba.org/samba/archives.html`
Samba documentation in Fedora	`/usr/share/doc/samba*/docs`

Continued

Table 15-1: *(continued)*

Samba Configuration and Log Files

`/etc/samba/smb.conf`	Primary configuration file for Samba servers
`/etc/samba/smbpasswords`	Stores Samba user passwords
`/etc/samba/smbusers`	Maps SMB usernames into Linux usernames
`/etc/samba/lmhosts`	Used to identify hosts Samba will communicate with that can't be obtained through broadcast, DNS, or other methods (similar to the TCP/IP `/etc/hosts` file)
`/var/log/samba`	Contains individual log files for nmbd (NetBios name server daemon), smbd (Samba server daemon), and each client that connect to the Samba server

Samba Daemons

`smbd`	The main Samba daemon
`nmbd`	The NetBIOS nameserver
`winbindd`	The `winbind` daemon

Samba Administrative Utilities

smbcontrol	Sends control messages to Samba daemons
smbpasswd	Manages SMB passwords
SWAT	Samba web configuration tool
net	Administers Samba and remote CIFS servers
pdbedit	Samba user account management tool
tdbbackup	Tool for backing up TDB databases

Samba Client Tools

rpcclient	Command-line MS-RPC client
smbtar	SMB back-up tool
smbclient	Command-line SMB client
smbmnt	Helper utility for mounting SMB file systems on Linux hosts
smbmount	User space tool for mounting SMB file systems under Linux
smbspool	Command-line SMB print client
smbumount	Userspace tool for unmounting SMB file systems under Linux
ntlm_auth	Allows external programs to use NTLM authentication
smbcquotas	Gets or sets quotas on NTFS5 shares
smbsh	Allows access to remote SMB shares with a UNIX shell

| smbtree | Text-based SMB network browsing |
| smbspool | Sends a print job to an SMB printer |

Samba Utilities	
smbstatus	Monitors the Samba service
testparm	Validates the `smb.conf` configuration file
testprns	Tests printer configuration
nmblookup	NetBIOS name query tool
wbinfo	Obtains `winbind` information
profiles	Migrates profiles from one domain to another
log2pcap	Generates `pcap` files from Samba log files

Summary

Samba, the Linux implementation of the Server Message Block protocol, is the best way to configure and manage heterogeneous networks that include Windows machines as well as those running Linux or Unix. Samba is included with most Linux distributions as part of a general server-level installation, and is easy to configure through the `smb.conf` file. You can administer Samba at the command line or through the SWAT web interface. Since Samba is a relatively straightforward service, troubleshooting is minimal. With Samba, no Linux administrator need fear a mixed network that incorporates Windows desktops into a secure Unix environment.

✦   ✦   ✦

NFS Troubleshooting

One of the most popular ways of sharing files among Linux and other UNIX systems is with the network file system (NFS) facility. Even Mac OS X can act as both an NFS client and a server. The fact that an NFS from a remote computer is connected to a local computer can be nearly invisible to a local user. To a systems administrator, however, there are lots of opportunities for configuring and tuning NFS.

This chapter takes you through some of the basics of setting up an NFS server, sharing file systems from that server to NFS clients, and tuning and troubleshooting the results.

Configuring NFS

In many ways, an NFS is treated like any other file system that might be available on your computer from hard disk partitions, a CD, a floppy disk, or other medium. To use an available NFS, you should follow two basic steps:

✦ *Mount it*—Using the `mount` command (with some special options), you identify the location in your local file system tree where you want the remote file system connected. For example, you might know that the `/var/chris` directory is being shared from a computer named daylight. To make the NFS-shared `/var/chris` available to your local computer, you might mount it on a local directory named `/var/daylight-chris`.

✦ *Access it*—Once a remote NFS is mounted locally, you access the contents of that file system as you would any other directory on your computer. To continue with the example, you could change to the mounted NFS directory (`cd /var/daylight-chris`), and then open files or run applications that are located in that directory.

The permissions to access data files, applications, and directories are determined by the computer that owns those items. Therefore, when a directory is shared using NFS, permissions from the computer using the shared NFS directory (the client) need to be mapped into those of the computer holding those assets (the server).

To continue with the example, let's say that the remote directory `/var/chris/docs` from the machine named daylight is restricted so that only the owner chris can access it (700 permissions). Someone trying to change to that directory or list its contents from the local mount point (`/var/daylight-chris/docs`) would have access denied, except in two cases. If the computer daylight mapped its user permissions in such a way that the local user trying to access that directory was mapped into the permissions of the computer daylight's user named chris, then access would be allowed. Likewise, if user permissions were set up to allow root user on a client machine to have the same privileges on the server, access would also be allowed.

To use NFS, you need at least two computers that are connected together by a common network. Because NFS is not considered a particularly secure network protocol, it is typically just run on a company's or other organization's local LAN. To run the example in this chapter, I use two computers on the same Ethernet LAN that are configured to use TCP/IP to communicate.

The NFS Server

On the NFS server, Fedora and Red Hat Linux systems have a graphical user interface that makes it easy to set up directories to be shared with other computers over your LAN. You start the NFS Server Configuration window by selecting System Settings ⇨ Server Settings ⇨ NFS. Or you can run `redhat-config-nfs` to launch the window on your desktop in Fedora Core 1.

Adding a Shared NFS Directory

To add a shared directory using the NFS Server Configuration window, click Add and enter information in the Add NFS Share window that appears. Figure 16-1 shows the NFS Server Configuration window with the pop-up window for adding a shared directory.

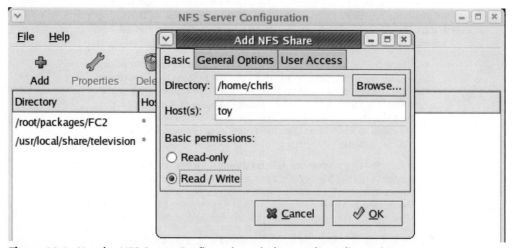

Figure 16-1: Use the NFS Server Configuration window to share directories.

In this example, I identify the directory /home/chris as being made available to be shared by the computer named toy as a read/write file system. A client (in this case, only the computer named toy) that mounts that directory could potentially have access to all files and directories below /home/chris. Of course, that depends on the read, write, and execute permissions set on those files and directories, as well as how users from the client are mapped into those permissions.

Here's a quick rundown of the information you can set from the Basic, General Options, and User Access tabs in the Add NFS Share window:

✦ *Directory*—You can add any directory you choose.

✦ *Host(s)*—Instead of entering a single TCP/IP host name, you can enter a fully qualified domain name (such as `toys.linuxtoys.net`), all hosts in an IP subnet (such as `10.0.0.0/255.255.255.0`), all hosts in an NIS netgroup (@`mynisgrp`), or all hosts in a domain (such as `*.linuxtoys.net`). Instead of an asterisk (to match all characters), you can use question marks to match any single character (for example, `???.linuxtoys.net` would match any three-character host name in the `linuxtoys.net` domain). To leave access open to all hosts, simply put a single asterisk (*) in this field.

✦ *Basic permissions*—Selecting read-only restricts access and so a client can only mount the directory read-only. Selecting read/write lets the client mount the directory with either full read/write permission or read-only (as the client chooses).

✦ *Allow connections from ports 1024 and higher*—Choose this option to allow a client to connect to the server from a request that originates from a port number higher than 1024. (See the `insecure` option on the exports man page.)

✦ *Allow insecure file locking*—This causes NFS to not authenticate locking requests from remote users of this shared directory. (See the `insecure_locks` option on the exports man page.)

✦ *Disable subtree checking*—With this feature on, NFS won't verify that the file requested by the client is actually in the shared directory. The server will only check that the file is in the file system. (See the `no_subtree_check` option on the exports man page.)

✦ *Sync write operations on request*—This forces a remote client write operation to be synced on your local disk at the client's request. (See the `sync` option on the exports man page.)

✦ *Force sync of write operations immediately*—This forces writes to the shared directory to be immediately synced to hard disk (when no loss of data is acceptable). (See the `no_wdelay` option on the exports man page.)

✦ *Treat the remote root user as local root*—This maps the permission of the root user on the client machine into the root user on the server. With this on, the client's root user has full control over the files and directories on the shared file system, and so use this feature with caution. (See the `no_root_squash` option on the exports man page.)

✦ *Treat all client users as anonymous users*—Use this feature to grant the same user and group privileges to everyone that accesses the shared directory. Then choose which user ID (UID) and group ID (GID) the clients are mapped into on the server for that shared directory. (See the `anonuid` and `anongid` options in the exports man page.)

After you have saved the information, it is written to the `/etc/exports` file. Some people who prefer to edit configuration files will bypass the NFS Server Configuration window and go straight to the `/etc/exports` file. Here's an example of the entry I just created as it appear in the `/etc/exports` file:

```
/usr/local/share/television toy(rw,sync,all_squash,anonuid=507,anongid=507)
```

As shown, the `/usr/local/share/television` directory is being made available to only one computer (named `toy`). The client will be able to mount the directory with read/write permissions (`rw`). The `sync` option indicates that writes only from the client have to be synced to the hard disk when the client requests it.

The last three options have to do with how user permissions are assigned. With `all_squash` set, every user who tries to access the directory from the host `toy` will be assigned to a single, anonymous user account. I then specifically set the anonymous user to UID 507 and GID 507 on the server (`anonuid=507` and `anongid=507`).

Starting the NFS Service

To make the directory that you just configured (and all other configured shared directories) available to client computers, type the following as root user:

```
#  chkconfig nfs on
#  service nfs start
Starting NFS services:       [ OK ]
Starting NFS quotas:         [ OK ]
Starting NFS daemons:        [ OK ]
Starting NFS mountd:         [ OK ]
```

At this point, you should be able to connect to the shared directory from the computer named toy by mounting it on toy's local file system.

The NFS Client

To use the files, applications, and directories that an NFS server makes available through a shared NFS directory, a client computer has to mount that directory. Like mounting a disk partition or CD, mounting a shared NFS directory results in that directory being connected to some point in the client computer's file system.

There are several different ways you can mount an NFS directory on a client computer:

✦ *Manual*—Run the `mount` command (as root user) from a Terminal window to identify the remote NFS directory, local mount point, and other information needed to complete the mount.

✦ *Boot time*—Add a line identifying the mount information to the `/etc/fstab` file. Unless you specifically indicate not to immediately mount the remote NFS directory, your computer will try to mount that directory when the computer boots up.

✦ *Automount*—Using the automount facility, you can configure the mounting of the NFS directory to occur when someone tries to access the contents of the local mount point directory.

These three procedures are explained in the following subsections.

Although there is NFS client and server software that runs on other platforms, for our purposes I'm going to show how a Fedora or Red Hat Linux client can connect to a shared NFS directory. The `mount` command and other procedures should work much the same way on any Linux or UNIX-like operating system (including MAC OS X and BSD systems).

Note

NFS client and server software is also available for Windows platforms. NFS is in Microsoft Windows Services for UNIX (`www.microsoft.com/windows/sfu`). There are also third-party NFS clients for Windows. For example, you can get a free trial of NFS software for Windows from XLink Technology, Inc. NFS client software starts at $89 to purchase a copy.

Mounting an NFS Directory Manually

Although the options may differ slightly among different operating systems, the mount command is the common way of mounting an NFS directory on a client. If the server has made a shared NFS directory available to your computer (either specifically, or by allowing all or a group of computers to access it), you use the mount command with the -t nfs option to mount the directory locally.

Following the example started in the NFS Server section, from the client computer named toy, you could type the following commands to mount the directory /var/chris from the computer daylight on a local mount point directory /var/daylight-chris. Run them as root user from a Terminal window:

```
#  mkdir /var/daylight-chris
#  mount -t nfs daylight:/var/chris /var/daylight-chris
```

If the mount was successful, you should silently see a new command prompt. Then you can type ls /var/daylight-chris to see if the contents of that directory show up. (If this doesn't happen for you, don't worry. Most of this chapter is devoted to troubleshooting the process.)

Mounting an NFS Directory at Boot Time

After you have successfully mounted an NFS directory manually, if you want that shared directory to be always available on your system, you can set it to be mounted automatically at boot time. You do this by adding an entry to the /etc/fstab file.

Following our example, this line shows what you could add to the /etc/fstab file on the computer named toy so that the directory /var/chris from the computer daylight is automatically mounted each time the toy computer is booted:

```
daylight:/var/chris /var/daylight-chris nfs rsize=8192,wsize=8192 0 0
```

There are six fields here. The daylight:/var/chris identifies the remote host and share names. The /var/daylight-chris identifies the local mount point. The nfs identifies this as an NFS. The rsize=8192,wsize=8192 are just two options I chose to add to the mount command (based on recommendations from the nfs man page). You can add other comma-separated options as well. The last two fields (0 0) tell the operating system not to dump the contents of the file system or run fsck, as you would do on a normal local file system.

With this entry in place, the NFS shared directory will automatically mount (if all goes well) the next time the client computer boots up.

There are many other options you can pass to the mount command to adjust how the NFS shared directory is mounted. We'll get into some of those later. For the moment, however, I want to mention the noauto option. For example, if you had put noauto, rsize=8192, wsize=8192 as options to mount, the directory would not be mounted automatically at boot time. However, when you go to mount it manually later, you can type the mount command using only some of the options. For example:

```
#  mount /var/daylight-chris
```

Using this command line, the mount command would go to the /etc/fstab file and figure out that the directory is associated with daylight:/var/chris, that it is an NFS directory (nfs), and that the rsize, wsize, and any other mount values listed should be used. This just saves you some typing for NFS shared directories you use often, but don't want to mount automatically.

Mounting an NFS Directory Using Automount

The autofs package is the default automounter used in Fedora and Red Hat Linux systems. (This package is described in Chapter 9.) Another automount package available with Fedora and Red Hat Linux systems is the am-utils package. The am-utils package has some good features that you can use with NFS.

In large installations where a lot of computers are offering and using NFS shared directories on a network, it can become difficult to manage them all. One way to deal with that problem is to use the am-utils automounter service (amd daemon) that comes with Fedora and Red Hat Linux (as well as other Linux and UNIX systems).

Using amd, an NFS can be mounted only when it is accessed. Then, after a period of inactivity, it is unmounted. In Fedora and Red Hat, a nice set of configuration files allows you to start up the automounter, and then change to list the contents of, or run a command from, the remote directory (/net by default).

Starting with the example shared directory we've been using in this chapter (daylight: /var/chris), here is how you would start the automounter to access that directory from a client machine (assuming the client is a Fedora or Red Hat Linux system):

```
#  service amd start
#  chkconfig amd on
```

Once the service is turned on (service command) and set to turn on at every reboot (chkconfig command), the /net directory should appear. If all goes right (and there are a lot of things that can go wrong along the way), in our example you should be able to type the following:

```
#  ls /net/daylight/var/chris
```

For this to work, I assume that:

✦ Your local computer can resolve the IP address for the computer named daylight (either through DNS, /etc/hosts, or some other mechanism).

✦ The /var/chris directory has been shared by daylight and made available to this local computer.

✦ Permissions on /var/chris are open to the extent that listing the contents of /var/chris will return something.

Notice that the system name follows the /net. You will have to traverse the full /net/ daylight/var/chris/ to get to the shared content. Also, typing ls /net/daylight/var will not show other directories from the server that exist in its /var directory.

To free up resources, after a period of not being accessed, the shared NFS directory will be unmounted. The mount will occur again, however, the next time someone tries to access any component of the shared NFS directory.

NFS User Permissions

You can control who can mount your NFS shared directory when you export it (from the information you added to the entry in /etc/exports). However, controlling how users can access the files, directories, and programs from the client computers that mount that shared directory is a bit trickier. The following subsections explain some means for controlling how users from the remote NFS client computer can access the files and directories on your NFS share.

Sharing Read-Only

There are a few ways to keep remote users from adding files to or changing files within a shared NFS directory from your server. The first way is to simply share the directory read-only from the server.

For an NFS directory that is shared read-only when it is mounted by the client, the client cannot change any file on the shared directory. Alternatively, if the client mounts a directory read-only (whether it was shared read-only or read/write), no user from the client will be able to write to the directory.

Anonymous Users

Using the all_squash option when the directory is shared in the /etc/exports file on the server, all users from the client computer are mapped into a single user and group ID on the server. By default, the anonymous UID is 65534 (nfsnobody) and GID is also 65534 (nfsnobody).

Because nfsnobody is not a real user on the server, the only files, directories, and programs users from client hosts will have access to on the shared directory are those that are either world read, write, and executable or those that were created by a user from the NFS client.

An administrator on the NFS server can assign any user ID and group ID to act as the anonymous NFS user. This is done by assigning appropriate ID numbers to the anonuid= and anongid= options when the directory is exported. You must use the UID numbers (from the /etc/passwd file) and GID numbers (from the /etc/group file), rather than using user or group names, when you assign the anonymous users and groups.

Mapped User IDs

When you don't designate all users to be assigned to an anonymous user account, the default user and group mappings are a bit strange. In that case, each user will have ownership and group permissions to files and directories based on their user and GID assignments on the client.

What exactly does this mean? Well, if your UID and GID numbers on the NFS client were 501, then you would be considered the owner of any files on the shared directory that was owned by the user number 501. This can cause some confusion (as well as a security breakdown) when the user named sally on the server has UID 501 and the user named joe on the client has UID 501. Once that directory is shared using NFS, files and directories owned exclusively by sally on the server are now also owned by joe (provided the directory was mounted with read/write permissions).

Because ownership is set by the UID and GID numbers, an ls -l of a file owned by sally will appear as follows when done on the server:

```
#  ls -l file.txt
-rw-rw-r--  1 sally    sally   34322 Mar    9 02:10 file.txt
```

A listing of the same file, mounted on a client computer using NFS, however, will appear to be owned by whatever user on the client machine has the same UID and GID as sally does on the server machine. You can see the numeric user and GIDs using ls -ln as follows:

```
#  ls -ln file.txt
-rw-rw-r--  1 501    501   34322 Mar    9 02:10 file.txt
```

Now, with joe, who is assigned UID 501 and GID 501 on the client machine, here's how a listing of the same file would appear when `ls -l` is run on the NFS client:

```
# ls -l file.txt
-rw-rw-r-- 1 joe   joe   34322 Mar   9 02:10 file.txt
```

In the old UNIX days, this type of user mapping made more sense. A company might have had only a handful of computers, each of which might have 100 user accounts on it. A small team of system administrators might be responsible for administering all those computers. The administrators could then share /etc/passwd files among those computers, allowing a set of users to easily maintain the same rights to files and directories across all those host computers.

With today's less centralized system administration and the proliferation of personal computers, a single /etc/passwd file is harder to maintain across a group of computers. So, the person who owns the computer may be assigned to the first user account on that computer (with UID and GID 500 in Fedora and Red Hat Linux systems by default).

As an administrator, you need to understand the potential lack of security that can arise by users from multiple computers with the same UID and GID, all sharing files from the same shared NFS resource.

One way in which a bit of security is built in by default is that the root user from the client does not have root permission to modify files on the NFS server. The root user is mapped to the permissions of the anonymous NFS user. You can override that, if you like, by adding the `no_root_squash` option to the exported directory (in the /etc/exports file on the server).

Troubleshooting NFS

It's possible (even likely) that the first time you try to share and mount an NFS shared directory, it will fail. The following section takes you through some problems and issues that can arise as you try to use the NFS facility.

Export Failures

To make sure that you have properly exported an NFS shared directory, you need to be able to see if any errors occurred when the export was done. Unfortunately, the NFS Server Configuration window will not always tell you when it creates an exported NFS directory entry that doesn't work.

If you launch the NFS Server Configuration window from a Terminal window, you will be able to see error messages that occur. As you add or modify shared directories in the NFS Server Configuration window, error messages and informational messages will appear in the Terminal window from which you launched NFS Server Configuration window. Here are some examples:

```
# redhat-config-nfs
exportfs: /etc/exports: 3: bad anonuid "anonuid=chris"
exportfs: toy has non-inet addr
exportfs: toy has non-inet addr
```

In this example, after I launched the NFS Server Configuration window, I added a shared directory. Although the action successfully saved the entry to /etc/exports (and didn't complain), error messages that showed up in the Terminal window where I launched the window show a few errors. First, I entered a user name to be used as the anonymous user and the option requires a UID number (such as 505). Second, the name of the computer I was allowing to share the directory (toy) failed to have its address resolved (my DNS server couldn't find toy and it was not listed in my /etc/hosts file).

Because the NFS Server Configuration window mostly writes to the /etc/exports file and runs the exportfs command, you can do those things by hand and find out if there were any problems. For example:

```
# exportfs -v -a
exportfs: /etc/exports: 3: bad anonuid "anonuid=chris"
exporting *:/usr/local/share/television
exporting *:/root/packages/FC2
```

Here you can see that running the exportfs command in verbose mode (-v) displays the failures and successes exporting the shared NFS directories in the /etc/exports file. The first attempt to export my /home/chris directory failed because I entered the anonymous user I wanted to use as the user name instead of the UID number. The other two exports in the file (/usr/local/share/television and /root/packages/FC2) both succeeded, as indicated by the exporting lines. You can verify that by typing the following:

```
# showmount -e
/usr/local/share/television *
/root/packages/FC2          *
```

Here you can see the two directories that have been successfully exported and that they are available to any host computer (*).

Unmount Failure

You try to unmount a remote NFS directory (using the umount command) and the unmount fails with a "device is busy" message such as the following:

```
# umount /mnt/whatever
umount: /mnt/whatever: device is busy
```

Most likely, there is a process holding the directory open. You can type the lsof command, along with the directory name, to see if any processes are currently accessing the shared directory:

```
[root@shuttle one]# lsof /mnt/whatever
COMMAND PID   USER FD   TYPE DEVICE SIZE NODE    NAME
lsof    3893  root cwd  DIR  0,12   4096 1079267 /mnt/whatever (duck:/tmp)
lsof    3894  root cwd  DIR  0,12   4096 1079267 /mnt/whatever (duck:/tmp)
bash    31558 root cwd  DIR  0,12   4096 1079267 /mnt/whatever (duck:/tmp)
```

Here you can see that the bash shell is using /mnt/whatever as the current working directory. Since I ran the lsof command from that same shell, that command is also showing /mnt/whatever. In this case, I can simply change to a different directory, and then try the umount command again. In some cases, you might need to kill a process that is holding open the device before the directory can be unmounted.

Often, instead of running the lsof command, I will just look for the shell I have opened to the shared directory after an unmount fails.

Mount Failures

The most common reasons for failures when you try to mount an NFS share are:

✦ Wrong share information

✦ Firewalls are blocking NFS ports

Mount failures can also occur if a mount request comes from a client that is making the request from an insecure port. The following sections describe each of these issues.

Wrong Share Information

So as not to give away information about NFS shares from inquiring clients, the same failure message from an NFS server when you try to mount an NFS share can result from any of several different problems. The basic failed NFS mount request looks like the following:

```
# mount -t nfs toy:/home/chris /mnt/toy
mount: toy:/home/chris failed, reason given by server:
Permission denied
```

This message indicates that you did contact the server, but you are not requesting a shared directory that is available for you to mount. Reasons that the mount might have failed include:

✦ *Directory is not being exported*—The directory may exist, but it is not currently being exported from the server. Check with the server that the directory is being shared from the server. If it is, make sure that you typed the name of the directory correctly.

✦ *You don't have proper permission*—The NFS server may have exported the directory, but you may not be on the list of clients.

In either case, the error message indicated that the NFS service is running on the server, so you should contact the system administrator of the NFS server to make sure you have the correct name of the share and the rights to mount it. If the NFS service had not been running on the server, you would have seen a message like the following when the mount failed:

```
mount: RPC: Program not registered
```

Firewalls Are Blocking NFS Ports

A restrictive firewall on the server might mistakenly be blocking NFS clients from mounting your NFS shares. If you are seeing RPC failures from NFS clients trying to mount NFS shares, it may be because the firewall rules (iptables) are not allowing requests to RPC and/or NFS ports.

To remedy this problem, be sure to open access, using the `iptables` command, to ports 111 (RPC) and 2049 (NFS) on the server. This should allow access from the NFS client systems.

Mount Fails from MAC OS X

You try to mount an NFS directory from your Linux computer on an iMAC and it fails. The problem might be that some versions of MAC OS X make the request to mount your NFS shared directory from a port higher than port 1024. By default, NFS in Fedora and Red Hat Linux will refuse to honor NFS mount requests that originate from ports above 1024.

You can get around this problem by adding the `insecure` option to your exported file system (in the `/etc/exports` file) when you export the file system from the server. This will allow requests for NFS mounts (which come from insecure ports by default on MAC OS X systems) to succeed.

File and Directory Permissions

Here are a few tips for those times when you can't access files and directories as you might expect:

✦ *Can't access NFS directory as root user*—By default, when someone shares a directory using NFS, the root user is always mapped into the anonymous user (which is the nfsnobody user and group with a 65534 UID and GID). This is true even if all other users are mapped into their same UID and GID numbers on the server. If you need to access a remote file system as the root user, the server must share that directory with the no_root_squash option added to the /etc/exports definition for the shared directory.

✦ *Can't write files to the remote NFS directory*—Here's a quick checklist of reasons why you might not be able to write to a remote NFS directory from an NFS client computer:

✦ *Shared directory was shared read-only*—Even if you mounted an NFS directory as read/write, you won't be able to write to it if it was shared read-only.

   • *Shared directory was mounted read-only*—A shared NFS directory that is available with read/write permissions still has to be mounted with read/write permission to allow writing.

   • *File and directory permissions prevent you from changing or creating files*—By default, you will be able to create or change only those files and directories that are owned by the anonymous NFS user (nfsnobody by default) or that are open for writing to everyone. If you need to create and change other files and directories on the shared directory, the NFS server needs to specifically allow you to do that. (*See the NFS User Permissions* section.)

   • *File locking requests fail from client*—Some older NFS clients may not be able, by default, to successfully request file locking on a shared NFS directory. The reason is that the NFS client may not be passing credential information about the user to the NFS server because the feature wasn't implemented in the client. To get around this problem, the server can add the insecure_locks option to the definition of the share in the /etc/exports file.

Performance Is Slow

Changing mount and export settings can have some effect on how NFS directories perform when they are shared with client computers:

✦ *Syncing writes to disk*—By default, an exported NFS directory is shared with the sync option on, causing writes to be committed to hard disk before an NFS request is completed. Setting the async option for the shared directory (in /etc/exports) can improve performance of writes to that shared directory, although it can pose some risk to data loss if the server crashes before the data moves from cache to hard disk. Not only can this result in corrupted data, but you may not know the data was corrupted until a later time when you return to use that data.

✦ *Delaying writes to disk*—With the sync option on, the wdelay option is also on by default, causing the disk to save several write requests before committing them to disk to improve performance. Because this can actually hurt performance on systems where many small, unrelated writes are occurring, you can disable the wdelay option by setting the no_wdelay option for the shared directory (in the /etc/exports file).

✦ *Improving general disk performance*—There are many standard disk performance techniques that will help the performance of your NFS server. See Chapter 9 for information on using the hdparm command, as well as other utilities, to tune your hard disk.

✦ *Changing read and write sizes*—On the client side, there are options you can add to the mount command (or the /etc/fstab file) when you mount the NFS share directory that can improve performance. The nfs man page recommends rsize= (the number of bytes for each data read) and wsize= (the number of bytes of each data write) be increased from the default 1024 to 8192 in both cases. The larger data reads and writes can be of particular value for transactions that transfer large blocks of data on networks that experience few data collisions.

✦ *Requests to an NFS server are timing out*—Whether from a slow network, slow server, or multiple subnet hops to get to the server, it's possible for operations to time out to an NFS server that is actually available. If a remote NFS share is mounted with the soft option, if no response occurs after a time-out period, the request fails. With the hard option (default), read and write requests will wait forever for the server to become available. After the time-out period with a hard-mounted NFS share, the time-out is logged, but NFS continues to make the request forever.

Here are a few options you can adjust to prevent time-outs:

• If you are getting slow response from an NFS server, increasing the RPC time-out value might improve overall performance. The timeo= option to the mount command lets you change the value of the first RPC time-out from the default 7-tenths of a second (timeo=7) to a larger number (in tenths of seconds). If the RPC request fails to get a response within the first timeo value, the time-out is doubled and the transmission is repeated until the maximum of 60 seconds is reached.

• If the read or write requests themselves are timing out, you can increase the number of minor time-outs that occur before a major time-out occurs and the request is abandoned. By default, the value of retrans= is set to 3. This causes the operation to fail after three minor time-outs when the directory is soft mounted.

✦ *Skip subtree checking*—You can gain some performance improvements with NFS by not verifying that a requested file is actually in the shared directory. Instead, you can have NFS only check that the file is in the correct file system. You can tell NFS to skip subtree checking by adding the no_subtree_check option to the /etc/exports file for the shared directory.

Unexpected NFS Behavior

Because a file system may exhibit different behavior when it is mounted locally than when it is mounted remotely, some unexpected behavior can occur. Here are some examples of NFS behavior that you might not expect:

✦ *Can't see contents of a subdirectory*—You mount a remote NFS directory and change to a subdirectory, only to find that the subdirectory appears to be empty. You go to the server and see that the directory is full of files that are world readable, but you still can't see them from the client. It may be that the subdirectory is on a separate partition on the server. For example, if you share the root directory (/) of a server that has separate /boot and /home directories, an ls of the boot and home directories from the client will show those directories on the server as empty.

To make it so you can traverse to the /boot and /home directories of the shared root directory just described, you have to do two things. First, you must add the nohide option to the export definition of the NFS-shared root files system. Second, you must explicitly share the /boot and /home directories as well in the /etc/exports file. For example:

```
/     *(ro,nohide)
/home *(ro)
/boot *(ro)
```

Caution

Take care when using the nohide option. Apparently multiple partitions on the same NFS-mounted directory structure are at some risk of having conflicting inode numbers, which can result in NFS becoming confused.

✦ *NFS requests hanging*—Here's where you have to consider how critical it is that your data stay in sync between your NFS client and server. If, for example, the client is performing a write operation and the server goes down or otherwise become inaccessible on the network, by default (using the hard mount option) the client process will hang until the write is completed. You will not be able to break out of that request without killing the process doing the write.

As an alternative, you can specify the soft option when you mount the directory (to allow the operation to time out eventually) or specify the intr option. (You can add these options when you mount the NFS directory, either from the mount command line or in the /etc/fstab file.) With the intr option set, a Ctrl+C on the command line should let you break out of a command that is waiting for an NFS resource to come back.

✦ *NFS mounts hanging on boot*—If you are automatically mounting an NFS at boot time (typically from the /etc/fstab file) and the NFS shared directory is temporarily unavailable, by default the boot process will not continue until that NFS directory becomes available.

This behavior might be acceptable if you don't have a working system without that directory (say, for example, if you are remotely mounting your /home directory). However, in many cases, you might just want the system to put the mount request in the background and continue booting the machine.

To have a mount request go into the background after the first mount request times out, add the bg option to the mount options in the /etc/fstab for that entry. To explicitly continue to try the mount in the foreground, you can add the fg option to the mount options in the /etc/fstab entry.

Monitoring NFS Behavior

Tools like the showmount and nfsstat commands can help you monitor the behavior of your NFS server. Here are some examples of ways you can check out what's happening with your NFS server:

✦ *Check who is mounting your directories*—You can find out which host computers are mounting your shared NFS directories and which directories they are mounting using the showmount command as follows:

```
#showmount -a
All mount points on daylight.linuxtoys.net:
toys:/usr/local/share/television
duck:/root/packages/FC2
```

To see just the host names of computers that are mounting your shared directories, type the following:

```
# showmount
Hosts on daylight.linuxtoys.net:
toys
duck
```

To see just the directories that are being shared, type the following:

```
# showmount -d
Directories on daylight.linuxtoys.net:
/usr/local/share/television
/root/packages/FC2
```

✦ *Check available disk space on remote NFS directories*—To find out how much disk space is available on any NFS directories that you have currently mounted, you can use the df command along with the NFS file type (-F NFS) and request for human-readable form (-h):

```
# df -hF nfs
Filesystem          Size Used Avail Use% Mounted on
daylight:/home/chris  16G  13G  1.7G  89% /var/daylight-chris
```

This output shows the disk space (size, used and available) for all remote NFS shared directories that are mounted on the local system. It also shows the computer and directory name for each remote file system and where on the local system the remote directory is mounted.

✦ *Monitoring NFS calls*—Using the nfsstat command, you can monitor the activity of various parts of the NFS service. The nfsstat command displays statistics on data being written in both client and server services related to NFS. Using the -o option, nfsstat can display information for the following services related to NFS:

- *-o nfs*—Displays NFS statistics based on each RPC call made to the NFS service. (RPC, which stands for *remote procedure calls*, is a method created by Sun Microsystems for making network requests and transferring data.)

- *-o rpc*—Displays general RPC call information.

- *-o net*—Displays network layer statistics, related to lower level data transfer.

- *-o fh*—Displays file handle data, such as file look-ups and cache hits.

- *-o rc*—Displays information relating to hits on the NFS server's request reply cache.

The following is an example of the nfsstat command showing NFS client statistics:

```
# nfsstat -c
Client rpc stats:
calls       retrans     authrefrsh
145         4           0
```

```
Client nfs v2:
null       getattr     setattr  root     lookup  readlink
0      0% 49     62%   0       0% 0    0% 18   22% 3    3%
read       wrcache     write        create remove  rename
0      0% 0      0%    0       0% 0    0% 0    0% 0    0%
link       symlink     mkdir        rmdir   readdir fsstat
0      0% 0      0%    0       0% 0    0% 0    0% 9    11%

Client nfs v3:
null       getattr     setattr  lookup  access   readlink
0      0% 38     57%   0       0% 1    1% 6    9% 0       0%
read       write       create       mkdir   symlink mknod
12    18% 0      0%    0       0% 0    0% 0    0% 0       0%
remove     rmdir       rename       link    readdir readdirplus
0      0% 0      0%    0       0% 0    0% 0    0% 2       3%
fsstat     fsinfo      pathconf commit
4      6% 3      4%    0       0% 0    0%
```

Under the rpc stats, you can see that 145 RPC calls were made and there were 4 retransmissions. If the number of retransmissions goes over 5 percent of the total number of calls, it indicates that the server is having trouble keeping up with your requests for data or that your requests are simply not reaching it.

NFS version 2 and version 3 calls reflect the type of activity going on between the NFS client and the NFS servers it is accessing. Many of the attributes here are those you would expect when reading, writing, and accessing file systems. Here is an example of nfsstat statistics for an NFS server:

```
# nfsstat -s
Server rpc stats:
calls      badcalls    badauth    badclnt    xdrcall
69997      0           0          0          0
Server nfs v2:
null       getattr  setattr  root     lookup    readlink
1    100%  0      0% 0     0% 0     0% 0     0% 0       0%
read       wrcache  write    create   remove    rename
0    0%    0      0% 0     0% 0     0% 0     0% 0       0%
link       symlink  mkdir    rmdir    readdir   fsstat
0    0%    0      0% 0     0% 0     0% 0     0% 0       0%
Server nfs v3:
null       getattr  setattr lookup  access     readlink
1    0%    714    1% 64    0% 379  0% 870    1% 0       0%
read       write    create  mkdir   symlink    mknod
67523 96%  252    0% 58    0% 0    0% 0      0% 0       0%
remove     rmdir    rename  link    readdir    readdirplus
58   0%    0      0% 21    0% 0    0% 30     0% 0       0%
fsstat     fsinfo   pathconf commit
12   0%    12     0% 0     0% 2      0%
```

The server statistics (nfsstat -s) reflect the result of calls made to the server related to NFS requests. Read and write requests reflect the amount of data being read and written to the NFS server. In the rpc stats, look for badcalls (which indicate requests that were rejected by the RPC layer) and badauth (which indicates requests for authentication that were rejected by the server).

NFS Troubleshooting References

Table 16-1 provides a reference for finding resources and troubleshooting NFS.

Table 16-1: NFS Troubleshooting References

General NFS Information	
NFS project	`http://nfs.sourceforge.net`
NFS documentation	`http://nfs.sourceforge.net/nfs-howto` NFS HOWTO
NFS e-mail archive	`http://sourceforge.net/mailarchive/forum.php?` `forum_id=4930`
NFS documentation in Fedora	`/usr/share/doc/nfs-utils*`
NFS 4 development	`www.citi.umich.edu//projects/nfsv4`

NFS Configuration and Log Files	
`/etc/fstab`	General file for mounting file systems at boot time or later, including NFS file systems.
`/etc/exports`	Contains exported NFS shares that are made available to clients.
`/etc/rc.d/init.d/nfs`	Start-up script for launching the NFS server.
`/etc/rc.d/init.d/nfslock`	Provides file-locking functions for the NFS service.
`/var/lib/nfs/*`	Several files in this directory contain information about NFS activities. The `etab` file lists the files that are currently exported and who they are exported to. The `rmtab` file lists file systems that are mounted at the moment. The `xtab` file contains information on which file systems are currently exported (duplicating information in the `/proc/fs/nfs/exports` file).

NFS Commands	
`Exportfs`	Tool for exporting NFS file systems.
`Rpcinfo -p`	Displays all RPC services, including NFS and related services, that are registered on the local computer.
`Nfsstat`	Check status of shared NFS resources.
showmount	Show which computers have mounted file systems from the NFS server.

Summary

While protocols such as Samba (for file sharing with Windows systems) have made NFS a less prominent file sharing protocol, NFS is still quite often used among computing environments made up primarily of Linux and UNIX systems. Troubleshooting techniques for NFS focus on both the server side (where a directory is exported for use by other computers) and the client side (where shared NFS directories are mounted on client file systems).

Basic NFS configuration in Fedora and Red Hat Linux systems can be done using graphical tools, such as the NFS Server Configuration window and commands. On the server side, the `exportfs` command and the `/etc/exports` configuration file are the primary tools for sharing NFS directories. On the client side, the `mount` command is used to connect an NFS directory to the client computer's local file system.

✦   ✦   ✦

Troubleshooting External Services

✦ ✦ ✦ ✦

Web Server Troubleshooting

The Apache web server is the most popular web server software in the world. It is provided by default as part of the server installation of Fedora Core, and most other Linux distribution today. Whether you serve thousands of virtual hosts offering completely dynamic content or a single site serving only static files, you can configure Apache to suit your needs.

In this chapter, we introduce the features new to the Apache 2.0 release. We show you the basics of Apache configuration, and offer some tricks culled from the best practices of professional web administrators. Finally, we provide some resources for further study, should you be interested in delving into the inner workings of the server.

Apache 2.0: An Overview

Although millions of websites are still hosted successfully on Apache 1.3 and earlier, Fedora Core supplies Apache 2.0, first released in 2001. The 2.0 version brought significant changes to Apache installations, including improvements in security, process management, and administrative ease. This section describes some of these improvements in detail.

Tip   There are a few reasons to run Apache 1.3 on your Fedora Core machine (such as some needed module compatibility). However, this is not a concern for most people. We offer some tips on making the transition from 1.x to 2.0 in the *Migrating from Apache 1.x to 2.0* section later.

UNIX Threading

Apache can take full advantage of POSIX threads support on UNIX systems to improve scalability. Unfortunately, this feature is not fully implemented in the Apache package included with the current version of Fedora Core, which is based on an older version of Apache optimized for stability when serving dynamic content.

Tip The Fedora Core Apache package can be recompiled to take advantage of the POSIX threads option, though in a limited implementation. See the MPM links in Table 17-2, and look at the "worker" MPM if you need fully implemented threads capability. Just be aware that use of the "worker" MPM is less stable and less compatible with some modules (for example, PHP).

New Build System

The build system in Apache 2.0 was completely rewritten and is now based on autoconf and libtool. This change makes compiling Apache more like working with other Linux packages than it used to be. This change does not affect Fedora Core users who use the default binary RPMs included with the Fedora Core distribution, but if you want to compile Apache from scratch, you'll find that the procedure for 2.0 is different than it was for Apache 1.x versions.

Tip Whenever recompiling packages from source on any Red Hat-based system, try to use source RPMs instead of less regulated tarball methods. By keeping your system on RPM, you maintain more flexibility and control over things like patching and revision-related packages.

Multiprotocol Support

Apache now has infrastructure that allows it to support serving multiple protocols, that is, protocols other than HTTP. For example, the mod_2echo module embeds a server that echoes whatever is sent to it, using this multiprotocol support.

Better Support for Non-UNIX Platforms

Apache 2.0 is faster and more stable than Apache 1.x on non-UNIX platforms. While this is not particularly important for those running UNIX- or Linux-only networks, those readers who administer multi-OS networks will find Apache 2.0 to be far more reliable on other operating systems since it is now implemented in native APIs for almost all platforms in general use.

New Apache API

The API for Apache modules has changed significantly under Apache 2.0. Most modules written for Apache 1.3 will not work under 2.0. The good news is that if you've been experiencing module ordering or priority problems under 1.x the API used for 2.0 modules will solve those issues.

Caution If you upgrade your Apache installation from 1.x to 2.0, you will probably need to download new 2.0 versions of all your installed modules. Although a given module may have the same name under each version, only the 2.0 modules will run reliably under the new server version.

IPv6 Support

Apache now gets IPv6 listening sockets by default on systems where IPv6 is supported by the Apache Portable Runtime library. Certain Apache directives, including Listen and NameVirtualHost, can now take numeric address strings.

Filtering

Apache now permits the use of modules that filter a stream of content as it travels past the web server. This may speed up your server's response. For example, the `mod_include` module checks file content before it is delivered to the client and parses it for Server Side Include directives, using the `INCLUDES`. You might also be interested in the `mod_ext_filter` module, which allows external programs to act as filters.

Multilanguage Error Responses

Error messages can be sent to the browser in multiple languages, depending on the Server Side Include documents called by the requesting browser. This may be of particular interest to those who administer sites that contain documents in different character sets.

Simplified Configuration

Many directives are easier to understand under 2.0 version than they were under Apache 1.x. For example, the `Port` and `BindAddress` directives have been removed and the `Listen` directive is now the only one used to bind IP addresses.

Separate Configuration Files for Apache Applications

Beginning with Apache 2.0, any file ending with the `.conf` suffix and located in `/etc/httpd/conf.d` will automatically be processed as if it were part of the main configuration file. This allows the administrator to separate configuration files for easier editing. This feature is intended to simplify configuration of Apache modules and helper programs. For example, `/etc/httpd/conf/perl.conf` can be used to configure the `mod_perl` module, `/etc/httpd/conf/php.conf` for PHP, and so on.

Updated Regular Expression Library

In order to take advantage of Perl 5's more powerful regular expression syntax, Apache 2.0 includes the Perl Compatible Regular Expression library, or PCRE. All Apache 2.0 regexp evaluation now follows Perl 5 syntax.

Apache on Fedora Core

If you're used to running Red Hat 7.x, then there are some differences in the Apache packages included with your Fedora Core distribution. Since Red Hat 8.0, the package names have changed from the RPM base name of `apache-1.3...rpm`. Now, you'll find your Apache packages under the base package name of `httpd-2.0...rpm`.

In addition, Fedora Core includes a number of useful packages for web server administrators and even for those who administer mail servers. Two programs of particular interest are Webalizer, which analyzes Apache log files and generates web server access reports, and SquirrelMail, a web-based IMAP e-mail client. Check your installation disks for the appropriate packages.

Apache Configuration

For such a powerful service, Apache configuration is remarkably simple. The main configuration file, that is `httpd.conf`, controls almost all run time settings. Under Apache 2.0, most external programs are controlled by separate configuration files, which are treated as part of `httpd.conf` when the daemon is running. You can read and edit Apache configuration and log files in your favorite text editor; the files are clearly laid out, and you'll be up to speed in no time.

Configuration Files

Most Apache configuration files are stored in the `/etc/httpd/conf/` directory, including `httpd.conf`, the main Apache configuration file (see the *httpd.conf* section later in this chapter for more details). This directory also contains a number of subdirectories that are used to manage SSL transactions:

✦ `ssl.key`—Store SSL keys in this directory. Each SSL-based virtual host should get its own SSL private-key/certificate pair. That way, if a domain served by a virtual host on your network moves to a different server, it can take its certificate/key pair to the new machine.

✦ `ssl.csr`—After creating an SSL certificate request, place them in this directory. Creating CSRs requires an SSL key and a domain or website's FQDN.

✦ `ssl.crt`—This directory contains SSL certificates. A SSL certificate is the *electronic notarization* that certifies a website and company as who they say they are. You get such *cert files* from *certificate authorities* such as GeoTrust (`www.geotrust.com`) or Verisign (`www.verisign.com`) after generating an SSL key and certificate request. Each certificate requires a matching SSL key.

The `/etc/httpd/conf.d/` directory is also quite important if you're going to add dynamic content. Any files located in this directory and named with `.conf` extension are processed as if they were part of the main configuration file `/etc/httpd/conf/httpd.conf`. This is done so that when new web-related packages are installed or upgraded, they can modify their own mini-conf file and not touch `httpd.conf`. If you make changes to any files in this directory, or to the main `httpd.conf`, you must restart or reload the Apache server process.

Note   The older configuration files `srm.conf` and `access.conf`, used under Apache 1.x, are no longer part of Apache 2.0. Their functions have been incorporated into the main `httpd.conf`.

Log Files

Although Apache generates a number of log files, there are three logs of particular importance:

✦ `/var/log/httpd/access_log`—This file logs all activity connected with access to the server. File access, client access, and any other attempts to reach or obtain files from the Apache process are documented here. Reporting packages like Urchin or Webalizer usually use data from this file. However, each vhost may have its own access file in its own area.

✦ /var/log/httpd/error_log—This file logs all error messages from Apache and is the best place to look when trying to diagnose a run time problem. Most problems with website content and related files, including missing files or modules, are reported here.

✦ /var/log/messages—This is the main server log file. If you are having problems starting Apache at all, look here. For example, if there is a typo in your httpd.conf file that keeps Apache from starting, you would see related errors in this file, identified with the httpd: ID tag.

Other Files

Along with the configuration and log files, there are three other directories of interest to the Apache administrator:

✦ /var/www/html/—This is the default location for Apache's default site's directory or *document root* (where the actual web content for the main server is stored).

✦ /var/www/cgi-bin/—This is the default location for the main site's CGI files, or what's called the *script alias* directory. It is the path parallel to the document root where script and binary executables (such as perl and python) can safely reside, separate from the main HTML content.

✦ /home/httpd/—Versions of Red Hat Linux predating version 7.0 used this directory instead of /var/www/.

httpd.conf

The /etc/httpd/conf/httpd.conf file is the main Apache server configuration file. In this section, we show you the main elements of a well-managed httpd.conf. The file is divided into three general sections: global environment, main server configuration, and virtual hosts.

Global Environment

Apache's global environment configuration, or *Section 1* area, controls the way in which Apache globally interacts with the server, operating system, and network stack on the server itself. This section contains entries that affect how long the server waits before a timeout, the number of child processes and simultaneous users allowed, and so on. This section also controls which global modules are loaded and the main server IP and port bindings.

In practice, once a web server is up and running, this section of httpd.conf is rarely edited. Changes made to this part of the file are usually done during performance tuning or in response to unusual traffic or load conditions. For most users, the default values set during Fedora Core installation, shown here, are sufficient.

```
### Section 1: Global Environment

ServerTokens OS
ServerRoot "/etc/httpd"
PidFile run/httpd.pid
Timeout 300
KeepAlive Off
MaxKeepAliveRequests 100
KeepAliveTimeout 15

<IfModule prefork.c>
```

```
StartServers        8
MinSpareServers     5
MaxSpareServers     20
MaxClients          150
MaxRequestsPerChild 1000
</IfModule>

<IfModule worker.c>
StartServers         2
MaxClients          150
MinSpareThreads      25
MaxSpareThreads      75
ThreadsPerChild      25
MaxRequestsPerChild  0
</IfModule>

Listen 80

LoadModule access_module modules/mod_access.so
LoadModule auth_module modules/mod_auth.so
[...]
Include conf.d/*.conf
#ExtendedStatus On
```

Tip

The settings under the prefork block are the settings one would adjust on a stock Apache installation to adjust how many simultaneous sessions can be established. The settings shown here permit 150 simultaneous clients. The Apache "compiled in" maximum is 256. However, since the stock Fedora Core/Red Hat kernel can now handle many thousands of processes (see /proc/sys/kernel/pid_max), you can safely recompile the source RPM for Apache to increase this, then adjust MaxClients in the httpd.conf file up to around 1,024, if you think that you really need this level of server capacity. For more information on this see http://httpd.apache.org/docs/mod/core.html#maxclients. If you have enabled the "server-info" feature, you can see the current setting of Max-Clientsat the http://localhost/server-info. This feature can be found in your httpd.conf file by searching for "server-info."

With MaxClients set to 1,024 and an average session time of 20 seconds, your Apache server could potentially serve up to 4.4 million hits a day. This is far above what 98 percent of sites need. The stock 150 MaxClients setting will allow over 648,000 hits per day, which is still more than what most of us actually need.

Caution

Be very careful about making this type of web server adjustment if you have other daemons on the server that compete for process or file handler resources (especially Sendmail, PostFix, or qmail), or if you do not have lots and lots of RAM (2GB or more).

Main Server Configuration

Section 2 of httpd.conf configures the main server settings that need to be configured but are not explicitly defined within any VirtualHost block. This part of the configuration file controls the default security settings, network *access control lists* (ACLs), the default locations of files, and any other setting that pertains to system-wide defaults.

Note

Any setting defined in the Section 2 main server configuration can be overridden for a given VirtualHost block with an explicit setting within that individual virtual host.

In particular, this section can be used to set the user and group under which Apache runs; this is important, since running as the root user is a bad thing. You can also use this section to control the location of the default server's document root, language settings, browser sensitivity, and system-wide error page files. Log file formats are also determined in this section; you may want to change the level of verbosity in your logs if you are trying to diagnose a particular problem. The default settings, minus the comments, are as follows:

```
### Section 2: 'Main' server configuration
User apache
Group apache
ServerAdmin root@localhost
UseCanonicalName Off
DocumentRoot "/var/www/html"
<Directory />
    Options FollowSymLinks
    AllowOverride None
</Directory>
<Directory "/var/www/html">
    Options Indexes FollowSymLinks
    AllowOverride None
    Order allow,deny
    Allow from all
</Directory>

<IfModule mod_userdir.c>
    UserDir disable
</IfModule>

DirectoryIndex index.html index.html.var
AccessFileName .htaccess
<Files ~ "^\ .ht">
    Order allow,deny
    Deny from all
</Files>

TypesConfig /etc/mime.types
DefaultType text/plain
<IfModule mod_mime_magic.c>
    MIMEMagicFile conf/magic
</IfModule>
HostnameLookups Off
ErrorLog logs/error_log
LogLevel warn
LogFormat "%h %l %u %t \ "%r\ " %>s %b \ "%{Referer}i\ "
\ "%{User-Agent}i\ "" combined
```

```
LogFormat "%h %l %u %t \ "%r\ " %>s %b" common
LogFormat "%{Referer}i -> %U" referer
LogFormat "%{User-agent}i" agent
  CustomLog logs/access_log combined
ServerSignature On
Alias /icons/ "/var/www/icons/"
<Directory "/var/www/icons">
    Options Indexes MultiViews
    AllowOverride None
    Order allow,deny
    Allow from all
</Directory>
AliasMatch ^/manual(?:/(?:de|en|fr|ja|ko|ru))?(/.*)?$
"/var/www/manual$1"
<Directory "/var/www/manual">
    Options Indexes
    AllowOverride None
    Order allow,deny
    Allow from all
    <Files *.html>
        SetHandler type-map
    </Files>
[...]
</Directory>

<IfModule mod_dav_fs.c>
    # Location of the WebDAV lock database.
    DAVLockDB /var/lib/dav/lockdb
</IfModule>

ScriptAlias /cgi-bin/ "/var/www/cgi-bin/"

<Directory "/var/www/cgi-bin">
    AllowOverride None
    Options None
    Order allow,deny
    Allow from all
</Directory>

[...language, icons, and browser settings]

#<Location /server-status>
#    SetHandler server-status
#    Order deny,allow
#    Deny from all
#    Allow from .example.com
#</Location>
```

The settings shown in bold italic are those that you are most likely to consider changing. The DirectoryIndex directive controls the type of files that are registered with the system to serve web content. This is useful if, for example, you want to move .htm files from a Windows IIS-based web server to your Apache server. The HostnameLookups and CustomLog directives, respectively, control whether IP addresses or FQDNs are used to represent web hits in the log files and the log file format. If you plan to do web-log report analysis on commercial websites with packages such as Urchin, Webalizer, or Webtrends, you will probably need to change these settings.

The Directory Directive

The `Directory` directive is very important. This Apache directive allows you to configure the way in which directories behave with regard to user access, network ACLs, symbolic links, and other operating system and network-based elements. These settings prescribe default behavior not only for the default site (in Section 2) but also for all virtual hosts controlled by this `httpd.conf` file (in Section 3).

Apache 2.0 is more secure out of the box than previous versions were. Default settings for directory access are more secure. If you want to allow greater access than the default setting permits, you will need to use a `Directory` directive block to change the level. For example, if an `index.html` file is not found in the `DocumentRoot` of the default host or of any virtual host, Apache will no longer send a directory listing to the requesting browser. This prevents a web user from hitting a new (nonlive) website and getting a file map of that website's file system. (Note that, depending on the exact Apache configuration, it may be possible for a visitor to browse subdirectories of the default site.)

For more information on the `Directory` directive and the options it takes, see the Apache 2.0 documentation at `http://httpd.apache.org/docs-2.0/mod/core.html#directory`.

Virtual Hosts

As a web administrator, the odds are good that most of the time you spend configuring Apache will be spent modifying Section 3 of the Apache configuration file, the `VirtualHost` section. The term *virtual host* refers to the fact that it is possible to host more than one domain on a single server machine. One type of virtual hosting is *name-based hosting*, which means that web servers are identified both by IP address and by fully qualified domain name, or FQDN. The HTTP protocol (since version 1.1) on both the web server and web browser (clients) together allows name-based hosting to work. Under name-based hosting, it is theoretically possible to host an infinite number of domains under a single IP address.

The `VirtualHost` section of `/etc/httpd/conf/httpd.conf` is where you set up each virtual host website on your server. IP addresses, document roots, log file locations, and other information unique to each host are specified in a separate block for each virtual host.

Caution   When setting up virtual hosts, if you do not uncomment and use the `NameVirtualHost` directive as seen in the succeeding block of code, then all virtual hosts (virtual websites) on the server will be served their content from the first virtual host set up in this section. This is a common mistake.

The following code shows the `VirtualHost` section of `/etc/httpd/conf/httpd.conf`.:

```
### Section 3: Virtual Hosts
#
# Use name-based virtual hosting.
#
#NameVirtualHost *:80
```

```
#
# VirtualHost example:
# Almost any Apache directive may go into a VirtualHost
# container.
# The first VirtualHost section is used for requests
# without a known server name.
#
#<VirtualHost *:80>
#     ServerAdmin webmaster@dummy-host.example.com
#     DocumentRoot /www/docs/dummy-host.example.com
#     ServerName dummy-host.example.com
#     ErrorLog logs/dummy-host.example.com-error_log
#     CustomLog logs/dummy-host.example.com-access_log common
#</VirtualHost>
```

Now that you have seen the basic layout of `httpd.conf`, let's look at a sample of how to set up virtual host name-based websites in the Section 3 vhost area of the configuration file. There are ample comments to explain the settings. Note that this file configures two websites on a single IP address:

```
NameVirtualHost 10.1.1.1

<VirtualHost 10.1.1.1>
##This is all that is needed to set up a basic vhost web
##site...
DocumentRoot /home/mike/web/html
ServerName mydomain.com
##Now all that is needed is an index.html file in the
##DocumentRoot.
</VirtualHost>

<VirtualHost 10.1.1.1>
##Bob's vhost has a few more options configured, but is
##sharing the same IP
DocumentRoot /home/bob/web/html
ServerName example.com
ServerAlias www.example.com
ErrorLog /home/bob/web/logs/example.com-error_log
CustomLog /home/bob/web/logs/example.com-access_log combined
##These "combined" web logs are important if you are going to
##be doing any web log reports via something like Webtrends
##orWebalizer (the latter is included with Linux for free).
```

(Note that the `CustomLog` line is wrapped. Do not wrap it in the configuration file.)

```
<Directory /home/bob/web/html>
##This directory block will allow us to use symlinks inside
##our vhost
Options +FollowSymLinks
##As well as move out all directory options out to be
##controlled via an external .htaccess file that a common
##user can edit himself
AllowOverride All
order allow,deny
```

```
##This defines who (what hosts/IPs, etc) can do all of this.
allow from all
</Directory>
##Always remember to close your config tags...
</VirtualHost>
```

The Red Hat HTTPD GUI Config Tool

Part of Red Hat's new development strategy is to provide the user with GUI tools for all of the console and flat file configuration settings. In Red Hat 8.0, 9, EL3, and now in Fedora Core, you can see many of these tools by typing redhat- and hitting the tab key twice. This will show you all of the GUI configuration tools. The GUI config tool for Apache is called redhat-config-httpd.

Back up your httpd.conf file before playing with this GUI tool! It will overwrite your /etc/httpd/conf/httpd.conf file with the stock httpd.conf file that comes with Apache/Fedora. If you choose to use this GUI tool, then you must use ONLY this tool going forward as it will save all changes in an XML backend that you do not normally edit by hand. If you do happen to lose your configuration file after experimenting with this tool, the utility is at least smart enough that it backs up your previous file to /etc/httpd/conf/httpd.conf.bak for safe keeping.

We do not recommend using most of these GUI configuration tools under Red Hat or Fedora Core, as they are still being tested and worked on for Red Hat's Enterprise Linux offering. Some of the tools (such as in apache, SAMBA, and others) can have small quirks that can cause additional issues.

Common Apache Usage

As an alternative to using redhat-config-httpd to configure and control Apache, we recommend that you still edit the httpd.conf file by hand and use command-line instructions to control the Apache httpd service. Table 17-1 shows some common Apache management commands based on the SysV initialization scripts now common across many Linux distributions.

Table 17-1: Common Apache Commands

Command	Action
/etc/init.d/httpd start	Start the web daemon
/etc/init.d/httpd stop	Stop the web daemon
/etc/init.d/httpd restart	Stop the daemon and then start it quickly
/etc/init.d/httpd reload	Reload the configuration files (safer and faster to use if no IP binding changes have been made)
/etc/init.d/httpd status	Obtain the daemon status
/etc/init.d/httpd -help	Obtain a listing of init script options
/etc/init.d/httpd configtest	Test your Apache configuration file changes *before* reloading/restarting

These commands call daemon initialization scripts that are actually located in the `/etc/rc.d/init.d/` directory. A shortcut (symlink) to this directory is `/etc/init.d/`. As listed here, the commands are invoked with the shorthand absolute path of `/etc/init.d/httpd` instead of `/etc/rc.d/init.d/httpd`.

The `service httpd start` and `/etc/init.d/httpd start` forms are equivalent. The format you use is entirely a matter of preference, but the former is a Red Hat standard. Many administrators prefer the latter form because they're used to it and because they can use tab completion to "remember" the name of a given daemon.

Once you have configured Apache to behave in the way you prefer, added your websites, and used the `configtest` command to verify you don't have any typos, you can use the `chkconfig` command to define the run levels in which Apache (or httpd) will start (and thus at boot time also). When you first look at Apache's run level settings with `chkconfig`, you see this:

```
# chkconfig --list httpd
httpd   0:off  1:off  2:off  3:off  4:off  5:off  6:off
```

This means that `Apache/httpd` is not configured to start in any run level at boot time, including the typical default runlevels of either 3 or 5 (in Red Hat–based distros). So in short, `httpd` will not automatically come up with these settings.

To add `httpd` to all of its default run levels (in Red Hat or Fedora Core Linux), simply tell `chkconfig` to add it for you:

```
# chkconfig httpd on
```

If you check again, you'll now see `httpd` included in runlevels 2 through 5:

```
# chkconfig --list httpd
httpd   0:off 1:off  2:on   3:on   4:on   5:on   6:off
```

Or, you could have also configured it to come up at specific runlevels like this:

```
# chkconfig --level 35 httpd on
# chkconfig --list httpd
httpd   0:off  1:off  2:off  3:on   4:off  5:on   6:off
```

Now that the run levels are configured, you can start Apache and check to see that it's running:

```
# /etc/init.d/httpd status
httpd is stopped
# /etc/init.d/httpd start
Starting httpd:                                    [  OK  ]
# /etc/init.d/httpd status
httpd (pid 5653 5652 5651 5650 5649 5648 5647 5646 5643) is running...
```

Always remember to check that your production services or daemons are set up to run in the appropriate run levels. When web and e-mail administrators look to see why a service or daemon has stopped responding, or to restart said daemon, they sometimes forget to see if the daemon boot time configuration, or init script settings, are configured correctly via `chkconfig`. Even if you fix what originally crashed the daemon, you may have the same problem the next time the machine is rebooted or changes run levels if you do not verify that it is set to come back up. If you use chkconfig as shown earlier, you can be sure that the service will come up after any system state change.

Migrating from Apache 1.x to 2.0

Those readers who are accustomed to working with Apache 1.x may find the transition to Apache 2.0 somewhat confusing. While the new version is much more robust and secure, there are some changes which you'll need to know about before you start performing your habitual tasks.

One common problem for 1.x administrators involves Apache 2.0's added security. By default, Apache now displays a standardized error page when a request is made for a nonexistent page. The document root OptionIndexes is disabled, even for virtual hosts and for / (each site's own document root). This means that a new VirtualHosts entry with no index.html file will display the default error page, which looks like the old server default index.html file. While this prevents malicious users from browsing part of your web server's file system by hitting a site with no index file, it can be annoying, especially if you're trying to just set up an HTTP-based file share.

Note   When moving or migrating between Apache 1.x systems and 2.x systems, as noted earlier in this chapter, the Apache RPM *base package name* is no longer apache with 2.0. Instead, it's httpd. Use these commands to search for both package names on a newer system:

```
# rpm -qa|grep apache
# rpm -qa|grep httpd
httpd-devel-2.0.46-25.ent
httpd-2.0.46-25.ent
```

Another area for confusion is the DirectoryIndex directive. Under Apache 2.0, the default number of DirectoryIndex file types (that is, the number of web page filenames and extensions that are considered the home page for a directory) is less than what it was under 1.x. Where there used to be five to seven supported file types, the default is now only two. To change this setting, look for the following line in httpd.conf:

```
DirectoryIndex index.html index.html.var
```

If you've migrated from Apache 1.x to 2.0 and many of your old pages suddenly stop functioning, then this is probably the reason.

Note   Before you modify the DirectoryIndex defaults, check the new outsourced /etc/httpd/conf.d/ directory to see if the directory index is now being handled by an external configuration file located there. For example, PHP is now handled by /etc/httpd/conf.d/php.conf, Python by /etc/httpd/conf.d/python.conf, and so on.

Finally, when you migrate from Apache 1.x to 2.0, you should copy all your Section 3 VirtualHost blocks from the old httpd.conf file into the new httpd.conf.

Caution   Do not copy your old 1.x files into the new 2.0 directories, and do not copy/paste an entire Apache 1.3 configuration contents (Section 1 or Section 2 content) into an Apache 2.0 daemon configuration file. Doing so will break Apache, create multiple migration-related problems, and possibly even require you to wipe and reinstall Apache from scratch.

Apache 2.0 Tips and Tricks

Once you've got Apache up and and it starts running with its default settings, you can begin to tinker. Because Apache is so configurable, it's likely that any two given installations differ greatly. You will learn, through testing and experience, what settings work best for your particular web server's needs. Here are some ideas and tricks that the Internet/Linux Administrators at Rackspace have come to rely on over the years.

Testing the Configuration File

Apache allows you to test your configuration file for syntax errors, invalid commands, and other problems. It's always a good idea to do this before restarting the Apache process with a new configuration, rather than bringing up the server with a problem that may cause it to crash. Test the Apache configuration file with the -t flag to httpd:

```
# httpd -t
Syntax error on line 1205 of /etc/httpd/conf/httpd.conf:
Invalid command ':wq', perhaps mis-spelled or defined by a
module not included in the server configuration
```

In this example, you can see the :wq command not an Apache command or directive at all, but a common typing mistake from the vi text editor, which "somehow" made its way into the configuration file. (Of course, nobody reading this book has ever made such a mistake, but it never hurts to be aware of the problems that your coworkers may face.)

If you attempt to restart the service with such errors present in the configuration file, the service will refuse to start back up and all of the websites hosted on that Apache installation will go down. As any administrator knows, downtime generates phone calls and phone calls are rarely pleasant. It's so easy to test httpd.conf before bringing up Apache that it should be a regular part of your routine.

Controlling User Access

Sometimes it is preferable to let nonroot users define their own access control rules for user and host access to their sites. This can be done with the .htaccess file, which allows you to delegate control of specific per-directory access to your users. If this file is used in conjunction with an .htpassword file to contain username and hashed passwords, the website owner can fully control nonsystem username and password access into their own site. This is good for security reasons, as you never want to allow website owners access to real system accounts other than their own.

The following VirtualHost example contains a Directory directive that enables the use of this user-level .htaccess control file:

```
<VirtualHost 10.1.1.1>
...
<Directory /home/bob/web/html/private-dir/>
```

```
AllowOverride All
      order allow,deny
      allow from all
</Directory>
...
</VirtualHost>
```

Tip

The `allow from all` line can be used to lock access down this `Directory` level directive to particular IP addresses or ranges. If you are especially concerned about security, this is a useful tool.

In this instance, you will need files named `.htaccess` (for delegated access control) and `.htpasswd` (to house nonsystem username/passwords). These files, working together, will create password protection for the `/home/bob/html/private-dir/` directory. For this to work, the `.htaccess` file should be placed in the directory defined in the `Directory` directive as shown earlier. To enable password protection, you must insert the following directives into the site owner's `.htaccess` file:

```
order allow,deny
allow from all
require valid-user
AuthName "My Directory Name"
AuthType Basic
AuthUserFile /home/bob/web/.htpasswd
```

Note

Note that the final line of `.htaccess` points to the `.htpasswd` file, and that it is in a secure directory that is not accessible from the website's document root. This is an important security setting.

Now you, or the website owner, must create the user/password file `/home/bob/web/.htpasswd`. Do so with the `htpasswd` command and the `-c` (create) flag the first time you do this:

```
$ cd /home/bob/web/
$ htpasswd -c .htpasswd bob
New password: <type password once>
Re-type new password: <type password again>
Adding password for user bob
```

If you want to add additional users to the file, use `htpasswd` without the flag:

```
$ htpasswd .htpasswd mike
New password:
Re-type new password:
Adding password for user mike
```

Once some users have been added to the file, the contents of `.htpasswd` will look something like this:

```
$ cat /home/bob/web/.htpasswd
bob:B2pw3uEPLrHO6
mike:HrwaYn6BZDSAQ
guest:zjsOB1XCVoa7U
```

Note each user has his or her own username entry and hashed password.

The `.htaccess` **and** `.htpasswd` **files should be set with permissions 755, or** `rwxr-xr-x`**. You do this on the example file with the command** `chmod 755 /home/bob/web/.htpasswd/home/bob/web/html/private-dir/.htaccess`**.**

It is always safer to place the `.htpasswd` file on the server somewhere outside the virtual host's own web space. Then, if a deviant websurfer gets into the file content of the website, there is no password file in a compromised location. As long as you define `.htpasswd`'s location properly in `.htaccess`, its location is not an issue to Apache.

By default, Apache does not authenticate against any of the main system authentication files such as `/etc/passwd` **or** `/etc/shadow`**. This is good security practice, as access to these files should be limited as much as possible. However, if your system has particular need to authenticate in this way, Apache modules like Radius or LDAP can be configured to work with other forms of centralized and centrally monitored login access.**

Restarting versus Reloading Apache

Earlier, in the *Apache Configuration* section we mentioned that it is necessary to restart Apache after you make configuration changes. There are two common init script methods of doing this: `restart` and `reload`. The difference is that `restart` is more like a reboot of the Apache daemon itself. The `restart` command gracefully stops all Apache processes, reloads the configuration file, and restarts the daemon. This can cause up to several seconds of downtime on large websites, so it is not recommended unless absolutely necessary. The `reload` command, however, merely asks Apache to reparse and reload the Apache daemon, using the new parameters in the configuration file. It is almost always faster than restarting and causes no downtime of the Apache daemon.

The `restart` command is a more complete method of implementing changes to websites after a configuration file change. However, it takes longer and will create some downtime for sites hosted on that machine, as well as possibly lose client session data. Unless you're changing IP or port bindings, the `reload` command is probably sufficient and will cause least inconvenience to your users. It will also warn you if there is a typo in the configuration file, such as the `:wq` that we saw when we tested our `httpd.conf` file previously.

Here's what the syntax and output of these commands look like on Red Hat and Fedora Core based systems:

```
# service httpd restart
Stopping httpd:                          [  OK  ]
Starting httpd:                          [  OK  ]
```

or

```
# service httpd reload
Reloading httpd:                         [  OK  ]
```

For non-Red Hat based systems try `/etc/init.d/httpd reload` **or** `restart`**.**

Again, if you get a [FAILED] reply and don't get a message to your console, then check the system log file /var/log/messages for an httpd:-related error.

Listing Virtual Host Settings

If you run a number of virtual hosts on one machine, you may need to see a complete listing of those hosts on a regular basis. An easy way to get such a vhost listing is to use the -S flag to the httpd daemon.

```
# httpd -S
VirtualHost configuration:
10.1.1.1:*            is a NameVirtualHost
        default server mydomain.com (/etc/httpd/conf/httpd.conf:1057)
        port * namevhost mydomain.com (/etc/httpd/conf/httpd.conf:1057)
        port * namevhost example.com.com (/etc/httpd/conf/httpd.conf:1062)
wildcard NameVirtualHosts and _default_ servers:
_default_:443        localhost.localdomain
(/etc/httpd/conf.d/ssl.conf:99)
Syntax OK
```

Note

Commands like httpd -S or httpd -t are quite different from other Apache commands, such as /etc/init.d/httpd configtest. With the former, you're actually calling the Apache binary daemon (/usr/sbin/httpd in most cases; the latter simply calls a SysV init script that takes in options like configtest, restart, and reload and then calls the binary on your behalf. Partly the reason for system initialization scripts is to standardize the location, method, and syntax of system startup scripts. However, sometimes you still need to call the daemon binary directly.

Listing Apache Compile-Time Options

If you did not compile the Apache binary yourself, or you need a listing of the compiled-in modules, you can use the httpd binary to list such modules. Do so with the -l flag, as follows:

```
# httpd -l
core.c
prefork.c
http_core.c
mod_so.c
```

If you need more information, such as the compile time options and settings use the -V flag. With this flag, you'll see more data about the flags used at compilation, along with other relevant and useful information:

```
# httpd -V
Server version: Apache/2.0.47
Server built:   Oct 23 2003 06:48:44
Server's Module Magic Number: 20020903:4
Architecture:   32-bit
Server compiled with....
-D APACHE_MPM_DIR="server/mpm/prefork"
-D APR_HAS_SENDFILE
-D APR_HAS_MMAP
```

```
-D APR_HAVE_IPV6 (IPv4-mapped addresses enabled)
-D APR_USE_SYSVSEM_SERIALIZE
-D APR_USE_PTHREAD_SERIALIZE
-D SINGLE_LISTEN_UNSERIALIZED_ACCEPT
-D APR_HAS_OTHER_CHILD
-D AP_HAVE_RELIABLE_PIPED_LOGS
-D HTTPD_ROOT="/etc/httpd"
-D SUEXEC_BIN="/usr/sbin/suexec"
-D DEFAULT_PIDLOG="logs/httpd.pid"
-D DEFAULT_SCOREBOARD="logs/apache_runtime_status"
-D DEFAULT_LOCKFILE="logs/accept.lock"
-D DEFAULT_ERRORLOG="logs/error_log"
-D AP_TYPES_CONFIG_FILE="conf/mime.types"
-D SERVER_CONFIG_FILE="conf/httpd.conf"
```

Advanced Apache administrators should be aware of the two options highlighted in the preceding code: the MPM compile time setting (for multiprocessing module support) and the all-important SUEXEC_BIN compile time path. For the MPM setting, also check the output of httpd -l, as it shows that the prefork.c MPM support is compiled in. This is the default behavior on most distributions that include Apache. The suexec binary is the package that allows certain CGI-based systems to run securely. Server Appliance control panels such as Plesk modify this with their own version of suexec.

Tip   Two other useful system commands can be used to find the number of current Apache connections and the number of running Apache processes. To get the number of connections, issue this command:

```
# netstat -an | grep [:]80 | wc -l
```

To see the number of running Apache processes, issue the following command:

```
# ps auxw | grep [h]pptd | wc -l
```

Fedora Core and suexec

By default, the Fedora Core compilation of suexec allows executions only in the /var/www and /../ directories. This affects web-based CGI scripts. As the suexec man page states, "suexec is used by the Apache HTTP Server to switch to another user before executing CGI programs. In order to achieve this, it must run as root. Since the HTTP daemon normally doesn't run as root, the suexec executable needs the setuid bit set and must be owned by root. It should never be writable for any other person than root."

This means that, by default, CGIs on your virtual hosts must either be located in a subdirectory of /var/www/, as in /var/www/cgi/, or in a directory outside the web content calling the CGI, as in /../cgi/. This is a security setting. Do not try to get around this limitation, for your own sake and for the sake of your users, unless you know exactly what you're doing.

Defining Web Directory Permissions

One of the most common mistakes made in defining new virtual hosts involves file system permissions. If you don't set the content directory and file permissions correctly, then Apache can't see the web content stored in that vhost's document root web directory, and thus the content cannot be seen from the web. You'll know you have this problem if you see an error, like the following one, in your browser:

```
Forbidden
You don't have permission to access / on this server.
Additionally, a 403 Forbidden error was encountered while
trying to use an ErrorDocument to handle the request.

Apache/2.0.47 (Fedora) Server at mydomain.com Port 80
```

If you look at the home directory permissions for the user whose site is having trouble, you can see the reason for this error (shown in the bold italics):

```
# ls -la /home
total 24
drwxr-xr-x    6 root     root      4096 Jan 1 16:41 .
drwxr-xr-x   21 root     root      4096 Jan 1 16:05 ..
drwx------    4 bob      bob       4096 Jan 1 16:42 bob
drwx------    4 mike     mike      4096 Jan 1 16:42 mike
```

The user bob's home directory is locked down tight, with permissions of 700 or owner=rwx group= world=. This means that the owner, bob, has full read/write/execute permissions, but people in the group bob have no access to his files, and the rest of the world—including the apache user and group—also have no access. Without access, the files can't be seen by Apache/httpd service, and the error occurs.

The chgrp Solution

There are a few ways to fix this problem. An old school solution and first impulse might be to recursively make the apache group the default group of bob's home directory. Doing so would look like this:

```
# chgrp apache /home/bob
# chgrp -R apache /home/bob/web
# chmod 2775 /home/bob/web/html    <--"SGID" bit for group dirs
```

Then, you can relax the group permissions on /home/bob/ a bit so that Apache can get to the web content when it's requested:

```
# chmod 750 /home/bob
```

This yields the permissions owner=rwx group=r-x world=, and with the user apache being the group, the Apache/httpd can now see and serve this user's web content.

With these settings in place, the output of ls -la should now look like this:

```
# ls -la /home/
total 24
drwxr-xr-x    6 root     root      4096 Jan 1 16:41 .
drwxr-xr-x   21 root     root      4096 Jan 1 16:05 ..
drwxr-x---    4 bob      apache    4096 Jan 1 16:42 bob
drwx------    4 mike     mike      4096 Jan 1 16:42 mike
```

This is much better, at least from Apache's point of view. Any web content in this directory should now be available. However, this isn't the best solution to the file permissions problem since it involves changing the user bob's reliance upon his *User Private Group*, which may affect other non-web system functions on Red Hat–based systems.

Caution

Changing a user's User Private Group (UPG) violates several best-practice standards on Red Hat– and Fedora Core–based systems. It is advised that you not use the methodology outlined here unless you are running a non-UPG based system (like SuSE) or have first examined the feasibility of other methods (outlined in the following sections). You can tell which system you're using since a stock non-UPG system will usually have its group ownership set to something like "users" instead of the username (for UPG-based systems).

The Relaxed Permissions Solution

Another option (mainly for non-Red Hat/Fedora Core-based systems) is simply to open up world executable (*group=* $--x$ or 701) access to `bob`'s directory. Remember, the execute permission on a directory allows users (or web visitors in the case of our example) to only traverse a directory. If you leave world Read access turned off but eXecute turned on, then visitors can't get to files unless they know exactly where they are and what they are called. The layout of `bob`'s home directory remains secret, but Apache can get in to obtain requested files because it knows it needs to serve the content form `/home/bob/web/html/`. Use `chmod` to set these directory permissions:

```
# chmod 701 /home/bob
# ls -la /home/bob
total 40
drwx-----x   4 bob      bob         4096 Jan 1 16:42 .
drwxr-xr-x   6 root     root        4096 Jan 1 16:41 ..
-rw-------   1 bob      bob           84 Jan 1 16:44
.bash_history
-rw-r--r--   1 bob      bob           24 Jan 1 16:41 .bash_logout
-rw-r--r--   1 bob,     bob          191 Jan 1 16:41
.bash_profile
-rw-r--r--   1 bob      bob          124 Jan 1 16:41 .bashrc
-rw-r--r--   1 bob      bob          237 Jan 1 16:41 .emacs
-rw-r--r--   1 bob      bob          120 Jan 1 16:41 .gtkrc
drwxr-xr-x   3 bob      bob         4096 Jan 1 16:41 .kde
drwxrwxr-x   4 bob      bob         4096 Jan 1 16:41 web
```

Now, the user `apache` (or any user who knows the directory structure) should be able to get into `bob`'s home directory. However, no user will be able to get a directory listing (read) or modify (write) any files. But since Apache knows that it is going directly to `/home/bob/web/html/`, it has full read/write access in `web`, and it can get into the top `/home/bob/` directory to reach those directories (which are all already opened up to `rwxrwxr-x`), there should be no trouble accessing the web content now.

To test this, put a sample `index.html` file in place and check it. For purposes of speed, you can use the simple text web browser `links` or `lynx` (no use firing up a GUI browser for this test):

```
# echo "This is Bob's Web Site"
>/home/bob/web/html/index.html
# links --dump http://example.com
   This is Bob's Web Site
```

Problem solved—and in a much better way than it could have been by recursively changing all of the user's group and permission settings simply to fix an Apache problem.

One caveat of this approach is that it does create somewhat less secure environment. Such a method is often jokingly referred to as *Security Through Obscurity* (which implies that such a system is not secure at all, but just well-hidden). This is not something you want to implement if user home directory security is important to you. Instead, look into the next solution, especially if you're running Red Hat–, Fedora Core–, or Debian-based systems.

The User Private Groups Solution

Red Hat–based distributions use a user ID (UID) and group ID (GID) allocation scheme called *User Private Groups* (UPG). One of the features of this standardized methodology is that users get their own group with the same name as their username. One nice thing about this system is that you can put users in another user's group, such as putting mike in bob's group. bob can then control what the people in his group can access by adjusting his own home directory and subdirectory permissions. The alternatives to UPG, shown in the preceding sections, are far more messy from an administrative perspective, especially when multiple people want to share the same files.

To implement UPG for our Apache user example, we can simply place the user apache into bob's user private group (instead of changing the group /home/bob/ altogether, or changing permissions to 701). Do this with the following command:

```
# usermod -G bob apache
```

After doing this, verify that apache is in the bob group with one of these commands:

```
# cat /etc/group|grep bob:
bob:x:502:mike apache
#
# groups apache
apache : apache bob
```

Now you can see that the apache user is in bob's group (as is mike). The first method looks for the bob group in the system's group file /etc/group and displays the GID and users in the group bob. The second method, using the groups command, shows to the groups to which the user apache belongs.

> **Tip**
> Normally, you could use the Red Hat GUI tool redhat-config-users to carry out this change; however, this tool is for *real people* user accounts only (that is, UIDs starting at 500, like adding mike to bob's group) and is not currently able to allow modification of system accounts (like apache).

Can you see why this is the preferred methodology? Let's look at what this does for us. Here are the old hacked up permissions from the "security through obscurity" method:

```
# ls -la /home/
total 24
drwxr-xr-x    6 root     root       4096 Jan  1 16:41 .
drwxr-xr-x   22 root     root       4096 Apr  7 20:20 ..
drwx-----x   18 bob      bob        4096 Mar 18 12:40 bob
drwx------    5 mike     mike       4096 Jan 11 14:26 mike
```

Now try the convenience of UPGs by changing the group permissions of /home/bob/ back to what they should be:

```
# chmod 750 /home/bob/
# ls -la /home/
total 24
drwxr-xr-x    6 root     root       4096 Jan  1 16:41 .
```

```
drwxr-xr-x   22 root     root      4096 Apr  7 20:20 ..
drwxr-x---   18 bob      bob       4096 Mar 18 12:40 bob
drwx------    5 mike     mike      4096 Jan 11 14:26 mike
```

Now no one can even peek or get into bob's home directory without being given explicit permission (by being put in his UPG), creating a much more secure and user-controllable environment. Since the apache user has been added to bob's UPG, bob can serve web content out of his secured home directory as well as allow his group members to get in with read-only access, while keeping his content locked down from all other users. We now have the best security arrangement this side of file system-level ACLs.

To finish this exercise, you may have to restart Apache, and then use links again to test it:

```
# ls -lad /home/bob/
drwxrwx---   18 bob     bob       4096 Mar 18 12:40 /home/bob/
# /etc/init.d/httpd restart
Stopping httpd:                                     [  OK  ]
Starting httpd:                                     [  OK  ]
# links --dump http://example.com
                          This is Bob's Web Site
```

Now you're good to go.

Tweaking Apache for Higher Loads

The number of simultaneous connections allowed to Apache is defined by the MaxClients directive. By default, Apache on Fedora Core has a compile-time MaxClients hard limit of 256. However, some high-volume sites may need more simultaneous connections than this. To achieve simultaneous connections of more than 256, you must recompile Apache with special options.

Note   On heavily used web servers, professional web administrators at Rackspace often help customers set MaxClients to 1,024 or even 2,048. However, even the most high-volume web servers rarely see more than 1,500 simultaneous sessions. Note that 1,500 simultaneous sessions, with a 2 minute average session time, would yield over one million sessions per day! That's a busy web server indeed.

Even if you leave MaxClients set at 256 and expect a 2 minute average session time you still have a maximum sessions capacity of 176,000 sessions per day. Remember that content type greatly affects the average session duration, and thus affects the capacity of your server due to its simultaneous session limit. This setting is dictated by your content type. If you offer only text files or file downloads, your session duration will typically be much shorter than if you host an online bank, stock brokerage, or interactive forums, where your average session time may be up to 30 minutes. This is why there are so many administrator-adjustable variables in httpd.conf. Remember, before you make such adjustments, you need to have a good feel for how your customers behave in relation to your web content.

Tip   Ever wondered how the real webspace pros actively develop, monitor, and tweak their website content and server settings? Getting a feel for your average *client session time*, *entry* and *exit pages*, and *referring sites* can be tough if you've never tried to get your mind around these numbers before. Making content changes (banner ads, catalog entry points, and so on) and server adjustments (such as MaxClients, Timeout, and KeepAlive) without knowing this critical information is like taking potshots in the dark. Web log reporting suites such as Urchin, Webalizer, and Webtrends can help you make such determinations. On the basis this information you can make informed content and server changes and measure the results of your changes.

Server Loads and Hardware Requirements

The more sessions your sites generate per day, the more simultaneous daemon processes are required. In turn, daemon processes require RAM. If you don't have enough RAM, your server dips into *swap space*—the temporary overflow storage space for RAM on the hard drive. When a server must "dip into swap," the overall machine speed drops dramatically as the hard drive's speed is usually an order of magnitude slower than the RAM's native speed. In short, if you want a fast web server, always add RAM before adding processor speed. If you serve only static content, the overall machine performance of even a simple Fedora Core/Apache 1GHz server with only 256 or 512 MB of RAM and a 100 Mbps network connection can surprise you with its speed.

Dual-processor machines are rarely required for web servers unless the hosted sites require a lot of processor-intensive *dynamic content* operations, such as those found on a LAMP installation (Linux, Apache, MySQL, and PHP). While vast amounts of RAM are key for static-only content sessions, those who work with database access and dynamic content should do some system load testing, and based on the results consider upgrading to multiprocessor systems.

Tip If you think you might eventually provide PostgreSQL, MySQL, Oracle, or other database access to your users, or you plan to move toward dynamic content based on Perl, Python, or PHP, you should consider future hardware purchases in that light. Even if you're serving only static content right now, go ahead and purchase or lease a multiprocessor-capable or *SM-* based system. Just don't fully populate all the processors and RAM if initial cost is an issue. In this way, you'll have an *in place* upgrade option in place to serve for your future growth, but won't take a huge hit to your bank account. Another natural benefit of this strategy is that SMP-based systems usually also have higher quality server grade components, as well as more RAM expansion options.

SCSI versus ATA

Setting up an Apache or FTP-based file share? Planning on running streaming multimedia web content? When the question of new hardware comes up, you may find yourself in an age-old discussion: Which is better—SCSI or ATA/IDE? The general wisdom holds that SCSI is faster because of the dedicated processing power of controllers on both the hard drive and the SCSI card, and the built-in speed advantages of command queuing, but that the cost of this speed is often prohibitive.

Not necessarily the case! That is, SCSI hardware is still expensive, but it's not always faster than ATA/IDE hardware any more. Now that ATA drives use Ultra-DMA bus transfers and 33/66/133 MHz instead of the old Processor I/O mode—and can do so without tying up other system buses

Continued

Continued

or the processor itself—most UDMA-ATA systems can now match all but the highest-end SCSI and SCSI/RAID systems. Combined with the newer multibus ATA RAID cards (see www.3ware.com) and newer Serial-ATA hardware the ATA/SATA is quickly becoming the preferred high-speed low-cost solution. In some high-speed server configurations, Rackspace has actually achieved higher overall Linux application speed on a server-grade ATA/UDMA-based system than identically configured servers running on SCSI. In addition, with the newer SATA II specification drives with command queuing, this hardware platform is positioned to compete directly with high-end SCSI systems and outpace them in raw throughput by 2005, while undercutting the price of comparably configured SCSI-based systems.

Bottom line: cost isn't everything. Check the performance ratings for all the hardware that suits your needs. You may be surprised!

Benchmarking

If you're interested in web server performance tuning, you will need a way to track the effects of changes you make to the server daemon as well as your content. Apache provides its own benchmarking tool, called ab or Apache Benchmark. It's quite easy to use.

Tip

Unless you're just stress testing your hardware, use Apache Benchmark remotely to get "total throughput" testing. This way you'll be able to identify not only hardware/configuration limitations, but also bottlenecks in your network and provider connectivity issues as well. Whether you test an intranet server from a client on your LAN or an Internet server from a remote client located across the Internet, strive for system testing that simulates real-world hardware and infrastructure load testing as much as possible.

In the following sample session we invoke Apache Benchmark to test a web server across the network from a local Linux machine's command line:

```
# ab -d -t 10   http://www.example.com/
```

The -d flag tells Apache Benchmark to deliver less verbose output. The -t flag, combined with the number 10, tells the program to test the server (pull down as many pages as it can) for 10 seconds. The last option is the URL of the site to be tested, and it gives the following output:

```
This is ApacheBench, Version 1.3d <$Revision: 1.67 $> apache-1.3
Copyright (c) 1996 Adam Twiss, Zeus Technology Ltd, http://www.zeustech.net/
Copyright (c) 1998-2002 The Apache Software Foundation, http://www.apache.org/

Benchmarking www.example.com (be patient)
Finished 3150 requests
Server Software:        Apache/2.0.46
Server Hostname:        www.example.com
Server Port:            80

Document Path:          /
Document Length:        35 bytes
```

```
Concurrency Level:        1
Time taken for tests:     10.000 seconds
Complete requests:        3150
Failed requests:          0
Broken pipe errors:       0
Total transferred:        942149 bytes
HTML transferred:         110285 bytes
Requests per second:      315.00 [#/sec] (mean)
Time per request:         3.17 [ms] (mean)
Time per request:         3.17 [ms] (mean, across all concurrent requests)
Transfer rate:            94.21 [Kbytes/sec] received

Connnection Times (ms)
              min   mean[+/-sd] median    max
Connect:       0     0    0.0      0       0
Processing:    2     2    4.4      2      135
Waiting:       2     2    4.3      2      134
Total:         2     2    4.4      2      135
```

The output, by default, is printed to the local terminal. However, there's a better way to do this. Tell ab to run its test and format the output in HTML with the -w flag and then scp the results back to the web server being tested:

```
# ab -d -t 10 -w http://www.example.com/ >x
# scp x bob@example.com:/home/bob/web/html/test-output.html
Finished 3464 requests
bob@es.playground.crudnet.org's password:
x         100% | ****************************|    2189
00:00
```

Now, you can share the results with anyone who's interested by sending them to http://www.example.com/test-output.html:

```
...
    Requests per second:    348.47
...
```

Although these results are impressive, remember that your results will vary a great deal depending on the site's location in the network, network congestion, routing, server load levels, entry page size, static or dynamic content, and all the other variables that can affect web servers. The important thing is to use this tool for baseline data. It can help you identify misconfigurations, and give you something to work against for future comparisons.

After you get a baseline, you can use the information to adjust your server performance. Some changes are easier than others, such as adjusting the settings for MaxClients and SpareServers in httpd.conf.

In other cases, you may need such testing results to encourage your site and content designers to minimize the entry page size, including image size, or make other changes to site content.

Note   At the time we wrote this book, Fedora Core 1 CDs shipped with the Apache package httpd-2.0.47-10, which included the ab version 2.0.40-dev. This developmental version may not work properly for you. If this is the case and you have not run up2date yet, do so and the replacement version of httpd-2.0.48-1.2 should fix the problem for you. This can be done from the command line by running `up2date httpd` to upgrade and fix just Apache/ab, or `up2date` to update the whole system.

Using server-status to track performance

Apache Benchmark is good as an external testing, website hammering, baselining and bottleneck testing tool. However, if benchmarking doesn't give you all the information you need about the inner workings of the httpd service itself, consider using the `server-status` module (or `mod_status.so`) that comes with Apache. This will show you what's going on inside Apache. It will show you how many httpd processes are running, your CPU usage, httpd server uptime, traffic levels, and other useful server side information. To set up `server-status`, uncomment the following line in `httpd.conf`:

```
ExtendedStatus On
```

You must also uncomment this section of `httpd.conf`:

```
<Location /server-status>
    SetHandler server-status
    Order deny,allow
    Deny from all
    Allow from 192.168.127.
</Location>
```

Be sure to enter your IP or network address in the next-to-last line. Then only those IP addresses or networks will be able to access data from server-status. Now, restart the Apache daemon with the `/etc/init.d/httpd restart` command. When it restarts, you can open this URL in your browser:

```
http://example.com/server-status?refresh
```

This server-status page will show you real-time data about your server, autorefreshed regularly. By using this page, combined with occasional stress testing and baselining using Apache Benchmark, and making small adjustments to settings in `httpd.conf` and your website content, you will be well on your way to having a real understanding of what's going on with your web server. You'll have a working knowledge of what *your* server's bottlenecks are, and most importantly, will be able to react to and customize your Apache server when the need arises.

Tip   The autorefresh setting may cause some artificial inflation to your `server-status` output. If you just want to call up data as you need it, rather than running `server-status` constantly, issue the URL without the `?refresh` component.

Apache Troubleshooting

Just as there are many ways to configure Apache, there are many ways in which things can go wrong. Luckily, most errors fall into a few basic categories. Here are some of the common problems that Rackspace sees with some of our own customers' controlled Apache servers, along with simple solutions that will get you backup in no time:

✦ *Permission errors when viewing a user's site*—Permissions are set incorrectly on the public web directory. You can either change the web directory's group to the `apache` group or define the directory so that it is world executable. If on a Red Hat, Fedora, or

Debian system, you can use UPGs to allow the user `apache` into the site owner's web content. See the *File Permissions* section earlier in the chapter for more information.

✦ *Can't access* `www.example.com`—If you can get web files at `http://example.com` but not at `www.example.com`, then you have the wrong or missing `ServerAlias` setting for that virtual host. The correct block of code should be as follows:

```
<VirtualHost 10.1.1.1>
    DocumentRoot /home/bob/web/html/
    ServerName example.com
    ServerAlias www.example.com
</VirtualHost>
```

✦ *Apache won't start or generates run time errors*—If httpd is not starting correctly, you may have mistakes in the `httpd.conf` file that prevent the Apache process from starting properly. Check `/var/log/messages` with the command `grep httpd: /var/log/messages` to see if the problem can be easily tracked down (these messages are also echoed to the console). If Apache starts but you continue to get run time errors such as broken graphic images or inoperative links, then the run time errors will be logged to `/var/log/httpd/error_log`. Use `tail` to watch this log file in real time as you use a web browser to generate the errors:

```
# tail -f /var/log/httpd/error_log
```

✦ *DNS problems*—At least 50 percent of the time, new and migrating website problems are DNS related. Be sure you check DNS from the top of the DNS namespace to down. Use the `whois` command to discover who owns and does DNS for a given domain: `whois example.com | grep -iA3 "server"`. After you know the authoritative DNS server(s), query it directly for the FQDN or URL you're interested in: `dig www.example.com @the.nameserver.com`. Make sure that there are valid CNAME records (aliases) or A records (IPs) for each of the URLs defined by a virtual host's `ServerName` and `ServerAlias` directives.

✦ *A new virtual site doesn't work*—Jorge Arrieta, a Server Administrator and RHCE at Rackspace, has found that if you've configured a new virtual host but can't pull up the site in a browser, there are several possible causes. First, restart the server if you did not do so after adding the new host. Also, make sure that the httpd service is configured to have back up after reboots (via `chkconfig`). Next, make sure that the DNS record points to the appropriate IP address, remembering that any DNS changes may take some time to propagate. If DNS looks good, issue the command

```
# httpd -S
```

to parse `httpd.conf` and list the configured `VirtualHost` entries. If the new virtual host is not listed, then it is not configured correctly and you will have to correct the configuration or look through `/var/log/messages` for related errors.

Apache Resources

Because Apache is the most popular web server on the market, you will find help and insight around every corner. Be sure to check when the information that you are looking at was written and which version of Apache it assumes. It may be addressing issues with either version 1.3 or 2.0. Table 17-2 contains URLs for basic Apache resources. There are also a number of mailing lists and websites that contain individual users' and administrators' Apache experiences, which might help solve a particular problem on your own installation.

Table 17-2: Useful Apache Resources

Resource	Web Address
General Apache documentation	`http://httpd.apache.org/docs-2.0` `http://localhost/manual/`
Apache 2.0 features	`http://httpd.apache.org/docs-2.0/new_features_2_0.html`
Apache changelog	`http://images.buy-here.com/Apache_Group/Apache2/CHANGES/txt`
Apache Benchmark bug discussion	`www.mail-archive.com/dev@httpd.apache.org/msg18013.html`
Threading bug discussion	`http://bugzilla.redhat.com/bugzilla/show_bug.cgi?id=98979` `https://rhn.redhat.com/errata/RHSA-2003-320.html`
Maximizing MaxSessions	`http://info.ccone.at/INFO/Mail-Archives/redhat/Dec-2002/msg00157.html`
Apache MPM (multiprocessing module)	`http://httpd.apache.org/docs-2.0/mpm.html` `www.edoceo.com/liberum/?doc=apache-mpm`
SSL over Apache 2.0	`www.redhat.com/docs/manuals/linux/RHL-9-Manual/custom-guide/ch-httpd-secure-server.html` `http://localhost/manual/ssl`

Summary

When you choose to install and run the Apache web server, you have selected the most popular web server in the world. Apache is robust, highly configurable and, because it's Open Source and evolves so quickly, it is also one of the most mature and secure web servers available. You can run Apache to serve a single site or to serve thousands of virtual hosts, all from a single server. Apache works seamlessly with modern dynamic content tools such as PHP/Python and LAMP, and its open-ended nature allows it to be easily tweaked to provide maximum performance for your environment. If you have specific web server capacity requirements, Apache comes with included tools both for stress testing the system as a whole and for monitoring the innards of the daemon itself. Should you run into a problem with your Apache installation, the source of the trouble is usually fairly simple to locate or is spelled out clearly in the log files. In addition, the Apache administrative community has shared a number of helpful hints on websites and in e-mail archives, so you can find an answer quickly and get your sites back online in short order.

✦   ✦   ✦

File Transfer Troubleshooting

There are many ways to get a file from Machine A to Machine B, ranging from good old-fashioned floppy disks to modern secure protocols that involve multiple authentication levels and specialized clients. Your choice depends on your environment, security needs, and user requirements. In this chapter, we focus on several network file transfer methods that are included in the Fedora Core distribution: FTP, SCP/SFTP/SSH, and WebDAV.

In the old days, files moved across networks through File Transfer Protocol, or FTP. Because security was not of particular concern in the days of trusted networks, FTP is a *clear text protocol*. Neither the file transfer nor any login authentication is encrypted. Clear text transfer methods are rapidly being replaced by *encrypted text protocols*, which scramble the transferring data as it passes across insecure network connections. A number of encrypted FTPs have been developed to replace FTP, such as SecureFTP (sftp) and SecureCopy (both based on SSH), FTP-SSL, and WebDAV over SSL.

Note   Though this is a Linux book, this chapter contains some information about Microsoft FrontPage. Most Linux administrators consider FrontPage to be unstable, insecure, and broken, but we often have to administer it anyway. See the *File Transfer Resource* section at the end of the chapter for some help if you find yourself forced into this situation.

Which File Transfer Method To Use?

Since Fedora Core offers you several ways to move files around your network and from system to system, you will need to pick the method best suited to your environment and the task at hand. To make this decision, you'll need to determine the kinds of files your users move regularly, how your users and fellow administrators prefer to work, and what kind of security your environment requires.

FTP

We begin with FTP, because it is the most common file transfer method on the planet. Everyone has access to it, and most users are familiar with it. Unfortunately, FTP is also one of the most insecure services available, and it's annoying to administer in a security conscious environment, especially with client-side firewalls. Still, you should know the FTP basics even if you choose to run a more secure protocol.

In this chapter, we cover configuration and basic administration for vsftpd, the FTP daemon included with Fedora Core. We describe common clients, and offer some hints on keeping it as secure as you can. Though the protocol itself is insecure, the current version of vsftpd has some security enhancements that make it the lesser evil if you must run this dangerous legacy protocol.

scp and sftp

For general system-wide file transfers, OpenSSH's scp and sftp client programs, for the sshd server-side service, can't be beat. They are fully encrypted, run over a single port (22) that is easy to configure for firewalls, and permit you to read or write files anywhere on the system. For users, file transfer based on SSH's scp and sftp offers a number of options, including command line and graphical user interface (GUI) clients.

The OpenSSH protocol suite includes scp, a secure replacement for the old rcp (remote copy) command. sftp, as the name implies, is a secure FTP subsystem of the sshd daemon. Both are fully integrated with Fedora Core's GUI environment. If you allow trusted client systems, such as administrative desktop, access to your systems, then you can use these tools together with *key-based authentication*. Key-based authentication allows you to have a login-free GUI environment and enjoy remote browser-style access to SSH resources.

Caution   Whenever you implement key-based authentication, or any other form of password-free authentication, you effectively remove the need for a username/password login and its associated security. Some workplaces may frown on this security compromise, or even ban it outright. Before you enable such a feature, be sure it's okay for you to do so.

SSH-based logins and file transfers via scp and sftp offer great flexibility. With scp, users can transfer files to any part of the system where they have existing privileges. They use the ordinary system accounts and passwords, plus server public/private keys, to authenticate their presence, and the existing file system security, such as permissions and group settings, remains in place.

However, scp's system user flexibility can be a disadvantage. The user needs to exist on your system, with a real username and password. You may not want to enable everyone who needs your files, with such privileges. You must also grant valid login shell access to anyone who uses scp on your system, including a /bin/bash setting in the /etc/password file. Therefore, scp-based file transfer mechanisms are usually best suited for trusted users and administrators, rather than for random people who might want a publicly available file from one of your machines. That said, scp *is* a command-line utility, so it is probably more suited to "power users" than your average desktop user. (For a browser-based tool see the *User Clients* section later, which describes Konqueror. This KDE tool supports scp- aware URLs, and there's even a Windows-based client.) This makes scp a snap for users of any ability.

The sftp client also uses the SSH daemon sshd with the sftp-server subservice. It also requires a user shell login. This would be a good overall solution, but the client sftp is neither user friendly nor feature rich. With that warning, you may still prefer sftp to other pure FTP client/server options if your users prefer the traditional interface. Like its cousin scp, sftp can also be used in GUI mode through KDE's Konqueror.

Remember that SSH, `scp`, and `sftp` access have the same security risks as local login access unless you use a shell replacement such as `scponly` (see *Using SCP* section later in this chapter).

WebDAV

Don't have root privileges? Can't create new users and change their passwords? Just trying to grant access to web users who want to publish content? What to do? FTP's not a real solution. Perhaps WebDAV is the solution for you. WebDAV is a flexible client/server protocol that offers file access without requiring you to give actual system user access to remote clients. It even offers version tracking and file locking so that groups of users can work on the same files.

The advantage of WebDAV is that you don't need to investigate external users and add them to the system. WebDAV is an Apache module that uses Apache-based web users, and which, when fully configured and enabled, allows web-based read/write access to files on your system—even with secure SSL, when configured properly. When you run WebDAV with Apache, it will use the standard security settings that you defined for Apache and atop the file system's own security permissions. Users see only the files for which you give them web logins to see. Additionally, since they're restricted to the system account `apache`, they have less opportunity to run local exploits in an attempt to gain root privileges.

Fresh out of the box, WebDAV is almost ready to go. You need to add only a few minor configurations to get it started. That said, you *will* need to do some work if you want to implement WebDAV with discrete Apache-based user-level logins *and* have a reasonable level of user authentication over a secure SSL-based connection. It's not an overly difficult task, however, and we show you how to do it in the *WebDAV* section of this chapter.

Configuring and Using FTP

As we said above, FTP is probably the most common method of file transfer. However, it's also one of the most dangerous. Many new administrators enable anonymous FTP access *and* full-write access, to make it easy to load files onto their server. Then they wonder why their hard drives have filled up with illicit files.

Anonymous FTP isn't the problem—poor system administration is. Even though FTP is one of the oldest protocols on the books, a lot of people don't bother to learn how to run it safely and publicly. Those who don't want to take the time to implement FTP securely should switch to an inherently safer option, like the SSH-based methods or WebDAV/SSL.

For many years, the Red Hat Linux FTP default daemon was `wu-ftpd`, a notoriously insecure daemon. With Red Hat Linux 8, the default changed to `vsftpd`, the version that ships with Fedora Core. Of course, `vsftpd` is still based on the FTP with all its security problems, but the daemon does give the FTP administrator some extra control over worst-case scenarios.

Those who administer file transfer services should pay particular attention to the major security sites. Vulnerabilities, exploits, and patches make the news here first, before CNNfn picks them up and your boss starts asking questions. We rely on www.cert.org, www.securityfocus.com, and www.cve.mitre.org.

In the past, Linux FTP daemons actually ran as subdaemons to either `inetd` or `xinetd`. This meant that actually the `inetd` or `xinetd` service was listening on the FTP control port (21) for incoming FTP requests, not the FTP daemon itself. However, `vsftpd` now runs as a stand-alone daemon on most Red-Hat-based systems. If you turn on the stand-alone service, you will be able to see it running by itself in the output of `netstat`:

```
#  /etc/init.d/vsftpd start
Starting vsftpd for vsftpd:                          [ OK ]
#  netstat -natp
Active Internet connections (servers and established)
Proto Recv-Q Send-Q Local Address      Foreign Address State
PID/Program name
tcp     0      0 0.0.0.0:32770       0.0.0.0:*       LISTEN  3428/rpc.statd
tcp     0      0 127.0.0.1:32771     0.0.0.0:*       LISTEN  3639/xinetd
tcp     0      0 127.0.0.1:783       0.0.0.0:*       LISTEN  3732/spamd -d -c -a
tcp     0      0 0.0.0.0:111         0.0.0.0:*       LISTEN  3408/portmap
tcp     0      0 0.0.0.0:80          0.0.0.0:*       LISTEN  3754/httpd
tcp     0      0 0.0.0.0:21          0.0.0.0:*       LISTEN  4675/vsftpd
tcp     0      0 0.0.0.0:22          0.0.0.0:*       LISTEN  3623/sshd
tcp     0      0 127.0.0.1:631       0.0.0.0:*       LISTEN  3585/cupsd
tcp     0      0 127.0.0.1:25        0.0.0.0:*       LISTEN  3693/master
tcp     0      0 0.0.0.0:443         0.0.0.0:*       LISTEN  3754/httpd
tcp     1      0 192.168.128.25:32778   216.239.39.99:80  CLOSE_WAIT
 4587/esd
tcp     1      0 192.168.128.25:32777   216.239.39.99:80  CLOSE_WAIT
 4587/esd
tcp     0      0 192.168.128.25:32936   64.39.31.80:22 TIME_WAIT -
```

The `vsftpd` daemon is shown listening on port 21.

Note   FTP actually runs on two ports: 20 and 21. Port 20 carries FTP data, while port 21 manages FTP control information. Since an incoming request is control information, `vsftpd` listens on port 21. The actual data is sent over port 20.

If you've configured other network services on your Fedora Core system, you may think that you're good to go with `vsftpd` once the installation is finished. This is not quite the case. Even if you set up an FTP server by selecting the `ftp-server` package at installation and the `vsftpd` packages were installed properly, you can't start using the service right away. Fedora Core actually installs `vsftpd` differently than it does other daemons. For example, here's what happens when you install Sendmail and set up the SysV initialization scripts for the mail server:

```
# chkconfig --list sendmail
sendmail  0:off  1:off  2:on  3:on  4:on  5:on  6:off
```

As expected, when the system installs the boot-time (or `init`) scripts for the Sendmail daemon, they are configured to come on in the main runlevels. When you boot this machine, the mail transfer agent (Sendmail) will come online. Now, what happened when you installed `vsftpd`?

```
# chkconfig --list vsftpd
vsftpd  0:off  1:off  2:off  3:off  4:off  5:off  6:off
```

Hmm. Even though the commands were the same for Sendmail and `vsftpd`, `vsftpd`'s default install configuration is `off`. This is a simple default security measure that's relatively new, but appreciated, under Red Hat Linux products. In order to use FTP, you must first install the daemon and then intentionally configure the `init` scripts to turn the service on at boot time, as seen in the following command sequence:

```
# chkconfig --list vsftpd
vsftpd   0:off   1:off   2:off   3:off   4:off   5:off   6:off
# chkconfig vsftpd on
# chkconfig --list vsftpd
vsftpd   0:off   1:off   2:on    3:on    4:on    5:on    6:off
```

Now the daemon will come up after a reboot. To turn on the service without rebooting, issue the following command (in many Linux distributions):

```
#/etc/init.d/vsftpd start
Starting vsftpd for vsftpd:                          [ OK ]
#
```

On Red Hat or Fedora systems, you might opt for the following method:

```
#service vsftpd start
Starting vsftpd for vsftpd:                          [ OK ]
```

Issue the `netstat` command to check whether the service is running on port 21:

```
#netstat -antp | grep 21
tcp    0    0 0.0.0.0:21       0.0.0.0:* LISTEN 4675/vsftpd
```

Restricting Access to FTP

Once you've gotten `vsftpd` up and running, any known users (that is, not anonymous) who are not in the `vsftpd` blacklist file will be able to log in. If you have users who should not have access to FTP resources, open `/etc/vsftpd.ftpusers` and put their usernames in this file. You can also add system or new service accounts to this file to restrict FTP access for system accounts. In this sample `/etc/vsftpd.ftpusers` file, we have blocked FTP access for the user `mike`:

```
# cat /etc/vsftpd.ftpusers
#  Users that are not allowed to login via ftp
root
bin
daemon
adm
lp
sync
shutdown
halt
mail
news
uucp
operator
games
nobody

#Non-FTP users
mike
```

Caution   Your various system service related accounts should be listed in `/etc/vsftpd` `.ftpusers` by default. Normally, if you take root out of this file, you allow root to log into FTP on your server—you might as well hand out invitations to the hacker/cracker sniffers out there who are looking for root passwords via the `PASS` string. Luckily, `vsftpd` is compiled to deny access to root regardless of its setting in this file, but it's a good practice to keep all your service related system accounts, as well as problem users, in your `/etc/vsftpd.ftpusers` file.

Another useful security-related `vsftpd` file is the `/etc/vsftpd.user_list` user password prompt file. If a user is listed in this file, he will not even be offered a password prompt if he attempts to FTP into the machine. As with `/etc/vsftpd.ftpusers`, `/etc/vsftpd.user_list` is filled with system accounts and root. It's a good way to protect passwords for accounts that have no business logging into FTP from even being queried for a password. If there is no password prompt given, there's no way to sniff the password string as it's sent. For some environments, simple login denial is not secure enough.

Note   Unlike most other daemons' config files, you do not need to restart `vsftpd` for the user-based changes to take effect after you edit `/etc/vsftpd.user` and `/etc/vsftpd` `.ftpusers` They are adopted instantly, unlike changes to the main daemon config file, `/etc/vsftpd/vsftpd.conf`.

Configuring Environmental Variables

Once you've defined your user blacklist file, you can begin to configure `vsftpd` for your particular environment. Note that these settings create user-based restrictions only. In order to define restrictions for entire networks or hosts, see Chapter 11 to learn more about working with TCP-Wrappers and iptables.

The main `vsftpd` configuration file is `/etc/vsftpd/vsftpd.conf`. The first lines you should look for areas follows:

```
anonymous_enable=YES
local_enable=YES
write_enable=YES
local_umask=022
#anon_upload_enable=YES
#anon_mkdir_write_enable=YES
```

Note that anonymous FTP is turned on by default. Though it may seem unwise to have write access also turned on, note that anonymous upload, `mkdir`, and write are all commented out. This indicates that only valid system users will be able to write to the local file system(s).

Note   Anonymous FTP logins are directed to `/var/ftp`. If you want anonymous users to write to your drive, you must enable anonymous login, write, and create as well as change the permissions of `/var/ftp` to enable access. More frequently, administrators create an "incoming" directory with specific permissions for anonymous users. If you do so, consider setting it up as a symbolic link to removable media or a drive with quota control, and run regular `cron` jobs to purge the directory. Don't set up a quiet haven for illegal material.

As you continue to read through the configuration file, you'll notice entries for timeouts and other connection management details:

```
dirmessage_enable=YES
xferlog_enable=YES
connect_from_port-20=YES
#chown_uploads=YES
#chown_username=whoever
#xferlog_file=/var/log/vsftpd.log
xferlog_std_format=YES
#idle_session_timeout=600
#data_connection_timeout=120
#nopriv_user=ftpsecure
#async_abor_enable=YES
#ascii_upload_enable=YES
#ascii_download_enable=YES
#ftpd_banner=Welcome to blah FTP service.
#deny_email_enable=YES
#banned_email_file=/etc/vsftpd.banned_emails
```

Look for the following lines in the file:

```
chroot_local_user=YES
#chroot_list_enable=YES
#chroot_list_file=/etc/vsftpd.chroot_list
```

This is a useful trick that allows you to `chroot` users into their own home directories when they FTP in. When you have this turned on, users can't get out of their home directories and go browsing around your file system. In the old days, setting this up was a bit complex, but `vsftpd` does it automatically.

Next, find this section in `/etc/vsftpd/vsftpd.conf`:

```
#ls_recurse_enable=YES
pam_service_name=vsftpd
userlist_enable=YES
#enable for standalone mode
listen=YES
tcp_wrappers=YES
```

If you want to use TCP-Wrappers with your FTP service, this final line must be turned on. For those who dislike `iptables` for securing system services against certain hosts, TCP-Wrappers is a more simple user space form of service/host blocking. We cover TCP-Wrappers in Chapter 11.

Passive FTP

Traditionally, most FTP problems have come from server firewall settings, client settings, or passwords. Over the past few years, however, there has been a rise in the number of problems related to passive versus nonpassive FTP. These problems appear when someone inside a local LAN or behind a firewall attempts to use a nonpassive (or just plain old) FTP server elsewhere on the Internet. The authentication goes smoothly on port 21, but when the FTP server attempts to open port 20 back to the client, the client's local firewall often blocks the connection. While this is logical, since an attempt from the outside to open an incoming port is indicative of cracker activity from the client's perspective, it's irritating to someone who just wants to get a file. More modern, intelligent, stateful, and protocol-savvy firewalls are aware of things like FTP session tracking (such as iptables or netfilter on Linux). However, many firewalls out there still do not have such awareness.

The best solution is to have the user try making the connection in *passive FTP mode*. In passive mode, the FTP client sets up both the authentication connection and the data connection, rather than having the remote FTP service open the data port back to them. Most modern FTP servers support passive-mode sessions, including the vsftpd daemon found on Fedora Core.

Tip   Learn more about the differences between active and passive IP at www.linuxchix .org/content/courses/security/connection_tracking.

Passive FTP and iptables

Are you using iptables on Linux for your firewall? If so, good. Under iptables, you can use *stateful packet inspection* and protocol-aware session tracking, two features that make for smart firewall rules. The ip_conntrack kernel module examines packets to see whether they will need exceptions to regular firewall rules, such as those usually needed by nonpassive FTP. Learn more at www.sns.ias.edu/~jns/security/iptables/iptables_conntrack.html.

In order to use passive-mode FTP, the user will need to change settings in the user FTP client. Most modern user clients, whether GUI or command-line, have this option. (If your user's client does not, encourage an upgrade.) GUI users should check their configuration or preferences menu for the correct option, while those using command-line clients will need to invoke the proper command or set a variable. Those using the ncftp FTP client should log in and then use this command sequence to enable passive mode:

```
ncftp / > passive
passive                on
```

while those using the lftp client should issue the command

```
lftp bob@mydomain.com:~ > set ftp:passive-mode on
```

after logging in to the remote server.

Note   Many users have started to use Internet Explorer (IE) as an FTP client. While it works most of the time, IE will not handle passive FTP by default. Check Microsoft's configuration suggestions at http://support.Microsoft.com/?kbid=323446. In addition, make sure they're using the latest version of IE. There are documented problems with passive FTP on IE version 5.x.

Configuring and Using scp and sftp

If the security risks of FTP are simply too much for you to deal with, consider switching to the secure suite of tools distributed by OpenSSH. OpenSSH offers secure versions of all the old familiar remote access and transfer tools, like Telnet (replaced by ssh), FTP (replaced by sftp), and rcp (replaced by scp). The client and server for each of these tools is preconfigured so that it's ready to go as soon as you log in for the first time on most modern Linux distributions. OpenSSH tools are everywhere: Every version of Linux, Solaris, PalmOS, Mac OS X, and Windows all have functional ports and user clients.

Note OpenSSH is installed by default on all Fedora Core *server* installations. If you choose another type of installation, you will need to install OpenSSH by hand before you can use it.

OpenSSH tools are not just for logins and file transfers. They can even be used to make insecure protocols behave more securely in much the same way as SSL allows web traffic to travel safely between a browser and a server. In fact, many insecure protocols can be *tunneled* securely over a remote SSH to local SSH machine connection, including X11, POP3, Telnet, SMTP, rsync, and so forth.

OpenSSH and Fedora Core

Fedora Core gives you all the OpenSSH tools you need, straight out of the box. If you select the regular server installation, you'll see these packages on your system after installation is complete:

```
# rpm -qa *ssh* | sort
openssh-3.6.1p2-19
openssh-askpass-3.6.1p2-19
openssh-askpass-gnome-3.6.1p2-19
openssh-clients-3.6.1p2-19
openssh-server-3.6.1p2-19
```

You will have the base OpenSSH package, some password authentication programs for the X11 GUI environment, all the OpenSSH clients including ssh, scp, and sftp, and the OpenSSH server itself, sshd. Though you can start using the OpenSSH tools right away, it's best to spend a few minutes configuring sshd so that it does precisely what you want it to.

Configuring sshd

The sshd daemon takes its configurations from the /etc/ssh/sshd_config file. As you can see later, most of the file is commented out. If you read the comments in the configuration file, you'll realize that most of these options are the default-compiled settings, but the settings are left in the file for reference. If you want to change how sshd behaves on your system, just remove the hash marks to uncomment a setting, and then change the setting from its default-compiled setting. Read through the sample file to see some of our suggestions for change:

```
$OpenBSD: sshd_config,v 1.59 2002/09/25 11:17:16 markus Exp $

# This is the sshd server system_wide configuration file. See
# sshd_config(5) for more information.

# This sshd was compiled with
# PATH=/usr/local/bin:/bin:/usr/bin

# The strategy used for options in the default sshd_config
# shipped with OpenSSH is to specify options with their
# default value where possible, but leave them commented.
# Uncommented options change a default value.

#Port 22
#Protocol 2,1
```

This default setting indicates that when sshd runs, it first offers sessions in SSH v 2 protocol to the connecting client, and then falls back to the SSH v1 protocol if required by the client. SSH 2 is more secure than the older version 1, and v1 has many known vulnerabilities. The only reason to run it is that some older ssh-based commercial packages require it. Don't run SSH v1 on your server. If you uncomment and edit this line, you can force your SSH daemon to offer only SSH v 2 to incoming clients. To do this, remove the hash mark and the trailing ,1 so that the line simply reads Protocol 2.

```
#ListenAddress 0.0.0.0
#ListenAddress ::
```

By default, the sshd service binds to all IP addresses associated with your server. If sshd is running on a firewall or on a multi-LAN server, you might choose to remove the hash mark and change the line ListenAddress 0.0.0.0 to something like ListenAddress 10.1.1.1 to restrict SSH logins to a particular side of your network.

Note   This configuration file is longer and more complex than what you see here. We're showing you only the most commonly tweaked settings.

```
# HostKey for protocol version 1
#HostKey /etc/ssh/ssh_host_key
# HostKeys for protocol version 2
#HostKey /etc/ssh/ssh_host_rsa_key
#HostKey /etc/ssh/ssh_host_dsa_key

# Lifetime and size of ephemeral version 1 server key
#KeyRegenerationInterval 3600
#ServerKeyBits 768

# Logging
#obsoletes QuietMode and FascistLogging
#SyslogFacility AUTH
SyslogFacility AUTHPRIV
#LogLevel INFO

# Authentication:

#LoginGraceTime 120
#PermitRootLogin yes
#StrictModes yes

#RSAAuthentication yes
#PubkeyAuthentication yes
#AuthorizedKeysFile        .ssh/authorized_keys
```

The last two lines in the preceding code block enable *key-based authentication*. SSL, SSH, and other modern encryption methods use *dual-key encryption*, a method that requires both a public and a private key to encrypt and decrypt a secure session or data stream. If you turn on key-based authentication in sshd, you remove the username/password authentication step and allow access only with a known set of keys. This is not necessarily more secure, as it now ties security to the remote trusted host's own security. However, this setting is often the only viable solution if you need remote automation scripts and other back-end programs to log into systems without requiring a human to type in a password.

Caution   You probably should not enable key-based authentication unless you are in a provably secure environment AND you trust everyone on your LAN plus everyone who has access to the server AND your security honchos approve it as an acceptable security policy.

```
# rhosts authentication should not be used
#RhostsAuthentication no
# Don't read the user's ~ /.rhosts and ~ /.shosts files
#IgnoreRhosts yes
# For this to work you will also need host keys in
# /etc/ssh/ssh_known_hosts
#RhostsRSAAuthentication no
# similar for protocol version 2
#HostbasedAuthentication no
# Change to yes if you don't trust ~ /.ssh/known_hosts for
# RhostsRSAAuthentication and HostbasedAuthentication
#IgnoreUserKnownHosts no

# To disable tunneled clear text passwords, change to
# no here!
#PasswordAuthentication yes
#PermitEmptyPasswords no

# Change to no to disable s/key passwords
#ChallengeResponseAuthentication yes

# Kerberos options
#KerberosAuthentication no
#KerberosOrLocalPasswd yes
#KerberosTicketCleanup yes

#AFSTokenPassing no

# Kerberos TGT Passing only works with the AFS kaserver
#KerberosTgtPassing no

# Set this to 'yes' to enable PAM keyboard-interactive
# authentication
# Warning: enabling this may bypass the setting of
# 'PasswordAuthentication'
#PAMAuthenticationViaKbdInt no

#X11Forwarding no
X11Forwarding yes
```

The X11Forwarding yes setting permits users to tunnel server-side X11 client programs and output over SSH to the local X11 GUI (called the local X11 server). That is, you could ssh into a remote system, start the Mozilla browser from the command line on the server, and get the GUI window for the Mozilla program running on the remote server "painted" on your local desktop X GUI. Imagine being able to run GNOME, KDE, and Linux applications off your Fedora Core machine while sitting in front of a Windows PC in a lab across the country, or running a system load graph for each of your servers on your local desktop. This is a powerful feature. It's safe to leave this function enabled, even if you never use it. Just be aware that you might get an unexpected window on your local machine if you're issuing commands over an ssh session.

```
#X11DisplayOffset 10
#X11UseLocalhost yes
#PrintMotd yes
#PrintLastLog yes
#KeepAlive yes
#UseLogin no
#UsePrivilegeSeparation yes
#PermitUserEnvironment no
#Compression yes

#MaxStartups 10
# no default banner path
#Banner /some/path
#VerifyReverseMapping no

# override default of no subsystems
Subsystem       sftp    /usr/libexec/openssh/sftp-server
```

The final line in the file turns on the sftp subsystem of sshd. It is enabled by default in most modern Linux distributions. If you can get into your server via ssh, then you can probably access sftp resources with the sftp client as well.

Configuring OpenSSH Services

Once you've determined that all the appropriate packages are on your system and made your basic sshd configuration file changes, it's time to check the server-side service. Everything you need to run OpenSSH services is managed by the sshd daemon. Verify that the daemon is running with the command

```
#ps auxw|grep [s]shd
root 3615   0.0 0.5 5100 1252 ? S 10:37 0:00 /usr/sbin/sshd
```

or the optional Red Hat command

```
#/etc/init.d/sshd status
sshd (pid 3615) is running...
```

If the daemon is running, you can use this command to stop and restart it in order to reload the changes in your config file:

```
#/etc/init.d/sshd restart
Stopping sshd:                                       [ OK ]
Starting sshd:                                       [ OK ]
```

In fact, you can do this while connected to the server through an SSH connection, and never lose the session. Just another reason why OpenSSH tools *are* the new de facto standard for remote Linux/UNIX access.

Finally, you should ensure that sshd will come up when the machine is booted and when runlevels change. The easiest way to do this is with the init script control tool chkconfig. First, check the existing configuration for the sshd service:

```
# chkconfig --list sshd
sshd     0:off   1:off   2:on    3:on    4:on    5:on    6:off
```

Since most servers boot into runlevels 3 and 5 almost exclusively (on Red Hat—other distributions may use different runlevels), these settings are appropriate for almost all cases.

If you want to configure the server so that it will not run a service such as sshd at boot time, you can turn the service off in all runlevels like this:

```
# chkconfig sshd off
```

Check it again:

```
# chkconfig --list sshd
sshd    0:off   1:off   2:off   3:off   4:off   5:off   6:off
```

Note   This shows that the service will be started when the server comes up into runlevels 2, 3, 4, or 5 (levels 0, 1, and 6 are for shutting down, single user or "safe mode", and rebooting, respectively). See Chapter 5 for more information on runlevels.

When you're ready to configure it to be on at boot time again, use chkconfig to turn the service on and verify that the runlevels are correct (most network services are configured to come up in either 2-5 or 3-5):

```
# chkconfig sshd on
# chkconfig --list sshd
sshd    0:off   1:off   2:on    3:on    4:on    5:on    6:off
```

Note   The chkconfig control tool only defines boot and runlevel settings for a given service or daemon when the entire system changes state (boots or changes runlevels). It does not start or stop a service in real time. If you need to make sure that sshd does not start after a reboot (set it to "off"), as well as stop the sshd service now running, then you should use this command sequence:

```
# chkconfig sshd off
```

which will configure the daemon to be off at boot time or runlevel changes, and then run

```
# /etc/init.d/sshd stop
```

OR

```
# service sshd stop
```

to gracefully shut down a running daemon, such as sshd, in real time (the latter is the optional Red-Hat-based init script usage). The opposite of these commands would be the usage of "on" and "start" respectively.

Caution   If you use the /etc/init.d/sshd stop option remotely over ssh, it will also end your session. The only way to get back into a system with a stopped sshd service like this would be to visit the machine physically, since you have turned off the service that provides access.

Using SCP

You're fully configured and ready to go. How does scp work? Just like cp, or scp's older cousin rcp (remote copy), it works only through an encrypted network connection. For example, assume that the user bob wants to copy everything from his current desktop to a remote server at bobsdomain.org. In the current directory, he has the following files:

```
$ ls -l
total 92
-rw-r--r--    1 root    root     1877 Dec 16 12:12 anaconda-ks.cfg
-rw-r--r--    1 root    root       98 Dec 17 06:33 fedora-desktop-update-
notes.txt
-rw-r--r--    1 root    root    49546 Dec 16 12:12 install.log
-rw-r--r--    1 root    root     5496 Dec 16 12:12 install.log.syslog
-rw-r--r--    1 root    root      512 Dec 16 11:50 ORIG-MBR.img
drwxr-xr-x    4 root    root     4096 Dec 21 22:50 PACKAGES
-r-xr-xr-x    1 root    root     4590 Dec 30 14:39 pcmcia-STOCK-INIT
-rw-r--r--    1 root    root      400 Dec 23 17:17 SYS-CHANGELOG.txt
```

Bob doesn't have much more than a few files and some subdirectories. To copy the files, he issues the following command:

```
$ scp * bob@mydomain.com:/home/bob/tmp/
```

```
The authenticity of host 'mydomain.com (127.0.0.1)' can't be established.
RSA key fingerprint is 7f:0d:1c:44:56:3d:1a:6d:67:03:e4:34:6f:5c:fc:d9.
Are you sure you want to continue connecting (yes/no)? yes
Warning: Permanently added 'mydomain.com' (RSA) to the list of known hosts.
```

At this point, Bob must confirm that he wants to save the public key from the remote machine. This will speed connection to this site in the future. The remote machine prompts for a password, and the file transfer begins:

```
bob@mydomain.com's password:
anaconda-ks.cfg                  100% 1877     4.8MB/s    00:00
fedora-desktop-update-notes.txt  100%   98   385.8KB/s    00:00
install.log                      100% 48KB   15.6MB/s    00:00
install.log.syslog               100% 5496     8.5MB/s    00:00
ORIG-MBR.img                     100%  512     1.1MB/s    00:00
PACKAGES: not a regular file
pcmcia-STOCK-INIT                100% 22KB     6.9MB/s    00:00
SYS-CHANGELOG.txt                100%  400     5.5MB/s    00:00
```

Note that scp did not do a recursive copy, and rejected the PACKAGES subdirectory. So the files did not get copied. To do so, Bob must specify recursive scp when he issues the initial command:

```
$ scp -rp * bob@mydomain.com:/home/bob/tmp
bob@mydomain.com's password:
anaconda-ks.cfg                  100% 1877     4.7MB/s    00:00
fedora-desktop-update-notes.txt  100%   98   369.5KB/s    00:00
install.log                      100% 48KB   15.6MB/s    00:00
install.log.syslog               100% 5496     8.1MB/s    00:00
ORIG-MBR.img                     100%  512     1.2MB/s    00:00
xf43sav-27t.tgz                  100% 33KB     1.6MB/s    00:00
savage_drv.o                     100% 75KB     2.9MB/s    00:00
scanModem                        100% 103KB    7.9MB/s    00:00
ModemData.txt                    100% 9139     5.8MB/s    00:00
ModemData.txt.2                  100% 17KB     8.8MB/s    00:00
ModemDriverCompiling.txt         100% 22KB     6.9MB/s    00:00
pcmcia-STOCK-INIT                100% 22KB     6.9MB/s 00:00
SYS-CHANGELOG.txt                100%  400     5.7MB/s 00:00
```

In this instance, the contents of the PACKAGES subdirectory and the directory itself were also copied over.

> **Note** The second scp example used both the --r (recursive) and --p (permissions) switches. Remember that you adopt the username and UID of the remote user, but files retain your local permissions. If you're backing up a system and you want to preserve all user/group and UID/GID information, tar is probably a better solution.

The scp tool is best for pushing and pulling files between system accounts and across networks, especially when the receiving user is going to adopt ownership of the files. One common use is to match scp with cron to push common system files, like /etc/hosts, nsswitch.conf, or resolv.conf, out to multiple machines on a network.

> **Tip** If you want to offer scp access but don't want to give shell access, consider scponly. It's a bash shell replacement for scp. Just install and then add it to /etc/shells as a valid shell choice. You can now give remote users access over scp and sftp without giving them login privileges and a command line over SSH. Learn more at www.sublimation.org/scponly/.

Key-Based Authentication for ssh, scp, and sftp

In some cases, you may prefer to enable key-based authentication rather than require users to type username/password pairs at login. As explained above, key-based authentication can be quite handy. If used by itself, it is less secure; however, it is sometimes the only way to automate systems smoothly and remove human intervention from the process.

To turn on key-based authentication, open the /etc/ssh/sshd_config file and locate the line beginning with #RSAAuthentication. Make sure that it is commented out, and that the PubkeyAuthentication line is active and set to yes:

```
#RSAAuthentication yes
PubkeyAuthentication yes
AuthorizedKeysFile      .ssh/authorized_keys
```

After you change the configuration file, you'll need to restart sshd:

```
# /etc/init.d/sshd restart
Stopping sshd:                                      [ OK ]
Starting sshd:                                      [ OK ]
#
```

Now, when the user Mike requests ssh access, sshd will look in /home/mike/.ssh /authorized_keys to see whether this person has an authorized public key that can be trusted as Mike's key. How did the key get into his ~/.sshd/authorized_keys file in the first place? Someone put it there, probably either Mike or his root administrator.

Key Pairs

In order to work with key-based authentication, you must follow several steps. First, you need to generate a public/private key pair. Once you have a public key, you can put it into an ~/.ssh/authorized_keys file (where ~ = /home/username/) so that you can access the account. To generate a key pair, follow this command sequence:

```
$ ssh-keygen -t dsa -C "mike_home"
Generating public/private dsa key pair.
Enter file in which to save the key (/home/mike/.ssh/id_dsa):
```

```
Enter passphrase (empty for no passphrase):
Enter same passphrase again: <enter>
Your identification has been saved in /home/mike/.ssh/id_dsa.
Your public key has been saved in /home/mike/.ssh/id_dsa.pub.
The key fingerprint is:
f1:7b:a8:80:ca:6f:12:da:1f:87:e7:f9:6a:ab:98:36 mike_home
[mike@localhost mike] $
[mike@localhost mike] $ ls -la .ssh/
total 20
drwx------     2 mike      mike      4096 Jan 10 19:04 .
drwx------     5 mike      mike      4096 Jan 10 18:55 ..
-rw-------     1 mike      mike       672 Jan 10 19:04 id_dsa
-rw-r--r--     1 mike      mike       599 Jan 10 19:04 id_dsa.pub
-rw-r--r--     1 mike      mike       219 Jan 10 18:58 known_hosts
```

The output of `ls --la .ssh/` shows the user Mike's private and public (.pub) `dsa`-based key files on his home machine. Assume that Mike needs to log into the remote system at work `mydomain.com`, and do so without a password. In order to do this, Mike's home public key needs to be placed in his ~/.ssh/authorized-keys file on the remote machine at work. First, from home, Mike prints his home `dsa` public key file to the screen:

```
[mike@localhost mike]$  cat .ssh/id_dsa.pub
ssh-dss
AAAAB3NzaC1kc3MAAACBAPWOCP1/hI2gE/2Uk1lcaFPIvGC3DfCwHTPOxONRJv5u
Aws6W29pFp6yZc91vnBbnBbCOaN33DCZKMwfpFpO8YOQBOfpR8SRTXhTIVuC+Z2bTBM
RZoWkEo9ZSAOZG4RoO2fm21Mr6ez2b6/NXoyp4CzZeDgreC7IWTNvOqWLjD+yiUr
AAAAFQDvC1cZ5P/i8g3cGLUqNEMxuif4JQAAAIBGBshp6bsM1be3VsTlDmBiCH+s
XH6l1HSufcaflIL2GtQUyoTp8DGXO+JP7UhkOXVlTBZfj6dx5h5GBQTzvbpUWafW
UKVxad/ahS6mg1YQASgjUgI3ru1z93xQoT6hkgEt90dIA1i6Axt/ajHK2E+wGsia
S6CC876aQUTF5GUP1gAAAIEA8asyusN+QdTtjbEnCjtKkHEFZ2h+SDex6i4I+VUc
XNCa7gILLj3O3N28WNz3fCDxDiOgF6wTlGD2Edm/1nfQ+IAzN+McRQupLjVMO2MK
eO9XqeIw/+6XH8UDW4J/dFVq7eKaSTZt3mr92XdG5xipU/VddA4k2qKwq6m8UpxA
knI= mike_home
```

Tip
Notice the comment at the end that identifies this key as `mike_home`. **This is a very useful trick, as it is nearly impossible to identify keystrings merely by reading them. It's wise to create separate public keys for work, home, laptops, and so on; the more keys you use, the more you need to keep them clearly marked.**

Mike then highlights the public key with his mouse and copies the text. Next, Mike uses ssh to log into his remote account at work (a password is still required at this point):

```
[mike@localhost mike]$ ssh mike@mydomain.com
bob@mydomain.com's password:
```

Next, Mike edits his remote ~/.ssh/authorized_keys file, or creates it if it does not exist:

```
[mike@mydomain.com mike]$ vi .ssh/authorized_keys
```

Note
Notice how the prompt changes from Mike's home `[mike@localhost mike]$` to `[mike@mydomain.com mike]$` at his work account.

Mike now pastes the copied text of his public key, saves the file, and exits the text editor. His account now looks as follows:

```
[mike@mydomain.com mike]$ ls -la .ssh/
total 24
drwx------    2 mike     mike     4096 Jan 10 19:35 .
drwx-----x    6 mike     mike     4096 Jan 10 19:35 ..
-rw-rw-r--    1 mike     mike      602 Jan 10 19:35 authorized_keys
-rw-------    1 mike     mike      668 Jan 10 19:34 id_dsa
-rw-r--r--    1 mike     mike      603 Jan 10 19:34 id_dsa.pub
-rw-r--r--    1 mike     mike      223 Jan 10 18:36 known_hosts
```

The files look right, but the permissions are wrong. Both the authorized-keys file and the id_dsa (private key) should be readable only by the user who owns them. Use chmod authorized_keys to fix this:

```
[mike@mydomain.com mike]$ chmod 700 .ssh/authorized_keys
[mike@mydomain.com mike]$ ls -la .ssh/
total 24
drwx------    2 mike     mike     4096 Jan 10 19:35 .
drwx-----x    6 mike     mike     4096 Jan 10 19:46 ..
-rwx------    1 mike     mike      602 Jan 10 19:35 authorized_keys
-rw-------    1 mike     mike      668 Jan 10 19:34 id_dsa
-rw-r--r--    1 mike     mike      603 Jan 10 19:34 id_dsa.pub
-rw-r--r--    1 mike     mike      223 Jan 10 18:36 known_hosts
```

Note   This is probably the most common problem with key-based authentication. Both the authorized_keys file and the .ssh directory should be set to rwx------ (700). If you don't chmod them both to 700, sshd will simply ignore one or both, and key-based authentication won't work.

Mike logs out of his remote work machine and then logs back in to see if the authorized_keys entry worked. If login no longer requires a password, then the key-based ssh authentication is working:

```
[mike@mydomain.com mike]$ exit
[mike@localhost mike]$
[mike@localhost mike]$ ssh mike@mydomain.com
[mike@mydomain.com mike]$
```

With this in place, Mike can now automate almost anything between his home and work account, whether it's pushing web content, bookmark files, or daily logs.

Note   While this will allow Mike to easily push things to work, or pull them back home from work (using ssh, scp, or sftp), this will not allow the mike user at work (mydomain.com) to automatically push things home, or pull things from home to work. To do this, Mike would also need to put his work public key in his home's ~.ssh/authorized_keys file.

For example, Mike might set up a regular job that copies web content from his home machine to his work machine. The following crontab entry will tar-gzip Mike's home web content every Sunday at 1:37 A.M. and scp it to his work's ~/BACKUPS/ directory:

```
37 1 * * 1     tar czvf ~/mike-web_backup_$(date +%Y-%m-%d).tgz ~/web
        && scp -p ~/mike-web_backup_$(date +%Y-%m-%d).tgz
        bob@mydomain.com:~/BACKUPS/
```

User Clients

One of the nice things about OpenSSH's SSH suite is that users can use whichever client they prefer: scp, sftp, or ssh. You don't need a GUI client at all. For example, the stock OpenSSH command line sftp client works perfectly:

```
$ sftp mike@mydomain.com
Connecting to mydomain.com...
sftp>
```

When you installed the complete OpenSSH suite as part of the server installation, the openssh-clients package was included. It includes all the command-line clients. However, you and your users aren't limited to command-line clients. Both GNOME and KDE offer a number of GUI tools and clients that work with and use OpenSSH. For example, if you point KDE's Konqueror web browser to the URL sftp://mydomain.com and you don't pass key-based authentication, a login window automatically pops up (Figure 18-1).

Figure 18-1: KDE's Konqueror browser is SSH-aware.

Table 18-1 shows some popular clients for scp and sftp. No matter the platform they use, your *do* users have some choice.

Table 18-1: Common scp/sftp Clients

Windows	WinSCP (scp and sftp)
	`http://winscp.sourceforge.net/eng/about.php`
	WS-FTPPro (sftp)
	`www.ipswitch.com/Products/WS_FTP/features.html`
	PuTTY (SSH, scp, and sftp)
	`www.chiark.greenend.org.uk/~sgtatham/putty/`

UNIX/Linux	Konqueror (sftp) `http://konqueror.kde.org` GFTP (scp and sftp) *http://gftp.seul.org*
Mac OS X	Fugu (sftp) `http://rsug.itd.umich.edu/software/fugu` Rbrowser (scp and sftp) *www.rbrowser.com*

SSH and Firewalls

If the sshd daemon is running and you can't get in with ssh, sftp, or scp, you may have selected install-time firewall configurations that lock the box down to the point where it can't be used as a server. While it's always good to start as securely as possible and then grant access, a server machine needs some freedom in order to do its work. You can see whether you inadvertently blocked SSH sessions by asking iptables what rules it is running:

```
# iptables -L
Chain INPUT (policy ACCEPT)
target     prot opt source               destination
RH-Firewall-1-INPUT  all  -- anywhere             anywhere

Chain FORWARD (policy ACCEPT)
target     prot opt source               destination
RH-Firewall-1-INPUT all -- anywhere              anywhere

Chain OUTPUT (policy ACCEPT)
target     prot opt source               destination

Chain RH-Firewall-1-INPUT (2 references)
target     prot opt source       destination
ACCEPT     all -- anywhere    anywhere
ACCEPT     icmp -- anywhere    anywhere            icmp any
ACCEPT     ipv6-crypt-- anywhere    anywhere
ACCEPT     ipv6-auth-- anywhere       anywhere
ACCEPT     all -- anywhere    anywhere    state RELATED,ESTABLISHED
ACCEPT     tcp -- anywhere    anywhere    state NEW tcp dpt:http
REJECT     all -- anywhere    anywhere    reject-with icmp-host-prohibited
```

Since there are no ACCEPT rules for SSH/port22 connections in this output, your SSH connections are being killed by the final line (REJECT all). This is a very secure setup, but it defeats the purpose of the server. To get your SSH connections working, you need to edit the

`/etc/sysconfig/iptables` file (on Red-Hat-based systems) and insert the iptable rule for ssh so that it looks like this:

```
...
Chain RH-Firewall-1-INPUT (2 references)
target     prot opt source          destination
ACCEPT     all  --  anywhere        anywhere
ACCEPT     icmp --  anywhere        anywhere        icmp any
ACCEPT     ipv6-crypt-- anywhere    anywhere
ACCEPT     ipv6-auth-- anywhere     anywhere
ACCEPT     all -- anywhere          anywhere        state RELATED,ESTABLISHED
ACCEPT     tcp -- anywhere          anywhere        state NEW tcp dpt:http
ACCEPT     tcp -- anywhere          anywhere        state NEW tcp dpt:ssh
REJECT     all -- anywhere          anywhere        reject-with icmp-host-prohibited
```

The second line from the bottom shows that SSH is now a *trusted protocol* from anywhere. You must now restart the `iptables` service. When it restarts, people should be able to connect through SSH.

 Tip   For a more friendly version of this configuration on all Red-Hat-based systems (including Fedora Core), type `redhat-config-securitylevel` to get the GUI configuration tool. Check the box next to SSH, and click OK to enable this ruleset change. The new rule will be saved to `/etc/sysconfig/iptables`, implemented, and will be loaded and used after all reboots.

Configuring and Using WebDAV

If you have a number of users who simply need file upload access to website file system space, such as those who host their websites on your local server farm, the WebDAV protocol is an excellent alternative to more fully featured or system user-based FTPs. Setting up WebDAV on Apache and Linux *securely* is not the simplest of tasks, but once configured it allows users to drag and drop content into place, edit content through a browser, and—in some cases—share content directly from the server to their local PCs. Most users who work with WebDAV prefer it to dated and less friendly protocols like FTP for daily web content administrative tasks.

Unlike the other protocols described in this chapter, WebDAV is not its own daemon or service, but an extension to the HTTP 1.1 protocol itself. WebDAV on Linux is an Apache module that is installed and configured in the same way as any other Apache module is managed. The current version of WebDAV is quite reliable, and can be used to replace other FTPs that your site users may be accustomed to. WebDAV by itself is not secure, but can be made secure with other encryption technologies such as SSL/TLS. This provides a secure alternative to FTP and is both more secure and stable than Microsoft FrontPage server extensions for UNIX/Linux.

To set up access through WebDAV for a web customer, follow the following steps:

1. Define a DavLockDB and `Directory` directive, or Directory block, in the customer's `VirtualHosts` section of your Apache `httpd.conf` file.

2. Place `AllowOverride all` and `DAV On` directives in that `VirtualHost` Directory block.

3. Set up `.htaccess` and `.htpassword` files to allow and authenticate that customer to use WebDAV in this new WebDAV directory.

The `.htaccess` file is used by the `AllowOverride` directive, and the `.htpassword` file is used by the `.htaccess` file.

Since WebDAV is defined on a per-directory basis, you could have a single virtual host with three separate WebDAV directories in it. Each of these directories can be managed by a different webmaster on one website, giving each person a small area under his sole control. Not only does WebDAV offer this advantage, but these are not even real system users—they are Apache authenticated users. This is a huge advantage over traditional system user and file system-wide configurations used with `scp`, `sftp`, or FTP file transfer methods; at least from a web administrator's perspective.

Note   Since WebDAV uses `.htaccess` and `.htpassword` files for authentication, no system account information is sent across the network when a user logs into WebDAV. This is a great boon for security on Linux/Apache web servers. The same web user can even be given different passwords for different web directories. WebDAV offers greater flexibility *and* better security.

Defining a WebDAV Share

In Chapter 17 we set up a website for the user Bob, called `mydomain.com`. In this section, we set up a WebDAV share for this site. Bob can use his web browser to manage the content of his site without needing a separate FTP client.

Tip   You can use multiple URLs to point to the same directory on the server's file system. For example, you can point `dav.mydomain.com` and `www.mydomain.com` to the same IP address, but call a different `VirtualHost` block for each URL. In this example, however, we use the same `VirtualHost` block for both `dav.mydomain.com` and `mydomain.com`, and just set up a subdirectory that points to the `DocumentRoot` of this virtual host.

Begin configuring the WebDAV share by opening the Apache configuration file, `/etc/httpd/conf/httpd.conf`. If you host many sites, you may have a number of `VirtualHost` entries that define each site you host. Find the `virtual host` section quickly by searching for `Section 3`. Then find the `VirtualHost` entry that defines the site for which you want to set up a WebDAV share and follow the numbered steps in the previous section to build the following code:

```
<VirtualHost 10.1.1.1>
    DocumentRoot /home/bob/web/html/
    ServerName mydomain.com
DavLockDB /tmp/mydomainDavLock
<Directory /home/bob/web/html/dav>
    AllowOverride All
    Order allow,deny
    Allow from 192.168.128.
    DAV On
</Directory>
</VirtualHost>
```

As you can see, Bob's site is now configured to use `.htaccess` and `.htpassword` to manage authentication and all other security settings for that directory. We have also identified certain IP blocks that are permitted to access the WebDAV share (`192.168.128.*` here). You can use this line to limit the networks that can see the share, then use `.htaccess` to limit access even more.

Tip

Whenever you work on a test website that may not have a real-world DNS name, or has a name that conflicts with an existing DNS name (as does our `mydomain.com` site), you can place an entry in `/etc/hosts` on the server and client machines using it. This fools the local system into accepting this test setup. For the site `mydomain.com`, we added this line in `/etc/hosts`:

```
10.1.1.1              mydomain.com www.mydomain.com
```

You can override DNS on Windows boxes like this also. Their `hosts` file is located in `C:\winnt\system32\drivers\etc\hosts` on WinNT/2000/XP, and in `c:\windows\hosts` for Win9x/ME clients.

The `DavLockDB`, `Directory`, and `DAV On` directives are all in place now in `httpd.conf`. However, we're not finished. The `Directory` directive currently points to a directory that does not exist. In the next command sequence, we create a symbolic link to this nonexistent location that points back to the main directory:

```
# cd /home/bob/web/html/
[root@localhost html]# ls
index.html  pics
[root@localhost html]# ls -la
total 16
drwxrwsr-x    3 bob       apache    4096 Jan 11 15:50 .
drwxrwsr-x    4 bob       apache    4096 Jan  1 16:41 ..
-rwxrwxr-x    1 bob       apache     114 Jan  9 17:45 index.html
drwxr-sr-x    2 apache    apache    4096 Jan 11 15:50 pics
#
```

Follow that with

```
# ln -s . dav
# ls -la
total 16
drwxrwsr-x    3 bob       apache    4096 Jan 11 15:50 .
drwxrwsr-x    4 bob       apache    4096 Jan  1 16:41 ..
lrwxrwxrwx    1 root      apache       1 Jan 11 15:50 dav -> .
-rwxrwxr-x    1 bob       apache     114 Jan  9 17:45 index.html
drwxr-sr-x    2 apache    apache    4096 Jan 11 15:50 pics
```

Voila! A symlink pointing to its own parent directory.

Now, if someone uses a WebDAV-aware browser and goes to `WebDav://mydomain.com/dav/`, that person will get access to the same contents that make up the website `http://mydomain.com`. Note that the user must append `/dav/` to the URL. This is not required when setting up a WebDAV share. However, since the WebDAV directory is a different directory—even though it's virtual—the `/dav/` suffix lets us differentiate between `/home/bob/web/html`, which has no referenced `.htaccess` file, and `/home/bob/web/html/dav/`, which does have a referenced `.htaccess` file. Remember that the `.htaccess` file is the key to nonsystem authenticated logins.

Caution

Be careful. When you have a subdirectory link that points back to its own parent directory, like this one, you can run into problems during routine system backups, searches, and other tasks. Any automated activity in the web directories must be configured to *not traverse* symbolic links. This includes jobs like `tar`-based backups and `find` search routines. If this is an issue for you, you may want to omit this part of WebDAV configuration. Instead, run WebDAV through a separate `VirtualHost` block that points at something like `/home/bob/web` **instead of** `/web/dav`.

Next, create the `.htaccess` file that the `AllowOverride` directive will call when someone tries to log into the WebDAV share. Put this file in the `/home/bob/web/html/` directory. Take a look inside a working `.htaccess` file for this site:

```
order allow,deny
allow from all
require valid-user
Authname "Welcome Back Webmaster Bob..."
Authtype Basic
AuthUserFile /home/bob/.htpasswd
```

> While the `.htaccess` file controls and externalizes the authentication control away from the main `httpd.conf` file, it in turn points to the `.htpasswd` file, where the web username and hashed password are actually stored.

Notice where the `.htpassword` file is located? Outside the web directory. In fact, completely outside the reach of Bob's web space. This is good security practice, because the `.htpassword` file usually contains all of the site's usernames and encrypted passwords. Set up your `.htpassword` file with the following commands:

```
# htpasswd -c /home/bob/.htpasswd bob
New password:
Re-type new password:
Adding password for user bob
#
# cat /home/bob/.htpasswd
bob:QfeYlAUIQVSow
#
```

Now restart your apache `httpd` service:

```
# /etc/init.d/httpd restart
Stopping httpd:                              [ OK ]
Starting httpd:                              [ OK ]
```

If you're using KDE's Konqueror, then you should now be able to point your browser to this share, with the correct URL (`webdav://mydomain.com/dav/` in this case), and get a secured login prompt. If you see the error message

```
An error occured while loading webdav://mydomain.com/dav/:

The file or directory webdav://mydomain.com/dav/ does not exist.
```

then you probably have the wrong path in `httpd.conf`, one of the access files is missing or misconfigured, or the symlink is not set up or configured. Check the site's error log or the general error log in `/var/log/httpd/error_log` for more information.

> If your Apache `conf` file is not set to FollowSymLinks by default, the line to enable this option should look like this example. It should be located under `Section 2` of your `/etc/httpd/conf/httpd.conf` file:

```
<Directory />
    Options FollowSymLinks
    AllowOverride None
</Directory>
```

Securing WebDAV with SSL

Although the WebDAV share is now configured properly, the data is still flowing to the browser unencrypted and is thus as unsafe as FTP. Securing a WebDAV share is done in the same way as you would secure a web page, using SSL. Since each SSL site on an Apache server requires a unique IP address, you will need to get an IP to assign solely to Bob's WebDAV share. While you could run this setup on the site's main IP address, there are other SSL services that generally take priority over WebDAV for the main address's SSL function. Since you can have only one SSL site per IP address, you will need an additional IP address configured on your server for this purpose.

Configuring WebDAV shares over SSL is simple. In general, you can copy your old non-SSL VirtualHost block in httpd.conf, paste it just below, and change the IP/port binding to x.x.x.x:port, where x.x.x.x is the additional IP that you've configured on the system and *port* is the SSL port to which you're binding that IP address, as in 10.1.1.2:443. The result should look like this:

```
NameVirtualHost *:443
<VirtualHost 10.1.1.2:443>
    DocumentRoot /home/bob/web/html/
    ServerName dav.mydomain.com
  SSLEngine on
  SSLCertificateFile /etc/httpd/conf/ssl.crt/server.crt
  SSLCertificateKeyFile /etc/httpd/conf/ssl.key/server.key
DavLockDB /tmp/mydomainDavLock
<Directory /home/bob/web/html/>
    AllowOverride All
    Order allow,deny
    Allow from all
    DAV On
</Directory>
</VirtualHost>
```

Note   If you set up WebDAV as described in the previous section, we just created a totally different WebDAV share but in a different virtual host (for SSL). As such, if you're following along, you need to go back and remove the Directory block and the DavLockDB line in the main VirtualHost block. Also, remove the symbolic link /dav/ that you created in the /home/bob/web/html/ directory.

The method used here is better than the /dav/ symbolic link trick within the main VirtualHost block described earlier. However, this method does require an additional IP address and an SSL certificate.

Note   Here, we use the self-signed dummy SSL certificate and default SSL server key. If you're running a serious web business, you may want to pay for a signed certificate from a third-party company like Verisign or Geotrust, though you'll pay several hundred dollars a year for the privilege. Most system administrators feel that certificates for internal use, like this one, are a waste of resources. If you agree, stick with the built-in certificate/key pair as we have done here.

Once you have this all set up, you can test your configuration. Make sure that you have your DNS or /etc/hosts file set up to point dav.mydomain.com to the new IP address. Restart Apache, and then point your WebDAV-enabled browser to the correct URL. The URL varies, depending on the web client you use. For KDE's Konqueror, the correct URL is webdavs://dav.mydomain.com/. Other software just asks for the fully qualified domain name, as in dav.mydomain.com, and then asks which protocol to use: in this case, webdav-ssl. Table 18-2 shows some common WebDAV-aware clients.

Table 18-2: Common WebDAV Clients

Windows	Internet Explorer 5.5 or newer http://www.Microsoft.com/windows/ie/default.asp WebDrive www.southrivertech.com/products/webdrive/index.html
Linux	KDE Konqueror *http://konqueror.kde.org*
Mac OS X	Goliath http://www.webdav.org/goliath/

Tip   Try adding an HTML editor, like Quanta, to your desktop's toolbar. With some WebDAV-aware browsers such as Konqueror, you can drag and drop the file you want to edit onto the editor's toolbar icon and vice versa (see Figure 18-2). With Fedora Linux, if you have everything you need installed, then you can right-click on .html files and easily select the Quanta Plus HTML editor. Web editing with no uploading or downloading.

Other File Transfer Solutions

There are many other ways to get files from Machine A to Machine B over networks. You can use NFS drive mounting on a trusted network, synchronization tools like rsync, and even tar streams tunneled through secure SSH connections. In this section, we describe solutions to two common file transfer jobs.

Network-Based tar Backups

This command tars all the /home users on your system. Unlike the regular use of tar, however, the output is not sent to a file. Rather, it's sent as a compressed stream over SSH to a file on a remote machine on your network:

```
# tar cpzv /home | ssh -q root@all.yourbase.com "cat >
/root/home-hackup.tgz"
```

Your local drive could be at 99 percent of full capacity, and this tar archiving method would still work, since the output never goes to the local disk at all, but is piped directly out over the network to Machine B (all.yourbase.com).

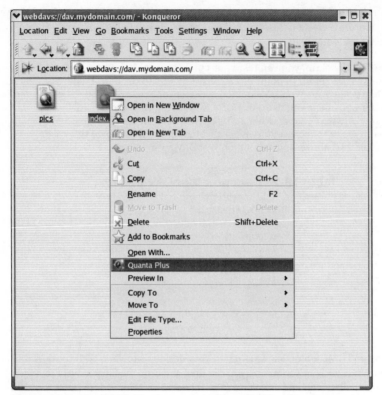

Figure 18-2: Use KDE's Konqueror to add an HTML editor to your toolbar.

Keeping Multiple Servers in Sync

If you run multiple servers on a network, you probably use common copies of your master files. Administrators running web farms or load-balanced web clusters often use a program like `rsync` to keep the common files under control. You can use `rsync` over an encrypted SSH session to enhance the security of this common operation. In fact, if you've set up key-based authentication, the entire process can be automated. Use the following commands:

```
rsync -e ssh -avuz /var/www/html/* webserver1.mydomain.com:/var/www/html/
rsync -e ssh -avuz /var/www/html/* webserver2.mydomain.com:/var/www/html/
rsync -e ssh -avuz /var/www/html/* webserver3.mydomain.com:/var/www/html/
```

Define a `cron` job that runs each of these commands nightly. It will send all changed files from your main machine to the multiple servers on the network. The first time you run this, all the files are pushed and will take a while; each time afterward, it only pushes files that have been changed. You can even configure a second instance and reverse the source and target directories to run it bidirectionally so that changes made on remote servers will be pulled back to the master machine.

Note If you rely on `rsync`, it's imperative that all server clocks are in sync. Do this by running `rdate` against a good time reference. Most big organizations have their own timeserver, but a common system `crontab` (run `crontab --e` to edit yours) for syncing the time at 1:13 every morning would be:

```
1 13 * * * rdate -s time.nist.gov
```

FISH

Fedora Core users (and Linux users in general) should be aware of the fish library and URL usage. fish provides graphical access to any SSH function. Under Fedora Core, it can be used within any KDE application. The easiest way to use fish is with the Konqueror web browser. Open Konqueror and type `FISH://username@localhost` in the Location box. An SSH login window will open. Once you have typed the appropriate system username and password, you can browse directories and transfer files over an SSH-encrypted connection (see the following figure).

Use fish to manage remote files graphically over an SSH connection.

File Transfer Troubleshooting

File transfer is a fairly straightforward process. If you run into trouble, the causes are easy to figure out, and the solutions are simple to implement. Here are some of the most common file transfer issues and a few hints to solve the problems:

✦ *SSH key-based authentication is not working*—There are two likely causes for key-based authentication failure. First, edit the sshd_config file on the target system (the one you are SSHing into), not on the local system. The target system's sshd_config needs these lines:

```
PubkeyAuthentication yes
AuthorizedKeysFile      .ssh/authorized_keys
```

Restart the target sshd service with the command service sshd restart or /etc/init.d/sshd restart. Next, be sure that the target user's ~/.ssh/authorized_keys file contains the public key of the client who is attempting to log into that user account, taken from ~/.ssh/id_dsa.pub. The file permissions of the target user's .ssh directory and authorized_keys file must be set appropriately:

```
#ls -lad /home/bob/.ssh/ /home/bob/.ssh/authorized_keys
drwx------ 2 bob bob 4096 Jan 10 19:35 /home/bob/.ssh/
-rwx------ 1 bob bob  602 Jan 10 19:35
/home/bob/.ssh/authorized_keys
```

✦ *Cannot log into running sshd daemon*—If the sshd service is running, but you can't log in, there are several possible causes. The first is quite simple to solve: verify (from the console) that sshd on the target server is actually running:

```
#/etc/init.d/sshd status
sshd (pid 4714) is running...
```

If you don't get the appropriate response, start the daemon. The solution to a more complex problem (if, for example, your firewall configuration is overly secure) is described earlier, under the *SSH and Firewalls* section. However a quick check on the target server may be to shut off the iptables service on the local and target systems altogether:

```
#/etc/init.d/iptables stop
Resetting built-in chains to the default ACCEPT policy: [ OK ]
```

✦ *"Permission denied" errors*—Unless you tell ssh, scp, or sftp differently, it will always attempt to log you into the remote system under the same username you are using locally. The solution is to log in with an explicit statement of the account you want to reach:

```
[amy@localhost amy]$ ssh mikey@192.168.128.3
```

✦ *Users should not be able to login as root*—For maximum security, administrators should login as themselves, then su - to the root account. With this method, you can track who's logging in and what they're doing. Edit /etc/sshd/sshd-config to deny root login:

```
PermitRootLogin no
```

Then restart the ssh service.

✦ *WebDAV doesn't work*—Try to get WebDAV running without SSL first. Lock down WebDAV so that it answers only specific IP addresses, using the `Allow from` line in the `Directory` directive block of `httpd.conf`. If you continue to get WebDAV error messages, consult the logs for a message like this:

```
# tail -f /var/log/httpd/error_log
.
.
.
[Sun Jan 11 21:26:41 2004] [notice] Apache/2.0.47 (Fedora)
configured -- resuming normal operations
[Sun Jan 11 21:26:55 2004] [error] [client 10.1.1.2] client
denied by server configuration: /home/bob/web/html/.htaccess
```

Such a message indicates that your `Allow from` line is probably misconfigured. Double-check the IP address block you entered.

File Transfer Resources

Because file transfer is so important when offering network-based services, there is a vast amount of information available to help you with file-transfer-related problems and questions. Table 18-3 shows some of the best places to start your search.

Table 18-3: File Transfer Resources

SSH/SCP/SFTP Suite (with OpenSSH)	
The OpenSSH suite	`http://openssh.org/`
The `ssh` and `sftp` daemon	`# man sshd`
The `sftp` client	`# man sftp`
SFTP (File Transfer Protocol)	`www.openssh.org/txt/draft-ietf-secsh-filexfer-02.txt`
SSH/SFTP Servers for Windows and Mac	`http://cygwin.com/`
	`http://openssh.org/windows.html`
	`www.f-secure.com/products/ssh`
WebDAV on Apache	
Apache Module mod_dav	`http://localhost/manual/mod/mod_dav.html` `http://httpd.apache.org/docs-2.0/mod/mod_dav.html`
	`www.webdav.org/mod_dav/`

Continued

Table 18-3: *(continued)*

WebDAV & Frontpage	`www.sambar.com/syshelp/webdav.htm`
WebDAV protocol	`www.faqs.org/rfcs/rfc2518.html`
VSFTPD	
Red Hat Enterprise Linux 3: Reference Guide, FTP	`www.redhat.com/docs/manuals/enterprise/RHEL-3-Manual/ref-guide/ch-ftp.html#S1-FTP-PROTOCOL`
`vsftpd` Configuration Options	`www.redhat.com/docs/manuals/enterprise/RHEL-3-Manual/ref-guide/s1-ftp-vsftpd-conf.html`
FrontPage on Apache ***(For Information Only)***	
Ready-to-Run Software's FrontPage Support	`www.rtr.com/fpsupport/`
Installing FrontPage Server Extensions to an Apache Server	`http://support.microsoft.com/default.aspx?scid=kb%3Ben-us%3B202198`

Summary

There are several protocols that can be used to move files from one location on a network to another. Though FTP, the original file transfer protocol, is still very common, it is not particularly secure and is generally discouraged for common use. Administrators increasingly prefer secure alternatives like those in the OpenSSH family, or web-based file transfer options like the WebDAV protocol or GUI SSH/FISH clients on the user side. Under Fedora Core, you can run a full array of FTPs and client programs to meet every user's need. As long as you keep an eye on secure configurations and track problems immediately, you should have little trouble managing file transfers across your networks and between your servers.

E-Mail Server Troubleshooting

The e-mail server software used to transmit e-mail across the Internet is called a *Mail Transfer Agent*, or MTA. There are several MTAs that run well on Linux: Sendmail, qmail, PostFix, and Exim among others. Sendmail is by far the most popular MTA on the planet and is the default MTA under Fedora Core. In this chapter, therefore, we focus on Sendmail configuration and troubleshooting. However, some users may prefer the PostFix MTA (also included with Fedora Core). At the end of this chapter, we introduce PostFix and provide basic information on configuring and running this alternative server.

> **Note**
>
> Sendmail is released in two versions: commercial and Free (speech, not beer). In this chapter, we address the Open Source version shipped with Fedora Core. If you need enterprise-level e-mail management, consider the sendmail.com commercial version. It provides a graphical interface, integrated spam control, and transparent antivirus protection.

You should know that Fedora Core or other Red Hat Linux installations do not automatically configure MTAs to detect incoming mail from the Internet. That is, the SMTP service or daemon binds only to localhost by default, so the mail server does not see incoming mail from the network. In order to get and distribute mail on your network, you'll need to configure your MTA of choice. Note that, by default, MTAs are designed only to gather mail from local scripts, programs, or users, and then to transfer those messages to other e-mail accounts (local or remote). If you want to run an MTA that listens to traffic from the network or the Internet, you must enable those functions. This is a security matter.

New to Mail Servers?

Because the focus of this chapter is on MTA configuration and troubleshooting, we assume that readers of this book already have a basic grasp of mail transfer agents and e-mail mechanisms in general. Basic mail concepts include mbox and MailDir formats, POP versus IMAP, port

Continued

Continued

assignment, and so on. If these concepts are unfamiliar to you, you might want to learn more before starting to run your own mail services. You can find a useful overview, slanted toward Red Hat Linux products, at `www.europe.redhat.com/documentation/HOWTO/Mail-Administrator-HOWTO-3.php3`.

Switching between MTAs with the alternatives System

Before you look at Sendmail or PostFix, you should know about a subsystem of Fedora Core and Red Hat Linux that controls which MTA the system uses. It is critical that you understand this MTA control system, since you need to know which MTA is in use before you can troubleshoot related e-mail problems.

Understanding the alternatives System

The *alternatives* system is a set of control scripts and symlinks that was developed by the Debian team to support application interoperability and dependency resolution. This system has been available on Red Hat installations since at least version 7.3. It usually goes unnoticed unless you need to track down a pesky MTA binary- or daemon-related problem.

Often, an e-mail server administrator has much more to contend with than just dealing with user-based e-mail. System scripts, web CGIs, user programs, and other parts of the system often send mail from the server. Each of these scripts and programs have their own method of sending automated e-mail. For example, many scripts send e-mail by calling the MTA directly. One may use `/usr/sbin/sendmail` while another may expect `/usr/sbin/postfix` to be installed, and still another may want `/usr/local/sbin/qmail`. If you don't offer these various MTAs to your users, you probably don't want to install and administer them all just for your automated scripts.

In order to deal with these multiple requests, many old-school mail administrators resort to ugly combinations of parallel binary installations and tricks involving scripts and aliases, all to gain a fraction of the functionality that alternatives provides out of the box. The problem with these customized designs is that only the designer knows how it works or how it fits together! While being the only one who can fix a crashing server may seem like good job security, it's not an optimal situation for the modern production enterprise-level e-mail environment. The alternatives system gives you the ability to use the MTA best suited to your situation, without the related headaches normally associated with multiple-MTA compatibility.

 Note   The alternatives system can be used to manage various overlapping binaries, such as redundant packages, daemons, or services. Under Fedora and Red Hat Linux, however, alternatives is currently used only to manage multiple MTAs and for CUPS/lpr printer daemon control and maintenance.

The theory behind the alternatives system is simple. Rather than rely on a single binary like `/usr/sbin/sendmail`, alternatives uses a set of symlinks that provide standard link names, all pointing to the ultimate MTA binary, like this:

```
/usr/sbin/sendmail -> /etc/alternatives/mta -> /usr/sbin/sendmail.sendmail
```

where the last filename is actually the Sendmail binary:

```
# ls -la /usr/sbin/sendmail.sendmail
-rwxr-sr-x 1 root smmsp 738752 Oct 2815:06 /usr/sbin/sendmail.sendmail
```

The /usr/sbin/sendmail binary has become a set of links that ultimately calls the "real" sendmail binary, /usr/sbin/sendmail.sendmail.

Why is this useful? User scripts, system packages, web CGI scripts, and other bits of code can now call your local MTA by the Sendmail legacy name and location, by the system MTA reference /etc/alternatives/mta, or by its legacy name, /usr/sbin/sendmail. For example, if the system were using PostFix under the alternatives system's control, the Sendmail symbolic link would look like this:

```
usr/sbin/sendmail -> /etc/alternatives/mta -> /usr/sbin/sendmail.postfix
```

The sendmail.postfix binary is actually the postfix binary with an additional Sendmail compatibility wrapper included that can take some Sendmail-formatted command-line options. Here is the actual file:

```
# ls -la /usr/sbin/sendmail.postfix
-rwxr-xr-x 1 root root 99776 Jul 22 14:45 /usr/sbin/sendmail.postfix
```

Compare this to the standalone PostFix binary shown here:

```
# ls -la /usr/sbin/postfix
-rwxr-xr-x 1 root root 62488 Jul 22 14:45 /usr/sbin/postfix
```

On an RPM-based system such as SuSE, Red Hat, or Fedora Core, you may notice that neither the PostFix nor the Sendmail RPM packages provide the symlink /etc/alternatives/mta. This link is dynamically created and switched by the alternatives system's control scripts. Curiously, both the Sendmail and PostFix RPMs "own" the symlink /usr/sbin/sendmail:

```
# rpm -qf /usr/sbin/sendmail
sendmail-8.12.10-1.1.1
postfix-2.0.11-5
```

At first glance, an experienced system administrator may see the alternatives system as one big mess of unneeded complexity and confusion that does not belong on a "properly managed" mail server. However, the more you study and use the alternatives system, the more you may begin to appreciate the genius of its layout and functionality.

To see what the alternatives system is doing for your MTA, issue the command alternatives -display mta and browse the output:

```
# alternatives --display mta
mta - status is auto.
link currently points to /usr/sbin/sendmail.sendmail
  /usr/sbin/sendmail.sendmail - priority 90
slave mta-pam: (null)
slave mta-mailq: /usr/bin/mailq.sendmail
slave mta-newaliases: /usr/bin/newaliases.sendmail
slave mta-rmail: /usr/bin/rmail.sendmail
slave mta-mailqman: /usr/share/man/man1/mailq.sendmail.1.gz
```

```
slave mta-newaliasesman:
sr/share/man/man1/newaliases.sendmail.1.gz
slave mta-aliasesman:
/usr/share/man/man5/aliases.sendmail.5.gz
   /usr/sbin/sendmail.postfix - priority 30
slave mta-pam: /etc/pam.d/smtp.postfix
slave mta-mailq: /usr/bin/mailq.postfix
slave mta-newaliases: /usr/bin/newaliases.postfix
slave mta-rmail: /usr/bin/rmail.postfix
slave mta-mailqman: /usr/share/man/man1/mailq.postfix.1.gz
slave mta-newaliasesman:
/usr/share/man/man1/newaliases.postfix.1.gz
slave mta-aliasesman:
/usr/share/man/man5/aliases.postfix.5.gz
Current 'best' version is /usr/sbin/sendmail.sendmail.
```

When you switch MTAs with the alternatives system, the entire system shifts gears. The manual page assignments for MTA binaries, mail queuing, system aliases, and even the PAM authentication system and SysV init (boot) scripts are reconfigured on the fly for the new MTA you have chosen (assuming, of course, that your new MTA is alternatives-aware). If you want to migrate from a Sendmail system to a PostFix system, all your mailing scripts, programs, and CGI scripts should work without major rewrites.

Using the alternatives System

Once you understand the concept behind alternatives, it is an easy system to use. In this section, we show you a simple command-line session. This output shows the process of switching between Sendmail and PostFix, using the `alternatives` or `redhat-switch-mail-nox` command, as well as some troubleshooting tips to make the switch easier.

Tip

Learn more about the alternatives system with the command man 8 alternatives.

To begin the process of switching MTAs, you should first verify that the system is using Sendmail as its mail transfer agent, and that alternatives is aware of this fact. Issue the command `alternatives -display mta`, as described in the previous section.

The line that shows the active MTA is `link currently points to ....` Remember, the actual Sendmail binary is `/usr/sbin/sendmail.sendmail` and the Sendmail/PostFix wrapper binary is `/usr/sbin/sendmail.postfix`.

When Sendmail is the active MTA, you'll also see that it is configured to come up as a service when the machine is booted via the `chkconfig` command:

```
# chkconfig --list|grep sendmail
sendmail  0:off  1:off  2:on  3:on  4:on  5:on  6:off
```

This shows that Sendmail will start up at boot time in runlevel 2, 3, 4, or 5. Once you have verified that Sendmail is active, you can issue the next set of commands, which notify the alternatives system to use PostFix as the MTA instead of Sendmail:

```
# alternatives --set mta /usr/sbin/sendmail.postfix
# alternatives --display mta
mta - status is manual.
link currently points to /usr/sbin/sendmail.postfix
/usr/sbin/sendmail.postfix - priority 30
slave mta-pam: /etc/pam.d/smtp.postfix
slave mta-mailq: /usr/bin/mailq.postfix
slave mta-newaliases: /usr/bin/newaliases.postfix
.
.
.
```

Now it's pointing to /usr/sbin/sendmail.postfix, the Sendmail compatibility wrapper for PostFix. Again, use chkconfig to see whether Sendmail is still set to run at boot time:

```
# chkconfig --list |grep sendmail
```

You should receive no output. Alternatives knew that you *had* Sendmail set up as the system MTA and switched to PostFix. The lack of output indicates that alternatives has not only changed the MTA, but has ensured that Sendmail will not be referenced at boot time or during runlevel changes.

Next, test whether the system also correctly set up PostFix as the system MTA and also configured it for the system's boot and runlevel changes:

```
# chkconfig --list |grep postfix
postfix   0:off  1:off  2:on   3:on   4:on   5:on   6:off
```

Now, when the system boots into either runlevel 3 or runlevel 5 (the default boot runlevels for Red Hat and Fedora Core), the Postfix MTA will start. It will also run if the runlevel is changed to anything from runlevels 2 to 5.

This all looks good, but the one thing that alternatives does not do for you is actually start and stop running daemons or services. In this example, Sendmail is still running. If you check the status of the MTA daemons before you stop Sendmail by hand, you will see something like this:

```
# /etc/init.d/sendmail status
sendmail (pid 5777 5768) is running
# /etc/init.d/postfix status
master is stopped
```

Stop the Sendmail daemon:

```
# /etc/init.d/sendmail stop
Shutting down sendmail:              [ OK ]
Shutting down sm-client:             [ OK ]
```

After you have seen the confirmation that Sendmail is stopped, you can start PostFix. PostFix can either be started manually or through runlevel change, as shown here:

```
# runlevel
N 3
# init 4
# init 3
# /etc/init.d/postfix status
master (pid 5904) is running
```

The first command showed the previous and current runlevels (N=unknown, or the system booted before your current runlevel was entered). On a headless or GUI-less server, this is runlevel 3 on Red Hat based systems. If you want to simulate a reboot without actually rebooting your system, just toggle over to another runlevel and then back to your production default runlevel. After doing this, anything set to run in your default runlevel should start up if not already running. The last command shows us that PostFix is now running.

Note

Changing runlevels is done here for illustrative purposes. Most administrators will not change runlevels on a production server unless they really have to. Most would simply issue the command /etc/init.d/postfix start. If you do want to simulate what happens when you boot a system, changing runlevels will get you as close as possible without doing an actual reboot.

Some experts consider the changing of runlevels (to test the ability of init script-configured services to properly start and stop on reboot) to be unduly dangerous on a production server. This is because a lot happens to a server when you toggle runlevels. Services across the system are checked for running process IDs (or PIDS), kill and start scripts are called, logs are written, and so on. However, the "boot survivability" of a service is best tested using this real world runlevel testing method. You just need to be sure that you know exactly what you have running (and not running) in each run level. If you are not intimately familiar with the configuration of all of the daemons on your server, or testing chkconfig controlled services like this makes you nervous on a live system, then just verify the proper per daemon configuration settings with chkconfig, manually start the service you're configuring, and then just check its status either with the init script or with ps, like this:

```
# chkconfig --list sendmail
sendmail      0:off   1:off   2:on   3:on   4:on   5:on   6:off
# /etc/init.d/sendmail status
sendmail is stopped
# /etc/init.d/sendmail start
Starting sendmail:                        [  OK  ]
Starting sm-client:                       [  OK  ]
# ps auxw| grep [s]endmail
root     31988  0.0  0.5   6320 2672 ?     S    18:46
0:00 sendmail:
accepting connections
smmsp    31997  0.0  0.4   6148 2340 ?     S    18:46
0:00 sendmail:
Queue runner@01:00:00 for /var/spool/clientmqueue
```

Once you get PostFix running, you may want to check the process to be sure that it is working correctly. You can use the /etc/init.d/postfix status method for testing (as we did previously), but if you instead use the ps command, you should see output like this when the PostFix MTA is functioning properly:

```
# ps auxw| grep [p]ostf
root     6123 ... /usr/libexec/postfix/master
postfix  6124 ... pickup -l -t fifo -u
postfix  6125 ... nqmgr -l -n qmgr -t fifo -u
```

Should you no longer want to work with PostFix, it is easy to reverse these commands and get back to Sendmail:

```
# /etc/init.d/postfix status
master (pid 5904) is running...
# /etc/init.d/postfix stop
Shutting down postfix:                       [ OK ]

# alternatives --set mta /usr/sbin/sendmail.sendmail
# chkconfig --list| grep sendmail
sendmail 0:off 1:off  2:on     3:on    4:on    5:on    6:off
# chkconfig --list| grep postfix
#
# /etc/init.d/sendmail status
sendmail is stopped
# init 4
# init 3
# runlevel
4 3
# /etc/init.d/sendmail status
sendmail (pid 5988 5979) is running...
```

This code block shows the complete process for using alternatives to change the server MTA, and then testing the change by switching runlevels. Be warned: changing runlevels can be dangerous if you don't know exactly what is going on in each runlevel. If you're not sure, just use the safer `/etc/init.d/sendmail start` command to start up Sendmail (or whichever service you're toggling) instead of `init 4` and `init 3`.

 Caution   Under Red Hat Linux 9, there was a bug in the stock alternatives system that makes Sendmail's `smtpauth` fail if you switch MTAs to PostFix and then back to Sendmail. Though it appears to have been fixed in Fedora Core 1, you should be aware of the potential problem. The bug is caused by a missing line in `/var/lib/alternatives/mta`:

```
/usr/sbin/sendmail.sendmail
90 sendmail
 /etc/pam.d/smtp.postfix  <--Add this line...
/usr/bin/mailq.sendmail
```

Add the line, change the default MTA to PostFix and then back to Sendmail, and turn on the `saslauthd` **service (don't forget to issue the** `chkconfig saslauthd on` **command), and it will work fine. If you continue to see error messages in** `/var/log/messages` **or** `/var/log/maillog`, **check** `http://bugzilla.redhat.com` **to find a fix or patch.**

Using GUI Configuration Tools for alternatives

Some people prefer to work with graphical user interfaces, and Red Hat has made a real commitment to providing GUI tools for the programs included with Red Hat Linux and Fedora Core. In some cases, a program may have both a GUI and a TUI (text-based user interface). All three options—GUI, TUI, or good old command line—will get the job done.

Under Fedora Core, the alternatives system has a Python-based graphical user interface, shown in Figure 19-1. Invoke it with the command `redhat-switch-mail`. If you prefer, you can invoke a text-based user interface, as seen in Figure 19-2, with `redhat-switch-mail-nox` (where `nox` stands for "no-X11").

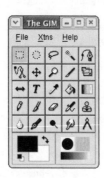

FC-1 i386

Figure 19-1: It's easy to manage the alternatives system with a point-and-click graphical interface.

Both these commands call the Python and XML underpinnings now used in Red Hat based systems to set up alternatives so that it runs properly with commands issued through the graphical or text-based configuration tools.

There is also a GUI for the chkconfig tool, shown in Figure 19-3. Note, however, that the chkconfig GUI only toggles the boot-time configuration for the runlevel that you are currently in (runlevel 5 if you are in the GUI). In contrast, chkconfig at the command line affects runlevels 2 through 5 when configuring services and daemons to be on and off. Invoke the chkconfig GUI with the command `redhat-config-services`.

If you are working on a Red Hat based system, you might prefer ntsysv, the ncurses, or text-based user interface for chkconfig, invoked with the ntsysv command. It is lightweight, fast, and does not require X11; you can use it via ssh over a text login. The ntsysv TUI is shown in Figure 19-4.

One nice feature of these tools is that you can use them to learn about the various services available on your server. For example, in the ntsysv TUI example, just highlight the service

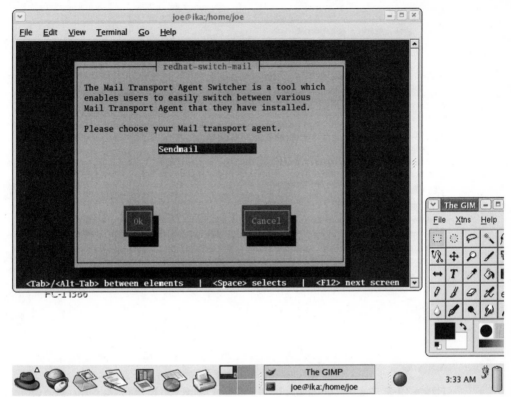

Figure 19-2: The text-based alternatives interface is a happy medium between command line and GUI.

that you're interested in and press F1 to see a Help window that describes that service. This is how many new Red Hat based sys-admins learn the ropes about system initialization services.

Sendmail Configuration

Setting up a new installation of Sendmail used to be a daunting task. While it is an intricate and challenging program and most people don't want to devote their lives to mining its depths, it has become much more user friendly in the past 4 or 5 years. Luckily, you can now get Sendmail to do what you need with a minimum of fuss, leaving the more complex questions to your copious spare time.

Tip   Those who run Sendmail should have handy a copy of *Sendmail* by Bryan Costales and Eric Allman (3rd edition, O'Reilly and Associates, 2002). It contains Everything you need to know about running this MTA—and then some.

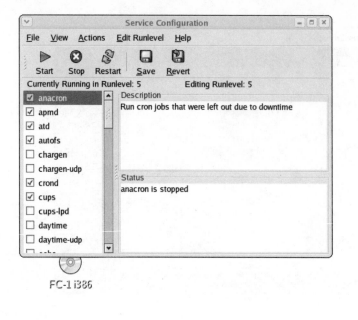
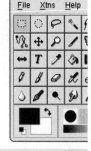

Figure 19-3: The chkconfig graphical interface helps you to manage services on various runlevels.

There are a few files that Sendmail administrators work with frequently. Some configuration files need to be edited before Sendmail runs properly, while you'll work with others on a regular basis. Sendmail log files are filled with useful information, and are a good resource for initial troubleshooting. Table 19-1 shows a list of these files with a brief description of each.

> **Note** The term *virtual hosting* describes the act of hosting more than one domain or host on a single server or IP address. With a single host and a single IP address, you could potentially host hundreds of domains or fully qualified domain names (FQDNs). In an e-mail context, this is usually called *vhosting*. When speaking of web servers, this is called *name-based hosting* and is supported under the HTTPv1.1 protocol.

The files in /etc/mail/ are critical for the Sendmail MTA. In a running domain, the most common file you'll edit is the /etc/mail/virtusertable file, as you'll see in the next section. If you need to block spammers and the like on a regular basis, /etc/mail/access may be your next most commonly edited file. The sendmail.mc file is used when you need to make MTA-wide changes to Sendmail, so be careful when editing this file—changes to the sendmail.mc file must be processed down to the sendmail.cf file using the m4 macro compiler. We'll make some basic changes to the sendmail.mc/cf pair in the *Turning on Public IP SMTP Bindings* section.

Figure 19-4: The ntsysv tool is a text-based interface for the chkconfig tool.

Table 19-1: Selected Sendmail Configuration Files

Configuration Files

/etc/aliases	The OS aliases file that connects local recipient accounts to other local or nonlocal accounts (root, postmaster, tom@yahoo.com, and so on). It also allows you to set up group-mail recipients, as well as route incoming e-mail to scripts and commands on the system
/etc/mail/sendmail.cf	The file that Sendmail uses (generated from the mc file) for all of its runtime settings. *Do not edit this file*
/etc/mail/sendmail.mc	The main human-editable macro config file that is m4-processed down to create the runtime .cf file. Also found in the /etc/mail/ directory in newer installs
/etc/mail/	Directory where most Sendmail individual settings files reside

Continued

Table 19-1: *(continued)*

/etc/mail/access	The setting file that is used to control e-mail flow to and through your server. Less common since SMTP-Auth has been implemented, but still used for some spam blocking or manually blacklisting people, domains, or IP address blocks
/etc/mail/virtusertable	This is the file that gives you control of domain-specific aliasing or virtual hosting of e-mail. For example, sending incoming mail for sales@mydomain.com to bob@mydomain.com, or creating catch-all e-mail addresses for entire domains
/etc//mail/domaintable	Includes a "domain table" that can be used to provide domain name mapping. Use of this should really be limited to your own domains. It may be useful if you change names (for example, your company changes names from oldname.com to newname.com)
/etc/mail/genericstable	This feature will cause certain addresses to be masqueraded or made to appear as another address
/etc/mail/mailertable	Can be used to override routing or provide DNS type routing for specific domains/ports. Used iwhen setting up a mail relay or mail hub for your domain(s)

Log Files

/var/log/maillog	The mail log file where SMTP, POP, and other runtime related Sendmail messages are logged. Look here first when you're having problems working with runtime related errors
/var/log/messages	Standard service related issues, authentication messages, service start errors, and so on

User/System Directories

/var/spool/mail/	Where users' e-mail spool files are stored
/var/spool/mqueue/	Where queued e-mail is stored

/etc/mail/virtusertable

Though Sendmail is a complex program that uses many configuration files, most administrators work with a small selection of those files on a regular basis and leave the rest alone. Of the many Sendmail configuration files, /etc/mail/virtusertable is the one you'll probably work with most frequently as an e-mail administrator. This file controls virtual hosting, domain-specific, and user-based aliasing. Here's a sample virtusertable file:

```
[...]
hire-me@mydomain.com        bsmith@mydomain.com
```

```
##--Local alias
bob@mydomain.com        bsmith

##--Local Junk mail accounts for Bob
bsmithjunk@mydomain.com     bsmith
bsmithjunk1@mydomain.com    bsmith

##--Local to Remote redirects
billmary@mydomain.com       wsmithok@earthlink.net
bill-n-mary@mydomain.com    wsmithok@earthlink.net
butch-n-mert@mydomain.com   wsmithok@earthlink.net

##--Multi-Domain Conflicting vhost addresses
sales@mydomain.com          bsmith
sales@yourdomain.com        mwalker
sales@homestarrunner.com    strongbad@aol.com

#-----Catch All Accounts-----
@mydomain.com               postmaster
```

Each section contains two columns. The first column contains the incoming address or address fragment that the MTA will actually see on incoming e-mail traffic, while the second column contains the actual local or remote address that should receive those messages.

Note that each section in the sample begins with a commented-out line describing the type of redirects in that section. Though your virtusertable file may be short, this is a good practice; the more traffic you get and the more redirects you manage, the harder it will be to find a problem in a virtusertable file without a roadmap.

Note   *Catch-all accounts* allow you to catch all unknown user (or undefined virtual user) e-mail and send it to one recipient—usually the domain administrator. The last line of the /etc/mail/virtusertable file shows a catch-all account. There are two important points to remember about these accounts. First, catch-all-accounts must appear below all other valid entries for that given domain. Second, if you enable a catch-all account for a given domain, all new e-mail addresses for that domain must now be placed in the virtusertable file in order for users to get their e-mail. Otherwise, a domain catch-all account will suck up all the e-mail going to users not defined in virtusertable.

If you edit /etc/mail/virtusertable, you will need to rebuild the binary database files that the running Sendmail MTA uses before the edits can take effect. There are two easy ways to do this:

```
# cd /etc/mail
# make
```

or (under Red Hat or Fedora-based Linux systems) simply restart the Sendmail service with

```
# service sendmail restart
Shutting down sendmail:                    [  OK  ]
Shutting down sm-client:                    [  OK  ]
```

/etc/aliases

The /etc/aliases file is a standard system file that maps incoming e-mail aliases to local or remote system accounts. One of the first jobs on a new system is usually to ensure that the root alias points to an actual e-mail address, whether local or remote. Other important aliases include postmaster, help, and abuse.

A sample /etc/aliases file might look like this:

```
[...]
# Person who should get root's mail
#root:                  marc
root:                   admin
postmaster:             root
mailman:                admin
mailman-owner:          mailman


# Shared addresses
webmaster:              admin, mike, mike@yahoo.com
helpdesk:               bob, mike, mike@yahoo.com
## xcssa mailman mail-list
## created: 04-Jun-2001 root
xcssa:          "| /usr/share/mailman/mail/wrapper post xcssa"
xcssa-admin:    "| /usr/share/mailman/mail/wrapper mailowner xcssa"
xcssa-request:  "| /usr/share/mailman/mail/wrapper mailcmd xcssa"
xcssa-owner:    xcssa-admin
```

Note that some of the aliases are mapped to other aliases, such as postmaster to root. In fact, the only actual person in the first section is admin, who ultimately receives all mail sent to root, postmaster, mailman, and mailman-owner.

As in most Linux config files, lines that start with a # are comments. It's a good idea to keep config files like this well-commented for clarity.

Note This file also includes other aliases, such as one for a mailing list called xcssa. The xcssa alias resolves to mailman list-server wrapper scripts, a useful trick but one that can be very dangerous. Such a function could be set up to accept an e-mail that triggers a local binary, such as the address reboot@example.net used to trigger the binary /sbin/reboot (see man smrsh for more details). Be careful when associating aliases with scripts or programs lest you leave back doors open, and future problems.

If you make changes to /etc/aliases, you will need to let Sendmail know that new aliases are available. You can do this with a simple command:

```
# newaliases
```

You must run this command to convert the human-readable /etc/aliases file into the binary format that the Sendmail MTA uses during runtime (/etc/aliases.db as a rule).

You can also use the sendmail command to enable /etc/aliases changes:

```
# sendmail -bi
```

Sendmail Tips and Tricks

While it's possible to administer Sendmail using nothing but guidance from the official program documentation, most administrators have collected shortcuts and ideas to help automate or streamline routine tasks. Since Sendmail has been around for so long and is so complex, new and experienced mail-admins alike just want a listing of the most commonly used tricks and shortcuts to do what they need to do with this powerful MTA. This section contains some useful Sendmail tricks used at Rackspace Managed Hosting to help customers out of tight.

Redirecting System Mail

When you set up a new system or a new mail server, there are several things that you should do right away to make your work life easier and your system more secure. One of these jobs is to redirect system mail so that it goes to someone other than the actual root user on the local system. This gets the system mail into the mailbox of a real person who can solve the problem, as well as keep the root mailbox from just sitting there and filling up the drive.

Tip

It's always a good idea to define your root alias so that it points both to your local administrative e-mail account and to a backup mail account on another server. If there are local problems such as a crashed mailbox, compromised root passwords, or other things that make it impossible for you to access root-related mail, you'll still be able to use the backup account to get system messages.

If you're using Sendmail, system e-mail is redirected with the /etc/aliases file. If you've switched to PostFix, you'll need to work in the /etc/postfix/aliases file. The syntax is the same for both MTAs:

```
[...]
# Person who should get root's mail
#root:               marc
root:                mylocalaccount, me@otherdomain.com
[...]
```

Once you've added the new information and saved the file, you must rebuild the alias database. Use the newaliases command:

```
# newaliases
/etc/aliases: 63 aliases, longest 10 bytes, 625 bytes total
```

Note

You should be able to use newaliases with Sendmail and with PostFix, even though the two MTAs use different newalias commands and configuration files. Why? It's the alternatives system at work again. Look at the output of alternatives-display mta and the results of ls -la $(which newaliases) to see how alternatives handles this situation.

What Are My Sendmail Settings?

Whether you're new to an existing Sendmail installation or you just want a quick overview, sometimes it's useful to get output that details every Sendmail configuration on the system. Get this information with the command:

```
# sendmail -vd0.015 < /dev/null
```

Securing User .forward Files

Individual users can create .forward files to redirect their e-mail to another address without needing root access to do so. These .forward files are processed by the procmail program. If you use .forward files (or allow your users to create them), be sure that the file's permissions are set securely. Otherwise, a .forward file will not work. Secure .forward files look like this:

```
$ cd /home/bob
$ ls -la .forward
-rwx------    1 bob    bob        27 Dec 25 00:04 .forward
$ cat /home/bob/.forward
bob@yahoo.com
```

This shows that the local user bob has all of his e-mail redirected to his Yahoo! account. Note that the file permissions must be set correctly, or it will not work. If you need to change the permissions of your .forward file, do so with the command chmod 700 .forward. Likewise, your home directory (/home/bob/ in this case) should also be locked down to at least rwxr-xr-x (755), or you may have .forward processing problems even if the file permissions are set properly.

Looking at the Outgoing Mail Queue

If you want to take a quick look at your system's outgoing mail queue, use this command:

```
# mailq
```

This command is actually a symbolic link to the sendmail binary, which is run internally as sendmail -bp:

```
# ls -la /usr/bin/mailq
lrwxrwxrwx  1 root    root    27 Dec 16 11:38 /usr/bin/mailq ->
    /etc/alternatives/mta-mailq
```

Changing Sendmail Options

To manage most Sendmail options, make changes in the /etc/mail/sendmail.mc macro configuration file. When the file has been saved, you must rebuild the .mc file down to the runtime configuration file /etc/mail/sendmail.cf with the m4 macro interpreter or processor. In this section, we describe three common Sendmail option changes and show the command sequences to accomplish each goal.

Rebuilding sendmail.cf

As we've said before, when you make a change to the sendmail.mc file, you must then follow up by rebuilding the sendmail.cf file with the m4 processor. First, we show you how to do this safely, and then show you how to make some common option changes to Sendmail.

Since you need to rebuild sendmail.cf each time you make configuration changes to the sendmail.mc file, here's an easy way to back up your critical system files, rebuild, and then restart Sendmail to take advantage of new settings. First, make a set of backup files:

```
# cd /etc/mail
# cp -a sendmail.cf sendmail.cf-BAK
# cp -a sendmail.mc sendmail.mc-BAK
```

Now that you have backup copies, you can make needed changes to the `sendmail.mc` file and then apply them to `sendmail.cf`:

```
# m4 sendmail.mc > sendmail.cf
#
```

Next, restart Sendmail to use the changes:

```
# /etc/init.d/sendmail restart
Shutting down sendmail:                    [  OK  ]
Shutting down sm-client:                   [  OK  ]
Starting sendmail:                         [  OK  ]
Starting sm-client:                        [  OK  ]
```

Turning on Public IP SMTP Bindings

Mail servers on Fedora Core and Red Hat Linux systems are bound, by default, only to the loopback IP address 127.0.0.1. This is done for security, since there are far more Linux machines out there that do *not* run as incoming mail servers than there are machines intended to accept incoming SMTP traffic. Leaving MTAs configured to loopback makes sense from a security perspective (fewer services exposed to the network means better security). If this were not the case, administrators would have to remember to turn off the mail server when configuring a nonmail server, which would make default Linux installations less secure everywhere.

However, if you need incoming Sendmail MTA services to run on a new machine, then you must manually configure Sendmail to listen on an external IP address.

Caution   Before you begin to configure Sendmail on a new machine, back up your existing `/etc/mail/` directory and all its configuration files. We'll wait here while you do it. Doing a quick backup has saved more than one mail administrator's job. Here's an easy back-up method that works for us:

```
# cp -a /etc/mail /etc/mail-BAK
# ls -lad /etc/mail-*
drwxr-xr-x  3 root    root      4096 Dec 16 12:16 /etc/mail-BAK
```

Once you have backed up your existing `/etc/mail/` dir and its configuration files, you can begin to work with `sendmail.mc`. Open `/etc/mail/sendmail.mc` in your favorite text editor and find the lines containing `127`:

```
[...]
dnl This changes sendmail to only listen on the loopback
device 127.0.0.1 dnl and not on any other network devices.
Comment this out if you want dnl to accept email over the
network.
DAEMON_OPTIONS('Port=smtp,Addr=127.0.0.1, Name=MTA')
[...]
```

Note   The lines that start with `dnl` are comments, like those beginning with # in configuration files. The `dnl` component tells the m4 macro processor to skip from here to the next line. (The excerpt above is actually line-wrapped.) Every line that is not a specific command for the m4 processor needs to start with `dnl`, or m4 will try to interpret it.

There are several ways to edit this file so that Sendmail will begin to listen for incoming SMTP traffic. You can add `dnl` to the beginning of the DAEMON_OPTIONS line, as in

```
dnl DAEMON_OPTIONS('Port=smtp,Addr=127.0.0.1, Name=MTA')
```

You can also leave the line as is, but change the IP address from 127.0.0.1 to the incoming IP address where you receive SMTP traffic. If you receive SMTP traffic on more than one IP address associated with this server, you can change 127.0.0.1 to 0.0.0.0 instead.

Note

Adding `dnl` to the start of the DAEMON_OPTIONS line is the same as changing the IP address to 0.0.0.0 (which means all IPs on the planet). Both methods bind SMTP to all IP addresses on the server. If you want a more restricted setting, set the IP address to a specific incoming IP address.

Not every system should bind SMTP to all incoming IP addresses. If you run internal services such as DHCP or DNS on a machine that also serves as the local firewall and router, you should probably only bind SMTP to a specific internal or external IP address (depending on your security model). Unless you need to bind to multiple IP addresses for vhosting purposes, it's good security policy to restrict SMTP and other services to a single interface or specific IP address.

Since you backed up the functioning `sendmail.cf` file before you edited `sendmail.mc`, it's safe to rebuild your `sendmail.cf` file now and test your new setting. Use the following commands to stop Sendmail, rebuild the `sendmail.cf` file from the edited `sendmail.mc` file, and restart Sendmail.

```
# cd /etc/mail
# /etc/init.d/sendmail stop
Shutting down sendmail:               [  OK  ]
Shutting down sm-client:              [  OK  ]
# m4 sendmail.mc > sendmail.cf
# /etc/init.d/sendmail start
Starting sendmail:                    [  OK  ]
Starting sm-client:                   [  OK  ]
# ps auxw| grep [s]endmail
root  4478 0.0  1.1 7660 2552 ?  S 23:25 0:00 sendmail:
accepting connections
smmsp 4487 0.0  1.0 7864 2252 ?  S 23:25 0:00 sendmail: Queue
runner@01:00:00 for /var/spool/clientmqueue
```

The output from `ps` shows that Sendmail restarted successfully. Now, you can check to see what IP address, or addresses, Sendmail is using to listen for incoming SMTP traffic:

```
# netstat -antp | grep :25
tcp 0 0 0.0.0.0:25 0.0.0.0:*  LISTEN  3780/sendmail: acce
```

Success! This shows us that Sendmail is bouncing to all IP addresses on port 25 (0.0.0.0:25), which is SMTP.

Turning on SMTP-Auth

With the ever-growing mountain of spam that overwhelms mail servers daily, many administrators have begun to implement controls to limit *mail relaying*.

Note

Mail relaying is the way in which someone can send mail through your mail server and out to other recipients not on your system at all. If you run open relays on your mail server, then spammers (who are always scanning for such gold mines) will lock onto your server and use it to send millions of e-mail messages from your server until you're eventually blacklisted by outfits such as www.ordb.org and www.spamhaus.org. Once you've been blacklisted, all of your legitimate e-mail will be blocked by all the big ISPs and hosters such as AOL, MSN, and Earthlink, your users' e-mail will all bounce, and you'll be in hot water. It is very difficult to get off some of these blacklists, so do your best to stay off them by never allowing mail relaying, except from people who can provide a valid username/password. This type of username/password SMTP restriction is called *SMTP-Auth,* and it is much preferred to older antirelaying methods such as pop-locks and manually updated whitelists.

If you have users who access their mail from dynamic IP addresses or who travel regularly so that you can't use IP-based access controls (or *whitelists*), you will probably want to enable SMTP-Auth on your Sendmail server. SMTP-Auth allows you to enforce client authentication before sending mail through your server.

To enable SMTP-Auth under Sendmail, open /etc/mail/sendmail.mc and make this edit:

```
define('confAUTH_OPTIONS', 'A')dnl
```

This should be the default on all newer Fedora Core and Red Hat based systems, but your mileage may vary on other distributions. After you have saved the file, rebuild sendmail.cf and restart Sendmail as described above.

Tip

Later in this chapter is an example of what SMTP-Auth will look like when you telnet directly into a Sendmail server's SMTP port.

Diagnosing Sendmail Problems

You may find yourself in a messy spot if you know there's a Sendmail problem but you can't figure out what it is. Since you need to know the problem before you can solve it, it's important to know how to diagnose Sendmail trouble. In this section, we show you two methods to do so.

Using Log Files to Diagnose Problems

Often the quickest and easiest way to diagnose a mail-related problem is to watch the Sendmail log file as you restart the service, test ports or passwords, or perform other functions that seem to be causing trouble for the MTA. Use the logs to monitor service start and stop errors, system errors in messages, and identify runtime errors. There are several ways to use logs to track Sendmail problems.

If you're having trouble with bad authentications (usernames and passwords) and you want to watch while a particular user logs in with the pop3 service (for example), then use the command

```
# tail -f /var/log/messages | grep username
```

The output will show exactly what's happening, and only for the username that you're interested in:

```
Dec 26 21:53:29 localhost pop(pam_unix)[7950]: authentication
failure; logname= uid=0 euid=0 tty= ruser= rhost=127.0.0.1
user=tweeks
Dec 26 21:53:31 localhost ipop3d[7950]: Login failed user=tweeks
auth=tweeks host=localhost.localdomain [127.0.0.1]
Dec 26 21:53:36 localhost ipop3d[7950]: Logout user=tweeks
host=localhost.localdomain [127.0.0.1]
```

Very useful indeed! If you suspect a bad password, you can filter the output even further to check only for login failures:

```
# tail -f /var/log/messages| grep 'Login failed'
Dec 26 22:00:39 localhost ipop3d[7958]: Login failed
user=tweeks auth=tweeks host=localhost.localdomain
[127.0.0.1]
```

Now you know that the client has forgotten his mail password, or is using a misconfigured mail client—possibly one of the most common mail administration problems seen.

To watch for bounced mail, mail relaying, and other connection issues, watch the Sendmail log file /var/log/maillog, grepping for a specific username or string with the command

```
# tail -f /var/log/maillog | grep bob2
Mar 26 02:55:18 localhost sendmail[8651]: i2Q8tFiJ008651:
to=bob2@fakebaddomain.com, ctladdr=tweeks (500/500),
delay=00:00:03, xdelay=00:00:02, mailer=relay, pri=30055,
relay=[127.0.0.1] [127.0.0.1], dsn=2.0.0, stat=Sent
(i2Q8tG0d008653 Message accepted for delivery)
Mar 26 02:55:18 localhost sendmail[8655]: i2Q8tG0d008653:
to=<bob2@fakebaddomain.com>,
ctladdr=<tweeks@localhost.localdomain> (500/500),
delay=00:00:02, xdelay=00:00:00, mailer=esmtp, pri=30365,
relay=fakebaddomain.com, dsn=5.1.2, stat=Host unknown (Name
server:
fakebaddomain.com: host not found)
```

Here we see that it could not find the domain name fakebaddomain.com: there lies your problem.

Tip

Always ask users with mail problems whether they've upgraded or changed their mail client or hardware lately. Most users let their mail clients remember the e-mail password; when new software is installed or new hardware is configured for them, they can't remember the password and blame the mail server or administrator for a problem. Though you'll probably need to change the client's password, you should explain the problem to the client (and to the client's manager, if you have that responsibility). Stored passwords defeat the purpose of password-protected e-mail accounts, and in some secure environments, client-side password storage may be actually against company security policy.

Diagnosing MTA Problems Using Telnet

Take a cue from those who troubleshoot MTAs for a living. The most common way to identify and track remote SMTP mail server problems is actually with Telnet: not Telnet as in a shell or login to the server, but running Telnet to the SMTP port (port 25) on the mail server itself and attempting to send a message directly to the server using the SMTP protocol. The resulting output will show you exactly what happens when a message is delivered on your machine, and is a good way to diagnose server issues, rule out or prove user/client-side issues, or identify things such as problems with SMTP-Auth.

This command session shows you how:

```
# telnet localhost 25
Trying 127.0.0.1...
Connected to localhost.
Escape character is '^ ]'.
220 playground.test.mydomain.com ESMTP Sendmail 8.11.6/8.11.6;
     Tue, 10 Sep 2002
14:11:41 -0500
ehlo mydomain.com  <--------------Initial Handshake & Option Listing
250-playground.test.mydomain.com Hello localhost [127.0.0.1],
     pleased to meet you
250-ENHANCEDSTATUSCODES
250-8BITMIME
250-SIZE
250-DSN
250-ONEX
250-ETRN
250-XUSR
250-AUTH LOGIN PLAIN   <------------------ Types of SMTP-Auth
250 HELP
mail from:tweeks@mydomain.com <-----------Email "From"
250 2.1.0 tweeks@mydomain.com... Sender ok
rcpt to:tweeks@mydomain.com <------------- Email "To"
250 2.1.5 tweeks@mydomain.com... Recipient ok
data  <--------------------------------- Go into "data mode"
354 Enter mail, end with "." on a line by itself
SUBJECT: This is a test from Playground
This is a test..

Tweeks
.  <------------------------------------- Terminating "."
250 2.0.0 g8AJBu004136 Message accepted for delivery
quit <-----------------------------------
221 2.0.0 playground.test.mydomain.com closing connection
Connection closed by foreign host.
```

This is what an e-mail client or another mail server does every time it connects to your e-mail server on port 25 and sends an e-mail. You could actually send e-mail like this if you were in a pinch!

Sendmail Troubleshooting

Though Sendmail servers can produce the same wide range of problems that any Unix server can generate, most daily Sendmail issues fall into just a few categories. Administrators spend a great deal of time resolving issues with client connections, passwords, with SMTP-Auth, with user mailboxes and POP3, and other such situations. In this section, you'll find some of the most common Sendmail troubleshooting problems and solutions.

Not Receiving Expected E-mail Volume

If you're not receiving incoming e-mail or are seeing less than you think you should, Sendmail may be listening on the wrong IP address. You may also have bound SMTP to a single IP address, though you receive incoming traffic on multiple IPs.

As seen previously, to check the IP address that Sendmail is using, issue this command:

```
# netstat -antp| grep :25
tcp  0  0 127.0.0.1:25   0.0.0.0:*   LISTEN   3780/sendmail: acce
```

The output should show the IP address defined by your settings in sendmail.mc and rebuilt sendmail.cf files. If you need to change the setting, use the process described in *Turning on Public IP SMTP Bindings* earlier in this chapter.

Note   An IP setting of 0.0.0.0:25 means that Sendmail listens for incoming SMTP traffic on all IP addresses associated with your system. Depending on your network configuration, this may be a security risk. 127.0.0.1:25 means that it is only listening to itself (web server CGI scripts, user programs, and so on).

Sendmail Not Accepting Connections

Sometimes Sendmail problems are simple in nature. If the server isn't running, you can't get mail. In other cases, Sendmail may have stopped running due to server load, as it is configured by default to stop accepting connections when server load reaches 8. Here's a simple test to check Sendmail's status:

```
# ps auxw| grep [a]ccepting
root 670 0.0 0.8 5628 2072 ? S Aug08 0:00 sendmail: accepting connections
```

Tip   If you want to check the IP addresses that Sendmail is using at the same time, you can append the command above with ; netstat-ant | grep:25 to get additional information.

E-mail Address Not Deliverable

Need to find out if a local or remote e-mail address accepts e-mail? This command will tell you whether a given e-mail address is deliverable (locally or remotely) and will use all the proper

/etc/aliases and virtusertable mappings assigned to it. It's an excellent way to weed out local problems as you diagnose a user's e-mail problems.

```
# sendmail -bv root@mydomain.com
root@mydomain.com... deliverable: mailer local, user bob
```

This shows that the root user is on the local system, and is aliased to the local user bob.

Trouble in the Queue

Although the queue contains a lot of useful information, it can be daunting to parse a lengthy queue yourself. Use this command to get a verbose parsing of the queue. It's particularly helpful when you have many e-mails queued due to DNS troubles or if you have persistent problems with third-party daemons rejecting your connections.

```
# mailq
/var/spool/mqueue (1 request)
-----Q-ID-----    --Size-- -Priority- ---Q-Time--- -----Sender/Recipient------
i202a4hb003780    5243        1655192 Mar 23 20:36 MAILER-DAEMON
               (Deferred: office100-235.sat.rackspace.com.: No route to host)
                        <root@office100-235.sat.rackspace.com>
               (Deferred: office100-235.sat.rackspace.com.: No route to host)
```

Total requests: 1This output shows a verbose listing of the mail queue and why it was queued. The following command will do the same, but also attempts to redeliver it:

```
# sendmail -v -q
```

This is a good command to run after you think that you've solved the problem.

> **Tip**   Combine this command with tail-f var/log/maillog in another shell or window to monitor the mail log file and help figure out complex local delivery issues, such as those involving procmail or vacation mail processing systems.

POP3 Not Running

POP3 is the protocol by which users are able to hit a mail server, authenticate, and pull their mail down to their client PC. Users love POP3 because POP3-based mail clients are usually feature-rich and simple to use. However, POP3 problems may be client-based or server-based, and aren't always easy to diagnose. This section offers a basic troubleshooting process for POP3, and it explains what to check to ensure that your POP3 daemon will come back up when the server is rebooted. First, you should ensure that the POP3 service is actually running. If it's not, user mail clients will be unable to connect to the server and download waiting messages. Use these commands to determine whether the service is up:

```
$ telnet localhost 110
Trying 127.0.0.1...
telnet: connect to address 127.0.0.1: Connection refused
$
$ netstat -ant | grep 110
$
```

The service doesn't seem to be running, so you need to turn it on:

```
# chkconfig --list| grep pop
        ipop2:   off
        ipop3:   off
        pop3s:   off
# chkconfig ipop3 on
# chkconfig --list| grep pop
        ipop2:   off
        ipop3:   on
        pop3s:   off
```

Note   Pop3 is currently one of the more popular mail retrieval protocols. However, if security is a concern, pop3s is better in that it runs over an encrypted SSL session.

Once the POP3 service is on, you can repeat the first command to see whether POP3 is now functional:

```
$ telnet localhost 110
Trying 127.0.0.1...
Connected to localhost.
Escape character is '^]'.
+OK POP3 localhost.localdomain v2003.83rh server ready
user tweeks
+OK User name accepted, password please
pass mY1337p45sw0rd
+OK Mailbox open, 3 messages
list
+OK Mailbox scan listing follows
1 122243
2 122247
3 122251
```

Note that the `ipop3` service on Red Hat based systems is a subservice of the `xinetd` daemon. The current running status of `xinetd` can be determined with the Red Hat based command

```
# service xinetd status
xinetd (pid 3747) is running...
```

and the boot-time configuration with

```
# chkconfig --list xinetd
xinetd   0:off   1:off   2:on   3:on   4:on   5:on   6:off
```

Be sure that `xinetd` is running, and that it is configured to run on at least runlevels 3, 4, and 5. The output of the `chkconfig -list xinetd` command, when `xinetd` is properly configured, will look like this:

```
xinetd   0:off   1:off   2:on   3:on   4:on   5:on   6:off
```

Top Sendmail Problems (and Solutions)

As with most client/server setups, mail experts see the same problems on a regular basis. With over 10,000 servers on line, Rackspace Managed Hosting sees a lot of Sendmail issues, and as a result has identified these as some of their top problems. Luckily for you, they've also supplied the solutions!

Dealing with Spam

Though spam itself isn't a Sendmail or PostFix problem, it's certainly an issue. Fedora Core includes the popular tool SpamAssassin, which many mail administrators have chosen to implement. SpamAssassin's not perfect, but with a 99%+ spam rejection rate, it certainly cuts down on the flood of unsolicited e-mail that cloaks the legitimate messages coming through your system.

Learn more about SpamAssassin through the documentation on your system with the command `more /usr/share/doc/spamassassin-2.60/README.spamd`.

Blacklisted IP Address

If you have a spammer on your system or you have allowed your system to be used as an open mail relay, you may find that your IP address has been blacklisted by an antispam organization. Note that being tagged as an open relay by entities such as `www.ordb.org` does not always mean that your SMTP daemon is open to the external world. Sometimes, things such as mail scripts on web servers have been identified as a possible opening for SMTP relaying abuse, such as `formmail.pl`. Just having such a file on your system can soil your reputation and brand you as an open relay or spam source. Several Rackspace techs use this quick check to quickly scan a system for this common—though vulnerable—web CGI file:

```
# find / -name "formmail*" -print 2>/dev/null
```

This scan may take a couple of minutes, but if this finds any instances of the `formmail` file, you can see whose file it is, remove it, and let them know that they cannot install that web CGI on your system for security reasons.

Note   Many mail server administrators use blacklists from spamcop.org or mail-abuse.org, or the open relay checker at ordb.org, to block incoming mail from IP addresses on such lists. If your IP is on one of these lists, then your users may not be able to successfully send e-mail to others on the Internet from your system. This makes you feel bad. You should occasionally check these lists to see if any of your servers or IP ranges are listed to stop such blacklisting problems from blindsiding you and reducing your organization's productivity.

Being blacklisted will cause a lot of e-mail bounces, delivered with various error messages, which can increase the traffic load on your server significantly.

Do you have a web user who has done something like upload a `formmail` script and has gotten you blacklisted? Maybe you have a regular user who just decided to try his or her hand at sending out spam from your system for some extra cash. Obviously, the first step to resolving this type of problem is to get rid of your spammer or problem web user, or to shut down the open relay if there is one. Next, you need to talk to your upstream provider; both of you should contact the blacklisting organization and ask them to release your IP from the blacklist after you've provided proof that the issue is resolved. However, this appeal process can often take days, or even weeks. A stopgap solution used by Jorge Arrietta, a Support Sys-Admin and RHCE at Rackspace Managed Hosting, involves redirecting your outgoing e-mail through an additional IP address using `iptables`. This is a good way to keep your critical mail flowing while your blacklist appeal process is pending. To do this, follow these steps:

1. Add a new IP address to your server that is not blacklisted.

2. Modify your MTA's configuration to send SMTP traffic over the new IP address, rather than the one that's blacklisted.

   While you can do this in your MTA's configuration files, it's easier to define a new outgoing SMTP rule with iptables on Linux. Use this command (replacing `<new.IP>` with the new IP address):

   ```
   # iptables -t nat -A POSTROUTING -p tcp --dport 25
   -j SNAT--to-source <new.IP>
   ```

   We recommend that you use iptables because you don't need to make permanent changes to your MTA configuration files. When the blacklist problem is fixed, you can flush the tables with `ptables -F` or `/etc/init.d/iptables restart` and return to normal.

If resolving the blacklist issue is taking longer than you expected and you need to reboot the system, you need to save the new setting to `/etc/sysconfig/iptables`. Before you do this, however, back up your current boot-time `iptables` settings with the command (on Red Hat/Fedora-based systems):

```
# cp -a /etc/sysconfig/iptables /etc/sysconfig/iptables-BAK
```

Make any `iptables` changes you want, and then save the currently running `iptables` settings into your boot-time settings with the command:

```
# iptables-save > /etc/sysconfig/iptables
```

or, on Red Hat/Fedora-based systems, with:

```
# service iptables save
Saving firewall rules to /etc/sysconfig/iptables:    [ OK ]
```

Mail Server Misconfiguration

AOL, Yahoo!Mail, HotMail, and other popular webmail hosts and ISPs have begun to bounce more and more of their incoming messages back to the originating domain. These messages are bounced for a number of reasons. If the bounce messages claim that your mail server is misconfigured, it may be due to a new method of detecting spam sources. Many service providers now use tools such as `nslookup` and `dig` to check the DNS entries of sites attempting to send mail to their users. If the forward and reverse DNS entries do not match, the message is sometimes rejected as potential spam.

For example, assume that the result of the command

```
$ nslookup yourdomain.org
```

is 10.1.1.2. The result of `nslookup 10.1.1.2` should then be yourdomain.org in order to match. However, if the result of `nslookup 10.1.1.2` is something like `www.yourdomain.org` or mail.yourdomain.org, or the command returns nothing at all, there is a good chance that your outgoing e-mail will be rejected.

To resolve this problem, configure your DNS servers to return matching information for both forward and reverse DNS checks.

Mail Bounces due to Dynamic IP Configuration

Another reason for the mail bounces described in the previous problem may be that your IP address is dynamic, rather than static, as with most dial-up, cable modem, and ADSL-based home or SOHO Internet connections. Spammers often try to spam through home broadband on dynamic IP addresses as their IP will eventually change, so this allows them to stay one step ahead of the blacklisters. As a result, big providers such as AOL and others just reject e-mail that is relayed directly from a dial-up or broadband dynamic IP range, but will usually accept mail from that provider's legitimate mail server(s). This is a particular problem when sending e-mail to AOL customers, as AOL enforces strict rules on source IP ranges as well as forward and reverse DNS checks.

For example, assume that a user is sending mail from a home office mail server connected to the Internet through a cable modem using the DHCP-assigned IP address 66.69.100.144. A reverse lookup on this IP may fail, or it might return a value such as cs6669199-144.satx.rr.com, which indicates a home user or a block of IPs known to be assigned dynamically. Since the address cannot be linked to an identifiable person or a machine without administrative—and in some cases legal—involvement, the message is therefore rejected.

The fix here? Never run a mail server on a dynamic IP address. We assume that those reading this book are able to use permanent or static IP addresses for their e-mail servers. If not, at least look into your provider's business offerings, which may offer some type of reprieve from this low-end connectivity. This problem is generally one that affects home users rather than administrators, but it's good to know why it happens. If you find that your office is actually on a noncommercial ADSL dynamic IP and is having this type of problem, at least now you can explain to your users (and your cheap boss) why all company e-mail is being bounced.

Tip

If you're having trouble with AOL rejections of your outgoing messages, check `http://postmaster.info.aol.com/trouble/trouble.html`. This page contains the steps AOL would like you to take before you contact it with a problem report.

PostFix Overview

For some administrators, PostFix is an excellent alternative to Sendmail. PostFix is installed by default on Fedora Core and Red Hat Linux systems, but not enabled by the alternatives system. It was developed as a more secure and modern alternative to Sendmail, and though it is compatible to Sendmail in almost areas, note that PostFix emulation of Sendmail command-line syntax is not 100% accurate. PostFix features include

✦ Multiple functional daemons that operate independently and without root level permission, enhancing MTA security

✦ Use of `/etc/aliases` as well as procmail-style `~/.forward` files

✦ Ability to deliver mail to mbox-style mailboxes in `/var/spool/mail/`

Though Sendmail is older and—in many cases—crankier than PostFix, it is still the default alternatives-enabled MTA on Red Hat Linux and Fedora Core based systems. Those who want to use PostFix must deliberately enable it. This section offers some basic configuration and feature information; for more detailed assistance, check the resources at the end of the chapter or visit www.postfix.org.

PostFix versus Sendmail

If you're new to PostFix but experienced with Sendmail, you probably want to know what's different between the two MTAs. One of the major differences is how each is configured straight out of the box on a stock system. If you telnet into SMTP on each MTA, you'll see this for Sendmail 8.12.10:

```
# telnet localhost 25
Trying 127.0.0.1...
Connected to localhost (127.0.0.1).
Escape character is '^]'.
220 es.playground.crudnet.org ESMTP Sendmail
8.12.10/8.12.10; Thu, 30
Oct 2003 22:42:38 -0500
ehlo t.net
250-playground.mydomain.com Hello localhost [127.0.0.1],
pleased to meet you
250-ENHANCEDSTATUSCODES
250-PIPELINING
250-8BITMIME
250-SIZE
250-DSN
250-ETRN
250-AUTH GSSAPI DIGEST-MD5 CRAM-MD5 LOGIN PLAIN
250-DELIVERBY
250 HELP
```

The output for PostFix 2.0.11 is a bit different.

```
# telnet localhost 25
Trying 127.0.0.1...
Connected to localhost (127.0.0.1).
Escape character is '^]'.
220 es.playground.crudnet.org ESMTP Postfix
ehlo t.net
250-es.playground.crudnet.org
250-PIPELINING
250-SIZE 10240000
250-VRFY
250-ETRN
250-XVERP
250 8BITMIME
```

As you can see, SMTP-Auth is not configured by default under PostFix. It can be turned on easily in the /etc/postfix/master.cf file, however. Neither Sendmail nor PostFix binds to anything other than localhost, by default, for incoming SMTP.

For more information on SMTP-Auth, see the local sample file `/usr/share/doc/` `postfix-2.0.11/samples/sample-auth.cf`, **or just see the line that contains the op-** **tion** `smtpd_sasl_auth_enable=yes` **in your** `/etc/postfix/master.cf` **file.**

Configuring PostFix

The true differences between PostFix and Sendmail begin to appear in configuration. While PostFix is "Sendmail-compatible," its design is quite unlike Sendmail's. PostFix splits up the various MTA functions and assigns each to a different program. These programs are configured and run as related, but are independent of each other. This is a more secure design than the large single-program Sendmail method.

Because each function is a separate program, you must configure each independently. This is more work at the start of a PostFix installation, but allows you a greater level of microconfiguration for your particular needs. PostFix configuration files are stored in `/etc/postfix`, and include:

+ `access`
+ `aliases`
+ `aliases.db`
+ `canonica`
+ `main.cf`
+ `main.cf.default`
+ `master.cf`
+ `pcre_table`
+ `postfix-files`
+ `postfix-script`
+ `post-install`
+ `regexp_table`
+ `relocated`
+ `transport`
+ `virtual`

Most of these files are relatively self-explanatory. Brief descriptions of the most important PostFix configuration files follow.

/etc/postfix/main.cf

The `/etc/postfix/main.cf` file is PostFix's primary configuration file. It is equivalent to `/etc/sendmail.cf`, but is editable like `/etc/sendmail.mc`. A sample `main.cf` file might look like this:

```
#soft_bounce = no
queue_directory = /var/spool/postfix
command_directory = /usr/sbin
```

```
daemon_directory = /usr/libexec/postfix
mail_owner = postfix
#default_privs = nobody
#myhostname = host.domain.tld
[...]
  inet_interfaces = localhost
#inet_interfaces = all
[...]
mydestination = $myhostname, localhost.$mydomain
[...]
#local_recipient_maps = unix:passwd.byname $alias_maps
[...]
unknown_local_recipient_reject_code = 450
[...]
#mynetworks = 168.100.189.0/28, 127.0.0.0/8
[...]
#relay_domains = $mydestination
#relayhost = $mydomain
[...]
#relay_recipient_maps =hash:/etc/postfix/relay_recipients
#in_flow_delay = 1s
alias_maps = hash:/etc/postfix/aliases
[...]
#alias_database = dbm:/etc/aliases
[...]
debug_peer_level = 2
debugger_command =
    PATH=/bin:/usr/bin:/usr/local/bin:/usr/X11R6/bin
    xxgdb $daemon_directory/$process_name $process_id
      & sleep 5
sendmail_path = /usr/sbin/sendmail.postfix
newaliases_path = /usr/bin/newaliases.postfix
mailq_path = /usr/bin/mailq.postfix
setgid_group = postdrop
manpage_directory = /usr/share/man
sample_directory = /usr/share/doc/postfix-2.0.11/samples
readme_directory = /usr/share/doc/postfix-2.0.11/README_FILES
alias_database = hash:/etc/postfix/aliases
```

When you first configure PostFix, you will need to change the inet_interfaces setting to pri, sec IP, or all for an Internet mail server. The default localhost setting will not allow PostFix to listen for incoming mail.

Many administrators will also want to add a setting for the "virtual maps" directive, the PostFix equivalent of the virtusertable file in Sendmail configuration. To do so, add this line:

```
virtual_maps = hash:/etc/postfix/virtual
```

After any configuration file change you should either reload or restart PostFix with the command

```
# /etc/init.d/postfix start
Starting postfix:                          [  OK  ]
```

Tip To learn more about the `/etc/postfix/main.cf` file, see `www.redhat.com/support/resources/howto/RH-postfix-HOWTO/x118.html`.

/etc/postfix/master.cf

PostFix's master process configuration file is located at `/etc/postfix/master.cf`. The master PostFix daemon is a supervisory application, run under root, which manages and monitors all other PostFix processes. The `master.cf` file contains various settings that affect all PostFix processes, such as message throttling, feature settings, and subdaemon configurations.

Each line in the `master.cf` file describes how a particular component or subdaemon is to run. Where the `main.cf` file controls MTA configurations for paths, aliases, options, and hostname or domain settings, `master.cf` manages the individual programs run by the master binary. These individual programs generally manage alternative services, such as SMTP, bounce management, mail queues, alternate mail engines, protocols, spam and virus filters, and so on.

The `stock /etc/postfix/master.cf` file looks much like this:

```
# ==========================================================================
# service type  private unpriv  chroot  wakeup  maxproc command + args
#               (yes)   (yes)   (yes)   (never) (100)
# ==========================================================================
smtp        inet  n       -       n       -       -       smtpd
#smtps      inet  n       -       n       -       -       smtpd
#  -o smtpd_tls_wrappermode=yes -o smtpd_sasl_auth_enable=yes
#submission  inet  n       -       n       -       -       smtpd
#  -o smtpd_enforce_tls=yes -o smtpd_sasl_auth_enable=yes
#628        inet  n       -       n       -       -       qmqpd
pickup      fifo  n       -       n       60      1       pickup
cleanup     unix  n       -       n       -       0       cleanup
#qmgr       fifo  n       -       n       300     1       qmgr
qmgr        fifo  n       -       n       300     1       nqmgr
#tlsmgr     fifo  -       -       n       300     1       tlsmgr
rewrite     unix  -       -       n       -       -       trivial-rewrite
bounce      unix  -       -       n       -       0       bounce
defer       unix  -       -       n       -       0       bounce
flush       unix  n       -       n       1000?   0       flush
proxymap    unix  -       -       n       -       -       proxymap
smtp        unix  -       -       n       -       -       smtp
relay       unix  -       -       n       -       -       smtp
#               -o smtp_helo_timeout=5 -o smtp_connect_timeout=5
showq       unix  n       -       n       -       -       showq
error       unix  -       -       n       -       -       error
local       unix  -       n       n       -       -       local
virtual     unix  -       n       n       -       -       virtual
lmtp        unix  -       -       n       -       -       lmtp
maildrop    unix  -       n       n       -       -       pipe
  flags=DRhu user=vmail argv=/usr/local/bin/maildrop -d ${recipient}
old-cyrus   unix  -       n       n       -       -       pipe
  flags=R user=cyrus argv=/cyrus/bin/deliver -e -m ${extension} ${user}
```

```
cyrus         unix -     n      n      -      -      pipe
   user=cyrus argv=/cyrus/bin/deliver -e -r ${sender} -m ${extension}
       ${user}
uucp          unix -     n      n      -      -      pipe
   flags=Fqhu user=uucp argv=uux -r -n -z -a$sender - $nexthop!rmail
       ($recipient)
ifmail        unix -     n      n      -      -      pipe
  flags=F user=ftn argv=/usr/lib/ifmail/ifmail -r $nexthop ($recipient)
bsmtp         unix -     n      n      -      -      pipe
  flags=Fq. user=foo argv=/usr/local/sbin/bsmtp -f $sender $nexthop $recipient
```

You will probably want to turn on SMTP-Auth rather than use the stock SMTP setting. To do so, comment out the `smtp` line in `master.cf` and replace it with this line:

```
smtp    inet   n    -    n    -    -    smtpd -o smtpd_sasl_auth_enable=yes
```

The `master.cf` file is extremely flexible, and offers a great deal of power in configuring a responsive and secure MTA. For example, here's a real-world `master.cf` modification written by Kevin Taylor, a Linux Sys-Admin and RHCE at Rackspace Managed Hosting. Kevin wanted to set up a `procmail` antivirus quarantine system, which used `master.cf`. The system needed to deliver incoming mail into `procmail` from the SMTP subdaemon, with a max thread count of 5. This is how he did it:

```
smtp    inet n    -    y    -    -    smtpd -o content_filter=filter:
filter  unix -    n    n    -    5    pipe user=filter
        argv=/usr/bin/procmail -m /etc/procmailrc ${sender} ${recipient}
```

This set up a filter entry in his `master.cf` file that formed a special user filter through which Kevin piped all incoming e-mail, using a `procmail` antivirus recipe. You'll find other `procmail` antivirus recipes at `http://agriroot.aua.gr/~nikant/nkvir/`.

/etc/postfix/virtual

The `/etc/postfix/virtual` file is the PostFix equivalent of Sendmail's `virtusertable` file.

> **Note** If you want to enable this feature, it must be added and turned on in the `main.cf` file before you begin to use it.

The main difference between the PostFix `virtual` file and Sendmail's `virtusertable` file is that `virtual` must have its virtual domains declared in the file before they can be used by the MTA. Entries in a PostFix `virtual` file might look like this:

```
mydomain.com                    Bob's virtual domain
bob@mydomain.com                bob
bob-home@mydomain.com           bsmith@yahoo.com
@mydomain.com                   bob
```

On the first line of the virtual file, the text after the virtual domain's domain name declaration is ignored by PostFix. Most administrators simply insert the word `VIRTUAL` for the sake of clarity.

One advantage that PostFix holds over Sendmail is that you no longer need to maintain a separate local-domains file to hold all of your local domain names, since you declare all virtual domains in `/etc/postfix/virtual`. In addition, you no longer need to add wildcard or catch-all accounts at the bottom of your virtual mapping file. For sysadmins who like to automate as many processes as possible, this is great because you can simply write a script that uses `cat` to append new users to the end of the virtual file without worrying about their location within the file.

Note Every time you modify `/etc/postfix/virtual`, whether it is for adding a new domain or a new address, you must rebuild the `virtual.db` hash file. Do so with the `postmap` command, as in

```
# postmap hash:/etc/postfix/virtual
```

Changes will be applied instantly, so you don't have to restart or reload the main PostFix daemon.

/etc/postfix/aliases

The `/etc/postfix/aliases` file is equivalent to Sendmail's `/etc/aliases` file. In fact, you should be able to use your `/etc/aliases` file as a direct replacement. However, because of the file's location under Sendmail, and because PostFix checks this file for system aliases, you will need to rebuild its hash file each time you add a new alias.

In PostFix, you rebuild the hash file from the command line with the postalias command, as in

```
# postalias hash:/etc/postfix/aliases
```

The hash file is also rebuilt automatically whenever the PostFix daemon is restarted, just as in Sendmail.

Sendmail and PostFix Resources

Because software problems and solutions evolve far more rapidly than the publication schedules of books or magazines, the best place to find the most up-to-date MTA assistance is on the web. Table 19-2 shows some of the best resources for your Sendmail or PostFix sources for help.

Table 19-2: Sendmail and Postfix Resources

Description	Location
Sendmail	
Sendmail Consortium	`www.sendmail.org`
Sendmail FAQ	`www.sendmail.org/faq`
Sendmail USENET newsgroup	`comp.mail.sendmail`
Server Side documentation (in the sendmail-doc RPM)	`/usr/share/doc/sendmail/README.cf`
Tom's Sendmail Cheat Sheet	`http://xcssa.org/files/sendmail-cheat-sheet-NONRACK.pdf`

Continued

Table 19-2: *(continued)*

Description	Location
Fedora Core 1 Release Notes	`http://fedora.redhat.com/docs/release-notes`
Red Hat 9 documentation	`www.redhat.com/docs/manuals/linux/RHL-9-Manual/ref-guide/s1-email-mta.html`
Enterprise (commercial) Sendmail	*`www.sendmail.com`*
Troubleshooting Sendmail	
Sendmail-related links	`www.sendmail.org/~ca/email`
Problems with relaying	`www.sendmail.org/~ca/email/relayingdenied.html`
PostFix	
PostFix command summary	`www.postfix.org/commands.html`
Review of Postfix	`http://homepages/tesco.net/~J.deBoynePollard/ReviewsUnixMTSes/postfix.html`
Postfix-related links	`www.postfix.org/big-picture.html` `www.postfix.org/docs.html`
Red Hat PostFix HOWTO	`www.redhat.com/support/resources/howto/RH-postfix-HOWTO/c108.html`

Summary

E-mail and MTA management is a core network administrative function. Under Fedora Core/Red Hat Linux, you can choose between two powerful mail transfer agents: Sendmail and PostFix. Though PostFix is gaining ground, Sendmail is still the most popular MTA on the planet, and is the default MTA on most Linux systems. It can be a complex and challenging service with multiple configuration requirements; however, once installed, it tends to run without much trouble and is usually robust and stable. Should you need or want to switch between Sendmail and PostFix, you can use the alternatives system, making an almost seamless change between the two and allowing you to use the strengths of each as necessary on your system.

As you set up your mail server, be sure to follow basic security guidelines. Set your server up on a static IP address, get rid of any open relays or scripts that exploit known security holes, and check the antispam blacklists to see if your IP address is questionable or on any blacklists. Use the aliases and `virtusertables`/virtual files to control important system messages and virtual domains. Be sure to enforce strong password control to maintain a secure e-mail environment.

If you run this server in an IT environment, check with other IT staff so that e-mail works with your other servers and client software. Do you need to implement collaborative e-mail solutions? What about CGI interfaces with your web servers? How do your users want to access their e-mail, and will you need to run both POP and IMAP services? Do you need to purchase an SSL certificate to ensure encrypted e-mail is secure? All these issues must be decided on a local level, and all require the active input of the person running the mail server.

✦   ✦   ✦

Fedora Software Repositories

This appendix provides information on some popular third-party software repositories that support Fedora Core. Although Fedora Core comes with thousands of software packages, there is still more software out there that people like to use with their Linux systems. It is virtually impossible for a distribution to include every piece of software that somebody might use, while still maintaining a high level of stability. Because of this, third party software repositories have sprung up to offer the extra software that is not included with Red Hat distributions. Table A-1 lists and describes many of these popular repositories.

Note   Many of these repositories are designed to be used alone, not mixed with other repositories. Some do make an effort to work with others. Please check the repository website for information about other repository interoperability.

Table A-1: Software Repositories that Support Fedora Core

Repository Name and Hompage	yum or apt Support	Description
Fedora.us www.fedora.us	Yum and apt	Fedora.us is a community project dedicated to building high-quality, third-party RPMs for the Red Hat Linux distribution.
rpm.livna.org http:// rpm.livna.org	Yum and apt	Because of legal questions, certain packages were removed from the Fedora.us site and can now be found on rpm.livna.org.
FreshRPMS www.freshrpms. net	Yum and apt	From its beginning in 2000, FreshRPMS has grown into one of the most popular software repositories for Red Hat Linux and now Fedora Core also.

Continued

Table A-1: *(continued)*

Repository Name and Hompage	yum or apt Support	Description
DAG http://dag.wieers.com/home-made/apt/	Yum and apt	Dag Wieers is a private citizen who enjoys packaging software for various Linux distributions, including Fedora Core.
Atrpms http://atrpms.physik.fu-berlin.de/	Yum and apt	ATrpms is a third-party RPM repository for Red Hat Linux distributions. Its original focus was on software used in natural sciences, but it now includes many nonscientific software titles such as system tools and multimedia packages.
NewRPMS http://newrpms.sunsite.dk	Yum and apt	NewRPMS is a noncommercial project. Its mission statement is to provide and maintain Red Hat and Fedora RPMs for software that is not included in the main distribution.
Jpackage www.jpackage.org	Yum and apt	JPackage Project has two primary goals: —To provide a coherent set of Java software packages for Linux, satisfying all quality requirements of other applications. —To establish an efficient and robust policy for Java software installation.
PlanetCCRMA ccrma-www-ccrma.stanford.edu/planetccrma/software/	Apt	Planet CCRMA (pronounced "karma") at Home is a collection of rpms for creating a multimedia workstation.
NyQuist http://people.ecsc.co.uk/~matt/repository.html	Yum and apt	NyQuist is a publicly accessible personal collection of RPMs.
KDE for Red Hat Linux http://kde-redhat.sourceforge.net/	yum and apt	The KDE for Red Hat project intends to promote the use of KDE and KDE-based applications on Red Hat Linux and Fedora Core through the creation and distribution of core and third-party KDE RPM packages.

Troubleshooting SUSE Linux

This appendix details the features of SUSE versions of Linux that may be unfamiliar to users of other distributions or versions of Linux.

SUSE Past and Present

SUSE has long been known in the Linux world for two particular features: (1) the typically German quality of the engineering which has gone into it and (2) YaST (*Yet another Setup Tool*)—the SUSE installation and administration tool.

SUSE's History

SUSE is the oldest existing commercial distribution of Linux. The company was founded in 1992, near Nuremburg in Germany, by four mathematics graduates. The first release of a Linux distribution by SUSE was in early 1993. SUSE rapidly gained support, particularly in Europe; language problems were an issue at first, and people still remember and joke about the early SUSE manuals, which were written in a language somewhat between German and English.

At the time that early versions of Red Hat (and Red Hat clones) were ubiquitous in the United States, SUSE Linux gained popularity in Europe. SUSE became a worldwide company with the establishment of offices in the United States (1997) and in the United Kingdom (1999).

Originally SUSE provided one product (SUSE Linux), which was released at least three times a year and was available only for the x86 platform. The current SUSE Professional is the direct descendent of this version—version numbers started at 4.2 and the current version of Professional is 9.1. In 2000, the SUSE offering was split into Professional and Personal versions, and versions for other hardware platforms (Alpha, Sparc, PPC, and IA-64) were released. The following year, SUSE released the Enterprise Server 7 version, and in due course, versions for IA64, PPC, S/390, and zSeries were released. SUSE developed powerful tools to aid in the process of porting Linux to other platforms and there was close collaboration with IBM in the production of versions for the PPC-based iSeries and pSeries and for the S/390 and zSeries mainframes.

SUSE also released a series of mail server products leading up to the current SUSE Linux OpenExchange Server 4.

Enterprise Server 7 was succeeded by Enterprise Server 8 (available on x86, IA-64, AMD64, iSeries, pSeries, and zSeries), and at the time this book was being written, Enterprise Server 9 was in beta testing.

At the time of the release of Enterprise Server 8 (in November 2002), the UnitedLinux consortium was established, with SUSE, Connectiva, TurboLinux, and SCO as members. UnitedLinux was an agreed core, developed by SUSE for enterprise distributions to be issued by the other vendors in the consortium. Following the defection of SCO from the Linux community and its extraordinary decision to take legal actions against IBM and Linux distributors and users, the UnitedLinux consortium lost its importance.

During roughly the same period, the other major commercial Linux vendor, Red Hat, also diversified its offerings to include high-value server versions. The reasons for these changes by both distributors were twofold: the vendors were keen to offer a high-value version of Linux with a paid-for software maintenance and update system, while business customers needed a Linux version with a longer life. As Linux began to be taken increasingly seriously by business, business customers needed to be able to plan for their implementations over a period of years with a guarantee that the versions employed would not become obsolete.

Historically, however, there were some differences between the two companies' philosophies. Both Red Hat and SUSE provided boxed versions of their "consumer" version for sale. While Red Hat offered ISO images identical to the CDs in the boxed product for download, SUSE did not, but allowed an FTP installation. SUSE somewhat controversially placed a licensing restriction on the redistribution of the YaST installation and administration tool; while the source remained open, it was not permissible to redistribute YaST on media offered for sale. This prevented a proliferation of SUSE clones in the way that there were numerous Linux distributions "based on Red Hat."

SUSE remained a private company, with capital from a group of investors. In late 2003, it was announced that SUSE had been sold to Novell. There was a general feeling that this was good for Novell (its share price rose very dramatically on news of the takeover) and good for Linux in general, and nothing has happened since that has dispelled this view.

Soon after the acquisition of SUSE by Novell, it was announced that future versions of YaST will be published under the GPL. It will also be possible for third-party vendors to write YaST modules to control the installation and behavior of their hardware or software on SUSE (see the *YaST* section of this appendix for more details).

Current SUSE Versions

SUSE divides its products into Home and Business versions. The Home versions are Professional and Personal; these are released twice yearly. The Business versions have a slower release cycle and a longer product life. They are sold bundled with a software maintenance agreement and full commercial support is available.

The current SUSE products are listed as follows:

✦ SUSE Linux Professional 9.1 (contains versions for x86 and AMD64)—The Professional 9.1 version contains "everything but the kitchen sink." It's a very full distribution with five CDs containing binary packages for x86, a two-sided DVD with the material from the

CDs on one side and the sources on the other, and an additional DVD from which you can install the x86-64 (AMD64) version.

Professional has all the server software contained in the Enterprise version (and more), but should be seen as essentially an unsupported version. It does, however, possess a very effective online update mechanism (YOU, or YaST Online Updater), and though SUSE makes no particular guarantees about this feature, security updates are issued in a very timely fashion.

✦ SUSE Linux Personal 9.1 (x86 only; includes a Live CD version)—Essentially intended as a desktop version, this is a subset of the Professional version. It now (since 9.1) includes a Live CD version, which is a bootable CD that boots a graphical Linux system without installing to the hard disk.

✦ SUSE Linux Enterprise Server 8 (9 as of Fall 2004)—Supported platforms for this version (by both the vendor and SUSE) are x86, IA-64, AMD64, iSeries, pSeries, and zSeries.

This is the flagship commercial version. One of the great strengths of SUSE is that the Enterprise Server is built in such a way that it is effectively identical on all the supported hardware platforms: SUSE Autobuild system produces all the packages in all the versions from the same source code.

✦ SUSE Linux Standard Server 8 (9)—The Standard Server differs from the Enterprise Server in that it is intended for a particular purpose and market: it fills essentially the same niche as the Microsoft Small Business Server. There is a web administration interface that allows for its configuration as a simple mail server, DHCP and DNS server, and file and print server for Windows clients. User information is held in an LDAP database.

If you need a single Linux server in a small office environment, the Standard Server is ideal and the built-in configuration defaults that are assumed by the web administration interface will generally be the right ones. But for a more flexible, general-purpose solution, you should use either the Professional version or the Enterprise Server, depending on your needs.

✦ SUSE Linux OpenExchange Server—The SUSE Linux OpenExchange Server is a hybrid product: a mail server based on well known, tried, and tested components; postfix as the Mail Transport Agent; cyrus for the IMAP server and mail storage; and OpenLDAP for the user and authentication information. At the same time it contains a powerful groupware component; this is a proprietary product from the Netline company. The groupware functionality can be accessed either through a web interface (which also offers webmail) or through Microsoft Outlook (in a similar way to Outlook in combination with a Microsoft Exchange server). A piece of add-on software is required on the Windows client to make this work. A PostgreSQL database holds the groupware data; the groupware server is provided by a java tomcat system and also provides a flexible WebDav interface.

The Open Exchange Server has gained a considerable reputation as a powerful contender in the commercial mail/groupware market.

✦ SUSE Linux Desktop—SUSE Linux Desktop is an enhanced Desktop version for business. It is a long-life maintained version with some additional features, notably the inclusion of the licensed copies of Crossover Office (which allows it to run a well defined set of Windows applications), StarOffice, and a Citrix client.

Licenses and Maintenance

SUSE distinguishes between the products that are regarded as being for business customers and those categorized as for the home user. This distinction is seen in the way the products are presented in SUSE publicity materials and on all SUSE websites.

Business Products

The business products are sold bundled with a software maintenance agreement and generally are not available separately from that agreement, except in certain cases on evaluation terms. They are also the products on which SUSE is prepared to offer commercial high-level support.

Note Details of SUSE's maintenance and support are available at www.suse.com/us/ business/services/support/index.html and www.suse.co.uk/uk/business/ services/support/index.html.

The business products have a long life (generally 5 years from initial release). In the case of the SUSE Linux Enterprise Server different versions are available and current at the same time: there is approximately a 2-year release cycle and a 5-year product life. This policy means that support and maintenance for SLES 8 will continue through the release of SLES 9 and will only cease after the release of SLES 10.

The OpenExchange server differs from most of SUSE's other offerings in that it is partly composed of proprietary software: the groupware functionality is provided by the ComFire application server from Netline. This software requires licenses for the groupware clients, with the license fee calculated according to the number of concurrent users who will be making use of the groupware functionality. Client access to the OpenExchange server purely as a mail server (POP3 or IMAP) is license free.

The SUSE Linux Desktop is offered on a per-machine license basis because it contains certain third-party licensed products, notably StarOffice and CodeWeavers Crossover office. The payment for the license for these is included in the initial maintenance payment.

Home User Versions

SUSE Linux Professional and Personal versions are unencumbered by restrictive licenses for the end user, apart from the one or two commercial demos that are not included in the FTP version.

The sysconfig Directory

One of the things people either love or hate about SUSE is the fact that all standard services can be configured via a central flat file repository of configuration settings. The old way (previous to SUSE 8) was to use the rc.config file, but this has been superseded by sysconfig.

Sysconfig is a directory beneath /etc, which is familiar to Red Hat users, and this is one of the reasons SUSE chose this layout. Because of technical and usability issues, the SUSE developers wanted to split out the configuration options of the ever-increasing services controlled by the SUSE configuration tool YaST (a more in-depth view of YaST is given later in this appendix) into separate files. As the sysconfig directory is something many Linux users are used to, this was a natural choice.

The system and services configuration is split into separate files. For example, to change kernel parameters (think `sysctl` parameters), you would edit the file `/etc/sysconfig/kernel`. Table B-1 provides a short overview of the most common files and their respective services.

Table B-1: Files under /etc/sysconfig/

File	Service	Description
Postfix	Postfix	Configuration of the standard SUSE mail server
apache	Apache	Configuration parameters for the Apache web server
Lang	System Language	Parameters to control language settings for the system
Keyb	Keyboard	Settings for keyboard, including keymap, rate, and delay
SuSEfirewall2	SUSE Firewall	The standard SUSE firewall configuration
windowmanager	[X|K|G]dm	Default window manager (KDE, GNOME, and so on)
Mouse	Mouse configuration	Mouse model, extensions, and so on

Note Editing these files will only set the scene for commitment to the running configuration. To commit any changes that are made in `/etc/sysconfig`, you will need to run SuSEconfig. SuSEconfig is detailed later in the chapter, but it is a very important tool that any SUSE user should learn to use.

Network Scripts

Keeping with the sysconfig theme, SUSE uses `/etc/sysconfig/network` to store configuration for networking.

A very important and useful file in `/etc/sysconfig/network` is the `config` file. Many options to control the way your network connection (and the system) functions can be found here. For example, if you use a laptop there are parameters to unmount any active NFS mounts before your network shuts down. Again, any `config` file settings that need to be committed should be done with SuSEconfig.

Each network interface that is configured on the system (either via YaST or manually) has an `ifcfg-`*interface* file. For a standard ethernet interface, we can use the `ifcfg-eth0` file to signify the first ethernet interface the system has found:

```
BOOTPROTO='static'
BROADCAST='192.168.255.255'
IPADDR='192.168.1.80'
NETWORK='192.168.0.0'
REMOTE_IPADDR="
STARTMODE='onboot'
UNIQUE='WL76.gUpZQ_u5zzC'
WIRELESS='no'
```

The configuration states the eth0 has a static configuration, with an IP of 192.168.1.80 and a network mask of 255.255.0.0. Setting BOOTPROTO to dhcp will tell the system to obtain an IP address and (if configured) other settings upon boot.

DHCP Configuration

If an interface has been configured as dhcp, the system will try to obtain an IP address when the system boots or via the rcnetwork control script. The values that the DHCP client will assign to various network-related settings can be controlled via the /etc/sysconfig/dhcp file.

DHCP allows an administrator to set the hostname of a client, routing tables and DNS servers to name a few. Most Linux DHCP clients allow a user to control whether those values are actually used. Table B-2 shows some options in the /etc/saysconfig/network/dhcp file.

Table B-2: Some Options in /etc/saysconfig/network/dhcp

Parameter	Description
DHCLIENT_SET_HOSTNAME	Should the hostname passed to the DHCP request be honored?
DHCLIENT_MODIFY_RESOLV_CONF	Should resolver parameters be saved in /etc/resolv.conf?
DHCLIENT_DEFAULT_ROUTE	Should the gateway/default route be honored?

As with most things that can be configured directly through the SUSE management system, the parameters are well documented and their value is either yes|no or a specific value. This gives users the ability to configure common services for "normal" use. The definition of *normal* has led to some controversy over the central configuration system that SUSE uses. Many power users of Linux prefer to configure services directly via the services' own configuration files. The reasoning behind the SUSE philosophy is that for new and intermediate users who need services configured as soon and as simply as possible, the central configuration is extremely useful. From a technical standpoint, YaST is able to store common changes that control services in a flat file.

Regardless of which camp you are in, the configuration element of SUSE provides power users the opportunity to configure services directly in the configuration file native to the service and lets novices/intermediates edit standardized files quickly and commit those changes.

The next section gives an introduction to another way of configuring the system: YaST, the SUSE management tool.

rc Scripts

Every Linux system has scripts that are used to start, stop, and query the status of a service, and SUSE is no different. As well as the standard init scripts for services being stored in /etc/init.d/, they are linked to *rc* scripts in /sbin and /usr/sbin.

To control a service, use the following commands:

✦ *rcservice* start—Start the service.

✦ *rcservice* stop—Shutdown the service.

- ✦ `rcservice status`—Check the status of the service (whether it is running).

- ✦ `rcservice reload`—This is service dependant, but is similar to sending a HUP signal to the process to reload its configuration files.

A problem many people new to SUSE have is how to find out what the name of a service is. There a few methods to this, but the best is to run the following command (again taking postfix as an example):

```
# rpm -ql postfix | grep rc
```

This will `grep` through the listing of all files in the postfix rpm that has been installed, to find the `rc` script. Once you know this you can use it to control the service.

chkconfig

The boot up process of a Linux system is usually controlled by run level scripts (stored in `/etc/init.d`) linked into run level directories. To stop system administrators from going made with symbolic links, the *chkconfig* utility is used to control the startup and precedence of system services.

Running *chkconfig* with no parameters will list all services and whether the service is on in the current runlevel. For a more in-depth look at services and their runlevels, adding the *list* parameter will display all services, all runlevels, and whether the service is on or off in those levels.

A SUSE service init script contains a header to tell the system what the default runlevels this script should reside in and default actions for those runlevels. To turn on postfix in its default runlevels (3 and 5), the command

```
# chkconfig -a postfix
```

will setup the links needed to start postfix by default in runlevel 3 and 5, along with the respective kill script to shut the service down in the correct priority.

The same is true for the reverse, removing a service from the init sequence.

```
# chkconfig -d postfix
```

`chkconfig` will then remove links in runlevel directories, and signify this with a listing of the postfix runlevel status.

`chkconfig` is a powerful utility to manage services from a scripted management system, and also for one off configurations by the administrator. For more information on `chkconfig`, see the `chkconfig(8)` man page.

X Configuration with SAX

SUSE's configuration tools help the user at every step, and with its history in X server development, SUSE has provided the sax2 tool to automatically configure X windows for a user environment.

Why sax2? The original sax tool was written for XFree86 version 3, and with the release of Xfree86 version 4, SUSE had to rewrite a lot of the sax tool as the underlying configuration of X changed so drastically.

During installation, sax is used to configure the video hardware. If for any reason (new graphics card or monitor) the display needs to be reconfigured, sax2 can be used to reinitialize display parameters and tweak the display to the user's requirements.

To start sax, issue *sax2* at the command line in an init level other than 5 or with no X server or display manager running. Figure B-1 shows the sax2 initial screen.

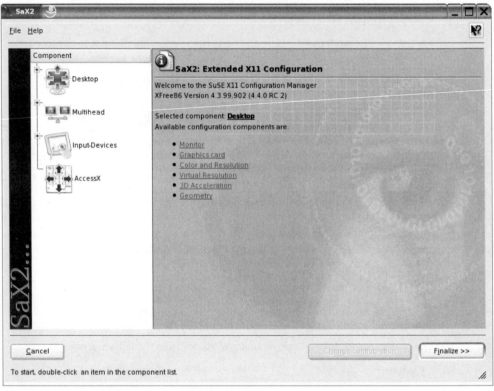

Figure B-1: sax2 initial screen.

Once started, you will be able to configure display parameters (video card, monitor, and so on), input parameters (mouse, keyboard, tablet), multihead display, and AccessX.

Selecting Graphics Card will allow you to provide specific information to sax that will enable accelerated features of your graphics card (extended 2D features). In our case we will select the framebuffer device (see Figure B-2) as this is the catch (nearly!) all setting that can be used with VESA 2.0 capable cards.

Once the graphics card has been configured, the resolution and monitor configuration needs to be set. Sax is capable of selecting a default monitor configuration based on DCE feedback during sax2 initialization. If your monitor is not DCE aware, you will need to use parameters from your monitor manual to configure it safely.

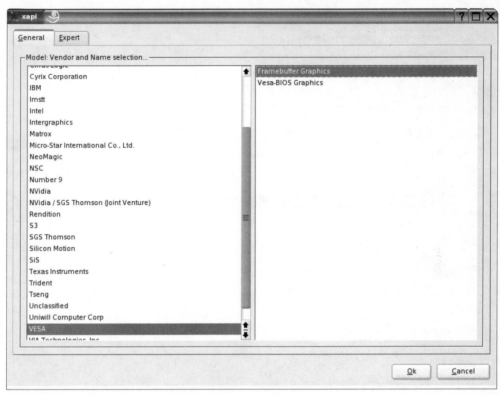

Figure B-2: sax2 graphics card configuration.

Selecting Monitor will provide you with the option of selecting the currently used monitor. Figure B-3 shows the sax2 monitor configuration screen. Clicking on properties will allow you to set parameters such as resolution and frequency settings.

Once configured you will then need to configure the color depth and resolution of your graphics card. If using the framebuffer device, most of the screen drawing routines will be carried out by the processor of the main system, so the higher the bit depth used for displays, the more work the processor will have to do. To combat this, the lowest screen depth possible for day-to-day work should be selected. This is usually 8 bits (256 colors).

Selecting Color and Resolution allows you to set the screen depth and also resolution of X, as shown in Figures B-4 and B-5.

Once configured, it is advisable to check the virtual resolution settings, as it is quite possible that the annoying feature may have been enabled.

3-D configuration is beyond the scope of this chapter, but you should take a look at the SUSE documentation for more information on configuring your system to take advantage of these features.

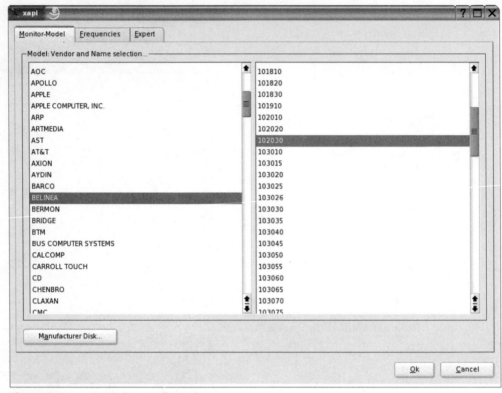

Figure B-3: sax2 monitor configuration.

After you have saved your configuration, it is advisable to take Sax's advice and test your new settings. If you are running a default runlevel of 5, and the configuration of X is incorrect, your system will keep trying to initialize the display until the respawn threshold has been met. If there are problems at a later date, you can boot your Linux system into runlevel 1 (single-user mode) without X by passing a value of "1" to the grub boot loader when the system starts up.

YaST

As noted above, the feature of SUSE Linux that is most distinctive is YaST. YaST (*Yet another Setup Tool*) is both the installer and a complete configuration tool for all the most important features of the system. YaST is designed in a modular way: when used for system configuration tasks, it loads a particular module according to the task being undertaken, but it is also possible to run a particular module separately without loading the entire YaST menu system. YaST can be run both in graphical mode and in text mode (ncurses interface). The functionality in either mode is identical: you can think of the two YaST user interfaces as alternative "skins" exhibiting the same underlying logic. What is important is that you can run YaST with all features in a text-only ssh session for remote system administration purposes.

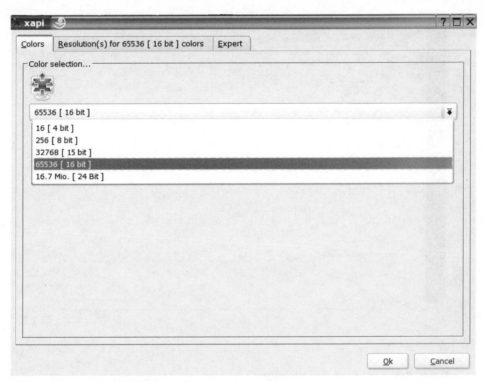

Figure B-4: sax2 color depth configuration.

Note You can also enable VNC in YaST (even during installation). This allows access to a graphical session from a remote VNC client, but should be considered less secure than ssh.

YaST has always been the distinguishing feature of SUSE Linux, and it has grown organically with the SUSE distribution. In earlier versions, YaST was a monolithic program; with the release of YaST 2 it became modular. Traditionally the YaST license has been a controversial issue; YaST was released under a license that, although it made the source available, restricted redistribution of the program by third parties. This had two important effects: it made it illegal to resell unofficial copies of SUSE CDs, and it made it impossible for third parties to create a distribution based on SUSE.

At the Novell Brainshare event in March 2004, Novell announced that future versions of YaST will be released under the GPL. This change was first made in SUSE Personal and Professional version 9.1.

Installing the System Using YaST

A normal SUSE installation follows the following pattern: Booting from the installation medium loads ISOLINUX, which in turn starts YaST. At the start of the initial boot, you are offered the opportunity to enter boot parameters, and to vary the defaults in other ways. In particular,

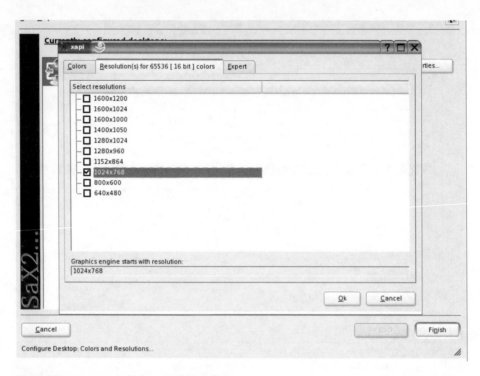

Figure B-5: sax2 resolution configuration.

you can change the screen resolution of the graphical installer or choose a text mode install. You can also choose to make use of a different installation medium.

There are a number of built-in boot options (including a "safe settings" installation and the rescue system). The bottom of the initial boot screen offers several options using function keys, as listed in Table B-3.

Table B-3: Function Keys at the Installation Boot Screen

Key	Function
F1	Help
F2	Change screen resolution or choose text-based install
F3	Choose where to load the installation files from (CD-ROM, SLP, FTP, HTTP, NFS, SMB, hard disk)
F4	Choose language
F5	Verbosity
F6	Choose to load an external driver

In rare cases the screen may go blank as soon as it tries to start the framebuffer graphics display used throughout the rest of the installation. If this happens, you may need to choose a different resolution using the F2 key, or if nothing else works, choose a text-based installation. If you are forced to take this option, it does not necessarily mean that you will not be able to get graphics to work after installation.

The F3 key offers the option to get the installation files from somewhere other than the CD or DVD, which you booted from. SUSE has always offered an FTP installation option for the Professional version—you can download a minimal boot CD (or set of boot and modules floppies) from the FTP site and start the install, which you then point elsewhere to get the installation files for the main part of the installation. Any of the protocols listed will work, so the installation DVD could be shared from a Windows machine on the network (the SMB option) or the files could be on an NFS, FTP, or HTTP (web) server somewhere. You can also install from a copy of the DVD on a hard disk partition; you could create that partition and copy the files onto it by first booting the rescue system before you start the installation. New in SUSE 9.1 is the SLP (*service location protocol*) option. Also known as *zeroconf* and based on the same standard as Apple's *rendezvous* feature, this allows a server to use the SLP protocol to advertise itself as containing an installation source; the SLP option will automatically find and use that service.

In addition to using a remote source for the SUSE distribution rpm files, you can also create an installation source for third-party software that YaST can understand. You can find details on this process at `http://portal.suse.de/sdb/en/2004/02/yast_instsrc.html`.

Creating a Swap Partition to Install on a Low-Memory Machine

YaST is a big program. If you are trying to install on a machine with insufficient memory (less than 128MB), you may have difficulties. In such cases it is useful to create a swap partition manually before starting the installation and configure the system to use it during installation; you should also run the installation in text mode. You will see a message that reads "Your computer does not have enough memory to run YaST. To continue, configure some swap space." You are then given the opportunity to activate an existing swap partition on the disk. If there is no swap partition, you should abort the installation and create one; you can do this by rebooting into the rescue system and using fdisk to create a suitably sized partition that should be given the partition ID 82 (Linux swap). You then need to run the `mkswap` command to format the partition as a swap partition. So typically you would do something like this:

```
# fdisk /dev/hda
```

Then in the fdisk program, press the **n** key to create a new partition, followed by the **p** key for a primary partition, then select the partition number (1 if there are no partitions on the disk), then press **t** to change the partition type (choose 82 for swap).

Write out the partition table with the `w` command, exit fdisk, and reboot to restart installation.

Once the installer has started and the language has been selected, a screen loads which summarizes a proposal for installation. The proposal includes a a suggested set of defaults together with a suggestion for partitioning based on the partitions found on the disk. This suggestion may or may not be useful; in a simple case (one Windows partition found which fills the whole disk), it will suggest a sensible choice (resize the Windows partition and create Linux swap and root partition). In more complicated cases where there are already Linux partitions on the disk, the suggestion may be a "destructive" one. In any case, you can choose an option giving you full control over the partitioning.

YaST's partitioning tool provides a graphical interface to the task of partitioning the disk(s) and choosing the filesystems: it supports the creation of swap, ext2, ext3, reiserfs, xfs, and jfs partitions. It also contains a very user friendly interface for the setting up LVM (the logical volume manager) and software RAID.

Note   If you are resizing a Windows partition it is advisable to use the Windows disk tools first (the scandisk and defragmentation tools). Although the resizer is very reliable, as with any such software, you are advised to back up first.

The other item in the summary screen that you may wish to change is the software selections default. You can make broad changes to this by choosing one of a number of software groups (such as "gnome system" or "kernel development") and you can make detailed changes at the level of individual packages. If you are using SUSE Linux Professional, the default options are a reasonably good choice for a desktop system (with KDE as the desktop), which you can build on later. The software selections screen allows you to choose according to a SUSE-designed set of installation scenarios or by package groups (based on the information contained internally within the actual RPM packages). Package dependencies should be handled intelligently; if you choose two packages that are incompatible or packages that have alternative dependencies, you will be offered a "conflict resolution" window in which to choose how to solve the problem.

Before proceeding with the installation, the main screen also offers the following setting options:

✦ System—A hardware detection tool. This will report all the hardware that YaST can find on your system; it's useful as a way of checking possible problems with particular devices.

✦ Keyboard—Choose your keyboard type and language. Usually this will have been correctly detected and/or assumed based on your language choice, but you may need to change it here.

✦ Booting—Choose grub or lilo for booting. By default, SUSE will boot the system with grub. If a Windows partition is present, the grub configuration will include it in the grub menu. Note that on SUSE, the grub apparatus is all in /boot/grub. The file /etc/grub.conf is required only for the functionality of the grub-install command: the grub menu is stored in the file /boot/grub/menu.1st. There are certain cases (in particular if you are booting from certain raid arrays or other types of disk that grub cannot directly read) where you may need to use lilo rather than grub for booting.

✦ Time zone—If the installer has not guessed your time zone correctly on the basis of the language information you gave it, you can set it here.

✦ Default runlevel—This setting defaults to 5 (that is, full networking with graphics and graphical login). If you wish to set up a server system without graphics, you should set this to runlevel 3.

Once you have agreed to all the choices in this screen and have chosen to go on, a confirmation dialogue appears. If you agree to proceed, YaST creates the partitions and file systems, and then starts the package installation. The package installation takes the bulk of the time needed for installation; exactly how long depends heavily on the speed of your processor and CD drive (and of course, the number of packages you have selected), but YaST will display a running estimate for the time remaining.

If you are installing from CDs, the system will reboot after package installation from the first CD is complete. On rebooting, a simple dialogue box will prompt you for the second CD and package installation will continue. If you are using another method, then the first reboot will take place at the end of the installation.

After the package installation is complete, there are certain other formalities to be completed. You need to set the root password, and provide networking details. In the networking setup, be sure that you complete all sections: the menu system here is not as well designed as it could be. If you are using a laptop with a PCMCIA network card, be sure to click the PCMCIA check box. YaST will then offer to do a first online update; you should do this provided the network configuration was successful and gives you access to the Internet. You are then invited to create an initial nonroot user. Note that on some versions of SUSE (including 9.1) in this screen "autologin" is the default. This may not be what you want; in that case you need to uncheck this check box (it's easy to forget to do this and annoying too; you then need to look at the kdm configuration file to fix it.)

After displaying the release notes, the last task is the setup of specific hardware including graphics cards, printers, and sound. In most cases an intelligent guess will already have been made for the graphics and sound setup, and you can simply accept the defaults.

Using YaST as a System Administration Tool

YaST has gradually gained more features and capabilities over time. It is able to control and configure most of the functions of the system. Its modular design means that new features can easily be added, and the recent announcement of its new GPL license and the publishing of open APIs will enable third-party vendors to write YaST modules to configure their own hardware and software. Figure B-6 shows the YaST startup screen.

If you are using the KDE desktop you can start YaST from the KDE menu. If you are not running as root, you will be prompted for the root password and the graphical version of YaST will start.

From the command line, the command yast (as root) will start the YaST in test mode, while yast2 will start it in graphical mode. If you are running the graphical display as a nonroot user, you should switch user to root with the sux command (rather than su) to make it possible for the graphical version to run.

You can start an individual YaST module without starting the YaST control centre, for example, the command

```
# yast2 printer
```

will start the printer configuration module.

You can get a list of all the installed YaST modules with this command:

```
# yast2 -l
```

Note that it's possible that not all available YaST modules are installed on the system. You can check this by searching for "yast" in the software installation module.

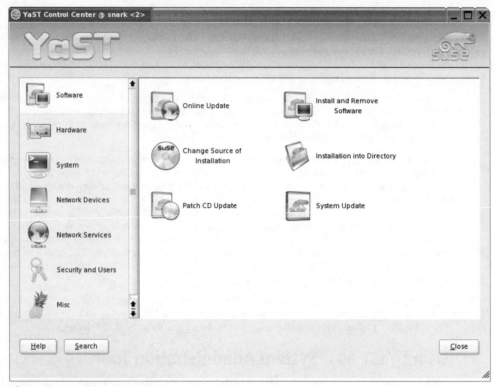

Figure B-6: YaST startup screen.

YaST and SuSEconfig

When YaST is used to configure the system, it makes changes to a set of files under the directory /etc/sysconfig/. Before YaST exits, it runs a tool called SuSEconfig that propagates those changes across the system to "do the right thing". Like YaST, SuSEconfig is modular. It contains a script for each YaST function, and these scripts can be run independently. They are found in the directory /sbin/conf.d/. If you make a manual change in a particular file in /etc/sysconfig/, you can run the relevant script in that directory.

The YaST Menus

When YaST is started, whether in text (ncurses) or graphical mode, exactly the same menus are available. The most important menus are listed below, grouped by category.

Software

✦ Online Update—Start and configure the Online Update mechanism. In the case of the business products, a username and password is required to make this work; these are issued when you register the product.

✦ Change source of installation—This menu allows you to enable a different source of packages apart from the CD or DVD that you installed from. This could be a network resource on your local network or it could be the SUSE FTP site or one of its mirrors. In the case of the Professional version, the packages are placed on the FTP site a few weeks after the release of the boxed version and choosing a fast mirror as your installation source is very convenient if you have a fast Internet connection.

✦ Install and Remove software—This menu does exactly what it says—YaST will calculate all necessary dependencies and install them automatically. There is a very useful search feature that allows you to search for available packages by name or to search for words in the package descriptions.

✦ Patch CD Update—This menu allows you to use one of the add-on or patch CDs that are issued from time to time by SUSE.

✦ Install to directory—This menu allows you to install a new, independent SUSE system under a directory in your existing installation.

✦ System Update—This menu allows you to update from an earlier version of SUSE.

Hardware

✦ CD-ROM drives menu and disk controller menu—Normally, you will not need to use either of these menus; the hardware will already have been correctly set up. In the case of CD-ROM drives, you can configure a newly added device here or remove or alter the mount points that have been set. Certain disk controllers have configuration options that can be controlled here.

✦ Graphics card and monitor—This menu calls the sax2 program from within YaST to set up or change the graphics configuration. Slightly more control is possible if you call sax2 from the command line when the system is in runlevel 3 and this way you can also control the resolution in which the sax2 tool itself runs (which may be necessary in difficult cases). If you are having serious difficulty getting the graphics to work, you should almost always be able to use framebuffer graphics. There is a useful SUSE support article at `http://portal.suse.com/sdb/en/2002/11/wessels_fbdev_grub.html`.

✦ Hardware information—This calls a program that scans all your hardware and reports on it. You have the option of saving the entire report to a file.

✦ IDE DMA mode—This menu allows you to set or unset DMA (direct memory access) modes for your IDE disks. By default SUSE makes a reasonable guess and sets DMA by default on hard disks, but not CD devices.

✦ Printer—This menu allows you to set up a local or network printer.

✦ Scanner—This menu allows you to set up a USB or SCSI scanner.

Network Devices

This section describes setting up network cards, modems, DSL devices, ISDN devices, fax machines, and also setting up a phone answering machine.

Network Services

The modules here will allow you to do a simple and straightforward set up of a variety of network services. The fact that these modules exist does not prevent you from configuring these services in more detail by editing the standard configuration files. You may want to use the YaST module to create a simple setup, which you modify in detail later. There are modules here for the following servers: DHCP, DNS, HTTP (using apache2), NFS, NIS, TFTP, postfix, and samba. You can also set up the machine as a samba, NFS or NIS client, and configure those network services that are started by the xinetd superserver.

Security and Users

✦ Edit and Create groups and Edit and Create users—These two menus give a graphical interface to the configuration of users and groups.

✦ Firewall—This module configures and activates the built-in firewall known as SuSEfirewall2.

✦ Security settings—This menu offers a choice of three preset security levels and the ability to configure each security feature in detail. Among other things, it controls the requirements for passwords and the encryption method, whether the Ctrl+Alt+Del and Magic SysRQ key combinations will be honored, and the setting of system file permissions (according to the schemes in the files /etc/permissions.*).

System

✦ Boot loader configuration—This menu allows you to switch between lilo and grub as boot loader and to edit the configuration files. In most cases working with the raw files will probably be preferable; if you don't understand how the boot loaders work, you probably shouldn't be trying to use this tool.

✦ Timezone—Allows you to adjust time zone settings. Normally this will not be necessary, provided that the settings made during installation were correct. (Note: the system should adjust automatically and correctly for Daylight Savings Time.)

✦ Choose language—You are unlikely to need to change the original setting here.

✦ Select keyboard layout—These menus allow you to change these localization settings.

✦ LVM—Allows you to configure and adjust logical volume settings.

✦ Partitioner—These menus give you access to the same disk partitioning tools that were offered during the installation. Note that you cannot resize or change mounted partitions with them.

✦ Profile manager—This is a graphical front end to SCPM (the system control profile manager), which allows you to set up and easily switch between different configuration profiles on the same machine. This is particularly useful for laptop users who are move between different networks with (for example) different network setups, printer types, and locations on each network.

✦ Powertweak configuration—This menu allows you to configure powertweak options. Powertweak is a program that gives you control over a wide variety of low-level options that control the kernel's interaction with the hardware and low-level networking settings. These are stored in the /etc/powertweak/tweaks file and then applied to the running kernel.

✦ Runlevel editor—This menu allows you to set the default runlevel and to set runlevels for individual services; it is thus an easy interface with the functionality of the chkconfig and insserv programs.

✦ Editor for `sysconfig` files—This menu allows you directly to change certain detailed settings in the files under `/etc/sysconfig`.

✦ Create a boot, module, or system floppy—This menu allows you to write out the standard boot and modules floppies from the installation media; it also allows to create a rescue boot floppy disk.

✦ Restore system—This menu allows you to restore the system from a backup.

Misc

This menu with the delightful pineapple icon includes the following:

✦ Load vendor driver CD—This allows the installation of third-party drivers through a standard interface.

✦ View start up log—The log file viewer is loaded with a copy of the startup log.

✦ View system log—The same log file viewer is loaded with a choice of log files to view, which it offers as a drop-down list.

✦ Post a support query—This option offers an automated way to send a support message back to SUSE.

✦ Autoinstallation—This option allows you to create an autoinstallation control file.

Autoyast: Automated Installations

Autoyast is a powerful tool for controlling unattended automated installations. The principles are similar to those of the Red Hat kickstart tool, but a very high degree of control over the automatic installation is possible. The installation is controlled by an xml file; this can be generated and written out by the YaST autoyast module, but for finer control you can edit the file by hand (preferably with an editor that understands XML and DTDs, such as emacs with the psgml package). Documentation is available on the system in `/usr/share/doc/packages/autoyast2/` and at `www.suse.com/~nashif/autoinstall/`.

The installation files can be offered across the network by NFS or HTTP. It is possible to boot the installation using PXE or a boot floppy or CD (which can be the first CD of the installation set). If you use PXE, you will also need to setup a TFTP server; the client that is being installed will get its initial kernel from this to boot the installation process.

In the case of SLES 8 and related products, the layout required on the server is complicated. This is because of the modular nature of these versions, which consist of a common set of three CDs (the UnitedLinux distribution) together with an additional CD (CD1 of SLES, Standard Server or SLOX). If you plan to use autoinstallation with SLES 8 via HTTP, you must use the SLES 8 Service Pack 3 to start the installation.

The YaST Online Updater (YOU)

YOU is the YaST Online Updater. In the case of the SUSE business products, YOU is one way for the administrator to take advantage of the SUSE maintenance system of package updates. The default KDE desktop contains a tray icon for susewatcher, which checks whether any relevant updates are available; the icon changes its appearance if you need to do an online update.

Installing Non-SUSE packages

If you are looking for packages that are not included in a SUSE distribution, you may find packages that have been prepared for Red Hat or Fedora rather than for SUSE. In some cases this will not be an issue: they will install by rpm without problems. In other cases you may need to install them with the rpm options -nodeps and/or -force; they may then run correctly, but might not. It's certainly well worth looking for packages built for SUSE first. Good sources for these include the following:

✦ http://packman.links2linux.de/

✦ www.usr-local-bin.org/

✦ http://lenz.homelinux.org/RPMs/

✦ http://gaugusch.at/susepackages.shtml

If you want to install Debian packages, that is also possible—the package alien allows conversion of Debian packages to RPM format. Again, there are no guarantees here: some packages will convert, install, and run perfectly, while others will cause problems. It is also possible to install the package deb, which contains the Debian package management tools and allows you to install Debian packages natively using dpkg. In general, this is a bad idea unless you have a very good reason for it and know exactly what you are doing; if you run two package managers in parallel, neither of them can have a full knowledge of the overall state of the system.

You may, however, want to use the Debian package commands with rpm. This is possible on SUSE Professional if you download the apt4rpm package. Repositories of SUSE packages designed to work with apt4rpm are available and more information can be found at http://linux01.gwdg.de/apt4rpm/home.html.

Also of interest is the *fou4s* project, "Fast Online Update for SuSE," which can be found at http://fou4s.gaugusch.at/. This provides an alternative lightweight interface to the functionality of the YOU, with certain additional features including the ability to access third-party packages from some of the sources listed in this appendix.

Finding More Information

There is plenty of information specific to SUSE Linux out there.

✦ SUSE's official websites include basic product information and links to other sources of help. www.suse.com, www.suse.co.uk, and www.suse.de/en/ are the U.S., U.K., and the English-language European sites, respectively.

✦ The SUSE portal is at http://portal.suse.com. This includes a searchable archive of support articles. If you have a business version, this is also where you register it to gain access to customer areas including the "maintenance web."

✦ There is a hardware database at: http://hardwaredb.suse.de/. It is by no means comprehensive (in fairness to SUSE, it would be extremely difficult to make it so), but it is a good place to start when looking for hardware compatibility information.

✦ Information about hardware and software certifications for the Enterprise Server can be found at www.suse.com/us/business/certifications/.

✦ Specific information about running Oracle on SUSE is at `www.suse.com/oracle/`.

✦ There are many public mailing lists run by SUSE: see `www.suse.com/us/private/ support/online_help/mailinglists/`. The archives are at `http://lists.suse.com/`.

✦ There is an unofficial SUSE FAQ at `http://susefaq.sourceforge.net/`.

Troubleshooting Debian GNU/Linux

This appendix is intended for those of you who would like to take some of the skills you've learned in the body of this book and apply them to a Debian installation. While the body of this book is focused on Fedora and Red Hat, I encourage you to read it if you haven't already, as it provides the fundamentals required for any problem-solving endeavor. In this appendix you'll find explanations of those portions of Debian that catch many Fedora or Red Hat troubleshooters by surprise.

The Debian Family Tree

Debian is a multi-purpose distribution that aims to be "the universal operating system." Though the phrase itself is said tongue-in-cheek by Debian Developers, it's true that we maintain multiple distributions for different purposes. Each tree is independent of the others, and when somebody is running Debian, they're running exactly *one* of the trees described in the following sections.

Debian/stable—currently codenamed *Woody*

Once every year or two, Debian releases what we call a *stable* release. CDs are pressed, mirrors are updated, and the announcement is made. Only the stable release of Debian has official CDs. The software contained in the stable release should be free of serious bugs, should be installable without difficulty, and has been proven reliable in the field.

Beware, though—Debian has its own meaning for the term *stable*. When we make a release, it's set in stone. The only updates we make to that software, once released, are of critical importance—bugs which affect security, data integrity, or the user's ability to install and use the package. We refer to these bugs as *release-critical*.

Once every three to six months, a *revision* for the last stable release is made. This is somewhat akin to a Windows service pack. In this revision, all security fixes that were released since the last revision or release are bundled together, and any other known release-critical bugs are fixed.

However, individual software packages aren't simply upgraded to the newest version available. Instead, the version that was released gets a patch that fixes only the serious problem(s). This allows for the most stable platform available, whether you're a developer, a systems integrator, a systems administrator, or even a user who really can't be bothered to go through a traumatic upgrade every six months. It may seem counterintuitive, but when you spend a few weeks working on a system and dealing with any oddities so that everything will work when you roll it out in a large environment, it's kind of a pain to have to do the same thing again six months down the line.

Debian/stable is primarily targeted at those individuals who want a stable platform to run their services on, whatever those might be—desktop, server or embedded device. Consider that even Debian/stable's relatively slow release cycle, one major release every year or two, isn't slow enough for everybody. Imagine a poor systems administrator with 2,000 individual systems that work perfectly fine, needing to upgrade them even once a year. That can be pretty time-consuming and expensive for even the largest of companies. Debian mitigates this issue by making sure that upgrades from an old Debian/stable to a newly-released Debian/stable can be done remotely without a great deal of effort on the part of the systems administrator.

As of this writing, the current Debian release is codenamed *Woody*, and rests at version 3.0r2. "3.0r2" translates to Debian 3.0, revision 2.

See the "Debian Archives Revisited—Official versus Unofficial" section of this appendix for a pointer on how to add updated packages to your Debian/stable installation via a popular unofficial Debian package repository.

Debian/testing—currently codenamed *Sarge*

Debian's *testing* tree isn't intended for use by regular end-users. It's a tree kept self-consistent and in a releasable state at all times. It doesn't get timely security updates. The exception to this rule is right before a release is going to be made; at that point, users are encouraged to test Debian/testing in an effort to find any last-minute bugs which might have slipped through quality assurance procedures.

I won't go into much detail about how Debian testing works, but it's worth mentioning that when it's decided that Debian is ready to make another stable release, this tree is given a version number and released. Right now, the testing tree is called *Sarge*. When our next release is made, Sarge will be released as the new Debian/stable. After this happens, a new Debian/testing tree will be created (a copy of the Debian/Sid tree described below), and it will be given a new codename.

When Sarge becomes Debian/stable, the old Debian/stable (currently Woody) will become Debian/old-stable. It will only be supported for a limited amount of time, typically a year, after which users are expected to seek external support or upgrade their systems.

I'll say again that this tree isn't meant for end-users. When it's safe for an end-user to install, public betas will be released. That happens nearer the end of a release cycle. Before the end of the release cycle, Debian/testing sees no timely security updates, and critical bugs in packages can go unfixed for weeks or longer.

Debian/unstable—the *Sid* tree

The *Sid* tree, often referred to as the *unstable* tree, is the constantly-evolving branch of Debian which most Debian Developers and desktop users prefer. This tree contains the latest versions of software available in Debian, compared to Debian/stable, which contains older, tried-and-proven software. When a Debian Developer uploads a new or updated software package, they upload it to Sid.

 Caution It's rare, but very occasionally software packages will be updated in the Sid tree which might break a user's machine. Users commonly guard against this by asking other users if anything bad has happened to them, by checking for bug reports, or by tracking mailing lists or discussion groups. See the "Getting Help" section of this appendix for useful suggestions on how to track information which pertains to Sid.

Sid's codename is never changed; it will remain Sid for the foreseeable future. Only Debian/stable and Debian/testing change codenames.

The Debian CD-ROMs

Another aspect of Debian confusing to those unfamiliar with it is which CD images they need to download or which pre-pressed CDs they need to purchase to complete an installation. You can install Debian in a number of ways, but the common course is to install from CDs you burn yourself or CDs you purchase. The site `www.debian.org/CD/` contains links to the different Debian CD images as well as a link to a list of vendors who sell ready-made CD sets.

The current Debian release as of the time of writing, version 3.0r2 (Woody), contains a full seven installation CDs for Intel-compatible computers. The next release is expected to include thirteen installation CDs. Don't despair! Debian goes to great lengths to ensure that only the first CD is required for a common installation. If your computer has an Internet connection, you don't even need the first CD (see the last part of this subsection).

 Note Unlike other distributions, which commonly require most if not all of their CDs for a standard installation, Debian puts the most commonly-used software on the first CD. If your computer doesn't have an Internet connection, you may very well want more CDs (the higher the CD number, the less popular the software contained therein), but if you have an Internet connection you'll do just fine with the first CD.

Rescue CDs

If your installation isn't working properly, you can use your Debian installation CD as a rescue utility. Upon booting with the CD in the CD-ROM drive, press F1 to see a help screen. Within it you'll see some pointers on the rescue mode of the CD-ROM.

Complete, full-featured, purpose-built rescue CDs are also available for download or purchase. By far the most popular is KNOPPIX, which happens to be based on Debian. While KNOPPIX was intended as a showcase for Free and Open Source Software, it serves as an excellent rescue CD. KNOPPIX is a *live* CD—all the software runs right off the CD, so there's no need for an installation process (which might destroy the data you're trying to recover). See `http://www.knoppix.net/` for more information. The official download site is `www.knopper` `.net/knoppix/index-en.html`.

Alternative installation CDs

Some Debian versions offer mini-CDs, also known as *netinst* CDs, which allow you to download a relatively small (185 megabyte) CD image and burn it. Only the basic Debian system will be installed from the CD, allowing you to use Debian's standard packaging tools to download and install any further software you require via the Internet. The mini-CDs are quite popular, as few people use all of the 650MB on the first Debian CD. Though the current Debian/stable has no official mini-CD, there are a few unofficial mini-CDs documented at `www.debian.org/` `distrib/netinst`.

Installation Notes

This section is not intended to document the Debian installation procedure. It's meant to point out some common difficulties that arise when somebody more familiar with Fedora or Red Hat attempts to install Debian.

The full installation manual is available at `http://www.debian.org/releases/stable/` `installmanual`. Be warned that it's very complete, and a pretty dry read. If you're using an Intel PC-compatible computer, you want the Intel x86 installation manual.

Hardware detection and setup

Simply put, there is no hardware autodetection during the installation for the current release of Debian . The next stable release of Debian, slated for release in the second quarter of 2004, will have full hardware detection support during the installation process.

In the meantime, the installation will ask you to load drivers for your hardware manually. Since the installation is text-based, the only drivers that must be installed are drivers for any hard drive controllers you may have which don't have support built into the installation kernel (most do), as well as any network drivers if you want to install packages over the network during the installation.

It's common for users to first load only those modules that are crucial for the installation, and then to load any remaining modules after the installation is complete, using the `modconf` command. However, while this is the common method, it isn't the only one. Rudimentary support for hardware detection can be added after the installation is complete by installing the `discover`, `read-edid`, `mdetect`, and `hotplug` packages. Some Debian packages will use these facilities when they're installed, so if you wish to use them, install them right after the initial (minimum) installation.

Picking packages (or not) during installation

The Debian installer will, by default, install only the most basic system. No compiler, no big editors, no graphical desktop. I recommend that you follow these defaults, and when the installer asks you if you'd like to run package installation programs (`tasksel` and `dselect`), answer No. Unlike some other operating systems or Linux distributions, it's trivial to install packages in Debian after the installation.

If you wish to upgrade your Debian/stable installation to Sid, you want to have as few packages installed as is feasible. The fewer packages you have installed during an upgrade from Debian/stable to Debian/Sid, the fewer chances there are for something to go wrong.

Likewise, if you're trying to troubleshoot why a package won't install, it's far easier to do so when it's the only package being installed at that time, rather than hundreds at once.

After the base installation is in place, you can use apt-get (a very popular tool) to install packages as you go, and the tasksel program allows you to install large numbers of related applications at once (these "tasks" are akin to Red Hat's Workstation and Server pre-selected package installation lists).

Common post-installation tasks

One of Debian's strengths—or weaknesses, depending on your administration style—is that it doesn't try to second-guess the administrator. If you followed my directions above, you'll have quite the anemic installation in some respects. As such, I would recommend you perform a few tasks you might not need to do when using another distribution:

1. Install a full-featured kernel. Debian installation kernels are geared towards installation, not routine workloads. To see a list of available kernels, run apt-cache search kernel-image. (With the next release of Debian (Sarge), this step won't be required.)

2. After installing your new kernel, double-check that all your hardware is functioning properly. If it is not, run the modconf program again to load any drivers that need to be loaded. They'll be loaded during any future reboots as well.

3. Install basic package sets that meet your needs. tasksel is a great way to do this.

4. If your computer is connected to the Internet full-time, install the ntpdate and ntp-simple packages. These two packages, working together, will ensure that your computer's clock is always accurate.

Debian Basics

In this section you'll get a crash course in finding and managing packages, as well as a few other systems administration topics. These areas are where differences between RPM-based distributions (like Fedora and Red Hat) and Debian are most evident.

Note   When you've been using an RPM-based distribution like Fedora or Red Hat for years, your first instinct when you want to install a piece of software is likely to be to hit www.rpmfind.net/ and look for an RPM to download. RESIST THIS URGE.

Debian archives

All the software that is officially packaged for Debian is contained in what's termed a *Debian archive*. How you access that archive can vary: you may have a set of Debian CDs (which contain a copy of the archive), you may have your own local copy of the archive on a server or on your hard drive, or you may use one of the many Debian archive mirrors.

These archives are not small. There are currently some 13,000 packages in Debian, available for you to install via apt-get or one of the many other packaging front-ends (introduced below).

When a package is created by a packager (also referred to as a *maintainer*), it gets uploaded to the Debian archive. If it isn't available in the Debian archive, thus available to you through apt-get and friends, chances are that it's a really poorly-made or poorly-maintained package (see the "Debian Archives Revisited—Official versus Unofficial" section for an exception to this rule). So if you're unable to install the package via any of the packaging front-ends, you're likely best off compiling from source. You shouldn't need to do this often, however, as so much is already available in the Debian archive.

Finding packages

Given that all this software is available, a problem arises—how do you know the names of the packages you want? How do you find them? There are multiple ways, but we'll treat only the most common here: `tasksel`, `apt-cache`, `aptitude`, and `http://packages.debian.org`.

Let's start with a working example. Say you want to install a bunch of packages related to a particular role. Perhaps it's a desktop machine. Go ahead and fire up the `tasksel` program from your command-line.

Among the first choices should be *Desktop environment*. Use your arrow keys to navigate the cursor to highlight the checkbox beside that entry, and then hit the i key. This will display a longer description of the task, as well as a list of packages that will be installed if you select it. Press the Enter key to exit the information screen, and then hit either the spacebar or Enter key to actually mark the task for installation. An asterisk (*) should appear in the checkbox beside the entry.

When you've selected the tasks you want installed, press the f key to finish the task selection phase and move onto the installation phase.

While `tasksel` is useful for setting up a basic system, what happens when you need a specific application that isn't already included in the task? This is where the more advanced front-ends come in.

`apt-cache` is part of the apt family of tools, which are described in more detail later. `apt-cache` has many options, but we'll only discuss its searching functionality here (see its man page for full documentation). Let's assume that you'd like an e-mail client, and you prefer using applications that integrate well with the K Desktop Environment:

```
#  apt-cache search kde email
kgpgcertmanager - KDE Certificate Manager
kmail - KDE Email client
ksig - graphical tool for managing multiple email signatures
#
```

As you can see, our search returns three useful results. The first column lists the package name, and the rest of the line is devoted to a short description of each package. The one you're probably looking for is `kmail`, which is the standard KDE e-mail client.

If, in your searching, you get more results than you can shake a stick at, you can look more closely at a package with `apt-cache show packagename`. Among other things, this prints the full description of the package, the individual who maintains it and their e-mail address, the amount of hard drive space the package uses when it's installed, and the package's version.

Though `apt-cache` is a great tool for finding packages, it isn't the only one. `aptitude` (feel free to run `apt-cache show aptitude`) is a full-screen, full-featured package management front-end. It presents the full list of available packages in a categorized, hierarchical format. You can also tell it to change the way it sorts, filters, and displays packages. `aptitude` can also serve as a drop-in command-line replacement for `apt-get`. For more information, see aptitude's manual, `/usr/share/doc/aptitude/README` (you may need to install it first, if you're using Woody).

If you prefer using a Web browser to search for packages and display their information, `http://packages.debian.org/` is an excellent resource. Not only does it offer all the functionality of `apt-cache`, but it also allows you to view much of the information about a package that would normally only be available to you if you installed the package. You can also search for which package(s) provide a particular file, for instance `/usr/lib/libasound .so.2`. With `http://packages.debian.org/`, your searches aren't limited to the current package set that's available in the Debian tree which you installed—you can search other trees (and other architectures, like PPC) as well.

If you find a package on `http://packages.debian.org/`, don't download the package file that's linked in the results page and try to install it manually. This will almost certainly result in pain and suffering. Instead, just run `apt-get install packagename`. Use `http://packages .debian.org/` only to help you find the names of packages; it should not be used as a download site.

Managing Packages

Now that we've discussed finding the name of the package you actually want, let's look at what having the package name actually lets you do. Since Debian serves as a central repository for all software that's built well for Debian (as opposed to other distributions where it's common to have many third-party package providers), simply knowing the name of the package lets you install it, remove it, and in some cases configure it. There's no need for lengthy URLs or a long list of download sites that must be checked manually for software updates.

Installing packages

Let's take a look at an example session. We'll install `vim`, a popular console-based text editor:

```
#  apt-get install vim
Reading Package Lists...
Building Dependency Tree...
The following extra packages will be installed:
  libgpmg1
The following NEW packages will be installed:
  libgpmg1 vim
0 packages upgraded, 2 newly installed, 0 to remove and 0 not upgraded.
Need to get 3796kB of archives. After unpacking 12.3MB will be used.
Do you want to continue? [Y/n]  y
Get:1 http://http.us.debian.org stable/main libgpmg1 1.19.6-12 [45.2kB]
Get:2 http://http.us.debian.org stable/main vim 6.1.018-1 [3751kB]
Fetched 3796kB in 15s (252kB/s)
Selecting previously deselected package libgpmg1.
(Reading database ... 9047 files and directories currently installed.)
Unpacking libgpmg1 (from .../libgpmg1_1.19.6-12_i386.deb) ...
Selecting previously deselected package vim.
Unpacking vim (from .../vim_6.1.018-1_i386.deb) ...
Setting up libgpmg1 (1.19.6-12) ...
```

```
Setting up vim (6.1.018-1) ...
```

\#

Note that apt-get told us it would be installing an extra package along with vim. This is Debian's vaunted automatic dependency-resolution at work. Observe:

```
#  apt-cache show vim | grep ^Depends:
Depends: libc6 (>= 2.2.4-4), libgpmg1 (>= 1.19.6-1), libncurses5
(>= 5.2.20020112a-1)
#
```

Though we already had appropriate versions of libc6 and libncurses5 installed (they're included in the base installation), we did not have libgpmg1 installed. Because the vim package is well-built and declares its requirements, apt-get is able to install every package required to use vim, and in an automated manner no less. This isn't as unique as it once was. apt-rpm is now included in several distributions, as is yum. Both apt-rpm and yum are relatively new, but they provide users of Fedora and Red Hat with similar functionality to the Debian tools they were modeled after.

What's most important is that the packages themselves are of high quality. They must properly declare their relationships to other packages—whether they require another package (Depends:), whether another package can't be installed at the same time as the one you're installing (Conflicts:), and so on. Additionally, it's important that all the packages follow the same policies and conventions. It doesn't help if the package you're trying to install depends on the package vim6, but the vim package you have installed is named vim. This is also why it's important to stick with packages from the standard Debian archives.

However, should you for some reason need to work with a .deb file manually (.deb is the underlying package file format), you can do so:

```
#  dpkg -i /var/cache/apt/archives/vim_6.1.018-1_i386.deb
(Reading database ... 9926 files and directories currently installed.)
Preparing to replace vim 6.1.018-1 (using .../vim_6.1.018-1_i386.deb) ...
Unpacking replacement vim ...
Setting up vim (6.1.018-1) ...
```

\#

Note   We just used the dpkg command for the first time. Roughly, this is equivalent to the rpm command Red Hat users may already be familiar with. dpkg's role in a Debian system is much the same as rpm's role in a Fedora or Red Hat system. However, use of dpkg directly in Debian is frowned upon unless you're careful and know what you're doing, as we provide other tools (such as apt-cache and apt-get) that are intended for direct use.

Notice that the output of this command looks strikingly similar to some of the output in our apt-get install invocation. This isn't surprising, because apt-get (and every other packaging front-end in Debian) just calls dpkg to handle the onerous task of unpacking the package, moving the new files in place, and running any pre- and post-installation scripts which are required.

For more information, refer to the dpkg and apt-get man pages. They're pretty complete and should answer any questions you might have.

Removing packages

Removing packages is a pretty easy task. Just use the apt-get remove command, like so:

```
# apt-get remove vim
Reading Package Lists...
Building Dependency Tree...
The following packages will be REMOVED:
  vim
0 packages upgraded, 0 newly installed, 1 to remove and 0 not upgraded.
Need to get 0B of archives. After unpacking 12.2MB will be freed.
Do you want to continue? [Y/n]
(Reading database ... 9926 files and directories currently installed.)
Removing vim ...
dpkg - warning: while removing vim, directory '/etc/vim' not empty so not
removed.
#
```

See how only vim was removed, and not libgpmg1 as well? apt-get can install additional packages automatically, but it doesn't try to remove them automatically. This behavior is considered dangerous, as the packaging system really doesn't know whether you're using a package for some other reason. aptitude has the ability to automatically track which packages were installed manually. See the aptitude manual (/usr/share/doc/aptitude/README) for an in-depth look at this excellent tool.

You can also use dpkg to remove packages. In fact, sometimes you must use dpkg. Only dpkg allows you to force package removals. Take a look at dpkg removing a package:

```
# dpkg -r vim
(Reading database ... 9926 files and directories currently installed.)
Removing vim ...
dpkg - warning: while removing vim, directory '/etc/vim' not empty so not
removed.
#
```

Caution   Please read the dpkg man page before you force a package removal, as this command can be quite dangerous.

Again, you see that this output was included in the apt-get remove run. You might have noticed that dpkg issues a warning: It claims that /etc/vim isn't empty and thus can't be removed. Take a look and see if there really is anything in /etc/vim:

```
# ls /etc/vim
gvimrc vimrc
#
```

Here you see two configuration files. They weren't deleted as part of the package removal, which brings us to our next topic, configuration file handling.

Configuration file handling

This is another area where people coming from Fedora or Red Hat might be thrown for a loop. Debian is almost zealous in its attitude about configuration files. They are sacrosanct. If any package tromps on a user's configuration, that package is tarred and feathered and beaten to a bloody pulp.

That's only a slight exaggeration. Configuration file handling is a very serious topic when it comes to Debian maintainers and their users. Briefly:

✦ A package may not blindly overwrite a configuration file that was put in place by the administrator before the package was installed.

✦ Any changes the administrator makes to a configuration file must be preserved, for instance when the package is being upgraded.

✦ Removing a configuration file is considered a change to that configuration file, and as such must be preserved.

✦ Unless the administrator explicitly says "remove the configuration files for this package," they are to be left in the filesystem.

We've seen that simply removing a package doesn't also remove its configuration files. Our example package, vim, has two configuration files left, /etc/vim/gvimrc and /etc/vim/vimrc. Let's use the dpkg -purge command to get rid of them:

```
# dpkg --purge vim
(Reading database ... 9056 files and directories currently installed.)
Removing vim ...
Purging configuration files for vim ...
# ls /etc/vim
#
```

As you can see, the configuration files have been removed. Now the packaging system, for all intents and purposes, thinks that vim has never been installed. Now take a look at what happens when you install a brand new package, but you already have a configuration file in place:

```
# ls /etc/vim/vimrc
ls: /etc/vim/vimrc: No such file or directory
# echo test > /etc/vim/vimrc
# ls /etc/vim/vimrc
/etc/vim/vimrc
# apt-get install vim
Reading Package Lists...
Building Dependency Tree...
The following NEW packages will be installed:
  vim
0 packages upgraded, 1 newly installed, 0 to remove and 0 not upgraded.
Need to get 0B/3751kB of archives. After unpacking 12.2MB will be used.
Selecting previously deselected package vim.
(Reading database ... 9053 files and directories currently installed.)
Unpacking vim (from .../vim_6.1.018-1_i386.deb) ...
Setting up vim (6.1.018-1) ...

Configuration file '/etc/vim/vimrc'
==> File on system created by you or by a script.
==> File also in package provided by package maintainer.
  What would you like to do about it ? Your options are:
```

```
  Y or I : install the package maintainer's version
  N or O : keep your currently-installed version
    D    : show the differences between the versions
    Z    : background this process to examine the situation
 The default action is to keep your current version.
*** vimrc (Y/I/N/O/D/Z) [default=N] ?
```

Here we are, at one of the standard Debian configuration file handling prompts. According to the package management system, this file is on the system because either we created it (and we did, that's what the echo command was for). It's also in the package we're trying to install.

At this point we have a number of options. We can say, "yes, don't worry about my configuration file, go ahead and overwrite it." We can say, "no, do not install the new configuration file, the one I have is fine." The D option is particularly useful on upgrades. The D option lets you see the differences between the current configuration file, and the one the package offers. The Z option is also generally useful; it drops you into a shell so you can more closely examine the situation. Perhaps you'll edit the current version of the configuration file before proceeding with the installation. Perhaps you'll make some minor changes to the new version, and then replace the old version with it. The possibilities are endless, as you're able to do pretty much whatever you like.

You will get similar prompts in other situations, but you will not get such a prompt when you remove a configuration file. Remember, removing a configuration file is considered a change to that configuration file, and it's a major one. Anyway, back to the configuration file prompt. Go ahead and press the Y key at the prompt to install the new configuration file to complete the installation, and then observe the results:

```
#  apt-get remove vim
Reading Package Lists...
Building Dependency Tree...
The following packages will be REMOVED:
  vim
0 packages upgraded, 0 newly installed, 1 to remove and 0 not upgraded.
Need to get 0B of archives. After unpacking 12.2MB will be freed.
Do you want to continue? [Y/n]  y
(Reading database ... 9926 files and directories currently installed.)
Removing vim ...
dpkg - warning: while removing vim, directory '/etc/vim' not empty so not
removed.
#  ls /etc/vim/vimrc
/etc/vim/vimrc
#  rm /etc/vim/vimrc
#  ls /etc/vim/vimrc
ls: /etc/vim/vimrc: No such file or directory
#  apt-get install vim
Reading Package Lists...
Building Dependency Tree...
The following NEW packages will be installed:
  vim
0 packages upgraded, 1 newly installed, 0 to remove and 0 not upgraded.
Need to get 0B/3751kB of archives. After unpacking 12.2MB will be used.
Selecting previously deselected package vim.
(Reading database ... 9056 files and directories currently installed.)
```

```
Unpacking vim (from .../vim_6.1.018-1_i386.deb) ...
Setting up vim (6.1.018-1) ...

#  ls /etc/vim/vimrc
ls: /etc/vim/vimrc: No such file or directory
#
```

To narrate the above session, the first thing we did was remove vim. We then confirmed that its configuration file /etc/vim/vimrc was still in place. We then removed it (for demonstration purposes), and confirmed it was gone. Then we installed vim again, and confirmed that our configuration file was still gone. You should now be asking, "How do I get that configuration file back?!" Good question, and here's the trick:

```
# dpkg --force-confmiss -i/var/cache/apt/archives/vim_6.1.018-1_i386.deb
(Reading database ... 9926 files and directories currently installed.)
Preparing to replace vim 6.1.018-1 (using .../vim_6.1.018-1_i386.deb) ...
Unpacking replacement vim ...
Setting up vim (6.1.018-1) ...

Configuration file '/etc/vim/vimrc', does not exist on system.
Installing new config file as you request.

#  ls /etc/vim/vimrc
/etc/vim/vimrc
#
```

As you can see, we needed to use the underlying dpkg tool with a forceful option to restore the configuration file. In this case, we used the -force-confmiss option. This tells dpkg to ignore any missing configuration files, and act as if they weren't removed. The package's new version of the configuration file will be installed instead.

You can also purge the package—that will also tell dpkg that any future installations should be done as if the package had never been installed:

```
# apt-get remove vim
Reading Package Lists...
Building Dependency Tree...
The following packages will be REMOVED:
  vim
0 packages upgraded, 0 newly installed, 1 to remove and 0 not upgraded.
Need to get 0B of archives. After unpacking 12.2MB will be freed.
Do you want to continue? [Y/n] y
(Reading database ... 9926 files and directories currently installed.)
Removing vim ...
dpkg - warning: while removing vim, directory '/etc/vim' not empty so not
removed.
# ls /etc/vim
gvimrc vimrc
# rm /etc/vim/vimrc
# ls /etc/vim
gvimrc
# dpkg --purge vim
(Reading database ... 9056 files and directories currently installed.)
```

```
Removing vim ...
Purging configuration files for vim ...
#  apt-get install vim
Reading Package Lists...
Building Dependency Tree...
The following NEW packages will be installed:
  vim
0 packages upgraded, 1 newly installed, 0 to remove and 0 not upgraded.
Need to get 0B/3751kB of archives. After unpacking 12.2MB will be used.
Selecting previously deselected package vim.
(Reading database ... 9053 files and directories currently installed.)
Unpacking vim (from .../vim_6.1.018-1_i386.deb) ...
Setting up vim (6.1.018-1) ...

#  ls /etc/vim
gvimrc vimrc
#
```

Configuring packages with debconf

You've seen what happens when you change or remove a configuration file. The next point is how to actually configure packages. Though Debian doesn't have a central application that can be used to configure the system, like Fedora and Red Hat do, many Debian packages use debconf, Debian's configuration framework. Individual packages can contain debconf scripts that prompt the user for information, and then create a default configuration file based upon the answers it received.

When a package uses debconf, the package provides a consistent and well-defined method of configuration. When you install or upgrade a package that uses debconf, the packaging system (specifically debconf) may display one or more questions for you to answer. You can decide what sorts of questions you'd like to answer; if you want, you can avoid all but the most critical questions. If you're a control freak like me, you can opt to answer even the lowest-priority questions.

An example of a critical debconf question can be found in the passwd package, which is responsible for setting the default system passwords at installation. In its debconf script, passwd asks for the root password, and this is a critical-priority question for obvious reasons. Also in the passwd package is a low-priority question regarding whether passwords should be stored separately from the username database. Roughly speaking, critical-priority questions must be answered by the user or the system will be nonfunctional or severely broken. Low-priority questions are those that have safe defaults and are only of interest to those who basically want to see every knob and have a chance to twiddle them. So taking our passwd package as an example, it's not safe to have a default root password, or anybody can use it to gain administrator access on the machine. However, there are very few reasons for keeping the password database merged with the username database, so it's safe to assume that the user wants them separate.

Though debconf is primarily useful as it asks questions automatically during package installation, you can also reconfigure a package later by invoking the dpkg-reconfigure command. (dpkg-reconfigure is part of the debconf package, so be sure that debconf is installed before you try to use it.) For example, to reconfigure the debconf package itself, issue the following command:

```
#  dpkg-reconfigure debconf
```

When you invoke a package's `debconf` configuration in this manner, it will assume that you wish to see every question again. If you want to override this behavior, you can use `dpkg-reconfigure`'s `-p` option:

```
# dpkg-reconfigure -p critical debconf
```

The available priorities, as of this time of writing, are low, medium, high, and critical. Priorities are inclusive, so if you've opted to see all low-priority questions, you'll also see all medium-, high-, and critical-priority questions. If a package doesn't have any questions to ask, you will simply be returned to your prompt.

`debconf` has numerous interfaces available, as you can see in `debconf`'s own configuration. As of this writing, Debian/stable has GNOME, readline (console line-based), dialog (console full-screen), and editor interfaces. The next Debian/stable release (Sarge) will add a K Desktop Environment interface.

Other basic dpkg commands

Now that you know how to install and remove packages, and how to work with their configuration files, let's take a look at some of the other commonly used commands for examining packages.

The first thing you might want to do is list packages. You can use `dpkg -l` without supplying a package name to get a list of all your packages. Unlike the various apt-related commands, which will tell you a great deal about any package which is either installed or available for installation, `dpkg` only knows about packages which you've installed or removed—similar to `rpm`. Observe the output:

```
# dpkg -l vim
Desired=Unknown/Install/Remove/Purge/Hold
| Status=Not/Installed/Config-files/Unpacked/Failed-config/Half-installed
| / Err?=(none)/Hold/Reinst-required/X=both-problems (Status,Err:
Uppercase=bad)
| | /Name            Version          Description
+++-=================-================-=====================================
ii vim               6.1.018-1        Vi IMproved - enhanced vi editor
#
```

`dpkg -l` will list packages you have installed, as well as some information about each package. The first column is the status column. In the example, we see that vim is fully-installed (the `ii` indicates this). Let's remove vim again, and then look at our package system database:

```
# dpkg -r vim
(Reading database ... 6944 files and directories currently installed.)
Removing vim ...
dpkg - warning: while removing vim, directory '/etc/vim' not empty so not
removed.
# dpkg -l vim
Desired=Unknown/Install/Remove/Purge/Hold
| Status=Not/Installed/Config-files/Unpacked/Failed-config/Half-installed
| / Err?=(none)/Hold/Reinst-required/X=both-problems (Status,Err:
uppercase=bad)
| | /Name            Version          Description
+++-==============-================-=========================================
rc vim               6.1.018-1        Vi IMproved - enhanced vi editor
#
```

The output is the same, except that the first column now shows rc rather than ii. This stands for "removed, but configuration files remain." Remember, removing packages doesn't automatically get rid of their configuration files. You must purge the package, explicitly telling dpkg that it's okay to nuke your configuration files, as in the following code:

```
# dpkg --purge vim
(Reading database ... 6074 files and directories currently installed.)
Removing vim ...
Purging configuration files for vim ...
#  dpkg -l vim
Desired=Unknown/Install/Remove/Purge/Hold
| Status=Not/Installed/Config-files/Unpacked/Failed-config/Half-installed
| / Err?=(none)/Hold/Reinst-required/X=both-problems (Status,Err:
uppercase=bad)
| | /Name              Version            Description
+++-==================-==================-================================
pn vim                <none>             (no description available)
#
```

Now dpkg doesn't know anything about versions and descriptions, all it knows is that the package's status is pn, in other words, "purged, not installed." You can run dpkg -l without any arguments at all to list all the packages that it's aware of.

Next you may want to take a look at the files that make up a package. Supplying -L to dpkg tells it to list package contents.

```
# dpkg -L libgpmg1
/.
/usr
/usr/lib
/usr/lib/libgpm.so.1.19.6
/usr/share
/usr/share/doc
/usr/share/doc/libgpmg1
/usr/share/doc/libgpmg1/copyright
/usr/share/doc/libgpmg1/changelog.gz
/usr/share/doc/libgpmg1/changelog.Debian.gz
/usr/lib/libgpm.so.1
#
```

dpkg -L is a pretty simple command. It lists any files that the package contains which dpkg knows about.

You can use dpkg -I to examine a package file that you've downloaded (via apt-get, not manually, if possible):

```
# dpkg -I /var/cache/apt/archives/sudo_1.6.6-1.1_i386.deb
new debian package, version 2.0.
size 134728 bytes: control archive= 2213 bytes.
      33 bytes,    2 lines         conffiles
     508 bytes,   12 lines         control
    1124 bytes,   18 lines         md5sums
    1852 bytes,   66 lines       * postinst         #!/usr/bin/perl
     159 bytes,    7 lines       * postrm           #!/bin/sh
     325 bytes,   12 lines       * prerm            #!/bin/sh
```

```
Package: sudo
Version: 1.6.6-1.1
Section: admin
Priority: optional
Architecture: i386
Depends: libc6 (>= 2.2.4-4), libpam0g (>= 0.72-1), libpam-modules
Installed-Size: 248
Maintainer: Bdale Garbee <bdale@gag.com>
Description: Provides limited super user privileges to specific users.
 Sudo is a program designed to allow a sysadmin to give limited
 root privileges to users and log root activity. The basic philosophy is
 to give as few privileges as possible but still allow people to get their
 work done.
#
```

This gives much of the same information as the apt-cache show command, shown earlier, as well as some information about any packaging scripts embedded in the package.

Another common operation is determining which file belongs to which package. You can use dpkg's -S option for this:

```
#   dpkg -S /etc/crontab
cron: /etc/crontab
#
```

If you want to check the integrity of the packages you have installed, you'll need to install an additional package called debsums. After you've installed it, feel free to run the debsums command.

Tip   Use debsums -q to list only errors and warnings, instead of telling you about every file that's perfectly all right.

Upgrading your installation

Upgrading your Debian installation is as simple as installing a package. In the example below, I just finished installing a Debian 3.0 Woody system from a CD. I've made sure the system can connect to the Internet, so we know it will be able to contact the Debian archive. I first run apt-get update, which freshens the local database of available packages using Debian's archives:

```
# apt-get update
Get:1 http://ftp.us.debian.org stable/main Packages [1774kB]
Get:2 http://non-us.debian.org stable/non-US/main Packages [44.5kB]
Get:3 http://security.debian.org stable/updates/main Packages [181kB]
Get:4 http://non-us.debian.org stable/non-US/main Release [102B]
Get:5 http://non-us.debian.org stable/non-US/main Sources [18.7kB]
Get:6 http://non-us.debian.org stable/non-US/main Release [104B]
Get:7 http://security.debian.org stable/updates/main Release [110B]
Get:8 http://ftp.us.debian.org stable/main Release [95B]
Get:9 http://ftp.us.debian.org stable/main Sources [729kB]
Get:10 http://ftp.us.debian.org stable/main Release [97B]
Fetched 2748kB in 11s (250kB/s)
Reading Package Lists... Done
```

```
Building Dependency Tree... Done
#
```

Then, I run apt-get to see what's in the upgrade and to start the upgrade:

```
# apt-get -u upgrade
Reading Package Lists... Done
Building Dependency Tree... Done
The following packages will be upgraded
  perl-base
1 packages upgraded, 0 newly installed, 0 to remove and 0 not upgraded.
Need to get 496kB of archives. After unpacking 102kB will be freed.
Do you want to continue? [Y/n] y
Get:1 http://security.debian.org stable/updates/main perl-base 5.6.1-8.6
 [496kB]
Fetched 496kB in 3s (126kB/s)
(Reading database ... 6065 files and directories currently installed.)
Preparing to replace perl-base 5.6.1-8.3 (using .../perl-base_5.6.1-
8.6_i386.deb) ...
Unpacking replacement perl-base ...
Setting up perl-base (5.6.1-8.6) ...

#
```

In my case, there was only one package (perl-base) available for upgrade. This is a fresh installation, with almost nothing installed. On a production machine, you can expect to see more upgrades. If you only want to upgrade a single package, just apt-get install *packagename*. You can actually supply multiple package names, if you'd like, to either install or upgrade more than one package at a time.

If you're running Debian/stable, you want go through this upgrading process about once a day, just to be sure that your installation is up-to-date with respect to any security issues. If you're running Sid, you will likely also want to upgrade once a day—but in this case, the upgrade will include many new versions of packages which are unrelated to any security vulnerabilities.

As mentioned earlier, automatically removing packages is generally considered a bad idea. As such, if an upgrade requires a package to be removed (for instance, if it's been replaced by another), you need to use a different form of the apt-get command. Instead of apt-get upgrade, use apt-get dist-upgrade.

The -u option, incidentally, tells apt-get to show us what it will be doing. This will be the default for the next Debian release (and already is the default, for people using Sid), but if you're still using Woody you should remember to add it.

Should you wish to stop a package from being upgraded, you can inform dpkg and the apt family of tools to put that package *on hold*, as shown in this example:

```
# echo perl-base hold | dpkg --set-selections
# apt-get -u upgrade
Reading Package Lists... Done
Building Dependency Tree... Done
The following packages have been kept back
  perl-base
0 packages upgraded, 0 newly installed, 0 to remove and 1 not upgraded.
#
```

Note that I put `perl-base` on hold, and now apt-get won't upgrade it. There are any number of reasons why you don't want to upgrade a particular package—for instance, perhaps you have compiled your own version and don't wish its files to be overwritten. The following example shows the commands to allow the package to be upgraded:

```
# echo perl-base install | dpkg –set-selections
#  apt-get -u upgrade
Reading Package Lists... Done
Building Dependency Tree... Done
The following packages will be upgraded
  perl-base
1 packages upgraded, 0 newly installed, 0 to remove and 0 not
 upgraded.
Need to get 0B/496kB of archives. After unpacking 102kB will be freed.
Do you want to continue? [Y/n]
```

`apt-get` is perfectly willing to upgrade that package, now that I've told the package subsystem that it's allowed to do so.

Debian commands: quick reference

Table C-1 provides a comparison between some of the most commonly used Debian and Red Hat commands.

Table C-1: Debian Command Reference

Operation	Debian Command	Red Hat Equivalent
Search for a package	`apt-cache search` *terms*	`rpm -qa` *packagename*
Show a package;s details	`apt-cache show` *packagename*	`rpm -qi` *packagename*
Install a package	`apt-get install` *packagename*, **or** `dpkg -i` */path/to/file.deb*	`rpm -ihv` *packagename*
Remove a package	`apt-get remove` *packagename*, **or** `dpkg -r` *packagename*	`rpm -e` *packagename*
Purge a package	`apt-get –purge remove` *packagename*, **or** `dpkg –purge` *packagename*	-------
Install a package, while replacing any missing configuration files	`dpkg –force-confmiss -i` */path/to/file.deb*	`rpm -Ihv –allfiles/` *packagename*
Reconfigure a package which uses `debconf`	`dpkg-reconfigure` *packagename*	-------
Quick list of an installed package	`dpkg -l` *packagename*	`rpm -qa`*packagename*

Operation	Debian Command	Red Hat Equivalent
Quick list of all installed packages	`dpkg -l`	`rpm -qa`
List files contained in a package	`dpkg -L` *packagename*	`rpm -ql` *packagename*
Find which package contains a file	`dpkg -S` */path/to/a/file*	`rpm -qf` */path/to/a/file*
Examine a downloaded .deb	`dpkg -I` */path/to/file.deb*	`rpm -qp -l` */packagename*
Refresh local package lists	`apt-get update`	`rpm -Uhv -justdb` */packagename*
Upgrade installed packages	`apt-get -u upgrade`	`rpm -freshen` *packagename*
Upgrade installed packages, while allowing package removals	`apt-get -u dist-upgrade`	-------
Put a package on hold so it won't get upgraded	`echo` *packagename* `hold | dpkg -set-selections`	-------
Allow a package which was previously on hold to be upgraded	`echo` *packagename* `install | dpkg -set-selections`	-------

Managing Runlevels

Another big difference between Debian and RPM-based distributions is the runlevel system. The default runlevel in Debian is 2, not 5 as it is in Fedora and Red Hat. This isn't to say that you don't get a GUI by default in Debian. You don't, but it's not because you're in runlevel 2.

By default, runlevels 2 through 5 in Debian are all identical. If you have a graphical login manager installed, it will be run regardless of which of those runlevels you're in. I've seen many a new Debian user go through the relatively onerous task of switching the default runlevel to 5, only to find that it changed absolutely nothing.

You can customize those runlevels to do whatever you'd like (include emulating Red Hat's default runlevel setup), but they all start out identical.

Enabling and disabling services

Another stumbling point is Debian's lack of `chkconfig`. Personally, I find this irritating as well. Debian has `update-rc.d` that can be used to set the runlevels a particular service starts in, but it's meant primarily for packages to use automatically, and isn't particularly easy for an administrator to use.

The easiest way to manage runlevels in Debian is to simply add and remove symlinks from the `/etc/rc[2-5].d/` directories manually. I agree, it's a pain.

Managing the symlinks in the Debian SysV init directories is documented in detail as part of the Debian Reference Manual, and is available on-line at `www.debian.org/doc/debian-policy/ch-opersys.html#s-sysvinit`.

On the other hand, you're not forced to use symlinks to control which services start and stop—you can instead use a simple, plain configuration file.

Alternative init systems

There's a solid following of people who enjoy the use of the file-rc package. It's not currently available to Woody users, but will be included in Sarge. Instead of using a symlink tree in /etc/rc*.d/, it allows you to control runlevel information via a simple file, /etc/runlevels.conf. It's a pretty decent alterative to symlink-style management. Thanks to update-rc.d, packages that automatically add symlinks will instead add lines to that configuration file.

Graphical administration systems

Debian doesn't have any centralized set of GUI administration tools. About the closest Debian has is debconf. Since Debian places such a high priority on preserving user/administrator changes to configuration files, most Debian users are quite comfortable using them.

If you wish to have a nice front-end to common system configuration tasks, feel free to explore the webmin packages. webmin is a Web-based configuration/administration system that many people like. It's pretty complete, and does a much better job at preserving any manual changes you've made to configuration files when compared to most other such centralized configuration tools.

You can get a list of available webmin modules by running apt-cache search webmin—the list isn't reproduced here as it's quite long. The webmin package itself installs a basic set of webmin modules, and you can install more manually if you'd like. After you've installed the webmin package, you can read the quick startup guide, available in /usr/share/doc/webmin/README.Debian.

Package conventions

Because Debian's archive is so complete, because it contains virtually every piece of software that a user might want, and because we apply very strict policies and standards to packages, there's a lot you can find out if you simply know the package's name.

✦ Many packages provide a Debian-specific README file, which often provides a quick startup guide. This is available as /usr/share/doc/*packagename*/README.Debian or /usr/share/doc/*packagename*/README.Debian.gz.

✦ Change logs for the software can be found in /usr/share/doc/*packagename*/changelog.gz and/or /usr/share/doc/*packagename*/changelog.Debian.gz (if the latter exists, it documents Debian-specific changes).

✦ http://packages.debian.org/*packagename* allows you to view all sorts of data about the package, without needing to install it.

Debian Archives Revisited—Official versus Unofficial ArchivesSo far in this appendix, I've been doing my best to impress upon you the importance of using the standard Debian archives. There are many reasons to do this, but there are times when using an unofficial archive is warranted. The two main reasons would be installing more up-to-date packages on a Debian/stable system, and installing patent-encumbered software.

Feel free to open up `/etc/apt/sources.list` in your favorite editor. My file looks like this:

```
# cat /etc/apt/sources.list
deb http://ftp.us.debian.org/debian/ stable main
deb-src http://ftp.us.debian.org/debian/ stable main

deb http://non-us.debian.org/debian-non-US stable/non-US main
deb-src http://non-us.debian.org/debian-non-US stable/non-US main

deb http://security.debian.org/ stable/updates main
#
```

Yours should look quite similar, though it won't be identical. Each line that starts with `deb` refers to an archive that houses binary packages (what you get when you `apt-get install` something), and each line that starts with `deb-src` refers to an archive that houses the sources for those binary packages (which can be downloaded via `apt-get source` *packagename*). The two different lines are often identical after that initial difference, as most archives host both binaries and sources. After the initial component of the line (either `deb` or `deb-src`) comes the archive's URL. This is a standard URL that refers to the location of the archive. Following the URL are one or more space-separated *components* which refer to which parts of the archive you're interested in.

I have two unofficial archives to recommend. They're both run by people I know, and in my experience the quality of the packages are acceptable, typically as good as what you'll find in the standard Debian archives (unlike most unofficial archives out there).

If you're running a Debian/stable installation, but you desperately need a newer version of a package than what is available in that tree, and you aren't willing to upgrade to Sid, then I would suggest `http://www.backports.org/`. Instructions on its usage are available at `www.backports.org/installation.html`.

If you want to use mplayer (a popular media player) or any mp3 encoders (which are patent-encumbered in countries which have weak patent offices), you can use Christian Marillat's archive, available at `deb ftp://ftp.nerim.net/debian-marillat/` *dist* `main`. (Substitute the *dist* appropriate for your installation: `stable`, `unstable`, or `testing`. Note that the various components of the line are separated by spaces.) You can also check `http://marillat.free.fr/`; that's where Christian posts news about his archive.

Troubleshooting Tips and Tools

This section provides an overview of some of the most common troubleshooting packages used in Debian. Since one of the biggest parts of an administrator's job is knowing the right tool to use for the job, you may find yourself making your own list of "essential packages" for easy reference.

When moving from Fedora or Red Hat

Earlier in this appendix, I described the most confusing aspects of Debian, at least for those readers who are moving from Fedora or Red Hat. Here's a refresher:

✦ Use `dpkg -L` to find files—especially configuration files. Some will be in different places on Debian when compared to Fedora or Red Hat.

✦ `/usr/share/doc/packagename/README.Debian` (sometimes with an added `.gz` extension) should be the first thing you check when you run into a problem with a given package.

✦ Always install packages via apt-get. Don't download a random package file from the Web; it will likely break your system badly.

✦ When in doubt, ask somebody who is more familiar with the system than yourself. The "Getting Help" section of this appendix will give you a good walkthrough of, well, getting help. Debian is not only a software distribution, it's also a rich community. Don't shun the community around Debian, as it's one of the most powerful tools available to you.

Troubleshooting tools

Aside from the simple pointers above, you'll mainly be working with the same software, diagnosing the same problems, and using the same tools as with Fedora or Red Hat. In my experience, the hardest part of any transition is just learning which packages provide which troubleshooting facilities (remember that with Debian, all you need to know is a package's name). So the following tables offer lists of package names with descriptions and tips on further documentation, just to get you started on your transition. Table C-2 covers file system tools; Table C-3 lists network tools; Table C-4 addressed system integrity tools; and Table C-5 offers debugging tools. Unless otherwise specified, full man pages for all the commands are included in the package.

Table C-2: File System Tools

Package Name	Relevant Commands	Description
e2fsprogs	fsck.ext2, fsck.ext3, mkfs.ext2, mkfs.ext3, resize2fs, tune2fs	Standard utilities for working with ext2 and ext3 filesystems. Of particular note is the resize2fs utility, which allows you to resize an unmounted ext2 or ext3 filesystem.
xfsprogs	mkfs.xfs, fsck.xfs, xfs_repair, xfs_growfs	These are the standard utilities for working with an XFS filesystem. xfs_growfs allows you to expand the size of an XFS filesystem while it's in-use (shrinking is not possible at all). xfs_repair can only be used on an unmounted XFS filesystem.
xfsdump	xfs_fsr	Among other commands, this package includes xfs_fsr—the defragmenter for the XFS filesystem.
reiserfsprogs	mkreiserfs, resize_reiserfs	The reiserfsprogs package includes the standard utilities for working with ReiserFS filesystems—including mkreiserfs (to create such filesystems), and resize_reiserfs (to resize such filesystems).
util-linux	fdisk, cfdisk	fdisk is the traditional filesystem partitioning utility, while cfdisk is a full-screen version which provides for a more pleasant experience.
parted	parted	parted is a newer partitioning utility, and is quite good. It's also capable of resizing many filesystems and partitions. Basic manual pages are provided in the parted package, while full documentation is contained in the parted-doc package.

Table C-3: Network Tools

Package Name	Relevant Commands	Description
iputils-tracepath	tracepath, tracepath6	iputils-tracepath contains modern versions of the venerable traceroute commands. They allow you to view the route any of your Internet packets take on the way to their destination. tracepath6 is IPv6-compatible.
iputils-ping	ping, ping6	Modern versions of the ping command. ping6 includes IPv6 support.
tcptraceroute	tcptraceroute	Similar to tracepath, tcptraceroute allows you to view the route your Internet packets take on the way to their destination. Unlike tracepath, tcptraceroute uses TCP, which allows it to circumvent misconfigured routers.
mtr-tiny	mtr	mtr is an excellent tool for diagnosing connectivity problems at a distance. It is similar to tracepath and traceroute in that it examines each step on a packet's journey, but it's different in that it collects a great deal of statistics and presents them in an organized manner.
monit	monit	monit is a "hearbeat" system. It allows you to monitor your computers and the services running on them in an automated manner. It allows for numerous reporting methods, including pages and e-mail. Documentation for monit is contained in /usr/share/doc/monit/.
netcat, netcat6	nc, nc6	netcat is a versatile tool for network analysis, whose full capabilities can't even be touched here. It's often referred to as "the Swiss Army knife of networking."
ssh	ssh, sshd	The Debian ssh package contains both the OpenSSH client and server. OpenSSH is a secure remote-login protocol that allows for unattended non-interactive logins.
telnet-ssl	telnet	While telnet's usage as a remote login protocol has been diminished in recent years (namely falling due to the convenience of SSH), it's still useful to talk to a network server "in the raw."
dnsutils	dig, nslookup	dnsutils contains dig and nslookup, two stalwart utilities used commonly in diagnosing Domain Name System problems.
openssl	openssl	The openssl package provides a command-line interface to the OpenSSL libraries, which export a large number of cryptographic-related functions.

Table C-4: System Integrity Tools

Package Name	Relevant Commands	Description
aide	aide	AIDE stands for "advanced intrusion detection environment." It keeps track of any changes to files on your system, and will notify you if something has changed when it shouldn't have. It can be difficult to set up and maintain, but the results are quite worth it. Man pages, as well as documentation in /usr/share/doc/aide/.
chkrootkit	chkrootkit	chkrootkit performs some rudimentary tests to check to see if a *root kit* has been installed on your Debian installation. A root kit is used by malicious crackers to maintain control over an installation they have cracked into.
checksecurity	checksecurity	checksecurity runs automatically each day and will notify you of any changes in setuidor setgid applications. setuid and setgid applications are those which always run with elevated user privileges, regardless of the user who actually runs them.
debsums	debsums	Many Debian packages include cryptographic "hashes" of files that allow one to identify whether a file has been changed since it was installed. debsums is a utility to ensure that no files have been changed. Be warned, though—if an intruder is able to change a file that came from a package, they're also able to change the database of cryptographic hashes. debsums can be thought of as an easy-to-use version of AIDE. (Note: this package is Debian-specific, unlike the others listed in these tables.)
tar	tar	tar is a venerable backup utility, which archives multiple files into a single, optionally compressed file. It can be difficult to use, but its archives are usable on pretty much any modern platform (and several obsolete platforms).
rsync	rsync	rsync is a file-transfer application which allows you to transfer sets of files between two machines. Even more impressive, however, is its ability to keep those two repositories synchronized—it implements a very efficient transfer algorithm which only transfers those parts of the files which have changed.
amanda-client, amanda-server	Too many to list.	Amanda is a popular client/server backup solution that works over a network. Documentation is available via man pages, /usr/share/doc/amanda-client/, and /usr/share/doc/amanda-server/.
duplicity	duplicity	duplicity is a flexible and secure backup/archiving solution. It supports encryption and incremental backups. It uses the same partial-change algorithm as rsync, meaning incremental backups are quite small in size.

Table C-5: Debugging Tools

Package Name	Relevant Commands	Description
strace	strace	strace allows you to monitor the internal workings of an application. This is particularly useful when the application fails to function but doesn't provide a helpful error message.
ltrace	ltrace	ltrace is similar to strace, but instead of intercepting system calls it intercepts library calls.
gdb	gdb	gdb is the GNU Debugger. It's a very complex debugger used to closely analyze, interactively, the inner workings of an application. It's primarily useful to developers, as knowledge of the application's source code is required. gdb documentation is in texinfo format, contained in the package. To view it, install the info package and then run `info gdb`.
ddd	ddd	ddd stands for Data Display Debugger. It's a graphical front-end to gdb. ddd documentation is in texinfo format, contained in the package. To view it, install the info package and then run `info ddd`.

Getting Help

As mentioned in the last section, one of the most powerful tools at your disposal is a community of people who have had the same problems you're having. However, like any tool, you need to be sure to use it properly and carefully.

Debian has a large, vibrant community of developers and users who often devote countless hours of their own time to helping other people troubleshoot their problems. Most of these people are not only generous enough to help you solve your problem, but they're also practical enough to make sure that you leave with a better understanding of how things went wrong in the first place and how to avoid such a situation in the future.

Common sources of documentation

As mentioned, the canonical location for a Debian package's documentation is `/usr/share/doc/packagename/`. Additionally, Debian Policy requires that all shell commands contain manual pages. Run `apt-get install man-db manpages` to install both the man page reader (`man-db`) and a set of common, shared man pages (`manpages`).

Sometimes, however, if the documentation is particularly disk-space-intensive, the package's documentation will be put into a second package. If `/usr/share/doc/packagename/` doesn't contain what you're looking for, and the manual page was either nonexistent or inappropriate, you should run `apt-cache search packagename doc`. That will show you any relevant documentation packages.

Last but not least are on-line sources of documentation. Debian provides a portal page for common documentation resources at `www.debian.org/doc/`. From that Web page, you'll also find links to The Linux Documentation Project (LDP), which deserves special mention. It contains many thousands of pages worth of guides and references for the documentation-hungry user. The Linux Documentation Project's official website is available at `www.tldp.org/`, and you can download and install the documentation for local use—just `apt-cache search doc-linux` and install any packages you think are appropriate.

Free on-line support

One of the more often-overlooked aspects of getting support, whether free or paid, is etiquette. Everybody has limits, both support personnel and users, and either side being demanding can quickly wear down patience and result in a poor experience on all sides. In that vein, here are some pointers you might want to keep in mind when you're getting support:

✦ Above all, be polite.

✦ If the person who's helping you asks you to run commands and provide them with the output, try to do so reasonably quickly so that nobody is left waiting.

✦ If you're being helped over the phone or in person or via some other real-time communications medium and you need to take a break, don't be afraid to say as much. Chances are, the person who's helping you wouldn't mind the chance for a coffee break either.

✦ If you have a question, go ahead and ask it—in a forum dedicated to support, permission to ask questions is implicit.

✦ Instead of telling somebody that "it doesn't work," try to give some details. It'll save you some time, as the first question the person providing the support will always ask is, "in what way doesn't it work?"

✦ Not everybody is created equal, and if you find that somebody who's supposedly trying to help you is either being offensive or giving bad advice, try to get in touch with the individual responsible for that particular support forum. Tell them about your encounter so that others don't have the same experience.

Now that you know the basic ground rules, let's go over your options for free support. As I've stressed, there are all sorts of people who enjoy spending some free time helping others.

Collecting information

The first thing anybody helping you will need to do is diagnose the problem. To assist in that process, you want to try to collect as much information related to your problem as possible. Not only will it be quicker for you, but it will be less stressful for the individual who's helping.

If you're getting an error of some sort, have it handy. If you can, copy and paste the error to a file for easy reference. Avoid writing things manually at all costs—even the slightest typo can cost hours worth of false leads. Also be sure to include the full command-line you're running, or document the steps required to reproduce the error. These are the first things you'll be asked when somebody tries to help out, and being able to answer their questions quickly and easily will likely make them quite happy.

If the application which is giving you the error is console-based, and doesn't require any user input, you can redirect all of its output to a log file:

```
# command -all --options here > command.log 2>&1
```

This will create a file called `command.log` in the current directory. If the application requires user input, you'll need to copy and paste all the relevant output manually.

If the application has any configuration files, be sure to have those handy as well. You can and should edit out any sensitive information (such as passwords), but tell the person who's helping that you did so.

Mailing lists

Mailing lists are a primary source of support for many people. While the answers won't necessarily be prompt (though many of the simpler questions are answered within minutes), it's a fairly convenient method of communication. A mailing list is a special e-mail address which, when sent an e-mail, forwards the message to many recipients. It's like a broadcast, in a way, except that it goes to only those people who are interested. These are the people who have subscribed to the list.

The primary Debian technical support and user mailing list is `debian-user@lists.debian.org`. You can subscribe to it via a web form at `http://lists.debian.org/debian-user/`. This list is very high-traffic, so you may not want to subscribe to it unless you like lots of e-mail. You can still send an e-mail to the list, but mention that you aren't subscribed and that people should send any replies directly to you (instead of through the list).

There are many other Debian mailing lists, some of which are versions of `debian-user@lists.debian.org`, except for specific languages. For a complete index, check out `http://lists.debian.org/`.

Websites

Mailing lists have been around for many years, and common Free/Open Source Software e-mail applications deal with them extremely well. However, most commercial e-mail applications are quite lacking in this respect. One of the side-effects of this has been a rise in the popularity of so-called "web boards."

These have been pretty slow to catch on in Debian, as mailing lists are simply so well-supported that many don't have the need to use anything else. However, at some point in the future there may be an official Debian web board for technical support. In the meantime, you can use an unofficial web board at `www.debianforum.com/`. At the time of writing, this forum has just been opened, so it doesn't have many active users. You may or may not get help there.

Real-time chat

A popular option for people looking for help is the use of IRC, which stands for *Internet Relay Chat*. Like mailing lists, IRC has been around for well over a decade. It's a near-real-time protocol, meaning that when you type out a message, others see it within a second or two.

There are many popular IRC networks, and most of them have a Debian "channel." A channel is a group chat, where many people see every message sent to the channel. The most official of these channels is `#debian` on `irc.debian.org`. If you wish to access this network, you'll need to download and install an IRC client. If you have Internet access for your Debian installation (meaning your networking is working, of course), I would suggest either the `irssi` (for a console environment) or `xchat` (for a graphical environment) packages. They're both good IRC clients. They'll also both connect you to irc.debian.org by default. When you've connected, simply issue the `/join #debian` command, wait for the channel to appear, and then start talking.

When you're using IRC and speaking in a channel, you should avoid pasting large amounts of text at once, and avoid hitting your enter key too often. Be sure to type full and complete sentences. Both of these suggestions help improve the channel's usability for everybody else—if everybody hits Enter after every third word and pastes 10 or 20 lines of text every few seconds, nobody will be able to follow any conversations. Instead, put your text in a file and place it somewhere from which it can be downloaded. If you don't have a readily-accessible server for this purpose, `www.pastebin.de/` allows you to paste your text and provide a URL for others to follow.

Reporting bugs

The quickest and easiest way to report bugs in Debian is via the reportbug package. This provides a console-based, step-by-step procedure that walks you through reporting a bug. After installing the package, however, you do need to tell it your name and e-mail address. I've included a sample `~/.reportbugrc` below:

```
# cat ~/.reportbugrc
realname "Your Name Here"
email "your@email.address"
#
```

Create that file with whatever editor you prefer—the file format should be self-explanatory, but if you need more information, consult its manual page via `man reportbug`.

After this, simply run `reportbug packagename`. It will walk you through reporting a bug step-by-step.

After you report a bug, the maintainer of the package will hopefully be getting in touch with you shortly. Be warned, though; package maintainers are sometimes quite busy, and if your bug report is particularly thorough, the only response you'll get is an e-mail telling you the bug has been fixed.

Using Sid

If you've decided to run Sid, you probably wish to keep abreast of any developments.

If you are administering a large number of Sid machines, then by far the best option is to have one or more "prototype" machines with every package you have installed on all your various Debian machines. Test each upgrade before you roll it out to the other machines, and you'll get a really good feel for what the upgrade entails (they're typically quite painless).

In addition to a test/prototype machine (or in lieu of one, if you don't have one handy), the packages apt-listchanges and apt-listbugs are helpful. apt-listchanges allows you to view packages' changelogs and news items before they're installed. apt-listbugs allows you to view any major bugs that have been filed against a package since it was last upgraded.

At the time of this writing, there's discussion revolving around a daily "State of Sid" mailing list, which will allow users to subscribe and receive daily notifications on any known breakage. Check `http://lists.debian.org/` to see if this mailing list exists yet.

`http://people.debian.org/~dbharris/tracking-sid/` has some links, documentation, and scripts that you might like to look at if you run Sid.

Commercial Support

If you're running a company, chances are you're interested in paying somebody to provide a guaranteed level of service. This is quite understandable, and you have a couple of options—in-house support and commercial support.

Most small- and large-scale Debian users prefer to use in-house support for its cost-effectiveness and quality. Since Debian is built by the systems administrators who use it, self-support is without a doubt the preferred support method. If you're interested in hiring individuals familiar with Debian to support your systems (as opposed to training your own pre-existing staff), you can send an e-mail to `debian-jobs@lists.debian.org` detailing the responsibilities and compensation of the position. Alternatively, if the position is of a sensitive nature, you can e-mail `debian-private@lists.debian.org`, which is read only by official Debian Developers. Messages sent to `debian-private@lists.debian.org` are kept in confidence.

If you'd rather pay a third party maintain your Debian systems, there are two primary options: Hewlett-Packard Services and Progeny. Both of these support vendors deal with each client on a case-by-case basis. You can contact Hewlett Packard Services via `www.hp.com/hps/`, and you can negotiate a support contract with Progeny by sending an e-mail to `sales@progeny.com`.

Summary

Debian is a complex topic and this appendix can't do it justice, but I hope that after reading it you'll have grasped a basic understanding of the concepts most important to Debian systems administration. We like to say that the various Linux distributions are "similar enough to look the same, but different enough to give you a headache." After reading this appendix, you should have be well-prepared to face those problems which most often confront people migrating from Fedora or Red Hat to Debian, such as finding and managing Debian packages and getting extra help when you need it.

Index